Race and Ethnic Conflict

SECOND EDITION

Race and Ethnic Conflict

Contending Views on Prejudice, Discrimination, and Ethnoviolence

edited by
Fred L. Pincus
University of Maryland, Baltimore County

Howard J. Ehrlich
The Prejudice Institute

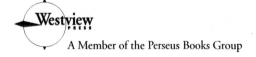

Westview Press
A Member of the Perseus Books Group

Published in 1999 in the United States of America by Westview Press, 5500 Central Avenue, Boulder, Colorado 80301-2877, and in the United Kingdom by Westview Press, 12 Hid's Copse Road, Cumnor Hill, Oxford OX2 9JJ

Library of Congress Cataloging-in-Publication Data
Race and ethnic conflict : contending views on prejudice,
discrimination, and ethnoviolence / edited by Fred L. Pincus, Howard
J. Ehrlich. — 2nd ed.
p. cm.
Includes bibliographical references.
ISBN 0-8133-3498-5 (pbk.)
1. United States—Race relations. 2. United States—Ethnic
relations. 3. Prejudices—United States. 4. Discrimination—United
States. 5. Violence—United States. I. Pincus, Fred L.
II. Ehrlich, Howard J.
E184.A1R23 1999
305.8'00973—dc21 98-28116
CIP

The paper used in this publication meets the requirements of the American National Standard for Permanence of Paper for Printed Library Materials Z39.48-1984.

To our sons,
Josh Pincus-Sokoloff
and Andrew Webbink

Contents

Credits

2. Excerpted from Joan Ferrante and Prince Brown, Jr., "Classifying People by Race," *The Social Construction of Race and Ethnicity in the United States,* pp. 109–119. Copyright © 1998 by Addison-Wesley Educational Publishers, Inc. Reprinted by permission.

3. Excerpted from Charles A. Gallagher, "White Racial Formation: Into the Twenty-first Century," in Richard Delgado and Jean Stefancic, eds., *Critical White Studies: Looking Behind the Mirror* (Philadelphia: Temple University Press, 1997), pp. 6–11.

4. Reprinted from Bob Blauner, "Talking Past Each Other: Black and White Languages of Race," *The American Prospect* 10 (Spring 1992):55–64, by permission of the publisher and the author.

5. Excerpted, with notes renumbered, from Joe R. Feagin and Clairece Booher Feagin, "Theoretical Perspectives in Race Relations," *Racial and Ethnic Relations, 4th Edition.* Copyright © 1993, pp. 26–47. Reprinted by permission of Prentice-Hall, Inc., Upper Saddle River, NJ.

6. Excerpted from James M. Jones, "The Changing Nature of Prejudice," *Prejudice and Racism, 2nd Edition* (Hightstown, NJ: McGraw-Hill, 1997), pp. 93–100, 123–130. Copyright © 1997. Reprinted with permission of The McGraw-Hill Companies.

7. Excerpted from Byron Roth, "Racism and Traditional American Values," *Studies in Social Philosophy and Policy* 18:119–140. Copyright © 1994 by Transaction Publishers. All rights reserved. Reprinted by permission of Transaction Publishers.

8. Excerpted from Lawrence E. Harrison, "The Fortunes of Ethnic Groups in America," *Who Prospers? How Cultural Values Shape Economic and Political Success* (New York: Basic Books, 1992), pp. 192–212. Copyright © 1992 by Lawrence E. Harrison. Reprinted by permission of Basic Books, a member of the Perseus Books Group.

9. Excerpted from William Julius Wilson, "Societal Changes and Vulnerable Neighborhoods," *When Work Disappears* (New York: Knopf, 1996), pp. 25–35, 37–38, 48–50. Copyright © 1996 by William Julius Wilson. Reprinted by permission of Alfred A. Knopf, Inc.

11. Excerpted from Douglas S. Massey, "America's Apartheid and the Urban Underclass," *Social Service Review* (Dec. 1994):471–487. Copyright © 1994 The University of Chicago. Reprinted with permission.

12. Excerpted from Marc Bendick, Jr., Charles W. Jackson, and Victor A. Reinoso, "Measuring Employment Discrimination Through Controlled Experiment," *The Review of Black Political Economy* (Summer 1994):24–48. Copyright © 1994 by Transaction Publishers. All rights reserved. Reprinted by permission of Transaction Publishers.

13. Excerpted, with notes renumbered, from Joleen Kirshenman and Kathryn M. Neckerman, "'We'd Love to Hire Them, But . . .': The Meaning of Race for Employers," in C. Jencks and P. E. Peterson, eds., *The Urban Underclass* (Washington, DC: Brookings Institution, 1991), pp. 203–232 as edited. Reprinted with permission of the Brookings Institution.

14. Excerpted from Karen J. Hossfeld, "Hiring Immigrant Women: Silicon Valley's 'Simple Formula,'" in Maxine Baca Zinn and Bonnie Thornton Dill, eds., *Women of Color in U.S. Society*, pp. 65–68, 71–82, 85–93. Copyright © 1994 by Temple University. Reprinted by permission of Temple University Press.

15. Excerpted from Joan Moore and Racquel Pinderhughes, "Introduction," *In the Barrios: Latinos and the Underclass Debate*, pp. xii–xx, xxv–xxxvii. Copyright © 1993 Russell Sage Foundation. Used by permission of Russell Sage Foundation.

16. Excerpted from Pyong Gap Min, "Major Issues Relating to Asian American Experiences," *Asian Americans: Contemporary Trends and Issues*, pp. 38–57. Copyright © 1995 by Sage Publications, Inc. Reprinted by permission of Sage Publications, Inc.

18. Excerpted, with notes renumbered, from Saskia Sassen, "America's Immigration 'Problem,'" *World Policy Journal* 6, no. 4 (Fall 1989):811–832.

19. Excerpted from Milton M. Gordon, "Models of Pluralism," *the Annals of the American Academy of Political and Social Science* 454 (1981):178–188. Reprinted by permission of the author and the publisher. Copyright © 1981 by the American Academy of Political and Social Sciences.

20. Excerpted from Peter Brimelow, "Introduction" and "Doing the Right Thing? The Morality of Immigration," *Alien Nation*, pp. 3–11, 241–254. Copyright © 1995 by Peter Brimelow. Reprinted by permission of Random House, Inc.

21. Excerpted from David Cole, "Five Myths About Immigration," *The Nation* (October 17, 1994):411–412. Reprinted with permission. Copyright © 1994.

22. Excerpted from Geoffrey Nunberg, "Lingo Jingo: English-Only and the New Nativism, *The American Prospect* 33 (July/August 1997):40–47. Reprinted with permission of the publisher and the author.

24. Excerpted from Thomas Sowell, "'New Racism' and Old Dogmatism," *Inside American Education: The Decline, the Deception, the Dogmas* (New York: Free Press, 1993), pp. 132–133, 155–173. Copyright © 1993 by Thomas Sowell.

25. Excerpted from Ronald Takaki, "Multiculturalism: Battleground or Meeting Ground?" *Annals of the American Academy of Political and Social Sciences* 530 (Nov. 1993):109–121. Copyright © 1993 by Sage Publications, Inc. Reprinted by permission of Sage Publications, Inc.

28. "White Supremacist Movement in the U.S. Today" by Abby L. Ferber is based on research for Abby L. Ferber, *White Man Falling: Race, Gender, and White Supremacy* (Lanham, MD: Rowman and Littlefield, 1998).

29. Excerpted from Stephen Thernstrom and Abigail Thernstrom, "Politics," *America in Black and White: One Nation Indivisible* (New York: Simon & Schuster, 1997), pp. 286–312. Copyright © 1997 by Stephen Thernstrom and Abigail Thernstrom. Reprinted by permission of Simon & Schuster.

30. Excerpted, with notes renumbered, from Howard Zinn, "Representative Government: The Black Experience," *Declarations of Independence* (New York: Knopf, 1991), pp. 231–258. Copyright © 1991 by Howard Zinn. Reprinted by permission of HarperCollins Publishers.

31. Excerpted from Deborah L. Toler, "Black Conservatives—Part Two," *The Public Eye Newsletter* 7, no. 4 (Dec. 1993):1–6, 9.

32. Excerpted from Mark Toney, "Power Concedes Nothing Without a Demand," in John Anner, ed., *Beyond Identity Politics: Emerging Social Justice Movements in Communities of Color* (Boston: South End Press, 1996), pp. 17–18. Reprinted with permission from South End Press.

34. Excerpted from Dinesh D'Souza, "Rethinking Racism," *The End of Racism: Principles for a Multiracial Society* (New York: Free Press, 1995), pp. 537–545. Copyright © 1995 by Dinesh D'Souza. Reprinted with the permission of The Free Press, a Division of Simon & Schuster.

35. Excerpted from A. Salz and J. Trubowitz, "It Was All of Us Working Together," *The Education Forum*, 62 (Fall 1997):82–90. Reprinted by permission of Kappa Delta Pi, an International Honor Society in Education.

36. Excerpted from Charles Jaret, "Changing the Whole System," *Contemporary Racial and Ethnic Relations*, pp. 562–577. Copyright © 1995 by HarperCollins College Publishers. Reprinted by permission of Addison-Wesley Educational Publishers, Inc.

Introduction

Much has happened in the area of race and ethnic relations since the first edition of our book was published in 1994. The changes in this edition reflect the changes in society and the writing about it.

We begin this book by summarizing our own observations. The first is that *prejudice and discrimination against racial/ethnic groups in American society is still a serious problem.* In spite of considerable civil rights legislation and government programs intended to minimize inequality, white Americans still have greater opportunities than all others. Discrimination persists; group tensions are on the rise.

The second observation is that *there has been a change in the dominant mode of expression of prejudice.* The ethnic group stereotypes of an earlier day were rooted in beliefs about the biological differences among people. Today, there is no longer a widespread or strongly held sense of biological inferiority. There is, rather, a sense of "cultural" difference. So, for example, minority groups are not rejected because they are seen as innately inferior but because their "lifestyle" is unacceptable. Further, the stereotypes of an earlier day were far more hateful and far more cruel than those of today. Today one seldom encounters people who regard the Japanese as cruel, sly, and treacherous or who fear Jews because they kidnap young children for ritual blood sacrifices. Fewer people today accept the gross, negative ethnic group stereotypes than at the time of the civil rights movement.

Third, *there has been a reduction in the amount of discrimination.* Changes have occurred in the motivation of people to discriminate against others in everyday settings. In public accommodations, in schools and in workplaces, in voting and political officeholding, major improvements have occurred in this society. To be sure, neighborhood segregation persists in almost all cities and has gotten worse in many. School segregation continues, although it is based more on residential patterns than on legal mandates. Intergroup friendships that cross ethnic and racial lines are still not as frequent as intragroup friendships. Although the prevailing social norms still prescribe considerable social distance between many ethnically different people in intimate settings, much less distance is prescribed in public and casual settings. This, too, is a major change in norms from the period of the civil rights movement. Remember that the civil rights struggles of the 1950s began over issues of where to sit in a bus or at a lunch counter. Public transportation and restaurants are now open to all. Barriers to participation in electoral politics have mainly been removed.

The fourth observation is that *the level of violence motivated by prejudice is high and has been increasing through the 1980s and 1990s.* This form of violence, which we call "ethnoviolence," ranges from psychologically damaging slurs and name-calling through graffiti and group defamation, telephone harassment, intimidating acts and personal threats to property damage, arson, and physical assaults. Increased ethnoviolence, however, is not so much a result of increasing prejudice as it is a result of increasing violence in society. As violent behavior has increased in society, so violence as a response to intergroup contacts has increased.

Fifth, *the number of players on the race and ethnic stage has increased.* In the past, most concern has been directed, appropriately, toward black-white relations. By the 1990s, mainly as a consequence of immigration, Hispanic and Asian populations had dramatically increased so that any thorough discussion of race/ethnic conflict had to include them. Native Americans are also making stronger demands to be heard. Conflict *between* minority groups has also been on the increase.

Sixth is the fact that *American "minorities" are more empowered than at earlier times.* Acts of discrimination and violence that would have been "overlooked" in the past are now being actively opposed.

Finally, *the news media are paying more attention to race/ethnic relations than ever before.* The 1996 arson attacks on black churches, for example, were widely covered in the national news media, as were the charges of CIA involvement in drugs sales in black areas of American cities and the violent activities of the militia and skinhead groups. Charges of discrimination against major corporations were also covered. In 1997, for example, the print media covered cases brought against Prudential, Liberty Mutual, Travelers, Aetna, First Union, Eddie Bauer, Denny's, Texaco, and Continental Airlines, among others. The coverage was mixed and not very analytical. On television, C-SPAN, the PBS series *Point of View* and *Frontline,* and ABC's *Nightline* have all provided intermittent coverage of intergroup problems and conflicts.

In our judgment, then, the problem of race and ethnic conflict is still quite serious and, in all probability, will continue to remain so. We strongly disagree with those who say that the basic problems have been solved and all that is left is a kind of mopping-up operation.

CAUSES OF PREJUDICE AND CONFLICT IN THE LATE 1990s

Why does prejudice and group conflict still exist in the United States in the 1990s? Although the contributors to this anthology present varying answers, we would like to describe five sets of social conditions that operate to maintain prejudice and its manifestation in discrimination, conflict, and ethnoviolence: (1) the history of prejudice and discrimination, (2) economic restructuring in the 1980s and 1990s, (3) political polarization, (4) a culture of denial of prejudice, and (5) the differentials of power in society.

The first contributing factor is the historical tradition of prejudice and its current manifestations in society. We need to make this observation explicit: Every child born into this society comes to learn its traditions and norms. Prejudice and discrimination are a part of those traditions and norms. They are a part of our cultural heritage. To be sure, not everyone accepts this part of the cultural heritage, but no one can escape dealing with it. This then is our starting point.

The second of these conditions is the economic restructuring in the 1980s and 1990s. By the 1980s, the American occupational and income structure began to change. The major growth in new jobs were those in lower-paying, nonunionized industries, while substantial numbers of higher-paying unionized manufacturing jobs were made obsolete or were exported. In the opening years of the 1990s, the United States was losing an average of one million jobs a year. The number of temporary and part-time jobs, most of which have low salaries, no benefits, and no security, also increased.

Further, the distribution of income became more polarized, with the top 20 percent gaining more income and the bottom 20 percent actually losing income. Finally, the growth of corporate mergers gave more power to the wealthy and powerful and increased feelings of insecurity and helplessness in the majority of the population. The size of the middle class shrunk. The result of these changes is that the 1990s saw the first American generation that could not realistically expect to do better than their families of origin. This economic climate creates fertile soil for the growth of race and ethnic hostility

The growth of political polarization is the third contributing factor to race and ethnic conflict in the 1990s. In the 1960s, the country experienced its first televised war (the American war in Indochina) and the modeling of violence on prime-time TV programming for family and children's viewing pleasure. The movements for social change that flourished in the late sixties had two lasting consequences. A new political consciousness evolved with a strong commitment to egalitarianism and to a democratic activism. However, the strong oppositional and countercultural trends of the "new left" of that period, which extended through the early 1970s, so threatened traditional values and existing power arrangements that a serious opposition developed. The 1970s brought what some observers termed a mean-spirited reaction to the liberal reformist programs of the sixties—the civil rights acts, medicare, and massive programs of educational assistance. The altruism of the sixties was replaced by a "me-first" orientation that carried with it a rejection of those programs designed to help African Americans and the poor.

The new left created the new right. The presidential administrations of Ronald Reagan and George Bush saw the rise of a powerful conservative movement and a new era of rightist, white supremacist organizations. By the end of the 1980s, America had become more politically polarized than at any time since the Great Depression of the 1930s. This continued through the 1990s with a conservative Supreme Court, a conservative Congress, and centrist President Bill Clinton, who often seemed more interested in pleasing conservatives than in pleasing the liberals who elected him.

It would not be unfair to say that there is no national resolve among religious leaders or within the business or political elites to deal with the problems of intergroup relations. Many Americans believe that antiminority discrimination is no longer a major problem. *This culture of denial is the fourth of the social forces that contribute to the maintenance of patterns of prejudice, discrimination, and conflict.* Like all cultural patterns, the culture of denial is transmitted across families and friends, through parents and teachers, and is authorized and maintained by the legitimate authorities in the government, the church, and the mass media. This pattern was exemplified by President Ronald Reagan asserting that civil rights leaders exaggerate racial problems in order to keep their organizations alive (CBS News, "60 Minutes," January 15, 1989). The function of such presidential pronouncements is to tell the country that there are no racial problems of serious concern. Certainly if issues are not mentioned they do not become part of the public agenda. For example, despite the four days of intergroup violence in Los Angeles (April 29 through May 2, 1992), issues of race and ethnic group relations were not, nor did they become, part of the political dialogue in the 1992 presidential campaign. This has to be regarded as a form of elite denial. Support for programs of prejudice reduction is not on the agenda of the major philanthropic foundations in the country, and one would be hard-pressed to create a substantial list of business, political, or religious elites who have been outspoken in their support of such programs. In mid-1997, President Clinton appointed an advisory commission to engage the country in a public dialogue on "racism." Although the event garnered considerable media coverage, much of it unfavorable, the commission and the president were intent on changing priorities on the public and elite agenda and breaking the pattern of national denial. National polls reveal that close to one of every two white Americans believes that blacks are as well-off or have the same life chances as do whites. (Less than one out of five blacks shares this belief.) In fact, as we show in our section on discrimination, black disadvantage has been historically stable and in many cases can still be described as extreme—in health, housing, income, and justice, among other comparisons.

This culture of denial has so permeated the patterns of American thought that it has had a deep impact on the way in which many whites think about prejudice. Many white people deny that discrimination against minorities persists, and they have concluded that any intervention designed to equalize opportunities is uncalled for. Further, they believe that given a "level playing field," any intervention, such as affirmative action, actually disadvantages whites. The result of this line of thought has been the increasing polarization of blacks and whites and the increasing white opposition to programs of social action. This opposition has also become central to the appeals of the right-wing white supremacist movement, which defines the differences that do exist as "cultural" and calls for a white-only society in order to maintain "true Christian American" culture.

The final condition that supports the development of prejudice and its manifestation in discrimination, conflict, and ethnoviolence is the differential of power in society. Americans differ extraordinarily in their life chances, and these life chances are determined by the resources of power that people have at their disposal as individuals or as members of a group. It is our premise that the greater the differences of power in a society, the greater the discrimination of minorities. The power differential is maintained through social class membership and through bureaucratic organization.

Bureaucracy requires that participants accept two basic principles of organization. The first is that it is necessary for some people to have power and authority over others. Bureaucracy also requires that participants accept an impersonal orientation, that is, treat people as objects. Those in authority in a bureaucratic organization therefore have a license to manipulate the behavior and lives of others without regard to them as individuals. This depersonalization, the process of treating persons as objects, is a necessary condition of discrimination and ethnoviolence. Participation in bureaucratic organization serves to validate both inequality and depersonalization as acceptable modes of behavior.

The social class system is built on differences in wealth and power and the lifestyles that accompany those differences. Why social classes persist is a central problem of sociology, but one of the reasons for its persistence is relevant here. People are socialized to accept the basic structures and norms of their society. And most Americans believe that our class system is basically fair—that the differences in wealth and power are just and that it is appropriate for families to pass along their privileges to their children.

However, although most people appear to accept the class system, the *extent* of the inequalities that characterize social classes is not regarded as fair. Many people would agree, for example, that it is not fair that the average chief executive officer of a large corporation earns more than two hundred times more than factory workers and that it is not fair that more than twice as many black infants die before they are one year old than do white infants. There is, in fact, an underlying tension about the American class system, but this tension is mediated by the beliefs—some would say mythological beliefs—that anyone can achieve wealth and power through individual effort. The tension is also mediated by the deeply rooted fear concerning the alternatives to the political and economic design of American society, a fear fostered by those who benefit most from its present structure.

The inequalities of social classes are closely connected to the inequalities among ethnic groups in two ways. First, disproportionate numbers of "minority" Americans occupy lower-middle, working-, and lower-class positions. Because of the large overlap between class and color and other ethnic identifications, the acceptance of the class system as legitimate and fair is equivalent to accepting the system of minority stratification as legitimate and fair.

Second, the class system fosters the development of prejudice, discrimination, and conflict because it is a system of inequality. From a social psychological perspective, treating people differently because of social class is very much like treating people differently because of ethnicity. There is a fundamental disjunction between economic inequality and the acceptance of racial and ethnic equality. This is a built-in paradox of modern society.

American society has clearly changed rapidly and dramatically. With these changes has come, for many, a sense of alienation: powerlessness in the face of such changes and confusion about what the new norms of behavior are in such a changing world. For many others, these changes have led to the reaffirmation of their value orientations, orientations ranging across the political spectrum. It is in this social context that Americans are taking sides on the issues of ethnic group relations.

ABOUT THE BOOK

We decided to produce this anthology because we were not satisfied with the texts and anthologies that were available for undergraduate courses in intergroup conflict. Like many other instructors, we found ourselves using more and more photocopied articles as texts for our classes. As the number of articles increased and the department budget decreased, we began to copy and sell the articles to students through the campus bookstore. Several court decisions have made this practice too expensive and of questionable legality.

After many discussions, we decided to publish a supplementary anthology, that is, one that is relatively short and inexpensive and that can be used with another textbook. The principles that guided us in selecting articles for the first edition also guided us for the second edition:

1. *We wanted to combine social psychological analyses of attitudes with sociological analyses of social structure and policy.* Section Two contains two articles about attitudes and the remainder of the book is more sociological in orientation. When possible, we tried to select articles that combined both levels of analysis.

2. *We wanted the articles to be theoretically diverse.* It is important for students to understand some of the important theoretical debates in the field so that they can arrive at their own decisions. Some of the articles were written by conservative authors, such as Dinesh D'Souza and Thomas Sowell, whereas others are by more radical authors, such as Howard Zinn and Joe and Clairece Feagin. Many articles were written by liberal authors from a variety of different race and ethnic perspectives. This theme of theoretical diversity runs throughout the book. In the discussion of attitudes in Section Two, for example, one article argues that white opposition to "forced busing" and "reverse discrimination" is one manifestation of "modern prejudice," whereas another article strongly disagrees. We also included debates on the causes of black poverty, the nature of race/ethnic conflict on campus, and the viability of electoral politics.

Of course, we have our own views about these debates and those appear in our signed articles. However, we have tried to be evenhanded in terms of presenting substantive and well-reasoned articles on both sides.

3. *The articles had to be readable by the majority of college and university undergraduates.* Many articles from professional journals, while important, are written so technically and with so much jargon and such complex statistics that most undergraduates could not be expected to understand them. Although we tried to select articles that were substantive and based on empirical research, we eliminated many simply because of their writing style.

4. *The articles had to be on subjects that were relevant to undergraduates.* "Relevance" is a term that was often used in the turbulent 1960s and referred to courses that spoke to the felt concerns of students at that time. As a result of our own teaching experience, we selected articles that were important in the field and that should be of general interest. Section Six, for example, includes three articles about tensions on college campuses.

THE POLITICS OF INEQUALITY

There are pivotal differences between conservative, liberal, and radical approaches to inequality. These differences become more apparent in the selected readings. The conservative tends to accept the basic forms of social organization, contending that the organizational processes that have developed through time are essentially sound and self-regulating. What is needed, in the conservative view, is a change in the lifestyle and behavior of those at the lower levels of the class and organizational systems. Government intervention is seen as counterproductive. The liberal tends also to be accepting of the basic social forms but emphasizes the need for the government to intervene in order to change the opportunity structure of society to more closely approximate an equality of outcome. Thus the major ameliorative programs of liberal administrations have involved the government strengthening civil rights laws, desegregating schools, and supporting affirmative action and progressive taxation. For conservatives and liberals, then, the basic class and organizational systems are sound; they differ, however, in the means they adopt to achieve group equality and in what they are willing to accept as a final outcome.

From the radical perspective, the existing patterns of inequalities are built into the social system. The class structure and bureaucratic forms of social organization are construed as having been built upon social inequality and operate so as to socialize people into the acceptance of inequality in principle and in practice. It is unrealistic, say radicals, to accept the inequities of wealth and power while realistically expecting equality in intergroup relations. Their response is that these inequalities are all mutually supportive and that all power differences need to be minimized, if not totally eradicated.

We hope that this book will help to stimulate thinking about the nature of intergroup conflict in the United States and about policies that could help to alleviate that conflict. Information is always better than ignorance, although solutions are not always simple or straightforward.

PART 1

Perspectives in Race and Ethnic Relations

1

The Study of Race and Ethnic Relations

FRED L. PINCUS AND HOWARD J. EHRLICH

One major goal of this anthology is to expose students to some of the diverse perspectives in the study of race and ethnic relations. Like scholars in other fields of inquiry, those who study race relations often disagree on many major issues. This is sometimes confusing to students. In 1968, when Fred Pincus first started teaching, a troubled student came up to him and said, "You and Dr. R. disagree on racial inequality." "I know," Pincus responded. The student, appearing even more troubled, said, "Maybe you didn't hear me. You and Dr. R. said different things in class." It took a while to calm her down and reassure her that it was normal for sociologists to disagree about important issues.

Today's students are not so naive and are more used to the fact that experts often disagree. However, students are still confused about what to make of these disagreements. It is often difficult to take the time to understand different arguments and to assess their strengths and weaknesses. Our goal is to make sure that diverse views are clearly presented so that the students can come to their own conclusions. Of course, we have our own views, which we express when appropriate.

These problems exist even when we begin discussing the basic terminology that social scientists generally use. Even simple definitions can be controversial.

A **majority group** *is a social group that controls the political, economic, and cultural institutions of a particular society.*

A **minority group** *is a social group that lacks control of the political, economic, and cultural institutions of a particular society.*

The central idea of these two concepts is *power,* not numbers. In the United States, the two go together since whites have the power and are also in the numerical majority. In most societies, the numerical majority also has power. In South Africa before the fall of apartheid in 1991, however, the black numerical majority would be referred to as the "minority group" because they lacked power.

There are some controversies about the use of these terms. First, some scholars have suggested that the terms *dominant group* and *subordinate group* be used because they are more descriptive. This would avoid the problem of the black South African majority being called a minority group. Second, some people object to that label because it is too geographically restrictive. For example, although Hispanics may be a minority group in the United States, they are the majority group in Latin America. Finally, since most members of minority groups in the United States are not white, there are other broad terms that can be used to describe them—*nonwhite* and *people of color.* Unfortunately, there are pros and cons for both of these. Since we have to use something, we will stick to the traditional concept of minority group.

There is much more controversy about two other concepts that are commonly used in the study of race and ethnic relations.

A **racial group** *is a social group that is socially defined as having certain biological characteristics that set them apart from other groups, often in invidious ways.*

An **ethnic group** *is a social group (1) that has certain cultural characteristics that set them off from other groups and (2) whose members see themselves as having a common past.*

Social scientists concerned with ethnicity direct most of their attention to different groups of whites in the United States either in terms of nationality (Italian, Irish, Greek) or religion (Protestant, Catholic, Jewish).

Most social scientists do not view racial groups as biological entities since there have always been major questions about the degree of biological "purity" and problems of categorization. In the 1950s, a UNESCO consortium of biologists, geneticists, and physical anthropologists issued a statement rejecting the usefulness of race as a biological concept. During the past ten years or so, there has been increasing discourse on what has been called "the social construction of race." The important issues in that discourse are how racial categories are defined and redefined, how different groups have different definitions of the same categories, and finally, how definitions of race change over the years.

Three of the chapters in this section are directly concerned with the concepts of race and ethnicity. Joan Ferrante and Prince Brown, Jr. ("Classifying People by Race") describe how the U.S. Bureau of the Census has defined racial categories over the past 300 years. Many of these definitions have been arbitrary rather than scientific. One theme that runs throughout American history is the attempt to separate whites from those who are not white. In addition, the census has always had problems in categorizing people of mixed-race backgrounds. In the 2000 census, people will be able to check more than one category for the first time. Finally, Hispanics have never been treated as a separate racial group in the census. Since 1970, a separate question has been asked about whether or not a person is Hispanic. Therefore, Hispanics can be members of any racial group.

In discussions of race and racial identity, much has been written about blacks, Asians, and Native Americans. Their group identities in the United States were influenced by their visible differences from the white majority, their oppression, and their struggles for equality. The implicit assumption was that whites were "raceless." When most people talked about *race,* they were talking about people who were not white. Even the census used a category of "nonwhite."

All that has changed in the past ten years with an increasing amount of scholarship being devoted to "whiteness" in the United States. Charles A. Gallagher ("White Racial Formation: Into the Twenty-First Century") argues that as whites have lost their *ethnic* identities over the past few decades, people who are white have become more concerned with their own cultural identity and political mobilization. Gallagher sees many working-class whites now struggling for a new identity combining a defense of past privilege with the present perception of being under attack.

Bob Blauner ("Talking Past Each Other: Black and White Languages of Race") addresses the issues of race and ethnicity and asserts that black Americans are both a racial group and an ethnic group. He argues that when black college students group together on college campuses, whites often define this behavior as a type of racial segregation. Blauner argues that blacks seek out other blacks for their common *cultural* characteristics just as other ethnic groups have done and continue to do.

Other concepts are also important in the study of race and ethnic relations.

Prejudice *is an attitude toward a group of people that can be either positive or negative.*

Discrimination *refers to actions that deny equal treatment to persons perceived to be members of some social category.*

Although we discuss both of these concepts later in the book, what we want to emphasize here is that prejudice refers to what people feel or believe, whereas discrimination refers to the actions that they take.

Another term that is often used in discussing race and ethnic conflict is **racism**. This terms presents a major dilemma because of its many different meanings. Bob Blauner, in the chapter mentioned above, describes six different ways that the term racism has been used over the past 150 years. None of them is wrong, says Blauner, although different people often have different definitions in mind when they use the term. He suggests that social scientists drop the term due to its imprecision. We agree with Blauner, and we do not provide a working definition of racism in this book. We use the term *prejudice* when we are describing what people think and feel and the term *discrimination* when we are talking about what people or institutions do. Since not all of the contributors to this book agree with this position, we clarify terms for students as we go along.

In addition to these disagreements about basic concepts, social scientists tend to have different theoretical perspectives about the study of race and ethnic relations. Unfortunately, most textbooks spend little if any time discussing their own theories, much less competing theories. This makes it difficult for students to be able to critically analyze any given author's point of view. The final chapter in Part One, by Joe R. Feagin and Clairece Booher Feagin ("Theoretical Perspectives in Race and Ethnic Relations"), discusses a wide variety of theoretical perspectives that are used in the field.

2

Classifying People by Race

JOAN FERRANTE AND
PRINCE BROWN, JR.

On a variety of official documents, citizens are requested to state their race or ethnicity. In census tabulations, they are asked to respond, indeed, to confess to their race, to examine their skin color, the color of their blood, their type of hair, and the breadth of their nostrils to allocate themselves to racial groups.

—Yehudi O. Webster, *The Racialization of America* (1993:44)

Most people in the United States equate race with physical features. In their minds, the term *race* refers to a group of people who possess certain distinctive and conspicuous physical traits. Racial categories are assumed to represent "natural, physical divisions among humans that are hereditary, reflected in morphology, and roughly but correctly captured by terms like Black, White, and Asian for Negroid, Caucasoid, and Mongoloid" (Haney López 1994:6). This three-category classification scheme has many shortcomings, which immediately become evident when we imagine using it to classify the more than 5.6 billion people in the world. If we attempted this task, we would soon learn that three categories are not enough—especially when we consider that for the 1990 U.S. Census, respondents wrote in the names of 300 alleged races and 75 combinations of multiracial ancestry (Morganthau 1995).

The refusal on the part of the government of the United States to acknowledge the obvious conclusion that their categories only very poorly capture the range of human features is driven by long-standing historical and social reasons. "The idea that there exist three races, and that these are 'Caucasoid', 'Negroid', and 'Mongoloid', is rooted in the European imagination of the Middle Ages, which encompassed only Europe, Africa, and the Near East. The peoples of the American continents, the Indian subcontinent, East Asia, Southeast Asia, and Oceania—living outside the imagination of Europe—are excluded from the three major races for social and political reasons, not for scientific ones. Nevertheless, the history of science has long been the history of failed efforts to justify these social beliefs" (Haney López 1994:13–14).

Adding more categories, however, would not ease the task of classifying the world's billions of people because racial classification rests on the fallacy that clear-cut racial categories exist. Why is this a fallacy? First, many people do not fit clearly into a racial category because no sharp dividing line distinguishes characteristics such as black skin from white skin or curly hair from wavy. This lack of a clear line, however, has not discouraged people from trying to devise ways to make the line seem clear-cut. For example, a hundred years ago in the United States there were churches that "had a pinewood slab on the outside door . . . and a fine tooth comb hanging on a string . . . " (Angelou 1987:2). People could go into the church if they were no darker than the pinewood and if they could run the comb through their hair without it snagging. At one time in South Africa, the state board that oversaw racial classification used a pencil test to classify individuals as white or black. If a pencil placed in the person's hair fell out, the person was classified as white (Finnegan 1986).

A second problem with the idea of clear-cut racial categories is that boundaries between races can never be fixed and definite, if only because males and females of any alleged race can produce offspring. Millions of people in the world have mixed ancestry and possess physical traits which make it impossible to assign them to any of the four narrow racial categories currently used by the U.S. government. The media often presents mixed ancestry as a recent phenomenon connected to the dismantling of laws forbidding interracial marriages in 1967 and a subsequent societal openness to interracial marriage (which produce mixed race children—*see* Beech 1996 as one example). Since colonial days in the United States, however, "there has been intermixture between White and Indian, between White and Negro, and between Negro and Indian. While the offspring of such unions could not be biologically classified (and by their very existence defy the popular meaning of race), many of them did undoubtedly become accepted and identified with one of the three recognized stocks" (Pollitzer 1972:720). Evidence of this intermixing before 1967 and of the fact that people become identified as belonging to one "racial" stock in spite of their mixed ancestry is reflected in 1929 and 1949 studies of the racial ancestry of college students attending historically black universities. In the 1929 study, 78% of Howard University students were of mixed "racial" ancestry. In the 1949 study, 84% of the college students studied were of mixed ancestry (Meier 1949). The widespread existence of intermixing, however, seemed to have little effect on dismantling beliefs that distinct racial categories exist.

A third shortcoming in systems of racial classification is that racial categories and guidelines for placing people in them are often vague, contradictory, unevenly applied, and subject to change. . . .

As [one] example of the arbitrary nature of classification rules, consider that for the 1990 Census coders were instructed to classify as white those who classified themselves as "white-black" and to classify as "black" those who classified themselves as "black-white" (U.S. Bureau of the Census 1994). Likewise the National Center for Health Statistics (1993) has changed the guidelines for recording race on birth and death certificates. Before 1989, a child born in the United States was designated as white if both parents were white; if only one parent was white, the child was classified according to the race of the nonwhite parent; if the parents were of different nonwhite races, the child was assigned to the race of the father.[1] If the race of one parent was unknown, the infant was assigned the race of the parent whose race was known. After 1989, the rules for classifying newborns changed: Now the race of the infant is the same as that of the mother (Lock 1993), as if identifying the mother's race would present no challenges. . . .

Finally, in trying to classify people by race, we would find a tremendous amount of variation among people designated as belonging to a particular race. For example, people classified as Asian or Mongoloid include, among other groups, Chinese, Japanese, Malayans, Mongolians, Siberians, Eskimos, and Native Americans. Likewise, there is considerable heterogeneity within the population labeled as "black" in the United States. Green (1978) identified at least nine distinct "cultural-ecological areas" for the nativeborn black population including areas of Native American influence (Oklahoma and parts of Arkansas and Kansas) and French tradition (Louisiana, eastern Coastal Texas, and southwestern Mississippi). In addition,

> the black population includes immigrants from the Caribbean area and the African mainland. Almost half a million persons in the 1990 census indicated that they were of sub-Saharan African ancestry. The black population from the Caribbean basin countries is diverse and includes Spanish-speaking persons from Cuba, the Dominican Republic, and Panama; French-speaking persons from Haiti and other French-speaking Caribbean areas; Dutch-speaking persons from the Netherlands Antilles; and English-speaking persons from the former British colonies. (Williams, Lavizzo-Mourey, and Warren 1994:33)

Perhaps the strongest evidence that race is not a biological fact but a social creation is the different rules for classifying people into racial categories across societies and the shifting rules for classifying people within a single society. In the United States, not only have the rules governing classification changed but so have the categories. For example, in the United States a question about race has appeared on every census since 1790, although it was not until 1850 that the government included a question that clearly attempted to distinguish the black population from the white. Prior to 1850, except for the category free whites, the other categories could include people of any race. Over the past 200 years, the U.S. Bureau of the Census has used as few as three racial categories and as many as 14. (See Table 2.1) Although the rationale for determining the number and names of categories is the subject of a separate book, we can be sure that the various racial classification schemes reflect the prevailing ideologies of their times, and that to understand the various schemes and the changes in those schemes, one must place them in a larger social context.

Based on the information presented in Table 2.1 one can readily identify at least two themes. (1) There has only been one category reserved for the population classified as white. In other words, there has been no attempt to further subdivide this white population even though the majority of people in the United States are classified as such. (2) At various times in history, the federal government has been preoccupied with identifying subdivisions within one broad racial category. In 1890, for example, there was an unusual emphasis placed on categorizing people according to degree of blackness. Notice that half the categories listed are devoted to this task. In 1930, five subcategories of "other race" were designated for people of Asian heritage, which at that time constituted only less than one-quarter of one percent (.002%) of the population (Lee 1993).

TABLE 2.1 Categories Used by the U.S. Bureau of the Census to Designate Race: 1790–1990

1790, 1800, 1810	
Free Whites	Slaves
All other Free Persons, except Indians not taxed	

1820, 1830, 1840	
Free Whites	Free Colored
Foreigners, not naturalized	Slaves

1850, 1860	
White	Mulatto
Black	Black slaves
	Mulatto slaves

1870, 1880, 1890, 1900, 1910, 1920	
White	Chinese
Black	Indian
Mulatto	Quadroon*
	Octoroon*
	Japanese

1930	
White	All other
Negro	Indian
	Japanese
	Filipino
	Hindu
	Korean

1940	
White	Japanese
Negro	Filipino
Indian	Hindu
Chinese	Korean

1950	
White	Japanese
Negro	Chinese
American Indian	Filipino

1960	
White	Hawaiian
Negro	Part Hawaiian
American Indian	Aleut
Japanese	Eskimo
Chinese	

1970	
White	Chinese
Negro/Black	Filipino
Indian	Hawaiian
Japanese	Korean

1980	
White	Indian (American)
Black or Negro	Asian Indian
Japanese	Hawaiian
Chinese	Guamanian
Filipino	Samoan
Korean	Eskimo
Vietnamese	Aleut

1990	
White	Asian or Pacific Islander
Black or Negro	
Indian (American)	
Eskimo	Chinese
Aleut	Hawaiian
	Korean
	Vietnamese
	Japanese
	Asian Indian
	Samoan
	Guamanian
	Other API

*Category applied to 1890 Census only.

SOURCE: U.S. Bureau of the Census 1989.

Sharon Lee (1993) points out that although the classification schemes in the United States have changed in significant ways over time, four dominant themes prevailed:

1. a pattern of separating the population into two groups: white and nonwhite

The federal government's attempt to categorize people into two broad racial groups is the most enduring theme in the history of the United States. As mentioned above, there has been "a chronic concern with populations defined as non-White. As many as 13 categories have been used to classify the numerically smaller population designated as nonwhite with no corresponding effort to do the same with the majority population classified as white. Although definitions of who belongs to white and non-white categories have shifted over time,[3] up until 1980, rules for the bureau of the census in classifying persons of mixed biological heritage had never specified the white category as an option. In other words, according to the bureau of the census "any mixture of white and nonwhite should be reported according to the nonwhite parent."

2. a belief in racial purity

The belief in the idea of racial purity is reflected in the absence of a mixed-race or multiracial category and in the absence of instructions to "check all that apply." In the United States, categories are treated as mutually exclusive—that is, it is not possible for someone to belong to more than one category. Even the 1990 Census asks respondents to "fill in ONE circle" for the race they consider themselves (and persons living within the same household) to be. If the person does not follow directions, census enumerators make every effort to assign people to one racial category even in instances where people give other kinds of responses.

Table 2.1 shows that there have been only a few attempts to identify multiracial populations. In 1890, the U.S. Bureau of the Census included the categories "Mulatto," "Quadroon," and "Octoroon" in an attempt to identify the "partly Black" population[4] and also gave special emphasis for identifying segments of the Native American population.[5] In the subsequent census, the categories "Quadroon" and "Octoroon" were dropped, never to appear again. The 1920 Census was the last time the term "Mulatto" appeared. Since 1920, with the exception of an attempt in 1950 to count "special communities" and an attempt in 1960 to identify those who are "part Hawaiian," the U.S. government has not attempted to identify "partly white" or "mixed-race" populations. Such changes and omissions reflect the general acceptance of the "one-drop rule" in defining who is black or, for that matter, who is not white in the United States. These changes and omissions also reflect a belief in the idea of racial purity—that people can be, or rather are, assigned to one racial category no matter what the facts are with regard to ancestry. . . .

In making the decision to assign children of mixed parentage to the race the "nonwhite" parent has been assigned, the government asks people to accept the idea that one parent contributes a disproportionate amount of genetic material to the child, so large a genetic contribution that it negates the genetic contribution of the other parent. It also serves to establish the category "white" as the ideal/standard category. As one indicator that the category "white" has been treated as the ideal/standard by which all others are measured, consider that of the many court cases in U.S. history related to "wrongful classification," no persons have gone to court to prove they are something other than white.

The predominance of the one-drop rule in the United States suggests that other ideas about race were never considered or were dismissed as possibilities. Other ideas include assigning people of mixed "race" to the same race as the "white" parent,[7] creating new racial categories to accommodate mixed ancestry, dropping the idea of race as a valid way to categorize people (Scales-Trent 1995), and adopting the French and Spanish models.

> During the time Louisiana was a French or a Spanish colony—a time when liaisons between white men and black women were widespread and in some cases nearly formalized—the offspring was treated according to a Latin view of race that left room for a spectrum of colors between black and white. The French had eight terms to calibrate the spectrum—from "mulatre," for the product of a union between a black and a white, to words like "marabout" and "metis," to describe more complicated combinations. The Spanish managed to come with sixty-four terms. Then, in 1803, Louisiana was taken over by the Americans, who imposed what Edmonson refers to as a Germanic view of descent, common to Northern Europe and England: "When it comes to mixing between in-group and out-group, the offspring is flawed, and becomes a member of the out-group." (Trillin 1986:66–67)

3. a pattern of transforming many ethnic groups into one racial group

"Federal Statistical Directive No. 15," an Office of Management and Budget document issued in 1977 and still in use today, outlines the standards for record-keeping, collection, and presentation of data on race and ethnicity. The directive names four official racial categories and two official ethnic categories. The four races are umbrella terms. That is, each is a supercategory under which aggregates of people who vary according to nationality, ethnicity, language, generation, social class, and time of arrival in the United States are forced into one category (Gimenez 1989). Those supercategories are listed below.

American Indian or Alaska Native (any person having origins in any of the original peoples of North America which by some estimates includes more than 2000 distinct groups);

Asian or Pacific Islander (any person having origins in any of the original peoples of the Far East, Southeast Asia, the Indian subcontinent, or the Pacific Islands;

Black (any person having origins in any of the black racial groups of Africa); and

White (a person having origins in any of the original peoples of Europe, North Africa, or the Middle East).

It is significant that the definition of the Black category, unlike the definitions for the other three categories, omits the words "original peoples" and substitutes "black racial groups of Africa." If "original peoples" were included in the definition of black, every person in the United States would have to check this category. In the view of evolutionary biologists all people evolved from a common African ancestor. Moreover, how many people know enough about the original peoples of a geographic area to know whether they are descendants?

Judy Scales-Trent (1995) maintains that we are asking the wrong questions. The questions should not be where did your people originate? "but rather 'What countries did your people travel through on their way here from Africa?' Or maybe 'What was the most recent stop your people made on their trek to this place from Africa? Was it Denmark? Turkey? Bolivia? Vietnam?'" (p. 140).

4. no sharp distinction between race, ethnicity, and national origin

Sociologist Martha E. Gimenez (1989) points out that the race question is poorly constructed in that it offers respondents racial, ethnic, and national origin categories as possible responses. As one example, in the Asian or Pacific Islander category, the bureau of the census lists as examples eight national origin groups plus a category labeled Hawaiian, which gives the impression that race, country of birth, and/or national origin are one and the same. The national origin groups include Chinese, Filipino, Korean, Vietnamese, Japanese, Asian Indian, Samoan, and Guamanian. Consider the confusion these categories might pose for someone of Chinese ancestry who was born outside of China (in Peru or Saudi Arabia, for example) and then immigrated to the United States. The point of these examples is to show that when a person checks "Chinese," we don't know if it is because he or she is of Chinese ancestry or because he or she was *born in* China (not everyone born in China is of Chinese ancestry). Does the word "Chinese" trigger in respondents associations of biological heritage or associations related to their country of birth or their ancestors' country of birth before their arrival to the United States? It is not clear whether respondents should think about race as something related to their ethnicity, physical appearance, biology, country of birth, or national origin.

This critique of the U.S. system of racial classification tells us that there is no such thing as race. Yet, the belief that physical appearance denotes one's race seems so obvious that it is difficult for us to accept this conclusion. "The central intellectual challenge confronting those who recognize that races are not physical fact [is]: Why do we easily recognize races when walking down the street if there is no morphological basis to race? Why does race seem obvious if it is only a fiction?" (Haney López 1994:19). Not knowing the details of other people's lives, we search a person's physical features looking for the telltale "Negroid," "Caucasian," or "Mongoloid" features and proceed to assign them to racial categories on the basis of their most superficial traits—skin color, hair texture, hair color, cheekbone structure, eye color, eyelids, and so on (Piper 1992). Given the importance of the idea of race as a fixed, objective phenomenon which dominates most people's thinking—what anthropologist Ashley Montagu (1964) called the "most dangerous myth of our time, and one of the most tragic" (p. 23)—it is appropriate that we review the evidence discrediting the idea that race is a biological fact. In the reading "Biology and the Social Construction of the 'Race' Concept," by Prince Brown, Jr., we learn why most biologists and social scientists have come to agree that race cannot be a biological fact. Further, we see clearly the systematic and persistent refusal of those assigned the task of racial classification in the United States to consider genetic reality. This failure to consider genetic reality is not unique to the United States. In "Comparing Official Definitions of Race in Japan and the United States," David M. Potter and Paul Knepper (1996) show that no scientific or logical basis exists for determining and assigning "race." Both societies nevertheless have an official ideology of "race" upon which they base their assumptions and practices. The United States claims to be a nation of distinct "racial" groups, while Japan describes itself as "racially pure." In both societies, powerful groups define the categories and make policies and laws to support their views.

Ian F. Haney López cautions that even if race has no biological basis, we cannot call it an hallucination. *Biological race* is the illusion; *social race* is not. Haney López (1994) defines race in social terms as "a vast group of people loosely bound together by historically contingent, socially significant elements of their morphology and/or ancestry" (p. 7). In evaluating this definition, we must keep in mind that a race is not created simply because a subset of people share just any characteristic (height, hand size, eye color or ancestry). It is the social significance ascribed to certain physical features and to certain ancestors, such as Africans, Europeans, or Asians, which define races. In "Passing for White, Passing for Black," Adrian Piper (1992) states, "What joins me to other blacks, then, and other blacks to another, is not a set of shared physical characteristics, for there is none that all blacks share. Rather, it is the shared experience of being visually or cognitively *identified* as black by a white racist society, and the punitive and damaging effects of that identification" (pp. 30–31). If those physical features we associate with a specific race are *absent* in a person who claims to be of that race, or if those physical features are present in a person who claims *not* to be of that race, we accuse him or her of being "underhanded or manipulative, trying to hide something, pretending to be something [they were not]" (Piper 1992:23).

Even the U.S. Office of Management and Budget (OMB), which sets racial and ethnic classification policy and standard in the United States, acknowledged the social significance of race in *Federal Statistical Policy Directive No. 15*. The directive states that a person's mixed race or ethnic background was to be reported in a standard category which most closely reflects how others in the community recognize that person (Hunt 1993).

In the reading "The Mean Streets of Social Race," Ian F. Haney López (1994) expands on the social significance of race through the case of Piri Thomas, a Puerto Rican of mixed Indian, African, and European descent, who finds himself transformed into a Black person upon moving to the United States with his family. López argues that race is *not* a fixed, inherited attribute, free of human intervention—something parents pass on to their off-spring through their genes. Rather, race is a product of at least three overlapping and inseparable factors: chance (physical features and ancestry), context (historical, cultural, and social setting), and choice (everyday decisions).

In view of the shortcomings associated with the U.S. system of racial classification and the fact that race is not a fixed, inherited attribute, we should not be surprised to learn that the U.S. Office of Management and Budget is under pressure to modify the classification scheme outlined in *Federal Statistical Policy Directive No. 15*.

NOTES

1. There was one exception to this rule. If either parent was Hawaiian, the child was assigned to the Hawaiian category (National Center for Health Statistics 1993).

3. Before 1980, Asian Indians were considered white. Mexicans were considered a separate race in 1930 but in the 1940 Census were classified as white. (*Ed.'s note:* In the 2000 Census, mixed race people can check multiple categories.)

4. A *mulatto* is a person with one white and one Negro parent or any person with mixed Caucasian and Negroid ancestry. A *quadroon* is a person with one-quarter Negro ancestry. An *octoroon* is a person with one white parent and one parent who is one-eighth Negro.

5. The 1880 and 1890 Censuses gave the following instructions for coding responses related to Native American identity.

If this person is of full-blood of this tribe, enter "/." For mixture with another tribe, enter name of latter. For mixture with white, enter "W.;" with black, "B.;" with mulatto, "Mu."

If this is a white person adopted into the tribe, enter "W.A.;" if a negro or mulatto, enter "B.A."

If this person has been for any time habitually on the reservation, state the time in years or fractions.

If this person wears citizen's dress state the time in years or fractions since he or she has habitually so worn it.

If other than native language is spoken by this person, enter for English, "E.;" Spanish, "S.;" French, "F.;" &c.

7. Beginning in 1989, the National Center for Health Statistics (1993) changed the rules for classifying mixed-race newborns so that this possibility existed. Prior to 1989, the child was assigned the same race as the nonwhite parent. In 1989, the baby was assigned to the same racial category as the mother, which means the baby was declared "white" even if the father was not. According to NCHC statistics, the majority of mixed race births were to mothers classified as white.

REFERENCES

Angelou, Maya. 1987. "Intra-Racism." Interview on the *Oprah Winfrey Show.* (Journal Graphics transcript #W172):2.

Beech, Hannah. 1996. "Don't You Dare List Them As 'Other.'" *U.S. News and World Report.* http://www.usnews.com/usnews/issue/birace.htm.

Brown, Prince, Jr. Unpublished. "Biology and the Social Construction of the 'Race' Concept." Northern Kentucky University.

Finnegan, William. 1986. *Crossing the Line: A Year in the Land of Apartheid.* New York: Harper & Row.

Forbes, Jack D. 1990. "The Manipulation of Race, Caste and Identity: Classifying Afro Americans, Native Americans and Red-Black People." *The Journal of Ethnic Studies* 17(4):23–25.

Gimenez, Martha E. 1989. "Latino/'Hispanic'—Who Needs a Name?: The Case Against a Standardized Terminology." *International Journal of Health Services* 19(3):567–571.

Green, V. 1978. "The Black Extended Family in the United States: Some Research Suggestions." pp. 378–387 in *The Extended Family in Black Societies,* edited by D. B. Shimkin, E. M. Shimkin, and D. A. Frate. The Netherlands: Mouton DeGruyter.

Haney López, Ian F. 1994. "The Social Construction of Race: Some Observations on Illusion, Fabrication, and Choice." *Harvard Civil Rights-Civil Liberties Law Review* 29:39–53.

Hunt, William M. 1993. *U.S. General Accounting Office Data Collection: Measuring Race and Ethnicity is Complex and Controversial.* "Testimony Before the Subcommittee on Census, Statistics, and Postal Personnel." Washington, DC: U.S. Government Printing Office.

Knepper, Paul. 1995. "Historical Origins of the Prohibition of Multiracial Legal Identity in the States and the Nation." *State Constitutional Commentaries and Notes: A Quarterly Review* 5(2):14–20.

Lee, Sharon M. 1993. "Racial Classification in the U.S. Census: 1890–1990." *Ethnic and Racial Studies* 16(1):75–94.

Lock, Margaret. 1993. "The Concept of Race: An Ideological Construct." *Transcultural Psychiatric Research Review* 30:203–227.

Meier, August. 1949. "A Study of the Racial Ancestry of the Mississippi College Negro." *American Journal of Physical Anthropology* 7(1):227–240.

Montagu, Ashley, ed. 1964. *The Concept of Race.* Toronto: Free Press.

Morganthau, Tom. 1995. "What Color is Black?" *Newsweek* (February 13): 63–65.

National Center for Health Statistics. 1993. "Advanced Report of Final Natality Statistics." *Monthly Vital Statistics Report* 41(9).

Piper, Adrian. 1992. "Passing for White, Passing for Black." *Transition* 58:4–32.

Pollitzer, William S. 1972. "The Physical Anthropology and Genetics of Marginal People of the Southeastern United States." *American Anthropologist* 74(1–2):719–734.

Poston, Dudley L., Jr., Michael Xinxiang Mao, and Mei-Yu Yu. 1994. "The Global Distribution of the Overseas Chinese Around 1990." *Population and Development Review* 20(3):631–645.

Potter, David M., and Paul Knepper. 1996. "Comparing Official Definitions of Race in Japan and the United States." *Southeast Review of Asian Studies* 28(1):103–118.

Scales-Trent, Judy. 1995. "Choosing Up Sides." Pp. 61–65 in *Notes of a White Black Woman: Race, Color, Community.* University Park: The Pennsylvania State University.

Strickland, Daryl. 1996. "Interracial Generation: 'We Are Who We Are'." *The Seattle Times.* http://webster3.seattletimes.com/topstories/browse/html/race_050596.html.

Trillin, Calvin. 1986. "American Chronicles: Black or White." *The New Yorker* (April 14):62–78.

U.S. Bureau of the Census. 1989. *200 Years of U.S. Census Taking: Population and Housing Questions, 1790–1990.* Washington, DC: U.S. Government Printing Office.

______. 1994. *Current Population Survey Interviewing Manual.* Washington, DC: U.S. Government Printing Office.

______. 1996. "Race." In *Appendix B: Definition of Subject Characteristics.* http://www.census.gov/td/stf3/append_b.html.

Webster, Yehundi O. 1993. *The Racialization of America.* New York: St. Martin's Press.

Williams, David R, Risa Lavizzo-Mourey, and Rueben C. Warren. 1994. "The Concept of Race and Health Status in America." *Public Health Reports* 109(1):26–41.

3

White Racial Formation

Into the Twenty-first Century

CHARLES A. GALLAGHER

Whiteness is in a state of change. One only need browse book stands or news racks for examples of how the idea of whiteness is being interpreted, defined, reinterpreted, and contested by popular writers and journalists. Whites perceive themselves, according to one account, as being part of a distinctly different, color-blind, sympathetic generation that has learned to look beyond "the color of the skin" to "the beauty within."[1]

Whereas some whites see a common humanity with their nonwhite counterparts, others see whiteness as a liability. A white sergeant with the Los Angeles County Sheriff's Office announced creation of the Association of White Male Peace Officers, with the goal of defending the rights of white officers who are "distinctly averse to the proposal that, as a class, we be punished or penalized for any real or purported transgressions of our forbears."[2] This "class" of white men seeks the same types of legal protection afforded to other groups organized around their race or gender. Samuel Francis, an editorial writer for the *Washington Times* and advisor to Patrick Buchanan's presidential campaign, declared that "whites must reassert our identity and our solidarity . . . in explicitly racial terms through the articulation of racial consciousness as whites."[3] Francis believes whites have ignored or disregarded their racial identity and must (re)unite as whites to stop the influx of non-white immigrants. It is no wonder many whites feel confused and overwhelmed about who they are racially and how they fit into American race relations.

The meaning of whiteness is not to be found in any single one of the preceding descriptions of how whites imagine themselves or come to understand their racial identity. The contemporary meaning is an amalgamation of these white narratives. Whites can be defined as naïve because they attach little meaning to their race, humane in their desire to reach out to nonwhites, defensive as self-defined victims, and reactionary in their calls for a return to white solidarity.

It is not surprising, then, that my respondents would generate similar disparate (and at times schizophrenic) renderings when asked what meaning they attach to their race. As in the anecdotes above, the extent to which whiteness was a salient form of identity for my respondents varied greatly, ranging from the naïve, to the reactionary, to the situational. Some described their sense of whiteness as being partially veiled, becoming visible and salient only when they felt they were a racial minority. This momentary minority status and the anxiety often associated with this experience colored how respondents saw themselves and their relationship to other racial groups. For other respondents, whiteness had been made explicitly visible at some earlier point in their lives. Their understanding of the concept was often no more than a list of what they were not, why they should not feel guilty about being white, or why their race was now being held against them. The extent to which a sense of whiteness was just emerging for some and had already evolved as an overt identity for others obscures an obvious and important finding: If whiteness was ever invisible for these respondents, it no longer is.

What, however, have we learned about the social, political, and cultural construction of whiteness? How is the construction of whiteness linked sociologically to the structural elements that shape those meanings? Respondents may "know they are white," but what does that mean and what are its political and social consequences? A number of patterns emerged in my data, each of which delineates a particular facet of how white racial identity is constructed and made salient. These patterns point to one clear and significant finding: Whiteness is in the midst of fundamental transformation. White identity is not only a reaction to the entrance of historically marginalized racial and ethnic groups into the political arena and the ensuing struggle over social resources. The construction of whiteness is based, at least among the respondents in my study, on a perception of current and future material deprivation and the need to delineate white culture in a nondemonized fashion. The majority of whites in this study have come to understand themselves and their interests as white. Many of my respondents now think about themselves as whites, not as ethnics; they see themselves as individuals who are members of a racial category with its own particular set of interests. They have attached new meanings to being white and have used those meanings as the basis for forging an identity centered around race. They have, to borrow Michael Omi and Howard Winant's term, gone through the process of racialization. The factors shaping white racialization include the decline of ethnicity, the rise of identity politics, the perception that whiteness is a social and economic liability, and the precepts of neoconservative racial politics. While I do not suggest whiteness is constructed in a uniform, linear fashion, I do believe that white racialization has emerged at this particular moment due to a confluence of these trends. I see them as being linked in the following ways.

THE ETHNIC VACUUM

A lack of ethnic identity among my respondents has created an emptiness that is being filled by an identity centered on race. Almost fifty years ago, W. Lloyd Warner observed: "The future of American ethnic groups seems to be limited; it is likely that they will quickly be absorbed. When this happens one of the great epochs of American history will end, and another, that of race, will begin."[4] My interviews and survey data bear out Warner's prediction. For the majority of the white respondents in my study, little is left in the way of ethnic solidarity, ethnic identity, or even symbolic nostalgia for the ethnic traditions of their older kin. When asked to define themselves in ethnic or racial terms (or both), the majority of students labeled themselves as white or Caucasian, ignoring such labels as Italian-American. Like most whites their age, these students have undergone such extensive generational assimilation and convergence of cultural experiences that only a few chose to describe themselves as "plain old American," "mutt," or "nothing." The young whites I interviewed were so removed from the immigrant experience that even the small minority who defined themselves in ethnic terms acknowledged that their ethnicity was in name only. As one remarked, he thought of his mixed Polish heritage only when he ate kielbasa at Christmas. Ethnicity is a subjective series of choices (or, as Mary Waters writes, an "option") in constructing an identity, but the majority of white students I interviewed and surveyed came from families where very little in the way of "ethnic options" existed because the symbolic ethnic practices had all but died out.

Young whites selectively resurrect their ethnicity through "immigrant tales" mainly when they feel white privilege is being contested, even though their perceived ethnic history does not necessarily concern a specific nation but rather a generalized idea of a European origin. This common, yet fuzzy, connection to the "old country" provides the historical backdrop and cultural space for the construction of white identity, or "a yearning for a usable past."[5] As the importance of ethnicity wanes in the lives of young whites, the immigration experience of older (or dead) kin becomes a mythologized narrative providing a historical common denominator of passage, victimization, and assimilation. As white students often tell it, blacks can point to the middle passage and slavery; Japanese and Chinese can speak of internment and forced labor, respectively; and whites have the immigrant experience. In a sense, past group victimization or hardship is part of the American experience; young whites, when confronted by real or perceived charges of racism, can point to the mistreatment of their older relatives when they were newly arrived immigrants in the United States.

Although whites did experience prejudice and discrimination when they arrived in the United States, it is unlikely that their descendants encounter anything remotely similar today. Unlike the case of the white ethnic revival movement of the 1960s and 1970s, it is now impossible to mobilize young whites politically based on their ethnicity; an ethnic identity no longer exists, as it did for their parents or grandparents.

The markers of ethnic identity have all but disappeared. A "subjective belief in common descent" did not exist for the majority of my respondents. These students could not speak, nor had they been exposed to, a "mother tongue." They did not feel obligated to marry or date people from similar ethnic backgrounds. Nor did they derive a "sense of honor" from being part of an ethnic group or draw on their heritage to become "a carrier of 'interests,' economic or political, which the members of an ethnic group lay claim to or defend."[6] The generation of older whites who were part of the "ethnic revival" and who used their ethnicity as the basis for group claims has been displaced by one that feels increasingly comfortable using their racial identity as the sole carrier of their interests.

Race matters for my respondents because it is racial, not ethnic, identity that is bound up in popular culture and the political order. As David Roediger sees it, "*Among whites,* racial identity (whiteness) and ethnic identity are distinct."[7]

I would argue, on the contrary, that for many respondents there is no distinction because ethnic identity has all but vanished. After generations of assimilation, only whiteness is left as an identity with any real social or political import. The decline of ethnicity among later-generation whites has created an identity vacuum, one that has been at least partially replaced by an identity grounded in race.

WHITE IDENTITY POLITICS

The second influence on white racialization is how identity politics has raised white consciousness. The generation of whites I studied, born around 1975, grew up with a brand of racial politics and media exposure that are unique. This generation is the first to witness the full social, political, and cultural effects of identity politics. As Herbert Blumer puts it, "To characterize another racial group is, by opposition, to define one's own."[8] The political and cultural mobilization of racially defined minorities has forced many of my white respondents to think about who they are racially in relation to other racial groups.

The racially charged and politically conservative environment of the late 1980s and 1990s has reinterpreted whiteness as a liability. The cultural mythology that has become today's commonsense understanding of race relations is a definition of society that is color blind. The ascendancy of color blindness as the dominant mode of race thinking and the emergence of liberal individualism as a source of white entitlement and racial backlash was a central finding in my work. It is, I believe, a view that is not specific to the student population at Urban University. Stanley Fish sums up how color blindness has been twisted politically to maintain white privilege. "When the goal was to make discrimination illegal," he argues, color blind meant lifting barriers to full citizenship, but the term now means blind to the effects of prejudice on people because of their color.[9]

The social movements that challenged the racial status quo unfolded over twenty-five years. The first "revolution" my respondents witnessed, however, was President Reagan's attack on civil rights legislation in the name of democracy and fair play. They grew up hearing that the United States was a color-blind nation, saw the rise of a black and Asian middle class, and were told stories about a federal government that "blocks opportunities for white workers."[10] Whites of this generation "have no knowledge of the disciplined, systematic, and collective *group* activity that has structured white identities in American society."[11]

RACIAL POLITICS: THE RIGHT AND WHITE VICTIMIZATION

The belief that whites were subject to racial discrimination (reverse discrimination) appeared as a dominant theme throughout my research. One example of this belief was the perception that a racial double standard exists on campus. In the majority of my interviews and focus groups, white students felt that race-based organizations at Urban University were a form of reverse discrimination. Twenty-nine of 119 campus organizations used race as their primary organizing principle. Mainly cultural and political, these groups encourage an affirmation of racial identity and provide a safe, supportive space for students of color to develop social and professional networks. The latent effect of these organizations, however, is that they transform and contribute to redefining the meaning of racial identity for whites on campus. When they are excluded, white students get a taste of what it is like to be reduced to a racial category. They are generally unnerved by this experience and quickly slip into reactionary, defensive posturing. The resentment, anger, and frustration white students express because they are excluded provide the foundation for a white identity based on the belief that whites are now under siege. Student groups like the Black Pre-Law Society or the Korean Cultural Club were sanctioned by the university, but, as was said many times in my interviews, if whites tried to establish an organization and it had "white" in the title a major controversy would ensue and the group and its members would be labeled racist. Nor could white respondents retreat into an Italian-American House or a Hibernians Club, because there was no basis for solidarity around an ethnic identity.

If a loss of ethnic identity has created a void among many of my respondents, and if identity politics has made whiteness a visible racial category, then the perception that being white is now a social liability has most certainly raised white consciousness. The social cost of whiteness arose whenever issues of affirmative action on and off campus were discussed. The majority of white students felt that contemporary affirmative action measures were unfair because issues of overt racism, discrimination, and equal opportunity had been addressed by their parents' generation in the 1960s. A majority of white students argued that the United States is a meritocracy where nonwhites have every advantage whites do (and in some cases more because of affirmative action). Most of my respondents want to believe the United States is an egalitarian, "color-blind" society because to think otherwise would raise the irritating issue of white privilege. The working- and middle-class young people I interviewed do not see themselves as privileged or benefiting from their skin color. It becomes difficult for working-class college students to think about white privilege when they are accumulating college debt, forced to live with their parents, working twenty-five hours a week on top of their studies, and are concerned that Starbucks or the Gap may be their future employer.

A fundamental transformation of how young whites define and understand themselves racially is taking place. The white students I interviewed believe that the American class system is fair and equitable: Anyone who delays gratification, works hard, and follows the rules will succeed regardless of color. Black television stars, the media's treatment of the black middle class, and stereotypes of Asians as model minorities have provided young whites with countless nonwhite success stories. For many of them, the "leveled playing field" argument has rendered affirmative action policies a form of reverse discrimination and a source of resentment. White students who believe social equality has been achieved are able to assert a racial identity and not regard themselves as racist—they are merely affirming their identity in ways similar to the language and actions of other racially defined groups. On the individual level, the racism most prevalent among the respondents was not the cultural stereotypes some white students used to counter charges of white privilege but the racist projections many made about how blacks perceive whites.

In large part, white identity is a reaction to the entry of historically marginalized racial and ethnic groups into the political arena and the ensuing struggle over social resources. But it is not only that. Whiteness as an explicit cultural product may be taking on a life of its own, developing its own racial logic and essence as it is molded by the political right. The rhetoric of neoconservatives serves to legitimate the benefits that accrue to whites based on skin color. Starting with the false premise of social equality and equal opportunity, neoconservatives can speak of America's Western roots and traditions in racial terms but not appear racist. This ostensibly nonracist "white" space that is being carved out of our cultural landscape allows whites to be presented like any other racial contender in the struggle over political and cultural resources and self-definition.

NOTES

1. Benjamin Demott, *The Trouble with Friendship: Why Americans Can't Think Straight About Race* (New York: Atlantic Monthly Press, 1995), p. 45.

2. "Police Officer Starts Group to Defend White Men," *New York Times,* November 19, 1995, § 1, at 36.

3. *New York Times,* February 23, 1995, at A23.

4. Quoted in Michael Banton, *Racial and Ethnic Competition* (London: Cambridge University Press, 1983), p. 64.

5. Bob Blauner, "Talking Past Each Other: Black and White Languages of Race," in *Race and Ethnic Conflict,* edited by Howard J. Ehrlich and Fred L. Pincus (Boulder, Colo.: Westview Press, 1994), p. 27.

6. Richard Alba suggests that these beliefs are the fundamental benchmark of what it means to be part of an ethnic group. See *Ethnic Identity: The Transformation of White America* (New Haven, Conn.: Yale University Press), p. 313.

7. David Roediger, *Towards the Abolition of Whiteness* (New York: Verso Press, 1994), p. 182.

8. Herbert Blumer, "Race Prejudice as a Sense of Group Position," 1:1 *Pac. Soc. Rev. 4.*

9. Stanley Fish, "How the Right Hijacked the Magic Words," *New York Times,* August 13, 1995, § 4, at 15.

10. Frederick R. Lynch, "Race Unconsciousness and the White Male," *29:2 Society 31.* Lynch is quoting the pollster Stanley Greenberg.

11. George Lipsitz, "The Possessive Investment in Whiteness: Racialized Social Democracy and the 'White' Problem in American Studies," *47:3 American Quarterly 369* (September 1995).

4

Talking Past Each Other

Black and White Languages of Race

BOB BLAUNER

For many African-Americans who came of age in the 1960s, the assassination of Martin Luther King, Jr. in 1968 was a defining moment in the development of their personal racial consciousness. For a slightly older group, the 1955 lynching of the fourteen-year-old Chicagoan Emmett Till in Mississippi had been a similar awakening. Now we have the protest and violence in Los Angeles and other cities in late April and early May of 1992, spurred by the jury acquittal of four policemen who beat motorist Rodney King.

The aftermath of the Rodney King verdict, unlike any other recent racial violence, will be seared into the memories of Americans of *all* colors, changing the way they see each other and their society. Spring 1992 marked the first time since the 1960s that incidents of racial injustice against an African-American—and by extension the black community—have seized the entire nation's imagination. Even highly publicized racial murders, such as those of African-American men in two New York City neighborhoods—Howard Beach (1986) and Bensonhurst (1989)—stirred the consciences of only a minority of whites. The response to the Rodney King verdict is thus a long-overdue reminder that whites still have the capacity to feel deeply about white racism—when they can see it in unambiguous terms.

The videotaped beating by four Los Angeles police officers provided this concreteness. To be sure, many whites focused their response on the subsequent black rioting, while the anger of blacks tended to remain fixed on the verdict itself. However, whites initially were almost as upset as blacks: An early poll reported that 86 percent of European-Americans disagreed with the jury's decision. The absence of any black from the jury and the trial's venue, Simi Valley, a lily-white suburban community, enabled mainstream whites to see the parallels with the Jim Crow justice of the old South. When we add to this mixture the widespread disaffection, especially of young people, with the nation's political and economic conditions, it is easier to explain the scale of white emotional involvement, unprecedented in a matter of racial protest since the 1960s.

In thirty years of teaching, I have never seen my students so overwrought, needing to talk, eager to do something. This response at the University of California at Berkeley cut across the usual fault lines of intergroup tension, as it did at high schools in Northern California. Assemblies, marches, and class discussions took place all over the nation in predominantly white as well as nonwhite and integrated high schools. Considering that there were also incidents where blacks assaulted white people, the scale of white involvement is even more impressive.

While many whites saw the precipitating events as expressions of racist conduct, they were much less likely than blacks to see them as part of some larger pattern of racism. Thus two separate polls found that only half as many whites as blacks believe that the legal system treats whites better than blacks. (In each poll, 43 percent of whites saw such a generalized double standard, in contrast to 84 percent of blacks in one survey, 89 percent in the other.)

This gap is not surprising. For twenty years European-Americans have tended to feel that systematic racial inequities marked an earlier era, not our own. Psychological denial and a kind of post-1960s exhaustion may both be factors in producing the sense among mainstream whites that civil rights laws and other changes resolved blacks' racial grievances, if not the economic basis of urban problems. But the gap in perceptions of racism also reflects a deeper difference. Whites and blacks see racial issues through different lenses and use different scales to weigh and assess injustice.

I am not saying that blacks and whites have totally disparate value systems and worldviews. I think we were more polarized in the late 1960s. It was then that I began a twenty-year interview study of racial consciousness published in 1989 as *Black Lives, White Lives.* By 1979 blacks and whites had come closer together on many issues than they had been in 1968. In the late 1970s and again in the mid-to-late 1980s, both groups were feeling quite pessimistic about the nation's direction. They agreed that America had become a more violent nation and that people were more individualistic and less bound by such traditional values as hard work, personal responsibility, and respect for age and authority. But with this and other convergences, there remained a striking gap in the way European-Americans and African-Americans evaluated *racial* change. Whites were impressed by the scale of integration, the size of the black middle class, and the extent of demonstrable progress. Blacks were disillusioned with integration, concerned about the people who had been left behind, and much more negative in their overall assessment of change.

In the 1990s this difference in general outlook led to different reactions to specific racial issues. That is what makes the shared revulsion over the Rodney King verdict a significant turning point, perhaps even an opportunity to begin bridging the gap between black and white definitions of the racial situation.

I want to advance the proposition that there are two languages of race in America. I am not talking about black English and standard English, which refer to different structures of grammar and dialect. "Language" here signifies a system of implicit understandings about social reality, and a racial language encompasses a worldview.

Blacks and whites differ on their interpretations of social change from the 1960s through the 1990s because their racial languages define the central terms, especially "racism," differently. Their racial languages incorporate different views of American society itself, especially the question of how central race and racism are to America's very existence, past and present. Blacks believe in this centrality, while most whites, except for the more race-conscious extremists, see race as a peripheral reality. Even successful, middle-class black professionals experience slights and humiliations—incidents when they are stopped by police, regarded suspiciously by clerks while shopping, or mistaken for messengers, drivers, or aides at work—that remind them they have not escaped racism's reach. For whites, race becomes central on exceptional occasions: collective public moments such as the recent events, when the veil is lifted, and private ones, such as a family's decision to escape urban problems with a move to the suburbs. But most of the time European-Americans are able to view racial issues as aberrations in American life, much as Los Angeles Police Chief Daryl Gates used the term "aberration" to explain his officers' beating of Rodney King in March 1991.

Because of these differences in language and worldview, blacks and whites often talk past one another, just as men and women sometimes do. I first noticed this in my classes, particularly during discussions of racism. Whites locate racism in color consciousness and its absence in color blindness. They regard it as a kind of racism when students of color insistently underscore their sense of difference, their affirmation of ethnic and racial membership, which minority students have increasingly asserted. Many black, and increasingly also Latino and Asian, students cannot understand this reaction. It seems to them misinformed, even ignorant. They in turn sense a kind of racism in the whites' assumption that minorities must assimilate to mainstream values and styles. Then African-Americans will posit an idea that many whites find preposterous: Black people, they argue, cannot be racist, because racism is a system of power, and black people as a group do not have power.

In this and many other arenas, a contest rages over the meaning of racism. Racism has become the central term in the language of race. From the 1940s through the 1980s new and multiple meanings of racism have been added to the social science lexicon and public discourse. The 1960s were especially critical for what the English sociologist Robert Miles has called the "inflation" of the term "racism." Blacks tended to embrace the enlarged definitions, whites to resist them. This conflict, in my view, has been at the very center of the racial struggle during the past decade.

THE WIDENING CONCEPTION OF RACISM

The term "racism" was not commonly used in social science or American public life until the 1960s. "Racism" does not appear, for example, in the Swedish economist Gunnar Myrdal's classic 1944 study of American race relations, *An American Dilemma.* But even when the term was not directly used, it is still possible to determine the prevailing understandings of racial oppression.

In the 1940s racism referred to an ideology, an explicit system of beliefs postulating the superiority of whites based on the inherent, biological inferiority of the colored races. Ideological racism was particularly associated with the belief systems of the Deep South and was originally devised as a rationale for slavery. Theories of white supremacy, particularly in their biological versions, lost much of their legitimacy after the Second World War due to their association with Nazism. In recent years cultural explanations of "inferiority" are heard more commonly than biological ones, which today are associated with extremist "hate groups" such as the Ku Klux Klan and the White Aryan Brotherhood.

By the 1950s and early 1960s, with ideological racism discredited, the focus shifted to a more discrete approach to racially invidious attitudes and behavior, expressed in the model of prejudice and discrimination. "Prejudice" referred (and still does) to hostile feelings and beliefs about racial minorities and the web of stereotypes justifying such negative attitudes. "Discrimination" referred to actions meant to harm the members of a racial minority group. The logic of this model was that racism implied a double standard, that is, treating a person of color differently—in mind or action—than one would a member of the majority group.

By the mid-1960s the terms "prejudice" and "discrimination" and the implicit model of racial causation implied by them were seen as too weak to explain the sweep of racial conflict and change, too limited in their analytical power, and for some critics too individualistic in their assumptions. Their original meanings tended to be absorbed by a new, more encompassing idea of racism. During the 1960s the referents of racial oppression moved from individual actions and beliefs to group and institutional processes, from subjective ideas to "objective" structures or results. Instead of intent, there was now an emphasis on process: those more objective social processes of exclusion, exploitation, and discrimination that led to a racially stratified society.

The most notable of these new definitions was "institutional racism." In their 1967 book *Black Power*, Stokely Carmichael and Charles Hamilton stressed how institutional racism was different and more fundamental than individual racism. Racism, in this view, was built into society and scarcely required prejudicial attitudes to maintain racial oppression.

This understanding of racism as pervasive and institutionalized spread from relatively narrow "movement" and academic circles to the larger public with the appearance in 1968 of the report of the commission on the urban riots appointed by President Lyndon Johnson and chaired by Illinois Governor Otto Kerner. The Kerner Commission identified "white racism" as a prime reality of American society and the major underlying cause of ghetto unrest. America, in this view, was moving toward two societies, one white and one black (it is not clear where other racial minorities fit in). Although its recommendations were never acted upon politically, the report legitimated the term "white racism" among politicians and opinion leaders as a key to analyzing racial inequality in America.

Another definition of racism, which I would call "racism atmosphere," also emerged in the 1960s and 1970s. This is the idea that an organization or an environment might be racist because its implicit, unconscious structures were devised for the use and comfort of white people, with the result that people of other races will not feel at home in such settings. Acting on this understanding of racism, many schools and universities, corporations, and other institutions have changed their teaching practices or work environments to encourage a greater diversity in their clientele, students, or work force.

Perhaps the most radical definition of all was the concept of "racism as result." In this sense, an institution or an occupation is racist simply because racial minorities are underrepresented in numbers or in positions of prestige and authority.

Seizing on different conceptions of racism, the blacks and whites I talked to in the late 1970s had come to different conclusions about how far America had moved toward racial justice. Whites tended to adhere to earlier, more limited notions of racism. Blacks for the most part saw the newer meanings as more basic. Thus African-Americans did not think racism had been put to rest by civil rights laws, even by the dramatic changes in the South. They felt that it still pervaded American life, indeed, had become more insidious because the subtle forms were harder to combat than old-fashioned exclusion and persecution.

Whites saw racism largely as a thing of the past. They defined it in terms of segregation and lynching, explicit white supremacist beliefs, or double standards in hiring, promotion, and admissions to colleges or other institutions. Except for affirmative action, which seemed the most blatant expression of such double standards, they were positively impressed by racial change. Many saw the relaxed and comfortable relations between whites and blacks as the heart of the matter. More crucial to blacks, on the other hand, were the underlying structures of power and position that continued to provide them with unequal portions of economic opportunity and other possibilities for the good life.

The newer, expanded definitions of racism just do not make much sense to most whites. I have experienced their frustrations directly when I try to explain the concept of institutional racism to white students and popular audiences. The idea of racism as an "impersonal force" loses all but the most theoretically inclined. Whites are more likely than blacks to view racism as a personal issue. Both sensitive to their own possible culpability (if only unconsciously) and angry at the use of the concept of racism by angry minorities, they do not differentiate well between the racism of social structures and the accusation that they as participants in that structure are personally racist.

The new meanings make sense to blacks, who live such experiences in their bones. But by 1979 many of the African-Americans in my study, particularly the older activists, were critical of the use of racism as a blanket explanation for all manifestations of racial inequality. Long before similar ideas were voiced by the black conservatives, many blacks sensed that too heavy an emphasis on racism led to the false conclusion that blacks could only progress through a conventional civil rights strategy of fighting prejudice and discrimination. (This strategy, while necessary, had proved very limited.) Overemphasizing racism, they feared, was interfering with the black community's ability to achieve greater self-determination through the politics of self-help. In addition, they told me that the prevailing rhetoric of the 1960s had affected many young blacks. Rather than taking responsibility for their own difficulties, they were now using racism as a "cop-out."

In public life today this analysis is seen as part of the conservative discourse on race. Yet I believe that this position originally was a progressive one, developed out of self-critical reflections on the relative failure of 1960s movements. But perhaps because it did not seem to be "politically correct," the left-liberal community, black as well as white, academic as well as political, has been afraid of embracing such a critique. As a result, the neoconservatives had a clear field to pick up this grass-roots sentiment and to use it to further their view that racism is no longer significant in American life. This is the last thing that my informants and other savvy African-Americans close to the pulse of their communities believe.

By the late 1970s the main usage of racism in the mind of the white public had undoubtedly become that of "reverse racism." The primacy of "reverse racism" as "the really important racism" suggests that the conservatives and the liberal-center have, in effect, won the battle over the meaning of racism.

Perhaps this was inevitable because of the long period of backlash against all the progressive movements of the 1960s. But part of the problem may have been the inflation of the idea of racism. While institutional racism exists, such a concept loses practical utility if every thing and every place is racist. In that case, there is effectively nothing to be done about it. And without conceptual tools to distinguish what is important from what is not, we are lost in the confusion of multiple meanings.

BACK TO BASICS

While public discourse was discounting white racism as exaggerated or a thing of the past, the more traditional forms of bigotry, harassment, and violence were unfortunately making a comeback. (This upsurge actually began in the early 1980s but was not well noticed, due to some combination of media inattention and national mood.) What was striking about the Bernhard Goetz subway shootings in New York, the white-on-black racial violence in Howard Beach, the rise of organized hate groups, campus racism, and skinhead violence is that these are all examples of old-fashioned racism. They illustrate the power and persistence of racial prejudices and hate crimes in the tradition of classical lynchings. They are precisely the kind of phenomena that many social analysts expected to diminish, as I did.

If there was one positive effect of this upsurge, it was to alert many whites to the destructive power of racial hatred and division in American life. At the same time, these events also repolarized racial attitudes in America. They have contributed to the anger and alienation of the black middle class and the rapid rise of Afrocentrism, particularly among college students.

As the gap in understanding has widened, several social scientists have proposed restricting the concept of racism to its original, more narrow meaning. However, the efforts of African-Americans to enlarge the meaning of racism is part of that group's project to make its view of the world and of American society competitive with the dominant white perspective. In addition, the "inflated" meanings of racism are already too rooted in common speech to be overturned by the advice of experts. And certainly some way is needed to convey the pervasive and systematic character of racial oppression. No other term does this as well as racism.

The question then becomes what to do about these multiple and confusing meanings of racism and their extraordinary personal and political charge. I would begin by honoring both the black and white readings of the term. Such an attitude might help facilitate the interracial dialogue so badly needed and yet so rare today.

Communication can only start from the understandings that people have. While the black understanding of racism is, in some sense, the deeper one, the white views of racism (ideology, double standard) refer to more specific and recognizable beliefs and practices. Since there is also a cross-racial consensus on the immorality of racist ideology and racial discrimination, it makes sense whenever possible to use such a concrete referent as discrimination, rather than the more global concept of racism. And reemphasizing discrimination may help remind the public that racial discrimination is not just a legacy of the past.

The intellectual power of the African-American understanding lies in its more critical and encompassing perspective. In the Rodney King events, we have an unparalleled opportunity to bridge the racial gap by pointing out that racism and racial division remain essential features of American life and that incidents such as police beatings of minority people and stacked juries are not aberrations but part of a larger pattern of racial abuse and harassment. Without resorting to the overheated rhetoric that proved counterproductive in the 1960s, it now may be possible to persuade white Americans that the most important patterns of discrimination and disadvantage are not to be found in the "reverse racism" of affirmative action but sadly still in the white racism of the dominant social system. And, when feasible, we need to try to bridge the gap by shifting from the language of race to that of ethnicity and class.

RACE OR ETHNICITY?

In the American consciousness the imagery of race—especially along the black-white dimension—tends to be more powerful than that of class or ethnicity. As a result, legitimate ethnic affiliations are often misunderstood to be racial and illegitimate.

Race itself is a confusing concept because of the variance between scientific and common sense definitions of the term. Physical anthropologists who study the distribution of those characteristics we use to classify "races" teach us that race is a fiction because all peoples are mixed to various degrees. Sociologists counter that this biological fiction unfortunately remains a sociological reality. People define one another racially, and thus divide society into racial groups. The "fiction" of race affects every aspect of peoples' lives, from living standards to landing in jail.

The consciousness of color differences, and the invidious distinctions based on them, have existed since antiquity and are not limited to any one corner of the world. And yet the peculiarly modern division of the world into a discrete number of hierarchically ranked races is a historic product of Western colonialism. In precolonial Africa the relevant group identities were national, tribal, or linguistic. There was no concept of an African or black people until this category was created by the combined effects of slavery, imperialism, and the anticolonial and Pan-African movements. The legal definitions of blackness and whiteness, which varied from one society to another in the Western hemisphere, were also crucial for the construction of modern-day races. Thus race is an essentially political construct, one that translates our tendency to see people in terms of their color or other physical attributes into structures that make it likely that people will act for or against them on such a basis.

The dynamic of ethnicity is different, even though the results at times may be similar. An ethnic group is a group that shares a belief in its common past. Members of an ethnic group hold a set of common memories that make them feel that their customs, culture, and outlook are distinctive. In short, they have a sense of peoplehood. Sharing critical experiences and sometimes a belief in their common fate, they feel an affinity for one another, a "comfort zone" that leads to congregating together, even when this is not forced by exclusionary barriers. Thus if race is associated with biology and nature, ethnicity is associated with culture. Like races, ethnic groups arise historically, transform themselves, and sometimes die out.

Much of the popular discourse about race in America today goes awry because ethnic realities get lost under the racial umbrella. The positive meanings and potential of ethnicity are overlooked, even overrun, by the more inflammatory meanings of race. Thus white students, disturbed when blacks associate with each other, justify their objections through their commitment to *racial* integration. They do not appreciate the ethnic affinities that bring this about or see the parallels to Jewish students meeting at the campus Hillel Foundation or Italian-Americans eating lunch at the Italian house on the Berkeley campus.

When blacks are "being ethnic," whites see them as being "racial." Thus they view the identity politics of students who want to celebrate their blackness, their *chicano-ismo,* their Asian heritages, and their American Indian roots as racially offensive. Part of this reaction comes from a sincere desire, almost a yearning, of white students for a color-blind society. But because the ethnicity of darker people so often gets lost in our overracialized perceptions, the white students misread the situation. When I point out to my class that whites are talking about race and its dynamics and the students of color are talking about ethnicity and its differing meaning, they can begin to appreciate each other's agendas.

Confounding race and ethnicity is not just limited to the young. The general public, including journalists and other opinion makers, does this regularly, with serious consequences for the clarity of public dialogue and sociological analysis. A clear example comes from the Chicago mayoral election of 1983. The establishment press, including leading liberal columnists, regularly chastised the black electorate for giving virtually all its votes to Harold Washington. Such racial voting was as "racist" as whites voting for the other candidate because they did not want a black mayor. Yet African-Americans were voting for ethnic representation just as Irish-Americans, Jews, and Italians have always done. Such ethnic politics is considered the American way. What is discriminatory is the double standard that does not confer the same rights on blacks, who were not voting primarily out of fear or hatred as were many whites.

Such confusions between race and ethnicity are exacerbated by the ambiguous sociological status of African-Americans. Black Americans are *both* a race and an ethnic group. Unfortunately, part of our heritage of racism has been to deny the ethnicity, the cultural heritage of black Americans. Liberal-minded whites have wanted to see blacks as essentially white people with black skins. Until the 1960s few believed that black culture was a real ethnic culture.

Because our racial language is so deep-seated, the terminology of black and white just seems more "natural" and commonsensical than more ethnic labels like African-American or European-American. But the shift to the term African-American has been a conscious attempt to move the discourse from a language of race to a language of ethnicity. "African-American," as Jesse Jackson and others have pointed out, connects the group to its history and culture in a way that the racial designation, black, does not. The new usage parallels terms for other ethnic groups. Many whites tend to dismiss this concern about language as mere sloganeering. But "African-American" fits better into the emerging multicultural view of American ethnic and racial arrangements, one more appropriate to our growing diversity. The old race relations model was essentially a view that generalized (often inappropriately) from black-white relations. It can no longer capture—if it ever could—the complexity of a multiracial and multicultural society.

The issue is further complicated by the fact that African-Americans are not a homogeneous group. They comprise a variety of distinct ethnicities. There are the West Indians with their long histories in the U.S., the darker Puerto Ricans (some of whom identify themselves as black), the more recently arrived Dominicans, Haitians, and immigrants from various African countries, as well as the native-born African-Americans, among whom regional distinctions can also take on a quasi-ethnic flavor.

Blacks from the Caribbean are especially likely to identify with their homeland rather than taking on a generic black or even African-American identity. While they may resist the dynamic of "racialization" and even feel superior to native blacks, the dynamic is relentless. Their children are likely to see themselves as part of the larger African-American population. And yet many native-born Americans of African dissent also resist the term "African-American," feeling very little connection to the original homeland. Given the diversity in origin and outlook of America's largest minority, it is inevitable that no single concept can capture its full complexity or satisfy all who fall within its bounds.

For white Americans, race does not overwhelm ethnicity. Whites see the ethnicity of other whites; it is their own whiteness they tend to overlook. But even when race is recognized, it is not conflated with ethnicity. Jews, for example, clearly distinguish their Jewishness from their whiteness. Yet the long-term dynamic still favors the development of a dominant white racial identity. Except for recent immigrants, the various European ethnic identities have been rapidly weakening. Vital ethnic communities persist in some cities, particularly on the East Coast. But many whites, especially the young, have such diverse ethnic heritages that they have no meaningful ethnic affiliation. In my classes only the Jews among European-Americans retain a strong sense of communal origin.

Instead of dampening the ethnic enthusiasms of the racial minorities, perhaps it would be better to encourage the revitalization of whites' European heritages. But a problem with this approach is that the relationship between race and ethnicity is more ambiguous for whites than for people of color. Although for many white groups ethnicity has been a stigma, it also has been used to gain advantages that have marginalized blacks and other racial minorities. Particularly for working-class whites today, ethnic community loyalties are often the prism through which they view their whiteness, their superiority.

Thus the line between ethnocentrism and racism is a thin one, easily crossed—as it was by Irish-Americans who resisted the integration of South Boston's schools in the 1970s and by many of the Jews and Italians that sociologist Jonathan Rieder describes in his 1985 book *Canarsie.*

White students today complain of a double standard. Many feel that their college administrations sanction organization and identification for people of color, but not for them. If there can be an Asian business organization and a black student union, why can't there be a white business club or a white student alliance? I'd like to explain to them that students of color are organized ethnically, not racially, that whites have Hillel and the Italian theme house. But this makes little practical sense when such loyalties are just not that salient for the vast majority.

Out of this vacuum the emerging identity of "European-American" has come into vogue. I interpret the European-American idea as part of a yearning for a usable past. Europe is associated with history and culture. "America" and "American" can no longer be used to connote white people. "White" itself is a racial term and thereby inevitably associated with our nation's legacy of social injustice.

At various California colleges and high schools, European-American clubs have begun to form, provoking debate about whether it is inherently racist for whites to organize as whites—or as European-Americans. Opponents invoke the racial analogy and see such organizations as akin to exclusive white supremacist groups. Their defenders argue from an ethnic model, saying that they are simply looking for a place where they can feel at home and discuss their distinctive personal and career problems. The jury is still out on this new and, I suspect, burgeoning phenomenon. It will take time to discover its actual social impact.

If the European-Americans forming their clubs are truly organizing on an ethnic or panethnic rather than a racial model, I would have to support these efforts. Despite all the ambiguities, it seems to me a gain in social awareness when a specific group comes to be seen in ethnic rather than racial terms. During the period of the mass immigration of the late nineteenth century and continuing through the 1920s, Jews, Italians, and other white ethnics were viewed racially. We no longer hear of the "Hebrew race," and it is rare for Jewish distinctiveness to be attributed to biological rather than cultural roots. Of course, the shift from racial to ethnic thinking did not put an end to anti-Semitism in the United States—or to genocide in Germany, where racial imagery was obviously intensified.

It is unrealistic to expect that the racial groupings of American society can be totally "deconstructed," as a number of scholars are now advocating. After all, African-Americans and native Americans, who were not immigrants, can never be exactly like other ethnic groups. Yet a shift in this direction would begin to move our society from a divisive biracialism to a more inclusive multiculturalism.

To return to the events of spring 1992, I ask what was different about these civil disturbances. Considering the malign neglect of twelve Reagan-Bush years, the almost two decades of economic stagnation, and the retreat of the public from issues of race and poverty, the violent intensity should hardly be astonishing.

More striking was the multiracial character of the response. In the San Francisco Bay area, rioters were as likely to be white as nonwhite. In Los Angeles, Latinos were prominent among both the protesters and the victims. South Central Los Angeles is now more Hispanic than black, and this group suffered perhaps 60 percent of the property damage. The media have focused on the specific grievances of African-Americans toward Koreans. But I would guess that those who trashed Korean stores were protesting something larger than even the murder of a fifteen-year-old black girl. Koreans, along with other immigrants, continue to enter the country and in a relatively short time surpass the economic and social position of the black poor. The immigrant advantage is real and deeply resented by African-Americans, who see that the two most downtrodden minorities are those that did not enter the country voluntarily.

During the 1960s the police were able to contain riots within the African-American community. This time Los Angeles police were unable to do so. Even though the South Central district suffered most, there was also much destruction in other areas including Hollywood, downtown, and the San Fernando Valley. In the San Francisco Bay area the violence occurred primarily in the white business sections, not the black neighborhoods of Oakland, San Francisco, or Berkeley. The violence that has spilled out of the inner city is a distillation of all the human misery that a white middle-class society has been trying to contain—albeit unsuccessfully (consider the homeless). As in the case of an untreated infection, the toxic substances finally break out, threatening to contaminate the entire organism.

Will this widened conflict finally lead Americans toward a recognition of our common stake in the health of the inner cities and their citizens, or toward increased fear and division? The Emmett Till lynching in 1955 set the stage for the first mass mobilization of the civil rights movement, the Montgomery bus boycott later that year. Martin Luther King's assassination provided the impetus for the institution of affirmative action and other social programs. The Rodney King verdict and its aftermath must also become not just a psychologically defining moment but an impetus to a new mobilization of political resolve.

5

Theoretical Perspectives in Race and Ethnic Relations

JOE R. FEAGIN AND
CLAIRECE BOOHER FEAGIN

In the United States, explanatory theories of racial and ethnic relations have been concerned with migration, adaptation, exploitation, stratification, and conflict. Most such theories can be roughly classified as either *order* theories or *power-conflict* theories, depending on their principal concerns. *Order theories* tend to accent patterns of inclusion, of the orderly integration and assimilation of particular racial and ethnic groups to a core culture and society, as in the third and fourth of the outcomes just described. The central focus is on progressive adaptation to the dominant culture and on stability in intergroup relations. *Power-conflict* theories give more attention to the first and fifth outcomes—to genocide and continuing hierarchy—and to the persisting inequality of the power and resource distribution associated with racial or ethnic subordination. In the United States most assimilation theories are examples of order theories. Internal colonialism theories and class-oriented neo-Marxist viewpoints are examples of power-conflict theories. There is considerable variation within these broad categories, but they do provide a starting point for our analysis.

ASSIMILATION AND OTHER ORDER PERSPECTIVES

In the United States much social theorizing has emphasized assimilation, the more or less orderly adaptation of a migrating group to the ways and institutions of an established group. Hirschman has noted that "the assimilation perspective, broadly defined, continues to be the primary theoretical framework for sociological research on racial and ethnic inequality." The reason for this dominance, he suggests, is the "lack of convincing alternatives.[1] The English word *assimilate* comes from the Latin *assimulare*, to make similar."

Robert E. Park

Robert E. Park, a major sociological theorist, argued that European out-migration was a major catalyst for societal reorganization around the globe. In his view intergroup contacts regularly go through stages of a *race relations cycle.* Fundamental social forces such as out-migration lead to recurring cycles in intergroup history: "The race relations cycle which takes the form, to state it abstractly, of *contacts, competition, accommodation* and eventual *assimilation,* is apparently progressive and irreversible."[2] In the contact stage migration and exploration bring people together, which in turn leads to economic competition and thus to new social organization. Competition and conflict flow from the contacts between host peoples and the migrating groups. Accommodation, an unstable condition in the race relations cycle, often takes place rapidly. It involves a forced adjustment by a migrating group to a new social situation. . . . Nonetheless, Park and most scholars working in this tradition have argued that there is a long-term trend toward assimilation of racial and ethnic minorities in modern societies. "Assimilation is a process of interpenetration and fusion in which persons and groups acquire the memories, sentiments, and attitudes of other persons or groups, and, by sharing their experience and history, are incorporated with them in a common cultural life."[3] Even racially subordinate groups are expected to assimilate.[4]

Stages of Assimilation: Milton Gordon

Since Park's pioneering analysis in the 1920s, many U.S. theorists of racial and ethnic relations and numerous textbook writers have adopted an assimilationist perspective, although most have departed from Park's framework in a number of important ways. Milton Gordon, author of the influential *Assimilation in American Life,* distinguishes a variety of initial encounters between race and ethnic groups and an array of possible assimilation outcomes. While Gordon presents three competing images of assimilation—the melting pot, cultural pluralism, and Anglo-conformity—he focuses on Anglo-conformity as the descriptive reality. That is, immigrant groups in the United States, in Gordon's view, have typically tended to give up much of their heritage for the dominant, preexisting Anglo-Saxon core culture and society. The touchstone of adjustment is viewed thus: "If there is anything in American life which can be described as an overall American culture which serves as a reference point for immigrants and their children, it can best be described, it seems to us, as the middle-class cultural patterns of, largely, white Protestant, Anglo-Saxon origins, leaving aside for the moment the question of minor reciprocal influences on this culture exercised by the cultures of later entry into the United States."[5]

Gordon notes that Anglo-conformity has been substantially achieved for most immigrant groups in the United States, especially in regard to cultural assimilation. Most groups following the English have adapted to the Anglo core culture. Gordon distinguishes seven dimensions of adaptation:

1. *cultural assimilation:* change of cultural patterns to those of the core society;

2. *structural assimilation:* penetration of cliques and associations of the core society at the primary-group level;
3. *marital assimilation:* significant intermarriage;
4. *identification assimilation:* development of a sense of identity linked to the core society;
5. *attitude-receptional assimilation:* absence of prejudice and stereotyping;
6. *behavior-receptional assimilation:* absence of intentional discrimination;
7. *civic assimilation:* absence of value and power conflict.[6]

Whereas Park believed structural assimilation, including primary-group ties such as intergroup friendships, flowed from cultural assimilation, Gordon stresses that these are separate stages of assimilation and may take place at different rates.

Gordon conceptualizes structural assimilation as relating to primary-group cliques and relations. Significantly, he does not highlight as a separate type of structural assimilation the movement of a new immigrant group into the *secondary groups* of the host society—that is, into the employing organizations, such as corporations or public bureaucracies, and the critical educational and political institutions. The omission of secondary-structural assimilation is a major flaw in Gordon's theory. Looking at U.S. history, one would conclude that assimilating into the core society's secondary groups does *not necessarily* mean entering the dominant group's friendship cliques. In addition, the dimension Gordon calls *civic assimilation* is confusing since he includes in it "values," which are really part of cultural assimilation, and "power," which is a central aspect of structural assimilation at the secondary-group level.

Gordon's assimilation theory has influenced a generation of researchers. . . . In a recent examination of Gordon's seven dimensions of assimilation, J. Allen Williams and Suzanne Ortega drew on interviews with a midwestern sample to substantiate that cultural assimilation was not necessarily the first type of assimilation to occur. For example, the Mexican Americans in the sample were found to be less culturally assimilated than African Americans, yet were more assimilated structurally. Those of Swiss and Swedish backgrounds ranked about the same on the study's measure of cultural assimilation, but the Swedish Americans were less assimilated structurally. Williams and Ortega conclude that assimilation varies considerably from one group to another and that Gordon's seven types can be grouped into three more general categories of structural, cultural, and receptional assimilation.[7]

In a later book, *Human Nature, Class, and Ethnicity* (1978), Gordon has recognized that his assimilation theory neglects power issues and proposed bringing these into his model, but so far he has provided only a brief and inadequate analysis. Gordon mentions in passing the different resources available to competing racial groups and refers briefly to black-white conflict, but gives little attention to the impact of economic power, inequalities in material resources, or capitalistic economic history on U.S. racial and ethnic relations.[8]

Focused on the millions of white European immigrants and their adjustments, Gordon's model emphasizes *generational* changes within immigrant groups over time. Substantial acculturation to the Anglo-Protestant core culture has often been completed by the second or third generation for many European immigrant groups. The partially acculturated first generation formed protective communities and associations, but the children of those immigrants were considerably more exposed to Anglo-conformity pressures in the mass media and in schools.[9] Gordon also suggests that substantial assimilation along certain other dimensions, such as the civic, behavior-receptional, and attitude-receptional ones, has occurred for numerous European groups. Most white groups have also made considerable progress toward equality at the secondary-structural levels of employment and politics, although the dimensions of this assimilation are neither named nor discussed in any detail by Gordon.

For many white groups, particularly non-Protestant ones, structural assimilation at the primary-group level is underway, yet far from complete. Gordon suggests that substantially complete cultural assimilation (for example, adoption of the English language) along with structural (primary-group) pluralism form a characteristic pattern of adaptation for many white ethnic groups. Even these relatively acculturated groups tend to limit their informal friendships and marriage ties either to their immediate ethnic groups or to *similar* groups that are part of their general religious community. Following Will Herberg, who argued that there are three great community "melting pots" in the United States—Jews, Protestants, and Catholics—Gordon suggests that primary-group ties beyond one's own group are often developed with one's broad socioreligious community, whether that be Protestant, Catholic, or Jewish.[10]

In his influential books and articles Gordon recognizes that structural assimilation has been retarded by racial prejudice and discrimination, but he seems to suggest that non-European Americans, including African Americans, will eventually be absorbed into the core culture and society. He gives the most attention to the gradual assimilation of middle-class non-Europeans. In regard to blacks he argues, optimistically, that the United States has "moved decisively down the road toward implementing the implications of the American credo of [equality and justice] for race relations"—as in employment and housing. This perceived tremendous progress for black Americans has created a policy dilemma for the government: should it adopt a traditional political liberalism that ignores race, or a "corporate liberalism" that recognizes group rights along racial lines? Gordon includes under corporate liberalism government programs of affirmative action, which he rejects.[11]...

Some assimilation-oriented analysts such as Gordon and Alba have argued that the once prominent ethnic identities, especially of European American groups, are fading over time. Alba suggests that there is still an ethnic identity of consequence for non-Latino whites, but declares that "a new ethnic group is forming—one based on a vague *ancestry* from anywhere on the European continent.[12] In other words, such distinct ethnic identities as English American and Irish American are gradually becoming only a vague identification as "European American," although Alba emphasizes this as a trend, not a fact. Interestingly, research on intermarriages between members of different white ethnic groups has revealed that large proportions of the children of such marriages see themselves as having multiple ethnic identities, while others choose one of their heritages, or simply "American," as their ethnic identity.[13]

Ethnogenesis and Ethnic Pluralism

Some theorists working in the assimilation tradition reject the argument that most European American groups have become substantially assimilated to a generic Anglo-Protestant or Euro-American identity and way of life. A few have explored models of adjustment that depart from Anglo-conformity in the direction of ethnic or cultural pluralism. Most analysts of pluralism accept some Anglo-conformity as inevitable, if not desirable. In *Beyond the Melting Pot,* Glazer and Moynihan agree that the original customs and home-country ways of European immigrants were mostly lost by the third generation. But this did not mean the decline of ethnicity. The European immigrant groups usually remained distinct in terms of name, identity, and, for the most part, primary-group ties.[14]

Andrew Greeley has developed the interesting concept of *ethnogenesis* and applied it to white immigrant groups, those set off by nationality and religion. Greeley is critical of the traditional assimilation perspective because it assumes "that the strain toward homogenization in a modern industrial society is so great as to be virtually irresistible."[15] Traditionally, the direction of this assimilation in the United States is assumed to be toward the Anglo-Protestant core culture. But from the ethnogenesis perspective, adaptation has meant more than this one-way conformity. The traditional assimilation model does not explain the persistence of ethnicity in the United States—the emphasis among immigrants on ethnicity as a way of becoming American and, in recent decades, the self-conscious attempts to create ethnic identity and manipulate ethnic symbols.[16]

. . . Greeley suggests that in many cases host and immigrant groups had a somewhat similar *cultural* inheritance. For example, some later European immigrant groups had a cultural background initially similar to that of earlier English settlers. As a result of interaction in schools and the influence of the media over several generations the number of cultural traits common to the host and immigrant groups often grew. Yet late in the adaptive process certain aspects of the heritage of the home country remained very important to the character of the immigrant-ethnic group. From this perspective, ethnic groups share traits with the host group *and* retain major nationality characteristics as well. A modern ethnic group is one part home-country heritage and one part common culture, mixed together in a distinctive way because of a unique history of development within the North American crucible.[17]

A number of research studies have documented the persistence of distinctive white ethnic groups such as Italian Americans and Jewish Americans in U.S. cities, not just in New York and Chicago but in San Francisco, New Orleans, and Tucson as well. Yancey and his associates have suggested that ethnicity is an "emergent phenomenon"—that its importance varies in cities and that its character and strength depend on the specific historical conditions in which it emerges and grows.[18]

Some Problems with Assimilation Theories

Most assimilation theorists take as their examples of ethnic adaptation white European groups migrating more or less voluntarily to the United States. But what of the adaptation and assimilation of non-European groups beyond the stage of initial contact? Some analysts of assimilation include nonwhite groups in their theories, despite the problems that arise from such an inclusion. Some analysts have argued that assimilation, cultural and structural, is the necessary, if long-term, answer to the racial problem in the United States. . . .

More optimistic analysts have emphasized progressive inclusion, which will eventually provide black Americans and other minority groups with full citizenship, in fact as well as principle. For that reason, they expect ethnic and racial conflict to disappear as various groups become fully assimilated into the core culture and society. Nathan Glazer, Milton Gordon, and Talcott Parsons have stressed the egalitarianism of U.S. institutions and what they view as the progressive emancipation of non-European groups. Gordon and others have underscored the gradual assimilation of middle-class black Americans over the last several decades. Full membership for black Americans seems inevitable, notes Parsons, for "the only tolerable solution to the enormous [racial] tensions lies in constituting a single societal community with full membership for all."[19] The importance of racial, as well as ethnic, stratification is expected to decline as powerful, universalistic societal forces wipe out the vestiges of earlier ethnocentric value systems. White immigrants have desired substantial assimilation, and most have been absorbed. The same is expected to happen eventually for non-European groups.

Assimilation theories have been criticized as having an "establishment" bias, as not distinguishing carefully enough between what *has* happened to a given group and what the establishment at some point felt *should have* happened. For example, a number of Asian American scholars and leaders have reacted vigorously to the application of the concept of assimilation to Asian Americans, arguing that the very concept originated in a period (1870–1925) of intense attacks by white Americans on Asian Americans. The term was thus tainted from the beginning by its association with the dominant European American group's ideology that the only "good groups" were those that assimilated (or could assimilate) in Anglo-conformity fashion.

Unlike Park, who paid substantial attention to the historical and world-economy context of migration, many of today's assimilation theorists do not analyze sufficiently the historical background and development of a particular racial or ethnic group within a national or world context. In addition, assimilation analysts such as Gordon tend to neglect the power imbalance and inequality in racial and ethnic relations, which are seen most clearly in the cases of non-European Americans. As Geschwender has noted, "they seem to have forgotten that exploitation is the driving force that gives meaning to the study of racial and ethnic relations."[20]

Biosocial Perspectives

Some U.S. theorists, including assimilationists, now accent a biosocial perspective on racial and ethnic relations. The idea of race and ethnicity being deeply rooted in the biological makeup of human beings is an old European and American notion that has received renewed attention from a few social scientists and biologists in the United States since the 1970s. In *Human Nature, Class, and Ethnicity,* for example, Gordon suggests that ethnic ties are rooted in the "biological organism of man." Ethnicity is a fundamental part of the physiological as well as the psychological self. Ethnicity "cannot be shed by social mobility, as for instance social class background can, since society insists on its inalienable ascription from cradle to grave." What Gordon seems to have in mind is not the old racist notion of the unchanging biological character and separateness of racial groups, but rather the rootedness of intergroup relations, including racial and ethnic relations, in the everyday realities of kinship and other socially constructed group boundaries. Gordon goes further, however, emphasizing that human beings tend to be "selfish, narcissistic and perpetually poised on the edge of aggression." And it is these selfish tendencies that lie behind racial and ethnic tensions.[21] Gordon is here adopting a Hobbesian (dog-eat-dog) view of human nature. . . .

Although decidedly different from the earlier biological theories, the modern biosocial analysis remains problematical. The exact linkages between the deep genetic underpinnings of human nature and concrete racial or ethnic behavior are not spelled out beyond some vague analysis of kin selection and selfish behavior. . . .

Another difficulty with the biosocial approach is that in the everyday world, racial and ethnic relations are *immediately social* rather than biological. As Edna Bonacich has pointed out, many racial and ethnic groups have mixed biological ancestry. Jewish Americans, for example, have a very mixed ancestry: as a group, they share no distinct biological characteristics. Biologically diverse Italian immigrants from different regions of Italy gained a sense of being Italian American (even Italian) in the United States. The bonds holding Jewish Americans together and Italian Americans together were not genetically based or biologically primordial, but rather the result of real *historical* experiences as these groups settled into the Untied States. Moreover, if ethnicity is primordial in a biological sense, it should always be a prominent force in human affairs. Sometimes ethnicity leads to recurring conflict, as in the case of Jews and Gentiles in the United States; in other cases, as with Scottish and English Americans, it quietly disappears in the assimilation process. Sentiments based on common ancestry are important, but they are activated primarily in the concrete experiences and histories of specific migrating and host groups.[22]

Emphasizing Migration: Competition Theory

. . . The *human ecology* tradition in sociological thought draws on the ideas of Park and other ecologists and emphasizes the "struggle of human groups for survival" within their physical environments. This tradition, which highlights demographic trends such as the migration of groups and population concentration in cities, has been adopted by competition analysts researching racial and ethnic groups.[23]

Competition theorists such as Susan Olzak and Joane Nagel view ethnicity as a social phenomenon distinguished by boundaries of language, skin color, and culture. They consider the tradition of human ecology valuable because it emphasizes the stability of ethnic population boundaries over time, as well as the impact of shifts in these boundaries resulting from migration; ethnic group membership often coincides with the creation of a distinctive group niche in the labor force. Competition occurs when two or more ethnic groups attempt to secure the same resources, such as jobs or housing. Competition theorists have accented the ways in which ethnic group competition and the accompanying ethnic solidarity lead to collective action, mobilization, and protest.[24]

According to competition theorists, collective action is fostered by immigration across borders and by the expansion of once-segregated minorities into the same labor and housing markets to which other ethnic groups have access. A central argument of these theorists is that collective attacks on a subordinate ethnic group—immigrant and black workers, for instance—increase at the local city level when the group moves up and out of segregated jobs and challenges other groups and not, as one might expect, in cities where ethnic groups are locked into residential segregation and poverty. . . .

Competition theorists explicitly contrast their analyses with the power-conflict views we will discuss in the next section, perspectives that emphasize the role of capitalism, economic subordination, and institutionalized discrimination. Competition theorists write about urban ethnic worlds as though institutionalized racism and capitalism-generated exploitation of workers are not major forces in recurring ethnic and racial competition in cities. As we have seen, they emphasize migration and population concentration, as well as other demographic factors. . . .

POWER-CONFLICT THEORIES

The last few decades have witnessed the development of power-conflict frameworks explaining U.S. racial and ethnic relations, perspectives that place much greater emphasis on economic stratification and power issues than one finds in assimilation and competition theories. Within this broad category of power-conflict theories are a number of subcategories, including the internal colonialism viewpoint, and a variety of class-based and neo-Marxist theories. . . .

Internal Colonialism

Analysts of internal colonialism prefer to see the racial stratification and the class stratification of U.S. capitalism as *separate but related* systems of oppression. Neither should be reduced in social science theories to the other. An emphasis on power and resource inequalities, particularly white-minority inequalities, is at the heart of the internal colonialism model.

The framework of internal colonialism is built in part upon the work of analysts of *external colonialism*—the worldwide imperialism of certain capitalist nations, including the United States and European nations.[25] For example, Balandier has noted that capitalist expansion has affected non-European peoples since the fifteenth century: "Until very recently the greater part of the world population, not belonging to the white race (if we exclude China and Japan), knew only a status of dependency on one or another of the European colonial powers."[26] External colonialism involves the running of a country's economy and politics by an outside colonial power. Many colonies eventually became independent of their colonizers, such as Britain or France, but continued to have their economies directed by the capitalists and corporations of the colonial powers. This system of continuing dependency has been called *neocolonialism*. Neocolonialism is common today where there are few white settlers in the colonized country. Colonies experiencing a large in-migration of white settlers often show a different pattern. In such cases external colonialism becomes *internal colonialism* when the control and exploitation of non-Euopean groups in the colonized country passes from whites in the home country to white immigrant groups within the newly independent country.[27]

Non-European groups entering later, such as African slaves and Mexican farm workers in the United States, can also be viewed in terms of internal colonialism. Internal colonialism here emerged out of classical European colonialism and imperialism and took on a life of its own. The origin and initial stabilization of internal colonialism in North America predate the Revolutionary War. The systematic subordination of non-Europeans began with "genocidal attempts by colonizing settlers to uproot native populations and force them into other regions."[28] Native Americans were killed or driven off desirable lands. Slaves from Africa were a cheap source of labor for capital accumulation before and after the Revolution. Later, Asians and Pacific peoples were imported as contract workers or annexed in an expansionist period of U.S. development. Robert Blauner, a colonialism theorist, notes that agriculture in the South depended on black labor; in the Southwest, Mexican agricultural development was forcibly taken over by European settlers, and later agricultural development was based substantially on cheap Mexican labor coming into what was once northern Mexico.[29]

In exploiting the labor of non-European peoples, who were made slaves or were paid low wages, white agricultural and industrial capitalists reaped enormous profits. From the internal colonialism perspective, contemporary racial and ethnic inequality is grounded in the economic *interests* of whites in low-wage labor—the underpinning of capitalistic economic exploitation. Non-European groups were subordinated to European American desires for *labor* and *land*. Internal colonialism theorists have recognized the central role of *government* support of the exploitation of minorities. The colonial and U.S. governments played an important role in legitimating slavery in the sixteenth through the nineteenth centuries and in providing the government soldiers who subordinated Native Americans across the nation and Mexicans in the Southwest.

Most internal colonialism theorists are not concerned primarily with white immigrant groups, many of which entered the United States after non-European groups were subordinated. Instead, they wish to analyze the establishment of racial stratification and the control processes that maintain persisting white dominance and ideological racism. Stokely Carmichael and Charles Hamilton, who in their writings in the 1960s were among the first to use the term *internal colonialism,* accented institutional racism—discrimination by the white community against blacks as a group.[30] From this perspective African Americans are still a "colony" in the United States in regard to education, economics, and politics. . . .

A Neo-Marxist Emphasis on Class

Analysts of racial and ethnic relations have combined an internal colonialism perspective with an emphasis on class stratification that draws on the Marxist research pioneered by [black sociologists W.E.B.] Du Bois and [Oliver] Cox. Mario Barrera, for example, has suggested that the heart of current internal colonialism is an interactive structure of class *and* race stratification that divides our society. Class, in the economic-exploitation sense of that term, needs to be central to a colonialism perspective. Basic to the U.S. system of internal colonialism are four classes that have developed in U.S. capitalism:

1. *capitalists:* that small group of people who control capital investments and the means of production and who buy the labor of many others;
2. *managers:* that modest-sized group of people who work as administrators for the capitalists and have been granted control over the work of others;
3. *petit bourgeoisie:* that small group of merchants who control their own businesses and do most of their work themselves, buying little labor power from others;
4. *working class:* that huge group of blue-collar and white-collar workers who sell their labor to employers in return for wages and salaries.

The dominant class in the U.S. political-economic system is the capitalist class, which in the workplace subordinates working people, both nonwhite and white, to its profit and investment needs. And it is the capitalists who decide whether and where to create jobs. They are responsible for the flight of capital and jobs from many central cities to the suburbs and overseas.

Barrera argues that each of these classes contains important segments that are set off in terms of race and ethnicity. Figure 5.1 suggests how this works. Each of the major classes is crosscut by a line of racial segmentation that separates those suffering institutionalized discrimination, such as black Americans and Mexican Americans, from those who do not. Take the example of the working class. Although black, Latino, and other minority workers share a similar *class* position with white workers, in that they are struggling against capitalist employers for better wages and working conditions, they are *also* in a subordinate position because of structural discrimination along racial lines within that working class. Barrera notes that the dimensions of this discrimination often include lower wages for many minority workers, as well as their concentration in lower-status occupations. Many Americans suffer from both class exploitation (as wage workers) and racial exploitation (as workers of color).

Ideology and Oppositional Culture

Internal colonialism theorists have studied the role of cultural stereotyping and ideology in limiting the opportunities of subordinate groups of color. A racist ideology dominates an internal colonialist society, intellectually dehumanizing the colonized. Stereotyping and prejudice, seen in many traditional assimilation theories as more or less temporary problems, are viewed by colonialism analysts as a way of rationalizing exploitation over a very long period, if not permanently. Discrimination is a question not of individual bigots but rather of a system of racial exploitation rationalized by prejudice.[31]

In his book on the English colonization of Ireland, Michael Hechter has developed a theory of internal colonialism that emphasizes how the subordinate group utilizes its own culture to *resist* subordination. Hechter argues that in a system of internal colonialism, cultural as well as racial markers are used to set off subordi-

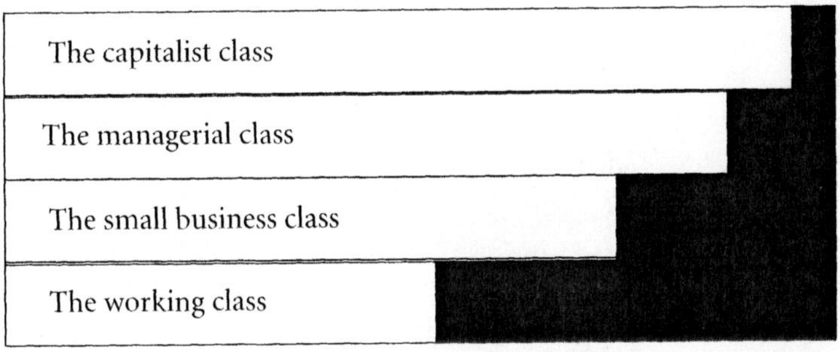

FIGURE 5.1 The Class and Race Structure of Internal Colonialism
Note: Shaded area represents nonwhite segment.

nate groups such as African Americans in the United States and the Irish in the United Kingdom. Resistance to the dominant group by the subordinate group often takes the form of cultural solidarity in opposition to the dominant culture. This solidarity can become the basis for protest movements by the subordinated group.[32]

Beginning in the 1960s, a number of power-conflict scholars and activists have further developed this idea of *oppositional culture* as a basis for understanding the resistance of non-European groups to the Euro-American core culture. Bonnie Mitchell and Joe Feagin have built on the idea of oppositional culture suggested in the work of Hechter and Blauner.[33] They note that in the centuries of contact before the creation of the Untied States, Mexico, and Canada, North America was populated by a diverse mixture of European, African, and Native American cultures. The U.S. nation created in the late 1700s encompassed African enslavement and the genocide of native Americans. Faced with oppression, these and other victims of internal colonialism have long drawn on their own cultural resources, as well as their distinctive knowledge of Euro-American culture and society, to resist oppression in every way possible.

The cultures of those oppressed by European Americans have not only provided a source of individual, family, and community resistance to racial oppression and colonialism but have also infused, albeit often in unheralded ways, some significant elements into the evolving cultural mix that constitutes the core culture of the United States. The oppositional cultures of colonized groups such as African Americans, Latino Americans, and Native Americans have helped preserve several key elements of U.S. society, including its tradition of civil rights and social justice. Another key element, ironically enough given the usual white image of minority families, is the value of extended kinship relations. The tendency toward extended kin networks is both culturally encouraged and economically beneficial for oppressed minority groups. For example, research on black and Latino communities has found extensive kinship networks to be the basis of social and economic support in difficult times. Native American groups have also been known for their communalism and extended family networks.[34]

. . . This reality contrasts with the exaggerated stereotypes of endemic family pathology in these groups. Internal colonialism theories accent both the oppression of minority Americans and the oppositional cultures that enable minority groups not only to survive but also to resist oppression, passively and actively.

Criticism of Internal Colonialism Theories

. . . Joan Moore has criticized the term *neocolonialism.* As we have noted, a neocolonial situation is one in which a Third World country (for example, an African country) has separated itself politically from a European colonial power but continues to be dependent on that country. The former colony needs "foreign experts." It has a class of indigenous leaders who help the former colonial power exploit the local population. It has a distinct territorial boundary. Moore suggests that this neocolonialism model does not apply very well to subordinate nonwhite groups in the United States, in that these groups are not generally confined to a specific bounded territory, nor do they contain the exploitative intermediary elite of Third World neocolonialism. This space-centered critique has been repeated by Omi and Winant, who argue that the social and spatial intermixing of white and nonwhite groups in the United States casts serious doubt on the internal colonialism argument about territorially bounded colonization.[35]

However, most internal colonialism researchers have recognized the differences between internal colonial and neocolonial oppression. These theorists note that the situations of minority groups in the United States are different from those of, for instance, Africans in a newly independent nation still dependent on a European country. In response to Moore's critique, internal colonialism analysts might argue that there are many aspects of colonialism evident in U.S. racial and ethnic relations; they might emphasize that non-European groups in the United States (1) are usually residentially segregated, (2) are typically "superexploited" in employment and deficient in other material conditions when compared with white immigrants, (3) are culturally stigmatized, and (4) have had some of their leaders co-opted by whites. While these conditions in the United States are not defined as precisely as they are in the case of Third World neocolonialism, they are similar enough to allow the use of the idea of colonialism to assess racial and ethnic relations in the United States.

The Split Labor Market View: Another Class-Based Theory

Colonialism analysts such as Blauner are sometimes unclear about whether all classes of whites benefit from the colonization of nonwhites, or just the dominant class of capitalist employers. A power-conflict perspective that helps in assessing this question is the *split labor market* view, which treats class in the sense of position in the "means of production." This viewpoint has been defended by Edna Bonacich. She argues that in U.S. society the majority-group (white) workers do not share the interests of the dominant political and economic class, the capitalists. Yet both the dominant employer class and the white part of the working class discriminate against the nonwhite part of the working class.[36]

. . . Bonacich emphasizes that discrimination against minority workers by ordinary white workers seeking to protect their own privileges, however limited these may be, is important. Capitalists bring in nonwhite laborers to decrease labor costs, but white workers resist because they fear job displacement or lower wages. For example, over the last century white workers' unions have restricted the access of black workers to many job ladders, thus splitting the labor market and reducing black incomes. . . . White workers gain and lose from this structural racism. They gain in the short run, because there is less competition for privileged job categories from the nonwhites they have excluded. But they lose in the long run because employers can use this cordoned-off sector of nonwhites to undercut them.[37]

"Middleman" Minorities and Ethnic Enclaves

Drawing on insights of earlier scholars, Bonacich has explored the in-between position, in terms of power and resources, that certain racial and ethnic groups have occupied in stratified societies. These groups find their economic niche serving elites and workers as small-business people positioned between producers and consumers. Some ethnic and racial groups become small-scale traders and merchants doing jobs that dominant groups are not eager to do. For example, many first-generation Jewish and Japanese Americans, excluded from mainstream employment by white Protestants, became small-scale merchants, tailors, restaurant operators, or gardeners. These groups have held "a distinctive class position that is of special use to the ruling class." They "act as a go-between to this society's more subordinate groups."[38]

Bonacich and Modell have found that Japanese Americans fit the middleman minority model. Before World War II Japanese Americans resided in highly organized communities. Their local economies were based on self-employment, including gardening and truck farming, and on other nonindustrial family businesses. The group solidarity of the first generation of Japanese Americans helped them establish successful small businesses. However, they faced hostility from the surrounding society, and in fact were driven into the businesses they developed because they were denied other employment opportunities. By the second generation there was some breakdown in the middleman position of Japanese Americans, for many of that generation moved into professional occupations outside the niche economy.[39]

Some middleman minorities, such as Jewish and Korean American merchants in central cities, have become targets of hostility from less well off groups, such as poor African Americans. In addition, strong ethnic bonds can make the middleman group an effective competitor, and even Anglo-Protestant capitalists may become hostile toward an immigrant middleman minority that competes too effectively. Thus Jewish Americans have been viewed negatively by better-off Anglo-Protestant merchants, who have the power to discriminate against them, as well as by poor black renters and customers with whom Jews deal as middleman landlords and merchants. . . .

A somewhat similar perspective, *enclave theory*, examines secondary-structural incorporation into the economy, especially the ways in which certain non-European immigrant groups have created social and economic enclaves in cities. Both the middleman and the enclave perspectives give more emphasis to economic inequality and discrimination than assimilation perspectives, and they stress the incorporation of certain groups, such as Asians and Cubans, into the United States through the means of small businesses and specialized ethnic economies. The major differences between the two viewpoints seem to stem from the examples emphasized. Groups accented by enclave theorists, such as Cuban Americans, have created ethnic enclaves that are more than merchant or trading economies—they often include manufacturing enterprises, for example. In addition, ethnic enclaves usually compete with established Anglo-Protestant business elites. In contrast, the middleman minorities and those described as enclave minorities develop trading economies and are likely to fill an economic niche that *complements* that of established white elites. However, the aforementioned research of Bonacich on Jewish Americans suggests that there is little difference between the real-world experiences of those described as middleman minorities. . . .

Women and Gendered Racism: New Perspectives

Most theories of racial and ethnic relations have neglected gender stratification, the hierarchy in which men as a group dominate women as a group in terms of power and resources. In recent years a number of scholars have researched the situations of women within racial and ethnic groups in the United States. Their analyses assess the ways in which male supremacy, or a patriarchal system, interacts with and operates within a system of racial and ethnic stratification. Discussing racial and ethnic cultures around the globe, Adrienne Rich has defined a *patriarchal system* as "a familial-social, ideological, political system in which men—by force, direct pressure, or through ritual, tradition, law and language, customs, etiquette, education, and the division of labor—determine what part women shall or shall not play, and in which the female is everywhere subsumed under the male."[40]

Asking whether racism or patriarchy has been the primary source of oppression, social psychologist Philomena Essed examined black women in the United States and the Netherlands.[41] She found racism and sexism interacting regularly. The oppression of black women can be seen as *gendered racism.* For example, under slavery African American women were exploited not only for labor but also as sex objects for white men. And after slavery they were excluded from most job categories available to white men and white women; major employment changes came only with the civil rights movement of the 1960s. Today racism has many gendered forms. In the U.S. mass media the white female is the standard for female beauty. Minority women are often stereotyped as matriarchs in female-headed families and are found disproportionately in lower-status "female jobs," such as typists. Some women of color are closely bound in their social relations with those who oppress them in such areas as domestic employment ("maids") and other low-paid service work.[42]

In her book *Black Feminist Thought* Patricia Hill Collins argues that a black feminist theoretical framework can help highlight and analyze the negative stereotypes of black women in white society—the stereotypes of the docile mammy, the domineering matriarch, the promiscuous whore, and the irresponsible welfare mother. These severely negative images persist among many whites because they undergird white discrimination against black women in the United States.[43]

Scholars assessing the situations of other women of color, including Native American, Asian, and Latino women, have similarly emphasized the cumulative and interactive character of racial and gender oppression and the necessity of liberating these women from white stereotypes and discrimination. For example, Denise Segura has examined labor-force data on Mexican American women and developed the concept of "triple oppression," the mutually reinforcing and interactive set of race, class, and gender forces whose cumulative effects "place women of color in a subordinate social and economic position relative to men of color and the majority white population.[44]

Class, the State, and Racial Formation

Looking at the important role of governments in creating racial and ethnic designations and institutionalizing discrimination, Michael Omi and Howard Winant have developed a theory of *racial formation.* Racial tensions and oppression, in their view, cannot be explained solely in terms of class or nationalism. Racial and ethnic relations are substantially defined by the actions of governments, ranging from the passing of legislation, such as restrictive immigration laws, to the imprisonment of groups defined as a threat (for example, Japanese Americans in World War II). Although the internal colonialism viewpoint gives some emphasis to the state's role in the exploitation of nonwhite minorities, it has not developed this argument sufficiently.

Omi and Winant note that the U.S. government has shaped the politics of race: the U.S. Constitution and a lengthy series of laws openly defined racial groups and interracial relationships (for example, slavery) in racist terms. The U.S. Constitution counted each African American slave as three-fifths of a person, and the Naturalization Law of 1790 explicitly declared that only *white* immigrants could qualify for naturalization. Many non-Europeans, including Africans and Asians, were prevented from becoming citizens. Japanese and other Asian immigrants, for example, were until the 1950s banned by law from becoming citizens. In 1854 the California Supreme Court ruled that Chinese immigrants should be classified as "Indians"(!), therefore denying them the political rights available to white Americans.[45]

For centuries, the U.S. government officially favored northern European immigrant groups over non-European and southern European groups such as Italians. For example, the Immigration Act of 1924 was used to exclude Asian immigrants and most immigrants from southern and eastern Europe, whom political leaders in Congress saw as racially inferior and as a threat to their control of the society. North European Americans working through the government thereby shaped the subsequent racial and ethnic mix that is the United States.

Another idea accented by Omi and Winant is that of *social rearticulation,* the recurring historical process of rupturing and reconstructing the understandings of race in this country. The social protest movements of various racial and ethnic groups periodically challenge the government's definition of racial realities, as well as individual definitions of those realities. The 1960s civil rights movement, for instance, rearticulated traditional cultural and political ideas about race in the United States, and in the process changed the U.S. government and broadened the involvement of minority Americans in the politics of that government. New social movements regularly emerge, sometimes bringing new identities and political norms.[46]

Resistance to the Dominant Group

Recent research has highlighted the many ways in which powerless groups fight back against the powerful. One power-conflict theorist who has made an important contribution to our understanding of how the oppressed react to oppression is James Scott. Influenced by the work of scholars such as John Gaventa on the many "faces of power," Scott has shown that at the heart of much interaction between the powerless and the powerful is intentional deception.[47] For example, the African American slaves were not free to speak their minds to their white masters, but they did create a crucial discourse among themselves that was critical of their white oppressors. Scott cites a proverb of African slaves on the Caribbean island of Jamaica: "Play fool, to catch wise." Looking closely at the lives of slaves and the poor everywhere, Scott has developed the idea of a backstage discourse by the oppressed that includes views that cannot be discussed in public for fear of retaliation. In addition to secret ideological resistance on the part of slaves and other poor people, a variety of other resistance tactics are used, including foot-dragging, pilfering, dissimulation, and flight. Scott cites Afro-Christianity as an example of how African American slaves resisted the "ideological hegemony" (attempts to brainwash) of white slavemasters. In public religious services African American slaves controlled their gestures and facial expressions and pretended to accept Christian preaching about meekness and obedience. Backstage, where no whites were present, Afro-Christianity emphasized "themes of deliverance and redemption, Moses and the Promised Land, the Egyptian captivity, and emancipation."[48] For slaves the Promised Land meant the North and freedom, and the afterlife was often viewed as a place where the slaves' enemies would be severely punished.

Historian Sterling Stuckey has noted that slave spirituals, although obviously affected by Christianity, "take on an altogether new coloration when one looks at slave religion on the plantations where most slaves were found and where African religion, contrary to the accepted scholarly wisdom, was practiced." The religion of African Americans mixed African and European elements from the beginning. Yet at its core the expressive, often protest-inclined African values prevailed over the European values.[49] Stuckey has shown that African culture and religion were major sources of the slaves' inclination to rebellion. The work of Scott and Stuckey can be linked to the analyses of Hechter and Mitchell and Feagin that we cited previously, for they too have accented the role of an oppositional culture in providing the foundation of resistance to racial oppression.

We can conclude this discussion of the most important critical power-conflict theories by underscoring certain recurring themes:

1. a central concern for racial and ethnic inequalities in economic position, power, and resources;

2. an emphasis on the links of racial inequalities to the economic institutions of capitalism and to the subordination of women under patriarchal systems;
3. an emphasis on the role of the government in legalizing exploitation and segregation and in defining racial and ethnic relations;
4. an emphasis on resistance to domination and oppression by those oppressed.

NOTES

1. Charles Hirschman, "America's Melting Pot Reconsidered," *Annual Review of Sociology* 9 (1983): 397–423.

2. Robert E. Park, *Race and Culture* (Glencoe, Ill.: Free Press, 1950), p. 150 (italics added).

3. Robert E. Park and Ernest W. Burgess, *Introduction to the Science of Society* (Chicago: University of Chicago Press, 1924), p. 735.

4. Janice R. Hullum, "Robert E. Park's Theory of Race Relations" (M.A. thesis, University of Texas. 1973), pp. 81–88; Park and Burgess, *Introduction to the Science of Society*, p. 760.

5. Milton M. Gordon, *Assimilation in American Life* (New York: Oxford University Press, 1964), pp. 72–73.

6. Ibid., p. 71.

7. Silvia Pedraza, *Political and Economic Migrants in America: Cubans and Mexicans* (Austin: University of Texas Press, 1985), pp. 5–7; Richard Alba, *Ethnic Identity: The Transformation of White America* (New Haven: Yale University Press, 1990), p. 311; J. Allen Williams and Suzanne T. Ortega, "Dimensions of Assimilation," *Social Science Quarterly* 71 (1990): 697–709.

8. Milton M. Gordon, *Human Nature, Class, and Ethnicity* (New York: Oxford University Press, 1978), pp. 67–89.

9. Gordon, *Assimilation in American Life*, pp. 78–108.

10. See Will Herberg, *Protestant—Catholic—Jew*, rev. ed. (Garden City, N.Y.: Doubleday, Anchor Books, 1960).

11. Milton M. Gordon, "Models of Pluralism: The New American Dilemma," *Annals of the American Academy of Political and Social Science* 454 (1981): 178–88.

12. Alba, *Ethnic Identity*, p. 3.

13. Stanley Lieberson and Mary Waters, "Ethnic Mixtures in the United States," *Sociology and Social Research* 70 (1985): 43–53; Cookie White Stephan and Walter Stephan, "After Intermarriage," *Journal of Marriage and the Family* 51 (May 1989): 507–19.

14. Nathan Glazer and Daniel P. Moynihan, *Beyond the Melting Pot* (Cambridge: M.I.T. Press and Harvard University Press, 1963).

15. Andrew M. Greeley, *Ethnicity in the United States* (New York: John Wiley, 1974), p. 293.

16. Ibid., pp. 295–301.

17. Ibid., p. 309.

18. William L. Yancey, D. P. Ericksen, and R. N. Juliani, "Emergent Ethnicity: A Review and Reformulation," *American Sociological Review* 41 (June 1976): 391–93. See also Greeley, *Ethnicity in the United States*, pp. 290–317.

19. Talcott Parsons, "Full Citizenship for the Negro American? A Sociological Problem," in *The Negro American,* ed. Talcott Parsons and Kenneth B. Clark (Boston: Houghton Mifflin, 1965–66), p. 740.

20. James Geschwender, *Racial Stratification in America* (Dubuque, Iowa: Wm. C. Brown, 1978), p. 58.

21. Gordon, *Human Nature, Class, and Ethnicity,* pp. 73–78. See also Clifford Geertz, "The Integrative Revolution," in *Old Societies and New States,* ed. Clifford Geertz (New York: Free Press, 1963), p. 109.

22. Edna Bonacich, "Class Approaches to Ethnicity and Race," *Insurgent Sociologist* 10 (Fall 1980): 11.

23. Frederik Barth, "Introduction," in *Ethnic Groups and Boundaries: The Social Organization of Culture Difference* (Oslo: Universitets Forlaget, 1969), pp. 10–17.

24. Susan Olzak, "A Competition Model of Collective Action in American Cities," in *Competitive Ethnic Relations,* ed. Susan Olzak and Joane Nagel (Orlando, Fla.: Academic Press, 1986), pp. 17–46.

25. Ronald Bailey and Guillermo Flores, "Internal Colonialism and Racial Minorities in the U.S.: An Overview," in *Structures of Dependency,* ed. Frank Bonilla and Robert Girling (Stanford, Calif.: privately published by a Stanford faculty-student seminar, 1973), pp. 151–53.

26. G. Balandier, "The Colonial Situation: A Theoretical Approach," in *Social Change,* ed. Immanuel Wallerstein (New York: John Wiley, 1966), p. 35.

27. Pablo Gonzalez-Cassanova, "Internal Colonialism and National Development," in *Latin American Radicalism,* ed. Irving L. Horowitz et al. (New York: Random House, 1969), p. 130; Bailey and Flores, "Internal Colonialism," p. 156.

28. Bailey and Flores, "Internal Colonialism," p. 156.

29. Blauner, *Racial Oppression in America,* p. 55. Our analysis of internal colonialism draws throughout on Blauner's provocative discussion.

30. Stokely Carmichael and Charles Hamilton, *Black Power* (New York: Random House, Vintage Books, 1967), pp. 2–7.

31. Guillermo B. Flores, "Race and Culture in the Internal Colony: Keeping the Chicano in His Place," in *Structures of Dependency,* ed. Bonilla and Girling, p. 192.

32. Michael Hechter, *Internal Colonialism* (Berkeley: University of California Press, 1975), pp. 9–12; Michael Hechter, "Group Formation and the Cultural Division of Labor," *American Journal of Sociology* 84 (1978): 293–318; Michael Hechter, Debra Friedman, and Malka Applebaum, "A Theory of Ethnic Collective Action," *International Migration Review* 16 (1982): 412–34. See also Geschwender, *Racial Stratification in America,* p. 87.

33. Joe Feagin and Bonnie Mitchell, "America's Non-European Cultures: The Myth of the Melting Pot," in *Toward the Multicultural University,* ed. Benjamin Bowser, Gale Auletta, and Terry Jones (Westport, CT: Greenwood Publishing Group, 1995).

34. Carol B. Stack, "Sex Roles and Survival Strategies in an Urban Black Community," in *Women, Culture and Society,* ed. Michelle Zimbalist Rosaldo and Louise Lamphere (Stanford, Calif.: Stanford University Press, 1974), p. 128; Ronald Angel and Marta Tienda, "Determinants of Extended Household Structure: Cultural Pattern or Economic Need? *American Journal of Sociology* 87 (1981–82): 1360–83.

35. Joan W. Moore, "American Minorities and 'New Nation' Perspectives," *Pacific Sociological Review* 19 (October 1976): 448–55; Michael Omi and Howard Winant, *Racial Formation in the United States* (New York: Routlege & Kegan Paul, 1986), pp. 47–49.

36. Bonacich, "Class Approaches to Ethnicity and Race," p. 14.

37. Barrera, *Race and Class in the Southwest,* pp. 201–3; Bonacich, "Class Approaches to Ethnicity and Race," p. 14

38. Bonacich, "Class Approaches to Ethnicity and Race," pp. 14–15.

39. Edna Bonacich and John Modell, *The Economic Basis of Ethnic Solidarity* (Berkeley: University of California Press, 1980), pp. 1–37. For a critique, see Eugene Wong, "Asian American Middleman Minority Theory: The Framework of an American Myth," *Journal of Ethnic Studies* 13 (Spring 1985): 51–87.

40. Quoted in Michael Albert et al., *Liberating Theory* (Boston: South End Press, 1986), p. 35.

41. Philomena Essed, *Understanding Everyday Racism* (Newbury Park, Calif.: Sage Publications, Inc., 1991), pp. 30–32.

42. Ibid., p. 32.

43. Patricia Hill Collins, *Black Feminist Thought: Knowledge, Consciousness, and the Politics of Empowerment* (Boston: Unwin Hyman, 1990), pp. 40–48.

44. Denise A. Segura, "Chicanas and Triple Oppression in the Labor Force," in *Chicana Voices: Intersections of Class, Race and Gender,* ed. Teresa Cordova et al. (Austin, Tex.: Center for Mexican American Studies, 1986). p. 48.

45. Omi and Winant, *Racial Formation in the United States,* pp. 75–76.

46. Howard Winant, "Racial Formation Theory and Contemporary U.S. Politics," in *Exploitation and Exclusion,* ed. Abebe Zegeye, Leonard Harris, and Julia Maxted (London: Hans Zell, 1991), pp. 130–40.

47. James C. Scott, *Domination and the Arts of Resistance* (New Haven: Yale University Press, 1990); John Gaventa, *Power and Powerlessness* (Urbana, Ill.: University of Illinois Press, 1980).

48. Scott, *Domination and the Arts of Resistance,* p. 116.

49. Sterling Stuckey, *Slave Culture* (New York: Oxford University Press, 1987), pp. 27, 42–46.

PART 2

Prejudice

One common problem for students is that words used by social scientists often take on a different meaning than the same words used in our everyday language. There are numerous reasons for this, including the need of sociologists and psychologists to share precisely the critical definitions of their theory. In informal discussion such precision is seldom necessary. However, for social scientists whose goal is to construct a theory of prejudice and to devise techniques of measuring prejudice, a high degree of specificity is required.

Students are sometimes further confused by the fact that different social scientists use different definitions of the same term. Again, there are numerous reasons for this, but the central reason is that different theorists want a concept to take on a meaning specific to their particular theory. This is what we do here. That is, we specify a definition of prejudice that is in common usage. For a review of definitions of prejudice, see Ehrlich (1973). The way prejudice is defined has some important implications for understanding the chapters that follow.

We define prejudice as an *attitude toward a category of people.* Note that we are not talking about an attitude toward a particular person. There is an obvious difference between hating your boss and hating all bosses. There is a difference between hating Salim because he is an obnoxious person and hating Salim because he is an Asian Indian.

Attitudes can be favorable or unfavorable, positive or negative. However, when we talk about prejudice, most of the time we are talking about unfavorable attitudes. Therefore we specify the direction of prejudice only when it is positive.

Quite obviously, the key to understanding the concept of prejudice requires understanding the meaning of the term "attitude." An attitude is an interrelated set of beliefs, feelings, and motivations about some object or class of objects. Beliefs, feelings, and motivations—all three are involved in an attitude; and all three are interrelated. To say a person is prejudiced against some group means that he or she holds a set of beliefs about that group; he or she has an emotional reaction to that group; and he or she is motivated to behave in a certain way toward that group. These components are all learned. We learn what people around us believe about a group. We learn how to respond emotionally to a group, and we learn how we should organize our behavior to that group.

Prejudice, then, is not something people are born with. One reason it looks that way is that beliefs about groups are learned very early. Children as young as three or four years of age often begin to learn the prevailing stereotypes of a group long before they can even identify the group or, for that matter, comprehend the full meaning of what they have learned. In the early years, parents are the major teachers of prejudice. Consider the white parent who tells the child that he cannot play with the children of color across the street because they are dirty. The parent is communicating a behavioral norm (cannot play with) and a stereotype (dirty). It does not take much repetition of similar messages before the child is motivated to not play with them and develops an aversive response to them (that is, an emotional feeling of avoidance). Think of all the messages you received in your family about others who were of a different background.

In order for a group to be a target of prejudice in society, there has to be some consensus in the society that the group is an "acceptable" target. For example, Episcopalians are not a socially acceptable target; Jews are. The reasons for this are social and historical. Who becomes a target of prejudice and the specific content of that prejudice are socially determined. It is the state of relations between groups in society that determines the dimensions of prejudice toward a specific group. Changing people's attitudes can be accomplished by changing the nature of intergroup relations in the society as well as by changing the individual's beliefs, feelings, or motivations. Clearly, it is easier to change the attitudes of a particular person than it is to change group relations in society. In the long run, both must be accomplished.

These three components of prejudice have common elements, yet paradoxically function differently. For example, one element is direction. Every belief, feeling, and motivation has a particular direction, that is, positive or negative, warm or cold, attractive or repulsive. An attitude is balanced if all of the elements are in the same direction. So if a person had very negative beliefs, a strong emotional response, and was motivated to avoid contact or to be openly hostile toward another person because of his or her ethnicity, we would say that person was highly prejudiced. But these elements do not always line up in the same direction. Take the case of a white person with favorable beliefs about blacks and with the intention to deal openly and without discrimination except that he or she feels very uncomfortable in personal encounters with blacks. This person's attitudes are unbalanced. Unbalanced attitudes are less stable and less predictive of behavior than are balanced attitudes. Further in this last example, the person may not even be fully aware of how their emotions influence their behavior. In various studies, for example, social psychologists have observed whites who unknowingly maintain greater physical distance, less eye contact, and even smile less often in a personal encounter with a dark-skinned other.

One of the more highly confirmed findings in the field of prejudice derives from this observation of balance and equilibrium: Prejudice is highly generalized. People who are prejudiced against one group tend to be prejudiced against others. This generality of prejudice even extends to attitudes toward oneself. People who have negative self-attitudes tend to have negative attitudes toward others. These findings have great implications for attitude change. They tell us that if we can change attitudes toward one group, we can likely change attitudes toward others. Further, if we can change attitudes toward oneself, we can also likely change attitudes toward others.

There is a "myth" about attitudes in general and prejudice in particular. That myth is the proposition that "attitudes are difficult to change." Although some individuals are closed-minded and their belief systems are highly resistant to change, for most people attitudes are relatively easy to change. The work of the advertising industry is a case in point. Advertising has become an application of attitude theory in which people have their emotions manipulated, are taught new beliefs, and are motivated to purchase the advertiser's product. With regard to prejudice, there is a substantial body of research that indicates such attitudes are relatively easy to manipulate.

We need to keep in mind that attitudes are not overt behaviors. The behavioral parallel to prejudice is what we generally refer to as *discrimination*. Generally, discrimination refers to actions that deny equal treatment to persons perceived to be members of some social category (such as ethnicity). The result is the restriction of opportunities and rewards available to others while maintaining those opportunities and rewards for one's own social group.

Attitudes tend to be consistent with behavior. People do behave in keeping with what they think, feel, and intend to do. However, the relation between prejudice and discrimination, between attitudes and behavior, is not a mechanical one. Often people need to learn how to express their attitudes in behavior and sometimes how to recognize behaviors that are incongruent with their attitudes. Further, in any given situation or role, there may contradictory expectations for behavior or the situation may evoke multiple attitudes that are not consistent. The complexity of this relationship is still under study, but what is important here is the understanding that for attitude changes to be maintained, the new attitudes have to be clearly expressible in behavior. Moreover, for changes in behavior to be lasting, underlying attitudes must also be changed.

In this section, we focus on some of the behavioral consequences of prejudice. In particular, we examine the societal implications of discrimination from a social psychological perspective. This is to say that we examine the relation of people's attitudes to the social context in which they occur. The contributions are themselves examples of how differing perspectives on prejudice lead to differing conceptions of social problems and human behavior.

The two chapters in this section cover an extraordinary range of issues centering on the question of how prejudice (labeled "racism" in these readings) is manifest. Byron Roth opens his argument with the caution that opposition to affirmative action, welfare policies, school busing, and the like should be taken at face value and not as an indicator of a disguised prejudice. That is, objection to government intervention may reflect an honest belief that these policies are intrinsically wrong or that government is unable to implement appropriate policies.

Why would social scientists misconstrue this opposition? Roth answers by pointing to studies that purport to show that social scientists are politically liberal or left of center. Because of these biases, such formulations as "symbolic racism," Roth argues, are untrustworthy. They confuse being "rationally motivated" with being "racially motivated."

James M. Jones provides a more traditional social psychological approach in his contribution. Like Roth, he speaks to the issue of substantial changes in intergroup attitudes in the United States. He provides data for both blacks and whites, dividing the responses into attitudes dealing with principles and attitudes dealing with policy implementation. For Jones, the disparity between the two sets of attitudes leads him to question the conceptualization of prejudice. For Roth, these same disparities lead him to question the conceptualization of policy. Roth argues that this conceptualization is based on the elitist and political bias of social scientists and that these disparities are "real." Jones argues that the expressions of prejudice have changed over time. From the research literature, he identifies three forms of expression—symbolic racism, modern racism, and aversive racism.

Symbolic racism is based on prejudice where the content of the attitude is the conjunction of (1) inappropriate beliefs and demands by blacks regarding civil rights and (2) the belief that discrimination has already been neutralized. Continuing black demands for government assistance are, therefore, seen as violating traditional norms of achievement and merit. Government policies such as court-ordered school busing and affirmative action are viewed as unnecessary and violating white civil rights. Modern racists, according to Jones, hold similar views regarding discrimination and the violation of norms. Both symbolic racists and modern racists believe that they are not prejudiced and that their beliefs are realistically grounded. The differences between the two conceptualizations are slight and are matters of emphasis. The modern racist tends to respond to the target of prejudice directly, in a more stereotyped manner and with a strong emotional loading. Symbolic racists tend to respond indirectly to the target of prejudice by focusing on social policies that affect group relations (busing, school desegregation, affirmative action). Aversive racists, in contrast, express their attitudes toward blacks in emotional responses—discomfort, disgust, fear, and so on. Like the others, aversive racists do not view themselves as being prejudiced.

The divergences of Roth and Jones illustrate three facets of the complexity of the study of prejudice. The first is how the changing relations between groups is reflected in the changes in the content of attitudes. The second is how these changing attitudes can be differently interpreted by scientists of differing political perspectives. Finally, both authors introduce the reader to the differences in the perceptions of blacks and whites. These differences are reflected in many of the selections in Part Three.

REFERENCES

Ehrlich, Howard J. (1973) *The Social Psychology of Prejudice.* New York: Wiley.

6

The Changing Nature of Prejudice

JAMES M. JONES

What do whites think about blacks? What do blacks think about whites? . . . By the 1970s, the development of large-scale survey methods by the National Opinion Research Center (NORC) and the Institute of Social Relations (ISR) made it possible to compare over time and, thereby, to detect trends in racial attitudes. ISR researchers Schuman, Steeh, and Bobo (1985) studied trends in racial attitudes from the 1950s through the 1970s. They focused on racial relations and social standing in U.S. society, examining primarily black-white attitudes. They divided attitudes into two categories: (1) *Broad principles,* which dealt with the major racial issues of the day (i.e., school integration, residential integration, integration of transportation, job discrimination, and racial intermarriage) and (2) *implementation* of those principles that related to the degree to which the government should intervene in order to combat discrimination or segregation, or to reduce racial inequalities in income or status.

WHITE RACIAL ATTITUDES

Table 6.1 shows trends in white racial attitudes in the category "broad principles" between 1960 and the late 1970s. On each question of principle, white respondents were more positive in the 1970s than they were in the 1960s. Attitudes were most positive on issues of school integration, job equity, and equal access to public facilities and transportation. Further, most whites, in the 1970s, believed that blacks should be able to live where they want (88%) and use public facilities freely (88%). They also felt that there should *not* be laws against intermarriage (71% opposed them), but it is not something of which they generally approved (33%). The desire to maintain 'residential choice' was supported by the small percentage of respondents (35%) who favored residential desegregation. Therefore, although there was an overall trend toward more positive endorsement of racial equality in principle, there remained evidence of boundaries that were not easily erased.

How much did respondents endorse strategies for implementing these principles? Table 6.2 illustrates trends in white respondents' attitudes toward implementation strategies.

TABLE 6.1 Trends in White Racial Attitudes, 1960s–1970s

Questioning Regarding Principles (Positive response trends)	*1960s*	*1970s*	*Trend*
Blacks and whites should attend same schools. (Yes)	65%	86%	+21%
Blacks should have an equal chance with whites for jobs. (Yes)	85%	97%	+12%
Transportation should be racially segregated. (No)	79%	88%	+9%
Blacks have the right to live wherever they can afford and want to. (Agree)	65%	88%	+23%
Blacks have rights to use the same parks, restaurants, and hotels as whites. (Yes)	73%	88%	+15%
There should be laws against racial intermarriage. (No)	38%	71%	+33%
Do you *approve* of interracial marriage? (Yes)	4%	33%	+29%
Do you favor strict segregation, desegregation, or something in between?			
Something in between	48%	60%	+12%
Desegregation	27%	35%	+8%

SOURCE: Adapted from Schuman, H., Steeh, C., and Bobo, L. *Racial Attitudes in America: Trends and Interpretations* (Cambridge, MA: Harvard University Press, 1985).

Whereas the trends in whites' attitudes toward general principles of racial equality were uniformly positive, attitudes toward implementation showed a growing belief that the government should do *less* to achieve the principles of racial equality. This pattern of attitudes among whites suggests some potential problems:

1. Principles of racial equality are positively endorsed, but government intervention to support these principles is becoming less desirable.
2. Social and economic inequality are not best reduced by resolving underlying issues of poverty and unemployment.
3. It is appropriate for government to protect the rights of blacks, but not to promote social arrangements in society.

Embedded in these attitude data are indications that racial groups are not likely to come closer together in practice, although beliefs about the desirability and appropriateness of such relationships seem clearly to be more positive. The light shines on the desire to *diminish* the role of government as social engineer in the United States.

Social psychologists were interested in understanding more about the behavioral consequences of these trends. A number conducted several investigations of their strength, character, and behavioral representations. . . .

TABLE 6.2 White Respondents' Attitudes Toward Government Role in Implementing Racial Equality

Questions Regarding Implementation of Racial Equality	*1960s*	*1970s*	*Trends*
Government in Washington should ensure fair treatment for blacks. (Yes)	38%	36%	–2%
Would vote for law that forbid homeowners to discriminate in sale of residence on basis of race. (Yes)	34%	37%	+3%
Government in Washington should see to it that black and white children go to same schools. (Yes)	42%	25%	–17%
Favor busing of black or white children to another school district. (Yes)	13%	17%	+4%
Government in Washington should support the right of black people to go to any hotel or restaurant they can afford. (Yes)	44%	66%	+22%
Are we spending too little on improving the conditions of blacks? (Yes)	27%	18%	–9%
Should government in Washington make every effort to improve the social and economic conditions of blacks and other minorities? (Yes)	22%	21%	–1%
The best way to address urban riots and unrest is to correct problems of poverty and unemployment. (Yes)	51%	41%	–10%

SOURCE: Adapted from Schuman, H., Steeh, C., and Bobo, L. *Racial Attitudes in America: Trends and Interpretations* (Cambridge, MA: Harvard University Press, 1985).

BLACK RACIAL ATTITUDES

The survey researchers at the Institute of Social Research also assessed black racial attitudes during the 1970s. There were signs then of differing viewpoints on racial matters. For example, Table 6.3 shows divergent trends between blacks and whites in responses to questions about the progress of blacks in the United States. Black respondents were nearly unanimous in their endorsement of racially integrated schooling and neighborhoods. Moreover, they were largely in favor of interracial marriages, though not unanimously. However, although desegregation had been favored by 78 percent of black respondents in the 1960s, it was favored by only 39 percent in the 1970s. Desegregation implies bringing races together, and this evidence suggests that it lost some of its appeal among blacks during the 1970s.

Turning our attention now to the question of implementing strategies to reduce racial inequality, Table 6.4 reveals both disparities and, surprisingly, similar trends between blacks and whites. First, in the 1970s blacks had a much more positive view of the need for action by the government than did whites. This was true in the 1960s, and was still true in the 1970s. For example, 66 percent of whites felt the federal government should support the rights of blacks to go to any hotel or

TABLE 6.3 Trends in Black Racial Attitudes, 1960s–1970s

Questions Regarding Principles (Positive response trends), Blacks	*1960s*	*1970s*	*Trend*
Blacks and whites should attend same schools. (Yes)	96%	98%	+2%
Blacks have the right to live wherever they can afford and want to. (Agree)	98%	99%	+1%
Do you approve of interracial marriage? (Yes)	76%	98%	+22%
Do you favor strict segregation, desegregation, or something in between?			
Something in between	17%	56%	+39%
Desegregation	78%	39%	–39%

SOURCE: Adapted from Schuman et al. (1985).

TABLE 6.4 Black Respondents' Attitudes Toward Government Role in Implementing Racial Equality

Questions Regarding Implementation, Blacks	*1960s*	*1970s*	*Trend*
Government in Washington should see to it that black and white children go to same schools. (Yes)	82%	60%	–22%
Favor busing of black or white children to another school district. (Yes)	46%	49%	+3%
Government in Washington should support right of black people to go to any hotel or restaurant they can afford. (Yes)	89%	91%	+2%
Are we spending too little on improving the conditions of blacks? (Yes)	83%	84%	+1%
Should government in Washington make every effort to improve the social and economic conditions of blacks and other minorities? (Yes)	78%	57%	–18%
The best way to address urban riots and unrest is to correct problems of poverty and unemployment. (Yes)	74%	64%	–10%

SOURCE: Adapted from Schuman et al. (1985).

restaurant they could afford. By contrast, 91 percent of blacks believed this should be the case. Blacks believed that the federal government should see to it that black and white children went to the same schools (60%); whites were less likely to support this idea (25%). This general discrepancy reflects the fact that blacks and whites have different expectations for how racial equality can be redressed.

But the second point these data show is that the trend of the 1970s was for a decline in positive attitudes regarding government's role in creating racial equality

TABLE 6.5 Perception of Racial Progress Is in the Eye of the Beholder

Questions Regarding Progress for Black Americans	*1966*	*1976*	*Trend*
1. How much real change do you think there has been in the position of black people in the past few years? (A lot)			
Blacks	41%	32%	–9%
Whites	40%	65%	+25%
2. Do you think that civil rights leaders are trying to push too fast, are going too slowly, or are moving at about the right speed? (Too slow)			
Blacks	22%	40%	+18%
Whites	2%	3%	+1%

SOURCE: Adapted from Schuman et al. (1985).

by *both* blacks and whites. For example, both black and white respondents reduced their support for the idea that government should make every effort to improve the social and economic conditions of blacks and other minorities—blacks by 21 percent (from 78% agreement in the 1960s to 57% in the 1970s) and whites by 1 percent (from 22% in the 1960s to 21% in the 1970s). Both blacks and whites were less inclined to believe that the way to handle urban riots is to correct problems of poverty and unemployment—both groups showed a 10 percent decline in support. Finally, both blacks and whites showed reduced support for the idea that government should see to it that black and white children go to the same schools (black support declined by 22%, white, by 17%).

Therefore, although blacks continued to see things differently in an absolute sense, both blacks and whites were becoming disenchanted with the prospects for, or appropriateness of, federal government intervention in matters of racial equality.

Finally, we may ask about the general view of the progress of black Americans as a result of the efforts made to implement the promise of the civil rights movement in the 1960s. Table 6.5 suggests that "progress may be in the eyes of the beholder."

From 1966 to 1976, blacks and whites had an increasingly different view of progress in equalizing the position of black Americans. With respect to progress itself, whites felt a lot had been accomplished in the 10-year period that ended in 1976. Specifically, 65 percent felt a lot of progress had been made, compared to only 40 percent in 1966, an increase of 25 percent. However, among blacks in 1976, only 32 percent felt a lot of progress had been made, an actual decline of 9 percent from 1966. For whites, the glass of the nectar of progress was filling up and, by 1976, was seen as two-thirds full. For blacks, the same glass was seen as slowly leaking out possibilities and, by 1976, was two-thirds empty!

This feeling among blacks of inadequate progress was reflected by impatience with the pace of change. "Are things moving too fast or are they moving too slowly?" the surveyors asked. In 1966, 22 percent of blacks felt that things were moving too slowly, but, in 1976, 40 percent felt this way—an 18 percent increase in impatience. For whites, in 1966, there were almost none who felt things were moving too slowly (2%) and, by 1976, that number had hardly changed (3%).

By the end of the 1970s, blacks were growing frustrated by what they perceived as a lack of progress. They began to endorse strategies that were increasingly being rejected by whites. Whites perceived that progress was being made, that the rate of progress was about right or, at least, not too slow.

BEHAVIORAL EXPRESSIONS OF RACIAL BIAS

Because many of the attitude trends among whites from the 1940s through the 1970s showed consistently positive movement, many came to believe that racial animosities had significantly declined. Some even believed that prejudice was a thing of the past. Although this rosy interpretation of the effects of the civil rights legislation of the 1960s and of the greater residential and educational mobility for blacks was spreading among ordinary people, social psychologists were detecting sinister signs of negativity. Crosby, Bromley, and Saxe (1980, p. 560) summarized several "unobtrusive studies of discrimination" and concluded that "antiBlack prejudice is still strong among American Whites."...

MICROLEVEL MANIFESTATIONS OF RACIAL BIAS

The racial divide grew broader and deeper in the 1980s. In spite of this, the popular belief that race relations and racial attitudes were no longer a problem persisted. . . . That was a belief held by whites, primarily. It was illustrated in their responses to questions about the degree of bias in U.S. society and the consequences of bias for blacks and other minority groups. This belief was not widely shared by blacks and, to a lesser extent, Hispanics. This comfortableness with race relations was somewhat illusory, as events of the 1990s would point out.

Afrocentrism increased the ideological differences between blacks and whites because it emphasized an experience that was largely outside the purview of whites. To a large degree, white acceptance was predicated on the notion that, except for skin color, blacks and whites were alike—both were American and both were searching for that American dream: "Eliminate racial discrimination and we can all be one happy family." Race runs deeper than that. However, even in the 1980s there was ample sociopsychological evidence that whites not only held deep-seated racial attitudes and beliefs, but also reacted with emotion and affect to blacks in ways that contradicted what they purported to feel.

In the remainder of this chapter, we will take a brief look at three of these ideas: symbolic racism, modern racism, and aversive racism. Each of these ideas proposes, in different ways, that deep-seated (perhaps unconscious), negative attitudes persist in people who may believe themselves to be purely nonprejudiced. They also share the view that this deep-seated negativity derives from a conflict between important values of the Protestant work ethic and humanitarian-egalitarianism beliefs and concur that these semiconscious or unconscious processes can influence thoughts and behavior of people who might think of themselves as nonprejudiced.

Symbolic Racism

Sears (1988) suggests that traditional forms of racial bias are reflected in hostility, antagonism, and derogation of blacks as a group, as a people, and as a culture. This negativity was further indicated by endorsement of formal inequality based on the fundamental antiblack sentiment and beliefs (Sears and Kinder, 1970). However, with the gains of the civil rights movement of the 1960s and the growing role of the government in advancing black rights and enforcing their legitimate expression, those traditional antagonisms lost public acceptance and "went underground," persisting in the form of symbolic racism (Sears, 1988).

Symbolic racism was defined as the intersection of antiblack sentiment and feeling and a strong endorsement of the traditional U.S. values of individualism reflected in the Protestant work ethic. Explicitly stated, symbolic racism was a new form of racial attitude, consisting of

> a blend of anti-Black affect and the kind of traditional American moral values embodied in the Protestant Ethic . . . a form of resistance to change in the racial status quo based on moral feelings that Blacks violate such traditional American values as individualism and self-reliance, the work ethic, obedience, and discipline. (Sears, 1988, p. 56)

Symbolic racism is an attitude that is expressed in three domains, as follows:

1. Antagonism toward blacks' demands
   - A. "Blacks are getting too demanding in their push for equal rights."
   - B. "Blacks shouldn't push themselves where they're not wanted."
   - C. "It is not easy to understand the anger of black people today."
2. Resentment over special favors for blacks
   - A. "Over the past few years, blacks have got more economically than they deserve."
   - B. "The government should *not* help blacks and other racial minor ties—they should help themselves."
3. Denial of continuing discrimination

   "Blacks have it better than they ever have before."

The more respondents agree with each of these comments, the more they can be characterized as holding symbolic racist attitudes. Such respondents (symbolic racists) share a basic antiblack sentiment and endorsement of traditional U.S. values.

Underlying the symbolic racism category concept is the proposition that these attitudes result from preadult socialization of normative values and beliefs. The traditional values are embraced without question, the target group is disliked, and a reason for the dislike is rationalized as a failure of the group's members to uphold core values.

Later, as adults, one can embrace the core values, reject anyone who fails to reflect them (in one's own view), and thus, without declaring oneself to be racially motivated, oppose issues that are favorable to blacks—or whatever target group is in question.

Using responses to questions such as those presented above, research has shown that symbolic-racism attitudes of whites could reliably predict opposition to busing, affirmative action, and bilingual education, and voting against Tom Bradley (mayor of Los Angeles) and Jesse Jackson (in his 1984 bid for the presidency), as well as positions on marginally racial issues, such as tax reduction.

Sears argues that symbolic racism has a far greater effect on white attitudes and behavior than does the old-fashioned, hostility-antagonism racial hatred. Symbolic racism is highly correlated with traditional racism in that both have a strong antiblack component. However, it is different in that it incorporates a focus on traditional values, whereas traditional racism does not. Research showed that the frequency of old-fashioned racism among subjects was much lower, in general, than that of symbolic racism (Kinder and Sears, 1981) and that, for the most part, symbolic racism scores predicted whites' behavior more reliably than measures of old-fashioned racism did.

In addition, symbolic racism distinguishes itself from other types of negative racial attitudes—specifically, those based on perceived realistic threat. So, for example, opposing busing as a means of achieving racial balance might reflect a symbolic-racism influence, but only to the degree that self-interested concern is not involved (e.g., if one has no children in the school system). Many data support the observation that symbolic-racist attitudes predict opposition to busing but that perceived personal racial threat does not (e.g., Kinder and Sears, 1981).

. . . The symbolic-racism approach argues that looking for racism under the same old rocks and in the same old utterances will result in misleading data. These theorists propose that racism has taken on a new mantle, cloaked to some extent in patriotism and a conservative return to good, old-fashioned values. . . .

Modern Racism

McConahay (1986) offers four principles of *modern racism:*

1. Discrimination is a thing of the past, because blacks now have the freedom to compete in the marketplace and enjoy those things they can afford.
2. Blacks are pushing too hard, too fast, and into places where they are not wanted.
3. These tactics and demands are unfair.
4. Therefore, recent gains are undeserved, and the institutions are giving blacks more attention and status than they deserve.

If these ideas reflect modern racism, McConahay (1986) shows us why people who hold these beliefs do *not* consider themselves to be racists. First, people accept the idea that racism is *bad;* however, they claim they are not racists, because these traditional values are not racially inspired beliefs but *empirical facts.* Second, racism, in their view, is only what can be classified as "old-fashioned racism"—that is, holding negative black stereotypes such as believing them to be characterized by ignorance, laziness, and dishonesty, and supporting racial segregation and open acts of discrimination. Modern racists, according to McConahay, do not identify themselves as racists, because (1) they see their beliefs as factual and (2) they do *not* hold old-fashioned racist views.

The net effect of this thinking is that whites can embrace attitudes that reflect the above reasoning while rejecting beliefs associated with old-fashioned racism. However, negative racial affect, according to McConahay (1986), lingers on and influences how relevant information is interpreted and how such information affects "modern racists" when they are called on to interpret new events or to engage in activities such as voting, giving opinions, serving on juries, or interacting with blacks on a day-to-day basis. Is this really racism? McConahay and colleagues set out, first of all, to measure modern racism, then to show that it reliably predicts whites' attitudes and/or behavior in just such situations.

Measuring Modern Racism

After several years of testing numerous items that tap white attitudes toward blacks, a six-item Modern Racism Scale (MRS) was developed. These six items, answered on a five-point scale that indicated strong disagreement to strong agreement, follow:

1. Over the past few years, the government and news media have shown more respect to blacks than they deserve to be shown. (Strongly agree = 5)
2. It is easy to understand the anger of black people in the United States. (Strongly disagree = 5)
3. Discrimination against blacks is no longer a problem in the United States. (Strongly agree = 5)
4. Over the past few years, blacks have received more economically than they deserve. (Strongly agree = 5)
5. Blacks are getting too demanding in their push for equal rights. (Strongly agree = 5)
6. Blacks should not push themselves where they are not wanted. (Strongly agree = 5)

Old-fashioned-racism items consisted of blatant forms of discrimination—such as opposition to open housing, opposition to racial intermarriage, opposition to the 1954 Supreme Court desegregation ruling, opposition to having black neighbors even of equal income and education, and opposition to full racial integration. One of the important distinguishing principles of the modern and old-fashioned forms of racism is that the latter is *reactive* (i.e., people do *not* consider themselves racist, because they reject these blatant attitudes), whereas the former is *nonreactive* (i.e., respondents do not consider them to reflect racism, and, therefore, endorse them willingly and openly.)

To test this reactivity assumption, McConahay, Hardee, and Batts (1981) had white male undergraduates fill out a "student opinion" survey that consisted of items that reflect both the modern and the old-fashioned racism. The questionnaires were administered by either a black or white female experimenter. The experimenter left subjects alone to fill out the scales and had them place the completed surveys anonymously in a folder before her return. It was expected that, for the old-fashioned items, subjects would be more conscious of the racial content when there was a black, as opposed to a white, experimenter and would possibly moderate their answers to be more positive, even though the surveys were anonymous. It was also expected that this would not happen for the modern racism items, because, it was argued, they were not perceived to be racist! The results confirmed these predictions. There was a significant difference in answers between the black and white experimenter conditions for the old-fashioned items such that the racial attitudes were more positive when the experimenter was black. There was no experimenter difference for the modern racism items. The authors interpret this finding as support for the nonreactivity of the MRS.

There is substantial similarity between the symbolic and modern racism concepts. Both argue that negative affect (expressed emotion) is attached to black people early in life. This negative affect lurks in the hearts and minds of whites and influences judgments and perceptions in their adulthood. Modern racism, more than symbolic racism, emphasizes the cognitive aspect of the attitude and suggests that the splitting apart of old-fashioned and modern racial beliefs is a more conscious cognitive process. The MRS has become a standard for measuring racial prejudice. It is short, has been extensively validated, and has proved to be reliable.

Aversive Racism

Gaertner and Dovidio (1986, p. 62) define *aversive racism* as ". . . a particular type of ambivalence in which there is conflict between feelings and beliefs associated with a sincerely egalitarian value system and unacknowledged negative feelings and beliefs about Blacks." This ambivalence arises from the assimilation of both an egalitarian value system and the opposing feelings and beliefs derived from the historical, as well as contemporary, cultural context of racism. That is, as children, people become socialized to the dominant racial biases of this society. Second, these biases are further ingrained via mechanisms of human cognitive processes that facilitate the formation of stereotypes and the production of prejudicial judgments.

As with symbolic and modern racism before, the foundation of aversive racism is laid by a cultural context of racist attitudes, values, and beliefs. The resultant prejudices, stereotypes, and negative feelings then become attached to members of racial groups as judged by society. This negative affect, though, is not hostility or hate (rather like what we have called "old-fashioned racists," and what Gaertner and Dovidio call "*dominative* racists." Instead, the aversive racist feels discomfort, uneasiness, disgust, and sometimes fear in the presence of blacks or of race issues. These feelings tend to motivate avoidance rather than intentionally aggressive, destructive, and hostile behaviors directed at blacks.

When is aversive racism most easily and accurately detected? Gaertner and Dovidio (1986) argue that aversive racists are strongly motivated by egalitarian values, as well as antiblack feelings. Therefore, they should be most vulnerable to behaving in a racist fashion when normative structures that clearly define acceptable egalitarian behavior are weak, ambiguous, or conflicting. To test this proposition, Frey and Gaertner (1986) had white female college students work on a task with either a black or white female partner (the experimental confederate). The subject was asked for help by her partner for reasons that were either self-induced (*internal locus*—the partner had not worked on the task very hard) or beyond the person's control (*external locus*—the task was unusually difficult). The subject was able to help by giving the partner Scrabble letters and bonus points to help them win a prize. Frey and Gaertner (1986) reasoned that the race of the partner would not matter when norms were clearly in support of helping (external locus). When the norms were not supportive of helping—that is, when the partner had been lazy (internal locus) and still asked for help—they expected that the partner's race would matter, with blacks receiving less help than whites received. The results strongly support these predictions.

These findings show that when conditions are favorable for positive interactions and "obvious" choices, people will "do the right thing." But when there is "wiggle room," the possibility of negative attitudes giving rise to racially biased behavior becomes more likely. . . .

The symbolic, modern, and aversive racism analyses show a variety of ways in which racial bias persisted in a time when it was believed to have substantially subsided. This is not to accept the view that nothing had changed, but it does make a compelling case for the persistent effects of cultural socialization, lingering affective reactions, and the subtle influences of these processes on attitudes and behavior. The effects are not always obvious, and one may easily mistake his or her feelings of openness and nonhostile attitudes as evidence of a lack of prejudice.

The important similarities in these lines of argument include the following:

1. Negative affective associations to black people
2. Ambivalence between feelings of nonprejudice or egalitarianism and those negative feelings
3. A tendency for people who aspire to a positive, egalitarian self-image to nevertheless show racial biases when they are unaware of how to appear nonbiased

The net effect of these studies is to suggest that there is a profound undercurrent of racial animosity not only in those overt bigots who got so much attention in the 1960s, but among more overtly friendly and reassuring people.

REFERENCES

Crosby, F., Bromley, S., and Saxe, L. (1980). "Recent Unobtrusive Studies of Black and White Discrimination and Prejudice: A Literature Review." *Psychological Bulletin*, 87, 546–563.

Frey, D., and Gaertner, S.L. (1986). "Helping and the Avoidance of Interracial Behavior. A Strategy That Can Perpetuate a Non-Prejudiced Self Image." *Journal of Personality and Social Psychology*, 50, 1083–1090.

Gaertner, S.L., and Dovidio, J.F. (1986). "The Aversive Form of Racism." In J.F. Dovidio and S.L. Gaertner (eds.), *Prejudice, Discrimination and Racism* (pp. 61–90). Orlando, FL: Academic Press.

Kinder, D.R., and Sears, D.O. (1981). "Prejudice and Politics: Symbolic Racism versus Racial Threats to the Good Life." *Journal of Personality and Social Psychology,* 40, 414–431.

McConahay, J.B. (1986). "Modern Racism, Ambivalence, and the Modern Racism Scale." In J.F. Dovidio and S.L. Gaertner (eds.), *Prejudice, Discrimination and Racism* (pp. 91–126). Orlando, FL: Academic Press.

McConahay, J.B., Hardee, B.B., and Batts, V. (1981). "Has Racism Declined in America? It Depends upon Who's Asking and What Is Asked." *Journal of Conflict Resolution,* 25, 563–579.

Schuman, H., Steeh, C., and Bobo, L. (1985). *Racial Attitudes in America: Trends and Interpretations.* Cambridge, MA: Harvard University Press.

Sears, D.O. (1988). "Symbolic Racism." In P.A. Katz and D.A. Taylor (eds.), *Eliminating Racism: Profiles in Controversy* (pp. 53–84). New York: Plenum.

Sears, D.O., and Kinder, D.R., (1970). "Racial Tensions and Voting in Los Angeles." In W.Z. Hirsch (ed.), *Los Angeles: Viability and Prospects for Metropolitan Leadership* (pp. 53–84). New York: Praeger.

7

Racism and Traditional American Values

BYRON M. ROTH

INTRODUCTION

Gunnar Myrdal's thesis that the racial prejudices of white Americans are the primary cause of the problems confronting black Americans continues to dominate debate on race relations. If this understanding, certainly correct at the time when it was formulated by Myrdal, is no longer sound, its continued endorsement only serves to block the development of alternative and more realistic explanations upon which to base social policy. A good deal of research effort, for instance, is devoted to finding the causes of white prejudice, a task that may not be very useful if whatever prejudice remains among whites is relatively unimportant for an understanding of black difficulties.

This is well illustrated by recent research in social psychology that follows the logic of *The Authoritarian Personality* in attempting to link prejudice with adherence to free-market and other traditional American values. This research tries to show that the traditional values of individualism and self-reliance, for example, are mainly a cloak for prejudice and are used to justify opposition to policies designed to promote racial equality.

People who express disagreement with affirmative action policies favoring minorities in university admissions, for instance, and who justify their objections on the basis of a commitment to the American values of self-reliance and equal treatment, are said to use those traditional values as a disguise for opposition to equality. This new understanding, ironically, turns Myrdal's thesis on its head. Myrdal argued that a true commitment to America's traditional values was the best antidote to discrimination against blacks. Today those selfsame traditional values are said to be the primary hindrance to racial equality. . . .

Many social scientists interpret whites' rejection of policies of preferential treatment for minorities as evidence of continued widespread racism. This general view is expressed in numerous books and articles which in recent years have lamented the fact that although whites increasingly seem to support the general principles of racial equality, they seem to resist strategies, such as employment guidelines, which many social scientists claim are necessary to implement those principles.

The view of University of Michigan political scientist Donald Kinder is representative of many. He acknowledges that few white Americans today express support for discrimination. According to Kinder, "[d]enial of equal rights and opportunities to blacks no longer enjoys majority support. On voting rights, public accommodations, housing, and employment practices, racist sentiment has drastically diminished; in some cases it has virtually disappeared. . . . This is a striking change and a momentous achievement." However, Kinder continues, conflict over racial matters still troubles American society:

> Indeed, affirmative action, racial quotas, "forced busing," and the "welfare mess" are among the most contentious public issues of our time. Forty years after Myrdal, in the wake of dramatic changes in public opinion and social custom, *why do so many white Americans continue to resist efforts designed to bring about racial equality?* (Emphasis added)[15]

Instead of interpreting opposition to affirmative action policies, current welfare policies, quotas, and school busing as reflecting honest disagreements over how best to achieve racial equality, many social scientists agree with Kinder in seeing such opposition as an attempt to resist racial equality.

It is important to note that the policies and programs being discussed were in large measure conceived and supported by social scientists. But that hardly justifies an *ad hominem* attack on people who disagree—an attack which portrays that disagreement as a disingenuous attempt to forestall racial progress. So firmly rooted is the belief that it is improper to look to blacks themselves for some of the causes of their difficulties that even in the face of very strong evidence of declining racism, many researchers continue to insist that there *must* be some sort of racism at work if blacks fail to achieve full equality as quickly as some thought they would.

For instance, in *Racial Attitudes in America,* Howard Schuman, Charlotte Steeh, and Lawrence Bobo report that 90 percent of whites support integrated education.[16] Yet 90 percent oppose school busing and almost that many oppose federal intervention to achieve racial balance in the schools.[17] In the area of equal employment, almost 100 percent support equal job opportunities.[18] At the same time, approximately 65 percent oppose federal intervention to assure fair employment practices.[19] And white Americans generally oppose quotas in employment and university admissions, whereas academic social scientists tend to support these policies.

Schuman, Steeh, and Bobo summarize their analysis as showing that insofar as the principles of equal opportunity are concerned, white Americans exhibit "a much lower level of support for government intervention to promote principles than for the principles themselves." Furthermore, they point out that "the level of support for intervention is almost always low in absolute terms." They report that the only case where a majority of white Americans support government intervention is to assure equal access to hotels and restaurants.[20]

RACISM AND TRADITIONAL AMERICAN VALUES

The majority of social scientists who express unhappiness with these findings seem unwilling to allow for the possibility that most white Americans support equal opportunity, but oppose various implementation policies out of a sincere belief that those policies *do not* forward the principles of racial equality, that such policies are in fact unfair and violate important values. What's more, white Americans are not alone in holding these beliefs. Black Americans are not uniform in their support of preferential policies. Depending on the question asked, a sizable minority of blacks, and sometimes a majority, oppose such policies.

Many researchers seem unwilling to entertain the possibility that Americans who hold these beliefs may be right about the shortcomings of government intervention. After all, much has happened since the passage of the Civil Rights Act of 1964 and the Voting Rights Act of 1965. Americans have been witness to various efforts undertaken by the federal government since the 1960s, many coercive and unpopular, in the name of racial justice. Many of these efforts went beyond attempting to equalize opportunities for blacks and whites and instead seemed to require the imposition of statistically equal outcomes in ways that many thought violated the work ethic. Perhaps the majority who express opposition to federal intervention do so because they have come to believe that many of those efforts were ill advised. Social scientists, on the other hand, seem reluctant to acknowledge that some of their original policy prescriptions may be counterproductive today.

Part of the reluctance of social scientists to grant simple rationality to those who oppose their positions on civil rights is undoubtedly rooted in the Freudian and behaviorist beliefs to which many social scientists subscribe. Rationality assumes conscious awareness of needs and desires, an awareness which Freudian theory denies. Rationality also assumes that behavior is purposive and directed toward ends that have been planned and thought through. In classic behaviorist theory, such as that of B. F. Skinner, behavior is the product of reinforcement and is largely a matter of habit. Planned, thoughtful action is therefore of little significance in explaining behavior in the behaviorist model.

Whatever the reason, there has been a pervasive resistance among social scientists to accepting the possibility that many people might oppose various government policies that affect blacks because their logic or experience leads them in good conscience to question the value of those policies. Too often such objections are dismissed as crude Freudian rationalizations for simple selfishness or racial prejudice. The overwhelmingly liberal political orientation of social scientists also helps explain their frustration with those who reject liberal remedies for racial problems. The left-leaning orientation of social scientists is no recent development. In their important 1958 book *The Academic Mind,* sociologists Paul Lazarsfeld and Wagner Thielens, Jr. (then at Columbia University) reported on a large-scale survey of American academic and social scientists undertaken in 1955.[23] They reported that 58 percent of social scientists voted for the liberal Democratic candidate Adlai Stevenson in the 1952 presidential election, while only 30 percent voted for Eisenhower. . . .[24]

Recent data collected for the Carnegie Commission on Higher Education by the Survey Research Center at Berkeley University reveals little change in the political attitudes of social scientists. In 1989, 72 percent of social scientists at all types of colleges and universities characterized themselves as liberal and only 14 percent as conservative. The most liberal faculties were those specializing in public affairs, with fully 88 percent describing themselves as liberal and none as even moderately conservative. Sixty-eight percent of psychology faculty described themselves as liberal, as did 63 percent in economics. By way of contrast, only 54 percent of physical scientists, 47 percent of those in mathematics, 40 percent of those in engineering, and 31 percent of those in business and management characterized themselves as liberal. . . .[33]

Not only are social scientists overwhelmingly left and liberal in their politics, but in addition they tend to take a condescending view of members of the general public, who often disagree with them and who are much less likely to be characterized as liberal. For instance, many social scientists accept left-wing economic thinking and reject free-market economics as a mere rationalization for injustice and inequality, and think Americans who accept market principles are at best naive and lacking in social sophistication. Adherence to conventional middle-class values and middle-class concerns is seen as evidence of intellectual shallowness. The "Protestant work ethic," by which is meant a belief that effort and hard work will in time be rewarded by material and spiritual well-being, is held as evidence of an endemic simple-mindedness. Social scientists, by and large, favor large-scale government programs to correct what they see as the inadequacies of the market. The misgivings that many white Americans express about the virtues and efficiency of government programs are usually dismissed as reflecting ignorance of the way things *really* work in America. Many of those in the social sciences seem unwilling to accept the possibility that the majority of white Americans hold the beliefs they do out of good and sound reasons, and social scientists are quick to attribute the anti-statism of most whites to naiveté or, when it relates to government policies on race, to thinly veiled racial animosity. . . .

Paul Sniderman of Stanford and Michael Hagen of Berkeley, in their 1985 book *Race and Inequality*, feel that white Americans do not really understand the American class system of stratification and do not really understand the difficulties that blacks and other minorities face in their efforts to achieve equality. To the dismay of Sniderman and Hagen, Americans really *do* believe in what the authors characterize as the "folk ideology" of the Protestant work ethic and are beset by a naive faith in individualism. According to Sniderman and Hagen, individualism involves "a bedrock belief in the ethic of self-reliance." In this ethic "[i]ndividuals must take care of themselves. They must not pretend to be victims of circumstance, or ask for special favors, in an effort to get others to do for them what they should do for themselves. . . ."[38]

The authors argue that individualism is, in their words, an "ungenerous idea," since "it refuses to acknowledge that some are in fact handicapped and must overcome obstacles that are not of their making and that others do not face. In this sense the individualist lacks empathy for those disadvantaged by race or by poverty or by gender. . . ."[39]

According to the authors, "there is something extraordinary . . . about the individualists' understanding of equality of opportunity."[40] They express surprise that people really believe in the Protestant work ethic and claim that this must be because they do not understand the difficulties some people face. Sniderman and Hagen comment that "so far as the individualist can make out . . . everyone can get ahead, regardless of whether he or she is black, female, or poor."[41] Their condescension toward the average American's understanding clearly influences the way Sniderman and Hagen interpret the questionnaires they designed to assess public opinion. For instance, people were asked the extent of their agreement with the following two statements:

> It's a lack of skill and abilities that keeps *many* black people from getting a job. It's not *just* because they are black. When a black person is trained to do something, he is able to get a job. (Emphasis added)
>
> Black people *may not have the same opportunities* as whites, but *many* blacks haven't prepared themselves enough to make use of the opportunities that come their way. (Emphasis added)[42]

Those who agreed with the above statements were, according to Sniderman and Hagen, betraying an "ungenerous individualism." On the other hand, those who agreed with the following statement exhibited, in the view of the authors, a more sophisticated and generous understanding:

> Even with the new programs, minorities still face the same old job discrimination once the program is over.[43]

In other words, those who disagreed with the view that discrimination is widespread were, by definition, characterized as ungenerous and resistant to racial equality. The authors do not acknowledge the possibility that the "wrong" answers to the above questions may be closer to reality than the alternatives which they think correct. Given the widespread application of affirmative action rules and guidelines, it is hardly unreasonable for people to reject the assertion that "minorities still face the same old discrimination."

Furthermore, given well-known problems among blacks in the inner cities, it seems hardly irrational to conclude that many blacks suffer "a lack of skill and abilities" that "keeps many black people from getting a job." Similarly, is it not true that "[w]hen a black person is trained to do something, he is able to get a job"? Statistics reviewed elsewhere clearly suggest that blacks who are trained for employment find employment. The belief that blacks with job training can find jobs does not suggest antipathy toward blacks, but rather, simple familiarity with the facts.

It is instructive to note that a 1989 survey by ABC News and the *Washington Post* found very little difference between blacks and whites who were asked questions similar to those given above. Sixty percent of whites and 60 percent of blacks agreed with the statement: "If blacks would try harder, they could be just as well off as whites." Fifty-six percent of whites and 52 percent of blacks agreed with the statement: "Discrimination has unfairly held down blacks, but many of the problems which blacks have today are brought on by blacks themselves."[44]

Other researchers also explain opposition to quotas and set-asides in terms of Americans' naiveté. In a 1983 paper on attitudes toward affirmative action, James Kluegel and Eliot Smith argue that while whites recognize that blacks suffered from discrimination in the past, and therefore support programs "offering to help blacks acquire skills," they nevertheless oppose preferential hiring quotas "because they are thought to violate dominant equity norms." The authors continue:

> The premise that affirmative action programs are necessary to equalize opportunity requires that whites believe that the stratification system currently does not provide equal opportunity for all persons and groups. In this regard the seeming insensitivity of whites to the socioeconomic disadvantage of blacks may stem more from racial

segregation, and the resulting limited and naive perspective whites have on blacks' circumstances, than from prejudice and racism.[45]

To assert that people who disagree with you are naive or callous is, of course, to engage in fairly obvious *ad hominem* rhetoric, a tactic that has become all too common among social scientists working in this area. It is grossly unfair to attack people on such grounds without any independent evidence of naiveté or callousness, and yet researchers such as Sniderman and Hagen, and Kluegel and Smith, offer no such independent evidence. They merely assume that those who do not agree with their views *must* be naive. The evidence indicates, however, that it is more reasonable to charge these researchers with a lack of understanding, rather than to so charge the "unsophisticated" people who disagree with them. Perhaps the public has viewed the events of the last twenty-five years and has drawn different conclusions than social scientists have about the effectiveness of government programs? Unfortunately, the obvious ideological bias evidenced by these social scientists makes it difficult for them to accept the possibility that such disagreement may, in fact, be well reasoned.

This bias, of course, makes it even harder for social scientists to consider the possibility that blacks themselves might be ill served by the various policies designed to help them. Those policies that encourage reliance upon government support may, if anything, make their situation worse. Furthermore, social scientists rarely deal with the possibility that incorrect social science theories might cause harm. How can we expect young black Americans to struggle to succeed when we keep telling them that the system is so stacked against them that they are bound to fail? Even if the social scientists are right and American society is stacked against blacks, defeatist attitudes are not likely to be helpful and may be self-confirming. Very few social scientists seem to entertain the possibility that the "naive" credo which urges people to "stand on their own two feet" might, even in the face of serious discrimination, be the best advice for young people to follow.

SYMBOLIC RACISM

The most striking example of the continuing influence of the association between traditional values and bigotry is contained in recent work that attributes the continuing opposition to many civil rights policies to a subtle new form of racism. David Sears, Donald Kinder, and John McConahay, along with various colleagues and independent researchers, have generated a sizable and influential research literature which purports to confirm the existence of this new type of racism.[46]

The main difficulty for this group is showing how racism is the problem when all objective measures on white American attitudes reveal a steady decline in racist attitudes. They have developed an elusive theory, clearly reminiscent of the thesis of *The Authoritarian Personality,* that people develop prejudiced attitudes in childhood and thereafter carry a "racial affect" with them into adult life. When confronted with programs designed to help blacks, they oppose those programs because of this new form of racism. The opposition is in turn rationalized in terms of a commitment to traditional American values.

Donald Kinder, a political scientist whom I quoted earlier, and social psychologist David Sears have written widely on the problem of symbolic racism among whites. They agree that in wide areas of American life, white opposition to equal opportunity for blacks has declined sharply: "On voting rights, schools, public accommodations, housing, and employment practices, segregationist sentiment has all but disappeared. White America has become, in principle at least, racially egalitarian—a momentous and undeniably significant change." Kinder and Sears argue, however, that opposition to equality still remains, but can no longer be based on the discredited "explicitly segregationist, white supremacist view." In its place, they suggest,

> is a new variant that might be called symbolic racism. This we define as a blend of antiblack affect and the kind of traditional American moral values embedded in the Protestant ethic. [It is] . . . a form of resistance to change in the racial status quo based on moral feelings that blacks violate such traditional American values as individualism and self-reliance, the work ethic, obedience, and discipline.[47]

The authors go on to argue that white Americans feel that "individuals should be rewarded on their merits, which in turn should be based on hard work and diligent service." This is of course the view of things embodied in the Protestant ethic. Kinder and Sears argue that since opposition to equality is now based on the Protestant ethic, "symbolic racism should find its most vociferous expression on political issues that involve 'unfair' government assistance to blacks . . . ," including welfare, reverse discrimination and racial quotas, forced busing, and government-funded abortions for the poor.[48]

In other words, agreement with traditional American values is, in the view of these authors, actually an expression of deeply felt prejudice and is therefore evidence of racial hostility. But how is this startling assertion validated—that is, how do Kinder and Sears know whether people who hold traditional views do so out of racism, rather than simply because they believe traditional values are important and worthwhile?

In order to distinguish opposition based on racial animosity from opposition based on political belief, one would need separate and independently validated measures of each. For instance, one would have to show, first, that there is a correlation between a belief in something like self-reliance and an expressed hatred toward blacks. Second, one would have to demonstrate that the belief in self-reliance is adopted *because* it is a way of criticizing blacks, who are thought to be lacking in self-reliance. This Kinder and Sears did not do. Rather, they used a questionnaire which, in effect, confused rationally motivated and racially motivated opposition to affirmative action policies. The questionnaire was originally administered in 1969 and 1973, during a period of considerable turmoil produced by Vietnam War protests and the rash of riots in black inner-city neighborhoods. The following questions were asked (items with an asterisk were not used in the 1969 study):

1. Do you think that most Negroes/blacks who receive money from welfare programs could get along without it if they tried, or do they really need the help?

2. Negroes/blacks shouldn't push where they're not wanted.
3. *Because of past discrimination, it is sometimes necessary to set up quotas for admission to college of minority group students.
4. Do you think Los Angeles city officials pay more, less or the same attention to a request or complaint from a black person?
5. Of the groups on the card are there any which you think have gained more than they are entitled to?
6. *It is wrong to set up quotas to admit black students to college who don't meet the usual requirements.
7. Over the past two years blacks have got more than they deserve.
8. In Los Angeles, would you say many, some, or only a few blacks miss out on jobs or promotions because of racial discrimination?
9. Busing elementary school children to schools in other parts of the city only harms their education.
10. In some cases it is best for children to attend elementary schools outside their neighborhood.
11. *Are you in favor or opposed to the busing of children to achieve racial desegregation?
12. *If the supreme court ordered busing to achieve racial desegregation of public schools would you be opposed to it?
13. *If necessary, children should be bused to achieve racial desegregation.[49]

A person's "score" on this symbolic-racism scale is determined by how many questions he answers in the "wrong" way. Those who oppose busing and quotas are therefore guaranteed to score high on symbolic racism, even if they disagreed with all the other items, since seven of the thirteen questions deal with busing and quotas. If, on top of that, respondents did not like welfare policies (item 1) and objected to special treatment for blacks in general (items 4, 5, and 7), they would be scored hopelessly racist in the "symbolic" sense. Item 2, "[B]lacks shouldn't push . . . ," does seem to suggest agreement with segregationist attitudes. But this is not clear, for while 64 percent of respondents agreed with that statement, 70 percent said they would not mind if a black moved next door to them, in response to a question on another questionnaire whose results were reported in the same article. On the other hand, the item "[B]lacks shouldn't push" may have tapped the strong feelings generated by the Watts riot of 1965. It is interesting in this regard that there were no questions about riots in the questionnaire, even though the riots were much discussed and created divisions even among liberal civil rights activists. In any case, just about anyone who disagreed with the liberal policy agenda of the time would have been classified as a symbolic racist by this questionnaire, and it is hardly surprising that so many of the respondents were so labeled. How could it be otherwise when popular opinion was, and still is, against coercive, as opposed to opportunity-enhancing, affirmative action policies? . . .

How did the authors verify the assertion that these attitudes were racist—that is, how did they measure the validity of the questionnaire? They did so by showing that there was a correlation between respondents' answers and their votes in the 1969 and 1973 Los Angeles mayoral elections, elections that happened to pit a black Democrat against a white Republican. In other words, the assertion that people who opposed busing and hiring quotas were racist was proven by the fact that they voted for a white conservative candidate who also opposed these policies, and against a black liberal who was thought more likely to support them.[57]

It is important to stress that the only independent validation of Kinder and Sears's symbolic-racism scale was the voting behavior of the respondents. Those who scored high on symbolic racism (i.e., expressed prevailing moderate to conservative views) were found to be more likely to vote for the white Republican, Sam Yorty, in the mayoral elections of 1969 and 1973 than for the black Democrat, Tom Bradley. This perfectly rational voting pattern was characterized by Kinder and Sears as "antiblack voting behavior." From the authors' data it is impossible to determine whether the voters chose the white conservative because he was white or because he was conservative. Kinder and Sears did not attempt to empirically answer that question but merely asserted that it must have been a vote based on race. . . .

IGNORING THE UNDERCLASS

One of the glaring weaknesses in the social science research literature assessing racial attitudes is its failure to come to grips with the growing pattern of pathology within underclass black communities. Most researchers ignore the possibility that the attitudes of many white Americans toward civil rights policies may have been affected by the trends so evident over the past thirty years in the inner cities. Maybe those trends explain why many white Americans have become reluctant to support a continuation of the policies which many interpret as causing those problems. Consider three important books on racial attitudes written in the 1980s by respected scholars: *Race and Inequality* by Paul Sniderman and Michael Hagen; *Racial Attitudes in America* by Howard Schuman, Charlotte Steeh, and Lawrence Bobo; and *Beliefs about Inequality* by James Kluegel and Eliot Smith.[64] In all three the topics of crime and illegitimacy are completely ignored, and neither term appears in any of the indexes. It is a serious weakness of these books about white attitudes toward blacks that they fail to address some of the most obvious reasons why whites might be having second thoughts about present policies.

The "American Public," whose responses to various questionnaires are analyzed in social science research, is generally a middle-class population, whose attachment to the Protestant ethic is well known. Also well known is the fact that middle-class Americans of all races place great value on home ownership, safe neighborhoods, and good schools as vehicles for the upward mobility of their children. In the questionnaires used to assess their attitudes, such people are asked to take positions on "blacks." But to which blacks are they supposed to refer? All the questionnaires are surprisingly vague on this point, especially in light of the widely acknowledged chasm that has developed between middle-class and underclass blacks. The former, in income, education, and lifestyle, are increasingly indistinguishable from their white counterparts. The latter, however, are marked by a degree of social pathology—in illegitimacy, crime, school failure, drug abuse, unemployment, etc.—that is highly disturbing to those, both black and white, in the middle class. This dichotomy within the black population goes completely without comment in the debates about the meaning of white attitudes toward busing, integration, and hiring and admissions quotas.

One obvious reason why so many whites reject the need for quotas and do not see black problems in terms of discrimination may be the *fact* that blacks, even *very poor* blacks, who have adopted middle-class behavior patterns—who postpone parenthood, finish school, avoid drugs and crime, etc., are doing quite well, while those in the underclass, who by their behavior appear to reject those values, are not. How, given this undeniable reality, is one supposed to respond to a request to choose between the following statements from Sniderman and Hagen's questionnaire?

A. Many blacks have only themselves to blame for not doing better in life. If they tried harder, they'd do better.
B. When two qualified people, one black and one white, are considered for the same job, the black won't get the job no matter how hard he tries.[65]

To choose "A" is to find yourself labeled "ungenerous" toward the plight of blacks, even though on its face it is a true statement. On the other hand, to agree with the second statement is to endorse what, at the present time, flies in the face of most people's experience. Affirmative action policies have meant that in recent years if a black and a white who are equally qualified apply for admission to an elite college or seek employment as police officers or firefighters, it is almost always the case that the black gets the admission notice or the job. The fact that people appear to give contradictory responses on such questionnaires does not imply that they are ambivalent about racial equality. But it does suggest that the usefulness of such questionnaires is limited indeed.

The failure to acknowledge the reality of the black underclass also makes problematic any easy assertions about the extent of real or "old-fashioned redneck racism." All researchers agree that support for segregation is a mark of real racism. It is typically measured by responses to such questions as the following in Gallup polls taken in 1978 and 1980:

1. Would you, yourself, have any objection to sending your children to school where a few of the children were black? [95 percent of respondents said no]
2. Would you, yourself, have any objection to sending your children to school where half the children were black? [76 percent said no]
3. Would you, yourself, have any objection to sending your children to school where more than half the children were black? [42 percent said no]
4. If a black person came to live next door would you move? [86 percent said no, 10 percent said they might, and 4 percent said yes]
5. Would you move if black people came to live in great numbers in your neighborhood? [46 percent said no, 33 percent said they might, and 21 percent said yes][66]

Is the fact that a majority of white parents object to their children attending a largely black school indicative of a lingering racial hostility? Or is it a response to the fact (and not merely the perception) that many such schools are dangerous places and have seriously compromised educational standards? Does the fact that 33 percent of respondents said they might move, and 21 percent said they would move, if large numbers of blacks came to live in their neighborhoods support the contention that a majority of whites reject integration "in practice"? Or does it reflect a concern that the "large numbers of blacks" may contain many members of the underclass? Very few people from the middle class, whether white or black, see such people as desirable neighbors. In fact, in a poll of residential preferences in the Detroit area in 1976, only 11 percent of *blacks* responded that they would prefer to live in a neighborhood where the residents were "all black" or "mostly black."[67] In truth, the hard data that forms the foundation for the current argument about racial attitudes is so fraught with difficulties that just about any interpretation can be gotten from it. And yet it is on these grounds that many social scientists charge white Americans with resisting racial equality. . . .

NOTES

15. Donald R. Kinder, "The Continuing American Dilemma: White Resistance to Racial Change Forty Years after Myrdal." *Journal of Social Issues,* vol. 42., no. 2 (1986), pp. 151–52.

16. Howard Schuman, Charlotte Steeh, and Lawrence Bobo, *Racial Attitudes in America* (Cambridge, MA: Harvard University Press, 1985), p. 77.

17. *Ibid.,* p. 88.

18. *Ibid.,* p. 74.

19. *Ibid.,* p. 91.

20. *Ibid.,* p. 197.

23. Paul F. Lazarsfeld and Wagner Thielens, Jr., with David Riesman, *The Academic Mind: Social Scientists in a Time of Crisis* (Glencoe, IL: Free Press, 1958).

24. *Ibid.,* p. 14.

33. "Politics of the Professoriate." *American Enterprise,* July/August 1991, p. 87.

38. Paul M. Sniderman and Michael Gray Hagen, *Race and Inequality: A Study in American Values* (Chatham, NJ: Chatham House, 1985), p. 97.

39. *Ibid.*

40. *Ibid.,* p. 93.

41. *Ibid.,* p. 96.

42. *Ibid.,* pp. 91–93.

43. *Ibid.*

44. "A Portrait in Black and White." *American Enterprise,* January/February 1990, p. 100.

45. James Kluegel and Eliot Smith, "Affirmative Action Attitudes: Effects of Self-Interest, Racial Affect, and Stratification Beliefs on Whites' Views." *Social Forces,* vol. 6. no. 3 (March 1983), p. 801.

46. See Kinder, "The Continuing American Dilemma."

47. Donald R. Kinder and David O. Sears, "Prejudice and Politics: Symbolic Racism versus Racial Threats to the Good Life." *Journal of Personality and Social Psychology,* vol. 40, no. 3 (1981), p. 416.

48. *Ibid.*

49. *Ibid.,* p. 420.

57. Kinder and Sears, "Prejudice and Politics," p. 417.

64. Sniderman and Hagen, *Race and Inequality;* Schuman, Steeh, and Bobo, *Racial Attitudes in America;* James R. Kluegel and Eliot R. Smith, *Beliefs about Inequality* (New York: Aldine De Gruyter, 1986).

65. Sniderman and Hagen, *Race and Inequality,* p. 93.

66. Schuman, Steeh, and Bobo, *Racial Attitudes in America,* pp. 106–8.

67. Gerald David Jaynes and Robin M. Williams, Jr., eds., *A Common Destiny: Blacks and American Society* (Washington, DC: National Academy Press, 1989), p. 133.

PART 3

Discrimination, Economic Restructuring, and Underclass Culture

Discrimination based on skin color has been a prominent and ugly reality in the United States for more than four centuries. People of color have been treated differently than whites and have suffered physically, economically, culturally, psychologically, and politically.

Blacks were forcibly brought over from Africa in the sixteenth and seventeenth centuries as indentured servants and slaves. After the abolition of slavery in the mid–nineteenth century, southern states imposed an all-encompassing system of legal segregation, which continued unabated until the 1960s. Even after the passage of the Civil Rights Act (1964), the Voting Rights Act (1965), and numerous other pieces of legislation and administrative guidelines, discrimination continues to be a widespread problem throughout the country.

Although never the victims of slavery, Hispanics were also the victims of white discrimination. The United States conquered Mexico during the nineteenth century and took over what is now the southwestern part of the United States. Puerto Rico, also annexed by war, has been an American colony since 1898. During the twentieth century, Hispanic immigrants have been disproportionately employed as migrant workers, low-paid restaurant and hotel workers, and workers in garment factory sweatshops.

American Indians were, of course, the targets first of new American colonists and then of subsequent generations as the country expanded westward. The military conquest and attempted extermination of Native Americans are infamous. The resettlement of conquered tribes on reservations was detrimental not only to both their economies and their cultures but also to the developing culture of the United States.

Asians have also been the victims of white discrimination. They were barely tolerated when they were imported as low-paid contract railroad workers in the mid–nineteenth century. A number of states passed laws prohibiting Chinese from owning property. After they were no longer needed, Congress passed the Chinese Exclusion Act in 1882, which prevented further Chinese immigration. American immigration legislation in the first half of the twentieth century gave small quotas to potential immigrants from Asia, as well as immigrants from

Africa and Latin America. During World War II, Japanese residents on the West Coast, both citizens and noncitizens, were forced into concentration camps as potential enemies of the state.

People of color, of course, have not been the only victims of discrimination. White immigrants, especially those from southern and eastern Europe, and non-Protestants also have a history of mistreatment. Irish, Italian, and Polish immigrants have been denied employment and housing. Catholics and Jews have suffered because of their religious beliefs. However, the discrimination against these white groups has not been as long lasting or intense as discrimination toward people of color.

STATISTICAL DISPARITIES

Statistics compiled by the federal government show the results of past and present discrimination against people of color. With the exception of Asians, people of color lag behind whites in all indicators of economic well-being.

The U.S. Bureau of the Census (1997d) provides the following data on median household income in 1995:

Asians	$40,614
Whites	$35,766
Hispanics	$22,860
Blacks	$22,393

Data for Native Americans were unavailable. According to these figures, black household income is only 63 percent of white income and Hispanic household income is 64 percent of white income.

The high income of Asian households is due, in part, to the large number of household members in the labor force. There are also great disparities in the median incomes of Asian households, with Vietnamese and Cambodian incomes being similar to black incomes.

Significant racial/ethnic differences also exist among individual workers. These statistics from the Bureau of the Census (1997a) are usually presented for year-round full-time workers, so part-time and intermittent full-time workers are excluded. In 1996, the median incomes for male year-round full-time workers were

Whites	$34,741
Blacks	$27,136
Hispanics	$21,265

Unfortunately, data for Asians and Native Americans were not reported. Black males made 78 percent of the income of white males and Hispanic males made only 61 percent of the income of white males.

Although female year-round full-time workers made less than comparable males, the racial/ethnic pattern for median income for females is the same:

Whites	$25,358
Blacks	$21,990
Hispanics	$19,272

The racial/ethnic gap among women is narrower than that among men. Black women made 87 percent of the income of white women and Hispanic women made 76 percent of the income of white women.

It is also important to note that within each race/ethnic group, men make considerably more than women. Among whites, women make only 73 percent of what men make. The comparable gender differences among blacks and Hispanics is 85 percent and 91 percent, respectively.

The disparities of wealth are even greater than those regarding income. Whereas income refers to the money that comes in each year (wages, salary, dividends, interest, transfer payments, etc.), wealth refers to the value of what a person or household owns (from clothing and cars to corporate stocks and bonds). In 1993, median household net worth (what one owns minus what one owes) was distributed as follows:

Whites	$45,740
Blacks	$4,418
Hispanics	$4,656

White households had more than ten times the wealth of black and Hispanic households (U.S. Bureau of the Census n.d.). The black-white gap in wealth has remained constant since 1984, but the Hispanic-white gap has increased substantially.

Unemployment differences between whites and people of color are also pronounced. The official 1996 unemployment rates (*Employment and Earnings* 1997) were as follows:

Whites	4.7%
Blacks	10.5%
Hispanics	8.9%

Blacks were 2.2 times more likely to be unemployed than whites, whereas Hispanics were 1.9 times more likely to be unemployed than whites.

It is also not surprising that significant racial/ethnic differences in poverty rates exist. In 1996, poverty rates for each race/ethnic group were as follows:

Whites	11.2%
Asians	14.5%
Blacks	28.4%
Hispanics	29.4%

In other words, blacks and Hispanics were about 2.5 times more likely to be poor than whites (U.S. Bureau of the Census 1997b). Asians also had higher poverty rates than whites, even though they had higher median household incomes.

Although these statistical disparities are troubling, the lack of progress in eliminating these disparities is even more troubling. For example, the government has kept statistics on family income, which is slightly different than household income, for many years. In 1996, the most recent figures, black families made 59 percent of what white families made; this is not much better than the 54 percent figure that existed in 1959. Hispanic families were *worse* off relative to whites in 1996 than they were in 1971 when the government first started keeping separate figures for Hispanics. The Hispanic/white family income figure was 58 percent in

1996 compared to 71 percent in 1971. The specific income figures are available in the statistical appendix at the end of this book.

The unemployment gap has also been relatively stable. Black unemployment has been double white unemployment since 1959. The black-white poverty gap has narrowed somewhat since 1959 although the Hispanic-white gap has remained constant since 1980.

In spite of the overall negative figures, there are several positive statistical trends. The educational gap between blacks and whites has declined (see Part Five). One striking indicator is that college-educated blacks now have median incomes that are 92 percent that of college-educated whites. In addition, the income gap between black two-parent families and comparable white families has been getting smaller. In 1996, black two-parent families made 84 percent of the income of white two-parent families; in 1970 the comparable figure was 70 percent. The implications of these findings are discussed below.

EXPLANATIONS OF STATISTICAL DISPARITIES

Social scientists of all political persuasions acknowledge the existence of these statistical disparities. The arguments have to do with *explaining* these disparities. Most scholars who study race and ethnic relations would agree that these disparities can largely be explained by past and present discrimination. Indeed, most of the readings in this section support this argument.

Some social scientists, however, argue that discrimination plays only a minor role. These scholars explain the statistical disparities by emphasizing either cultural differences, human capital differences, or the effect of structural changes in the larger society. We explain these competing arguments below.

Cultural Explanations

Conservatives such as Edward Banfield, Charles Murray, and Lawrence Harrison often argue that culture can account for most of the statistical disparities. The underclass culture, which is said to be passed on from generation to generation, emphasizes living in the present rather than planning for the future, being dependent on welfare rather than trying to get a job, and feeling powerless about the chances of being upwardly mobile. This culture of poverty, say conservatives, prevents people in the underclass from taking advantage of opportunities that might be available to them.

Using this analysis, conservatives argue that the black-white difference in family income can be attributed to the expectation and/or desire of poor women to bear and raise children without the help of a husband. Over 40 percent of black families are single-parent families that are headed by women.

The problem with saying that black families made only 59 percent of what white families made in 1996, say conservatives, is that one is comparing all black families, of which a large proportion are headed by women, with all white families, of which only a small proportion are headed by women. If, on the other hand, one looks only at two-parent families, black families make 84 percent of the income of white families. The conclusion, say conservatives, is that blacks who choose middle-class family structures are more economically similar to white families than those who do not choose middle-class family structures.

Human Capital Explanations

Rather than emphasizing cultural variables, some conservatives and a few liberals argue that differences in "human capital" (i.e., skills and credentials) can explain most of the statistical disparities. Black-white differences in unemployment and income, they argue, can be explained by differences in education. Blacks have lower levels of education and, therefore, can be expected to have fewer jobs and lower-paying jobs. Conservatives often use the culture argument to explain why black-white differences in human capital exist. Black female-headed families, according to this argument, are less able than white families to motivate their children to get an education and to help them while they are in school.

Unfortunately neither the culture argument nor the human capital argument is supported by the statistical evidence. For example, even though the income gap between white and black two-parent families is closing, the 84 percent gap is still quite substantial. This is especially significant since both partners in black two-parent families are much more likely to be working full-time than in white two-parent families. Finally, looking at the data for female-headed families only, black families make only 69 percent of the income of white families. At best, cultural differences in family structure explains only part of the statistical disparity between black and white family income.

Similarly, differences in human capital, as measured by years of education, cannot explain differences in individual income and unemployment. Even at the same level of education, blacks and Hispanics tend to have higher unemployment rates than whites. This is true for young high school graduates and those with some college. (See statistical appendix.) It is also true for Hispanic college graduates relative to comparable whites. Only among white and black college graduates are the unemployment rates relatively equal (*Employment and Earnings* 1997).

People of color also have lower incomes than whites, even at the same level of education. For example, consider the median incomes of year-round full-time workers who were twenty-five years old and older in 1995. Among high school dropouts, blacks made only 84 percent of what whites made. Among people with high school degrees and those with some college, blacks made only 80 percent of what whites made. Even among college graduates, blacks made only 78 percent of what whites made (U.S. Bureau of the Census 1997c). The earnings gap is greater among men than among women.

The same trend is true for Hispanics and Asians. In 1993, for example, Asian high school graduates made 87 percent of what comparable whites made, and Asian college graduates made only 90 percent of what whites made. Asians with some college, however, made 6 percent *more* than comparable whites (Carter and Wilson 1997). Like the cultural argument, the human capital argument can, at best, explain only part of the statistical disparities discussed above.

There are also conceptual problems with both arguments. First, they assume that you can separate culture and human capital from discrimination. Second, there is a problem with the causal relationship between variables.

Conservatives tend to argue that both family structure and years of education are *independent* of discrimination. They also assume that female-headed families and low levels of education among blacks are cultural choices rather than the result of discrimination. The correlation between female-headed families with low education and low income then becomes a causal relationship; that is, *culture* causes *female-headed families and low education*, which result in *low income*.

However, culture does not just fall from the sky; it is, in part, the result of socioeconomic conditions. It is also possible to argue that the large number of black female-headed families is a *result* of discrimination, not a cause. Unemployed and low-paid black men, for example, do not have enough money to support a family and, therefore, cannot fulfill one of the major social responsibilities associated with traditional definitions of masculinity. Fathering, without the responsibility for the children, may be an alternative source of masculinity.

Similarly, low levels of educational achievement are, in part, also the result of discrimination. Schools in poor black neighborhoods are notoriously bad, in part, because of low expectations on the part of teachers, a tracked curriculum, and a lack of financial resources. A good argument can be made that the schools, intentionally or not, are a major contributing factor to the low educational levels among poor blacks.

In addition, poor parents, who faced both educational and employment discrimination themselves, cannot provide the same help to their children that middle-class parents can. Again, this is not just a cultural factor but is also the result of prior discrimination.

Structural Changes

A third explanation of the statistical disparities that minimizes discrimination is associated with some liberal and radical social scientists, such as William Julius Wilson (1987, 1996). According to this argument, changes in the U.S. economy during the late twentieth century have disproportionately hurt poor people of color. In order to maintain profits in the face of foreign competition, many U.S. manufacturers have tried to reduce labor costs by moving their operations outside of the country where labor costs and taxes are lower and environmental regulations are more lax. This has dramatically reduced the number of available well-paying blue-collar jobs.

Since a high proportion of these jobs were unionized, membership in labor unions has declined. This trend, combined with the attacks of the Reagan and Bush administrations, has resulted in a weakened labor movement. Finally, the new jobs in the growing service sector of the economy are disproportionately nonunionized and low paying and the better-paying more-skilled jobs require job experience and/or educational credentials.

Although these trends hurt all workers, the argument continues, they hurt black and Hispanic workers the most. A greater proportion of minority families than white families were dependent on unionized blue-collar jobs. White displaced workers have fared better than minorities in terms of finding new jobs. The concentration of poor blacks in the inner city and the movement of jobs to the suburbs makes things even more difficult. Although these trends have little to do with discrimination, they exacerbate statistical disparities that may have been the result of previous discrimination.

We are sympathetic with the argument that these structural changes have a disproportionately negative impact on people of color. However, as the readings in this section show, discrimination is still a significant and independent problem. Both discrimination and the larger socioeconomic trends operate concurrently and both must be confronted if racial/ethnic equality is to become a reality.

* * *

The first two readings in this section take the view that discrimination has diminished in importance. Lawrence E. Harrison ("How Cultural Values Shape Economic Success") makes the conservative argument that cultural differences between whites and people of color can explain the economic differences. William Julius Wilson ("Societal Changes and Vulnerable Neighborhoods") argues that larger social changes are negatively impacting poor black inner-city neighborhoods.

The remaining eight readings, on the other hand, argue that discrimination is alive and well in the United States and has substantial negative impacts on people of color. Fred L. Pincus ("From Individual to Structural Discrimination") begins this section with a discussion of different types of discrimination. In addition to discussing intentional discrimination at both an individual and structural level, he argues that some social policies that appear to be race-neutral in intent have discriminatory *effects*.

Douglass S. Massey ("America's Apartheid and the Urban Underclass") argues that residential segregation against blacks is still a significant issue. This segregation causes concentrated poverty in black communities and limits opportunities for upward mobility.

The next three readings address the issue of employment discrimination. Marc Bendick, Jr., Charles W. Jackson, and Victor A. Reinoso ("Measuring Employment Discrimination Through Controlled Experiments") examine how Washington, D.C., employers reacted to black and white applicants with identical credentials. The good news is that most employers did not favor either the black or white applicant. The bad news is that when one was favored, it was usually the white that benefited.

Joleen Kirschenman and Kathryn M. Neckerman ("'We'd Love to Hire Them, But . . . ': The Meaning of Race for Employers") show that Chicago employers discriminate against poor black and Hispanic males because of the expectation that they will have poor work habits. Karen J. Hossfeld ("Hiring Immigrant Women: Silicon Valley's 'Simple Formula'") shows how California's high-tech employers discriminate on the basis of gender as well as race and ethnicity.

Since most of the research on discrimination is about blacks, we have included readings on two rapidly growing race/ethnic groups. Joan Moore and Raquel Pinderhughes ("Latinos and Discrimination") analyze the problems faced by Hispanics in the United States, and Pyong Gap Min ("Major Issues Relating to Asian American Experiences") does the same for Asians.

Among the various policies intended to combat employment discrimination and provide equal opportunity is affirmative action. Fred L. Pincus ("The Case for Affirmative Action") analyzes this controversial policy.

REFERENCES

Carter, Deborah J., and Reginald Wilson (1997) *Minorities in Higher Education: 1996–1997, The Fifteenth Annual Status Report*. Washington, D.C.: American Council on Education.

U.S. Bureau of the Census (1997a) Current Population Reports, Series P-60, No. 197, *Money Income in the United States, 1996*. Washington, D.C.: U.S. Government Printing Office.

U.S. Bureau of the Census (1997b) Current Population Reports, Series P-60, No. 198. *Poverty in the United States, 1996.* Washington, D.C.: U.S. Government Printing Office.

U.S. Bureau of the Census (1997c) Current Population Reports, Series P20–498. *The Black Population in the United States, March 1996 (Update).* Washington, D.C.: U.S. Government Printing Office.

U.S. Bureau of the Census (1997d) "Median Incomes for Selected Household Characteristics and Income Definitions, 1995" Available: http://www.census.gov/hhes/income/income95/in95med2.html.

U.S. Bureau of the Census (n.d.) *Asset Ownership of Households: 1993 Highlights.* Available: http://www.census.gov.hhes/www/wealth/highlite.html.

U.S. Department of Labor (1997) *Employment and Earnings*, January.

Wilson, William Julius (1987) *The Truly Disadvantaged: The Inner City, the Underclass, and Public Policy*. Chicago: University of Chicago Press.

Wilson, William Julius (1996) *When Work Disappears: The World of the New Urban Poor.* New York: Knopf.

8

How Cultural Values Shape Economic Success

LAWRENCE E. HARRISON

Since the Supreme Court's *Brown v. Board of Education* ruling against segregated schools in 1954, most black Americans have participated in a political, social, and economic revolution. In terms of political participation, education, upward employment mobility, and family income, huge strides have been made toward closing the gap between blacks and whites, above all for the two-thirds of America's blacks who have made it into the mainstream—and into the middle class. The condition of the one-third who have not made it, most of them in the ghetto, is a tragedy for them, in personal terms, as well as for the broader society, in terms of the heavy costs of lost creativity, crime, and welfare and other social programs.

But while racism still exists (there are many reasons to believe that it has declined sharply), in my view it is no longer the principal obstacle to progress for people in black ghettos. The just-cited statistic of two-thirds of America's blacks having moved into the mainstream is one compelling evidence of that assertion. I believe that the principal obstacle today is culture: a set of values and attitudes, strongly influenced by the slavery experience, perpetuated by the isolation enforced, historically, by the Jim Crow laws and, today, by the ghetto. Accordingly, antipoverty policies and programs must emphasize access to the mainstream. Affirmative action has contributed to the achievement of that access for the majority of blacks, but its costs increasingly outweigh its benefits, particularly since its focus shifted from equal opportunity to equal results. This evolution strengthens the position of those black leaders who, like the Hispanic leaders calling for bilingualism and biculturalism, would subordinate national—American—identity to racial/ethnic identity.

HISTORICAL OVERVIEW: BLACKS IN THE UNITED STATES

The first blacks arrived in Virginia in 1619. They were not slaves but, like so many whites, indentured servants who, in due course, earned their freedom. Slavery was not introduced in the colonies until the second half of the seventeenth century, by which time there was already an appreciable number of "free persons of color."[1]

The number grew as a result of the freeing of slaves by masters, or *manumission*, often following sexual liaisons; the purchase of freedom by slaves who enjoyed a salary or other income; or escape through the underground railway to the North.

By the outbreak of the Civil War, the number of "free persons of color" approached 500,000, more than 10 percent of the total black population at the time. Many lived in the North, particularly cities, or in the plantation-free Piedmont, and tidewater Virginia and Maryland. Large and dynamic free black (principally mulatto) communities also sprang up in New Orleans, where a third of the "free colored" families owned slaves,[2] and in Charleston, South Carolina. By the Civil War, most free blacks were literate and self-sufficient. Almost all black slaves were illiterate, since most slave owners believed that education would ultimately precipitate slave uprisings. The free blacks were increasingly acculturated to the white cultural mainstream. In many cases, white fathers of mulattoes facilitated their access. Their self-image—and expectation of upward mobility—had to be far more positive than that of the slaves.

Slaves were acculturated to a system that almost totally suppressed the idea of progress, along with any progressive values and attitudes. Moreover, they came to the New World from traditional African societies that practiced both slavery and religions based on magic and propitiation of spirits. (The roots of Haitian voodoo are in the Dahomey region of West Africa—today called Benin—whence came large numbers of American slaves, many of whom practiced it, calling it "Hoodoo.")

I accept Herbert Gutman's thesis that slavery did not destroy the black family.[3] But that does not gainsay slavery's inculcation of values that are impediments to work, saving, education, and upward mobility, impediments that operated with comparably stultifying effect for American *and* Latin American slaves. The Venezuelan writer Carlos Rangel has observed, "a number of factors inhibit the development of societies based on slavery: the passive resistance to work that is the earmark of the slave; the absurd prestige of idleness that afflicts his master; and . . . a rhythm of life so little concerned with punctuality."[5] The words of the liberal Brazilian economist Celso Furtado about the consequences of slavery in his country also merit our attention: "Through the first half of the twentieth century, the vast majority of the descendants of slaves continued to live within the limited system of 'necessities.' . . . Able to satisfy their living expenses with two or three days of work per week, [they] found it much more attractive to 'buy' leisure than to continue working when they already had enough to 'live.'"[6]

Thomas Sowell adds, "As workers, blacks had little sense of personal responsibility under slavery. Lack of initiative, evasion of work, half-done work, unpredictable absenteeism, and abuse of tools and equipment were pervasive under slavery, and these patterns did not suddenly disappear with emancipation."[7] According to John Dollard, "The slavery system was . . . a device for getting work done without regard to its effect on Negro personality. . . . The cultivation of dependence reactions by the slavery system . . . is quite extreme."[8] The historian Stephan Thernstrom speaks of a black "cultural pattern—an emphasis on consumption rather than saving, an aversion to risk-taking investment" that would logically have its roots in the slavery experience.[9]

Slavery undermines the focus on the future that is instrumental to planning, saving, and investing. For the slave, the present is the overwhelming reality. And, as Eugene Genovese notes, there are "some important cultural continuities [with Africa]. Traditional African time-reckoning focuses on present and past, not future."[10]

Freedmen and Their Descendants

It should not be surprising, then, that most black leadership and achievement in the nineteenth century and the first decades of the twentieth century came from the descendants of "free persons of color," who got a head start on acculturation to the American mainstream. The first great black leader, Frederick Douglass, had escaped from urban slavery in the South and lived for many years as a free man in the North, married to a white woman. In 1870, free persons of color established the first black high school in the United States, Dunbar High in Washington, D.C., whose students scored higher as a whole than any white high school in citywide tests in 1899 and for years thereafter, and which sent three-fourths of its graduates on to college. W.E.B. Du Bois was a descendant of free blacks. So were or are United Nations official Ralph Bunche, Supreme Court Justice Thurgood Marshall, and the politically prominent Andrew Young, Clifford Alexander, and Julian Bond.

Thomas Sowell notes that, through the first half of the twentieth century, descendants of free persons of color constituted the majority of black professionals and were far better educated and had smaller families than descendants of emancipated slaves. Sowell concludes, "As with other groups around the world, historic advantages in acculturation had enduring consequences for generations to come."[11]

To be sure, many descendants of freedmen are lighter in color, and it is probably true that they were somewhat less discriminated against for that reason. But in the heyday of anti-Negro prejudice in the United States, lighter skin was no guarantee of better treatment. For example, no American black of any shade played in the baseball major leagues until Jackie Robinson broke the barrier in 1947 (although some Latin Americans "of color" did—but they were labeled "Latins").

Except when it has mitigated discrimination and enhanced expectations of upward mobility, skin color is, I believe, largely a coincidence when it comes to the achievements of the descendants of "free persons of color." I believe that the principal reason that they have done better than the descendants of emancipated slaves is that they got a head start of several generations on acculturation. One evidence of this is the extent to which they speak unaccented English. The broader, more rapid acculturation of the last few decades has made standard English far more common among blacks.)

The West Indians

Further evidence of the significance of culture in black achievement is furnished by West Indian immigrants in America. Substantial West Indian immigration started in the early years of the twentieth century, principally from Jamaica, Barbados, Trinidad, and the Bahamas. Sowell observes that, by 1920, one-quarter of

Harlem's population was West Indian, although West Indians represent only about 1 percent of the national black population.[12] That 1 percent has produced an extraordinary number of leaders and achievers: Marcus Garvey, Stokely Carmichael, Malcolm X, James Farmer, Roy Innes, Shirley Chisholm, Kenneth B. Clark, W. Arthur Lewis, Sidney Poitier, Harry Belafonte, Godfrey Cambridge, and Ford Foundation president Franklin Thomas.

The parents of General Colin Powell, appointed Chairman of the Joint Chiefs of Staff in 1989, were Jamaicans. His father was a clerk, his mother a seamstress. In an interview at the time of his appointment, he said, "The key to opportunity in this country begins with education. My parents expected it. And in my family, you did what your parents expected of you."[13]

But beyond these celebrities, West Indians have also produced a standard of living and educational level that, by the second generation, have exceeded the national average (and average family size, unemployment, and crime rate *below* the national average). . . .

The experience of the West Indian immigrants refutes any argument that lighter skin color and consequent reduced discrimination are at the root of the success of the descendants of freedmen. Sowell observes that West Indian blacks are not racially distinct from American blacks. He explains the more progressive values and attitudes of the West Indian immigrants as the consequence of earlier emancipation (1838) and of the fact that, whereas slaves in the United States were usually fed from a common kitchen, slaves in the British colonies were usually given a small plot to grow their own food and a surplus to sell.[19] I think there is truth to those explanations, as well as in the likelihood that West Indian performance in the United States is in part a consequence of the self-selection of achievers and risk takers implicit in any decision to emigrate. But I also think that the postemancipation access to the respective cultural mainstreams was substantially greater for former British slaves, at least those who lived in urban areas, than for former American slaves, particularly as the institution of Jim Crow took hold on the latter. Acculturation of former slaves to British values, attitudes, and institutions has been complete in prosperous and democratic Barbados that the Barbadians (or "Bajans," as they call themselves) have been referred to as Afro-Saxons and Black Englishmen.[20] Harold Cruse observes, "West Indians are essentially conservatives fashioned in the British mold."[21]

One manifestation of the generally greater postemancipation access of West Indian blacks to the mainstream has been access to the most prestigious public- and private-sector jobs in the West Indian islands. High-achievement role models symbolizing upward mobility have thus been widely visible to young blacks. Until the past quarter-century, comparable role models for American blacks were proportionally much fewer, a point stressed by John Dollard in his 1937 classic, *Caste and Class in a Southern Town:* "A Negro plantation manager, a very rare specimen, said that the Negroes on his plantation tend to improve faster under a Negro manager. They say to themselves that what he can do, they can do; whereas with a white boss they feel that the gulf is too great and make no effort to improve."[22] Harold Cruse notes that Black Power leaders Stokely Carmichael and Lincoln Lynch, both West Indians, "emphasized the fact that in Jamaica and Trinidad there 'is a lot of poverty but we felt proud being black.' Moreover, the West Indians have political power (i.e., black policemen, civil servants, public officials, etc.)."[23]

Compared to 1937, black role models now abound in America, and the broad awareness of black achievement in politics, sports, business, the media, the arts, and other spheres, as well as the movement into the middle class of substantial numbers of blacks, means that a similar demonstration effect is now operating here, no doubt further contributing to the rapid growth of the black middle class.

Racism

In *A Piece of the Pie,* Stanley Lieberson argues that the overwhelming explanation for low levels of black achievement is racism and discrimination.[24] The bulk of his analysis addresses the differences between the experiences of the south, central, and Eastern European (he uses the acronym SCE) immigrants of the late nineteenth and early twentieth centuries—most of whom arrived penniless but most of whose descendants are now substantially established in mainstream America—and American blacks, many of whom are still outside that mainstream. Lieberson is uncomfortable with culture as an explanation for variations in performance between blacks and whites, and one of the criticisms I have of his book is that he fails to address the widely varying performance within the SCE group, for example, between Italians and Jews.

Using extensive data for Providence, Rhode Island, covering the years from 1880 to 1935, Joel Perlmann analyzed the differences in upward mobility among the Irish, Italian, Jewish, and black communities. While he concludes that discrimination is the overriding explanation for the condition of blacks, which is entirely credible to me given the time period of his study, he also concludes that "[t]he Providence data . . . strongly suggest that in the cases of the Italians and the Russian Jews . . . pre-migration cultural attributes cannot be dismissed or even treated as afterthoughts, but rather constitute an important part of the explanation for group differences in behavior."[25] As Stephan Thernstrom explains, "in Boston, the Irish and Italians moved ahead economically only sluggishly and erratically; the English and the Jews, on the other hand, found their way into the higher occupational strata with exceptional speed. . . . [T]here is some basis for believing . . . that the cultures the immigrants brought with them had some effect."[26]

Although I accept Lieberson's thesis that the discrimination problem has been greater and of longer duration for blacks than for Chinese or Japanese, I think he exaggerates the extent of that difference, making it easier to dismiss culture as an explanation of the striking differences in achievement among the nonwhite groups.

But whatever my reaction to *A Piece of the Pie,* Sowell's data on the performance of West Indian immigrants calls into serious question the validity of Lieberson's thesis. I accept that discrimination is an important part of the explanation of the black condition in the United States and was, in fact, the dominant cause, at least in the South, until the 1960s. But circumstances are very different today, and while racism and discrimination still exist, the principal obstacle to continued movement toward racial equality in America in my view is a cultural one, flowing principally from the black slavery experience perpetuated by the isolation and oppression of Jim Crow. . . .

AMERICA'S RACIAL REVOLUTION

The debate about the condition and future of blacks in the United States is often overgeneralized. Some black leaders so emphasize racism and discrimination that many white liberals have the sense that bigotry and injustice dominate the lives of most blacks—except perhaps certain athletes, politicians, and media and entertainment stars. The heavy media, academic, and political focus on the acute problems of the black ghetto has contributed to a white American view of race issues that is disproportionately influenced by the condition of a minority of blacks and is often accompanied by disproportionately guilty feelings.

Contrary to the image of broadly persistent racism and poverty, a racial and cultural revolution has occurred in the United States over the past thirty-five years on a par with the Spanish miracle of the same period and even the Meiji Restoration, which occurred in a comparable span of years. In 1950, about one of every six blacks was in the middle class. Today, as I mentioned previously, two of every three American blacks are middle class.[31] In response to the vastly increased opportunity available to them, the majority who are in the black middle class have adopted the future-oriented, progressive values of the American mainstream, sloughing off the present-oriented, static values and isolation inculcated by slavery and Jim Crow. A substantial percentage of American blacks now live in the suburbs.

The National Research Council's five-year study, *A Common Destiny: Blacks and American Society*, published in 1989, opens with the following words:

> Just five decades ago, most black Americans could not work, live, shop, eat, seek entertainment, or travel where they chose. Even a quarter century ago—100 years after the Emancipation Proclamation of 1863—most blacks were effectively denied the right to vote. A large majority of blacks lived in poverty, and very few black children had the opportunity to receive basic education; indeed, black children were still forced to attend inferior and separate schools in jurisdictions that had not accepted the 1954 decision of the Supreme Court declaring segregated schools unconstitutional.
>
> Today the situation is very different. In education, many blacks have received college degrees from universities that formerly excluded them. In the workplace, blacks frequently hold professional and managerial jobs in desegregated settings. In politics, most blacks now participate in elections, and blacks have been elected to all but the highest political offices.[33*]

In addition, there have been some sweeping changes in white American attitudes about race—in part because of the leadership of Harry Truman (who integrated the armed forces), Dwight Eisenhower, Earl Warren, John F. Kennedy, Martin Luther King, Jr., Lyndon Johnson, and the courts; in part because of the efforts of religious, academic, business, labor, and entertainment leaders throughout the society; in part because of the dramatically changed image of blacks on television and in the movies in recent decades; in part because of the black revolution in

---

*The book was published before Douglas Wilder was elected as governor of Virginia.

sports; and indeed as a consequence of desegregation, busing, and affirmative action programs (all of which have also had their costs).

In 1958, 55 percent of white Americans said they would not move if a black family moved in next door; in 1978, the figure had increased to 85 percent.[34] In 1958, 72 percent of Southern parents and 13 percent of Northern parents objected to desegregated schools; in 1980, 5 percent of parents in both South and North objected.[35] In 1958, 4 percent of whites approved of black-white intermarriage; in 1978, 32 percent did.[36] Shelby Steele, a black professor at San Jose State University who has written extensively about race relations from an integrationist point of view—and who is vilified by some black leaders—recently observed, "As a black person you always hear about racists but never meet any."[37]. . .

THE GHETTO TRAGEDY

The racial revolution has transformed the lives and prospects of two-thirds of America's blacks, but it has not significantly affected the lives of the other third, most of whom live in ghettos. Many of them came North in the vast waves of Southern black immigrants of the 1950s, 1960s, and 1970s. They are but a few decades removed from the typically hopeless poverty of sharecropping and tenant farming, or the humiliation and poverty of Jim Crow caste discrimination in towns and cities. They confront the intense stresses of ghetto life that have produced crime and other manifestations of social breakdown in many immigrant groups. They confront those stresses not only with little relevant experience but with the static, dependent, present-oriented culture of slavery perpetuated in Jim Crow.

The indicators of the waste and suffering of human beings in the ghetto are staggering. Unemployment among ghetto youths approximates 50 percent. The principal cause of death of young black males is homicide. The incidence of drug commerce and use in the ghetto appears to be far higher than in the society at large. In 1980, 48 percent of black infants were born to single mothers, compared with 11 percent of white infants. The rate of infants born to single mothers among black women ages fifteen to nineteen was 82 percent.[48] Almost 50 percent of prison inmates are black (blacks account for 11 percent of the population).[49] One in four black males is either in jail, on parole, or on probation.[50]

In *America Now,* the anthropologist Marvin Harris says, "A study of arrests in seventeen large American cities located in every region of the country, conducted under the auspices of the President's Commission on the Causes of Crime and Prevention of Violence, indicated that the 'race of offenders' was black in 72% of criminal homicides, 74% of aggravated assaults, 81% of unarmed robberies, and a whopping 85% of armed robberies."[51] These figures may exaggerate the extent of black participation in crime because of discriminatory police behavior, but if we could remove that distortion we would still surely be left with a disproportionate black crime rate.

Harris goes on to observe that whereas "we find there are proportionately five times more homicides, ten times more rapes, and eight times more robberies in the United States than in Japan," if one subtracts the crimes perpetrated by blacks and Hispanics from the U.S. total, "America's rates of violent crime are much closer to the rates found in [Japan]" (for example, the homicide rate in the United States would fall from five times to less than twice the Japanese rate).[52]

The Cultural Explanation

The conventional wisdom, typified by *A Common Destiny,* is to blame the persistent ghetto tragedy and racial inequality mostly on racism and discrimination, past and present:

> Foremost among the reasons for the present state of black-white relations are two continuing consequences of the nation's long and recent history of racial inequality. One is the negative attitudes held toward blacks and the other is the actual disadvantaged conditions under which many black Americans live. These two consequences reinforce each other. Thus, a legacy of discrimination and segregation continues to affect black-white relations.[53]

That approximates the explanation of many black leaders, and it reminds us of what Daniel Moynihan has called "a near-obsessive concern to locate the 'blame' for . . . Negro poverty . . . on forces and institutions outside the community concerned."[54] But if the opinion polls are to be believed, racism, and its concomitant, discrimination, have declined sharply in the United States to the point where only a small fraction of whites practices them in ways that impinge on opportunity for blacks. In fact, affirmative action—positive discrimination, if you will—has operated *for* significant numbers of blacks, albeit principally in the middle class. Surely, opportunities for blacks in the era of affirmative action psychology and poverty programs are at least as great as opportunities were for the ethnic groups that lived in ghettos early in this century, for example, the Chinese, the Jews, the Italians.

The black social scientist William Julius Wilson makes an apt observation:

> [I]t is not readily apparent how the deepening economic class divisions between the haves and the have-nots in the black community can be accounted for when [the racism/discrimination] thesis is invoked, especially when it is argued that this same racism is directed with equal force across class boundaries in the black community. Nor is it apparent how racism can result in a more rapid social and economic deterioration in the inner city in the post–civil rights period than in the period that preceded the notable civil rights victories.[55]

An intense debate about the causes of the ghetto tragedy, with strong ideological overtones, has followed in the wake of the 1965 Moynihan report, *The Negro Family: The Case for National Action.*[56] Charles Murray's *Losing Ground* has become the rallying point for what is often referred to as the "conservative" interpretation. Murray adduces extensive data, which have fomented great controversy among social scientists, to make the point that the social breakdown of the ghetto was the consequence of disincentive effects of the expansion of welfare programs, particularly, liberalized Aid for Families with Dependent Children and the introduction of food stamps.[57]

The "liberal" view has continued to emphasize racism and discrimination. But a more pragmatic liberalism has also emerged in the views of William Julius Wilson and others. Wilson suggests several other causes, including the young age profile of ghetto dwellers, the disproportionate impact on blacks of the decline of American industry, the departure from the ghetto of the middle-class blacks who gave the ghetto both structure and stability.

Although I fully acknowledge that some racism and some discrimination still exist, and although I believe there is truth in the views of both Murray and Wilson, another factor may be even more important in explaining the ghetto tragedy: *ghetto blacks still suffer from a world view, and the values and attitudes it propagates, that is significantly influenced by the slavery experience.* Their ancestors were denied access to the cultural mainstream first by slavery, then by Jim Crow. The current generation is barred by the invisible walls of the ghetto. In this respect, the problems of the ghetto are similar to the problems of Haiti, a former slave society that has lived much of its history isolated from the progressive currents that have moved other nations, including some neighboring islands, toward democracy, economic dynamism, and social justice. The problems of the ghetto also evoke, for the same reason of isolation, the acute problems of American Indians who live on reservations. . . .

From his studies of poor people, principally in Latin America, Oscar Lewis concluded that people who live in poverty often are embedded in a "culture of poverty." Among the characteristics of that culture, all of which would be inculcated or reinforced by slavery: "The lack of effective participation and integration of the poor in the major institutions of the larger society . . . present-time [orientation] . . . a minimum of organization beyond the level of the nuclear and extended family . . . the absence of childhood as a specially prolonged and protected stage in the life cycle . . . a strong feeling of marginality, of helplessness, of dependence, and of inferiority . . . fatalism and a low level of aspiration."[59] Those characteristics describe the centuries-old condition of the poor majority in Latin America; several of them are also relevant to the higher social strata there. The difference between Latin America and the United States is that, in the latter, one finds a far more progressive mainstream that embraces the large majority of the population.

"Assimilation" is another way of approaching the question of cultural isolation. Using Milton Gordon's seven measures of assimilation,[60] Calvin Schmid and Charles Nobbe drew the following conclusion in a 1965 study of assimilation by nonwhite groups:

> As far as the cultural and civic dimensions are concerned, Negroes . . . have evidenced a substantial degree of assimilation, but on the remaining five variables they have remained virtually unassimilated. [American] Indians, with an overwhelming proportion segregated on reservations, are even less culturally and "civically" assimilated than Negroes. . . . On the other hand, Chinese and especially Japanese show a higher degree of cultural and civic assimilation than any of the other minority races. Moreover, they have made some headway in the other dimensions of assimilation.[61]

The cultural explanation is largely dismissed in *A Common Destiny,* consistent with the taboo, common in political and academic circles, against anything that sounds like "blaming the victim,"[62] a taboo that surfaced violently in the response to Daniel Moynihan's 1965 study of the breakdown of the black family. I want to emphasize that a cultural interpretation of conditions in the ghetto is *not* blaming the victim. It is a way of understanding a grave problem that may contribute to the problem's solution. The idea of blame is essentially irrelevant: to the extent that something is to be blamed for the values and attitudes that get in the way of progress for ghetto dwellers, it would have to be slavery and Jim Crow, surely not those who have suffered from those two institutions.

In *A Common Destiny's* chapter on education, we find:

> Another possible reason for black-white achievement differences . . . is a black-white cultural difference in socialization. Studies of transracially adopted children provide empirical support for this hypothesis. [Four studies of] transracially adopted black children . . . found that these black children perform about as well as white children on intelligence tests . . . [and] that scores in measured intelligence were directly related to greater proximity to a white middle-class standard. [One of the social scientists] concluded that variation in the tested intelligence of black children on the basis of rearing in a black middle-class or white middle-class environment *is difficult to explain on any basis other than black-white cultural differences.*[63] [Italics added.]

A few pages later, the authors point to another phenomenon that evokes the "crabs-in-a-barrel" behavior typical of peasant cultures around the world:

> Recent ethnographic work . . . suggests that black student peer culture undermines the goal of striving for academic success. Among eleventh graders at a predominantly black high school in Washington, D.C., many behaviors associated with high achievement—speaking standard English, studying long hours, striving to get good grades—were regarded as "acting white." Students known to engage in such behavior were labeled "brainiacs," ridiculed, and ostracized as people who had abandoned the group.[64]

But *A Common Destiny* concludes with the judgment,

> In considering cultural characteristics, it is especially difficult to assess their independent causal significance. In any case the culture-of-poverty thesis by itself is inadequate to account for the most recent changes we are seeking to understand. . . . [I]f cultural differences have diminished over the years when family differences have increased more rapidly, there is at least some doubt that culture of poverty is a sufficient explanation.[65]

I was unable to find any data documenting a narrowing of cultural differences between people in the ghetto and those in the mainstream. I would obviously not be surprised to see a substantial narrowing of value and attitude differences between middle-class blacks and whites. But I would be both surprised and encouraged to note a significant shift toward mainstream values on the part of ghetto dwellers. Nor did I find reference to Thomas Sowell's work on the achievement of West Indian immigrants in *A Common Destiny.*

In dismissing the role of culture, *A Common Destiny* asks a question that I find astonishing: "the conventional notion of culture of poverty implies that given characteristics (values, beliefs, behaviors) are transmitted from one generation to another as self-perpetuating patterns. . . . How frequently does this occur?"[66] My answer, of course, would be, always. . . .

Those who blame the agony of the ghetto principally on racism and discrimination perform a double disservice. They send the message to the ghetto inhabitants that they have no control over their destinies, that their salvation depends on the benevolence and charity of whites. "Racism" thus has as paralyzing and destructive an effect on the ghetto as "dependency theory"—the view prevailing until recently in academic circles that Latin America's problems are principally attributable to Yankee imperialism—has had on Latin America.

The accusation of racism also increasingly antagonizes whites who have made a sincere effort—often over many decades—not only to live a color-blind life but also to support affirmative action. To those people, "racism" increasingly sounds like, "What have you done for me today?"

Bringing Ghetto Blacks into the Mainstream

If I am right that the black ghetto problem is now principally a cultural one—and I hasten to repeat that I accept that other factors, including discrimination, are also in play—then the solutions must emphasize access and acculturation to the mainstream. The process is obviously complicated, difficult, and time-consuming. But we should take heart from the vast movement from lower to middle class of most blacks in the past several decades, and from the experience of other ethnic groups in the ghetto.

. . . My ideas are, in many respects, parallel to those of many civil rights leaders. The main difference is that I want to send this message: "The opportunity is there. If you meet discrimination—and there's a fair chance you won't—you can overcome it. Go for it!" The message that permeates the ghetto is that the opportunity *isn't* there—instead, discrimination is—and that, short of antisocial behavior, ghetto people are impotent.

The kinds of programs that I think stand the best chance—and I appreciate how difficult and costly it can be to make them work—are those that focus on exposing children to the broader society. My list is far from exhaustive, but includes: Head Start/supervised play/day-care activities as early as possible; busing to schools where the student body composition includes significant numbers from the cultural mainstream—white and black—along the lines of magnet school programs; summer work and summer camp programs, perhaps combining the two; the use of university students as tutors of ghetto children;[68] courses that better prepare high school youngsters for effective child rearing.

. . . I also think that the acculturation process can be facilitated by more involvement by blacks who are in the mainstream culture with those who aren't. Their upward mobility is compelling evidence to ghetto blacks that the opportunity exists. The black middle class is also eloquent testimony to the capacity of human beings to modify values and attitudes.

NOTES

1. The divergent experiences of "free persons of color," emancipated blacks, and West Indians derive principally from Thomas Sowell, ed., *Essays and Data on American Ethnic Groups* (Washington, D.C.: The Urban Institute, 1978).

2. See David C. Rankin, "The Impact of the Civil War on the Free Colored Community of New Orleans," *Perspectives in American History* 11 (1977–78): 385, cited in Thomas Sowell, *Ethnic America* (New York: Basic Books, 1981), p. 205.

3. Herbert G. Gutman, *The Black Family in Slavery and Freedom, 1750–1925* (New York: Vintage Books, 1976).

5. Carlos Rangel, *The Latin Americans: Their Love-Hate Relationship with the United States* (New York and London: Harcourt Brace Jovanovich, 1977), p. 193.

6. Celso Furtado, *Formacáo Económica do Brasil,* 4th ed. (Rio de Janeiro: Editora Fundo de Cultura SA, 1961), p. 162; cited in Maria Lucia Victor Barbosa, *O Voto da Pobreza e a Pobreza do Voto* (Rio de Janeiro: Jorge Zahar Editor, 1988), p. 39.

7. Sowell, *Ethnic America,* p. 200.

8. John Dollard, *Caste and Class in a Southern Town* (Madison: University of Wisconsin Press, 1988), p. 417.

9. Stephan Thernstrom, *The Other Bostonians* (Cambridge: Harvard University Press, 1973), p. 217.

10. Eugene Genovese, *Roll, Jordan, Roll* (New York: Vintage Books, 1976) p. 289.

11. Thomas Sowell, *The Economics and Politics of Race* (New York: Quill, 1983), p. 128.

12. Sowell, *Ethnic America,* p. 216.

13. Quoted in *Parade,* 13 August 1989, p. 5.

19. Sowell, *Ethnic America,* pp. 216, 218.

20. See Lawrence Harrison, *Underdevelopment Is a State of Mind—The Latin American Case* (Lanham, MD: Harvard Center for International Affairs and University Press of America, 1985), chapter 5.

21. Harold Cruse, *The Crisis of the Negro Intellectual* (New York: Quill, 1984), p. 119.

22. Dollard, *Caste and Class in a Southern Town,* p. 66.

23. Cruse, *The Crisis of the Negro Intellectual,* p. 427. In contrast, Thomas Sowell observes, "Few children of rising ethnic groups have had 'role models' of their own ethnicity. Some of the most successful—notably the Chinese and Japanese—almost never did" (*Ethnic America,* p. 279).

24. Stanley Lieberson, *A Piece of the Pie* (Berkeley, Los Angeles, and London: University of California Press, 1980).

25. Joel Perlmann, *Ethnic Differences* (Cambridge: Cambridge University Press, 1988), p. 216.

26. Thernstrom, *The Other Bostonians,* pp. 250–51.

31. I use Franklin Frazier's definition of middle class, which includes white-collar and skilled blue-collar workers. In *The New Black Middle Class* (Berkley: University of California Press, 1987), Bart Landry's data indicate that black white-collar and skilled blue-collar workers, which accounted for 11 percent of the black population in 1910, accounted for 67 percent in 1981. In the 22 July 1991 *U.S. News & World Report,* the economists James Smith and Finis Welch conclude that "fully two thirds of blacks could be characterized as middle class" (p. 20).

33. Gerald David Jaynes and Robin M. Williams, Jr., eds., *A Common Destiny: Blacks and American Society* (Washington, D.C.: National Academy Press, 1989) p. 3.

34. Ibid., p. 12.

35. *The Gallup Report,* no. 185 (February 1981): 30.

36. *The Gallup Report,* 1958 and 1978.

37. Shelby Steele, "I'm Black, You're White, Who's Innocent? Race and Power in an Era of Blame," *Harper's* (June 1988): 48.

48. Charles Murray, *Losing Ground* (New York: Basic Books, 1984), pp. 126–27.

49. Jaynes and Williams, *A Common Destiny,* pp. 522, 461.

50. "One in Four," *The New Republic,* 26 March 1990, p. 5.

51. Marvin Harris, *America Now* (New York: Simon & Schuster, 1981), p. 123. Earlier data in this paragraph are from the same source.

52. Ibid., pp. 118, 123.

53. Jaynes and Williams, *A Common Destiny,* p. 5.

54. Daniel P. Moynihan, "The Professors and the Poor," in *On Understanding Poverty,* ed. Daniel P. Moynihan (New York: Basic Books, 1968), p. 33; quoted in Murray, *Losing Ground,* p. 33.

55. William Julius Wilson, *The Truly Disadvantaged* (Chicago and London: University of Chicago Press, 1987), p. 11.

56. Office of Policy Planning and Research, *The Negro Family: The Case for National Action* (Washington, D.C.: U.S. Department of Labor, March 1965).

57. Murray, *Losing Ground.*

59. Oscar Lewis, *Anthropological Essays* (New York: Random House, 1970), pp. 70–77, passim.

60. Milton M. Gordon, *Assimilation in American Life* (New York: Oxford University Press, 1964), pp. 70–75, lists cultural, structural, marital, identificational, attitude receptional, behavior receptional, and civic indicators.

61. Calvin F. Schmid and Charles E. Nobbe, "Socioeconomic Differences Among Non-White Races," *American Sociological Review* 30, no. 6 (December 1965): 909–22.

62. See, for example, William Ryan, *Blaming the Victim* (New York: Vintage Books, 1976).

63. Jaynes and Williams, *A Common Destiny,* p. 370.

64. Ibid., p. 372.

65. Ibid., pp. 543–44.

66. Ibid., p. 541.

68. This idea was advocated by William Raspberry in ". . . And a Plan That Just Might Work," *Washington Post,* 19 June 1991.

9

Societal Changes and Vulnerable Neighborhoods

WILLIAM JULIUS WILSON

The disappearance of work in many inner-city neighborhoods is partly related to the nationwide decline in the fortunes of low-skilled workers. Although the growing wage inequality has hurt both low-skilled men and women, the problem of declining employment has been concentrated among low-skilled men. In 1987–89, a low-skilled male worker was jobless eight and a half weeks longer than he would have been in 1967–69. Moreover, the proportion of men who "permanently" dropped out of the labor force was more than twice as high in the late 1980s than it had been in the late 1960s. A precipitous drop in real wages—that is, wages adjusted for inflation—has accompanied the increases in joblessness among low-income workers. If you arrange all wages into five groups according to wage percentile (from highest to lowest), you see that men in the bottom fifth of this income distribution experienced more than a 30 percent drop in real wages between 1970 and 1989.

Even the low-skilled workers who are consistently employed face problems of economic advancement. Job ladders—opportunities for promotion within firms—have eroded, and many less-skilled workers stagnate in dead-end, low-paying positions. This suggests that the chances of improving one's earnings by changing jobs have declined: if jobs inside a firm have become less available to the experienced workers in that firm, they are probably even more difficult for outsiders to obtain.

But there is a paradox here. Despite the increasing economic marginality of low-wage workers, unemployment dipped below 6 percent in 1994 and early 1995, many workers are holding more than one job, and overtime work has reached a record high. Yet while tens of millions of new jobs have been created in the past two decades, men who are well below retirement age are working less than they did two decades ago—and a growing percentage are neither working nor looking for work. The proportion of male workers in the prime of their life (between the ages of 22 and 58) who worked in a given decade full-time, year-round, in at least eight out of ten years declined from 79 percent during the 1970s to 71 percent in the 1980s. While the American economy saw a rapid expansion in high technology and services, especially advanced services, growth in blue-collar factory, transportation, and construction jobs, traditionally held by men, has not kept pace with the rise in the working-age population. These men are working less as a result.

The growth of a nonworking class of prime-age males along with a larger number of those who are often unemployed, who work part-time, or who work in temporary jobs is concentrated among the poorly educated, the school dropouts, and minorities. In the 1970s, two-thirds of prime-age male workers with less than a high school education worked full-time, year-round, in eight out of ten years. During the 1980s, only half did so. Prime-age black men experienced a similar sharp decline. Seven out of ten of all black men worked full-time, year-round, in eight out of ten years in the 1970s, but only half did so in the 1980s. The figures for those who reside in the inner city are obviously even lower.

One study estimates that since 1967 the number of prime-age men who are not in school, not working, and not looking for work for even a single week in a given year has more than doubled for both whites and nonwhites (respectively, from 3.3 to 7.7 percent and 5.8 percent to 13.2 percent). Data from this study also revealed that one-quarter of all male high school dropouts had no official employment at all in 1992. And of those with high school diplomas, one out of ten did not hold a job in 1993, up sharply from 1967 when only one out of fifty reported that he had had no job throughout the year. Among prime-age nonwhite males, the share of those who had no jobs at all in a given year increased from 3 percent to 17 percent during the last quarter century.

These changes are related to the decline of the mass production system in the United States. The traditional American economy featured rapid growth in productivity and living standards. The mass production system benefited from large quantities of cheap natural resources, economies of scale, and processes that generated higher uses of productivity through shifts in market forces from agriculture to manufacturing and that caused improvements in one industry (for example, reduced steel costs) to lead to advancements in others (for example, higher sales and greater economies of scale in the automobile industry). In this system plenty of blue-collar jobs were available to workers with little formal education. Today, most of the new jobs for workers with limited education and experience are in the service sector which hires relatively more women. One study found that the U.S. created 27 clerical, sales, and service jobs per thousand of working-age population in the 1980s. During the same period, the country lost 16 production, transportation, and laborer jobs per thousand of working-age population. In another study the social scientists Robert Lerman and Martin Rein revealed that from 1989 to 1993, the period covering the economic downturn, social service industries (health, education, and welfare) added almost 3 million jobs, while 1.4 million jobs were lost in all other industries. The expanding job market in social services offset the recession-linked job loss in other industries.

The movement of lower-educated men into the growth sectors of the economy has been slow. For example, "the fraction of men who have moved into so-called pink-collar jobs like practical nursing or clerical work remains negligible." The large concentration of women in the expanding social service sector partly accounts for the striking gender differences in job growth. Unlike lower-educated men, lower-educated women are working more, not less, than in previous years. The employment patterns among lower-educated women, like those with higher education and training, reflect the dramatic expansion of social service industries. Between 1989 and 1993, jobs held by women increased by 1.3 million, while those held by men barely rose at all (by roughly 100,000).

Although the wages of low-skilled women (those with less than twelve years of education) rose slightly in the 1970s, they flattened out in the 1980s, and continued to remain below those of low-skilled men. The wage gap between low-skilled men and women shrank not because of gains made by female workers but mainly because of the decline in real wages for men. The unemployment rates among low-skilled women are slightly lower than those among their male counterparts. However, over the past decade their rates of participation in the labor force have stagnated and have fallen further behind the labor-force-participation rates among more highly educated women, which continue to rise. The unemployment rates among both low-skilled men and women are five times that among their college-educated counterparts.

Among the factors that have contributed to the growing gap in employment and wages between low-skilled and college-educated workers is the increased internationalization of the U.S. economy. As the economists Richard B. Freeman and Lawrence F. Katz point out:

> In the 1980s, trade imbalances implicitly acted to augment the nation's supply of less educated workers, particularly those with less than a high school education. Many production and routine clerical tasks could be more easily transferred abroad than in the past. The increased supply of less educated workers arising from trade deficits accounted for as much as 15 percent of the increase in college–high school wage differential from the 1970s to the mid-1980s. In contrast, a balanced expansion of international trade, in which growth in exports matches the growth of imports, appears to have fairly neutral effects on relative labor demand. Indeed, balanced growth of trade leads to an upgrading in jobs for workers without college degrees, since export-sector jobs tend to pay higher wages for "comparable" workers than do import-competing jobs.

The lowering of unionization rates, which accompanied the decline in the mass production system, has also contributed to shrinking wages and nonwage compensation for less skilled workers. As the economist Rebecca Blank has pointed out, "unionized workers typically receive not only higher wages, but also more non-wage benefits. As the availability of union jobs has declined for unskilled workers, non-wage benefits have also declined."

Finally, the wage and employment gap between skilled and unskilled workers is growing partly because education and training are considered more important than ever in the new global economy. At the same time that changes in technology are producing new jobs, they are making many others obsolete. The workplace has been revolutionized by technological changes that range from the development of robotics to information highways. While educated workers are benefiting from the pace of technological change, involving the increased use of computer-based technologies and microcomputers, more routine workers face the growing threat of job displacement in certain industries. For example, highly skilled designers, engineers, and operators are needed for the jobs associated with the creation of a new set of computer-operated machine tools; but these same exciting new opportunities eliminate jobs for those trained only for manual, assembly-line work. Also, in certain businesses, advances in word processing have increased the demand for those who not only know how to type but can operate specialized software as well; at the same time, these advances reduce the need for routine typists and secretaries. In the new global economy, highly educated and thoroughly trained men and women are in demand. This may be seen most dramatically in the sharp differences in employment experiences among men. Unlike men with lower education, college-educated men are working more, not less.

The shift in demand has been especially devastating for those low-skilled workers whose incorporation into the mainstream economy has been marginal or recent. Even before the economic restructuring of the nation's economy, low-skilled African-Americans were at the end of the employment queue. Their economic situation has been further weakened because they tend to reside in communities that not only have higher jobless rates and lower employment growth but lack access to areas of higher employment and employment growth as well. Moreover, they are far more likely than other ethnic and racial groups to face negative employer attitudes.

Of the changes in the economy that have adversely affected low-skilled African-American workers, perhaps the most significant have been those in the manufacturing sector. One study revealed that in the 1970s "up to half of the huge employment declines for less-educated blacks might be explained by industrial shifts away from manufacturing toward other sectors." Another study reported that since the 1960s "deindustrialization" and the "erosion in job opportunities especially in the Midwest and Northeast . . . bear responsibility for the growth of the ranks of the 'truly disadvantaged.'" The manufacturing losses in some northern cities have been staggering. In the twenty-year period from 1967 to 1987, Philadelphia lost 64 percent of its manufacturing jobs; Chicago lost 60 percent; New York City, 58 percent; Detroit, 51 percent. In absolute numbers, these percentages represent the loss of 160,000 jobs in Philadelphia, 326,000 in Chicago, 520,000—over half a million—in New York, and 108,000 in Detroit.

Another study examined the effects of economic restructuring in the 1980s by highlighting the changes in both the variety and the quality of blue-collar employment in general. Jobs were grouped into a small number of relatively homogeneous clusters on the basis of job quality (which was measured in terms of earnings, benefits, union protection, and involuntary part-time employment). The authors found that both the relative earnings and employment rates among unskilled black workers were lower for two reasons: traditional jobs that provide a living wage (high-wage blue-collar cluster of which roughly 50 percent were manufacturing jobs) declined, as did the quality of secondary jobs on which they increasingly had to rely, leading to lower relative earnings for the remaining workers in the labor market. As employment prospects worsened, rising proportions of low-skilled black workers dropped out of the legitimate labor market.

Data from the Chicago Urban Poverty and Family Life Survey show that efforts by out-of-school inner-city black men to obtain blue-collar jobs in the industries in which their fathers had been employed have been hampered by industrial restructuring. "The most common occupation reported by respondents at ages 19 to 28 changed from operative and assembler jobs among the oldest cohorts to service jobs (waiters and janitors) among the youngest cohort." Fifty-seven percent of Chicago's employed inner-city black fathers (aged 15 and over and without undergraduate degrees) who were born between 1950 and 1955 worked in manufacturing and construction industries in 1974. By 1987, industrial employment in this group had fallen to 31 percent. Of those born between 1956 and 1960, 52 percent worked in these industries as late as 1978. But again, by 1987 industrial employment in this group fell to 28 percent. No other male ethnic group in the inner city experienced such an overall precipitous drop in manufacturing employment. These employment changes have accompanied the loss of traditional manufacturing and other blue-collar jobs in Chicago. As a result, young black males have turned increasingly to the low-wage service sector and unskilled laboring jobs for employment, or have gone jobless. The strongly held U.S. cultural and economic belief that the son will do at least as well as the father in the labor market does not apply to many young inner-city males.

If industrial restructuring has hurt inner-city black workers in Chicago, it has had serious consequences for African-Americans across the nation. "As late as the 1968–70 period," states John Kasarda, "more than 70 percent of all blacks working in metropolitan areas held blue-collar jobs at the same time that more than 50 percent of all metropolitan workers held white-collar jobs. Moreover, of the large numbers of urban blacks classified as blue-collar workers during the late 1960s, more than half were employed in goods-producing industries."

The number of employed black males ages 20 to 29 working in manufacturing industries fell dramatically between 1973 and 1987 (from three of every eight to one in five). Meanwhile, the share of employed young black men in the retail trade and service jobs rose sharply during that period (from 17 to almost 27 percent and from 10 to nearly 21 percent, respectively). And this shift in opportunities was not without economic consequences: in 1987, the average annual earnings of 20-to-29-year-old males who held jobs in the retail trade and service sectors were 25 to 30 percent less than those of males employed in manufacturing sectors. This dramatic loss in earnings potential affects every male employed in the service sector regardless of color.

The structural shifts in the distribution of industrial job opportunities are not the only reason for the increasing joblessness and declining earnings among young black male workers. There have also been important changes in the patterns of occupational staffing within firms and industries, including those in manufacturing. These changes have primarily benefited those with more formal education. Substantial numbers of new professional, technical, and managerial positions have been created. However, such jobs require at least some years of postsecondary education. Young high school dropouts and even high school graduates "have faced a dwindling supply of career jobs offering the real earnings opportunities available to them in the 1960s and early 1970s."

In certain urban areas the prospects for employment among workers with little education have fallen sharply. John Kasarda examined employment changes in selected urban centers and found that major northern cities had consistent employment losses in industries with low mean levels of employee education and employment gains in industries in which the workers had higher levels of education. For example, during the 1980s New York City lost 135,000 jobs in industries in which the workers averaged less than twelve years of education, and gained almost 300,000 jobs in industries in which workers had thirteen or more years of education. Philadelphia lost 55,000 jobs in the low-education industries and gained 40,000 jobs for workers with high school plus at least some college. Baltimore and Boston also experienced substantial losses in industries employing low-education workers and major gains in industries employing more educated workers.

Kasarda's study also documents the growing importance of education in nine "economically transforming" northern cities and in Los Angeles. The jobs traditionally held by high school dropouts declined in all nine northern cities between 1980 and 1990, while those held by college graduates increased. "Los Angeles, which experienced a 50 percent increase in city [urban] jobs held by college graduates, also experienced a 15 percent growth in jobs held by those who have not completed high school. The latter no doubt reflects the large immigration of Hispanic workers and other minorities" who have little education.

To some degree, these changes reflect overall improvements in educational attainment within the urban labor force. However, they "were not nearly as great as the concurrent upward shifts in the education of city jobholders." Moreover, much of the increase in the "college-educated" jobs in each city reflected the educational status of suburban commuters, while much of the decrease in the "less than high school" category reflected the job losses of city residents, few of whom could aspire to a four-year postsecondary degree.

As pointed out earlier, most of the new jobs for workers with limited training and education are in the service sector and are disproportionately held by women. This is even more true for those who work in social services, which include the industries of health, education, and welfare. As we have seen, within central cities the number of jobs for less educated workers has declined precipitously. However, many workers stayed afloat thanks to jobs in the expanding social service sector, especially black women with less than a high school degree. Robert Lerman and Martin Rein report that among all women workers, the proportion employed in social services climbed between 1979 and 1993 (from 28 to 33 percent). The health and education industries absorbed nearly all of this increase. Of the 54 million female workers in 1993, almost one-third were employed in social service industries. Social services tend to feature a more highly educated workforce. Only 20 percent of all female workers with less than a high school degree were employed in social services in 1993. (The figure for comparable males is even less. Only 4 percent of employed less educated men held social service jobs in 1993.) Nonetheless, the proportion of less educated female workers in social services is up notably from 1989.

Indeed, despite the relatively higher educational level of social service workers, the research of Lerman and Rein reveals that 37 percent of employed less educated black women in central cities worked in social services in 1993, largely in jobs in hospitals, elementary schools, nursing care, and child care. In central cities in the largest metropolitan areas, the fraction of low-educated African-American female workers in social services sharply increased from 30.5 percent in 1979 to 40.5 percent in 1993. Given the overall decline of jobs for less educated central city workers, the opportunity for employment in the social service industries prevented many inner-city workers from joining the growing ranks of the jobless. Less educated black female workers depend heavily on social service employment. Even a small number of less educated black males were able to find jobs in social services. Although only 4 percent of less educated employed males worked in social services in 1993, 12 percent of less educated employed black men in the central cities of large metropolitan areas held social service jobs. Without the growth of social service employment, the rates of inner-city joblessness would have risen beyond their already unprecedented high levels.

The demand in the labor market has shifted toward higher-educated workers in various industries and occupations. The changing occupational and industrial mix is associated with increases in the rates of joblessness (unemployment and "dropping out" of, or nonparticipation in, the labor force) and decreases in the relative wages of disadvantaged urban workers.

The factors contributing to the relative decline in the economic status of disadvantaged workers are not solely due to those on the demand side, such as economic restructuring. The growing wage differential in the 1980s is also a function of two supply-side factors—the decline in the relative supply of college graduates and the influx of poor immigrants. "In the 1970s the relative supply of college graduates grew rapidly, the result of the baby boomers who enrolled in college in the late 1960s and early 1970s in response to the high rewards for college degrees and the fear of being drafted for the Vietnam War," state Freeman and Katz. "The growth in supply overwhelmed the increase in demand for more educated workers, and the returns to college diminished." In the 1980s, the returns for college increased because of declining growth in the relative supply of college graduates.

Also in the 1980s, a large number of immigrants with little formal education arrived in the United States from developing countries, and affected the wages of poorly educated native workers, especially those who had dropped out of high school. According to one estimate, nearly one-third of the decline in earnings for male high school dropouts compared with other workers in the 1980s may be linked to immigration. However, although the increase in immigration contributed to the growing inequality, it is only one of several factors depressing the wages of low-skilled workers. As Sheldon Danziger and Peter Gottschalk point out in this connection, "Immigrants are heavily concentrated in a few states, such as California and Florida . . . inequality did rise in these states, but it rose in most areas, even those with very few immigrants."

* * *

Joblessness and declining wages are also related to the recent growth in ghetto poverty. The most dramatic increases in ghetto poverty occurred between 1970 and 1980, and they were mostly confined to the large industrial metropolises of the Northeast and Midwest, regions that experienced massive industrial restructuring and loss of blue-collar jobs during that decade. But the rise in ghetto poverty was not the only problem. Industrial restructuring had devastating effects on the social organization of many inner-city neighborhoods in these regions. The fate of the West Side black community of North Lawndale vividly exemplifies the cumulative process of economic and social dislocation that has swept through Chicago's inner city.

After more than a quarter century of continuous deterioration, North Lawndale resembles a war zone. Since 1960, nearly half of its housing stock has disappeared; the remaining units are mostly rundown or dilapidated. Two large factories anchored the economy of this West Side neighborhood in its good days—the

Hawthorne plant of Western Electric, which employed over 43,000 workers; and an International Harvester plant with 14,000 workers. The world headquarters for Sears, Roebuck and Company was located there, providing another 10,000 jobs. The neighborhood also had a Copenhagen snuff plant, a Sunbeam factory, and a Zenith factory, a Dell Farm food market, an Alden's catalog store, and a U.S. Post Office bulk station. But conditions rapidly changed. Harvester closed its doors in the late 1960s. Sears moved most of its offices to the Loop in downtown Chicago in 1973; a catalog distribution center with a workforce of 3,000 initially remained in the neighborhood but was relocated outside of the state of Illinois in 1987. The Hawthorne plant gradually phased out its operations and finally shut down in 1984.

The departure of the big plants triggered the demise or exodus of the smaller stores, the banks, and other businesses that relied on the wages paid by the large employers. "To make matters worse, scores of stores were forced out of business or pushed out of the neighborhoods by insurance companies in the wake of the 1968 riots that swept through Chicago's West Side after the assassination of Dr. Martin Luther King, Jr. Others were simply burned or abandoned. It has been estimated that the community lost 75 percent of its business establishments from 1960 to 1970 alone." In 1986, North Lawndale, with a population of over 66,000, had only one bank and one supermarket; but it was also home to forty-eight state lottery agents, fifty currency exchanges, and ninety-nine licensed liquor stores and bars.

The impact of industrial restructuring on inner-city employment is clearly apparent to urban blacks. The UPFLS survey posed the following question: "Over the past five or ten years, how many friends of yours have lost their jobs because the place where they worked shut down—would you say none, a few, some, or most?" Only 26 percent of the black residents in our sample reported that none of their friends had lost jobs because their workplace shut down. Indeed, both black men and black women were more likely to report that their friends had lost jobs because of plant closings than were the Mexicans and the other ethnic groups in our study. Moreover, nearly half of the employed black fathers and mothers in the UPFLS survey stated that they considered themselves to be at high risk of losing their jobs because of plant shutdowns. Significantly fewer Hispanic and white parents felt this way. . . .

The increasing suburbanization of employment has accompanied industrial restructuring and has further exacerbated the problems of inner-city joblessness and restricted access to jobs. "Metropolitan areas captured nearly 90 percent of the nation's employment growth; much of this growth occurred in booming 'edge cities' at the metropolitan periphery. By 1990, many of these 'edge cities' had more office space and retail sales than the metropolitan downtowns." Over the last two decades, 60 percent of the new jobs created in the Chicago metropolitan area have been located in the northwest suburbs of Cook and Du Page counties. African-Americans constitute less than 2 percent of the population in these areas.

In *The Truly Disadvantaged,* I maintained that one result of these changes for many urban blacks has been a growing mismatch between the suburban location of employment and minorities' residence in the inner city. Although studies based on data collected before 1970 showed no consistent or convincing effects on black employment as a consequence of this spatial mismatch, the employment of inner-city blacks relative to suburban blacks has clearly deteriorated since then. Recent research, conducted mainly by urban and labor economists, strongly shows that the decentralization of employment is continuing and that employment in manufacturing, most of which is already suburbanized, has decreased in central cities, particularly in the Northeast and Midwest. As Farrell Bloch, an economic and statistical consultant, points out, "Not only has the number of manufacturing jobs been decreasing, but new plants now tend to locate in the suburbs to take advantage of cheap land, access to highways, and low crime rates; in addition, businesses shun urban locations to avoid buying land from several different owners, paying high demolition costs for old buildings, and arranging parking for employees and customers."

Blacks living in central cities have less access to employment, as measured by the ratio of jobs to people and the average travel time to and from work, than do central-city whites. Moreover, unlike most other groups of workers across the urban/suburban divide, less educated central-city blacks receive lower wages than suburban blacks who have similar levels of education. And the decline in earnings of central-city blacks is related to the decentralization of employment—that is, the movement of jobs from the cities to the suburbs—in metropolitan areas. . . .

Also, since 1980, a fundamental shift in the federal government's support for basic urban programs has aggravated the problems of joblessness and social organization in the new poverty neighborhoods. The Reagan and Bush administrations—proponents of the New Federalism—sharply cut spending on direct aid to cities, including general revenue sharing, urban mass transit, public service jobs and job training, compensatory education, social service block grants, local public works, economic development assistance, and urban development action grants. In 1980, the federal contribution to city budgets was 18 percent; by 1990 it had dropped to 6.4 percent. In addition, the economic recession which began in the Northeast in 1989 and lasted until the early 1990s sharply reduced those revenues that the cities themselves generated, thereby creating budget deficits that resulted in further cutbacks in basic services and programs along with increases in local taxes.

For many cities, especially the older cities of the East and Midwest, the combination of the New Federalism and the recession led to the worst fiscal and service crisis since the Depression. Cities have become increasingly underserviced, and many have been on the brink of bankruptcy. They have therefore not been in a position to combat effectively three unhealthy social conditions that have emerged or become prominent since 1980: 1) the prevalence of crack-cocaine addiction and the violent crime associated with it; 2) the AIDS epidemic and its escalating public health costs; and 3) the sharp rise in the homeless population not only for individuals but for whole families as well.

Although drug addiction and its attendant violence, AIDS and its toll on public health resources, and homelessness are found in many American communities, their impact on the ghetto is profound. These communities, whose residents have been pushed to the margins of society, have few resources with which to combat these social ills that arose in the 1980s. Fiscally strapped cities have watched helplessly as these problems—exacerbated by the new poverty, the decline of social organization in the jobless neighborhoods, and the reduction of social services—have made the city at large seem a dangerous and threatening place in which to live. Accordingly, working- and middle-class urban residents continue to relocate in the suburbs. Thus, while joblessness and related social problems are on the rise in inner-city neighborhoods, especially in those that represent the new poverty areas, the larger city has fewer and fewer resources with which to combat them.

Finally, policymakers indirectly contributed to the emergence of jobless ghettos by making decisions that have decreased the attractiveness of low-paying jobs and accelerated the relative decline in wages for low-income workers. In particular, in the absence of an effective labor-market policy, they have tolerated industry practices that undermine worker security, such as the reduction in benefits and the rise of involuntary part-time employment, and they have "allowed the minimum wage to erode to its second-lowest level in purchasing power in 40 years." After adjusting for inflation, "the minimum wage is 26 percent below its average level in the 1970s." Moreover, they virtually eliminated AFDC benefits for families in which a mother is employed at least half-time. In the early 1970s, a working mother with two children whose wages equaled 75 percent of the amount designated as the poverty line could receive AFDC benefits as a wage supplement in forty-nine states; in 1995 only those in three states could. Even with the expansion of the earned income tax credit (a wage subsidy for the working poor) such policies make it difficult for poor workers to support their families and protect their children. The erosion of wages and benefits forces many low-income workers in the inner city to move or remain on welfare.

10

From Individual to Structural Discrimination

FRED L. PINCUS

People often think of racial discrimination in terms of the actions of individual prejudiced white people against individual people of color. However, as we have already shown, prejudice (an attitude) does not necessarily lead to discrimination (an overt behavior), and discrimination is not always caused by prejudice.

Group discrimination can exist at many different levels. An individual teacher who mistreats a Hispanic student is different from a school system that refuses to admit Hispanics. An individual personnel officer who decides not to hire a qualified black applicant is different from an entire state police department that refuses to hire black officers.

In their influential book *Black Power*, which was published more than a quarter of a century ago, Stokely Carmichael and Charles Hamilton differentiated "individual racism" from "institutional racism." The former involved the behavior of white individuals toward blacks and other minorities, and the latter involved the behavior of the entire white society and its institutions toward people of color.

Since *racism* is a pejorative word often used imprecisely, I shall modify the Carmichael/Hamilton typology and apply it to the concept of discrimination. My discussion here deals with three different types of race/ethnic discrimination: individual, institutional, and structural.

1. *Individual discrimination* refers to the behavior of individual members of one race/ethnic group that is intended to have a differential and/or harmful effect on the members of another race/ethnic group. This category includes a wide range of behavior by majority-group individuals or small groups—from anti-Asian graffiti and name calling, to an employer's refusal to hire blacks or a landlord's refusal to rent to Hispanics, to physical attacks against Native Americans.

According to this definition, actions by individual minority-group members against the majority group can also be characterized as "individual discrimination." Examples might include antiwhite graffiti by blacks, physical attacks against whites by Hispanics, or employment discrimination by Asians against whites. Each of these actions entails intentional antiwhite treatment that has a differential and/or harmful impact.

2. *Institutional discrimination* is quite different in that it refers to the policies of majority institutions, and the behavior of individuals who implement these policies and control these institutions, that are intended to have a differential and/or harmful effect on minority groups. A major goal of institutional discrimination is to keep minority groups in a subordinate position within society. Hence this concept is much broader than that of individual discrimination.

Sometimes, institutional discrimination is embodied in laws and government policy. From the 1890s until the 1950s, for example, most southern states had laws that *legally* discriminated between blacks and whites in all areas of life—from voting, education, and employment to religion, public accommodations, and restaurants. These laws had broad support among the white population and were even given the stamp of approval by the U.S. Supreme Court in 1896. Legal segregation, which has been referred to as the "Jim Crow System," is a clear example of institutional discrimination, and it goes far beyond the level of individual actions.

Blacks are not the only victims of institutional discrimination in the United States. Whites seized the land of Native Americans by brutally defeating them on the battlefield and then confining them to reservations. Treaties with Indian Nations were routinely broken by the government, and entire tribes were forcibly moved from one reservation to another, often with fatal results.

Asians have also been victims. After Japan attacked Pearl Harbor in 1941, all Japanese people on the West Coast were taken from their homes and placed in internment camps for the duration of the war. Both citizens and noncitizens were forced to sell their property at a great loss.

Although most discrimination by federal, state, and local governments is now illegal, examples of institutional discrimination can still be found. One such example is "gerrymandering," the illegal drawing of electoral districts in such a way as to intentionally minimize the electoral power of minority groups. Police and fire departments in many cities across the country have illegally refused to hire and promote *qualified* blacks and Hispanics at the same rate as comparably qualified whites. (This practice has resulted in a series of lawsuits and controversial affirmative action programs that we will discuss later in the book.) And even the prestigious Federal Bureau of Investigation illegally discriminated against black and Hispanic agents until 1992, when the FBI entered into a consent decree to end a lawsuit by black agents.

Institutional discrimination can be detected in the private sector as well. Real estate associations often "steer" blacks away from white neighborhoods and show them houses and apartments in predominantly minority neighborhoods. Banks in various cities have "redlined" certain minority areas (that is, they have refused to grant mortgages to people who live in these areas regardless of whether they meet the financial qualifications specified), and they have granted smaller mortgages at higher interest rates. Moreover, large corporations have been convicted of racial discrimination in hiring and promotion, and private social clubs often refuse to admit minority members.

Since the majority group generally controls the major institutions, institutional discrimination is almost always carried out by the majority group against the minority group—not the other way around. For the most part, minority groups lack the power with which to practice institutional discrimination. Nevertheless, the refusal by a black-controlled city government to hire whites would be an example of institutional discrimination.

3. Finally, there is a third type of discrimination that some would say is not really discrimination at all. *Structural discrimination* refers to the policies of majority institutions, and the behavior of the individuals who implement these policies and control these institutions, that are race-neutral in intent but have a differential and/or harmful effect on minority groups. The key element in structural discrimination is not the intent but the effect of keeping minority groups in a subordinate position.

Although it is sometimes difficult to determine whether a particular phenomenon is an example of institutional or structural discrimination, the differences between the two are important both conceptually and in terms of social policy. Both types have the *effect* of keeping minority groups subordinate, but only institutional discrimination is *intended* to keep minority groups subordinate. Some examples of structural discrimination follow.

It is well known that blacks and Hispanics are underrepresented on the nation's college campuses. Most colleges, however, have what appear to be race-neutral meritocratic entrance requirements: Anyone who meets the requirements will be admitted regardless of race, ethnicity, gender, and so on. Requirements usually include high school grades, scores on SAT or ACT tests, teacher recommendations, and the like. And most educators sincerely believe that schools with the most rigorous entrance requirements offer the highest-quality educations.

It is also well known that, for a variety of reasons, blacks and Hispanics on the average tend to get lower high school grades and to score lower on the SAT than do whites. Accordingly, a smaller proportion of blacks and Hispanics than whites are admitted to college, especially to the more prestigious schools. In this case, we can say that college entrance requirements constitute an example of structural discrimination because they have a negative effect on blacks and Hispanics.

The criteria that educators believe to be important are less accessible to black and Hispanic students than to whites. As a rule, college managers and faculty members do not intend to be racially discriminatory, and many even feel quite bad about the harm done to black and Hispanic students as a result of these requirements. However, most also do not want to change the requirements.

It is possible, of course, that the underrepresentation of blacks and Hispanics on college campuses is being caused by institutional discrimination. A few colleges may still refuse to admit any black students. Others may purposely inflate entrance requirements as a way of screening out most minority students. Individual discrimination may also be taking place, as when a recruiting officer chooses to avoid black high schools when looking for potential students.

Another example of structural discrimination can be found in the context of job qualifications. Many employers require new employees to have earned a bachelor's degree even though there may be no direct connection between a college education and the skills required for the job in question. The employer, of course, may *believe* that college-educated people will be better workers. Since a smaller percentage of blacks and Hispanics get bachelor's degrees than do whites, blacks will be underrepresented among those who qualify for the job. This is a case of structural discrimination because blacks and Hispanics are negatively affected by the educational requirement for the job, even though there may be no intent to subordinate them.

On the other hand, a large corporation that used the bachelor's degree requirement to intentionally screen out blacks and Hispanics would be committing a form of institutional discrimination. And an individual personnel manager who refused to hire a qualified black applicant would be guilty of individual discrimination.

Consider yet another example: Insurance rates for homes, businesses, and cars are generally higher in black communities than in white communities, in part because of the higher rates of street crime in lower-income black communities. Insurance companies argue that it is good business to charge higher rates in areas where they will have to pay out more in claims, and they insist that they charge high rates in high-crime white areas as well. Yet in spite of the apparently race-neutral determination of insurance rates, the average black ends up paying more than the average white. So this, too, is an example of structural discrimination.

The "good business" argument can also be seen in the banking practice of granting loans and mortgages. The lower an individual's income, the less likely that individual is to be able to pay back the loan. Banks, therefore, are reluctant to give loans to lower-income people; and if they grant any at all, the loans are likely to be small. Since blacks tend to earn lower incomes than whites, they find it more difficult to get loans. Consequently, they have a harder time buying homes and starting businesses. Accordingly, the lending practices of banks are examples of structural discrimination, even though the banks themselves may be following standard business procedures.

Although banks and insurance companies routinely use the "good business" argument to justify structural discrimination, they sometimes practice institutional discrimination as well. Banks often "redline" black communities, and insurance companies have been known to charge higher rates in black communities than in white ones, even after controlling for crime rates.

Many social scientists and much of the general public would be reluctant to apply the term *structural discrimination* to the examples listed here, given the absence in these examples of any intent to harm minority groups or keep them subordinate. I assert, however, that the negative *effects* constitute discrimination. Thus even policies that are intended to be race-neutral and are carried out by well-intentioned people can perpetuate racial inequality.

Like institutional discrimination, structural discrimination is almost always a matter of majority group against minority group, not the other way around. Again, since most social institutions work to the advantage of the majority group, few if any institutional policies favor the minority group. Groups with little power are generally unable to implement policies that are structurally discriminatory.

Although it is sometimes difficult to know whether a given policy that negatively affects minority-group members is a case of individual, institutional, or structural discrimination, an understanding of the conceptual differences among these three categories is important. Since the different types of discrimination have different origins, different policies are required for their elimination. In trying to eliminate individual and institutional discrimination, for example, activists can appeal to the moral and legal principles of equal opportunity and racial fairness. In particular, they might argue that race-neutral meritocratic policies that promote equal opportunity should be the rule in education, employment, housing, and so on.

Where structural discrimination is concerned, however, policies that are race-neutral in intent are not race-neutral in effect. Since policymakers involved with structural discrimination have not tried to harm or subordinate minorities, it makes no sense for activists to appeal to their sense of racial fairness. The policy-makers already believe that they are being racially fair. Instead, activists must convince these policymakers to reevaluate some of the fundamental policies upon which their institutions are based.

If banks are practicing institutional discrimination by "redlining" minority areas, for example, activists can demand that the banks treat each person in that area as a distinct individual. All individuals, inside or outside the redlined area, who meet the banks' universal credit requirements should receive a mortgage. Race or neighborhood should not be a factor.

Confronting the profit-oriented business practices of banks, which I have included in the category of structural discrimination, is more problematic. Even without redlining, banks grant fewer mortgages to blacks than to whites because of racial differences in income and wealth. Bankers can argue that they are simply being good race-neutral capitalists and may even express sincere regret that more blacks do not qualify for loans and mortgages. To deal with this problem, activists must confront the profit-oriented business practices themselves, not the racial views of the bank officials. Perhaps banks have to forgo some of their profits in order to help poor black communities. Perhaps the federal government must subsidize more loans to low-income blacks and create not-for-profit banks in low-income areas.

Alternative arguments are also needed to confront racial inequality in higher education. Colleges that refuse to admit Hispanics who meet their admissions standards are practicing institutional discrimination. If activists can successfully show that qualified Hispanics are not being admitted, they can try to bring public pressure on the colleges to get them to stop discriminating. If this effort failed, the activists could probably sue the colleges in a court of law.

Combating structurally discriminatory admissions standards in higher education requires a different approach. Educators can justify admissions standards by saying that certain grade-point averages and SAT scores are essential to the mission of academic excellence in their institutions, even though a relatively small percentage of Hispanics are able to qualify.

Activists must call on educators to modify their standards, not their racial views. (Certainly Hispanics do not benefit from the standards currently in place.) Indeed, colleges should devote more resources to remedial and support programs for Hispanics who do not meet the entrance requirements. Also needed are new pedagogical techniques, including a more multicultural curriculum, that would be more suited to Hispanic students. And perhaps colleges could shoulder some of the responsibility for improving the quality of high schools attended by Hispanic students.

All three types of discrimination coexist as major problems in American society. And all three must be confronted if racial equality is to be achieved. Individual and institutional discrimination are the most visible. Yet even if they were completely eliminated, the prospect of racial equality would be jeopardized by continuing structural discrimination.

11

America's Apartheid and the Urban Underclass

DOUGLAS S. MASSEY

Although the Kerner Commission of 1968 singled out the ghetto as a fundamental structural factor promoting black poverty in the United States, residential segregation has been overlooked in recent academic debates and policy discussions on the urban underclass. Despite the fact that a large share of African Americans continue to be segregated involuntarily on the basis of race, thinking within the policy establishment has drifted toward the view that race is declining in significance and that black poverty is largely a class-based phenomenon.

Given this emphasis, research into the causes of urban black poverty has focused largely on race-neutral factors such as economic restructuring, family dissolution, education, culture, and welfare. Although researchers often use the terms "ghetto," "ghetto poor," and "ghetto poverty," few see the ghetto itself as something problematic, and few have called for dismantling it as part of a broader attack on urban poverty. Despite its absence from policy discussions, however, residential segregation is not a thing of the past or some neutral fact that can be safely ignored. A large share of black America remains involuntarily segregated, and because life chances are so decisively influenced by where one lives, segregation is deeply implicated in the perpetuation of black poverty.

As a result of their residential segregation, African Americans endure a harsh and extremely disadvantaged environment where poverty, crime, single parenthood, welfare dependency, and educational failure are not only common but all too frequently the norm. Because of the persistence of white prejudice against black neighbors and the continuation of pervasive discrimination in the real estate and banking industries, a series of barriers is placed in the path of black social and geographic mobility. The federal government has not just tolerated this state of affairs; at key junctures over the past several decades it has intervened actively to sustain it. Residential segregation by race is an embedded feature of American life that is deeply institutionalized at all levels of U.S. society, and as long as high levels of racial segregation persist, black poverty will be endemic, and racial divisions will grow.

TRENDS IN BLACK-WHITE SEGREGATION

In the years following the civil rights movement of the 1960s, urban blacks came to experience one of two basic conditions. Those in metropolitan areas with large black populations experienced extremely high levels of segregation that showed little tendency to decline over time.[1] Levels of black suburbanization lagged well behind those of other groups, and those African Americans who did manage to achieve suburban residence remained racially isolated. In 16 metropolitan areas Nancy Denton and I observed, blacks were so highly segregated across so many dimensions simultaneously that we coined the term "hypersegregation" to describe their situation. Together these metropolitan areas—which included Baltimore, Chicago, Cleveland, Detroit, Los Angeles, Newark, Philadelphia, St. Louis, and Washington—contained more than one-third of all African Americans in the United States.[2]

In urban areas where blacks constituted a relatively small share of the population, such as Tucson, Phoenix, and Seattle, however, levels of black-white segregation *declined* after 1970, at times quite rapidly.[3] In these urban areas, African Americans dispersed widely throughout the metropolitan environment, and, in contrast to the situation of large urban black communities, suburbanization brought significant integration and interracial contact. Unfortunately, relatively few African Americans experienced these benign conditions.

The dividing line between these contrasting trends is a metropolitan black fraction of 5 percent. Below this level, desegregation occurred; above it, there was little change. Andrew Gross and I developed an index of the degree of segregation required to keep white neighborhoods at 5 percent black or less.[4] The difference between this index and the level of segregation actually observed in 1970 closely predicted the decline in segregation levels over the ensuing decade. During the 1970s, in other words, U.S. urban areas were moving toward precisely that level of segregation needed to keep the likelihood of white-black contact at 5 percent or less. In areas with small black populations, this pattern implied rapid desegregation; in areas with large black communities, it meant continued segregation and racial isolation.

Preliminary work on the 1990 census suggests that this split in the urban black experience has continued.[5] Urban areas with large black populations remain highly segregated and have shown little tendency toward a decline in segregation; areas with small black populations continue their move toward integration. Declines in segregation were especially rapid in urban areas of the South and West that contained sizable Hispanic populations and large military bases, in addition to small black populations. Although black access to suburbs increased, in areas with large African-American populations settlement was restricted to a small number of suburban communities whose racial segregation was increasing; the small number of blacks entering suburbs was not sufficient to affect the overall pattern of high racial segregation within the urban area as a whole. As a result, metropolitan areas that were hypersegregated in 1980 generally remained so in 1990, and some new areas were added to the list.[6]

The high degree of black residential segregation is unprecedented and unique. No other group in the history of the United States has ever experienced such high levels of segregation sustained over such a long period of time. Despite recent declines, the average level of black segregation is still 50 percent greater than that observed among Asians or Hispanics, and the lowest levels of black segregation generally correspond to the highest levels observed for Hispanics and Asians.

THE CAUSES OF RACIAL RESIDENTIAL SEGREGATION

This distinctive pattern of high black segregation cannot be attributed to socioeconomic factors, at least as of 1980 when the last study was carried out.[7] As of that date, black families earning over $50,000 were just as segregated as those earning under $2,500, and in metropolitan areas with large Hispanic as well as black populations, the poorest Hispanic families were *less* segregated than the most affluent blacks. Similar patterns are observed when data are broken down by education and occupation. Controlling for social class makes little difference in considering the level of black segregation: blacks in large cities are segregated no matter how much they earn, learn, or achieve.

Rather than a lack of income, high levels of black segregation are attributable to three other factors: prejudice, discrimination, and public policy. White racial prejudice yields a weak demand for housing in integrated neighborhoods and fuels a process of neighborhood racial transition. Pervasive discrimination in the real estate and banking industries keeps blacks out of most neighborhoods, providing prejudiced whites with an avenue of escape when faced with the prospect of black settlement in their neighborhoods. Finally, the federal government itself institutionalized the practice of mortgage redlining and supported state and local governments in their use of urban renewal and public housing programs as part of a deliberate attempt to segregate urban blacks.

White Prejudice

Although whites have now come to accept open housing in principle, survey data show that they are reluctant to accept it in practice. Whereas almost 90 percent of white respondents to national surveys agree that "black people have a right to live wherever they can afford to," only 40 percent would be willing to vote for a law stating that "a homeowner cannot refuse to sell to someone because of their race or skin color."[8]

When questions are posed about specific neighborhood compositions, moreover, it becomes clear that white tolerance for racial mixing is quite limited. One-third of whites responding to a 1992 Detroit survey said they would feel uncomfortable living in a neighborhood where 20 percent of the residents were black, and about the same percentage would be unwilling to live in such an area.[9] When the racial composition was increased to one-third black, 59 percent of all whites said they would be unwilling to live there, 44 percent would feel uncomfortable, and 29 percent would seek to leave. At a 50-50 racial mixture, neighborhoods become unacceptable to all but a small minority of whites: 73 percent said they would not wish to live there, 53 percent would try to leave, and 65 percent would feel uncomfortable.

In contrast. African Americans express strong support for integration in both principle and practice. Blacks are unanimous in agreeing that "black people have a right to live wherever they can afford to," and 71 percent would vote for a communitywide law to enforce this right.[10] When asked about specific neighborhood racial compositions, they consistently select racially mixed areas as most desirable. Although the most popular choice is a neighborhood that is half-black and half-white, 87 percent would be willing to live in a neighborhood that is only 20 percent black.[11]

Black respondents do express a reluctance to move into all-white neighborhoods; however, this apprehension does not indicate a rejection of integration per se, but stems from a well-founded fear of hostility and violence. Among black respondents to a 1976 Detroit survey who said they would be reluctant to move into an all-white area, 34 percent thought that white neighbors would be unfriendly and make them feel unwelcome, 37 percent thought they would be made to feel uncomfortable, and 17 percent expressed a fear of violence; four-fifths rejected the view that moving into a white neighborhood constituted a desertion of the black community.[12]

If it were up to them, then, blacks would live in racially mixed neighborhoods. But it is not solely up to them because their preferences interact with those of whites to produce the neighborhoods we actually observe. Whereas most blacks pick a 50-50 racial mixture as most desirable, the vast majority of whites are unwilling to live in such a neighborhood, and most would try to leave. This fundamental disparity has been confirmed by surveys conducted in Milwaukee, Omaha, Cincinnati, Kansas City, and Los Angeles, all of which show that blacks strongly prefer a 50-50 mixture and that whites have little tolerance for racial mixtures beyond 20 percent black.[13]

These contrasting attitudes imply a disparity in the demand for housing in integrated neighborhoods. Given the violence, intimidation, and harassment that historically have followed their moving into white areas, blacks are reluctant to be first across the color line. After one or two black families have entered a neighborhood, however, black demand grows rapidly given the high value placed on integrated housing. This demand escalates as the black percentage rises toward 50 percent, the most preferred neighborhood configuration; beyond this point, it stabilizes and falls off as the black percentage rises toward 100 percent.

The pattern of white demand for housing in racially mixed areas follows precisely the opposite trajectory. Demand is strong for homes in all-white areas, but once one or two black families have moved in, white demand begins to falter as some white families leave and others refuse to move in. The acceleration in residential turnover coincides with the expansion of black demand, making it very likely that outgoing white households are replaced by black families. As the black percentage rises, white demand drops more steeply and black demand rises at an increasing rate. By the time black demand peaks at the 50 percent mark, practically no whites are willing to move in and the large majority are trying to leave. Thus, racial segregation is fomented by a process of racial turnover fueled by antiblack prejudice on the part of whites.

Institutional Discrimination

Although prejudice is a necessary condition for black segregation, it alone is insufficient to maintain the residential color line. Active discrimination against black home seekers must also occur: some neighborhoods must be kept nonblack if whites are to have an avenue of retreat following black entry elsewhere. Racial discrimination was institutionalized in the real estate industry during the 1920s and well established in private practice by the 1940s.[14] Discriminatory behavior was open and widespread among real estate agents at least until 1968, when the Fair Housing Act was passed. After this date, outright refusals to rent or sell to blacks became rare, given that overt discrimination could lead to prosecution under the law.

Black home seekers now face a more subtle process of exclusion. Rather than encountering "white only" signs, they encounter a covert series of barriers surreptitiously placed in their way. Although each individual act of discrimination may be small and subtle, together they have a powerful cumulative effect in lowering the probability of black entry into white neighborhoods. Because the discrimination is latent, moreover, it is unobservable, and the only way to confirm whether it has occurred is to compare the treatment of black and white clients with similar social and economic characteristics.

Differences in the treatment of white and black home seekers are measured by means of a housing audit.[15] Teams of white and black auditors are paired and sent to randomly selected real estate agents to pose as clients seeking a home or apartment. The auditors are trained to present comparable housing needs and family characteristics and to express similar tastes; they are assigned equivalent social and economic traits by the investigator. After each encounter, the auditors fill out a report of their experiences, and the results are tabulated and compared to determine the nature and level of discrimination.

In 1987, George Galster wrote to more than 200 local fair housing organizations and obtained written reports of 71 different audit studies carried out during the 1980s: 21 in the home sales market and 50 in the rental market.[16] Despite differences in measures and methods, he concluded that "racial discrimination continues to be a dominant feature of metropolitan housing markets in the 1980s." Using a conservative measure of racial bias, he found that blacks averaged a 20 percent chance of experiencing discrimination in the sales market and a 50 percent chance in the rental market.

He also studied six real estate firms located in Cincinnati and Memphis and found that racial steering occurred in roughly 50 percent of the transactions sampled during the mid-1980s.[17] Racial steering occurs when white and black clients are guided to neighborhoods that differ systematically with respect to social and economic characteristics, especially racial composition. Homes shown to blacks tended to be in racially mixed areas and were more likely to be adjacent to neighborhoods with a high percentage of black residents. Whites were rarely shown homes in integrated neighborhoods unless they specifically requested them, and even then they were guided primarily to homes in white areas. Sales agents made numerous positive comments about white neighborhoods to white clients but said little about these neighborhoods to black home buyers. In a review of 36 different audit studies, Galster discovered that selective comments by agents are probably more common than overt steering.[18]

In 1988, the U.S. Department of Housing and Urban Development (HUD) carried out a nationwide audit survey.[19] Twenty audit sites were randomly selected from among metropolitan areas having a central city population exceeding 100,000 and a black percentage of more than 12 percent. Real estate advertisements in major metropolitan newspapers were randomly sampled, and real estate agents were approached by auditors who inquired about the availability of the advertised unit; they also asked about other units that might be on the market. The Housing Discrimination Study (HDS) covered both the rental and sales markets, and the auditors were given incomes and family characteristics appropriate to the housing unit advertised.

The HDS provides little evidence that discrimination against blacks has declined. Indeed, prior studies appear to have understated both the incidence and severity of housing discrimination in American cities. According to HDS data, housing was made systematically more available to whites in 45 percent of the transactions in the rental market and in 34 percent of those in the sales market. Whites received more favorable credit assistance in 46 percent of sales encounters and were offered more favorable terms in 17 percent of rental transactions. When housing availability and financial assistance were considered together, the likelihood of experiencing racial discrimination was 53 percent in both the rental and sales markets.

In addition to measuring the incidence of discrimination (i.e., the percentage of encounters where discrimination occurs), the HDS study also measured its severity (the number of units made available to whites but not blacks). In stark terms, the severity of housing discrimination is such that blacks are systematically shown, recommended, and invited to inspect far fewer homes than comparably qualified whites. As a result, their access to urban housing is substantially reduced.

Among advertised rental units, the likelihood that an additional unit was shown to whites but not blacks was 65 percent, and the probability that a shown unit was recommended to whites but not blacks was 91 percent.[20] The HDS auditors encountered equally severe bias in the marketing of nonadvertised rental units: the likelihood that an additional unit was inspected by whites only was 62 percent, whereas the probability that whites alone were invited to see another unit was 90 percent.[21] Comparable results were found in urban sales markets, where the severity of discrimination varied from 66 percent to 89 percent. Thus, no matter what index one considers, most of the housing units made available to whites were not brought to the attention of blacks.[22]

Although these audit results are compelling, they do not directly link discrimination to segregation. Using data from an earlier HUD audit study, however, Galster related cross-metropolitan variation in housing discrimination to the degree of racial segregation in different urban areas.[23] He not only confirmed an empirical link between discrimination and segregation, he also discovered that segregation had important feedback effects on socioeconomic status. Not only does discrimination lead to segregation, but segregation, by restricting economic opportunities for blacks, produces interracial economic disparities that incite further discrimination and more segregation.

Galster has also shown that white prejudice and discrimination are connected to patterns of racial change within neighborhoods.[24] In a detailed study of census tracts in the Cleveland area, he found that neighborhoods that were all white or racially changing evinced much higher rates of discrimination than areas that were stably integrated or predominantly black. Moreover, the pace of racial change was strongly predicted by the percentage of whites who agreed that "white people have a right to keep blacks out of their neighborhoods." That is, neighborhoods in which a large share of whites endorsed racial discrimination in principle tended to turn over racially most rapidly.

Public Policy

The final factor responsible for black residential segregation is government policy. During the 1940s and 1950s, the Federal Housing Administration (FHA) invented the practice of redlining and effectively established it as standard practice within the banking industry.[25] As a condition for underwriting a mortgage, the FHA required a neighborhood assessment; neighborhoods that contained black residents, were adjacent to black areas, or were thought to be at risk of attracting blacks at some point in the future were colored red on the agency's Residential Security Maps and systematically denied access to FHA-backed loans. Private lenders originating non-FHA loans took their cue from the government, and the practice of redlining became institutionalized throughout the lending industry.

Black and mixed-race areas were thus denied access to capital, guaranteeing that housing prices would stagnate, dwellings would steadily deteriorate, and whites would be unable to purchase homes in integrated areas. As a result of federal policy, therefore, racial turnover and physical deterioration became inevitable following black entry into a neighborhood. During the early 1970s, lawsuits and pressure from the civil rights community finally forced the FHA to open up its lending program to black participation. Since then, however, whites have deserted the FHA lending program in favor of conventional loans.

Studies show that blacks are still rejected for conventional loans at rates far higher than whites of comparable economic background.[26] Moreover, because of redlining, black and racially mixed areas do not receive the amount of mortgage capital that they would otherwise qualify for on economic criteria alone.[27] Paradoxically, the recent opening up of FHA lending to blacks has only fueled neighborhood racial transition, with FHA loans being used by blacks to buy homes from whites in racially mixed areas, who then flee to all-white neighborhoods using conventional loans that are denied to blacks.

During the period 1950–70, the federal government also promoted segregation through urban renewal and public housing programs administered by HUD. As black in-migration and white suburbanization brought rapid racial turnover to U.S. cities, local elites became alarmed by the threat that expanding ghettos posed to white institutions and business districts. With federal support, they used renewal programs to clear black neighborhoods encroaching on white districts and employed public housing as a means of containing those families displaced by "renewal." White city councils blocked the construction of minority housing projects outside of the ghetto, however, so most were built on cleared land in black areas, thereby driving up the degree of racial and class isolation.[28]

RACIAL SEGREGATION AND SOCIOECONOMIC MOBILITY

If segregation is imposed on African Americans involuntarily through an interlocking set of individual actions, institutional practices, and governmental actions that are prejudicial in their intent and discriminatory in their effect, then significant barriers are placed in the path of black social mobility. Because where one lives is such an important determinant of one's life chances, barriers to residential mobility inevitably end up being barriers to social mobility. If one group of people is denied full access to urban housing markets on the basis of skin color, then it is systematically denied access to the full range of benefits in urban society.

Housing markets are especially important because they distribute much more than a place to live; they also distribute any good or resource that is *correlated* with where one lives. Housing markets do not just distribute houses; they also distribute education, employment, safety, insurance rates, services, and wealth in the form of home equity; they also determine the level of exposure to crime and drugs and the formation of peer groups that children experience. Research consistently shows that, dollar for dollar of income, year for year of schooling, and unit for unit of occupational status, blacks achieve much less in the way of residential benefits than other racial and ethnic groups.[29]

Because of persistent segregation, blacks are far more likely than whites of the same income to experience inferior schools, isolation from jobs, crime and violence, excessive insurance rates, sagging home values, and environments where expectations run to gang membership and teenage pregnancy rather than college attendance. As a result, black families who have improved their lot are much less able than the upwardly mobile of other groups to consolidate their gains, move ahead further, and pass their achievements on to their children.

SEGREGATION AND THE CONCENTRATION OF POVERTY

Segregation not only harms the interests of individual people and families who experience barriers to residential mobility; it also undermines the community as a whole by concentrating poverty at extraordinary levels. Concentrated poverty occurs because segregation confines any general increase in black poverty to a small number of spatially distinct neighborhoods. Rather than being spread uniformly throughout a metropolitan environment, poor families created by an economic downturn are restricted to a small number of densely settled, tightly packed, and geographically isolated areas. Given a high level of residential segregation, any increase in the poverty rate *must* produce a spatial concentration of poverty; no other result is possible.[30]

Because rates of poverty and levels of segregation differ so much between whites, blacks, and Hispanics, individual members of these groups are structurally constrained to experience markedly different levels of neighborhood poverty. The geographic concentration of poverty is built into the experience of blacks but is alien to the experience of whites, even if they are quite poor themselves. Moreover, the basic effect of segregation in concentrating poverty is significantly exacerbated by public housing, which was used during the period 1950–70 in a racially discriminatory manner to confine and isolate urban blacks. Neighborhoods that contain public housing projects have concentrations of poverty that are at least double what they would be otherwise.[31]

In concentrating poverty, segregation acts simultaneously to concentrate anything that is correlated with poverty: crime, drug abuse, welfare dependency, single parenthood, and educational difficulties. To the extent that individual socioeconomic failings follow from prolonged exposure to concentrated poverty and its correlates, therefore, these disadvantages are ultimately produced by the structural organization of U.S. metropolitan areas. The mere fact that blacks are highly segregated as well as poor means that individual African Americans are more likely to suffer joblessness and to experience single parenthood than either Hispanics or whites, quite apart from any disadvantages they may suffer with respect to personal or family characteristics.

A growing body of research has linked individual socioeconomic difficulties to the geographic concentration of socioeconomic disadvantage that people experience in their neighborhoods.[32] One study has directly linked the socioeconomic disadvantages suffered by individual minority members to the degree of segregation their group experiences in urban society. Using individual, community, and metropolitan data from the 50 largest U.S. metropolitan areas in 1980, Andrew Gross, Mitchell Eggers, and I show that segregation and poverty interact to concentrate poverty geographically within neighborhoods and that exposure to neighborhood poverty subsequently increases the probability of male joblessness and single motherhood among individuals.[33] In this fashion, we link the structural condition of segregation to individual behaviors widely associated with the underclass through the intervening factor of neighborhood poverty.

According to our estimates, increasing the black poverty rate from 10 percent to 40 percent under conditions of no segregation has a relatively modest effect on the neighborhood environment that blacks experience, raising it modestly from about 8 percent to 17 percent. Although the probabilities of male joblessness and single motherhood are sensitive to the rate of poverty that people experience in their neighborhood, this modest change in neighborhood poverty is not enough to affect individual outcomes very much. The probability of male joblessness rises only from 36 percent to 40 percent as a result of increased poverty concentration, and the likelihood of single motherhood increases from 23 percent to 28 percent.

In a highly segregated urban area, in contrast, increasing the overall rate of black poverty causes a marked increase in the concentration of poverty within black neighborhoods. As the overall rate of poverty increases from 10 percent to 40 percent, the neighborhood poverty rate likewise goes from 10 percent to 41 percent. This sharp increase in neighborhood poverty has a profound effect on the well-being of individual blacks, even those who have not been pushed into poverty themselves because segregation forces them to live in neighborhoods with many families who are poor. As a result of the increase in neighborhood poverty to which they are exposed, the probability of joblessness among young black males rises from 40 percent to 53 percent, and the likelihood of single motherhood increases from 28 percent to 41 percent.

Thus, increasing the rate of poverty of a segregated group causes its neighborhood environment to deteriorate, which in turn causes individual probabilities of socioeconomic failure to rise. The same rise in poverty without segregation would hardly affect group members at all because it would have marginal effects on the neighborhoods where they live. Segregation, in other words, is directly responsible for the creation of a uniquely harsh and disadvantaged black residential environment, making it likely that individual blacks themselves will fail, no matter what their socioeconomic characteristics or family background. Racial segregation is the institutional nexus that enables the transmission of poverty from person to person and generation to generation and is therefore a primary structural factor behind the perpetuation of the urban underclass.

PUBLIC POLICY NEEDS

In the United States today, public policy discussions regarding the urban underclass frequently devolve into debates on the importance of race versus class. By presenting the case for segregation's role as a central cause of urban poverty, I seek to end this specious opposition. The issue is not whether race *or* class perpetuates the urban underclass, but how race *and* class *interact* to undermine the social and economic well-being of black Americans. I argue that race operates powerfully through urban housing markets and that racial segregation interacts with black class structure to produce a uniquely disadvantaged neighborhood environment for many African Americans, an environment that builds a variety of self-perpetuating processes of deprivation into black lives.

Public policies therefore must address both race and class issues if they are to be successful. Race-conscious steps need to be taken to dismantle the institutional apparatus of segregation, and class-specific policies must be implemented to improve the socioeconomic status of African Americans. By themselves, programs targeted to low-income blacks will fail because they will be swamped by powerful environmental influences arising from the disastrous neighborhood conditions that blacks experience as a result of segregation. Likewise, efforts to reduce segregation will falter unless African Americans acquire the socioeconomic resources that enable them to take full advantage of urban housing markets and the benefits they distribute.

The elimination of residential segregation will require the direct involvement of the federal government to an unprecedented degree, and two departments, Housing and Urban Development and Justice, must throw their institutional weight behind fair housing enforcement if residential desegregation is to occur. If the ghetto is to be dismantled, HUD, in particular, must intervene forcefully in eight ways.

1. The Department of Housing and Urban Development must increase its financial assistance to local fair housing organizations to enhance their ability to investigate and prosecute individual complaints of housing discrimination. Grants made to local agencies dedicated to fair housing enforcement will enable organizations to expand their efforts by hiring more legal staff, implementing more extensive testing programs, and making their services more widely available.
2. Housing and Urban Development should establish a permanent testing program capable of identifying real estate agents who engage in a pattern and practice of discrimination. A special unit dedicated to the regular administration of housing audits should be created in HUD under the assistant secretary for fair housing and equal opportunity. Audits of randomly selected real estate agents should be conducted annually within metropolitan areas that have large black communities, and when evi-

dence of systematic discrimination is uncovered, the department should compile additional evidence and turn it over to the attorney general for vigorous prosecution. Initially, these audits should be targeted to hypersegregated cities.

3. A staff should be created at HUD under the assistant secretary for fair housing and equal opportunity to scrutinize lending data for unusually high rates of rejection among minority applicants and black neighborhoods. When the rejection rates cannot be explained statistically by social, demographic, economic, credit history, or other background factors, a systematic case study of the bank's lending practices should be initiated. If clear evidence of discrimination is uncovered, the case should be referred to the attorney general for prosecution, and, if not, an equal opportunity lending plan should be negotiated, implemented, and monitored.
4. Funding for housing certificate programs authorized under Section 8 of the 1974 Housing and Community Development Act should be expanded, and programs modeled on the Gautreaux Demonstration Project in Chicago should be more widely implemented. Black public housing residents who have moved into integrated suburban settings through this project have been shown to experience greater success in education and employment than a comparable group who remained behind in the ghetto.[34]
5. Given the overriding importance of residential mobility to individual well-being, hate crimes directed against blacks moving into white neighborhoods must be considered more severe than ordinary acts of vandalism or assault. Rather than being left only to local authorities, such crimes should be prosecuted at the federal level as violations of the victim's civil rights. Stiff financial penalties and jail terms should be imposed, not in recognition of the severity of the vandalism or violence itself, but in acknowledgment of the serious damage that segregation does to our national well-being.
6. The Department of Housing and Urban Development should work to strengthen the Voluntary Affirmative Marketing Agreement, a pact reached between HUD and the National Association of Realtors during the Ford administration. The agreement originally established a network of housing resource boards to enforce the Fair Housing Act with financial support from HUD. During the Reagan administration, however, cuts in HUD's funding forced a redesign of the agreement that relieved real estate agents of their responsibility. New regulations also prohibited local resource boards from using testers and made secret the list of real estate boards that had signed the agreement. In strengthening this agreement, the list should once again be made public, the use of testers should be encouraged, and the responsibilities of real estate agents to enforce the Fair Housing Act should be spelled out explicitly.
7. The department should establish new programs and expand existing programs to train real estate agents in fair housing marketing procedures, especially those serving black neighborhoods. Agents catering primarily to white clients should be instructed about advertising and mar-

keting methods to ensure that blacks in segregated communities gain access to information about housing opportunities outside the ghetto, whereas those serving the black share of the market should be trained to market homes throughout the metropolitan area and should be instructed especially in how to use multiple listing services. Housing and Urban Development officials and local fair housing groups should carefully monitor whether real estate agents serving blacks are given access to multiple listing services.

8. Finally, the assistant secretary for fair housing and equal opportunity at HUD must take a more active role in overseeing real estate advertising and marketing practices, two areas that have received insufficient federal attention in the past. Real estate agents in selected metropolitan areas should be sampled, and their advertising and marketing practices regularly examined for conformity with federal fair housing regulations. The department should play a larger role in ensuring that black home seekers are not being systematically and deliberately overlooked by prevailing marketing practices.

For the most part, these policies do not require major changes in legislation. What they require is political will. Given the will to end segregation, the necessary funds and legislative measures will follow. For America, the failure to end segregation will perpetuate a bitter dilemma that has long divided the nation. If segregation is permitted to continue, poverty inevitably will deepen and become more persistent within a large share of the black community, crime and drugs will become more firmly rooted, and social institutions will fragment further under the weight of deteriorating conditions. As racial inequality sharpens, white fears will grow, racial prejudices will be reinforced, and hostility toward blacks will increase, making the problems of racial justice and equal opportunity even more insoluble. Until we decide to end the long reign of American Apartheid, we cannot hope to move forward as a people and a nation.

NOTES

1. Douglas S. Massey and Nancy A. Denton, *American Apartheid: Segregation and the Making of the Underclass* (Cambridge, Mass.: Harvard University Press, 1993), chap. 3.

2. Douglas S. Massey and Nancy A. Denton, "Hypersegregation in U.S. Metropolitan Areas: Black and Hispanic Segregation along Five Dimensions," *Demography* 26, no. 3 (August 1989): 373–93.

3. Douglas S. Massey and Nancy A. Denton, "Trends in the Residential Segregation of Blacks, Hispanics, and Asians," *American Sociological Review* 52, no. 6 (December 1987): 802–25.

4. Douglas S. Massey and Andrew B. Gross, "Explaining Trends in Residential Segregation, 1970–1980," *Urban Affairs Quarterly* 27, no. 1 (September 1991): 13–35.

5. Reynolds Farley and William H. Frey, "Changes in the Segregation of Whites from Blacks during the 1980s: Small Steps toward a More Integrated Society," *American Sociological Review* 59, no. 1 (February 1994): 23–45; Mark Schneider and Thomas Phelan, "Black Suburbanization in the 1980's," *Demography* 30, no. 2 (May 1993): 269–80.

6. Nancy A. Denton, "Are African Americans Still Hypersegregated in 1990?" in *Residential Apartheid: The American Legacy,* ed. Robert Bullard (Newbury Park, Calif.: Sage, 1994).

7. Nancy A. Denton and Douglas S. Massey, "Residential Segregation of Blacks, Hispanics, and Asians by Socioeconomic Status and Generation," *Social Science Quarterly* 69, no. 4 (December 1988): 797–817.

8. Howard Schuman, Charlotte Steeh, and Lawrence Bobo, *Racial Attitudes in America: Trends and Interpretations* (Cambridge, Mass.: Harvard University Press, 1985); Howard Schuman and Lawrence Bobo, "Survey-based Experiments on White Racial Attitudes toward Residential Integration," *American Journal of Sociology* 94, no. 2 (September 1988): 273–99.

9. Reynolds Farley, Charlotte Steeh, Tara Jackson, Maria Krysan, and Keith Reeves, "The Causes of Continued Racial Residential Segregation: Chocolate City, Vanilla Suburbs Revisited," *Journal of Housing Research* 4, no. 1 (1993): 1–38.

10. Lawrence Bobo, Howard Schuman, and Charlotte Steeh, "Changing Racial Attitudes toward Residential Integration," in *Housing Desegregation and Federal Policy,* ed. John M. Goering (Chapel Hill: University of North Carolina Press, 1986), pp. 152–69.

11. Farley et al. (n. 9 above).

12. Reynolds Farley, Suzanne Bianchi, and Diane Colasanto, "Barriers to the Racial Integration of Neighborhoods: The Detroit Case," *Annals of the American Academy of Political and Social Science* 441 (January 1979): 97–113.

13. William A. V. Clark, "Residential Preferences and Neighborhood Racial Segregation: A Test of the Schelling Segregation Model," *Demography* 28, no. 1 (February 1991): 1–19.

14. Massey and Denton, *American Apartheid* (n. 1 above), chap. 2.

15. John Yinger, "Measuring Racial Discrimination with Fair Housing Audits: Caught in the Act," *American Economic Review* 76, no. 5 (December 1986): 991–93.

16. George C. Galster, "Racial Discrimination in Housing Markets during the 1980s: A Review of the Audu Evidence," *Journal of Planning Education and Research* 9, no. 3 (March 1990): 165–75

17. George C. Galster, "Racial Steering by Real Estate Agents: Mechanisms and Motives," *Review of Black Political Economy* 19, no. 1 (Summer 1990): 39–63.

18. George C. Galster, "Racial Steering in Urban Housing Markets: A Review of the Audit Evidence," *Review of Black Political Economy* 18, no. 3 (Winter 1990): 105–29.

19. John Yinger, *Housing Discrimination Study: Incidence of Discrimination and Variations in Discriminatory Behavior* (Washington, D.C.: U.S. Department of Housing and Urban Development, Office of Policy Development and Research, 1991), and *Housing Discrimination Study: Incidence and Severity of Unfavorable Treatment* (Washington, D.C.: U.S. Department of Housing and Urban Development, Office of Policy Development and Research, 1991).

20. Yinger, *Housing Discrimination Study: Incidence of Discrimination and Variations in Discriminatory Behavior* (n. 19 above), table 42.

21. Ibid.

22. Ibid., table 44.

23. George C. Galster, "More than Skin Deep: The Effect of Housing Discrimination on the Extent and Pattern of Racial Residential Segregation in the United States," in Goering, ed. (n. 10 above), pp. 119–38; George C. Galster and W. Mark Keeney, "Race, Residence, Discrimination, and Economic Opportunity: Modeling the Nexus of Urban Racial Phenomena," *Urban Affairs Quarterly* 24, no. 1 (September 1988): 87–117.

24. George C. Galster, "The Ecology of Racial Discrimination in Housing: An Exploratory Model," *Urban Affairs Quarterly* 23, no. 1 (September 1987): 84–107, "White Flight from Racially Integrated Neighbourhoods in the 1970s: The Cleveland Experience," *Urban Studies* 27, no. 3 (March 1990): 385–99, "Neighborhood Racial Change, Segregationist Sentiments, and Affirmative Marketing Policies," *Journal of Urban Economics* 27, no. 3 (March 1990): 344–61.

25. Kenneth T. Jackson, *Crabgrass Frontier: The Suburbanization of the United States* (New York: Oxford University Press, 1985), chap. 11.

26. Harold A. Black and Robert L. Schweitzer, "A Canonical Analysis of Mortgage Lending Terms: Testing for Lending Discrimination at a Commercial Bank," *Urban Studies* 22, no. 1 (January 1985): 13–20.

27. Louis G. Pol, Rebecca F. Guy, and Andrew J. Bush, "Discrimination in the Home Lending Market: A Macro Perspective," *Social Science Quarterly* 63, no. 4 (December 1982): 716–28; Gregory D. Squires, William Velez, and Karl E. Taueber, "Insurance Redlining, Agency Location, and the Process of Urban Disinvestment," *Urban Affairs Quarterly* 26, no. 4 (June 1991): 567–88; Harriet Tee Taggart and Kevin W. Smith, "Redlining: An Assessment of the Evidence of Disinvestment in Metropolitan Boston," *Urban Affairs Quarterly* 17, no. 1 (September 1981): 91–107.

28. Arnold R. Hirsch, *Making the Second Ghetto: Race and Housing in Chicago, 1940–1960* (Cambridge: Cambridge University Press, 1983); John F. Bauman, *Public Housing, Race, and Renewal: Urban Planning in Philadelphia, 1920–1974* (Philadelphia: Temple University Press, 1987); Ira Goldstein and William L. Yancey, "Public Housing Projects, Blacks, and Public Policy: The Historical Ecology of Public Housing in Philadelphia," in Goering, ed. (n. 10 above); Douglas S. Massey and Shawn M. Kanaiaupuni, "Public Housing and the Concentration of Poverty," *Social Science Quarterly* 74, no. 1 (March 1993): 109–22.

29. Richard D. Alba and John R. Logan, "Variations on Two Themes: Racial and Ethnic Patterns in the Attainment of Suburban Residence," *Demography* 28, no. 3 (August 1991): 431–53; Douglas S. Massey and Nancy A. Denton, "Spatial Assimilation as a Socioeconomic Process," *American Sociological Review* 50, no. 1 (February 1985): 94–105; Douglas S. Massey and Eric Fong, "Segregation and Neighborhood Quality: Blacks, Hispanics, and Asians in the San Francisco Metropolitan Area," *Social Forces* 69, no. 1 (September 1990): 15–32; Douglas S. Massey, Gretchen A. Condran, and Nancy A. Denton, "The Effect of Residential Segregation on Black Social and Economic Well-being," *Social Forces* 66, no. 1 (September 1987): 29–57.

30. Douglas S. Massey, "American Apartheid: Segregation and the Making of the Underclass," *American Journal of Sociology* 96, no. 2 (September 1990): 329–58; Massey and Denton, *American Apartheid* (n. 1 above), chap. 5.

31. Massey and Kanaiaupuni (n. 28 above).

32. Christopher Jencks and Susan E. Mayer, "The Social Consequences of Growing Up in a Poor Neighborhood," in *Inner City Poverty in the United States*, ed. Laurence E. Lynn, Jr., and Michael G. H. McGeary (Washington, D.C.: National Academy Press, 1990), pp. 111–86; Dennis P. Hogan and Evelyn M. Kitagawa, "The Impact of Social Status, Family Structure, and Neighborhood on the Fertility of Black Adolescents," *American Journal of Sociology* 90, no. 4 (January 1985): 825–55; Frank F. Furstenburg, Jr., S. Philip Morgan, Kristin A. Moore, and James Peterson, "Race Differences in the Timing of Adolescent Intercourse," *American Sociological Review* 52, no. 4 (August 1987): 511–18; Jonathan Crane,

"The Epidemic Theory of Ghettos and Neighborhood Effects on Dropping Out and Teenage Childbearing," *American Journal of Sociology* 96, no. 5 (March 1991): 1226–59.

33. Douglas S. Massey, Andrew B. Gross, and Mitchell L. Eggers, "Segregation, the Concentration of Poverty, and the Life Chances of Individuals," *Social Science Research* 20, no. 4 (December 1991): 397–420.

34. James E. Rosenbaum and Susan J. Popkin, "Employment and Earnings of Low-Income Blacks Who Move to Middle Class Suburbs," in *The Urban Underclass*, ed. Christopher Jencks and Paul E. Peterson (Washington, D.C.: Brookings Institution, 1991), pp. 342–56; James E. Rosenbaum, "Black Pioneers—Do Their Moves to the Suburbs Increase Economic Opportunity for Mothers and Children?" *Housing Policy Debate* 2, no. 4 (1991): 1179–1214.

12

Measuring Employment Discrimination Through Controlled Experiments

MARC BENDICK, JR.,
CHARLES W. JACKSON, AND
VICTOR A. REINOSO

To what extent does discrimination operate in the American labor market today? Has the United States achieved a color-blind society, or do personal characteristics still condition the rewards to personal qualifications?

This paper utilizes a new technique for empirical research on these questions, employment "testing" or "auditing." The paper first outlines gaps in empirical information that testing can address. It then describes the testing approach and illustrates its power with results from initial applications. These results demonstrate that hiring discrimination remains far more prevalent than is commonly assumed. The paper concludes with suggested directions for future public and private efforts against bias.

WHAT IS KNOWN ABOUT EMPLOYMENT DISCRIMINATION

During the past several decades, substantial research has been conducted on employment discrimination, the vast majority of it suggesting that racial and ethnic bias survives to a significant extent.

This conclusion is reinforced by the continued operation of race/ethnic distinctions throughout American society. These patterns include wide-spread segregation in housing and social life, as well as incidents of discrimination experienced by minorities in daily living. Additionally, public opinion surveys indicate that substantial segments of the American population continue to hold stereotyped beliefs and prejudiced attitudes toward minority groups.[1]

Studies of the labor market also suggest the continued presence of discrimination. While some racial and ethnic gaps have diminished over recent decades, econometric research continues to find that minorities do less well than equally qualified nonminorities on such employment outcomes as representation in higher-level occupations, wages, returns on investment in educational credentials, and rates of job dismissal.[2] Public agencies enforcing antidiscrimination laws continue to receive a large flow of complaints annually. In 1988 (the latest year for which detailed data have been released), 50,477 charges alleging race, ethnic, or national origin discrimination in employment were filed with the federal Equal Employment Opportunity Commission (EEOC) and its state and local counterparts.[3]

This accumulated evidence is limited in two important ways. First, much of the information is indirect; rather than observing discriminatory behavior itself, that behavior is inferred from observing its preconditions or its consequences. Second, the magnitude of discrimination remains controversial. Some studies confirm the presence of discrimination but do not estimate its magnitude; others provide quantitative estimates, but these estimates often are not robust with respect to changing assumptions.

Among all aspects of employment, perhaps the greatest uncertainty surrounds estimates of bias in *hiring.* If a job applicant is told that an advertised position has already been filled or that another applicant has been hired who is more qualified, the disappointed job seeker typically does not have sufficient information to confirm or contradict these assertions. Probably reflecting this difficulty in verification, among all race/ethnicity employment discrimination charges filed with the EEOC in 1988, only 6.4 percent concerned hiring.[4]

THE METHODOLOGY OF EMPLOYMENT TESTING

In this context of information gaps, testing represents a promising new empirical technique. Employment testing may be defined as a social science procedure creating controlled conditions under which to measure employers' candid responses to the personal characteristics of job seekers. Its approach is that of a laboratory experiment in which one condition varies while other factors likely to affect a measured outcome are systematically held constant. Testing achieves this circumstance by sending matched pairs of research assistants to apply simultaneously for the same job vacancy. Economists define employment discrimination as "valuation in the labor market of personal characteristics which are unrelated to productivity."[5] In employment testing, applicant characteristics related to productivity are controlled by selecting, training, and credentialing testers to create pairs of job applicants who appear equally qualified for the job they seek. Simultaneously, the effect of characteristics unrelated to productivity are subjected to experimentation by pairing testers who differ in one personal characteristic (in the present case, minority and nonminority). When the testers in these pairs experience substantially different responses to their applications, few assumptions and little analysis are required to infer that the difference is caused by that personal characteristic.

The Fair Employment Council of Greater Washington, Inc. (FEC) has implemented this concept by conducting race-based tests in the Washington, D.C. metropolitan area since the fall of 1990.[6] At that time, six pairs of testers were recruited from among upper-level university undergraduates or recent graduates. Each pair teamed one African American research assistant with a white research assistant of the same sex, approximate age, personal appearance, articulateness, and manner. Testers received training of approximately one week, including an explanation of testing,[7] information on the job-seeking process, coaching on how to be an effective applicant, and practice interviews.

During training, FEC staff worked with each tester pair to develop fictional biographies specifying personal histories, education, work experience, and job-relevant skills. Reflecting information on typical prerequisites for common entry-level occupations,[8] these biographies were designed to make all testers strong candidates for the positions for which they were to apply. Biographies for each pair of testers were made equivalent, with only slight variations to keep their pairing from being apparent to potential employers. A typical pair of testers consisted of persons who were actually recent graduates from the same Ivy League university. However, their testing biographies described both as having completed two years of college at different nonprestigious schools and possessing approximately two years' entry level work experience in retail and office positions. For vacancies where skills such as typing were relevant, testers offered similar levels of proficiency.

Once trained, testers were dispatched to apply for jobs picked through random sampling[9] from the region's largest-circulation newspaper, the *Washington Post;* from among employment agencies in the telephone "Yellow Pages"; and from other public lists of firms in an industry, such as a directory of local hotels published by the Washington Conventions and Visitors Bureau. From November 1990 to August 1991, six teams of FEC testers completed a total of 149 audits.

In assessing the results of these tests, the most central measure of discrimination is differences in rates of job-seeking success: Who proceeds furthest in the job application process? Who receives a job offer? The hypothesis of an absence of discrimination would be confirmed if equally qualified minority and nonminority testers met with success at equal rates, and discrimination is measured by the extent to which minorities are treated less favorably than their nonminority partners. Of course, instances also arise in which minority job candidates are selected over nonminority candidates, reflecting either random effects where two equally qualified candidates compete for a single opening or employer preference in favor of minorities. Therefore, in this paper, testing outcomes are analyzed by computing the proportion of job applications in which nonminority applicants are successful, the proportion of applications in which minorities are successful, and subtracting the latter from the former to generate a net rate of discrimination against minority job seekers.

While this net rate is an important summary measure of the magnitude of discrimination, testing generates more empirical information than is captured in any single number. Testing allows the recording of detailed information about employer-applicant interactions—for example, what questions are asked, what information is volunteered, and what degree of encouragement is expressed to job candidates. Thus, testing generates behavioral data on institutional and psychological mechanisms of bias that have previously been examined only in case studies. But because testing is structured to eliminate explanations of differences in treatment other than discrimination, the complexity that leads case studies to be difficult to interpret is sharply reduced. At the same time, by repeating the same procedure in dozens or hundreds of job applications, testing moves beyond isolated case studies to statistically analyzable samples.

TABLE 12.1 Characteristics of Six Testing Studies of Racial/Ethnic Discrimination in Hiring, 1989–1992

	African American–White Pairs			*Latino–Anglo Pairs*		
Characteristic	*FEC*	*UI*	*UC*	*FEC*	*UI*	*UC*
Method of application	In person	In person	In person	In person	Telephone/ Mail	In person
Number of tests	149	300	145	498	300	140
Tester gender	Male & Female	Male	Male	Male & Female	Male	Male
Labor market	Washington	Washington Chicago	Denver	Washington	San Diego Chicago	Denver
Source of job sample	newspaper industry lists walk-ins	newspaper	newspaper	newspaper industry lists walk-ins	newspaper	newspaper
Location						
City	60%	—	24%	21%	—	23%
Suburbs	40	—	76	79	—	77
Employees						
< 15	17%	—	22%	—	12%	19%
≥ 15	83	—	78	—	88	81
Education claimed in resume						
High school graduate		100%	100%		100%	100%
1–2 years college	100%			50%		
college graduate				50%		
Employment Cluster						
Retail	22%	23%	37%	34%	16%	37%
Office	5	21	20	46	10	17
Service	63	37	32	4	56	35
Other	10	19	11	16	18	11

The testing approach can be applied to a range of demographic groups and sample of jobs, and that process is well underway. Table 12.1 profiles six studies completed by three different research organizations—the Fair Employment Council of Greater Washington, the Urban Institute, and the University of Colorado—implementing variations of the same core testing design.[10] The table indicates that 1,532 tests have been accumulated in four metropolitan labor markets: Chicago, Denver, San Diego, and Washington, D.C. The job vacancies tested typically have been for entry-level positions ranging in qualifications from less-than-high-school-graduate to college graduate and drawn from a variety of industries. Discrimination against both African Americans and Hispanics has been

TABLE 12.2 Selected Outcome Measures in Four Testing Studies, 1989–1992

	White–African American Pairs		*Anglo–Hispanic Pairs*	
Outcome Measure	*FEC*	*UI*	*FEC*	*UI*
Applicants experienced a substantial difference in treatment or outcome				
Non-minority favored	29%	20%	25%	31%
Minority favored	– 5	– 7	– 3	–11
DIFFERENCE	24%	13%@	22%	20%
Probability an applicant received a job offer				
Non-minority	15%	15%	—#	22%
Minority	– 4	– 5	—	– 8
DIFFERENCE	11%	10%	—	15%

@ Includes only differences in the stage to which job applicants advanced; does not include any differences in treatment.

Applications were not pursued to the job offer stage.

Details may not add to totals due to rounding.

explored using both male and female testers and job applications by mail and telephone as well as in-person.

THE OVERALL PREVALENCE OF DISCRIMINATION

Selected results from four of these six studies are presented in Table 12.2[11] These results indicate that many firms today do operate as equal opportunity employers. This conclusion is based on instances in which a pair of testers contacted companies, and the equal qualifications of the two testers were reciprocated by equal treatment. In some cases, both were turned away because the job had already been filled. In other cases, both were interviewed and then offered equivalent jobs. In cases where only one position was available, even-handedness was reflected in an equal probability that the minority or the nonminority applicant would be chosen. In the four studies reviewed in Table 12.2, even-handed treatment was observed between 70 and 80 percent of the time.

In the remaining tests, however, the outcomes were different. The first row of Table 12.2 reports the proportion of tests in which one or more substantial differences in treatment or outcome were encountered by tester teams. It indicates that African American testers were treated significantly worse than their white partners at a net rate of 24 percent in the FEC study;[12] in tests pairing Anglo and Latino applicants, the corresponding figure for net disadvantage to Latinos ranged from 22 percent in the FEC study to 20 percent in the Urban Institute effort. In other words, discrimination adversely affected minority job seekers in more than one job application in five.

The second section of Table 12.2 focuses on a particularly important outcome measure—the probability that a person applying for a position eventually is offered that position. The table indicates that the net difference between nonminority and minority applicants—all to the disadvantage of minorities—ranges from 10 percent (in the Urban Institute's African American/white study) to 15 percent (in the Urban Institute Hispanic/Anglo study), with the FEC's figure of 11 percent for its African American/white tests falling in between.

The rates displayed in Table 12.2 incorporate the effects of discrimination operating in several different ways and at several different stages of the job-seeking process. In the FEC's African American/white tests, the following rates of prevalence were observed for five of these mechanisms:

- *Opportunities to Interview.* Although the testers in each pair presented their applications at virtually the same moment, one might be turned away "because the job is filled," while the other was interviewed. Overall, 48.3 percent of white testers received interviews, compared to 39.6 percent of their African American partners, a difference of 8.7 percentage points.
- *Job Offers or Referrals.* Although each pair of testers were selected and trained to be equally poised and articulate and carried resumes describing equivalent education and experience, one tester might be rejected while the other received a job offer. Some 46.9 percent of white testers who were interviewed received job offers, compared to 11.3 percent of their black counterparts, a difference of 35.6 percentage points.
- *Compensation.* In 16.7 percent of the tests in which both the African American tester and her/his white partner were offered the same job, the white was offered a higher starting wage; the reverse never occurred. In cases where both testers were offered the same job, the starting wage offered white applicants averaged $5.45 per hour, compared to $5.30 for their African American partners, a gap of $.15 per hour.
- *Steering.* Both applicants might be offered jobs, but one a well paid, upwardly mobile position and the other a low-pay, dead-end post. A total of 2.0 percent of white applicants were "steered" to an alternative job at a lower level than the position for which they initially applied, compared to 5.4 percent of African American applicants, a difference of 3.4 percentage points.
- *Access to Additional Opportunities.* When applying for one position, a job candidate is sometimes considered for other vacancies, often unadvertised ones, at the same level or higher than the job originally advertised. This situation was experienced by 4.0 percent of white testers but only 2.7 percent of African American testers, a gap of 1.3 percentage points.

Among these five differences, only that for job offers is large enough to be statistically significant (at the .01 level) in a sample of 149 tests. However, all five consistently operated to the disadvantage of minority applicants. Furthermore, when expressed as a proportion of the time nonminorities are favored over minorities when the mechanism potentially operates, the differences are substantial. The figures in the previous paragraphs translate into a rate of whites obtaining job interviews that is *22 percent* higher than that for their equivalently qualified African American counterparts; a rate for whites of receiving job offers at the interview stage that is *415 percent* the rate for African Americans; a *17 percent* probability that a white offered a job will receive a higher wage offer than an African American offered the same position; a likelihood for a white applicant of being steered to a lesser-quality job that is *37 percent* lower than that for an African American; and access to additional job vacancies that is *48 percent* greater for a white than an African American. Together, these effects make the labor market experiences of equally qualified minority and nonminority job applicants substantially different.

The following incidents[13] exemplify the forms of discriminatory treatment whose rates of incidence have just been presented:

- *Opportunities to Interview.* The *Washington Post* carried an advertisement for a restaurant supervisor in the Washington suburbs. An African American tester who went to the restaurant was told that he would be called if the restaurant wished to pursue his application. Minutes later, a white tester with equivalent credentials followed the same procedure. He was called later the same day to schedule an interview, interviewed the day after that, and subsequently offered the position. Meanwhile, the African American tester made four follow-up calls to reiterate his interest in the position, including one after the white tester refused the job offer. No response was received to these calls.
- *Job Offers or Referrals.* An African American female tester sought entry-level employment through a large employment agency in downtown Washington. After completing an application and being interviewed briefly, she was told that she would be called if a suitable vacancy became available. Shortly thereafter, her white testing partner arrived seeking similar opportunities. After she completed an application and was interviewed, she was told about a receptionist/sales position at an upscale health and grooming firm. She was coached on interviewing techniques and scheduled for an interview later that day; in that interview, she was offered the position.
- *Compensation.* A major department store chain advertised in the *Washington Post* for sales assistants in the women's clothing department of a branch in an affluent neighborhood. When a pair of female testers applied for the position, both were interviewed by the store's personnel department, and both were offered permanent, full-time employment. However, the starting salary offered to the African American tester was \$6.50 per hour, while her white partner was offered \$7.50 per hour.
- *Steering.* A major-brand auto dealer in the Washington suburbs advertised in the *Washington Post* for a car salesperson. An African American tester who applied was told that to enter the business, he should accept a position as a porter/car washer. Arriving shortly thereafter with identical credentials, his white testing partner was immediately interviewed for the sales position that had been advertised.
- *Access to Additional Opportunities.* A dating service in the Washington suburbs advertised in the *Washington Post* for a receptionist/typist. When

an African American tester applied for the position, she was interviewed but heard nothing further. When her white testing partner applied for the receptionist position and was interviewed, the employer offered to create a new position for her, that of personal assistant to the manager. This new position would pay more than the receptionist job, would lead to rapid raises and promotions, and would provide tuition assistance. Follow-up calls by the African American tester elicited no interest on the part of the firm, either for the receptionist position or the newly created opportunity, even after the white tester refused the offer.

RELATING THESE RATES TO THE OVERALL LABOR MARKET

A rate of discrimination exceeding twenty percent is unfortunate, particularly when that rate reflects behavior as blatant as that just illustrated. However, discrimination is even more insidious than these numbers suggest, for four reasons.

First, a typical job seeker applies for a number of jobs in the course of one search for employment.[14] If one job application in five is infected by discriminatory treatment, then the probability that a minority job seeker experiences discrimination during a multiple-application job search approaches 100 percent. Such findings suggest that virtually every minority participant in the non-professional American labor market is likely to be touched by discrimination at some time in her or his working life.

Second, inequality of opportunities often arise after initial hiring—as signaled, for example, by the 67,192 race/ethnic complaints alleging employment bias filed with the EEOC in 1988 that involved assignments, compensation, promotion, dismissal, or other treatment of persons already employed. Indeed, entry-level recruitment and hiring are believed to be the personnel processes in which minorities have made the most progress in many firms, with "glass ceiling" problems in retention and advancement remaining substantially more intractable.[15] Thus, posthiring practices undoubtedly produce instances of discrimination in addition to those counted through testing studies of hiring alone.

Third, while the effects of discrimination are serious for any worker, they are perhaps most destructive for job seekers just entering the world of work; being denied access to the bottom rung of "career ladders" can trap persons in a lifetime of "dead end," low-paying, unstable employment.[16] Testing results demonstrating that discrimination is common are based on samples of jobs disproportionately composed of such career-entry opportunities. Furthermore, the better the job, the greater the likelihood of discrimination. For example, in FEC African American–white tests where both applicants received a job offer, the average starting wage offered to whites was $5.45 per hour; in jobs where white applicants received an offer but their black partner did not, the starting wage averaged $7.13 per hour.

Finally, testing is most readily applied only to job vacancies that are relatively accessible because they are advertised in newspapers or listed with employment agencies. Such vacancies account for only about one-third of all employment opportunities, with the remaining two-thirds filled through more private means of recruitment such as word-of-mouth and personal referrals.[17] It is reasonable to assume that some employers utilize recruitment techniques in which information about vacancies is not publicized to keep away minority and other "undesirable" applicants. Therefore, the extent of discrimination in the overall labor market is almost certainly higher than the rate among vacancies that have been subject to testing. . . .

DIRECTIONS FOR PUBLIC POLICY

The persistence of substantial racial/ethnic bias in hiring, documented by testing, clearly implies the need for continued efforts toward its eradication. Enforcement of antidiscrimination laws—such as is carried out by the Equal Employment Opportunity Commission, its state and local counterparts, the Office of Federal Contract Compliance, and by private litigation—needs to be maintained. Indeed, testing enhances opportunities for such efforts in that testers can participate in litigation either as plaintiffs who are victims of discrimination or as witnesses corroborating allegations of discrimination by actual job seekers.[26]

Support by the American voting public and their elected representatives is prerequisite to such efforts. Accordingly, it is unfortunate that, while racial/ethnic minorities within the American population hold perceptions of the prevalence of discrimination matching the empirical findings in this paper, nonminorities predominantly do not. For example, a 1989 nationwide poll reported that 80 percent of African Americans thought that an African American applicant who is as qualified as a white applicant is less likely to win a job that both want—but only 37 percent of whites agreed; and 62 percent of African Americans felt that the chances of an African American to win a supervisory/managerial position were worse than those for whites—but only 41 percent of whites agreed.[27]

Given these perceptions, perhaps it is not surprising that, since the early 1980s, enforcement activities of the federal Equal Employment Opportunity Commission have stagnated under a combination of inadequate resources and leadership that was ambivalent about the agency's mission. Between fiscal year 1982 and fiscal year 1992, the EEOC's backlog of cases grew from 33,417 to 52,856; and the proportion of complaints dismissed by the EEOC for "no cause" rose from 29 percent in 1981 to 59 percent in 1986.[28] In the same era, considerable policy attention was paid to the contention that litigation in the United States on subjects such as employment discrimination was chronically overused and adversely affected the productivity and competitiveness of the American economy:[29] five Supreme Court rulings substantially reduced the power and scope of federal antidiscrimination laws; and passage of the Civil Rights Act of 1991 to reverse these rulings sparked protracted and bitter debate. Had testing studies indicating the continued prevalence of discrimination challenged public perceptions, this course of events might have been different.

While indicating the continuing need for traditional enforcement of civil rights laws, testing results also suggest the desirability of some refocusing of efforts. In particular, traditional enforcement often focuses on instances of blatant, conscious discriminatory behavior (for example, failure to interview minority job candidates) or the discriminatory impact of "objective" selection procedures (for example, racial/ethnic differences in pass rates on written examinations). While not denying the importance of such mechanisms, testing suggests that they represent only part of current problems. It is equally important to focus on the role of less blatant, often unconscious personal judgments and attitudes in generating differences in employment outcomes—for example, how accurately employers evaluate interviews with minority job candidates. The process of examining and modifying such cognitive processes is complex, involving individual consciousness-raising as well as changes in organizational cultures.[30] However, such difficult undertakings are required to address important forms of employment bias in the 1990s.

NOTES

This research was supported by grants to the Fair Employment Council of Greater Washington, Inc. from the Rockefeller, Ford, MacArthur, Public Welfare, and Norman Foundations. The authors are solely responsible for all findings and conclusions.

1. Gerald Jaynes and Robin M. Williams, eds., *A Common Destiny, Blacks and American Society* (Washington: National Academy of Sciences Press, 1989), chapters 2 and 3; Reynolds Farley, Charles Steeh, Tara Jackson, Maria Krysan, and Keith Reeves, "Continued Racial Segregation in Detroit: 'Chocolate City, Vanilla Suburbs' Revisited," *Journal of Housing Research*, Vol. 4, No. 1 (1993), pp. 1–38; Joe R. Feagin and Melvin P. Sikes, *Living with Racism, The Black Middle Class Experience* (Boston: Beacon Press, 1994); Louis Harris, *The Unfinished Agenda on Race in America* (New York: NAACP Legal Defense Fund, 1989); Tom Smith, *Ethnic Images* (Chicago: National Opinion Research Center, 1990).

2. Andrew Gill, "The Role of Discrimination in Determining Occupational Structure," *Industrial and Labor Relations Review*, Vol. 42, No. 4 (1989), pp. 610–623; Jaynes and Williams, *Common Destiny*, pp. 146–147; K.I. Wolpin, "The Determinants of Black-White Differences in Early Employment Careers: Search, Layoffs, Quits, and Endogenous Wage Growth," *Journal of Political Economy*, Vol. 100, No. 3 (1992), pp. 535–60; Glen Cain, "The Economic Analysis of Labor Market Discrimination: A Survey," in Orley Aschenfelter and Richard Layard, eds., *Handbook of Labor Economics* (New York: Elsevier, 1986), pp. 694–785: Craig Zwerling and Hilary Silver, "Race and Job Dismissal in a Federal Bureaucracy," *American Sociological Review*, Vol. 57, No. 5 (1992), pp. 651–660.

3. *Combined Annual Report, Fiscal Years 1986, 1987, and 1988* (Washington: U.S. Equal Employment Opportunity Commission, 1988).

4. EEOC, *Annual Report;* see also Jomills Braddock and James M. McPartland, "How Minorities Continue to Be Excluded from Equal Employment Opportunities: Research on Labor Market and Institutional Barriers," *Journal of Social Issues*, Vol. 43, No. 1 (1987), pp. 5–39.

5. Kenneth Arrow, "The Theory of Discrimination," in Orley Aschenfelter and Albert Rees, eds., *Discrimination in Labor Markets* (Princeton: Princeton University Press, 1973), p. 3.

6. *Annual Report, 1990–1992* (Washington: Fair Employment Council of Greater Washington, Inc., 1993). *Employment Testing Manual* (Washington: Fair Employment Council of Greater Washington, Inc., 1993). The same techniques are also applicable to demographic characteristics other than race and ethnicity. For example, using pairs of applicants age 32 and 57, testing has been applied to hiring discrimination based on age; see Marc Bendick, Jr., Charles Jackson, and Horacio Romero, *Employment Discrimination Against Older Workers: An Experimental Study of Hiring Practices* (Washington: Fair Employment Council of Greater Washington, 1993).

7. Tests might be conducted in a "double blind" format, that is, with testers not being told that discrimination is the subject of the study in which they are participating. This approach was implemented, for example, in a study of discrimination in auto sales practices; see Ian Ayres, "Fair Driving: Gender and Race Discrimination in Retail Car Negotiations," *Harvard Law Review,* Vol. 104, No. 4 (1991), pp. 817–872. However, it is unrealistic to assume that employment testers would not infer the subject of the study from the procedures they were following and the data they were asked to record. Instead, the FEC seeks to ensure the objectivity of tester-generated data by careful tester selection, extensive training, close supervision, data collection procedures that emphasize facts over judgments, and an organizational culture of social science objectivity.

8. *Dictionary of Occupational Titles* (Washington: U.S. Department of Labor, 1991); *Occupational Outlook Handbook* (Lincolnwood, IL: VGM Career Horizons, 1990).

9. In preparing sampling frames for random sampling, positions were excluded if they were part-time or temporary employment; were in government; or required advanced education, extensive experience, specialized skills, or occupational licenses. While sampling within each sampling frame was random, some sampling frames were selected, in part, because of hypotheses that firms in that frame might be particularly bias-prone (e.g., employment agencies). To the extent that this hypothesis was confirmed, caution should be exercised in applying the precise rate of bias estimated from this sample to the general labor market.

10. The core design is set forth in Marc Bendick, Jr., *Auditing Race Discrimination in Hiring: A Research Design* (Washington: Bendick and Egan Economic Consultants, Inc., 1989). For alternative designs, see Jerome Culp and Bruce Dunson, "Brothers of a Different Color: A Preliminary Look at Employer Treatment of Black and White Youth," in Richard Freeman and Harry Holzer, eds., *The Black Youth Employment Crisis* (Chicago: University of Chicago Press, 1986), pp. 233–259; P.A. Riach and J. Rich, "Measuring Discrimination by Direct Experimental Methods: Seeking Gunsmoke," *Journal of Post-Keynesian Economics,* Vol. 14, No. 2 (1991–92), pp. 143–50; Frank Bovenkerk, *A Manual for International Comparative Research on Discrimination on the Grounds of "Race" and Ethnic Origin* (Geneva: International Labour Organisation, 1992); and George Galster et al., *Sandwich Hiring Audit Pilot Program* (Washington: The Urban Institute, 1994).

Table 12.1 is based on the following sources: Column (a): FEC, *Annual Report,* chapter 3; Column (b): Margery Austin Turner, Michael Fix, and Raymond Struyk, *Opportunities Diminished, Opportunities Denied* (Washington: Urban Institute, 1991); Columns (c) and (f): Franklin James and Steve DelCastillo, *We May Be Making Progress Toward Equal Access to Jobs Evidence From Recent Audits* (Denver: University of Colorado, 1992); Column (d): Marc Bendick, Jr., Charles Jackson, Victor Reinoso, and Laura Hodges, "Discrimination Against Latino Job Applicants: A Controlled Experiment," *Human Resource Management,* Vol. 30, No. 4 (1991), pp. 469–484; Column (e): Harry Cross et al., *Employer Hiring Practices: Differential Treatment of Hispanic and Anglo Job Seekers* (Washington: Urban Institute, 1990).

11. The sources for Table 12.2 are the same as for Table 12.1 (see Footnote 10).

James and DelCastillo, *We May Be Making Progress,* report a testing study in the Denver labor market that estimated a two percent net rate of discrimination against African Americans compared to whites but a ten percent rate in favor of Hispanics over Anglos. These results are contaminated by methodological flaws, including inappropriate pairing of testers, inadequate supervision of field work, and compensation arrangements giving minority testers greater incentives to pursue job openings than nonminorities. These flaws led to differences in the level of effort expended by paired testers (e.g.; different numbers of follow-up calls) and also raised general concerns about data validity and reliability; see

Michael Fix and Raymond Struyk, eds., *Clear and Convincing Evidence: Measurement of Discrimination in America* (Washington: Urban Institute Press, 1993), appendix. Accordingly, this study is not included in Table 12.2.

12. The net rate of 24 percent is obtained by subtracting 5 percent of instances in which minorities were favored from the 29 percent of instances in which the nonminorities were favored. The comparable figure in Table 12.2 for the Urban Institute study of African Americans and whites—13 percent—refers only to differences in the stage of application to which the testers progress, not the full range of possible differences in treatment or outcome.

13. These examples, all involving African Americans, are drawn from FEC, *Annual Report*, pp. 5–6. Comparable incidents involving Latinos are presented in Bendick et al., "Discrimination Against Latinos," p. 475.

14. Marc Bendick, Jr., "Matching Workers and Job Opportunities," in D. Bawden and F. Skidmore (eds.), *Rethinking Employment Policy* (Washington: Urban Institute Press, 1989), pp. 81–108; Harry Holzer, "Informal Job Search and Black Youth Unemployment," *American Economic Review*, Vol. 77, No. 3 (1987), pp. 446–452; Steven M. Bortnick and Michele Harrison Ports, "Job Search Methods and Results: Tracking the Unemployed, 1991," *Monthly Labor Review*, Vol. 115, No. 12 (1992), pp. 29–35.

15. R. Roosevelt Thomas, *Beyond Race and Gender* (New York: American Management Association, 1991); Susan Jackson and Associates, *Diversity in the Work-place* (New York: Guilford Press, 1992); Mary Lou Egan and Marc Bendick, Jr., *Managing Greater Washington's Changing Workforce* (Washington: Greater Washington Research Center, 1991).

16. Freeman and Holzer, *Black Youth;* Marc Bendick, Jr., and Mary Lou Egan, *Jobs: Employment Opportunities in the Washington Metropolitan Area for Persons with Limited Employment Qualifications* (Washington: Greater Washington Research Center, 1988).

17. See Footnote 14.

26. Roderic Boggs, Joseph Sellers, and Marc Bendick, Jr., "Use of Testing in Civil Rights Enforcement," in Michael Fix and Raymond Struyk eds., *Clear and Convincing Evidence: Measurement of Discrimination in America* (Washington: Urban Institute Press, 1993), pp. 345–376; FEC, *Annual Report*, pp. 10–13; Michael Yelnosky, "Filling an Enforcement Void: Using Testers to Uncover and Remedy Discrimination in Hiring for Lower-Skilled, Entry-Level Jobs," *University of Michigan Journal of Law Reform*, Vol. 26, No. 2 (1993), pp. 404–459.

27. Harris, *Unfinished Agenda;* see also J.R. Kluegel and E.R. Smith, *Beliefs about Equality: Americans' Views of What Is and What Ought to Be* (Hawthorne, NY: Aldine de Gruyter, 1986).

28. Women Employed, *Compilation of EEOC District Office Reports* (Chicago: Women Employed, 1992); Claudia Withers and Judith A. Winston, "Equal Employment Opportunity," in *One Nation Indivisible: The Civil Rights Challenge for the 1990s* (Washington: The Citizens Commission on Civil Rights, 1989), pp. 190–214.

29. Walter Olson, *The Litigation Explosion* (New York: Truman Talley Books, 1992).

30. Thomas, *Beyond Race and Gender;* Jackson, *Diversity;* Egan and Bendick, *Managing.* Several social psychological studies have found that, in laboratory simulations of employment selections, individuals often discriminated in favor of minorities [Arvey and Campion, "The Employment Interview"; Braddock and McPartland, "How Minorities"]. These results contrast with the findings of testing studies involving actual job selections in firms. To understand this contrast, further research is needed to differentiate between discrimination reflecting the attitudes of individual staff members and that reflecting the policies and organizational culture of the firms that employ them.

13

"We'd Love to Hire Them, But . . ."

The Meaning of Race for Employers

JOLEEN KIRSCHENMAN
AND KATHRYN M. NECKERMAN

. . . In this paper we explore the meaning of race and ethnicity to employers, the ways race and ethnicity are qualified by—and at times reinforce—other characteristics in the eyes of employers, and the conditions under which race seems to matter most. Our interviews at Chicago-area businesses show that employers view inner-city workers, especially black men, as unstable, uncooperative, dishonest, and uneducated. Race is an important factor in hiring decisions. But it is not race alone: rather it is race in a complex interaction with employers' perceptions of class and space, or inner-city residence. Our findings suggest that racial discrimination deserves an important place in analyses of the underclass.

RACE AND EMPLOYMENT

In research on the disadvantages blacks experience in the labor market, social scientists tend to rely on indirect measures of racial discrimination. They interpret as evidence of this discrimination the differences in wages or employment among races and ethnic groups that remain after education and experience are controlled. With a few exceptions they have neglected the processes at the level of the firm that underlie these observed differences.[1] . . .

The theoretical literature conventionally distinguishes two types of discrimination, "pure" and "statistical." In pure discrimination, employers, employees, or consumers have a "taste" for discrimination, that is, they will pay a premium to avoid members of another group.[2] Statistical discrimination is a more recent conception that builds on the discussions of "signaling."[3] In statistical discrimination, employers use group membership as a proxy for aspects of productivity that are relatively expensive or impossible to measure. Those who use the concept disagree about whether employers' perceptions of group differences in productivity must reflect reality.[4] In this discussion, we are concerned with statistical discrimination as a cognitive process, regardless of whether the employer is correct or mistaken in his or her views of the labor force. . . .

The distinction between pure and statistical discrimination is a useful one. However, it is also useful to recognize the relationship between the two. There are several ways in which a taste for discrimination in employment practices may lead to perceived and actual productivity differences between groups, making statistical discrimination more likely. Social psychological evidence suggests that expectations about group differences in productivity may bias evaluation of job performance.[5] These expectations may also influence job placement. In particular, workers of lower expected productivity may be given less on-the-job training. Finally, and most important for our study, productivity is not an individual characteristic; rather, it is shaped by the social relations of the workplace. If these relations are strained because of tastes for discrimination on the part of the employer, supervisor, coworkers, or consumers, lower productivity may result.[6] Thus what begins as irrational practice based on prejudice or mistaken beliefs may end up being rational, profit-maximizing behavior.

DATA

This research is based on face-to-face interviews with employers in Chicago and surrounding Cook County between July 1988 and March 1989. Inner-city firms were oversampled; all results here are weighted to adjust for this oversampling. Our overall response rate was 46 percent, and the completed sample of 185 employers is representative of the distribution of Cook County's employment by industry and firm size.[7]

Interviews included both closed- and open-ended questions about employers' hiring and recruitment practices and about their perceptions of Chicago's labor force and business climate. Our initial contacts, and most of the interviews themselves, were conducted with the highest ranking official at the establishment. Because of the many open-ended questions, we taped the interviews.

Most of the structured portion of the interview focused on a sample job, defined by the interview schedule as "the most typical entry-level position" in the firm's modal occupational category—sales, clerical, skilled, semiskilled, unskilled, or service, but excluding managerial, professional, and technical. The distribution of our sample jobs approximates the occupational distribution in the 1980 census for Cook County, again excluding professional, managerial, and technical categories. In effect, what we have is a sample of the opportunities facing the Chicago job-seeker with minimal skills. . . .

Although we do not present our findings as necessarily representative of the attitudes of all Chicago employers, as the rules of positivist social science would require, they are representative of those Chicago employers who spoke to a particular issue. A standard rule of discourse is that some things are acceptable to say and others are better left unsaid. Silence has the capacity to speak volumes. Thus we were overwhelmed by the degree to which Chicago employers felt comfortable talking with us—in a situation where the temptation would be to conceal rather than reveal—in a negative manner about blacks. In this paper we make an effort to understand the discursive evidence by relating it to the practice of discrimination, using quantitative data to reinforce the qualitative findings.

WE'D LOVE TO HIRE THEM, BUT . . .

. . . Explanations for the high rates of unemployment and poverty among blacks have relied heavily on the categories of class and space.[8] We found that employers also relied on those categories, but they used them to refine the category of race, which for them is primary. Indeed, it was through the interaction of race with class and space that these categories were imbued with new meaning. It was race that made class and space important to employers.

Although some employers regarded Chicago's workers as highly skilled and having a good work ethic, far more thought that the labor force has deteriorated. When asked why they thought business had been leaving Chicago, 35 percent referred to the inferior quality of the work force. . . . Several firms in our sample were relocating or seriously considering a move to the South in a search for cheap skilled labor. Employers of less skilled labor can find an ample supply of applicants, but many complained that it was becoming more difficult to find workers with basic skills and a good work ethic.

These employers coped with what they considered a less qualified work force through various strategies. Some restructured production to require either fewer workers or fewer skills. These strategies included increasing automation and deemphasizing literacy requirements—using color-coded filing systems, for example. But far more widespread were the use of recruiting and screening techniques to help select "good" workers. For instance, employers relied more heavily on referrals from employees, which tend to reproduce the traits and characteristics of the current work force: the Chicago Association of Commerce and Industry has reported a dramatic increase in the use of referral bonuses in the past few years. Or employers targeted newspaper ads to particular neighborhoods or ethnic groups. The rationale underlying these strategies was, in part, related to the productivity employers accorded different categories of workers.

For instance, whether or not the urban underclass is an objective social category, its subjective importance in the discourse of Chicago employers cannot be denied. Their characterizations of inner-city workers mirrored many descriptions of the underclass by social scientists. Common among the traits listed were that workers were unskilled, uneducated, illiterate, dishonest, lacking initiative, unmotivated, involved with drugs and gangs, did not understand work, had no personal charm, were unstable, lacked a work ethic, and had no family life or role models.

Social scientists discover pathologies; employers try to avoid them. After explaining that he hired "the best applicant," the owner of a transportation firm added, "Probably what I'm trying to say is we're not social minded. We're not worried about solving the problems of sociology. We can't afford to." But despite not being worried about the "problems of sociology," employers have become lay social theorists, creating numerous distinctions among the labor force that then serve as bases for statistical discrimination. From their own experiences and biases, those of other employers, and accounts in the mass media, employers have attributed meaning to the categories of race and ethnicity, class, and space. These have then become markers of more or less desirable workers.

These categories were often confounded with each other, as when one respondent contrasted the white youth (with opportunities) from the North Shore with the black one (without opportunities) from the South Side. Although the primary distinction that more than 70 percent of our informants made was based on race and ethnicity, it was frequently confounded with class: black and Hispanic equaled lower class; white equaled middle class. And these distinctions also overlapped with space: "inner-city" and at times "Chicago" equaled minority, especially black; "suburb" equaled white. In fact, race was important in part because it signaled class and inner-city residence, which are less easy to observe directly. But employers also needed class and space to draw distinctions within racial and ethnic groups; race was the distinguishing characteristic most often referred to, followed respectively by class and space. . . .

Race and Ethnicity

When they talked about the work ethic, tensions in the workplace, or attitudes toward work, employers emphasized the color of a person's skin. Many believed that white workers were superior to minorities in their work ethic. A woman who hires for a suburban service firm said, "The Polish immigrants that I know and know of are more highly motivated than the Hispanics. The Hispanics share in some of the problems that the blacks do." These problems included "exposure to poverty and drugs" as well as "a lack of motivation" related to "their environment and background." A man from a Chicago construction company, expressing a view shared by many of our informants, said, "For all groups, the pride [in their work] of days gone by is not there, but what is left, I think probably the whites take more pride than some of the other minorities." (Interviewer: "And between blacks and Hispanics?") "Probably the same."

In the discourse of "work ethic," which looms large among the concerns of employers, whites usually came out on top. But although white workers generally looked good to employers, East European whites were repeatedly praised for really knowing how to work and caring about their work. Several informants cited positive experiences with their Polish domestic help. In the skilled occupations, East European men were sought. One company advertised for its skilled workers in Polish- and German-language newspapers, but hired all its unskilled workers, 97 percent of whom were Hispanic, through an employee network.

When asked directly whether they thought there were any differences in the work ethics of whites, blacks, and Hispanics, 37.7 percent of the employers ranked blacks last, 1.4 percent ranked Hispanics last, and no one ranked whites there. Another 7.6 percent placed blacks and Hispanics together on the lowest level; 51.4 percent either saw no difference or refused to categorize in a straightforward way. Many of the latter group qualified their response by saying they saw no differences once one controlled for education, background, or environment, and that any differences were more the result of class or space.

Although blacks were consistently evaluated less favorably than whites, employers' perceptions of Hispanics were more mixed. Some ranked them with blacks; others positioned them between whites and blacks. . . .

They also believed that a homogeneous work force serves to maintain good relations among workers. . . . A personnel manager from a large, once all-white Chicago manufacturing concern lamented the tensions that race and ethnic diversity had created among workers: "I wish we could all be the same, but, unfortunately, we're not." An employer of an all-white work force said that "if I had one [black worker] back there it might be okay, but if I have two or more I would have trouble." But although some employers found a diverse work force more difficult to manage, few actually maintained a homogeneous labor force, at least in terms of race and ethnicity.

Employers worried about tensions not only between white and minority workers but also between Mexicans and blacks, Mexicans and Puerto Ricans, and even African and American blacks. A restaurateur with an all-white staff of waiters and a Hispanic kitchen said, "The Mexican kids that work in the kitchen, they're not, they're not kids anymore, but they don't like to work with black guys. But they don't like to work with Puerto Rican guys either." . . .

Blacks are by and large thought to possess very few of the characteristics of a "good" worker. Over and over employers said, "They don't want to work." "They don't want to stay." "They've got an attitude problem." One compared blacks with Mexicans: "Most of them are not as educated as you might think. I've never seen any of these guys read anything outside of a comic book. These Mexicans are sitting here reading novels constantly, even though they are in Spanish. These guys will sit and watch cartoons while the other guys are busy reading. To me that shows basic laziness. No desire to upgrade yourself." When asked about discrimination against black workers, a Chicago manufacturer related a common view: "Oh, I would in all honestly probably say there is some among most employers. I think one of the reasons, in all honesty, is because we've had bad experience in that sector, and believe me, I've tried. And as I say, if I find—whether he's black or white, if he's good and, you know, we'll hire him. We are not shutting out any black specifically. But I will say that our experience factor has been bad. We've had more bad black employees over the years than we had good." This negative opinion of blacks sometimes cuts across class lines. For instance, a personnel officer of a professional service company in the suburbs commented that "with the professional staff, black males that we've had, some of the skill levels—they're not as orientated to details. They lack some of the leadership skills."

One must also consider the "relevant nots": what were some employers not talking about? They were not talking about how clever black workers were, they were not talking about the cultural richness of the black community, nor were they talking about rising divorce rates among whites. Furthermore, although each employer reserved the right to deny making distinctions along racial lines, fewer than 10 percent consistently refused to distinguish or generalize according to race.

These ways of talking about black workers—they have a bad work ethic, they create tensions in the workplace, they are lazy and unreliable, they have a bad attitude—reveal the meaning race has for many employers. If race were a proxy for expected productivity and the sole basis for statistical discrimination, black applicants would indeed find few job opportunities.

Class

Although some respondents spoke only in terms of race and ethnicity, or conflated class with race, others were sensitive to class distinctions. Class constituted a second, less easily detected signal for employers. Depending somewhat on the demands of the jobs, they used class markers to select among black applicants. The contrasts between their discourse about blacks and Hispanics were striking. Employers sometimes placed Hispanics with blacks in the lower class: an inner-city retailer confounded race, ethnicity, and class when he said, "I think there's a self-defeating prophecy that's maybe inherent in a lot of lower-income ethnic groups or races. Blacks, Hispanics." But although they rarely drew class distinctions among Hispanics, such distinctions were widely made for black workers. As one manufacturer said, "The black work ethic. There's no work ethic. At least at the unskilled. I'm sure with the skilled, as you go up, it's a lot different." Employers generally considered it likely that lower-class blacks would have more negative traits than blacks of other classes.

In many ways black business owners and black personnel managers were the most expressive about class divisions among blacks. A few believed poor blacks were more likely to be dishonest because of the economic pressures they face. A black jeweler said the most important quality he looked for in his help was "a person who doesn't need a job."

> (Interviewer: That's what you're looking for?)
> That's what we usually try to hire. People that don't need the job.
> (Interviewer: Why?)
> Because they will tend to be a little more honest. Most of the people that live in the neighborhoods and areas where my stores are at need the job. They are low-income, and so, consequently, they're under more pressure and there's more of a tendency to be dishonest, because of the pressure. . . .

Other employers mentioned problems that occur in the workplace when there are class divisions among the workers. These are reminiscent of the tensions created by the racial and ethnic diversity described earlier. One black businesswoman told of a program wherein disadvantaged youths were sent to private schools by wealthy sponsors. She herself was a sponsor and held the program in high regard, but she hired some of these youths and they did not get along with her other young employees: "Those kids were too smart 'cause they were from a middle-class background." (Interviewer: "So these were primarily middle-class kids?") "No, they're not middle class, but they have middle-class values because they're exposed to them all the time." They made excellent employees, she said, "if you kept your store filled with just them. They're more outgoing and less afraid of the customers. But they're very intimidating to the supervisors because they know everything by the time they get to be a sophomore in high school." . . .

Thus, although many employers assumed that black meant "inner-city poor," others—both black and white—were quick to see divisions within the black population. Of course, class itself is not directly observable, but markers that convey middle- or working-class status will help a black job applicant get through race-based exclusionary barriers. Class is primarily signaled to employers through speech, dress, education levels, skill levels, and place of residence. Although many respondents drew class distinctions among blacks, very few made those same distinctions among Hispanics or whites; in refining these categories, respondents referred to ethnicity and age rather than class.

Space

Although some employers spoke implicitly or explicitly in terms of class, for others "inner-city" was the more important category. For most the term immediately connoted black, poor, uneducated, unskilled, lacking in values, crime, gangs, drugs, and unstable families. "Suburb" connoted white, middle-class, educated, skilled, and stable families. Conversely, race was salient in part because it signaled space; black connoted inner city and white the suburbs. . . . When asked what it would take for their firm to relocate to the inner city, respondents generally thought it an implausible notion. They were sure their skilled workers would not consider working in those neighborhoods because they feared for their safety, and the employers saw no alternative labor supply there.

The skepticism that greets the inner-city worker often arises when employers associate their race and residence with enrollment in Chicago's troubled public education system. Being educated in Chicago public schools has become a way of signaling "I'm black, I'm poor, and I'm from the inner city" to employers. Some mentioned that they passed over applicants from Chicago public schools for those with parochial or suburban educations. If employers were looking at an applicant's credentials when screening, blacks in the inner city did not do well. As one employer said, "The educational skills they come to the job with are minimal because of the schools in the areas where they generally live."

A vice president of a television station complained of the inner-city work force:

> They are frequently unable to write. They go through the Chicago public schools or they dropped out when they were in the eighth grade. They can't read. They can't write. They can hardly talk. I have another opinion which is strictly my own and that is that people who insist on beating themselves to the point where they are out of the mainstream of the world suffer the consequences. And I'm talking about the languages that are spoken in the ghetto. They are not English.

Employers were clearly disappointed, not just in the academic content and level of training students receive, but in the failure of the school system to prepare them for the work force. Because the inner city is heavily associated with a lack of family values, employers wished the schools would compensate and provide students the self-discipline needed for workers socialization. Additionally, they complained that black workers had no "ability to understand work." . . . It is not only educational content per se that employers were looking for; some were concerned with the educational "experience." One talked about how it just showed "they could finish something." Thus inner city is equated with public school attendance, which in turn signifies insufficient work skills and work ethic.

. . . Another employer used space to refine the category of race: "We have some black women here but they're not inner city. They're from suburbs and . . . I think they're a little bit more willing to give it a shot, you know, I mean they're a little bit more willing [than black men] to give a day's work for a day's pay."

Employers readily distinguished among blacks on the basis of space. They talked about Cabrini Green or the Robert Taylor Homes or referred to the South Side and West Side as a shorthand for black. But they were not likely to make these distinctions among whites and Hispanics. They made no reference to Pilsen (a largely immigrant Mexican neighborhood), Humboldt Park (largely Puerto Rican), or Uptown (a community of poor whites and new immigrants).

For black applicants, having the wrong combination of class and space markers suggested low productivity and undesirability to an employer. The important finding of this research, then, is not only that employers make hiring decisions based on the color of a person's skin, but the extent to which that act has become nuanced. Race, class, and space interact with each other. Moreover, the precise nature of that interaction is largely determined by the demands of the job. . . .

CONCLUSION

Chicago's employers did not hesitate to generalize about race or ethnic differences in the quality of the labor force. Most associated negative images with inner-city workers, and particularly with black men. "Black" and "inner-city" were inextricably linked, and both were linked with "lower-class."

Regardless of the generalizations employers made, they did consider the black population particularly heterogeneous, which made it more important that they be able to distinguish "good" from "bad" workers. Whether through skills tests, credentials, personal references, folk theories, or their intuition, they used some means of screening out the inner-city applicant. The ubiquitous anecdote about the good black worker, the exception to the rule, testified to their own perceived success at doing this. So did frequent references to "our" black workers as opposed to "those guys on the street corner."

And black job applicants, unlike their white counterparts, must indicate to employers that the stereotypes do not apply to them. Inner-city and lower-class workers were seen as undesirable, and black applicants had to try to signal to employers that they did not fall into those categories, either by demonstrating their skills or by adopting a middle-class style of dress, manner, and speech or perhaps (as we were told some did) by lying about their address or work history.

By stressing employers' preconceptions about inner-city workers, we do not mean to imply that there are no problems of labor quality in the inner city: the low reading and mathematics test scores of Chicago public school students testify to these problems. But if the quality of the inner-city labor force has indeed deteriorated, then it is incumbent on employers to avoid hiring inner-city workers. This is precisely the result one would expect from William Julius Wilson's account of increased social dislocations in the inner city since the early 1970s. Because race and inner-city residence are so highly correlated, it would not be surprising if race were to become a key marker of worker productivity.

However, productivity is not an individual characteristic. Rather it is embedded in social relations. The qualities most likely to be proxied by race are not job skills but behavioral and attitudinal attributes—dependability, strong work ethic, and cooperativeness—that are closely tied to interactions among workers and between workers and employers. Our evidence suggests that more attention should be paid to social relations in the workplace. Antagonisms among workers and between workers and their employers are likely to diminish productivity. Thus employers' expectations may become self-fulfilling prophecies.

NOTES

1. One of the exceptions is Braddock and McPartland (1987).
2. Becker (1957).
3. Phelps (1972); Arrow (1973); and Spence (1973).
4. See, for example, Thurow (1975); Aigner and Cain (1977); and Bielby and Baron (1986).
5. See Bielby and Baron (1986) for a discussion.
6. Anderson (1980).
7. The sample and survey methods are described in more detail in the "Employer Survey Final Report," available from the authors.
8. Wilson (1980, 1987); and Kasarda (1985). We use the term "space" in the tradition of urban geography. We do this to draw attention to the way people categorize and attach meaning to geographic locations.

REFERENCES

Aigner, Dennis J., and Glen G. Cain. 1977. "Statistical Theories of Discrimination in Labor Markets." *Industrial and Labor Relations Review* 30 (January), pp. 175–87.

Anderson, Elijah. 1980. "Some Observations on Black Youth Employment." In *Youth Employment and Public Policy,* edited by Bernard E. Anderson and Isabel V. Sawhill. Prentice-Hall.

Arrow, Kenneth. 1973. "The Theory of Discrimination." In *Discrimination in Labor Markets,* edited by Orley Aschenfelter and Albert Rees. Princeton University Press.

Bielby, William T., and James N. Baron. 1986. "Men and Women at Work: Sex Segregation and Statistical Discrimination." *American Journal of Sociology* 91 (January), pp. 759–99.

Braddock, Jomills Henry II, and James M. McPartland. 1987. "How Minorities Continue to Be Excluded from Equal Employment Opportunities: Research on Labor Market and Institutional Barriers." *Journal of Social Issues* 43, pp. 5–39.

Kasarda, John D. 1985. "Urban Change and Minority Opportunities." In *The New Urban Reality,* edited by Paul E. Peterson. Brookings.

Phelps, Edmund S. 1972. "The Statistical Theory of Racism and Sexism." *American Economic Review* 62 (September), pp. 659–61.

Spence, Michael. 1973. "Job Market Signalling." *Quarterly Journal of Economics* 87 (August), pp. 355–74.

Thurow, Lester C. 1975. *Generating Inequality: Mechanisms of Distribution in the U.S. Economy.* Basic Books.

Wilson, William Julius. 1980. *The Declining Significance of Race: Blacks and Changing American Institutions.* 2d ed. University of Chicago Press.

______. 1987. *The Truly Disadvantaged: The Inner City, the Underclass, and Public Policy.* University of Chicago Press.

14

Hiring Immigrant Women

Silicon Valley's "Simple Formula"

KAREN J. HOSSFELD

I have a very simple formula for hiring. You hire right, and managing takes care of itself. Just three things I look for in hiring [entry-level, high-tech manufacturing operatives]: small, foreign, and female. You find those three things and you're pretty much automatically guaranteed the right kind of work force. These little foreign gals are grateful to be hired—very, very grateful—no matter what.

—a White male production manager and hiring supervisor in a Silicon Valley printed circuit board assembly shop

Trainers and employment agencies around town have this story we tell that explains why we prefer to invest our resources in groups with a good track record. If you tell people that there's a job call Monday morning downtown at nine, this is what happens: the Chinese and the Koreans show up the night before and camp outside the door, so they'll be the first in line. The Iranians used to show up at seven, but now they own everything so they don't need the jobs. Between eight and nine, the Whites show up. The Mexicans come in the afternoon, after their siesta, and the Blacks roll by—maybe—sometime the next day.

—a White male industrial training program and employment agency director in Silicon Valley

California's famed high-tech industrial region, Silicon Valley, is renowned for the great opportunities it has provided to live out the American dream. Since the 1970s, thousands have flocked there in hopes of getting rich quick by hitching their wagons (computerized ones, of course) to the lucrative high-tech revolution. In fact, thousands have indeed become millionaires in the process. Thousands more have successfully turned to the industry in search of new and exciting professional careers, at a time when most other industries in the country are declining. But not every group has had equal access to the preponderance of riches fueled by the region's rapid industrial growth. In fact, shoring up the simple formula of the American dream is another "simple formula" that is actually quite complex: many employers' predilection for basing hiring on gender, race, and nationality. This chapter examines this predilection on the "low-tech" side of high-tech industry: manufacturing assembly work. I explore the factors that peg workers who are "small, foreign and female" in the lowest paid jobs—factors that are not quite as obvious as they might appear.

The findings draw from my larger study of the lives and labors of Third World[1] immigrant women workers in Silicon Valley's semiconductor manufacturing industry (Hossfeld 1988, 1992). Empirical data come from conversations I had between 1982 and 1990 with over 200 workers, as well as with many of their family members, employers, managers, labor organizers, and community leaders. Extensive indepth interviews were conducted with eighty-four immigrant women representing twenty-one nationalities, and with forty-one employers and managers who represented twenty-three different firms. All but five of these management representatives are white men born in the United States. All of the workers and managers are employed at Santa Clara County, California, firms engaged in some aspect of semiconductor chip manufacturing assembly. I directly observed production at fifteen of these firms.

Silicon Valley's high-tech production labor force includes immigrants from at least thirty Third World nations. The primary informant sampling in the study reflects this diversity. Approximately 40 to 50 percent of the workers, in both the study and the larger labor force, are from Mexico, with other sizable groups representing Vietnam, the Philippines, South Korea, and Taiwan. Smaller numbers come from Cambodia, Laos, Thailand, Malaysia, Indonesia, India, Pakistan, Iran, Ethiopia, Haiti, Cuba, El Salvador, Nicaragua, Guatemala, and Venezuela. There is also a very small group of Southern European workers, mainly from Portugal and Greece, who are not considered in this study.

All of the women workers were first interviewed informally, in small groups, and then individually, following a formal interview schedule that lasted at least three hours. None of the workers were approached on the job or interviewed at the job site. Additional in-depth, open-ended interviews were conducted with thirty-six of the women at their homes, and were accompanied by group interviews with their household members. Access to worker informants was gained by three methods: through my established contacts in immigrant communities; by attending social, church, and neighborhood functions within these communities; and by attending advertised job calls at high-tech manufacturing firms. Many of my initial informants introduced me to their friends and coworkers. In order to ensure a broad sample, I did not interview more than five people who were introduced by the same source or who worked at the same plant.

In addition to interviews, many worker informants were also visited several times over an eight-year period. During these visits, I participated in household functions and helped deal with family, immigration, and work concerns. By far the most revealing data, from managers and workers alike, were gathered during informal conversations in homes or other social environments.

Managers and employers were identified and approached through personal contacts in the local high-tech industry. The three largest semiconductor manufacturing firms that dominate the industry are all represented in the management sample, as are the majority of the middle-sized firms that employ assembly workers. Managers and employers were formally interviewed for a minimum of one hour at their work site; most also were interviewed informally away from the work site for at least an hour.

HIRING DYNAMICS: THE CONTINUING SIGNIFICANCE OF RACE

Silicon Valley high-tech manufacturing companies' propensity to recruit and hire primarily Asian and Latina women for operative jobs has been documented by several researchers (Green 1980; Katz and Kemnitzer 1984; Siegel and Borock 1982; Snow 1986). It is well recognized that this pattern is not exclusive to the region but applies to the high-tech industry globally (Ehrenreich and Fuentes 1981; Grossman 1979; Lim 1978; Women Working Worldwide 1991). The microelectronics industry is, in fact, at the forefront of corporate capital's trend to relocate manufacturing production in peripheral and semi-peripheral areas where cheap, often state-controlled, women's labor is plentiful, particularly in Southeast Asia but also in Mexico, Puerto Rico, and other locations in Asia, Central America, South America, and Europe (Siegel 1980). Since the 1960s, large U.S. microelectronics manufacturers have been shifting the bulk of their production facilities to offshore locations but have maintained factories in core regions, such as Silicon Valley, in order to facilitate prototypic, custom-design, and short-term manufacturing.

Employers and labor market analysts frequently argue that individuals who are women and/or people of color and/or immigrants take low-paying jobs either because they are content with them, or because they are unqualified for and sometimes even undeserving of better-paying jobs. I refer to these ideologies—and the hiring strategies that accompany them—as racial, immigrant, and gender "logic." Whether employers are conscious of it or not, each of these logics serves as a form of "capital logic," that is, as strategies that increase profit maximization. Specifically, hiring patterns that are informed by racism, national chauvinism, and sexism increase class stratification and labor control, and decrease potential unity among workers.

White employers' use of racism to help establish a hierarchical and exploitative division of labor is not a new phenomenon, nor is it specific to high-tech industry. The contemporary textile industry, for example, also draws heavily on Third World women workers, an increasing trend in global capitalist development. In textiles, as in high-tech industry, employers have used sexist and racist stereotypes to help establish an international division of labor. For example, textile employers tell indigenous textile workers in Western Europe and North America that wage cuts and layoffs should be blamed on Third World women who are "naturally" willing to work for less and to tolerate more exploitative conditions than workers in the core, not on the skewed capitalist international division of labor (Chapkis and Enloe 1983)....

SILICON VALLEY'S DIVISION OF LABOR

Silicon Valley, as California's Santa Clara County is commonly referred to, is famed for its microelectronics industry and for the technological revolution it helped to generate. The region is renowned for its computer wizards and for the high-tech fortunes made and lost by venture capitalists and entrepreneurs. But behind Silicon Valley's celebrity is a less-known feature both of the specific region and of the world's fastest-growing industry in general. The microelectronics industry is predicated on a division of labor that is more sharply stratified by class, gender, race, and nationality than almost any other contemporary industry. The high-profile, high-paid engineers, executives, and investors are overwhelmingly White, male U.S. citizens. On the opposite end of the occupational spectrum, the majority of low-paid manufacturing workers are Third World women.

Close to 200,000 people, or 25 percent of employees in the San Jose Metropolitan Statistical Area labor force, work in Silicon Valley's microelectronics industry.[2] There are over 800 manufacturing firms that hire ten or more people each, including 120 large firms that each count over 250 employees. In addition, an even larger number of small firms hire fewer than ten employees apiece. Approximately half of this high-tech labor force—100,000 employees—are in production-related work.[3] An estimated one-quarter of all high-tech industry employees, or half of production-related workers (50,000–70,000), work in semiskilled operative jobs (Siegel and Borock 1982). This contrasts sharply with the majority of other manufacturing industries, where the workers directly engaged in production average from 70 to 80 percent of total employees (Gregory 1984). Semiconductor manufacturing, the industrial sector that is the focus of this study, involves the production of integrated circuits, the silicon "chips" that serve as the basic building block of microelectronics technology. Production includes a complex combination of engineering processes that are performed by highly skilled technicians, as well as finishing and assembly work that is classified as unskilled or semiskilled work. The division of labor within the industry is highly skewed by gender and race. Although women account for close to half of the total Santa Clara County paid labor force both within and outside the industry, only 18 percent of managers, 17 percent of professional employees, and 25 percent of technicians in the industry are female. Conversely, women account for at least 68 percent, and by some reports as much as 85–90 percent, of the operative jobs in high-tech work (California Department of Development 1983).

Similar disparities exist vis-à-vis minority employment, although there are established bourgeoisies among the immigrant communities in the region who have achieved financial prosperity.[4] According to the 1980 census, 73 percent of all employees in Santa Clara County are non-Hispanic White; 15 percent are Hispanic (all races); 7.5 percent are Asian or Pacific Islander; 3 percent are Black; and 0.5 percent are Native American (California Department of Development 1983:96–97). These work force figures are roughly equivalent to each group's regional population percentage, according to census estimates. However, the census does not adequately measure the county's thousands of undocumented residents. In addition, since the census, the region has seen a steady increase in the number of Third World immigrants arriving each year, due in part to influxes of refugees. The number of Indochinese living in Santa Clara County is thought to have quadrupled between 1980 and 1984 alone. It is in these groups of recent immigrants that high-tech employers find much of their production labor force.

Within the microelectronics industry, 12 percent of managers, 16 percent of professionals, and 18 percent of technicians are minorities, mainly concentrated at the lower-paying and less powerful ends of these categories. An estimated

50–75 percent of operative jobs are held by racial minorities, according to state estimates (California Department of Development 1983). Employers and industry analysts estimate that in the industry as a whole, approximately half of all operatives are Third World immigrants.

FINDINGS

Findings indicate that race, national origin, and gender have major significance in determining the class structure and division of labor of Silicon Valley's high-tech industry. High-tech industry managers still use race and nationality, in addition to gender, as primary categories in designating the division of labor. At each of the subcontracting firms I observed, between 80 and 100 percent of workers are Third World immigrants. These firms tend to specialize primarily in unskilled and semiskilled assembly work, which is subcontracted out from other firms. Subcontractors usually pay lower wages and offer fewer benefits than the larger, more vertically integrated, better-known semiconductor firms, such as Silicon Valley's "Big Three": Intel, National Semiconductor, and Advanced Micro Devices. Subcontractors provide an easily expandable and expendable labor force for the very volatile industry. These assembly shops, where immigrant women were the most highly concentrated, have the lowest job security in the business.

Both employers and workers interviewed in this study agree that the lower the skill and pay level of the job, the greater the proportion of Third World immigrant women tends to be. Assembly work, which is classified as the lowest skilled and is the lowest-paid production job, has the highest concentration of these workers. Entry-level electronics production workers, in job categories such as semiconductor processing and assembly, earn an average of from $4.50 to $5.50 an hour; experienced workers in these jobs earn from $5.50 to $8.50. At each of the small (less than 250 employees) subcontracting assembly plants directly observed, immigrant women account for at least 75 percent and up to 100 percent of the assembly labor force. At only one of these plants do White males account for more than 2 percent of the production workers. By contrast, 90 percent of managers and owners at these businesses are White males. The proportion of nonimmigrant women of all races and of immigrant and nonimmigrant minority men increases in skilled production work. Men are concentrated in higher-paying specialties, such as machine and tool operating and technician work. The nonimmigrant women who work in production tend to do semiskilled labor, such as semiconductor processing. This pays slightly more than assembly work but less than jobs where men are concentrated.

The large nonsubcontracting firms I observed have higher percentages of male and nonimmigrant women assemblers and operatives than do smaller subcontracting firms. But even at the big firms, Third World immigrant women typically account for at least 50 percent of the workers. Men are always in a minority on the assembly line, and White men are rare. The presence of some men, however, and of larger numbers of nonimmigrants at larger firms is probably related to the greater opportunities for advancement there. A personnel manager who had worked both at a subcontracting firm and at one of the Big Three told me that the larger, vertically integrated semiconductor firms, unlike subcontractors, try to hire "a certain percentage of 'regular' American workers." This, he says, enables personnel departments to have "an educated, more permanent, in-house work force that we can draw on for training and promotion for more skilled work."

GENDER LOGIC

The employers interviewed indicated that they prefer to hire immigrant women, as compared to immigrant men, for assembly work because of beliefs shared by workers and employers alike that women can afford to work for less. None of the employers had any concrete knowledge about their workers' families or arrangements. Yet almost all of the employers stated that they assumed that their women workers were attached to male workers who were earning more than the women were. In fact, 80 percent of the women workers I interviewed were the main income earners in their families.[5]

Approximately 75 percent of the managers and employers interviewed stated that immigrant women are better suited to high-tech assembly work than immigrant men. Their jobs are characterized by assembly line–style repetition of a small set of tasks. According to workers, the work is extremely tiring because it requires constant concentration and intensive eye-hand coordination to manipulate the tiny, intricate circuitry. Employers and managers consistently claimed that Third World immigrant women are particularly suited to the work because of their supposedly superior hand-eye coordination and their patience. One male manager claimed that the "relatively small size" of many Asian and Mexican women "makes it easier for them to sit quietly for long periods of time, doing small detail work that would drive a large person like [him] crazy." The workers this man supervised, however, thought he preferred to hire physically small women because he could then feel superior and intimidating, "more like a big man," as a Filipina employee put it.

"IMMIGRANT LOGIC" IN HIRING

> *If I had to pay higher wages. I wouldn't stay in business here. It's not that I couldn't "afford" it per se, but the profit margin would be smaller, obviously. In Singapore, labor costs one-fifth of what it does here.*
>
> **—a White male employer, subcontracting assembly plant**

According to employers, low-level production jobs in Silicon Valley probably would not exist unless there were workers available to work cheaply at insecure nonunionized jobs. Without such a reserve army of labor to call on, manufacturers might very well have developed the industry differently, with an even greater emphasis on automation and overseas location. An engineer in charge of production technology at a semiconductor manufacturing firm observed: "We already have the technology to fully automate everything we do here—it's just more expensive. We could definitely automate every step of the process if it ever becomes cheaper to do that than use human labor. Because of the large supply of unskilled immigrants in the area, labor is still cheaper for doing certain jobs than machines are." He later commented that two major factors could tip the balance in this equation: a curtailed immigration flow and unionization.

Employers interviewed in Silicon Valley electronics plants explain their penchant for hiring large numbers of immigrants in terms typical of employers everywhere who hire immigrants: they are more willing than nonimmigrants to work for low pay in "bad" jobs (i.e., jobs that are unsafe, monotonous, uncomfortable, and unsteady). Immigrants are seen—and see themselves—as being more desperate for work at any wage, because of lack of language, employable skills, or education.

Fifty percent of the employers interviewed offered some form of unsolicited moral legitimation for why they pay such low wages. The following remark from an assembly shop owner typifies this: "I don't want you to think I'm some kind of heartless ogre—my people really do seem to manage quite well on what they earn." The remaining 50 percent offered no personal legitimation: they simply indicated that their wage structures are the result of market supply and demand. This comment from an employer at a subcontracting assembly plant is unusually straightforward:

> Beats me how [entry level operatives] survive: they can't possibly do much more than eke by on these wages. But if they don't know the language, and some of them are illiterate even in their own language, and let's suppose, hypothetically of course, that they're not exactly here [in the U.S.] legally—just how many options have they got? We [employers] take advantage of this, but I'm not here to apologize for capitalism.

Employers (as well as the nonimmigrant White and African American workers with whom I talked) argue that immigrants from industrializing countries are better able to survive on very low wages than nonimmigrants. They surmise this is for two reasons. First, people from poor countries are viewed as skilled at and "used to" living on scant resources. Several employers and managers believed that "poverty management skills," as one assistant personnel manager termed it, are one of the "cultural values" that render certain minority groups more likely to succeed. A White male owner of a disk drive manufacturing facility reported:

> These people from Third World countries really are incredible: they're so resourceful! I have this one woman who works for me—she's Filipino, or from somewhere around there—and she supports three kids and her parents on \$5.65 an hour. Not only that, but she always makes the best of the situation, and she's always bringing in cakes and things for everyone. We only have one kid, and my wife says she can't make ends meet. And believe me, I make more than \$5.65 an hour!

A second explanation several employers offered in explaining immigrant workers' willingness and ability to live on low wages is that such workers' family members are probably still living in their countries of origin, to which the immigrants themselves are planning to return. What might seem like meager savings in the United States, these employers pointed out, stretch much farther in poorer countries.

Historically, employers and the public in the United States have viewed Third World immigrant workers as being able to survive on substandard wages because the immigrants' families were living "back home," where U.S. dollars went farther. Immigrants are seen as people—usually men—who live frugally now in order to live well when they return to their countries of origin. For some immigrants, this scenario is indeed true, but the majority of immigrants to the United States never return to their native countries to live. Today's immigrants to Silicon Valley are rarely planning to save money in order to return home: over 95 percent of the immigrant workers I interviewed reported that they plan to stay in the United States permanently. The great majority also came with families: the low wages they earn must support them on U.S., not Third World, prices. And although many are helping to support relatives in their countries of origin, all had immediate family members living in the United States.

Employers stressed that they are doing immigrant workers a favor by supplying them with any job at all, as the following quotes from two board shop owners reveal:

> I don't really prefer to hire immigrants, but they're usually the only ones willing to do the job. Most Americans would find it kind of boring work, but the Mexicans and the rest of them are grateful for whatever they can get. It beats welfare—both from their point of view, and from ours.
>
> Actually, it's a good deal all around. A lot of these people were starving before they came to the States, so to them this job is a real step up. They haven't got many skills and they don't speak much English, so they can't expect to be paid much. They're grateful for whatever they get, and I feel we're providing a service by employing them.

In general, employers feel that immigrants are not taking jobs away from U.S. citizens, because relatively few citizens apply for such low-paid and "boring" jobs. That U.S. citizens do not, by and large, take these jobs does indeed suggest that they do not want them, as long as they can get better-paying ones. Yet White North American workers of both sexes, and often men of color, are discouraged by management from applying for entry-level manufacturing jobs, and are more likely to be denied such jobs when they do apply. This was openly confirmed by the majority of hiring personnel interviewed, who claim that most men and White women are not well suited for these jobs.

All of the subcontracting employers interviewed think American-born workers, and particularly American men, would be so frustrated at the lack of mobility opportunity in assembly shops that they would soon quit. One of them explained: "I've had White guys come in here—mainly college kids on breaks wanting to pick up money for the summer. One of them I put in management, but I won't put them on the line. They wouldn't last a week, it's so boring."

When I applied for assembly jobs at various plants, I was repeatedly told by personnel directors that the work wouldn't suit me and that I'd be much happier at a professional job or in a training program, because I was "an American." Naomi Katz (like me, a college-educated, White, North American woman) told me she had the same experience when she looked for assembly work during her study of Silicon Valley workers (Katz and Kemnitzer 1984). While investigating *maquiladora* work in southern California, Maria Patricia Fernandez-Kelly, who speaks both Spanish and English fluently, found that when she made phone inquiries for production jobs in Spanish, she was told there were openings, but when she inquired in English, she was told there were not (Fernandez-Kelly 1985).

Adapting Fernandez-Kelly's technique, I had a team of nationally diverse male and female students call plants and inquire about entry-level production job openings. Female students with Asian, Pacific Islander, or Latino "accents" were told there might be jobs available for them three times more often than male students with Anglo accents.[6] One of the reasons for this bias, a personnel director told me, is that managers think the only educated Americans who would take such jobs must be either journalists or union organizers who were trying to get a story or stir up trouble.

Managers typically exclude American workers of color from their rationale that U.S. citizens are not appropriate for assembly jobs. The hiring personnel I interviewed tended to lump all applicants within a broad racial or ethnic grouping together in their hiring evaluation, whether the individuals were U.S. citizens, native-born or not, especially if the applicants speak with any kind of accent that managers perceived as "foreign." Thus, a third-generation Chicana worker who speaks with a "Spanish" accent may be classified with recent Mexican immigrants in terms of managers' racial and nationality categorizations about who is appropriate for a job.

One of the central reasons that employers "prefer" to hire immigrants rather than available nonimmigrants for low-skill, low-paid, and precarious jobs is that their worth is less valued in society in general. This is clearly expressed by one of the factory owners I interviewed: "This industry is very volatile: the market demand is constantly fluctuating. One month I may have to let a third of my production people go, and the next month I may need to double my work force. Let's face it, when you have to expand and contract all the time, you need people who are more expendable. When I lay off immigrant housewives, people don't get as upset as if you were laying off regular [*sic*] workers."

Employers also prefer Third World immigrants because they are often newly proletarianized, with little organizing experience in an industrialized setting. And as people who are insecure in their residential status, whether documented or not, immigrants are seen as unlikely to "make waves" against any part of the American system for fear of jeopardizing their welcome. Many of the production processes in semiconductor manufacturing involve the use of highly toxic chemicals, and the rate of reported occupational illnesses in the industry in California is three times the average for all industries (Olson 1984:71). Labor organizers interviewed believe that one of the reasons management prefers to hire immigrants is that they are less familiar with occupational health and safety laws than other workers, and less likely to seek their enforcement.

RACIAL LOGIC

As the quote about job trainers' racial hiring preferences at the beginning of this paper suggests, Silicon Valley employers and their colleagues distinguish not only between immigrants and nonimmigrants but also between different immigrant groups. A clear racial, ethnic, and national pecking order of management's hiring preferences emerges from interview findings. Most employers have a difficult time clearly distinguishing the myriad diverse races, ethnicities, and nationalities represented in their labor force. Yet this did not prevent many of them from making stereotypic assumptions about very broadly and usually incorrectly categorized groups. The two such broadly defined "groups" most prevalent in the immigrant work force, and thus most often compared by employers, are Asians and Pacific Islanders, to whom employers variously refer as "Asians" or "Orientals"; and Latinos, to whom employers variously refer as "Hispanics," "Latins," "South Americans," or, generically, "Mexicans." Asian immigrant women are clearly management's preferred production workers. Eighty-five percent of the employers and 90 percent of the managers interviewed stated that they believe Asian women make the best assembly-line workers in high-tech manufacturing.

Because employers tend to ascribe specific work characteristics to entire groups, they assign each group to jobs that emphasize these characteristics, thereby fulfilling their own prophecies. I observed hiring practices that appeared to be based on employers' racial and gender pecking orders. The training and employment agency director quoted at the beginning of this article assumes that different work characteristics exist according to race, and that members of some racial groups always show up late, and some always early, to job calls—not only to job calls, he implies, but also to work. Yet at none of the five large job calls I attended at high-tech manufacturing plants was this the case: Blacks, Whites, Latinos, and Asians all showed up early.

At the two job calls where I was able to obtain the relevant data, Asians were the most likely to obtain entry-level assembly jobs requiring no previous experience, and Whites and Blacks the least likely, regardless of nationality. Of those applying, approximately 20 percent of Asians, 12 percent of Latinos, 5 percent of Whites, and 5 percent of Blacks were hired. Although over 25 percent of the applicants for entry-level assembly jobs were male, they received only approximately 10 percent of the jobs. Three men who came specifically to apply for assembly jobs were hired as technicians, jobs for which they did not originally apply. Although data collection at these job calls did not control for other important factors—such as age, education, immigration status, language skills, and job experience—the heavily skewed hiring preferences clearly suggest racial discrimination.

Most managers interviewed consider African Americans to be the least desirable workers, not because they are believed to be too good for the jobs, as Whites are generally considered, but because they are not considered dependable enough for employment in general. Managers were mixed in their evaluation of Black immigrants: one production manager commented that Black Caribbean immigrants are "not usually as cocky" as African Americans. Management attitudes toward entry-level African American applicants are more negative than toward any other group. For working-class African Americans in Silicon Valley, this suggests, Wilson's prognosis of the declining significance of race in the labor market is not applicable. However, Silicon Valley hiring personnel repeatedly commented that there is a shortage of African American applicants at the professional level. I was told by several that they would like to find and hire well-credentialed African American engineers or programmers.[7] This suggests that White racism against

Blacks may indeed be partially mitigated by Blacks' class and educational status, as Wilson proposes (Wilson 1978), but I was unable to find African American high-tech professionals who could confirm or deny this. My impression from talking with both managers and workers is that White racism against Blacks is a strong factor in the structuring of the Silicon Valley labor force but that, unsurprisingly, it is more intensely (although certainly not exclusively) experienced by and directed toward working-class Blacks.

Three of the firms I talked with were considering opening plants in U.S. localities with large Mexican populations (Brownsville, Texas; Albuquerque, New Mexico; and Watsonville, California). When I suggested locations characterized by large reserve labor pools of Black workers, such as nearby Oakland and East Palo Alto, spokespersons at all three firms indicated that these areas did not have suitable labor climates. Black workers are hired by high-tech production facilities in North Carolina's Research Triangle, however. An organizer whose union was conducting an organizing campaign in the high-tech manufacturing industry at the time suggested that Silicon Valley firms would not consider locating in Oakland because of union strength in that largely Black area. A leader in a different union that was targeting a large local semiconductor manufacturing company believed the industry's avoidance of the region was directly rooted in racism.

Four employers who had no direct experience—either negative or positive—with hiring Blacks and Latinos in skilled positions told me that they would prefer not to do so unless no one else was available. Their preferences, according to the respondents, were not based on comparative productivity reports from colleagues but on what they had personally concluded about these groups outside of the workplace. "Blacks are troublemakers," explained one administrator. "I found that out when I was at [the University of California at Berkeley]. They don't like Whites and they don't like authority—and I'm both." Only two of the employers interviewed reported that they had no racial preferences in hiring for entry-level jobs. Only one of the two claimed to have absolutely no racial preference for hiring at any level, but even he amended his claim by adding, "as long as the secretaries are pretty, and personally, I don't find most Black women that attractive."

I was told several times by employers and managers that they prefer not to put Blacks and Hispanics in jobs that require much training, because, as one White manager worded it, "that would be throwing good money after bad—they tend to quit faster, so why invest in them?" Yet at none of the companies I observed was management able to provide me with a racial breakdown of turnover rates. A Black Jamaican woman who worked in the plant of the manager just quoted confided: "More Blacks would be likely to stick around if they gave us a chance at the better jobs, but they never do. So of course you're going to leave if you find a better offer, or if you just get tired knowing you'll stay at the bottom, no matter what you do."

Guadalupe Friaz's in-depth study of a large Silicon Valley electronics firm provides another example of how what appears to be a race distinction between workers may actually be a result of managers' racism. Friaz found that Asians had the lowest turnover rate of any group at the firm, and that Blacks and Latinos had the highest. She suggests that one possible explanation for this difference is the bias of racist supervisors, who treat workers differently and recommend promotions according to race (Friaz 1985).

Certainly not all employers and managers I interviewed and observed displayed blatant racism. Even those who admitted to personal racial preferences in hiring typically indicated that they knew it was illegal to institutionalize such preferences, as this executive's words illustrated: "It would be fine with me if I could simply advertise that I only wanted to hire certain groups. But nobody's that stupid—you'd get your butt sued off. But it's not against the law to choose where you post jobs—and where you don't. . . . I resent anybody telling me who I should hire, regardless of who does the best work, but I'm a stickler about doing everything by the law."

Less than 10 percent of the managers and employers in my study reported that they were aware of the Equal Employment Opportunity Commission (EEOC) investigating or reviewing their firms' hiring practices. One employer, however, pointed out that if his firm were being investigated, he probably would not admit it. An EEOC staff worker who was contacted for this study clarified that the agency mainly dealt with professional-level jobs and/or firms with government contracts. Even if someone filed a discrimination complaint, she explained, the regional office was backlogged well over a year in its investigations.

Interviews with White employers and administrators suggested that they are most comfortable when their workplace colleagues and office staff are also White, and their production work force is not. This makes it easier for management to construct an "us" and a "them" to help solidify the division of labor. It protects the white-collar Whites from having to confront their own racism, enabling them to view work relationships as occupationally, rather than racially, based. This is certainly not a unique situation. As a union organizer phrased it, "Historically, it has always been easier for bosses to exploit people they don't identify with." . . .

IMMIGRANT WOMEN WORKERS' CONSCIOUSNESS

It takes time . . . sometimes even years, before many Third World immigrants realize that racism stands in their way. . . . They tend to think their slow economic progress is just because they are new in this country, just as the Irish and the Italians and the Jews once were. It takes a while for them to realize the ramifications of the fact that although accents and citizenship and cultural customs can change in one or two generations, skin color does not. That is the main way that today's immigrants differ from yesterday's. When their newness wears off, they will still be non-Whites in a world dominated by Whites.

—a Chinese American social worker in San Francisco's Asian immigrant communities

Cross-nationally, working-class immigrants interviewed for this study concurred with employers' "immigrant logic" that all immigrants who arrive in the United States with little or no material wealth, and with little or no English or easily transferable job skills, will have to work their way up from near the bottom of the job and class ladders. Even those who arrive with transferable job skills do not expect to compete on an equal footing with nonimmigrant workers in the short run. There is a strong sense that as new immigrants, they must pay their dues by taking unpreferred jobs and living close to the poverty margin. Most do not view this as unfair or exploitative. It does not make them like their jobs, but they see their situation as something every family or ethnic group must go through upon immigration. They view their position in the U.S. labor force as part of a cycle of economic assimilation. They believe that any new immigrants who work hard and pay their dues will eventually move into the middle or upper middle class, or at least the stable working class, and that their low-level jobs will be filled by new waves of immigrants, who in turn can work their way up and be replaced by even newer waves. This is described by many as the "American way." Almost all believe that their families will be economically assimilated by their second generation in the United States, if not sooner.

The ideology that Third World immigrants "deserve less" is cut from a cloth similar to the ideology that devalues women's labor, and the two are often intertwined in the workplaces where immigrant women are employed. There is a major difference between the two ideologies, though. Immigrant status can be overcome, at least within one generation, but gender status is more permanent. And even in terms of immigrant status, the reality of U.S. society is that not every immigrant group has made equal inroads into the middle- and upperclass strata, even with time. Although most White groups have done so, many Third World groups have not.[9]

Many of the immigrant informants confirmed that they are indeed better off than they would be if they had stayed in their countries of origin. A Vietnamese community leader explained that my questions about the "quality of work" and "standard of living" are not very relevant to refugees who have brushed death so closely. The majority of immigrants interviewed were grateful to the United States and to their employers, an attitude I did not expect to find among such a low-paid work force. Even the immigrant workers who did not feel particularly grateful, mainly Latinos but also some Asians, agreed that whatever the shortcomings of their lives in the United States, they were economically worse off before they came here. A Mexican woman told me: "I don't earn enough here to support my family. If there weren't three of us working in our household, we wouldn't get by. But what choice do I have? [In Mexico] I had no job at all, and three babies to feed."

Regardless of how long they have been at their current jobs, all of the women workers interviewed believed that they would move on to better jobs within a few years. I found numerous workers who had been doing the same or similar work for over five years, yet still maintained that their jobs were temporary. Even individuals who had been on the job for as long as ten years still tended to view the job as a temporary stop, as a stepping-stone to somewhere else. Although this may prove to be the case, they have spent a substantial portion of their work lives "not getting involved" in trying to change unfavorable conditions because of this view. A union organizer commented:

> Six years ago, when we approached workers at [a large semiconductor firm], I met this very bright, articulate Mexicana who seemed pretty feisty, who I thought would be an excellent union advocate on the floor. I approached her about it, and she said no, that she believed in unions but she was going to be out of that place soon and didn't want to make any commitments there. This year I ran into her again—she's

> now at [a competitor firm] doing the same job, and she said the exact same thing. Maybe she'll go for it in another five years—if there's any jobs left here to be "about to quit" in the first place.

Excerpts from an interview with a young Filipina fabrication operator also illustrate this predicament. Asked about her attitudes toward unions, she replied: "Most of the women here are not interested in organizing a union. The work is pretty bad for the health, and we'd like to see that changed, and better benefits, but most of us don't expect to be here too long. Union drives take a long time—sometimes a couple of years—and I'll be gone by then." This statement takes on a new perspective when juxtaposed to an earlier part of the interview:

> *Interviewer (I):* How long have you been in this line of work?
> *Respondent (R):* Four years.
> *I:* How long did you plan on staying when you took the job?
> *R:* A year.
> *I:* When do you plan on leaving?
> *R:* Within a year. (laugh) This time I mean it!
> *I:* What kept you from leaving sooner?
> *R:* I was trying to save up enough to go to school to get a beautician's license.
> *I:* Have you saved almost enough?
> *R:* No, nothing. I spent it all on things my family needed.
> *I:* What will you do when you leave?
> *R:* Something more interesting—I don't know. Maybe we'll win the lottery! (laughter)

I later showed this woman her two sets of statements, and asked her to compare them. After reading her own words, she explained:

> You're probably thinking that in four years I could have worked to organize a union, or at least filed a grievance about the allergies I developed from the [processing chemicals]. But even though I didn't leave, I was ready to at any time, in case something else came along. And I want to stay ready to leave at any time—I don't want to feel committed and sucked in at a job I don't like. . . . This year I'm leaving for sure.

Two years later, this same woman was working at another semiconductor plant after being temporarily unemployed due to a layoff at her old plant.

Although small groups of immigrants suffered racial or ethnic oppression in their homelands, most of the immigrant workers interviewed were accustomed to being members of the majority racial group in their countries of origin. Thus, most of them did not grow up subject to internalized racial oppression, as Erica Sherover-Marcuse (1986) suggests is the case for people of color born and raised in the United States. This may help to explain why managers often make a pretense of disguising their racism as immigrant logic when dealing directly with workers. Many of the more recent immigrants deny the existence of discrimination and prejudice against their racial or national group in the United States. Informants who have been in the United States five years or less are much more likely to explain their experiences with discrimination as being based in their ignorance as, or others' ignorance of, foreigners rather than as race related. This is true for close to 70 percent of the Asian immigrants interviewed but for only 30 percent of the Mexican immigrants. Mexican immigrants are more likely to have heard explicit accounts of racism in the United States before immigrating, from friends and relatives who migrated back and forth between the two countries. A recently arrived, undocumented Mexican worker commented: "I already knew that 'gringos' don't like Mexicans before we came here, because my cousin lived in the States. But I also knew they would hire us for certain jobs, so we came anyway." Her observation is typical of those made by her compatriots. Latinos in general, as well as the few Black immigrants among the informants, are more likely than Asians to expect racism to deter their access to equitable jobs and incomes.

Most of the Asian immigrants were not very knowledgeable about U.S. racism when they immigrated, or at least did not realize it extends to Asians. A woman from India commented: "I knew that Americans [*sic*] did not like the Blacks, but I was surprised they don't like Indians too much, either." Remarks from a recently immigrated Chinese worker suggest that she is shocked by derogatory racial slurs when they are directed at her own national/racial group, but not when they are directed at certain others: "Why do they say these things to us?" she asked. "People treat us bad, like they do the Blacks or Mexicans. I don't understand. I thought Chinese culture is very respected here."

CONCLUSION

The main source of legitimation of both gender and racial hierarchy within the high-tech industry in Silicon Valley lies, obviously, in the existence of occupational and social stratification. Every day workers and managers view the gender-, class-, and race-tiered structure of the industry, and although some may consider it unfair, most believe that it is inevitable. As a Chicana who worked as a bonder in a large firm said of the company's racial and gender hierarchy: "Of course I don't like it, but there's nothing I can do about it—it's like that everywhere." An African American woman coworker agreed: "It's a White man's world—just look around the plant. I take the job I can get and I do it." The few who did challenge the hierarchy, during conversation, were mainly not immigrants: some of the White women workers questioned sexual hierarchies, and some nonimmigrant women of color questioned both sexual and racial boundaries. In general, though, as with sexism, employers can use "immigrant-specific" logic because it corresponds to workers' own consciousness of their limited options.[10]

In conclusion, the racial division of labor in the Silicon Valley high-tech manufacturing work force originates in the racially structured labor market of the larger economy, and in the "racial logic" that employers use in hiring. This "racial logic" is based on stereotypes—both observed and imagined—that employers have about different racial groups. One of the effects of this racial logic, vis-à-vis workers, is to reproduce the racially structured labor market and class structure that discriminates against minorities and immigrants. Another effect is that within the workplace, racial categories and racism become tools for management to divide and control workers. These are dynamics that individuals and organizations interested in social change must become more familiar with—not just in Silicon Valley but elsewhere. As for the situation in highly "innovative" Silicon Valley itself, to date, neither labor, women's, nor ethnic organizations have made major inroads in challenging the hiring hierarchy (Hossfeld 1991). But challenge it we must. Equality of opportunity, both at work and away from it, cannot be achieved unless we learn to recognize and reject practices that are based on "simple formulas" about gender, race, and nationality.

NOTES

1. As many recent scholars and activists have noted, the term "Third World" is problematic and imprecise. Yet so, too, are currently available substitute terms such as "postcolonial," "industrializing," and "developing." For references to the terminology debate from a feminist perspective, see Mohanty, Russo, and Torres, 1991. In this article, the term "Third World immigrants" refers to individuals who have migrated (in this case to the United States) from world regions with a history of colonial domination.

2. Statistical references in this study have not been updated to reflect the 1990 census because the research was conducted, and refers to conditions, during the 1980s.

3. These production jobs include the following U.S. Department of Labor occupational titles: semiconductor processor, semiconductor assembler, electronics assembler, and electronics tester. Entry-level wages for these jobs in Silicon Valley are $4.00–$5.50; wages for workers with one to two years' experience or more are $5.50–$8.00 an hour, with testers sometimes earning up to $9.50. California Department of Employment Development 1983.

4. This is especially true of Asian communities. The Vietnamese, for example, have founded several business associations, and own several blocks of businesses in downtown San Jose. Hispanic groups have a much smaller business ownership base, although there is a Hispanic Chamber of Commerce in the area.

5. For a more extensive discussion of how gender ideologies are used as the basis of both labor control and labor resistance in this work force, see Hossfeld 1990.

6. The student team was composed of University of California at Santa Cruz undergraduates, aged eighteen to twenty-five.

7. In Silicon Valley, the low proportion of Black workers correlates to the low proportion of Blacks in the overall county labor force, 3.11 percent.

9. Japanese Americans are among the top income earners in the United States, while Blacks and Hispanics are among the lowest in income. For evidence that Japanese and other Asian Americans have had to work harder for relatively lower economic status than Whites, see Woo 1985.

10. For discussion of how immigrant women workers resist managers' efforts to use racism and sexism as forms of labor control, see Hossfeld 1990. For discussion of barriers to labor organizing around these issues, see Hossfeld 1991.

REFERENCES

California Department of Employment Development. 1983. *Annual Planning Information: San Jose Standard Metropolitan Statistical Area 1983–1984.* San Jose.

Chapkis, Wendy, and Cynthia Enloe. 1983. *Of Common Cloth: Women in the Global Textile Industry.* Amsterdam: Transnational Institute.

Ehrenreich, Barbara, and Annette Fuentes. 1981. "Life on the Global Assembly Line." *Ms.*, January, pp. 52–59.

Fernandez-Kelly, Maria Patricia. 1985. "Advanced Technology, Regional Development and Hispanic Women's Employment in Southern California." Paper presented at the Women, High Technology and Society Conference, University of California, Santa Cruz, June 1.

Friaz, Guadalupe. 1985. "Race and Gender Differences in Mobility and Turnover in a Large Electronics Firm." Paper presented at the Women, High Technology and Society Conference, University of California, Santa Cruz, June 1.

Green, Susan S. 1980. *Silicon Valley's Women Workers: A Theoretical Analysis of Sex-Segregation in the Electronics Industry Labor Market.* Honolulu: Impact of Transnational Interactions Project, Cultural Learning Institute, East-West Center.

Gregory, Kathleen. 1984. "Signing-up: The Culture and Careers of Silicon Valley Computer People" Ph.D. dissertation, Northwestern University. Ann Arbor, Michigan: University Microfilms International.

Grossman, Rachel. 1979. "Women's Place in the Integrated Circuit." *Southeast Asia Chronicle* 66 and *Pacific Review* 9 (joint issue): 2–17.

Hossfeld, Karen. 1988. "Divisions of Labor, Divisions of Lives: Immigrant Women Workers in Silicon Valley." Ph.D. dissertation, University of California, Santa Cruz. Ann Arbor, Michigan: University Microfilms International.

———. 1990. "'Their Logic Against Them': Contradictions in Sex, Race and Class in Silicon Valley." In Kathryn Ward, ed., *Women Workers and Global Restructuring.* Ithaca, N.Y.: ILR Press.

———. 1991. "Why Aren't High-Tech Workers Organized?" In Women Working Worldwide, eds., *Common Interests: Women Organizing in Global Electronics.* London: Women Working Worldwide.

———. 1992. *Small, Foreign, and Female: Immigrant Women Workers in Silicon Valley.* Berkeley: University of California Press.

Katz, Naomi, and Davis S. Kemnitzer. 1984. "Women and Work in Silicon Valley: Options and Futures." In Karen Brodkin Sacks and Dorothy Remy, eds., *My Troubles Are Going to Have Trouble with Me: Everyday Trials and Triumphs of Women Workers.* New Brunswick, N.J.: Rutgers University Press.

Lim, Linda. 1978. *Women Workers in Multinational Corporations: The Case of the Electronics Industry in Malaysia and Singapore.* Michigan Occasional Papers in Women's Studies no. 9. Ann Arbor: University of Michigan.

Mohanty, Chandra, Ann Russo, and Lourdes Torres, eds. 1991. *Third World Women and the Politics of Feminism.* Bloomington: Indiana University Press.

Olson, Lynne. 1984. "The Silkwoods of Silicon Valley." *Working Woman* (July): 71–72, 106, 108, 110–111.

Sherover-Marcuse, Erica. 1986. *Emancipation and Consciousness.* London: Basil Blackwell.

Siegel, Lenny. 1980. "Delicate Bonds: The Global Semiconductor Industry." *Pacific Research* 1.

Siegel, Lenny, and Herb Borock. 1982. *Background Report on Silicon Valley.* Prepared for the U.S. Commission on Civil Rights. Mountain View, Calif.: Pacific Studies Center.

Snow, Robert. 1986. "The New International Division of Labor and the U.S. Workforce: The Case of the Electronics Industry." In June Nash and Maria Patricia Fernandez-Kelly, eds., *Women, Men and the International Division of Labor.* Albany: State University of New York Press.

Wilson, William Julius. 1978. *The Declining Significance of Race: Blacks and Changing American Institutions.* Chicago: University of Chicago Press.

15

Latinos and Discrimination

JOAN MOORE AND
RAQUEL PINDERHUGHES

THE UNDERCLASS DEBATE

It is clear that there is as yet no consensus about the term "underclass" or about the concepts behind it. The debate about whether the American urban poor can be characterized as an "underclass" is part of a larger debate about urban poverty in the United States. The terms of that debate have shifted significantly over the past two decades. In the sixties and seventies the debate focused on matters of labor-supply resources, tax rates, and equal opportunity. In the eighties, the emphasis shifted to dependency and joblessness, with emphasis on their radiating consequences (Ellwood 1988). Currently, the debate reflects a deep concern about a group of people who manifest a distinctive set of values, attitudes, beliefs, norms, and behaviors (Ricketts and Sawhill 1988; Morris 1989; Wilson 1987).

The underclass debate can also be seen as an extension of the debate about who is responsible for the condition of the poor—the individual or society? Is persistent poverty caused by behavioral pathology or the economic structure? . . .

No matter what the details, when one examines the history of the term among sociologists, it is clear that Wilson's 1987 work seriously jolted the somewhat chaotic and unfocused study of poverty in the United States. He described sharply increased rates of what he called "pathology" in Chicago's black ghettos. By this, Wilson referred specifically to female headship, declining marriage rates, illegitimate births, welfare dependency, school dropouts, and youth crime. The changes in the communities he examined were so dramatic that he considered them something quite new.

Two of the causes of this new poverty were particularly important, and his work shifted the terms of the debate in two respects. First, Wilson argued effectively that dramatic increases in joblessness and long-term poverty in the inner city were a result of major economic shifts—economic restructuring. "Restructuring" referred to changes in the global economy that led to deindustrialization, loss and relocation of jobs, and a decline in the number of middle-level jobs—a polarization of the labor market. Second, he further fueled the debate about the causes and consequences of persistent poverty by introducing two neighborhood-level factors into the discussion. He argued that the out-migration of middle- and working-class people from the urban ghetto contributed to the concentration of poverty. These "concentration effects" meant that ghetto neighborhoods showed sharply increased proportions of very poor people. This, in turn, meant that residents in neighborhoods of concentrated poverty were isolated from "mainstream" institutions and role models. As a result, Wilson postulates, the likelihood of their engaging in "underclass behavior" was increased. Thus the social life of poor communities deteriorated because poverty intensified. . . .

Scholars engaged in research on poverty in Latino communities were often critical of Wilson's framework, but intrigued by his analysis. Although he focused exclusively on black poverty, much of what Wilson described at the neighborhood level was familiar to scholars examining poverty in Latino communities—but it needed modification. Moore (1989) summarized the value of certain elements of the analysis and some of the potential modifications in an early overview of existing research evidence. She concluded that economic restructuring was clearly an important factor in understanding Latino poverty. However, since most Latinos are located outside the Rustbelt, analyses of their poverty needed to take into account the diverse forms that economic restructuring has taken in different parts of the United States. Then again, Wilson's emphasis on the importance of migration in contributing to the development of an urban black "underclass" fell short when applied to Latinos. Wilson was concerned with out-migration of middle-class residents from the ghettos: by contrast, any examination of Latino poverty needed to consider how the vast wave of new, poor immigrants affected poor neighborhoods. There was much evidence that immigration is not only important but often critical.

The overview also suggested that by contrast with Wilson's portrayal of the decay of the black family and other institutions, Latino institutions were generally viable. The evidence on familism was skimpy, but there was good reason to believe that in many areas Latino families still operate to support and control their members. The evidence about street problems was very mixed: certainly it is not generally an occasion for despair, bad as it is in some locales. . . .

THE LATINO POPULATION—SOME BACKGROUND

American minorities have been incorporated into the general social fabric in a variety of ways. Just as Chicago's black ghettos reflect a history of slavery, Jim Crow legislation, and struggles for civil and economic rights, so the nation's Latino barrios reflect a history of conquest, immigration, and a struggle to maintain cultural identity.

In 1990 there were some 22 million Latinos residing in the United States, approximately 9 percent of the total population. Of these, 61 percent were Mexican in origin, 12 percent Puerto Rican, and 5 percent Cuban. These three groups were the largest, yet 13 percent of Latinos were of Central and South American origin and another 9 percent were classified as "other Hispanic". Latinos were among the fastest-growing segments of the American population, increasing by 7.6 million, or 53 percent, between 1980 and 1990. There are predictions that Latinos will outnumber blacks by the twenty-first century. If Latino immigration and fertility continue at their current rate, there will be over 54 million Latinos in the United States by the year 2020.

This is an old population: as early as the sixteenth century, Spanish explorers settled what is now the American Southwest. In 1848, Spanish and Mexican settlers who lived in that region became United States citizens as a result of the Mexican-American War. Although the aftermath of conquest left a small elite population, the precarious position of the masses combined with the peculiarities of southwestern economic development to lay the foundation for poverty in the current period (see Barrera 1979; Moore and Pachon 1985).

In addition to those Mexicans who were incorporated into the United States after the Treaty of Guadalupe Hidalgo, Mexicans have continually crossed the border into the United States, where they have been used as a source of cheap labor by U.S. employers. The volume of immigration from Mexico has been highly dependent on fluctuations in certain segments of the U.S. economy. This dependence became glaringly obvious earlier in this century. During the Great Depression of the 1930s state and local governments "repatriated" hundreds of thousands of unemployed Mexicans, and just a few years later World War II labor shortages reversed the process as Mexican contract-laborers (*braceros*) were eagerly sought. A little later, in the 1950s, massive deportations recurred when "operation Wetback" repatriated hundreds of thousands of Mexicans. Once again, in the 1980s, hundreds of thousands crossed the border to work in the United States, despite increasingly restrictive legislation.

High levels of immigration and high fertility mean that the Mexican-origin population is quite young—on the average, 9.5 years younger than the non-Latino population—and the typical household is large, with 3.8 persons, as compared with 2.6 persons in non-Latino households (U.S. Bureau of the Census 1991). Heavy immigration, problems in schooling, and industrial changes in the Southwest combine to constrain advancement. The occupational structure remains relatively steady, and though there is a growing middle class, there is also a growing number of very poor people.

The incorporation of Puerto Ricans into the United States began in 1898, when the United States took possession of Puerto Rico and Cuba during the Spanish-American War. Although Cuba gained its independence in 1902, Puerto Rico became a commonwealth of the United States in 1952. Thus Puerto Rican citizens are also citizens of the United States. The colonial relationship strongly influenced the structure of the Puerto Rican economy and the migration of Puerto Ricans to the mainland. As a result of the U.S. invasion, the island's economy was transformed from a diversified, subsistence economy, which emphasized tobacco, cattle, coffee, and sugar, to a one-crop sugar economy, of which more than 60 percent was controlled by absentee U.S. owners (Steward 1956). The constriction of the sugar economy in the 1920s resulted in high unemployment and widespread poverty, and propelled the first wave of Puerto Rican migration to the United States (Rodriguez 1989).

Puerto Rican migration to the mainland took place in roughly three periods (Stevens-Arroyo 1974). The first, 1900–1945, was marked by the arrival of rural migrants forced to leave the island to find work after some of these economic transformations. Many migrants directly responded to U.S. companies who valued Puerto Rican citizenship status and experience in agriculture and recruited Puerto Rican laborers for agriculture and industry in the United States (Morales

1986; Maldonado 1972). Almost all settled in New York City, most working in low-skilled occupations.

The second period, 1946–1964, is known as the "great migration" because it was during this period that the greatest number of Puerto Ricans migrated. This movement reflected factors that included the search for work, artificially low fares between the island and New York arranged by the island government, labor recruitment, and the emergence of Puerto Rican settlements on the mainland. Though Puerto Ricans were still relegated to low-wage jobs, they were employed in large numbers.

The period after 1965 has been characterized by a fluctuating pattern of net migration as well as greater dispersion to parts of the United States away from New York City (Rodriguez 1989). It is known as the "revolving-door migration": during most of this period the heavy flow from the island to the mainland was balanced by equally substantial flows in the opposite direction. However, since 1980 the net outflows from Puerto Rico have rivaled those experienced in the 1950s.

Over the past three decades the economic status of Puerto Ricans dropped precipitously. By 1990, 38 percent of all Puerto Rican families were below the poverty line. A growing proportion of these families were concentrated in poor urban neighborhoods located in declining industrial centers in the Northeast and Midwest, which experienced massive economic restructuring and diminished employment opportunities for those with less education and weaker skills. The rising poverty rate has also been linked to a dramatic increase in female-headed households. Recent studies show that the majority of recent migrants were not previously employed on the island. Many were single women who migrated with their young children (Falcon and Gurak 1991). Currently, Puerto Ricans are the most economically disadvantaged group of all Latinos. As a group they are poorer than African Americans.

Unlike other Latino migrants, who entered the United States as subordinate workers and were viewed as sources of cheap labor, the first large waves of Cuban refugees were educated middle- and upper-class professionals. Arriving in large numbers after Castro's 1959 revolution, Cubans were welcomed by the federal government as bona fide political refugees fleeing communism and were assisted in ways that significantly contributed to their economic well-being. Cubans had access to job-training programs and placement services, housing subsidies, English-language programs, and small-business loans. Federal and state assistance contributed to the growth of a vigorous enclave economy (with Cubans owning many of the businesses and hiring fellow Cubans) and also to the emergence of Miami as a center for Latin American trade. Cubans have the highest family income of all Latino groups. Nevertheless, in 1990, 16.9 percent of the Cuban population lived below the poverty line.

In recent years large numbers of Salvadorans and Guatemalans have come to the United States in search of refuge from political repression. But unlike Cubans, few have been recognized by the U.S. government as bona fide refugees. Their settlement and position in the labor market have been influenced by their undocumented (illegal) status. Dominicans have also come in large numbers to East Coast cities, many also arriving as undocumented workers. Working for the lowest wages and minimum job security, undocumented workers are among the poorest in the nation.

Despite their long history and large numbers, Latinos have been an "invisible minority" in the United States. Until recently, few social scientists and policy analysts concerned with understanding stratification and social problems in the United States have noticed them. Because they were almost exclusively concerned with relations between blacks and whites, social scientists were primarily concerned with generating demographic information on the nation's black and white populations, providing almost no information on other groups. Consequently, it has been difficult, sometimes impossible, to obtain accurate data about Latinos.

Latinos began to be considered an important minority group when census figures showed a huge increase in the population. By 1980 there were significant Latino communities in almost every metropolitan area in the nation. As a group, Latinos have low education, low family incomes, and are more clustered in low-paid, less-skilled occupations. Most Latinos live in cities, and poverty has become an increasing problem. On the whole, Latinos are more likely to live in poverty than the general U.S. population: poverty is widespread for all Latino subgroups except Cubans. They were affected by structural factors that influenced the socioeconomic status of all U.S. workers. In 1990, 28 percent were poor as compared with 13 percent of all Americans and 32 percent of African Americans (U.S. Bureau of the Census 1991). Puerto Ricans were particularly likely to be poor. . . .

THE IMPORTANCE OF ECONOMIC RESTRUCTURING

. . . Rustbelt manufacturing decline and Sunbelt growth have come to epitomize what economic restructuring means. But in reality things are a lot more subtle, a lot more complex, and demand a more elaborate conceptualization, especially as these trends affect Latino poverty. Elements of a more complex model are being developed by a number of researchers, but as of this writing none is yet adequate to understand the shifts that are evident in the cities represented here. Several of these deserve particular emphasis.

First, there is the "Rustbelt in the Sunbelt" phenomenon. Some researchers have argued that deindustrialization has been limited to the Rustbelt, and that the causal chain adduced by Wilson therefore does not apply outside that region. But the fact is that many Sunbelt cities developed manufacturing industries, particularly during and after World War II. Thus Rustbelt-style economic restructuring—deindustrialization, in particular—has also affected them deeply. In the late 1970s and early 1980s cities like Los Angeles experienced a major wave of plant closings that put a fair number of Latinos out of work (Morales 1985; Soja, Morales, and Wolff 1983).

Second, there has been significant reindustrialization and many new jobs in many of these cities, a trend that is easily overlooked. Most of the expanding low-wage service and manufacturing industries, like electronics and garment manufacturing, employ Latinos (McCarthy and Valdez 1986; Muller and Espenshade 1986), and some depend almost completely on immigrant labor working at minimum wage (Fernandez-Kelly and Sassen 1991). In short, neither the Rustbelt nor the Sunbelt has seen uniform economic restructuring.

Third, Latinos are affected by the "global cities" phenomenon, particularly evident in New York and Chicago. This term refers to a particular mix of new jobs and populations and an expansion of both high- and low-paid service jobs (see Sassen-Koob 1984). When large multinational corporations centralize their service functions, upper-level service jobs expand. The growing corporate elite want more restaurants, more entertainment, more clothing, and more care for their homes and children, but these new consumer services usually pay low wages and offer only temporary and part-time work. The new service workers in turn generate their own demand for low-cost goods and services. Many of them are Latino immigrants and they create what Sassen calls a "Third World city . . . located in dense groupings spread all over the city": this new "city" also provides new jobs (1989, p. 70).

Los Angeles has experienced many of these patterns. The loss of manufacturing jobs has been far less visible than in New York or Chicago, for although traditional manufacturing declined, until the 1990s high-tech manufacturing did not. Moreover, Los Angeles' international financial and trade functions flourished (Soja 1987). The real difference between Los Angeles on the one hand and New York and Chicago on the other was that more poor people in Los Angeles seemed to be working. In all three cities internationalization had similar consequences for the *structure* of jobs for the poor. More of the immigrants pouring into Los Angeles were finding jobs, while the poor residents of New York and Chicago were not.

Fourth, even though the deindustrialization framework remains of overarching importance in understanding variations in the urban context of Latino poverty, we must also understand that economic restructuring shows many different faces. It is different in economically specialized cities. Houston, for example, has been called "the oil capital of the world", and most of the devastating economic shifts in that city were due to "crisis and reorganization in the world oil-gas industry" (Hill and Feagin 1987, p. 174). Miami is another special case. The economic changes that have swept Miami have little to do with deindustrialization, or with Europe or the Pacific Rim, and much to do with the overpowering influence of its Cuban population, its important "enclave economy", and its "Latino Rim" functions (see Portes and Stepick 1993).

Finally, economic change has a different effect in peripheral areas. Both Albuquerque and Tucson are regional centers in an economically peripheral area. Historically, these two cities served the ranches, farms, and mines of their desert hinterlands. Since World War II, both became military centers, with substantial high-tech defense industrialization. Both cities are accustomed to having a large, poor Latino population, whose poverty is rarely viewed as a crisis. In Tucson, for example, unemployment for Mexican Americans has been low, and there is stable year-round income. But both cities remain marginal to the national economy, and this means that the fate of their poor depends more on local factors.

Laredo has many features in common with other cities along the Texas border, with its substantial military installations, and agricultural and tourist functions. All of these cities have been affected by general swings in the American and Texan economy. These border communities have long been the poorest in the nation, and their largely Mexican American populations have suffered even more from recent economic downturns. They are peripheral to the U.S. economy, but the important point is that their economic well-being is intimately tied to the Mexican economy. They were devastated by the collapse of the peso in the 1980s. They are also more involved than most American cities in international trade in illicit goods, and poverty in Laredo has been deeply affected by smuggling. Though Texas has a long history of discrimination against Mexican Americans, race is not an issue within Laredo itself, where most of the population—elite as well as poor—is of Mexican descent. This fact is of particular importance in evaluating the underclass debate.

THE INFORMAL AND ILLICIT ECONOMIES

The growth of an informal economy is part and parcel of late twentieth-century economic restructuring. Particularly in the global cities, a variety of "informal" economic activities proliferates—activities that are small-scale, informally organized, and largely outside government regulations (cf. Portes, Castells, and Benton 1989). Some low-wage reindustrialization, for example, makes use of new arrangements in well-established industries (like home work in the garment industry, as seamstresses take their work home with them). Small-scale individual activities such as street vending and "handyman" house repairs and alterations affect communities in peripheral as well as global cities. These money-generating activities are easily ignored by researchers who rely exclusively on aggregate data sources: they never make their way into the statistics on labor-market participation, because they are "off the books". But they play a significant role in the everyday life of many African American neighborhoods as well as in the barrios.

And, finally, there are illicit activities—most notoriously, a burgeoning drug market. There is not much doubt that the new poverty in the United States has often been accompanied by a resurgence of illicit economic activities (see Fagan, forthcoming, for details on five cities). It is important to note that most Latino communities have been able to contain or encapsulate such activities so that they do not dominate neighborhood life. But in most of them there is also little doubt that illicit economic activities form an "expanded industry". They rarely provide more than a pittance for the average worker: but for a very small fraction of barrio households they are part of the battery of survival strategies. . . .

IMMIGRATION

Immigration—both international and from Puerto Rico—is of major significance for poor Latino communities in almost every city in every region of the country. Further, there is every reason to believe that immigration will continue to be important.

First, it has important economic consequences. Immigration is a central feature of the economic life of global cities: for example, Los Angeles has been called the "capital of the Third World" because of its huge Latino and Asian immigration (Rieff 1991). Those cities most bound to world trends (New York, Los Angeles, Chicago, Houston, and Miami) experienced massive Latino immigration in the 1980s. In the Los Angeles, Houston, and Miami communities, immigration is a major factor in the labor market, and the residents of the "second settlement"

Puerto Rican communities in New York and Chicago operate within a context of both racial and ethnic change and of increased Latino immigration. The restructured economy provides marginal jobs for immigrant workers, and wage scales seem to drop for native-born Latinos in areas where immigration is high. This is a more complicated scenario than the simple loss of jobs accompanying Rustbelt deindustrialization. Immigrants are ineligible for most government benefits, are usually highly motivated, and are driven to take even the poorest-paying jobs. They are also more vulnerable to labor market swings.

Though immigrants have been less important in the peripheral cities of Albuquerque, Laredo, and Tucson, each of these cities is special in some way. Albuquerque has attracted few Mexican immigrants, but it draws on a historical Latino labor pool—English-speaking rural *Manitos*—who are as economically exploitable as are Spanish-speaking immigrants from Mexico. Until recently Tucson was also largely bypassed by most Mexican immigrants. Instead, there is an old, relatively self-contained set of cross-border networks, with well-established pathways of family movement and mutual aid. Similar networks also exist in Laredo. Laredo's location on the border means that many of its workers are commuters—people who work in Laredo but live in Mexico.

In recent years, immigration has not been very significant in most African American communities, and as a consequence it is underemphasized in the underclass debate. It is also often interpreted as wholly negative. This is partly because the positive effects can be understood only by researchers who study immigrant communities themselves, partly because in some places large numbers of immigrants have strained public resources, and partly because immigrants have occasionally become a source of tension among poor minority populations. Though the specific contouring of immigration effects varies from place to place, immigration is a highly significant dimension of Latino poverty, both at the citywide level and also in the neighborhoods. It is an issue of overriding importance for the understanding of Latino poverty, and thus for the understanding of American urban poverty in general.

CONCENTRATION EFFECTS

One of the most important features of Wilson's analysis of black poverty in Chicago is his emphasis on the dramatic increase both in the number of poor neighborhoods between 1970 and 1980 and also in the proportion of poor people in already poor neighborhoods. Poverty became intensely concentrated. Not only did people have more difficulty getting jobs, but also, for the first time, middle- and working-class blacks were able to leave the ghettos and move into housing that was formerly closed to them. In Wilson's analysis, this concentration of poverty meant that achieving role models were gone, the marriage market was weakened, job networks were vitiated, and those remaining in the ghettos were deprived of the support that middle-class residents gave to churches, schools, and other stabilizing institutions.

Generally speaking, poverty did not become as concentrated in Latino neighborhoods during the 1970s as it did in black Chicago. An examination of trends in the sixty largest cities showed that it happened only in a few cities in the Northeast and Midwest (Massey and Eggers 1990). Translated into ethnic terms, this implies that it was primarily in some Puerto Rican communities that concentrated poverty became a serious problem. Most cities with large Mexican American populations did not experience an increased concentration of poverty in the 1970s; the large influx of immigrants in the 1980s may have changed this.

The concentration of poverty comes about not only because of market forces or the departure of the middle classes for better housing; in Houston, Rodriguez shows that restructuring in real estate had the effect of concentrating poverty. Concentrated poverty can also result from government planning. Chicago's decision decades ago to build a concentration of high-rise housing projects right next to one another is a clear case in point. Another is in New York's largely Latino South Bronx, where the city's ten-year-plan created neighborhoods in which the least enterprising of the poor are concentrated, and in which a set of undesirable "Not-In-My-Back-Yard" institutions, such as drug-treatment clinics and permanent shelters for the homeless, were located. These neighborhoods are likely to remain as pockets of unrelieved poverty for many generations to come (Vergara 1991). It was not industrial decline and the exodus of stable working people that created these pockets: the cities of Chicago and New York chose to segregate their problem populations in permanent buildings in those neighborhoods.

Some of the dynamics that Wilson identified as responsible for the concentration of black poverty are different in Latino neighborhoods. To be sure, they also saw jobs vanish, but two factors in particular tend to distinguish Latino from black communities: continual immigration and a historically lower level of housing discrimination. These two factors mean that there has been a continual traffic—both into and out of—most poor Latino urban communities. Immigrants from rural areas or from outside the United States move into the poorest neighborhoods, and those who can afford it move into somewhat better neighborhoods as the city's Latino *colonia* expands. To a superficial observer, the old neighborhood may look the same, but there is a continual population turnover.

Though this kind of population turnover may siphon off some of a neighborhood's achieving residents, this does not mean that cross-class linkages necessarily disappear, or that there is complete social isolation. Vélez-Ibáñez describes cross-class household clusters that transcend neighborhood boundaries and provide extensive resources to the poor. This topic urgently demands further research: many of the black as well as the Latino middle class come from humble roots, and it cannot be taken for granted that they cut themselves off from those roots.

In addition, these studies demonstrate that it is not just poverty that gets concentrated. Most immigrants are poor, and most settle in poor communities, thus further concentrating poverty. But, as Rodriguez shows, immigrant communities may be economically, culturally, and socially vital. Social isolation early in the immigration process, he argues, can strengthen group cohesion and lead to community development, rather than to deterioration. The Los Angeles studies also portray institution-building among immigrants in poor communities, and institutional "resilience" characterizes many of the communities studied in this volume—especially New York and Chicago. Vélez-Ibáñez's analysis of poverty in Tucson points to the overwhelming importance of "funds of knowledge" shared in interdependent household clusters. Although a priori it makes sociological sense that concentrated poverty should destroy communities, these studies offer evidence that a different pattern emerges under certain circumstances. To use Grenier and Stepick's term, "social capital" also becomes concentrated.

In short, the concentration of poverty need not plunge a neighborhood into disarray, and these authors identify structural resources that ward off despair. This line of reasoning raises other issues. If it isn't just demographic shifts that weaken neighborhoods, then what is it? These questions strike at the heart of the underclass debate. The old, rancorous controversy about the usefulness of the "culture of poverty" concept questioned whether the poor adhered to a special set of self-defeating values, and if so, whether those values were powerful enough to make poverty self-perpetuating. That argument faded as research focused more effectively on the situational and structural sources of poverty. We do not intend to revive this controversy. It is all too easy to attribute the differences between Latino and black poverty to "the culture". This line can be invidious, pitting one poor population against another in its insinuation that Latino poverty is somehow "better" than black poverty. (Ironically, this would reverse another outdated contention—i.e., that Latinos are poor *because* of their culture.) Too little is known about poor communities of *any* ethnicity.

OTHER ASPECTS OF URBAN SPACE

Where a poor neighborhood is located makes a difference. First, some are targets for "gentrification". This is traditionally viewed as a market process by which old neighborhoods are revitalized and unfortunate poor people displaced. But there is a different perspective. Sassen (1989) argues that gentrification is best understood in the context of restructuring, globalization, and politics. It doesn't happen everywhere. Gentrification, along with downtown revitalization and expansion, affects Latino neighborhoods in Chicago, Albuquerque, New York, and west side Los Angeles. In Houston, a variant of "gentrification" is documented. Apartment owners who were eager to rent to Latino immigrants when a recession raised their vacancy rates were equally eager to "upgrade" their tenants when the economy recovered and the demand for housing rose once again. Latinos were "gentrified" out of the buildings.

Second, Latinos are an expanding population in many cities, and they rub up against other populations. Ethnic succession is explicit in Albuquerque and in Chicago. It is implicit in East Los Angeles, with the Mexicanization of Chicano communities, and in Houston, with the immigration of Central Americans to Mexican American neighborhoods and the manipulated succession of Anglos and Latinos. In Albuquerque and East Los Angeles, Latinos are "filling in" areas of the city, in a late phase of ethnic succession. Ethnic succession is *not* an issue in Laredo because the city's population is primarily of Mexican origin. It is crucial in Miami, where new groups of immigrants are establishing themselves within the Latino community: newer immigrants tend to move into areas vacated by earlier Cuban arrivals, who leave for the suburbs. In Brooklyn a different kind of urban ecological function is filled by the Puerto Rican barrio—that of an ethnic buffer between African American and Anglo communities. Los Angeles' Westlake area is most strongly affected by its location near downtown: it is intensely involved in both gentrification and problems of ethnic succession. Here the Central Americans displaced a prior population, and, in turn, their nascent communities are pressured by an expanding Koreatown to the west and by gentrification from the north and from downtown.

These details are important in themselves, but they also have implications for existing theories of how cities grow and how ethnic groups become segregated (and segregation is closely allied to poverty). Most such theories take the late nineteenth-century industrial city as a point of departure—a city with a strong central business district and clearly demarcated suburbs. In these models, immigrants initially settle in deteriorating neighborhoods near downtown. Meanwhile, earlier generations of immigrants, their predecessors in those neighborhoods, leapfrog out to "areas of second settlement", often on the edge of the city.

In this discussion only New York and Chicago fit this pattern; all the other cities have evolved differently. In the Mexican American Southwest, Chicano barrios were historically scattered throughout metropolitan areas, and this pattern still remains. Many Mexican enclaves evolved out of early labor camps. Whole families emigrated or were imported into these camps to work at ranching, railway maintenance, citrus harvesting and packing, and brickmaking. As the population of southwestern cities boomed, many such settlements were wiped out, though some persisted, surrounded by new middle-class housing.

Thus it is no surprise that the "traditional" Rustbelt pattern of ethnic location and ethnic succession fails to appear in most cities. New Latino immigrants are as likely to settle initially in communities on the edge of town (near the new jobs) as they are to move near downtown; or their initial settlement may be steered by housing entrepreneurs, as in Houston. The new ecology of jobs, housing, and shopping malls has made even the old Rustbelt cities like Chicago less clearly focused on a central downtown business district.

Housing for the Latino poor is equally distinctive. Poor communities in which one-third to one-half of the homes are owner-occupied would seem on the face of it to provide a different ambience from public housing—like the infamous phalanx of projects on Chicago's South Side that form part of Wilson's focus. In fact, in many southwestern cities home ownership among the Latino poor is relatively high. There is not as much ownership in East Los Angeles as in Albuquerque, Laredo, and Tucson, but it is a realistic aspiration. By contrast, New York, Chicago, Houston, and Los Angeles' Westlake are the communities in our sample in which Latinos are primarily dependent on rental housing. In Houston the excessive manipulation of rental housing added to the vulnerability of nascent Latino communities.

Finally, space is especially important when we consider Mexican American communities on the border. Mexican Americans in most border communities have important relationships with kin living across the border in Mexico, and this is certainly the case in Tucson and Laredo. But space is also important in economic matters. Shopping, working, and recreation are conditioned by the proximity of alternative opportunities on both sides of the border. And in Laredo the opportunities for illicit economic transactions also depend on location. The Laredo barrios in which illicit activities are most concentrated are located right on the Rio Grande River, where cross-border transactions are easier.

In sum, when we consider poor minority neighborhoods, we are drawn into a variety of issues that go well beyond the question of how poverty gets concentrated because middle-class families move out. We must look at the role of urban policy in addition to the role of the market. We must look at the factors that promote and sustain segregation. We must look at how housing is allocated, and where neighborhoods are located within cities. And, finally, we must look at how the location of a neighborhood facilitates its residents' activity in licit and illicit market activities.

THE ROLE OF THE STATE

Most discussions of changes in poverty assume either a constant governmental role or a shrinking national welfare state, but there is evidence to contradict such a simple view. First, in many poor communities money derived from welfare makes a significant contribution to the local economy, and it is easy to forget that the underdeveloped American welfare state is more underdeveloped in some places—and for some people. California and New York supported welfare recipients at $850 and $806 a month for a family of three, respectively, in 1992—though of course living costs are also high. Illinois provides less, but is more generous than Arizona and Florida, whereas Texas is near the bottom, with a mere $476 a month (*New York Times,* July 5, 1992). The substantial differences in the amount of money available through AFDC means that poor families in Houston, Laredo, and Tucson may be driven to other expedients, and the patterns discerned in those cities should be viewed against this background. In addition, immigrants—whether documented or not—are not eligible for most welfare benefits, though their U.S.-born children are. Immigrant life and the search for work and housing are colored by this fact, and poverty at the neighborhood level is thus conditioned by policy made at the state and national levels.

Second, government has disinvested in these neighborhoods. During the War on Poverty, in the 1960s, community-based organizations appeared in most cities to serve a variety of needs unmet by welfare bureaucracies. These ranged from health care to services for families of prisoners. Most of those organizations disappeared during the 1980s. This aspect of welfare-state contraction—or government disinvestment—is easily overlooked. Once it was fashionable to criticize such organizations for their many inadequacies, but their departure meant that community resources were seriously depleted.

By contrast, the Cubans of Miami offer a prime example of government investment. Government spending during the early stages of settlement was essential in permitting Cubans to translate their substantial human and financial capital into a thriving enclave economy, with Cuban professionals and Cuban-owned businesses. Unlike other Latino groups, Cubans had the political clout to make this happen.

Third, government involvement in urban space and urban housing is critical to the well-being of many Latino communities. We have noted New York City's enhancement of permanent poverty neighborhoods in the South Bronx through its ten-year plan for the city. Some communities are also affected by downtown revitalization in which the role of government is all-important. The level of involvement varies substantially from city to city and from one period to another, and these variations affect the poor of all ethnic groups. They are more obvious for Latinos because so many live in states with a very short tradition of serious government help.

CONCLUSION

[We need to] respond directly to Wilson's work—to his conceptualization of an "underclass"; to his theory that urban poverty has become concentrated; that it has become concentrated as a result of the decline of the manufacturing sector and the out-migration of the middle class; and to his characterization of the underclass in relation to specific behaviors. But it is clear that to apply Wilson's analysis to the Latino situation requires considerable adaptation of the original formulation. For example, there is little debate that the nation as a whole has been profoundly affected by economic restructuring. But matters become more complicated when one looks at any given city—no matter what subpopulation is of concern—and even more complicated when one looks at Latinos. Again, though immigration is a relatively minor concern in understanding Wilson's subjects, it is a major phenomenon in most Latino communities, and is closely tied in with economic restructuring. It has a major bearing on Latino poverty. Finally, for Wilson urban space is largely a matter of "concentration effects", but for many communities matters become much more complex.

In sum, [we] conclude that economic restructuring has been critical in increasing poverty in Latino communities. But the emphasis is on the complexity of economic restructuring rather than on the constriction of the manufacturing sector alone. [Our studies] show how new Latino immigrants help to revitalize and stabilize impoverished Latino communities. They show how Latino communities may serve different ecological functions in the city—some as buffer zones between poor black and more affluent white communities, some as targets for gentrification. Although these studies document poverty and many problems, they do not portray the severe urban decay that Wilson describes in Chicago's ghettos. Some of the studies portray thriving ethnic enclaves with businesses owned by Latino residents, and strong interhousehold networks that cross class boundaries and mediate the effects of poverty. Finally, most authors describe poor Latino residents who are strongly attached to the labor market. Many of those who are unemployed are actively searching for work. Others are employed in the informal sector; there they work for wages so low it keeps them living below the poverty line. Still others are employed in the underground economy.

The "new poverty" described so effectively by Wilson for the black population of deindustrialized Chicago is directly applicable only to the New York and Chicago Puerto Rican communities [we discussed]; the deindustrialization framework simply does not work in cities that were never industrialized to begin with. Nevertheless, these studies indicate that national economic restructuring has affected all cities, even those most peripheral to mainstream trends. Again, immigration is of major importance even where there has not been deindustrialization, because most of the new jobs are in low-wage manufacturing and service occupations, and these jobs are easily filled by exploitable immigrants.

To apply to Latino populations, it is clear that, at the very least, the underclass/deindustrialization framework must be expanded to take into account both the traditional and modern mixes of industry and of the informal economy in any given locale, along with immigration, the niches in urban space into which Latinos fall, and the extent of government investment. Even with such modifications, the perspective does not account for important cultural and historical differences in social organization between Latinos and others at the community and family levels.

REFERENCES

Barrera, Mario 1979. *Race and Class in the Southwest.* Notre Dame, IN: University of Notre Dame Press.

Ellwood, David T. 1984. *The Impact of AFDC on Family Structure and Living Arrangements.* Washington, DC: U.S. Department of Health and Human Services, Assistant Secretary for Planning and Education.

Falcon, Luis, and Douglas Gurak 1991. "Features of the Hispanic Underclass: Puerto Ricans and Dominicans in New York." Unpublished manuscript.

Fagan, Jeffrey, ed. forthcoming. *The Changing Ecology of Crime and Drugs.*

Fernandez-Kelly, Patricia, and Saskia Sassen 1991. "A Collaborative Study of Hispanic Women in the Garment and Electronics Industries: Executive Summary." New York: New York University, Center for Latin American and Caribbean Studies.

Hill, Richard Child, and Joe R. Feagin 1987. "Detroit and Houston: Two Cities in Global Perspective." In Michael Peter Smith and Joe R. Feagin, eds., *The Capitalist City,* pp. 155–177. New York: Basil Blackwell.

Maldonado-Denis, Manuel 1972. *Puerto Rico: A Sociohistoric Interpretation.* New York: Random House.

Massey, Douglas, and Mitchell Eggers 1990. "The Ecology of Inequality: Minorities and the Concentration of Poverty." *American Journal of Sociology* 95:1153–1188.

McCarthy, Kevin, and R.B. Valdez 1986. *Current and Future Effects of Mexican Immigration in California.* Santa Monica, CA: Rand Corporation.

Moore, Joan, 1989. "Is There a Hispanic Underclass?" *Social Science Quarterly* 70:265–283.

Moore, Joan, and Harry Pachon 1985. *Hispanics in the United States.* Englewood Cliffs, NJ: Prentice Hall.

Morales, Julio 1986. *Puerto Rican Poverty and Migration: We Just Had to Try Elsewhere.* New York: Praeger.

Morales, Rebecca 1985. "Transitional Labor: Undocumented Workers in the Los Angeles Automobile Industry." *International Migration Review* 17:570–96.

Morris, Michael 1989. "From the Culture of Poverty to the Underclass: An Analysis of a Shift in Public Language." *The American Sociologist* 20:123–133.

Muller, Thomas, and Thomas J. Espenshade 1986. *The Fourth Wave.* Washington, DC: Urban Institute Press.

Portes, Alejandro, Manuel Castells, and Lauren A. Benton 1989. *The Informal Economy.* Baltimore: Johns Hopkins University Press.

Portes, Alejandro, and Alex Stepick 1993. *City on the Edge: The Transformation of Miami.* Berkeley: University of California Press.

Ricketts, Erol, and Isabel V. Sawhill 1988. "Defining and Measuring the Underclass." *Journal of Policy Analysis and Management* 7:316–325.

Rieff, David, 1991. *Los Angeles: Capital of the Third World.* New York: Simon and Schuster.

Rodriguez, Clara 1989. *Puerto Ricans: Born in the U.S.A.* Boulder: Westview Press.

Sassen, Saskia 1989. "New Trends in the Sociospatial Organization of the New York City Economy." In Robert Beauregard, ed., *Economic Restructuring and Political Response.* Newbury Park, CA.

Sassen-Koob, Saskia 1984. "The New Labor Demand in Global Cities." In Michael Smith, ed., *Cities in Transformation.* Beverly Hills, CA: Sage.

Soja, Edward 1987. "Economic Restructuring and the Internationalization of the Los Angeles Region." In Michael Peter Smith and Joe R. Feagin, eds., *The Capitalist City,* pp. 178–198. New York: Basil Blackwell.

Soja, Edward W., Rebecca Morales, and G. Wolff 1983. "Urban Restructuring: An Analysis of Social and Spatial Change in Los Angeles." *Economic Geography* 59:195–230.

Stevens Arroyo, Antonio M. 1974. *The Political Philosophy of Pedro Abizu Campos: Its Theory and Practice.* Ibero American Language and Area Center. New York: New York University Press.

Steward, Julian H. 1956. *The People of Puerto Rico.* Urbana, IL: University of Illinois Press.

U.S. Bureau of the Census 1991. *The Hispanic Population in the United States: March 1991.* Current Population Reports, Series P-20, No. 455. Washington, DC: U.S. Government Printing Office.

Van Haitsma, Martha 1991. "Attitudes, Social Context, and Labor Force Attachment: Blacks and Immigrant Mexicans in Chicago Poverty Areas." Unpublished manuscript presented at the University of Chicago Urban Poverty and Family Structure Conference.

Vergara, Camilo Jose 1991. "Lessons Learned, Lessons Forgotten: Rebuilding New York City's Poor Communities." *The Livable City* 15:3–9.

Wilson, William Julius 1987. *The Truly Disadvantaged: The Inner City, the Underclass, and Public Policy.* Chicago: The University of Chicago Press.

16

Major Issues Relating to Asian American Experiences

PYONG GAP MIN

This chapter introduces major issues relating to Asian American experiences.* Some are practical issues with policy implications, such as anti-Asian violence. Other issues concern Asian American experiences that have both theoretical and practical implications. For example, Asian Americans' degree of socioeconomic success is a question of interpretation, using a particular theoretical perspective, as much as a practical question concerning the economic well-being of Asian Americans. Therefore, whenever necessary, I will introduce a theoretical orientation useful for understanding the issue under consideration.

Depending on our ideological and/or theoretical position, we have different views about which issues are important to the experiences of Asian Americans. [This chapter] emphasizes structural factors such as institutional barriers, discrimination, and disadvantages facing Asian Americans, rather than the cultural mechanisms employed for their successful adjustment. This structural approach and the related theoretical perspectives have largely determined which issues concerning Asian Americans are presented in this chapter.

In the 1970s, the U.S. media and many scholars portrayed Asian Americans as successful minority groups that overcame disadvantages through hard work, family ties, and emphasis on children's education. Largely in reaction to this "model minority" thesis, Asian American scholars began to emphasize the structural barriers facing Asian Americans. The revisionist critique of the model minority thesis currently has a powerful influence in Asian American scholarship. The attack on the model minority thesis is not limited to academic research. Activists, social workers in Asian American communities, Asian American faculty members, and the U.S. Commission on Civil Rights have also expressed concerns about the negative consequences of the success image. This chapter will introduce many issues that revisionist critics of the model minority thesis consider important.

---

*Bibliographic references have been deleted unless they are associated with direct quotations.

ASIAN AMERICANS' UNDERREWARD AND UNDEREMPLOYMENT

Several topics discussed as major issues in this chapter concern socioeconomic adjustment. A question underlying all these issues is whether Asian Americans are socioeconomically successful. Traditionally, the U.S. media and many researchers have emphasized Asian American success stories. Those who considered Asian Americans successful focused on their high family incomes (relative to white family incomes) and their high educational levels.

However, revisionist critics claim that this traditional interpretation has little validity. They concede that Asian Americans excel in education and earn relatively high incomes. But they point out that to assess Asian American's success in socioeconomic adjustment, we must compare their incomes to their educational levels. Revisionist critics argue that Asian American workers do not receive economic rewards comparable to their education. To support this argument, many researchers have shown, using regression analysis, that Asian workers receive smaller economic rewards for their education than white workers. This means that Asian Americans need more education to maintain economic parity with white Americans.

Asian American workers' unequal rewards for their human capital investments suggest that they, like other racial minority members and women, encounter structural barriers in the labor market. Dual labor market theory is useful for understanding this social phenomenon. Dual labor market theory was created as an alternative to the human capital investment model to explain earnings. Dual labor market theorists distinguish between primary and secondary labor markets. The primary labor market is characterized by high wages, fringe benefits, job security, unionization, and opportunity for promotion; the secondary labor market has the opposite characteristics. The theory's central argument is that the kind of market a worker is located in is a more accurate predictor of his/her earnings than the worker's human capital investments.

Using dual labor market theory, several sociologists argue that a large proportion of minority members and new immigrants, regardless of their education, are trapped in the secondary labor market. Some revisionist scholars use dual labor market theory as a frame of reference to discuss Asian Americans' unequal rewards for their education. Partly because of racial discrimination, a higher proportion of Asian Americans work in the secondary labor market than their education levels might indicate. Some scholars show that even Asian workers in the primary labor market, such as Korean immigrant physicians and Asian American government employees, are concentrated in periphery specialty areas or less influential positions.

Moreover, revisionist critics also point out that Asian Americans' high median family income compared to whites is not a good indicator of their socioeconomic position. Critics provide three reasons for not using family income to measure Asian American economic success. First, the relatively high median family income among Asian Americans is misleading because all Asian ethnic groups have more workers per family than whites. Asian Americans generally need more workers per family to maintain parity with white Americans. Second, Asian ethnic groups' median family incomes do not accurately reflect their standards of living, because

Asian Americans are concentrated in San Francisco, Los Angeles, New York City, and Honolulu, where living expenses are much higher than in the United States as a whole. Finally, revisionist scholars argue that average family income is misleading because Asian ethnic groups are socioeconomically polarized. We will come back to this point in the next section.

Negative Effects of the Success Image on Welfare Benefits

Revisionist critics argue that the success image is not only invalid but also detrimental to the welfare of Asian Americans. They point out that because Asian Americans are assumed to be economically well-off, they are eliminated from affirmative action and other programs designed to help disadvantaged minorities. As Hurh and Kim (1989) forcefully argue, "Asian Americans are considered by the dominant group as 'successful' and 'problem free' and not in need of social programs designed to benefit disadvantaged minorities such as black and Mexican Americans" (p. 528). Nakanishi (1985–1986) points out that the alleged success of Asian Americans "disguises their lack of representation in the most significant national arenas and institutions" (p. 2). Several revisionist scholars also point out that the success stories of Asian Americans have stimulated anti-Asian sentiment and violence on college campuses and communities during recent years. In addition, Hurh and Kim claim that by defining Asian Americans as a model minority, the dominant group has led Asian Americans to develop "false consciousness." Many Asian Americans believe that they have attained middle-class status without realizing they are underemployed and overworked.

Revisionist scholars also point out that the positive stereotype of Asian Americans negatively affects other minority groups as well. By emphasizing the importance of cultural traits and values in Asians' successful adjustment, the success image in effect blames other less successful minority groups for their own failure. It thus legitimates the openness of American society. As one writer (Crystal, 1989) comments:

> The existence of a "model minority" supports the belief that democracy "works" and that the racism about which some ethnic groups complain is the product of their own shortcomings and is not inherent in society. To be able to make an assertion is, as one might imagine, extremely important to many persons in power. (p. 407)

The above criticism becomes significant because when politicians and journalists talk about the success stories of Asian Americans, they may intend to suggest that blacks and other minority groups have not succeeded because of their cultural deficiencies.

Revisionist critics have made us aware that the positive stereotypes of Asian Americans can have negative consequences. However, one could argue that the revisionist critics fail to recognize the positive effects the model minority thesis has had on Asian Americans while overemphasizing its negative effects. Positive stereotypes are likely to lead policy makers to be less sensitive to the needs of Asian Americans and to stimulate anti-Asian sentiments among less successful whites and minorities. However, positive stereotypes are also likely to lead many

Americans—managers, teachers, community leaders, and home owners—to hold more favorable views of Asian Americans and treat them more favorably. The connection between the positive stereotypes of Asian Americans and their favorable treatment in the classroom, job hiring, and housing is so obvious that we need not provide evidence to support this argument. Nevertheless, there is one empirical study that focused on the positive effects of these stereotypes. In her Westinghouse project, Choi (1988) showed that high school teachers expect Asian students to perform better in science and math and to be more motivated than white students. Based on the findings, she concluded that "the high expectation feedback the Asian students receive from their teachers might push them a little further than if teachers had a lower expectation of them" (Choi, 1988, pp. 17–18).

Underrepresentation in Executive and Managerial Positions

Another important issue regarding Asian Americans' socioeconomic adjustment is their underrepresentation in important administrative, executive, and managerial positions in corporate and public sectors. Asian Americans are well-represented in professional occupations mainly because they are highly educated and obtain professional certificates. However, they are severely underrepresented in high-ranking executive and administrative positions. For example, only two Asian Americans currently serve as presidents of major universities, although Asian American professors constitute a large proportion of the total faculty in American colleges and universities. Few Asian Americans hold important positions in local and federal governments.

Asian Americans may be at a disadvantage for these administrative positions because they lack communication and leadership skills, a result of the authoritarian child socialization techniques practiced in many Asian American families. However, it is also true that many well-qualified Asian Americans are not given these desirable positions because Asians are stereotyped as docile and lacking leadership skills. Compared to blacks, Asian Americans are severely underrepresented in leadership positions, particularly in higher education institutions and government, partly because affirmative action does not apply to them.

Closely related to the underrepresentation of Asian Americans in high-ranking executive and administrative positions is the so-called "glass ceiling." Glass ceiling refers to a situation in which people cannot advance beyond a certain level in their careers. The term can be applied to the mobility barrier facing women and minority members. However, the term is largely used to indicate the difficulty that highly educated Asian Americans encounter in reaching the top of the occupational ladder. For example, analyzing the career histories of 12,200 Caucasian and Asian engineers, Tang (1993) showed that there was more racial disparity in managerial representation and upward mobility than in earnings. The glass ceiling has been the topic of many seminars and conferences on Asian Americans' occupational adjustment.

CLASS HOMOGENEITY VERSUS CLASS DIVISION

When people claim that Asian Americans are socioeconomically successful, they assume that Asian Americans are more or less homogeneous in socioeconomic status. However, Asian Americans are not a socioeconomically homogeneous group. Indochinese refugees and immigrants from mainland China are far behind other Asian groups in socioeconomic status. There are also significant intraethnic differentials in socioeconomic status. Those who emphasize Asian American success in socioeconomic adjustment use statistical averages as the indicators. However, revisionist critics argue that averages are misleading because some Asian ethnic groups are socioeconomically polarized. Statistically speaking, Asian Americans have a bipolar distribution, with proportionally far more people both above and below the average. Occupationally, larger proportions of Asian Americans than white Americans occupy both the highest and the lowest tiers of the occupational hierarchy. Economically, a much larger proportion of Asian Americans than white Americans is at the poverty level, although proportionally more of them belong to the high-income brackets. The Chinese American community is extremely polarized along class lines.

Asian American children's educational performance is also polarized. Using standardized test results as indicators, Asian American students as a group do much better than other minority students, even better than white students. Asian Americans stand well above white Americans in college enrollment. However, as Hu (1989) indicates, Asian American students have the largest proportions of both the highest and the lowest Scholastic Achievement Test scores. Compared to whites, Asian American students include proportionally larger numbers of both super students and poor students. Revisionist scholars criticize the American media for focusing on Asian American students' success stories, giving the impression that most Asian American students are super students.

Ethnic Solidarity Versus Class Conflict

The issue of class homogeneity versus class division is closely related to another issue: the issue of ethnic solidarity versus class conflict. Researchers traditionally emphasized each Asian community's strong ethnic ties based on common culture and national origin. For example, in his study of the Japanese community in Seattle, Miyamoto (1939) described ethnic solidarity as its most conspicuous characteristic. However, since the late 1970s, an increasing number of Asian American scholars have shown class conflicts in Asian ethnic communities. The Chinatown study by Light and Wong (1975) highlighted the class division between business owners and ethnic employees and their conflicts over economic interests. Based on his analysis of the Chinese community in Toronto, Thompson (1979) also indicated that class conflict affected the structure of a North American Chinese community. In another article (Thompson, 1980), he discussed major classes in Chinatowns in North America and suggested that a modified Marxian class model best describes the current structure of Chinese ethnic communities.

In the 1980s, several researchers showed the economic disadvantages of Chinese workers employed in ethnic businesses in Chinatowns in New York and San Francisco, jobs characterized by low wages and poor working conditions. They suggested that Chinatown business owners achieve economic mobility largely by exploiting co-ethnic employees. The emphasis on economic exploitation is in sharp contrast with the enclave economy thesis, which emphasizes the economic benefits to both business owners and employees in an ethnic enclave. In his New

York Chinatown study, Kwong (1987) stressed the Chinese community's polarization into the working and professional classes. Other scholars consider class division in the Chinese community important in understanding the differences, not only in their life chances, but also in lifestyles, including their family system.

Japanese Americans are culturally and socioeconomically more homogeneous than Chinese Americans and may therefore be less suitable for class analysis. Nevertheless, researchers have recently criticized the research tradition for overemphasizing the homogeneity and solidarity of Japanese Americans. Researchers have increasingly emphasized the class conflict of the early Japanese community rather than its ethnic solidarity. For example, in his study of first-generation Japanese, Ichioka (1988) highlighted the exploitative relationship between Japanese labor contractors and Japanese labor immigrants. Glenn (1980, 1986) analyzed the difficulty of Japanese American women engaged in domestic service, who were doubly exploited both as Asian Americans and as women.

FAMILY TIES VERSUS FAMILY CONFLICTS

Traditionally, the U.S. media and researchers depict Asian Americans as maintaining strong family ties, which facilitate their adjustment in American society. They emphasize that the harmony between husband and wife and parents and children in Asian American families, particularly Asian immigrant families, is based on traditional family values brought from Asian countries.

To what extent Asian Americans maintain family ties is an empirical question that can be determined by comparing Asian American families with white American families. However, our perception may be shaped by our particular approach or theoretical orientation. The traditional interpretation—that family ties facilitate Asian immigrants' adjustment—is the cultural approach, in that it tries to explain Asian Americans' adjustment in terms of their cultural mechanism, family ties. In reaction, more and more researchers now apply the structural approach, paying great attention to the effects of structural conditions on Asian American families. As Kibria (1993) states in her introduction to Vietnamese immigrant families:

> In contrast to such cultural explanations, I suggest that immigrant families must be analyzed in relation to the external structural conditions encountered by immigrants in the "host" society. These structural conditions provide the fundamental parameters—opportunities and conditions—within which immigrants must construct their family life. (p. 22)

Kibria (1993) indicates that the increase in Vietnamese women's control over economic and social resources and the concomitant decline in Vietnamese men's earning power and social status contributed, along with other factors, to a shift in relative power from men to women. This shift in power, although desirable from the egalitarian point of view, brings about conflicts and tensions in marital relations as Vietnamese women challenge men's traditional patriarchal authority. The loss of parental social and economic resources and exposure to the American socioeconomic environment have also liberated Vietnamese children from parental control, increasing generational conflicts in Vietnamese immigrant families.

Glenn's (1983) study of Chinese families was probably the first significant work to examine Asian American families using a structural approach. She emphasized the "changing structure of Chinese-American families resulting from the interplay between shifting institutional constraints and the efforts of the Chinese Americans to maintain family life in the face of these restrictions" (p. 35). Based on a historical analysis, she described three types of Chinese American families that emerged in three different periods: split household, small producer, and dual-wage worker.

DISCRIMINATION IN COLLEGE ADMISSION

Their cultural tradition stressing education and their higher professional socioeconomic status enable Asian immigrants to successfully educate their children, although there are big intergroup differences in terms of socioeconomic status and national origin. Although the United States is an achievement-oriented society, Asian societies put more emphasis on children's education. Many Asian immigrants made the trans-Pacific migration mainly in search of a better education for their children. A disproportionately large number of recent Asian immigrants were able to send their children to elite universities. Also, a large number of Asian students annually come to major universities for undergraduate and graduate study. As a result, Asian American enrollment at many prestigious American colleges and universities has increased dramatically. Several campuses of the University of California system have witnessed a phenomenal increase in the number of Asian American students since the mid-1970s. Over the last 20 years, the proportion of Asian American students has also significantly increased in several private universities with national reputations.

Administrators in prestigious universities, perhaps concerned about the radical increase in Asian American students, have taken measures to lessen the increase. Asian American students, faculty members, and community leaders charge that these elite universities used quotas to limit the enrollment of Asian American applicants. Recent internal and external investigations suggest that these universities discriminated against Asian American students in granting admission. This is a controversial issue. . . .

Whether or not elite universities discriminated against Asian American students is a complicated issue that cannot be deciphered by statistical facts alone. As Takagi (1990) nicely analyzed, participants in the admissions controversy interpreted the same facts in different ways to justify their claims and counterclaims. In admissions policy, UC Berkeley and other universities combine strict academic criteria with supplemental criteria such as personal essays, extracurricular activities, and extra European foreign language courses. Asian American organizations argue that using supplemental criteria discriminates against Asian American students, who are generally disadvantaged in these areas. However, university officials justify the supplementary criteria in the name of student body *diversity.* That is, they claim that the supplemental criteria add diversity to the class by admitting students with more attributes than good grades and high test scores.

Conservative white politicians have used the Asian American student admissions controversy to attack affirmative action. They argue that elite universities use discriminatory quotas against Asian American students to create a floor for underrepresented black and Hispanic students. They suggest that abolishing affirmative action policies in admissions would eliminate discrimination against Asian American students. However, Asian American leaders object to the pairing of Asian American admissions with an attack on affirmative action. They argue that because Asian American students do not compete with black or Hispanic students, their admission is a separate issue from affirmative action.

When Jewish students in Ivy League schools increased in the first half of the 20th century, Jewish applicants encountered restrictive admission measures. Asian American students will continue to increase in major universities in the future. To lessen the increasing proportion of Asian American students, more restrictive measures may be taken in colleges and universities. However, any such restrictive measure is likely to meet a strong Pan-Asian opposition. If university officials attempt to use measures to curb the increase in Asian American students, it will be interesting to see what arguments they will use and how Asian American organizations will challenge their arguments.

ANTI-ASIAN VIOLENCE

Minority members in the United States are often subject to "hate crimes" or "bias crimes"—crimes motivated by animosity toward victims because of their race, religion, sexual orientation, or national origin. In the 1980s, civil rights laws and ordinances were passed to protect minority citizens. Nevertheless, there is evidence that hate crimes against Asian Americans have increased since the early 1980s. The U.S. Commission on Civil Rights monitors and collects data on the violations of minority rights. It regularly releases reports on cases of discrimination and violence against minority members. The reports on anti-Asian discrimination and violence released by the agency in 1986 and 1992 both concluded that anti-Asian violence is on the rise. Reports released by Los Angeles County in 1990 and 1991 also indicate that hate crimes against people of Asian ancestry have recently increased. Because the Hate Crimes Statistics Act enacted in 1990 requires the U.S. Attorney General to collect and report data on hate crimes, more accurate information on hate crimes against Asian Americans will be available in the future.

Several factors have contributed to the rise in hate crimes against Asian Americans. First of all, the great increase in the Asian American population has contributed to the rise in anti-Asian crimes. As previously noted, Asian Americans currently constitute a large proportion of the population in many cities. The increase in the Asian American population simply increases the likelihood that more Asian Americans will interact with members of non-Asian groups, and thus more of them will be targets of hate crimes. Moreover, the increase in Asian immigrants with language barriers and different customs is likely to increase the prejudice against Asian Americans.

Second, economic factors play an important role in the increase of anti-Asian violence. The economic recession that began in the mid-1970s coincided with the influx of Asian immigrants. Many Americans, both black and white, feel that new Asian immigrants took over their jobs and businesses, although research shows that this is not the case. Many Korean immigrants established businesses in black inner-city neighborhoods as living conditions of the black underclass became increasingly worse. Korean merchants all over the country have been targets of black hostility in the form of physical assault, boycott, arson, murder, and press attack. Black hostility toward Korean merchants culminated during the Los Angeles race riots in the spring of 1992, when more than 2,000 Korean-owned stores were burned and/or looted. Undoubtedly, black people's perception that Korean immigrants economically exploit them is mainly responsible for black hostility toward Koreans.

Another economic factor influencing the recent rise in anti-Asian violence cases is the trade deficit between the United States and Japan and the general perception that Japanese imports cause economic problems in the United States. Vincent Chin, a Chinese American, was murdered in 1982 by two white auto workers who, mistaking him for a Japanese, sought a scapegoat for their economic problems. As the U.S. economic situation further deteriorated in 1991, U.S. media and high-ranking politicians blamed the Japanese for the trade imbalance. The high unemployment rate and the political controversy over trade deficits heightened anti-Japanese sentiments all over the country. Recent Japan bashing culminated in the murder of a Japanese businessman in his home in Ventura County, California, in February 1992. Two weeks before he was stabbed to death, he was threatened by two white young men, who blamed Japan for causing economic problems in the United States.

Closely related to the economic factors in anti-Asian violence is the success image of Asian Americans. As previously discussed, both the U.S. media and scholars depict Asian Americans as "successful model minorities," which has negative effects on the interests of Asian Americans. The success image can heighten the resentment toward Asian American academic and economic success and in turn increase hate crimes against them. Many white Americans, particularly those in the lower tiers of the socioeconomic hierarchy, are jealous and resentful of Asian Americans' success. Out of their status anxiety, they believe that Asian Americans belong to an "inferior race." Asian Americans' success image only strengthens their status anxiety.

REFERENCES

Choi, M. (1988). *Race, gender, and eyeglasses: Teachers' perceptions of Asian, Black, and White students.* Paper submitted to Westinghouse Science Talent Search, Stuyvesant High School, New York City.

Crystal, D. (1989). Asian Americans and the myth of the model minority. *Social Casework, 70,* 405–413.

Glenn, E. N. (1980). The dialectics of wage work: Japanese-American women and domestic service, 1905–1940. *Feminist Studies, 6,* 432–471.

Glenn, E. N. (1983). Split household, small producer and dual wage earner: An analysis of Chinese American family strategies. *Journal of Marriage and the Family, 45,* 35–46.

Glenn, E. N. (1986). *Issei, Nisei, war bride: Three generations of Japanese American women in domestic service.* Philadelphia: Temple University Press.

Hu, A. (1989). Asian Americans: Model or double minority? *Amerasia Journal, 15*(1), 243–257.

Hurh, W. M., & Kim, K. C. (1982). Race relations paradigm and Korean-American research: A sociology of knowledge perspective. In Eui-Young Yu, E. Phillips, & Eun Sik Yang (Eds.), *Koreans in Los Angeles: Prospects and promises* (pp. 219–246). Los Angeles: Center for Korean and Korean-American Studies, California State University.

Ichioka, Y. (1988). *The Issei: The world of the first generation Japanese immigrants, 1885–1924.* New York: Free Press.

Kibria, N. (1993). *Family tightrope: The changing lives of Vietnamese Americans.* Princeton, NJ: Princeton University Press.

Kwong, P. (1987). *The new Chinatown.* New York: Noonsday.

Light, I. (1972). *Ethnic enterprise in North America: Business and welfare among Chinese, Japanese, and Blacks.* Berkeley: University of California Press.

Light, I., & Wong, C. C. (1975). Protest or work: Dilemmas of the tourist industry in American Chinatown. *American Journal of Sociology, 80,* 1342–1368.

Miyamoto, S. F. (1939). Social solidarity among the Japanese in Seattle. *Publications in the Social Sciences, 11*(21). Seattle: University of Washington.

Nakanishi, D. T. (1985–1986). Asian American politics: An agenda for research. *Amerasia Journal, 12*(2), 1–27.

Takagi, D. Y. (1990). From discrimination to affirmative action: Facts in the Asian American admissions controversy. *Social Problems, 37,* 578–592.

Tang, J. (1993). The career attainment of Caucasian and Asian engineers. *Sociological Quarterly, 34,* 467–496.

Thompson, R. H. (1979). Ethnicity vs. class: An analysis of conflict in a North American Chinese community. *Ethnicity, 6,* 306–326.

Thompson, R. H. (1980). From kinship to class: A new model of urban overseas Chinese social organization. *Urban Anthropology, 9,* 265–293.

17

The Case for Affirmative Action

FRED L. PINCUS

Affirmative action programs are at the center of an intense controversy. Proponents argue that programs that take race and gender into account are necessary to promote genuine equal opportunity and more equal outcomes. Opponents, on the other hand, argue that programs utilizing quotas and "reverse discrimination" are unfair to white males.

This thirty-year-old debate raises complex legal, political, and philosophical issues concerning the role that government should play to promote equal opportunity. Most citizens in the 1990s would agree that the government, especially the federal government, should protect individual citizens from discrimination on the basis of their race, ethnicity, or gender. In a *New York Times*/CBS News poll, for example, 88 percent of blacks and 65 percent of whites agreed that it was "necessary to have laws to protect minorities against discrimination in hiring and promotion"(Verhovak 1997).

There is a widespread belief that employment and educational decisions should be based on meritocratic criteria; that is, decisions should be based on an "objective" assessment of an individual's skills, abilities, and motivation. An individual's race, ethnicity, gender, or religion should not matter. Fair decisions, the argument continues, are "color-blind" and "gender-blind."

There are questions, however, about how to ensure that employers, educators, and public officials act in a meritocratic manner. There are even more questions about what to do if meritocratic policies do not result in equal outcomes. Should the government provide equal opportunity, or should it ensure equal outcomes? Finally, some people are even questioning the adequacy of the concept of meritocratic standards. Are they clear? Appropriate? Objective?

I define affirmative action as those policies intended to achieve race and gender equality that go beyond meritocratic decisionmaking by taking race and gender into account. In this chapter, I describe and analyze two policies in some detail: (1) goals and timetables administered by the Office of Federal Contract Compliance Programs and (2)court-ordered hiring and promotion quotas. Due to limitations of space, I cover the issues of college admissions and minority-owned business set-asides more briefly. I emphasize the racial aspects of affirmative action and discuss gender in less detail.

AFFIRMATIVE ACTION PROCEDURES ADMINISTERED BY THE OFFICE OF FEDERAL CONTRACT COMPLIANCE PROGRAMS

The only federal program legally called "affirmative action" is based on Executive Order 11246 issued by President Lyndon B. Johnson in 1965. Guidelines to implement this program were first issued in 1968 and revised in 1971.[1] The Office of Federal Contract Compliance Programs (OFCCP) is the agency that administers affirmative action guidelines. Since most discussions of affirmative action ignore these guidelines, I want to discuss them in some detail.

Federal contractors and subcontractors, excluding those in construction, who have fifty or more employees *and* a federal contract of $50,000 or more are required to develop an affirmative action plan within 120 days of receiving a contract. Failure to develop and implement an affirmative action plan could result in a contractor being debarred, that is, losing the current contract and being declared ineligible to receive additional contracts.

Contractors must first conduct a *utilization study* of their employees. Basically, they must count the number of employees in each department and in each occupational category and identify women and minority employees. The employer must be able to make the following types of statements: "In the maintenance department, X percent of skilled blue-collar workers are black" or "In the sales department, Y percent of the managers are Hispanic."

Next, the employer must determine the percentage of minorities and women who are in the "availability pool," that is, those who are *qualified* and potentially available for the job. This is a complex issue and requires some explanation.

For most clerical, sales, blue-collar, and service jobs, the availability pool is the labor force in the immediate geographical area of the employer. For less-skilled jobs, the availability is calculated as the percentage of minorities or women in the surrounding labor force. If the labor force is 10 percent Asian, for example, the availability of Asian clerical workers would be 10 percent. In more-skilled jobs, such as carpentry, the availability would be the percentage of minority workers employed in that occupation. The surrounding labor force may be 15 percent black, but the availability of black carpenters may only be 5 percent.

For professional and managerial jobs, however, the availability may well be statewide or even nationwide. For social workers, for example, the Hispanic availability might be defined as the percentage of Hispanics getting social work degrees in the entire state in the last five years. For college faculty, on the other hand, the availability of female sociologists might be the percentage of Ph.D.'s in sociology granted to women in the past five years in the entire country.

There are pages of regulations specifying how these figures are to be calculated. The important point here is that the availability pool is an estimate of the percentage of *qualified* minority and female workers in a particular job category.

Employers must then compare the distribution of minority or female employees in a specific job category in a specific department to the minority and female distribution in the availability pool. If the actual employment is equal to or greater than the availability (e.g., the availability of women accountants is 20 percent and 20 percent of the accountants actually employed are female), the employer is "in compliance." If, on the other hand, the actual employment distribution is below the availability figure (e.g., only 10 percent of the accountants are female), the employer is "underutilized." The employer must follow this same procedure for each job category in each department.

If a contractor is underutilized, a set of goals and timetables must be included in the affirmative action plan. The goal is to hire enough qualified female or minority employees to reach the percentage distribution stated in the availability pool. In the above example, the contractor tries to hire enough qualified female accountants so that 20 percent of all accountants are female. The timetable must be reasonable considering the conditions of that contractor. Employers with high turnovers might be able to reach the goal in a few months, whereas one with low turnover might take a few years.

Next, the contractor must specify procedures to achieve the goal. For the most part, this means trying to "expand the availability pool." This would include designing advertisements containing a statement like "Equal Opportunity Employer; Women and Minorities Encouraged to Apply." It would also include taking out advertisements targeted at women and minorities, sending letters to well-known women and minorities asking for referrals, sending letters to schools who train large numbers of *qualified* women and minorities, and making recruiting trips to conferences that might be attended by women and minorities.

After the contractor designates an employee as the affirmative action representative who oversees this process, the affirmative action plan is then complete. The contractor does *not* have to submit the plan to the OFCCP for approval; the plan must simply be kept on file in the contractor's office. However, the contractor is expected to make a "good faith effort" to implement the plan. This is quite different from the expectation that is associated with court-imposed hiring quotas discussed in the next section.

What happens if the contractor fails to meet the goal specified in the plan? Suppose the contractor had a goal to hire one black administrator but actually hired one white male. Does the contractor face the loss of the federal contract?

Probably not. First of all, no one but the employer is likely to know that the goal was not met. More importantly, the contractor was required only to make a good faith effort to achieve the goal, not to actually succeed. In the unlikely event that the employer was ever investigated by the OFCCP, all the contractor would have to do is show that he or she followed the procedures to encourage women and minorities to apply for the position. If the contractor can demonstrate that the white male who applied for the administrative position was more qualified than the black and female applicants, there is no problem. Affirmative action guidelines *require* meritocratic hiring. Given the relatively mild nature of these regulations, one can make a strong argument that they do not constitute even a moderate form of preferential treatment.

These affirmative action regulations involve a certain amount of effort and cost on the part of federal contractors. But they do not force contractors to hire unqualified people, nor do they permit reverse discrimination. All that contractors have to do is be able to justify why their employment levels are below the percentages in the availability pool. Some contractors, however, may pressure their personnel officers to hire unqualified underutilized minorities to avoid problems with OFCCP officials. It is difficult to determine how extensive this practice is.

Construction contractors are also required to establish goals and timetables. However, they are not required to have full affirmative action plans on file because they do not have the same kind of stable labor force as a manufacturer might have. Many construction contractors hire different people from one job to the next.

The OFCCP does conduct "compliance reviews" of certain contractors who are suspected of not fully complying with guidelines. A compliance officer spends about three weeks conducting one of these reviews. In 1996, the OFCCP conducted 3,476 compliance reviews, a 46 percent decline from the 6,232 reviews conducted in 1989. In two-thirds of these reviews, the contractor agreed to change some aspect of the affirmative action plan to bring it into compliance. This decline in compliance reviews is due, in part, to the 17 percent decline in staff between 1992 and 1997 (U.S. Dept. of Labor 1997).

Although this may seem like a large number of reviews, there were 192,500 contractors that fell under OFCCP regulations in 1995 (Wilcher 1995). At the rate of 3,476 reviews each year, it would take the OFCCP fifty-six years to review all contractors even once. Consequently, contractors do not really have to worry very much about being reviewed.

After the review, if the compliance officer and the contractor cannot reach an agreement, there are several levels of appeal available to the contractor. Recalcitrant contractors can ultimately be debarred; that is, they can lose their existing contracts and be declared ineligible to receive future contracts. However, this is extremely rare. According to the OFCCP, only forty contractors have been debarred since 1972.[2] These forty companies account for a tiny fraction of the hundreds of thousands of companies that have been government contractors since 1972. Twenty-five of the companies were declared ineligible during the 1972–1980 period, which covered the Nixon, Ford, and Carter administrations. Four were declared ineligible during the Reagan years, three during the Bush years, and eight during the Clinton years.

Data are available for thirty-two of the forty companies. The companies range in size from the Hesse Envelope Co. of Dallas, Texas, which employed 120 people, to major multinational corporations such as Firestone, Uniroyal, and Prudential Insurance. Fourteen of the contractors are in manufacturing, five in construction, three in food production, and two in financial services. The remaining eight are in individual or unknown industries.

What does a government contractor have to do to be debarred? Detailed information about the debarments was hard to come by, although I was able to get some limited data on twelve of them (Pincus 1993). Half of the contractors were debarred for flagrantly defying the OFCCP by refusing to even develop affirmative action plans and/or refusing to submit required statistical information about their employee records. Most of the rest refused to modify their plans sufficiently to comply with OFCCP guidelines or failed to make good faith efforts to meet their hiring goals. Only one contractor—Uniroyal—was debarred for failing to rectify discriminatory hiring patterns.

The reality is that the federal affirmative action regulations that are administered by the OFCCP do not put a great deal of pressure on federal contractors to increase their hiring of women and minority workers. If a contractor is willing to be even the least bit flexible, the chances are good that the OFCCP will sign off on their affirmative action plans. Even after being debarred, companies can be reinstated if they make the necessary changes. In fact, the median period of debarment for the thirty-two contractors was only eight months.

There is some evidence suggesting that these affirmative action policies had the intended effect of increasing the economic well-being of minority and female workers. Looking at national employment data since the 1960s, there has been a modest increase in the percentage of women and minorities in a variety of occupations that had been the nearly exclusive domains of white males.

Natalie Sokoloff (1992), for example, examined changes in the race/gender composition of fifty male-dominated professions between 1960 and 1980. The percentage of black males in these professions increased from 1.5 percent in 1960 to 2.7 percent in 1980. During the same period, black females in the male-dominated professions increased from 0.2 percent to 1.4 percent. White females increased from 6.2 percent to 18.1 percent.

In spite of this progress, the race and gender gaps are still substantial. In 1990, for example, white males still accounted for 59 percent of computer systems analysts, 65 percent of physicians, 71 percent of lawyers, and 79 percent of engineers (U.S. Bureau of the Census 1992).

The key question is whether these gains are due to affirmative action or to other factors. For example, the numerous federal programs intended to prevent employment discrimination (e.g., the Civil Rights Act of 1964) may have led to increased minority hiring.

In addition, structural changes in the labor force may have influenced these employment gains. For example, since professional, managerial, and technical jobs have been expanding at faster *rates* than other job categories, there is increased space for women and minorities to occupy those jobs. In addition, the increased educational attainment of women and minority workers has enabled more of them to qualify for these high-level jobs than in the past. Although it is likely that affirmative action has some positive impact, it is impossible to separate out the effects of these other factors.

Another way to address the question is to compare the race and sex employment distributions in firms that are covered by affirmative action regulations with comparable firms that are not covered. Presumably, if the employment of minorities and women in "covered" firms is growing faster than in "noncovered" firms, one can attribute much of the growth to affirmative action.

The results of the studies that have addressed this question on a national level are reasonably consistent: Blacks, both males and females, have shown faster rates of employment growth in covered firms than in noncovered firms. This is especially true in firms that have undergone compliance reviews (Donohue and Heckman 1991). The rate of employment of white women has also increased faster in covered than in noncovered firms, although compliance reviews do not have positive effects on their employment growth (Leonard 1986; Smith and Welch 1984). Firms with the biggest goals show the largest growth in minority employment. These findings, of course, are consistent with the view that affirmative action promotes minority and female employment.

However other evidence on the effects of affirmative action is inconclusive. For example, the available studies do not show consistent declines in black-white and male-female wage gaps in covered firms compared with noncovered firms. Similarly, there is no consistent evidence that blacks and women in covered firms have higher status jobs than in noncovered firms.

Critics (Beller 1978) have responded that it is not enough to show growth of minority employment in covered firms since employment may have dropped in noncovered firms. If this were true, the overall effect of affirmative action could be zero. Up to this point, however, there are no data to support this assertion. O'Neill and O'Neill (1992) argue that since most of the gains discussed above occurred prior to the time that the OFCCP began to enforce affirmative action, the gains may not be due to affirmative action. Clearly more research is needed to disentangle all of the variables that are involved. The best that can be said is that the available data suggest that affirmative action may have a modest but positive effect on increasing minority employment.

QUOTAS IN HIRING AND PROMOTION

The most controversial of all affirmative action policies are "quotas," that is, policies that reserve a certain number of positions for qualified minority or female candidates. Quotas specify a hiring or promotion *floor* designating a minimum number of women or minorities must be hired or promoted. (This is different from the historical use of anti-Semitic quotas as a *ceiling,* which specified that only a certain number of Jews could be hired.)

Quotas are highly unpopular among white Americans, although the degree of disapproval varies greatly by who the beneficiary is supposed to be and also by how the question is phrased. In 1995, for example, a Gallup Poll asked a national sample its opinions about affirmative action programs "designed to give preferential treatment to [women/minorities] in such areas as getting jobs and promotions, obtaining contracts, and being admitted to schools." Among whites, 61 percent disapproved of programs for minorities, while only 36 percent approved. On the other hand, whites were almost evenly split on affirmative action programs for women, with 49 percent disapproving and 46 percent approving. In both cases, most of those who approved of the programs wanted preferential treatment *without* quotas. If the phrase "to make up for past discrimination" is added to the question, the disapproval rate increases dramatically.

Responding to the same questions, people of color were strongly supportive of affirmative action. Sixty-six percent approved of affirmative action for minorities and 78 percent approved of it for women. Like whites, the majority of the people of color who approved of these programs wanted to implement them without quotas. (For a more detailed discussion, see Pincus [1998] and Steeh and Krysan [1996].)

Whatever one's views on quotas, however, one thing is clear: *Quotas and goals are not the same.* First, especially in court-imposed quotas, the employer or school must hire a minority or female for that position, under penalty of law. If no qualified minority or woman is found, either the position must remain empty or the employer must seek special permission to hire a white male. In the case of goals, in contrast to quotas, the employer must merely make a good-faith effort to hire a qualified minority or woman; if none is found, there are no legal consequences, and a white or male may be hired.

Second, in a quota situation, a white male with superior work experience or credentials could be passed over in favor of a qualified but less experienced minority or female applicant. For goals, a more qualified white male must be hired over a less-qualified minority or female applicant since the final hiring must be meritocratic.

Before a quota can be imposed by a court, a group of minority or female employees generally sues an employer for discrimination. For private employers, the suit is generally handled by the Equal Employment Opportunity Commission (EEOC). For public agencies, the suit is handled by the Civil Rights Division of the Justice Department. A disproportionate number of cases of public employers involve police and fire departments.

Sometimes, the government and the employer enter into a consent decree, which is a legal agreement, approved by a judge, that contains a quota system of hiring and/or promotion. In the early 1980s, there were at least fifty-one consent decrees involving public employers in effect. The quotas, for example, might require the hiring of one black for every white until the percentage of black employees reaches a certain percentage, which generally corresponds to the availability pool.

Even under quotas, employers are not forced to hire unqualified people. Generally, the employee has to qualify on the basis of some criteria set by the employer such as an educational credential, a minimum score on a test, or a minimum level of experience. Employees who do not meet these criteria cannot be considered for the position. All those who do meet the criteria are seen as being qualified and, hence, able to carry out the duties of the position.

Next in the process of a quota system, the qualified whites are ranked from "most qualified" to "least qualified" in terms of the criteria. The same is done for the qualified minorities. If only ten people can be hired or promoted and there is a 50–50 quota, then the top five whites and the top five minorities are chosen. Even though all of the selected minorities are qualified, it is possible that some of them may be less qualified than some of the whites who were not chosen. If there were only four qualified blacks on the list, the remaining position would either go unfilled or would go to the sixth white candidate.

There is a common belief, especially among whites, that quotas are widespread across the country and that any minority male and almost any female can get a job as long as they are breathing. White males, on the other hand, are seen to be at a disadvantage, no matter how qualified they are.

Government statistics demonstrate, however, that whites still have lower unemployment rates than blacks and Hispanics, even at the same level of education. The main exception is young college graduates, among whom the black and white unemployment rates were equal in 1996. Comparable Hispanics still had higher unemployment rates (U.S. Dept. of Labor 1996).

In fact, court-imposed quotas are few and far between. It is generally illegal for an employer to voluntarily adopt a quota hiring system without getting court approval. Courts impose quotas only when there is a long history of explicit discrimination and when the employer fails to take corrective action; that is, quotas are generally seen as policies of last resort.

Hiring and promotion quotas were declared constitutional by the U.S. Supreme Court in 1987, in spite of the fierce opposition of the administration of former president Ronald Reagan. Clarence Thomas, now a justice on the U.S. Supreme Court, joined the administration's opposition to affirmative action while he served as the head of the Equal Employment Opportunity Commission during the late 1980s.

In the landmark 1987 *U.S. v. Paradise* decision, which involved the Alabama State Police, the court outlined the criteria that must be present for a quota to be constitutional.

1. The attempt to remedy explicit past discrimination provides a compelling government interest.
2. Some form of quota system is the only way to achieve the goal of ending discrimination.
3. The program is narrowly tailored in terms of specific jobs in specific agencies.
4. The program is flexible, so, for example, whites could be hired if there were no qualified minorities.
5. The program is temporary; it exists for a certain period of time or until a certain percentage of employees are minority.
6. The program is fair to whites, who are not to be totally excluded from a position but whose chances are simply reduced.

The Court has also ruled that employers and schools can voluntarily decide to consider race and gender as one of many factors in hiring (*Regents of the University of California v. Bakke*, 1978, and *Johnson v. Transportation Agency of Santa Clara County*, 1987). This is not considered to be a quota since positions are not reserved for women or minorities. Race or gender can be *a* factor along with education, test scores, work experience, and so forth.

The 1996 *Hopwood v. Texas* decision suggests that the court may be reconsidering its stand on race as one of many factors (see below for details). During the same year, California voters approved Proposition 209, which banned the use of race and gender in employment decisions made by public employees.

Seniority presents another controversial issue in quota arrangements since promotions are often awarded on that basis. Since minorities tend to be the last hired, they often have less seniority than whites. Some consent decrees have suggested separate seniority lists for blacks and whites. In this case, it is possible that all blacks selected for promotion because they are at the top of the black seniority list have lower seniority than a white candidate who was not selected. Is this an equitable policy?

On the one hand, this could be seen as unfair to white workers because it violates the seniority principle, which is a part of many contracts, both union and nonunion. However, if an employer has a history of discrimination against blacks, the principle of seniority itself would hurt black workers since they tend to have less seniority than whites and would be less likely to be promoted for a number of years. A separate black seniority list may be the only way to overcome the effects of past discrimination and give black workers a fair chance of being promoted. The Supreme Court has ruled that separate seniority lists for promotions are constitutional in consent decrees.

Seniority presents another dilemma when it comes to layoffs. In many contracts, layoffs are done on a "last hired—first fired" basis. In this case, the effects of a quota consent decree in hiring can be reversed by seniority-based firings. Although some have suggested a quota system in layoffs to protect recently hired blacks, the U.S. Supreme Court has declared this unconstitutional (*Firefighters Local Union No. 1794 v. Stotts*, 1984). Quotas can only be used in hiring and promotions.

Another highly publicized case concerned layoffs when the two candidates were equal in both seniority and merit. Two Piscataway, New Jersey, schoolteachers, one black and one white, were judged by the school board to be equal in merit and had been hired on the same day. Faced with the need to lay off one teacher, the board laid off the white teacher to promote diversity since the school had never before employed a black teacher in the business department. The white teacher sued and won the case in two lower courts. Before the case could be decided by the Supreme Court, civil rights organizations agreed to an out-of-court settlement, fearing that the more conservative court would use this case to abolish all affirmative action.

Quotas do work to increase minority and female employment in specific firms. A study of police departments around the country, for example, confirms the view that quotas support hiring of policewomen (Warner and Steel 1989). Departments with no affirmative action plans or with voluntary plans were more likely to show a below-average utilization of women than departments with court-ordered plans or consent decrees.

ADMISSION TO HIGHER EDUCATION

The underrepresentation of blacks, Hispanics, and Native Americans in higher education has been a major national issue for four decades. Since the late 1970s, colleges and universities around the country have used the "race as one of many factors" principle that was articulated in the 1978 *Bakke* decision to help diversify their campuses. Although race cannot be considered as the *only* factor, it can be considered along with other factors, such as economic disadvantage, extracurricular activities, parents' alumni status, and so forth. This principle was used both at the undergraduate level and in graduate and professional schools.

Several developments during the mid-1990s led to restrictions on the use of this principle. In 1995, the regents of the University of California voted to ban the use of race in admission and hiring. The following year, voters approved Proposition 209, which banned the use of race in all public institutions throughout the state. The U.S. Supreme Court has declined to rule on a legal challenge to Proposition 209.

Similar propositions are under consideration in a number of other states, and time will tell whether California is in the vanguard of anti–affirmative action sentiment. In 1997, however, voters in Houston rejected a local ballot measure that would have outlawed affirmative action in that city.

Also in 1996, the U.S. Appeals Court for the Fifth Circuit issued the *Hopwood* decision, which involved the University of Texas law school. Four white students sued the university on the basis of reverse discrimination, alleging that they were passed over for admission while blacks and Hispanics with lower scores were admitted. The court held that the "race as one of many factors" principle was unconstitutional. Since the U.S. Supreme Court refused to rule on the case, none of the institutions in the Fifth Circuit (Texas, Mississippi, and Louisiana) can use the *Bakke* principle, whereas the rest of the country can.

The impact of these decisions was immediate. Black first-year enrollment at the University of Texas at Austin law school dropped from thirty-one in 1996 to four in 1997. Hispanic enrollment dropped from forty-eight to twenty-six. Similar patterns occurred at most other law schools and medical schools in the state. The patterns in the enrollment of first-time undergraduates across the state was more mixed (Campbell 1997). A similar drop in black and Hispanic enrollment took place at the law schools of the University of California at Berkeley and at UCLA.

There is some evidence that *Hopwood* and Proposition 209 may be affecting medical schools as well. The Association of American Medical Colleges reported an 11 percent decline in the number of black, Hispanic and Native American students who applied to medical schools around the country between 1996 and 1997. The white rate dropped only 8.7 percent and the Asian rate dropped 4.7 percent. In the four states where affirmative action in admissions is no longer permissible, there was a 17 percent decline in minority applications (Campbell 1997).

A second policy to increase minority enrollment in higher education has also come under fire. Some states and many individual colleges, both public and private, had established special scholarships for minority students; that is, whites could not even apply for them. According to the American Council on Education, in the late 1980s less than 3 percent of minority students received scholarships specially designated for minorities. This accounted for 2 percent of all aid to college students (DeWitt 1991).

In 1994, however, the U.S. Appeals Court for the Fourth Circuit ruled that these scholarships were unconstitutional. The U.S. Supreme Court declined to rule on the case. Many schools in Maryland and Virginia have opened these scholarships to nonminority students, and many others are reconsidering their policies on minority scholarships (Lederman 1996).

BUSINESS SET-ASIDES

During the late 1960s, the federal, state, and local governments began to develop programs in which a small percentage of government contracts would be set aside for minority contractors. In part, this was a reaction to pressure for equal opportunity from the minority business community. In addition, conservative politicians saw this as a way to strengthen minority businessmen, who, presumably, would be more conservative than militant civil rights activists. Many observers argue that these set-aside programs were a major reason for the expansion of minority-owned businesses in the 1970s and 1980s (Bates 1993).

In spite of the set-aside programs, minority businesses remained highly underrepresented among government contractors. In 1995, for example, they received only 5.5 percent of government contracts (Stout and Rodriguez 1997). Nevertheless, white businessmen began to bring a variety of lawsuits charging racial discrimination. In the 1989 *Crosen* decision, the U.S. Supreme Court severely restricted the ability of state and local governments to provide set-aside programs. The Court did say, however, the federal set-aside programs could continue. In 1995, the Court restricted federal set-aside programs in the *Aderand* decision. Now set-aside programs are constitutional only if discrimination can be proved, if set-aside programs are the only way to overcome discrimination, and if the program is time-limited. This is another example of how a more conservative Supreme Court is restricting affirmative action.

SUPPORT AFFIRMATIVE ACTION

Affirmative action is an essential weapon in the struggle for racial and gender equality in the United States. Given the history of racism and the current economic structure of the United States, minorities and women must be given special consideration if they are ever to achieve incomes and occupational statuses equal to those of white males.

Although racial discrimination is less of a problem than it was fifty years ago, it still exists. Meritocratic decisionmaking by employers is far from a reality. The goals and timetables that are administered by the Office of Federal Contract Compliance Programs help employers to set realistic hiring goals and establish criteria to monitor their progress. Employers who want to hire on meritocratic criteria find it easier to do so, whereas those who still prefer to discriminate find things more difficult.

Recalcitrant employers who insist upon discriminating can be punished by the federal government. The OFCCP can debar contractors who refuse to comply with affirmative action guidelines. The Justice Department and the EEOC can ask the courts to impose hiring and/or promotion quotas on employers who continue to discriminate. The federal government can also set aside a percentage of contracts and subcontracts for minority-owned businesses.

The U.S. Supreme Court has ruled these programs to be legal within certain guidelines. Empirical studies have shown that affirmative action programs probably have modest benefits for minorities in terms of providing more jobs and expanding their business opportunities, although more research is needed. Hence, affirmative action can help to mitigate the effects of continuing intentional racial discrimination.

Even if there were no intentional racial discrimination, however, some kind of affirmative action would still be needed to overcome the effects of past discrimination. Minority populations are disproportionately poor and, therefore, are less likely than whites to have the educational credentials and job training to qualify for many jobs. Given their history of past discrimination, minorities tend to have less seniority than whites. Hiring or promoting on the basis of the apparently neutral criteria of meritocracy and seniority leaves minorities at a disadvantage.

Carolyn Boyes-Watson (1994) argues that most Americans view the hiring process like the speed skating competitions in the Winter Olympics, in which there is a concrete universalistic criterion for success. In skating, the criterion would be speed, and in hiring it would be credentials.

However, Boyes-Watson argues that hiring more closely resembles figure skating, in which success requires a combination of skills, including strength, jumping, speed, grace, and creativity. Since different skaters have different combinations of skills, a group of judges must subjectively evaluate each skater. Employers, too, must balance many criteria: recommendation by a friend, relative, golf partner, or former classmate of employer; recommendation by another employee; political patronage; style of clothing; personality; and so forth. In other words, normal hiring procedures are far from objective.

Others argue that meritocratic criteria, in themselves, are not really objective but are intensely political. "For 'standards' do not fall from the sky. . . . What was not seen when such meritocratic standards were erected was that they incorporated then existing assumptions of what was meritorious . . . and that they thus institutionalized existing relations of power" (Lauter 1991: 214–216).

For example, the LSAT tests, which predict success in law school, were developed by whites during a period when blacks were not permitted to attend. During the past decade, there has been an intense debate over admissions standards.

> There is no neutral way to define "merit" or "qualifications" for legal study beyond a bare minimum of literacy skills. . . . The question of how to distribute the benefits of education, whether by limiting admission to those with a particular standardized test score or by practicing affirmative action, inevitably is political. The two possibilities simply would produce two different sets of lawyers and presumably two different professional cultures. But the choice between these alternatives cannot be predicated on the existing concepts of merit or qualification. (Peller 1991: B2)

A recent study also suggests that affirmative action students in medical schools turn out to be qualified doctors (Bonner 1997). A study at the University of California at Davis followed medical students admitted to the medical school between 1968 and 1987. Students who were admitted under regular criteria were compared with those who were admitted under "special circumstances." Most, but not all, of this latter group were minority students admitted under affirmative action. Investigators found that the two groups had similar graduation rates, similar completion rates for residency programs, similar evaluations from their residency supervisors, and were in similar medical practices. On the other hand, the special circumstance students had more trouble in first-year science classes, were less likely to graduate with honors, and were more likely to have to repeat their certification exams. In other words, the special circumstances students did what they had to do, even though they had more trouble doing it.

Simply ending discrimination is not enough to create genuine equal opportunity. The affirmative action programs discussed above are one way to deal with intentional discrimination, past and present, at both the institutional and individual levels.

Many of the problems faced by minority communities, of course, have nothing to do with intentional racial discrimination and cannot be solved by affirmative action. In fact, many of these problems are shared by the white working class.

Working people face the loss of jobs as employers move their plants in the search for cheaper labor, lower taxes, and less stringent environmental controls. Unions have come under attack from employers and the federal government and are less able to protect the jobs and living standards of their members. Government cutbacks have reduced both the quality and quantity of education, health care, welfare, housing, and other social services. Small businesses, regardless of the race of the owner, have high failure rates because they have trouble competing with the large multinational corporations, most of which are owned and controlled by wealthy white males.

Affirmative action cannot do anything about these. Only a multiracial working people's social movement, committed to race and sex equality, has the potential to turn the tide (see Part Seven). Affirmative action is simply one tool among many for combating present discrimination and the effects of past discrimination. For that, it should be strongly supported.

COMMENTS ON CRITICS

One major aspect of the conservative critique of affirmative action is that racial discrimination has been so significantly reduced that it is no longer a major barrier to blacks and other minorities. Policies such as affirmative action, the argument continues, are not necessary. An overwhelming majority of the white population accepts this viewpoint. In a 1997 poll, for example, 79 percent of whites believed that blacks in their community have as good a chance as whites to get a job for which they are qualified. Ninety-three percent believed that blacks in their community can get as good an education as whites (Gallup 1997). If discrimination is no longer seen as a problem, those who fail simply did not try hard enough (Kluegel and Smith 1986).

This book presents ample evidence that intentional racial discrimination is still a major problem and that white males are still the most privileged group, with the highest incomes and the best jobs. In addition, the cultural behavior of a group is shaped by the group's economic circumstances. An individual's motivation and self-discipline can be negatively affected if his or her racial group faces severe racial discrimination.

Conservative critics argue, further, that it is wrong to assume that the *absence* of historical discrimination would have resulted in a proportional representation of all racial/ethnic groups in the occupational distribution. We cannot know what would have happened in the absence of discrimination. It is irrational, they continue, to say that true equality of opportunity is present only when, for example, blacks make up 12 percent of managers or when Hispanics make up 9 percent of professionals.

Although it is true that it is impossible to determine what the occupational distribution would have been in the absence of discrimination (not to mention 200 years of slavery and genocide against Native Americans), we need some statistical guidelines to assess efforts to overcome the effects of past and continuing discrimination. Using statistical goals to move toward proportional representation, however mechanical it may appear, is not a bad place to start. If all discrimination is genuinely removed and disparities still exist, the guidelines can be reexamined.

It is also important to mention that the conservative argument against proportional representation does not apply to the concept of the "availability pool" in the affirmative action regulations administered by the OFCCP. Readers should recall that the availability pool is an estimate of the minority population that is *presently qualified* to do various jobs in a particular geographical region.

A third conservative criticism of affirmative action is that it costs individual corporations and the economy as a whole billions of dollars a year to comply with regulations (Beer 1987; Brimelow and Spencer 1993). This is said to hurt corporate profitability and, therefore, to reduce the competitiveness of U.S. corporations in the world economy.

Although the precise cost of affirmative action is unknown, spending money on *effective* policies to achieve racial equality is worthwhile. Historically, corporations have made billions from paying black workers lower wages than whites. Individual corporations can afford to spend thousands of dollars each year to make sure that minority and female workers have chances equal to white males. Perhaps highly paid executives, who are predominantly white males, could voluntarily take a few thousand dollars from their exorbitant salaries to fund their companies' affirmative action programs. Similarly, the federal government could build fewer high-priced weapons in order to fully fund the OFCCP.

Conservative critics also express concern about the effect of affirmative action on the loss of jobs for white male workers. Ten percent of white males report losing a job or promotion because of their race, whereas 13 percent report losses due to their sex (Morin and Warden 1995). This rate of perceived discrimination, which is probably exaggerated, is much lower than the 23 percent of women and the 44 percent of blacks who reported losses of jobs or promotions.

This is a difficult issue since it could easily be argued that most whites, as a group, have benefited from living in a racist society. However, some individual whites who are qualified for jobs and/or promotions are clearly hurt by affirmative action policies. Gertrude Ezorsky (1991), a supporter of affirmative action, has argued that such whites should receive financial compensation from the federal government since they have been forced to make sacrifices for the larger good.

Another conservative criticism is that affirmative action hurts successful minorities because there is always a cloud of doubt about their skills and qualifications (Carter 1991). Are they successful because of their own talents or because of affirmative action? This cloud is said to be perceived by both whites and minorities. I am not aware of any empirical studies of this question.

Although this cloud-of-doubt argument may be a problem, eliminating affirmative action is not the solution. Much of the cloud of doubt is due to racial prejudice. Successful minority individuals, especially blacks, have always been viewed with suspicion, even before affirmative action. Significantly, there has been little concern raised about the psychological well-being of the recipients, mostly white males, of other forms of preference. The children of alumni who get preference for college admission do not walk under any cloud. The relatives of bosses or the recipients of political patronage, both of whom have the inside track to certain jobs, are not troubled by the same doubts about their competence, particularly if they can show that they can do the job. Why single out minorities and females?

Consciousness-raising groups for white employees and support groups for black employees would go a long way toward creating an atmosphere that a given individual can succeed or fail on the basis of his or her own abilities. It is both unwise and unnecessary to eliminate affirmative action programs in order to strengthen the psychological well-being of successful black employees.

Criticisms of affirmative action do not come only from conservatives. Some liberal and Marxist critics have argued that race-specific policies such as affirmative action are undesirable because they tend to prevent the formation of multiracial political coalitions. What is needed, they argue, are universalistic policies that benefit everybody. Calls for a national public works program to provide more jobs for everyone, for example, would be preferable to demanding that blacks get preference for the few existing jobs.

What is really needed, in my judgment, is a combination of universalistic programs and affirmative action. Universalistic policies alone would still leave minorities at a disadvantage relative to whites. On the other hand, white support for affirmative action would send a signal to minorities that whites are genuinely interested in racial equality. This, in turn, would encourage minorities to join multiracial coalitions to fight for universalistic programs.

As long as race continues to be a dominant factor in American life, affirmative action will be a necessary tool in the struggle for racial equality.

NOTES

1. The following discussion is based on my review of federal affirmative action guidelines and on discussions with several OFCCP officials in 1992.

2. The following discussion of affirmative action violators is based on an annual list, "Companies Ineligible for Federal Contracts Under the Regulations of the Office of Federal Contract Compliance Programs," that is compiled by the OFCCP each year. See Pincus (1993) for full details.

REFERENCES

Bates, Timothy (1993) *Banking on Black Enterprise: The Potential of Emerging Firms for Revitalizing Urban Economies.* Washington, D.C.: Joint Center for Political and Economic Studies.

Beer, William R. (1987) "Resolute Ignorance: Social Science and Affirmative Action." *Society* (May-June): 63–69.

Beller, Andrea H. (1978) "The Economics of Enforcement of an Antidiscrimination Law: Title VII of the Civil Rights Act of 1964." *Journal of Law and Economics* 21 (2): 359–380.

Bonner, Ethan (1997) "Little Impact on Doctors' Careers Is Seen from Affirmative Action." *New York Times*, Oct. 8: A1, 22.

Boyes-Watson, Carolyn (1994) "False Dichotomies: Affirmative Action and Meritocratic Hiring in Academia." Paper presented at the 64th Annual Convention of the Eastern Sociological Society, Baltimore, MD, March 17–20.

Brimelow, Peter, and Leslie Spencer (1993) "When Quotas Replace Merit, Everybody Suffers." *Forbes*, Feb. 15: 80–102.

Campbell, Paulette Walker (1997) "Minority Applications to Medical School Drop in States Without Affirmative Action." *Chronicle of Higher Education,* Nov. 14: A46.

Carter, Steven L. (1991) *Reflections of an Affirmative Action Baby*. New York: Basic Books.

DeWitt, Karen. (1991) "Limits Proposed for Race-Based Scholarships." *New York Times*, Dec. 5: A26.

Donohue, John J., III, and James Heckman (1991) "Continuous Versus Episodic Change: The Impact of Civil Rights Policy on the Economic Status of Blacks." *Journal of Economic Literature* 29 (Dec.): 1603–1643.

Ezorsky, Gertrude (1991) *Racism and Justice: The Case for Affirmative Action*. Ithaca, NY: Cornell University Press.

Fisher, Anne B. (1985) "Businessmen Like to Hire by the Numbers." *Fortune*, Sept. 16: 23–29.

Gallup, George, Jr. (1997). *The 1997 Gallup Poll Social Audit on Black/White Relations*. Princeton: Gallup Organization.

Hugick, Larry (1991) "The 'Quotas' Issue: Advantage Bush." *Gallup Poll Monthly*, June: 32–35.

Kluegel, James R., and Eliot R. Smith (1986) *Beliefs About Inequality: Americans' Views of What Is and What Ought to Be*. New York: Aldine De Gruyer.

Lauter, Paul (1991) *Canons and Contexts*. New York: Oxford University Press.

Lederman, Douglas (1996) "The Impact of a Court Ruling Against Minority Scholarships: Two Years Later." *Chronicle of Higher Education*, Oct. 25: A38.

Leonard, Jonathan S. (1986) "What Was Affirmative Action?" *American Economic Review* 76 (May): 359–363.

Lloyd, Mark (1990) "Affirmative Action Victory." *Focus*, July: 3–4.

Morin, Richard, and Sharon Warden (1995) "Americans Vent Anger at Affirmative Action." *Washington Post*, Mar. 24: A1, A4.

O'Neill, Dave M., and June O'Neill (1992) "Affirmative Action in the Labor Market." *Annals of the American Academy of Political and Social Science* 523 (Sept.): 88–103.

Peller, Gary (1991) "Espousing a Positive Vision of Affirmative Action Policies." *Chronicle of Higher Education*, Dec. 18: B1–B2.

Pincus, Fred L. (1998) "Toward a Marxist View of Affirmative Action." *Critical Sociology*. Forthcoming.

______. (1993) "Enforcing Federal Affirmative Action Guidelines: Compliance Reviews and Debarment." *Journal of Intergroup Relations* 20 (Summer): 3–11.

Smith, James P., and Finis Welch (1984) "Affirmative Action and Labor Markets." *Journal of Labor Economics* 2 (Apr.): 269–301.

Sokoloff, Natalie J. (1992) *Black Women and White Women in the Professions*. New York: Routledge, Chapman and Hall.

Steeh, Charlotte, and Maria Krysan (1996) "Affirmative Action and the Public: 1970–1995." *Public Opinion Quarterly* 60: 128–158.

Stout, Hilary, and Eva M. Rodriguez (1997) "Government Contracts to Minority Firms Increase Despite Court's 1995 Curb on Affirmative Action." *Wall Street Journal*, May 7: A20.

U.S. Bureau of the Census (1992) *Detailed Occupation and Other Characteristics from the EEO File for the United States, 1990*. CP-S-1-1.

U.S. Department of Labor (1992) *Employment and Earnings*. Jan.

______. (1996) *Employment and Earnings*.

______. (1997) "Office of Federal Contract Compliance Programs (OFCCP) Quick Facts." Mimeo, Oct. 4.

Verhovak, Sam Howe (1997) "In Poll, Americans Reject Means but Not Ends of Racial Diversity." *New York Times*, Dec. 14: 1, 34.

Warner, Rebecca L., and Brent S. Steel (1989) "Affirmative Action in Times of Fiscal Stress and Changing Value Priorities: The Case of Women in Policing." *Public Personnel Management* 3 (Fall): 291–309.

Wilcher, Shirley J. (1995) "Statement of Shirley J. Wilcher, Deputy Assistant Secretary for Federal Contract Compliance, Employment Standards Division, U.S. Department of Labor, Before the House Committee on Economic and Educational Opportunities, Subcommittee on Employer-Employee Relations." Washington, D.C.: Office of Federal Contract Compliance Programs. June 21.

PART 4

Immigration

There have been several relatively distinct phases in the history of American immigration. These historical distinctions involved differences in the ethnic and racial composition of the people moving, differences in the sociological factors that impelled their movement, differences in their motives for migration and where they settled, and differences in the responses made to them by the resident populations. The dominant imagery of this country welcoming the newcomer was vital to maintaining the ideals of egalitarianism and, to some extent, the myth of representative government (see the essay by Howard Zinn in Part Seven). This imagery, along with that of economic opportunity, also served to attract people. Nevertheless, the resident populations, despite their own immigrant origins, have always been ambivalent to immigration while accepting of individual migrants. This ambivalence on open immigration has always been a part of American life. It is manifest today in concerns over new immigrants taking jobs from residents, costing taxpayers more money in public assistance, in conflicts over the likelihood of newcomers shifting the balance of political power away from established interests, and in an ambivalence about the value of providing political, religious, and other forms of sanctuary to those desiring to enter this country. These concerns of today are the same concerns that were expressed in the early nineteenth century in response to immigration. As a result, at times a given immigrant group would be welcomed, and at later times rejected; at times new restrictions would be placed on those who could enter, and at other times specific entrants were encouraged.

BRIEF HISTORY OF AMERICAN IMMIGRATION

At the time of the Revolution, the white American population was mainly English and Protestant in background. There were small representations of other groups, including German nationals, as well as Catholics and Jews. Figure P4.1 is a pie chart reprinted from the first census in 1790. It was clearly a different time and place.

Indians were not counted and were generally treated as subhumans to be eliminated as the colonists began a westward expansion. Blacks, who were mainly slaves, made up close to 20 percent of the colonial population. Like the Indians,

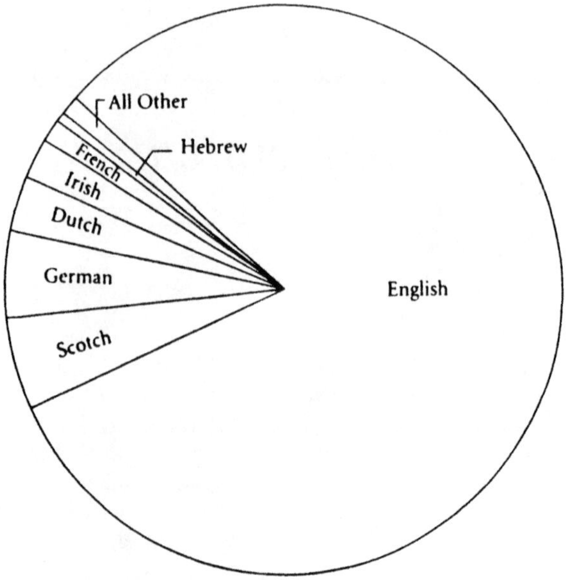

FIGURE P4.1 This pie chart appeared in the first U.S. census, conducted in 1790.

they were not counted or viewed as integral or assimilable or even desirable in this new country's settlement.

Whereas the post-Revolutionary phase of immigration set the stage for this new country to view itself as white, Anglo-Saxon, and Protestant, the pre–Civil War stage, 1815–1860, saw the rise of an ethnocentric ideology that foreshadowed the development of organized bigotry in the United States. This was the period of the rise of "nativist" third parties. The Native American Party became a national third party in 1840 and was succeeded by an even stronger organization in the 1850s.

The most prominent theme of this movement was the fear that the new foreign-born voters would wrest control of the political process and, because of their ignorance of American institutions, wreck the political system, if not the entire country. Labor competition also played a key element in the growth of this new bigotry. Possibly the most prominent theme, however, was the movement's anti-Catholicism. The growth of American Catholicism and the strong Irish Catholic inmigration reestablished earlier fears of a papal takeover of America. The number of Catholics in America had risen to from 35,000 in 1790 to 1.3 million fifty years later. Not only did the nativists fear that this country would fall into the hands of the Catholic hierarchy and its allies in the European monarchies, but they were fearful of the proliferating convents and monasteries as places of wickedness and vice. Although this may all seem hard to imagine, the lingering fear of the papal menace haunted even the presidential candidacy of John F. Kennedy in 1960.

The Civil War disrupted the nativist movement. In a new phase of immigration, from 1865 to 1890, approximately 11 million people arrived from mainly northern and western Europe, that is, from Great Britain, Germany, Scandinavia, and so on. In the following period, 1890 to 1930, the number of immigrants doubled, reaching 22 million. In this wave, migrants streamed from the countries of southern and eastern Europe. This was the migration from Austria, Bulgaria, Czechoslovakia, Finland, Greece, Hungary, Italy, Poland, Portugal, Romania, Spain, Turkey, the U.S.S.R., and Yugoslavia. Not only did these new migrants differ in their cultures and languages, they were substantially poorer and, unlike the preceding wave, began to settle in ethnic enclaves in the urban centers. This large inmigration was joined by the growth of a serious and powerful immigration restrictionist movement, a movement fueled by the sponsorship of political elites. Although it had started earlier with federal acts denying entry to Chinese and Japanese migrants, the opening of the century was accompanied by an increasing number of conditions to shut out people. Within the first two decades, Congress had ratified and established the precedence for screening people by health, social class, and political beliefs. The 1924 immigration act passed by Congress was openly designed to maintain the "racial preponderance [of] the basic strain on our people." A numerical limit was placed on annual immigration, and quotas were assigned to each national group in proportion to its representation in the existing population. By 1927, Congress established the basis of those quotas to be the United States' population of 1890. This was chosen as the baseline in order to limit the number of southern and eastern European migrants and to favor those from the north and west. World War II disrupted the rising bigotry, and the immigrant flow was reduced to a trickle of refugees and displaced persons.

Up until the start of World War II, these waves of semiskilled and unskilled immigrants were critical in this country's development. These newcomers were central to the building of American cities, to our westward expansion, and to providing the workforce for the growth of American industry.

Figure P4.2 displays the number of immigrants by census period. As the figure illustrates, the number of migrants increased following the end of World War II. A new pattern of immigration emerged in the 1980–1989 period, a pattern representing the second largest period of immigration in United States history. This new immigration reflects greater cultural diversity than in earlier periods. Mexican migrants were the largest group, followed by arrivals from the Philippines, China (the mainland, Hong Kong, and Taiwan), Korea, and Vietnam. Smaller but substantial numbers of Asian Indians and Dominicans arrived, followed in number by people from Jamaica, Cuba, Iran, Cambodia, the United Kingdom, Laos, the Arab countries, Canada, and Colombia. The foreign-born population of the United States at the end of 1990 was approximately 9 percent—considerably less than it had been in the late nineteenth and early twentieth centuries.

Another distinctive characteristic of this new phase of inmigration has been the concentration of settlement in a few states, mainly California and New York. These are followed by Texas, Florida, Illinois, and New Jersey. Almost three-quarters of all newcomers settled in these six states. The question of impact, obviously, has to be addressed separately by area of settlement. These areas have been affected disproportionately, and the rapid changes have intensified group tensions.

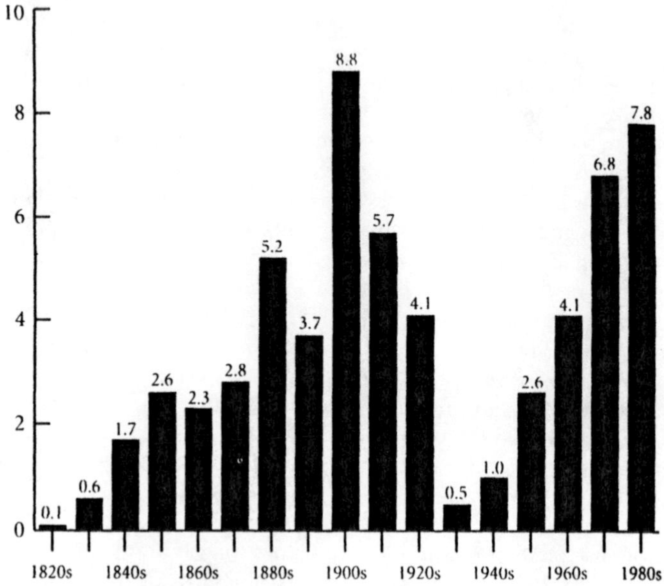

FIGURE P4.2 U.S. Immigration by Decade, 1821–1990 (in millions)

During the years after World War II, Congress enacted a series of immigration control bills reflecting a myriad of interests but essentially designed to codify political restrictions on who could enter this country. From the standpoint of intergroup tensions, the most significant of these bills were passed in 1986 and 1990. The Immigration Reform and Control Act of 1986 was intended to control the number of illegal immigrants and to rationalize immigration policy. It allowed for undocumented workers to legalize their status if they could prove continuous residence in the country since January 1, 1982, or before. At the same time, the bill sought to reduce employment opportunities for undocumented workers by subjecting employers to civil and criminal penalties for hiring them. However, the legislation has served mainly to increase discrimination against Hispanic workers without really reducing the flow of illegal entrants. The Immigration Act of 1990 was designed to favor entrants on the basis of their skills and education. People with the background needed by business and industry were to be given priority. Priority was also given to keeping families together, that is, to wives and husbands, children and parents, and siblings of newcomers. The result of this policy, however, has been to favor and increase the entry of western Europeans.

WHY DO PEOPLE MOVE AND WHAT HAPPENS WHEN THEY DO?

There are two facets of the question of why people move. First, there are the individual motivating factors. Second, there are those larger social factors that create these motives and figuratively push people to new destinations. Portes and Rumbaut (1990) identify four basic types of migrants that are independent of the immigrant's ethnicity.

The bulk of immigrants are *labor migrants.* They come to escape poverty and are attracted by the minimum wages of this country. *Professional migrants* are the well-educated elite who move to improve their socioeconomic status. This has recently been the case for immigrants from the Philippines, China, India, and Great Britain. *Entrepreneurial migrants* come with past experiences in business, often with access to capital and labor. They are more likely to settle in the ethnic enclaves, providing business services within the ethnic community. Current examples are Koreans, Cubans, and Chinese. Finally, there are the *refugees,* who are seeking asylum from the likelihood of political persecution and physical harm in their native country. Over the past thirty years these have included significant numbers of Laotians and Cambodians, Salvadorans and Guatemalans, and Iranians. International migration is a major and often traumatic episode in people's lives. The motivations to migrate are complex, and the myriad of decisions surrounding the move are highly stressful. Relatively few people do move, and many who do return to their homeland, often in disillusionment.

In her article in this section, Saskia Sassen writes that most countries with a large outmigration to the United States have a set of identifiable linkages to the United States, which, along with overpopulation, poverty, or unemployment, evokes migration. The thrust of her analysis is the identification of the nature of those linkages resulting from American investments in those countries. Among those identified are the disruption of traditional work structures, especially through the recruitment of young women, and the cultural identification with Americans as a consequence of working in American- or Western-managed businesses. Of course, for a migration flow to be practicable there have to be jobs for the newcomers. Sassen details how the rise of low-wage service sector jobs as well as downgraded manufacturing jobs in the United States fills this need. Thus, as manufacturing jobs have been shifted to less-developed countries, the effect in those countries is to promote emigration, while the growth of these new jobs in the United States has helped to absorb the new migrants.

Milton Gordon raises the question of how it is that new immigrants are assimilated into American society. He proposes that there are two basic models of assimilation: liberal pluralism and corporate pluralism. The difference between the two models rests on the degree to which new immigrant groups preserve their separate cultural practices and accommodate to the cultural practices of the new society. According to the liberal policy, multiculturalism is acceptable as long as minority groups do not demand state support or attempt to establish their own territory and language. The liberal model is basically assimilationist. Separate groups can retain their own cultural practices and identity as long as they also accept the dominant culture. Although it is expected that they will struggle politically for greater independence, that struggle must be contained within the operating rules of the state.

The corporate model depicts a substantial shift to a more pluralistic conception of the nation-state. Here some degree of multicultural separatism, including bilingualism and territorial exclusiveness, is accepted. The state is required to intervene actively in order to promote political and economic equality among the multiple ethnic groups seeking a discrete cultural—and legal—identity. The outstanding illustration of the corporate model is to be found in the political arrangements between Quebec and Canada.

Both models assume a central state government as well as an essentially stratified economic system. The liberal model is based on the acceptance of the existing stratification system. It views society as a meritocracy and does not question its economic system, although it requires equal opportunity and permits the state to intervene so that no group is totally oppressed. It is the role of the state managers to see that all group conflicts, whether class or ethnically based, are managed so as to maintain the order of the society. The corporate model adds a unique dimension. Economic and political equality are viewed as also being group characteristics. The role of the state is to assist each group in achieving parity. Theoretically, then, if the distribution of privilege, wealth, and power is the same in the minority society as it is in the majority society, then corporate pluralism has been achieved. The fact that both societies could have large numbers of poor people and great differences between the wealthy and the rest of the population is considered irrelevant to these models.

Beyond these models, economic and cultural differentials are generating considerable conflict. There is a general perception that immigrants are taking the jobs of native workers as well as competing for existing public and social services in the community. Consequently, the majority of Americans want to halt immigration, and they want also to declare English as the "official language."

Peter Brimelow, in the excerpt from his book, writes that an "ethnic and racial transformation" is taking place. As a consequence, American core values are seen as being threatened by the high immigration of so many diverse cultural groups. Brimelow views the new immigrant stream as less skilled than earlier streams, offering unneeded, unskilled labor power, providing no economic benefit to the society, while using health, education, and welfare services at the expense of the citizen taxpayers. For Brimelow, the United States has always "had a specific ethnic core. And that core has been white."

David Cole, in contrast, views Brimelow's position as the "New Know Nothingism" and presents a response to what he labels the five myths of immigration. Cole argues that the new immigrants, like their predecessors, are assimilating and that they pay more in taxes than they cost in benefits received.

Geoffrey Nunberg, in his essay "Lingo Gringo," focuses exclusively on the issue of learning the language. As the fulcrum of assimilation, language learning is critical. Nunberg reports that the majority of immigrant parents, in fact, want their children to learn English. Further, the writer refers to surveys of language usage indicating that perhaps as many as 97 percent are proficient in English. "English-only," he writes, "is an irrelevant provocation. It is a bad cure for an imaginary disease."

REFERENCES

Portes, Alejandro, and Ruben Rumbaut (1990) *Immigrant America: A Portrait.* Berkeley: University of California Press.

18

America's Immigration "Problem"

SASKIA SASSEN

Immigration has traditionally aroused strong passions in the United States. Although Americans like to profess pride in their history as "a nation of immigrants," each group of arrivals, once established, has fought to keep newcomers out. Over the past two centuries, each new wave of immigrants has encountered strenuous opposition from earlier arrivals, who have insisted that the country was already filled to capacity. (The single exception to this was the South's eagerness to import ever more slaves.) Similar efforts to shut out newcomers persist today. But those who would close the door to immigration are mistaken on two counts: not only do they underestimate the country's capacity to absorb more people, but they also fail to appreciate the political and economic forces that give rise to immigration in the first place.

U.S. policymakers and the public alike believe the causes of immigration are self-evident: people who migrate to the United States are driven to do so by poverty, economic stagnation, and overpopulation in their home countries. Since immigration is thought to result from unfavorable socioeconomic conditions in other countries, it is assumed to be unrelated to U.S. economic needs or broader international economic conditions. In this context, the decision on whether to take in immigrants comes to be seen primarily as a humanitarian matter; we admit immigrants by choice and out of generosity, not because we have any economic motive or political responsibility to do so. An effective immigration policy, by this reasoning, is one that selectively admits immigrants for such purposes as family reunification and refugee resettlement, while perhaps seeking to deter migration by promoting direct foreign investment, foreign aid, and democracy in the migrant-sending countries.

Although there are nuances of position, liberals and conservatives alike accept the prevailing wisdom on the causes of immigration and the best ways to regulate it. The only disagreement, in fact, is over how strictly we should limit immigration. Conservatives generally maintain that if immigration is not severely restricted, we will soon be overrun by impoverished masses from the Third World, although the demand for cheap agricultural labor at times tempers this position. Liberals tend to be more charitable, arguing that the United States, as the richest country in the world, can afford to be generous in offering a haven to the poor and oppressed. Advocates of a less restrictive policy also note the positive effects of immigration, such as the growth of cultural diversity and a renewed spirit of entrepreneurship.

Not surprisingly, U.S. immigration laws have reflected the dominant assumptions about the proper objectives of immigration policy. The last two major immigration reforms, passed in 1965 and 1986, have sought to control immigration through measures aimed at regulating who may enter legally and preventing illegal immigrants from crossing our borders. At the same time, the U.S. government has attempted to promote economic growth in the migrant-sending countries by encouraging direct foreign investment and export-oriented international development assistance, in the belief that rising economic opportunities in the developing world will deter emigration. Yet U.S. policies, no matter how carefully devised, have consistently failed to limit or regulate immigration in the intended way.

The 1965 amendment to the Immigration and Naturalization Act was meant to open up the United States to more immigration, but to do so in a way that would allow the government to control entries and reduce illegal immigration. It sought to eliminate the bias against non-Europeans that was built into earlier immigration law and to regulate the influx of immigrants by setting up a series of preference categories within a rather elaborate system of general quotas.[1] Under this system, preference was given to immediate relatives of U.S. citizens and, to a lesser extent, to immigrants possessing skills in short supply in the United States, such as nurses and nannies.

The 1965 law brought about major changes in immigration patterns, but not necessarily the intended ones. The emphasis on family reunification should have ensured that the bulk of new immigrants would come from countries that had already sent large numbers of immigrants to the United States—that is, primarily from Europe. But the dramatic rise in immigration after 1965 was primarily the result of an entirely new wave of migrations from the Caribbean Basin and South and Southeast Asia. The failure of U.S. policy was particularly evident in the rapid rise in the number of undocumented immigrants entering the country. Not only did the level of Mexican undocumented immigration increase sharply, but a whole series of new undocumented flows were initiated, mostly from the same countries that provided the new legal immigration.

The outcry over rising illegal immigration led to a series of congressional proposals that culminated in the 1986 Immigration Reform and Control Act. This law was intended to rationalize immigration policy and, in particular, to address the problem of illegal immigration. It features a limited regularization program that enables undocumented aliens to legalize their status if they can prove continuous residence in the United States since before January 1, 1982, among other eligibility criteria. A second provision of the law seeks to reduce the employment opportunities of undocumented workers through sanctions against employers who knowingly hire them. The third element is an extended guest-worker program designed to ensure a continuing abundant supply of low-wage workers for agriculture.

So far, the law's overall effectiveness has been limited. While some 1.8 million immigrants applied to regularize their status[2] (a fairly significant number, though less than expected), there is growing evidence that the employer sanctions program is resulting in discrimination against minority workers who are in fact U.S. citizens, as well as various abuses against undocumented workers. Meanwhile, illegal immigration has apparently continued to rise. Congressional efforts to correct the law's shortcomings have already begun. . . .

Yet even a modified version of the 1986 law has little chance of successfully regulating immigration for one simple reason: like earlier laws, it is based on a faulty understanding of the causes of immigration. By focusing narrowly on immigrants and on the immigration process itself, U.S. policymakers have ignored the broader international forces, many of them generated or at least encouraged by the United States, that have helped give rise to migration flows. . . .

THE NEW IMMIGRATION

Beginning in the late 1960s, immigration patterns to the United States began to change in several important ways. First, there was a significant rise in overall annual entry levels. From 297,000 in 1965, immigration levels increased to 373,000 in 1970, rose to 531,000 in 1980, and reached 602,000 in 1986. At the same time, there was a dramatic change in the regional composition of migration flows. As recently as 1960, more than two-thirds of all immigrants entering the United States came from Europe. By 1985, Europe's share of annual entries had shrunk to one-ninth, with the actual numbers of European immigrants declining from almost 140,000 in 1960 to 63,000 in 1985. Today, the vast majority of immigrants to the United States originate in Asia, Latin America, and the Caribbean.

Asians make up the fastest growing group of legally admitted immigrants. From 25,000 entries in 1960, annual levels of Asian immigrants rose to 236,000 in 1980 and 264,700 in 1985. While these figures were elevated somewhat by the flow of Southeast Asian refugees admitted in the aftermath of the Vietnam War, refugees account for only a small proportion of the overall rise in Asian immigration. In fact, it is the Philippines, South Korea, and Taiwan, not the refugee-sending countries of Vietnam and Cambodia, that have been the largest Asian sources of immigrants. . . . In the 1980s, the Asian immigration began to include new flows from nations such as Singapore, Malaysia, and Indonesia that had not previously been sources of emigration to the United States.

The increase in Hispanic and West Indian immigration, while not quite as dramatic, has nevertheless been significant. . . . The top 10 immigrant-sending countries today are all in Latin America, the Caribbean Basin, or Asia. Between 1972 and 1979, Mexico, with more than half a million entries annually, was by far the largest source of legally admitted immigrants, followed by the Philippines with 290,000, South Korea with 225,000, China (defined as including both Taiwan and the People's Republic) with 160,400, India with 140,000, and Jamaica with 108,400. With the single exception of Italy, all of the countries sending more than 100,000 immigrants each year were either in the Caribbean Basin or in Asia. Other important sources of immigrants outside these regions were the United Kingdom, West Germany, and Canada, sending about 80,000 each during the 1972–1979 period. By 1987, 43 percent of the 600,000 entries were from Asia, 35 percent from Latin America and the Caribbean Basin, and only 10 percent from Europe.

It is important to note that the new Asian immigration, often thought to consist predominantly of professional and middle-class individuals, is increasingly becoming working-class migration. In several cases, what began as middle-class migrations eventually paved the way for the migration of poorer strata as well as undocumented immigrants. This has been true of South Korean migration, for example, which now includes significant numbers of undocumented immigrants and sweatshop employees, as well as of Filipino migration.

Another feature of the new immigration is the growing prominence of female immigrants. During the 1970s, women made up 60 percent of all immigrants from the Philippines, 61 percent of South Korean immigrants, 53 percent of Chinese, 52 percent of Dominicans, 52 percent of Colombians, 53 percent of Haitians, and 52 percent of immigrants from Hong Kong. Even in the well-established, traditionally male-dominated migration flow from Mexico, women now make up almost half of all legal immigrants.[3] . . .

The new immigration is further characterized by the immigrants' tendency to cluster in a few key U.S. regions. . . . The states of California and New York receive almost half of all immigrants, while another one-fourth go to New Jersey, Illinois, Florida, and Texas.

Moreover, the new immigrants tend to cluster in the largest metropolitan areas, such as New York, Los Angeles, San Francisco, Chicago, Houston, and Miami. . . . About 40 percent of immigrants settle in the 10 largest U.S. cities. . . . In these cities, immigrants make up a considerably higher proportion of the population than they do of the U.S. population as a whole. . . .

THE INADEQUACY OF CLASSICAL EXPLANATIONS

The main features of the new immigration—in particular, the growing prominence of certain Asian and Caribbean Basin countries as sources of immigrants and the rapid rise in the proportion of female immigrants—cannot be adequately explained under the prevailing assumptions of why migration occurs. Even a cursory review of emigration patterns reveals that there is no systematic relationship between emigration and what conventional wisdom holds to be the principal causes of emigration—namely overpopulation, poverty, and economic stagnation.

Population pressures certainly signal the possibility of increased emigration. Yet such pressures—whether measured by population growth or population density—are not in themselves particularly helpful in predicting which countries will have major outflows of emigrants, since some countries with rapidly growing populations experience little emigration (many Central African countries fall into this category), while other countries with much lower population growth rates (such as South Korea), or relatively low density (such as the Dominican Republic), are major sources of migrants.

Nor does poverty in itself seem to be a very reliable explanatory variable. Not all countries with severe poverty experience extensive emigration, and not all migrant-sending countries are poor, as the cases of South Korea and Taiwan illustrate. The utility of poverty in explaining migration is further called into question by the fact that large-scale migration flows from most Asian and Caribbean Basin countries started only in the 1960s, despite the fact that many of these countries had long suffered from poverty.

The presumed relationship between economic stagnation and emigration is similarly problematic. It is commonly assumed that the lack of economic opportunities in less developed countries, as measured by slow growth of gross national product (GNP), plays a key role in inducing individuals to emigrate. But the overall increase in emigration levels took place at a time when most countries of origin were enjoying rather rapid economic growth. Annual GNP growth rates during the 1970s ranged from 5 to 9 percent for most of the leading migrant-sending countries. In fact, most of the key emigration countries were growing considerably faster than other countries that did not experience large-scale emigration. . . .

This is not to say that overpopulation, poverty, and economic stagnation do not create pressures for migration; by their very logic, they do. . . . The evidence suggests that these conditions are not sufficient by themselves to produce large new migration flows. Other intervening factors need to be taken into account—factors that work to transform these conditions into a migration-inducing situation.

Take, for example, the cases of Haiti and the Dominican Republic. At first glance, the high levels of emigration from these countries would seem to offer support for the argument that overpopulation, poverty, and economic stagnation cause migration. Yet one is struck by the fact that these conditions were present in both countries long before the massive outflow of emigrants began. What, then, accounted for the sudden upsurge?

In the case of the Dominican Republic, the answer seems to lie in the linkages with the United States that were formed during the occupation of Santo Domingo by U.S. marines in 1965 in response to the election victory of the left-wing presidential candidate Juan Bosch. The occupation not only resulted in the growth of political and economic ties with the United States but also produced a stream of middle-class political refugees who emigrated to the occupying country. The settlement of Dominican refugees in the United States in turn created personal and family linkages between the two countries. U.S.-Dominican ties were subsequently further consolidated through U.S. investment in Dominican agriculture and manufacturing for export. Migration to the United States began to increase soon thereafter, rising from a total of 4,500 for the period from 1955 to 1959 to 58,000 between 1965 and 1969. Thus, the new developments that appear to have coincided with the initiation of large-scale emigration were the establishment of close military and personal ties with the United States and the introduction of U.S. direct foreign investment.

Haiti, on the other hand, was not subjected to direct U.S. military intervention, but the establishment of linkages with the United States and the introduction of direct foreign investment seem to have played a similarly important role in producing emigration. Although Haiti has long been desperately poor, massive migration to the United States began only in the early 1970s. In this case, the key new development or intervening process appears to have been the adoption of an export-oriented economic growth policy by President Jean-Claude Duvalier in 1972. Haiti's economy was opened to foreign investment in export manufacturing and the large-scale development of commercial agriculture, with the United States serving as the key partner in this new strategy. The necessary labor supply for these new modes of production was obtained through the massive displacement of small landholders and subsistence farmers. This upheaval in Haiti's traditional occupational structure, in conjunction with growing government repression and the emergence of close political and economic links with the United States, coincided with the onset of a major migration flow to the United States.

In both cases, then, the establishment of political, military, and economic linkages with the United States seems to have been instrumental in creating conditions that allowed the emergence of large-scale emigration. Such linkages also played a key role in the migration of Southeast Asians to the United States. In the period following the Korean War, the United States actively sought to promote economic development in Southeast Asia as a way of stabilizing the region politically. In addition, U.S. troops were stationed in Korea, the Philippines, and Indochina. Together, U.S. business and military interests created a vast array of linkages with those Asian countries that were later to experience large migration flows to the United States. The massive increase in foreign investment during the same period, particularly in South Korea, Taiwan, and the Philippines, reinforced these trends.

In other words, in most of the countries experiencing large migration flows to the United States, it is possible to identify a set of conditions and linkages with the United States that, together with overpopulation, poverty, or unemployment, induce emigration. While the nature and extent of these linkages vary from country to country, a common pattern of expanding U.S. political and economic involvement with emigrant-sending countries emerges.

THE INTERNATIONALIZATION OF PRODUCTION

To understand why large-scale migrations have originated in countries with high levels of job creation due to foreign investment in production for export, it is necessary to examine the impact of such investment on the economic and labor structure of developing countries.

Perhaps the single most important effect of foreign investment in export production is the uprooting of people from traditional modes of existence. It has long been recognized that the development of commercial agriculture tends to displace subsistence farmers, creating a supply of rural wage laborers and giving rise to mass migrations to cities. In recent years, the large-scale development of export-oriented manufacturing in Southeast Asia and the Caribbean Basin has come to have a similar effect (though through different mechanisms); it has uprooted people and created an urban reserve of wage laborers. In both export agriculture and export industry, the disruption of traditional work structures as a result of the introduction of modern modes of production has played a key role in transforming people into migrant workers and, potentially, into emigrants.

In export manufacturing, the catalyst for the disruption of traditional work structures is the massive recruitment of young women into jobs in the new industrial zones. Most of the manufacturing in these zones is the sort that employs a high proportion of female workers in industrialized countries as well: electronics assembly and the manufacture of textiles, apparel, and toys. The exodus of young women to the industrial zones typically begins when factory representatives recruit young women directly in their villages and rural schools; eventually, the establishment of continuous migration streams reduces or eliminates the need for direct recruitment. The most obvious reason for the intensive recruitment of women is the firms' desire to reduce labor costs, but there are other considerations as well: young women in patriarchal societies are seen by foreign employers as obedient and disciplined workers, willing to do tedious, high-precision work and to submit themselves to work conditions that would not be tolerated in the highly developed countries.

This mobilization of large numbers of women into waged labor has a highly disruptive effect on traditional, often unwaged, work patterns. In rural areas, women fulfill important functions in the production of goods for family consumption or for sale in local markets. Village economies and rural households depend on a variety of economic activities traditionally performed by women, ranging from food preparation to cloth weaving, basket making, and various other types of crafts. All these activities are undermined by the departure of young women for the new industrial zones. . . .

For men and women alike, the disruption of traditional ways of earning a living and the ascendance of export-led development make entry into wage labor increasingly a one-way proposition. With traditional economic opportunities in the rural areas shrinking, it becomes difficult, if not impossible, for workers to return home if they are laid off or unsuccessful in the job search. . . . People uprooted from their traditional ways of life, then left unemployed and unemployable as export firms hire younger workers or move production to other countries, may see few options but emigration, especially if an export-led growth strategy has weakened the country's domestic market–oriented economy.

But the role played by foreign investment in allowing the emergence of large-scale emigration flows does not end there. In addition to eroding traditional work structures and creating a pool of potential migrants, foreign investment in production for export contributes to the development of economic, cultural, and ideological linkages with the industrialized countries. These linkages tend to promote the notion of emigration both directly and indirectly. Workers actually employed in the export sector—whether managers, secretaries, or assemblers—may experience the greatest degree of westernization and be most closely connected to the country supplying the foreign capital; they are, after all, using their labor power to produce goods and services for people and firms in developed countries. For these workers, already oriented toward Western practices and modes of thought in their daily experience on the job, the distance between a job in the offshore plant or office and a comparable job in the industrialized country itself is subjectively reduced. It is not hard to see how such individuals might come to regard emigration as a serious option.

In addition to the direct impact on workers in the export sector, the linkages created by direct foreign investment also have a generalized westernizing effect on the less developed country and its people. This "ideological" effect in promoting emigration should not be underestimated; it makes emigration an option not just for those individuals employed in the export sector but for the wider population as well. . . .

While foreign investment, along with other political, military, and cultural links, helps to explain how migration becomes an option for large numbers of individuals in some developing countries, it does not fully explain why the United

States has been overwhelmingly the main destination for migrants. After all, Japan, West Germany, the Netherlands, and Great Britain all have substantial direct foreign investment in developing countries. . . .

It is in this context that the 1965 liberalization of U.S. immigration law and the unfading image of the United States as a land of opportunity acquire significance. The conviction among prospective emigrants that the United States offers unlimited opportunities and plentiful employment prospects, at least relative to other countries, has had the effect of making "emigration" almost identical with "emigration to the United States." This has tended to create a self-reinforcing migration pattern to the United States. As new bridges for migrants are created by foreign investment (in conjunction with political and military activity) and strengthened by the existence of economic opportunities in the United States, the resulting new migrations create additional bridges or linkages between the United States and migrant-sending countries. These, in turn, serve to facilitate future emigration to the United States, regardless of the origin of the foreign investment that created the conditions for emigration in the first place. . . .

THE NEW LABOR DEMAND IN THE UNITED STATES

At first glance, both the heavy influx of immigrants into the United States over the past two decades and their clustering in urban areas would appear to defy economic logic. Why would an increasing number of immigrants come to this country at a time of high overall unemployment and sharp losses of manufacturing and goods-handling jobs? And why would they settle predominantly in the largest U.S. cities, when many of these were in severe decline as centers of light manufacturing and other industries that traditionally employed immigrants? The liberalization of immigration legislation after 1965 and the prior existence of immigrant communities in major urban centers no doubt played some role in attracting immigrants from the older, primarily European, emigration countries. But the most important reason for the continuation of large inflows among the new migrant groups has been the rapid expansion of the supply of low-wage jobs in the United States and the casualization of the labor market associated with the new growth industries, particularly in the major cities. . . .

The increase in low-wage jobs in the United States is in part a result of the same international economic processes that have channeled investment and manufacturing jobs to low-wage countries. As industrial production has moved overseas, the traditional U.S. manufacturing base has eroded and been partly replaced by a downgraded manufacturing sector, which is characterized by a growing supply of poorly paid, semi-skilled or unskilled production jobs. At the same time, the rapid growth of the service sector has created vast numbers of low-wage jobs (in addition to the better-publicized increase in highly paid investment banking and management consulting jobs). Both of these new growth sectors are largely concentrated in major cities such as New York and Los Angeles. Such cities have seen their economic importance further enhanced as they have become centers for the management and servicing of the global economy; as Detroit has lost jobs to overseas factories, New York and Los Angeles have gained jobs managing and servicing the global network of factories.

These trends have brought about a growing polarization in the U.S. occupational structure since the late 1970s. Along with a sharp decline in the number of middle-income blue- and white-collar jobs, there has been a modest increase in the number of high-wage professional and managerial jobs and a vast expansion in the supply of low-wage jobs. Between 1963 and 1973, nine out of 10 new jobs created were in the middle-earnings group, while the number of high-paid jobs was shrinking. Since 1973, by contrast, only one in two new jobs has been in the middle-income category. If one takes into consideration the increase in the number of seasonal and part-time workers, then the growing inequality within the labor force becomes even more pronounced. The proportion of part-time jobs increased from 15 percent in 1955 to 22 percent in 1977. By 1986, part-time workers made up fully a third of the labor force; about 80 percent of these 50 million workers earn less than $11,000 a year. . . .

TOWARD A WORKABLE IMMIGRATION POLICY

A workable U.S. immigration policy would be based on the recognition that the United States, as a major industrial power and supplier of foreign investment, bears a certain amount of responsibility for the existence of international labor migrations. The past policies of the United States toward war refugees might serve as a model for a refashioned immigration policy. Few people would argue that flows of refugees from Indochina were the result of overpopulation or economic stagnation, even though the region may in fact have suffered from these problems. Instead, it is widely recognized that U.S. military activities were to some degree responsible for creating the refugee flows. When the United States granted Indochinese refugees special rights to settle here, it was acknowledging this responsibility, at least indirectly. A similar acknowledgement is due in the case of labor migrations.

When drafting laws in most areas of foreign relations, lawmakers generally make an effort to weigh the differing degrees of responsibility of various actors and take into account such complex phenomena as the globalization of production and international flows of capital and information. Why, then, is it not possible to factor in similar considerations in the designing of immigration policy? To be sure, international migration poses special problems in this regard, since the relationship of immigration to other international processes is not readily apparent or easily understood. But the overly simplistic approach most policymakers have adopted until now has greatly hindered the fashioning of a fair and effective immigration policy. The precise features of such a policy will have to be elaborated through further study and debate. But one thing is clear: U.S. immigration policy will continue to be counterproductive as long as it places the responsibility for the formation of international migrations exclusively on the shoulders of the immigrants themselves.

NOTES

1. Earlier agreements barred Chinese labor immigration (1882), restricted Japanese immigration (1907), and culminated in the 1924 National Origins Act. This act was the first

general immigration law in that it brought together the growing number of restrictions and controls that had been established over a period of time: the creation of classes of inadmissible aliens, deportation laws, literacy requirements, etc. The 1965 immigration law ended these restrictions. In this sense it was part of a much broader legislative effort to end various forms of discrimination in the United Sates, such as discrimination against minorities and women.

2. About 1.8 million aliens applied under the main legalization program; in addition, 1.2 million applied under special legalization programs for agriculture. While the majority applying under the main program are expected to obtain temporary resident status, it is now becoming evident that a growing proportion may not be complying with the second requirement of the procedure, that of applying for permanent residence.

3. A similar trend is taking place in the undocumented Mexican migration. See R. Warren and J. S. Passel, *Estimates of Illegal Aliens from Mexico Counted in the 1980 U.S. Census* (Washington, D.C.: Bureau of the Census, Population Division, 1983).

19

Models of Pluralism

The New American Dilemma

MILTON M. GORDON

Over a generation ago, Gunnar Myrdal, in his monumental study of this country's greatest and most salient issue in race relations—what was then referred to as "the Negro problem"—wrote of "an American dilemma"—the gap and implicit choice between the religious and political ideals of the American Creed which called for fair and just treatment of all people, regardless of race, creed, or color, and the overt practices of racial discrimination and prejudice directed by Whites toward Blacks which took place in the daily life of the American people. Thus this country stood at a crossroads whence it could choose to follow the existing pathway of racial discrimination and hostility or, conversely, make the decision to honor its best ideals and eliminate differential treatment of its people on the basis of race. The tension of this choice, declared Myrdal, existed not only between Americans of varying attitudes and persuasion, but also within the heart of the individual citizen.[1]

It is my contention that, at least at the level of formal governmental action, the United States of America, in the three and one half decades since Myrdal published his great study, has moved decisively down the road toward implementing the implications of the American Creed for race relations, that this is a most important step (although it obviously does not remove all aspects of racially discriminatory treatment and prejudice from the institutions and private social relations of everyday American life), and that, with respect to racial and ethnic relations, America now faces a *new dilemma*—a dilemma which is oriented toward a choice of the *kind of group pluralism* which American governmental action and the attitudes of the American people will foster and encourage. . . .

A NEW DILEMMA

. . . In the dilemma which Myrdal presented [he] identified two divergent paths, one of them supported by the finest ideals of religious and civic morality, the other buttressed not by any well-understood moral and religious conviction, but by destructive and hateful practices arising out of the worst impulses in humankind. In the new American dilemma, however, which centers on the proper role of government in dealing with racial and ethnic relations, proponents of both sides can claim in good faith to derive their respective positions from standard moral and religious systems, one side emphasizing principles of equal treatment and individual meritocracy, the other principles that call upon group compensation for undeniable past injustices. It is my conviction that this controversy and the important choices involved can be discussed most expeditiously and with the optimum possibility for producing a useful, well-considered national debate rather than a simple emotional dismissal of one side or the other, in the larger context of types of pluralism and the choice of which type of pluralist society is most appropriate and most beneficial for a nation composed of many ethnic groups—and specifically, for the United States of America.

THE NATURE OF PLURALISM

What, indeed, is racial and ethnic pluralism? In its most generic aspects it refers to a national society in which various groups, each with a psychological sense of its own historical peoplehood, maintain some structural separation from each other in intimate primary group relationships and in certain aspects of institutional life and thus create the possibility of maintaining, also, some cultural patterns which are different from those of the "host" society and of other racial and ethnic groups in the nation. I have referred to these two dimensions as "structural pluralism" and, in the term suggested by Horace Kallen, "cultural pluralism."[2] Note that I use the phrase "create the possibility of maintaining" in reference to variations in cultural patterns. I use this construction advisedly, since racial and ethnic pluralism can exist without a great deal of cultural diversity; it cannot exist at all, however, without structural separation.

As I interpret the American historical experience, using these analytical distinctions, and also bringing into play the role of both the Anglo-conformity and the "melting pot" ideas, the dominant pattern with regard to our country's racial and ethnic diversity has been a composite consisting of a great deal of persistent structural pluralism, cultural pluralism in the case of the first generation of immigrants, and the overwhelming dominance of Anglo-conformity with regard to the cultural patterns of the second and successive generations, although not to the exclusion of the retention of symbolic elements of the ancestral tradition[3] and, of course, with the maintenance of religious differences from the original Protestant norm, that is, Roman Catholicism and Judaism (although both in Americanized form)—and all of this spiced up with a little and flavorful bit of "melting pot."[4]

LIBERAL AND CORPORATE PLURALISM

The new element in the situation—the one which creates the dilemma of choice currently before the American people—is the role of government in racial and ethnic relations, together with ethical and philosophical issues revolving around ideas of just rewards and whether to treat persons as individuals or as members of a categorically defined group. In combination, these issues point to the delineation of two alternative theoretical patterns or models of a racially and ethnically plural society, in which the issues of cultural and structural differences figure, but are now joined by other dimensions in order to incorporate the new considerations. I have called the two patterns thus distinguished *liberal pluralism* and *corporate pluralism*.[5] I wish now to portray and analyze these alternative models of pluralism in somewhat systematic form. For that purpose, I am denoting six dimensions with which to compare and contrast the two theoretical types of racial and ethnic pluralistic societies. These are (1) legal recognition and differential treatment, (2) individual meritocracy and equality of opportunity versus group rewards and equality of condition, (3) structural separation, (4) cultural differences, (5) area exclusivism, and (6) institutional monolingualism versus institutional bilingualism or multilingualism. I shall now proceed to a consideration of these two differing types of pluralism using these dimensions.

Legal Recognition and Differential Treatment

In liberal pluralism, government gives no formal recognition to categories of people based on race or ethnicity (and, of course, religion, which may be considered a possible component of ethnicity). Furthermore, it provides no benefits to nor exerts any penalty from any individual because of his or her racial or ethnic background. It does not stipulate segregation, nor does it formally promote integration, but allows individuals of all racial and ethnic groups to work things out by themselves on the basis of freedom of choice. It may, however, intervene legally through legislation or executive orders to *prevent* discrimination in such areas as employment, education, voting, public facilities, and public accommodations. But such prevention is focused on *specific acts which can be proven to be discriminatory* and not on the promotion of integration through direct governmental action. Thus a fair employment commission's investigation and adjudication of a complaint of racial discrimination in a particular firm, agency, or educational institution would fall within the framework of liberal pluralism, while an industry-wide investigation to ascertain and change particular percentages of racial and ethnic percentages of employees would not.

It is plausible to suggest that the just described pattern within the framework of "liberal pluralism" has been the general ideal and goal of the American experience, and that although, in practice, America has at times miserably failed to live up to this ideal—notably, though not exclusively, in the case of Blacks—nevertheless, recent advances in the race relations area have brought us close to full implementation of this set of desired patterns in the relationship of the American government toward its citizens.[6]

Corporate pluralism, on the other hand, envisages a nation where its racial and ethnic entities are formally recognized as such—are given formal standing as groups in the national polity—and where patterns of political power and economic reward are based on a distributive formula which postulates group rights and which defines group membership as an important factor in the outcome for individuals. In widely varying degree, nations like Belgium, the Netherlands, Switzerland, Canada, the Soviet Union, and Lebanon contain some aspects of a corporate pluralism model. In the United States, recently introduced measures, such as government-mandated affirmative action procedures in employment, education, and stipulated public programs, and court-ordered busing of school children across neighborhood district lines to effect racial integration, constitute steps toward the corporate pluralist idea. Many proponents of these measures support them simply as transitional and compensatory devices to rectify the effects of past racial discrimination; however, it is not clear what formulas would be used to measure the designated completion of the process and whether, in fact, these procedures, if left in place for any length of time, would not simply become eventually a permanent part of the national pattern of operation.

Individual Meritocracy and Equality of Opportunity Versus Group Rewards and Equality of Condition

These are basic philosophical ideas of equality and attribution which also definitely distinguish the two types of pluralism from each other. In liberal pluralism, the unit of attribution for equity considerations is always and irrevocably the individual. The individual gets what he deserves in economic and political rewards on the basis of his merit and accomplishment. Both in theory and practice, considerations of compassion and the need for basic minimal rewards usually shore up the bottom end of the scale, but above this minimal line individual merit prevails. Equality for citizens is defined as equality of opportunity (and, of course, equality before the law), but not in terms of results or condition, a matter which is left to the myriad workings of the competitive process. Racial and ethnic factors, in this paradigm, should play no role at all in the distributive process, either positive or negative. Proponents of this model insist that it represents traditional American ideals and the principles of the Enlightenment on which the American republic was founded.

Corporate pluralism postulates a reward system, both economic and political, which gives legitimacy to the standing and stake of racial and ethnic groups in the distributive process. Political bodies, such as legislatures, judiciaries, municipal councils, and even executive offices, must reflect, to a substantial degree, the numerical weight of the various racial and ethnic groups in the total population. In the economic arena, economic justice is not achieved until the income and occupational distributions of the various groups are approximately equal, and business, professional, and government units of significant size must each, individually, show a pattern of reward of differential income, power, and status to its employees which mirrors the national population distribution of racial and ethnic groups. Presumably, *within* the required ratios, individual merit considerations will be operative. Proponents of this system argue that, at the very least, it is necessary to institute such a model of rewards for a time in order to allow a minority group which has suffered heavy discrimination in the past to catch up with the other groups with any reasonable degree of rapidity. In this system also, equality is defined as equality of condition rather than simply equality of opportunity.

Structural Separation

Liberal pluralism's formula for the resolution of structure issues—deciding what cliques, clubs, and institutions to belong to—is strictly laissez faire. Its message to the minority group member is, "If you want to form your own ethnically enclosed network of primary group relations, and your separate institutional life, go ahead. That's your business. If you don't want to, that's equally all right. If you want to marry across racial or ethnic lines, there is no legal bar. The policy in all these matters is strictly 'hands off.'"

In the American historical experience, this policy, where it was implemented (it was, of course, distinctly not implemented in the southern states for Blacks and Whites until recently), gave members of racial and ethnic minorities the maximum amount of freedom of choice in these matters. Of course, we are referring here to government policy only. In the northern states, physical intimidation and custom did what government did not attempt to do: keep people of different races apart. Second-generation immigrants (most first-generation immigrants, quite understandably, wanted to stay within their own ethnic enclaves for primary group relations) who ventured out of the ethnic social network and looked for some "neutral" social structure found that the only alternative structures were white Protestant Anglo-Saxon in nature and reluctant or unwilling to let them in, anyway. The opening up of primary group networks, after all, requires two favorable decisions, one by the aspiring entrant, the other by the gatekeeper of the social structure in which one is seeking entrance. But as far as government was concerned, except for the now defunct Jim Crow laws, the gates were legally open, and private attitudes determined the outcome.

In the case of corporate pluralism, the situation is somewhat different. Structural separation is not necessarily legally mandated, but the logic of the reward system stipulating that group membership plays a large role in educational access, occupational placement, income, political power, and similar matters places distinct pressure on members of particular racial and ethnic groups to stay within the group for marriage, close personal friendship, institutional life, and social identity. After all, if a significant portion of one's rational interests are likely to be satisfied by emphasis on one's ethnicity, then one might as well stay within ethnic boundaries and at the same time enjoy the social comforts of being among "people of one's own kind," where prejudice and discrimination toward oneself are not present. Moving across ethnic boundaries to engage in significant interethnic social relationships is likely to lead to social marginality in a society where ethnicity and ethnic identity are such salient features. Thus the logic of corporate pluralism is to emphasize structural separation.

Cultural Differences

Very much as in the case of structural issues, liberal pluralism allows members of minority groups the maximum amount of freedom to make as much or as little as they please of their ancestral cultural heritage. There are no "bonus points" for perpetuating it and no penalties for drawing away from it. Groups and individuals from within the group can make their own decisions on these matters.

There are, of course, boundaries which indicate that a certain value consensus for all groups within the national framework is expected. The attempt to introduce polygamy in the American historical experience failed because it violated this consensus. No projected set of alternative values which advocated violence, murder, or theft as desirable patterns of behavior would obviously be tolerated. But within the normal range of nondestructive behavior, much variation is allowed, and conflicts over what norms shall constitute public policy are usually settled through the usual political processes—that is, the ballot box and judicial decisions. Or if the numbers are not great and civic policy is not essentially threatened, alternative value and behavior patterns are institutionalized as allowable exceptions or variations. An American case in point would be the provisions made in national legislation for conscientious objectors to war and military service, which stem, institutionally, from the value systems of British-descended Quakers and several religious sects of German origin whose ancestors were once immigrants to America. The issue of monolingualism versus bilingualism is also, of course, a cultural one, but it is so important in itself that I am considering it separately below.

Corporate pluralism, on the other hand, places a distinct positive value on cultural diversity and encourages its perpetration. Its viewpoint is that the preservation of its own ancestral cultural patterns by each racial and ethnic group is both an institutional right and a positive virtue. From this perspective, the culture of the nation is seen as a mosaic of subcultural patterns interacting in an overall framework of integration and harmony, thus providing a richer cultural life for the nation than is possible where one standard set of cultural patterns, established by the majority, constitutes the norm. Thus members of diverse racial and ethnic groups are encouraged to lay considerable emphasis on developing and honoring their own ancestral heritage even in successive generations of the original group.

Area Exclusivism

In the liberal pluralist model, no racial or ethnic group is able to lay legal claim to a particular piece of territory within the nation and to exclude people of other identities from access or residence. This is the case both in terms of large segments of national territory and in terms of particular neighborhoods in a specific community. Thus area exclusivism is legally forbidden. Area concentration, however, which reflects the voluntary choices of members of a particular racial or ethnic group to live in the same neighborhood or to settle in a particular city, is well within the liberal framework and is likely to occur, as the American experience has shown. However, if dubiously legal or extralegal attempts (that is, the once but no longer legally permissible "restrictive covenant," real estate brokerage practices, and physical intimidation) are made to exclude members of other groups from living in a particular neighborhood or portion of the city, then the principles of liberal pluralism are flagrantly violated. It is clear that American practices in this area, although improving, still have a long way to go to achieve full implementation of these principles.

Corporate pluralism does not demand area exclusivism, but is more tolerant of it as a possible variant arrangement in the domain of racial and ethnic relations. Its emphasis on group identity and group rights makes it less insistent on the principle of free access in travel or residence to any physical portion of the national collectivity, regardless of race, color, or creed.

Institutional Monolingualism Versus Institutional Bilingualism or Multilingualism

On the language issue, liberal pluralism and corporate pluralism stand at opposite poles. Liberal pluralism insists on institutional monolingualism—that is, that there shall be only one standard language in the nation, that this language shall be the publicly mandated language of the educational system and all legal documents and procedures, and that no other language shall have any public standing. This viewpoint does not sanction hostility to the teaching or learning of other languages as supplementary options, it does not militate against voluntary retention of other languages as taught in the home or in private supplemental schools, and in fact, may encourage bilingualism or multilingualism for cultural or pragmatic purposes. But it makes one language the standard of the nation and allows no other to assume any official status. It is a clearly delineated position which, in fact, has been basically the American position, historically and up to the very recent present, at which time it has been challenged by proponents of mandatory bilingual education in the public schools for children who are language handicapped as a result of coming from a non-English-speaking home.

Corporate pluralism, on the other hand, supports official or institutional bilingualism or multilingualism. Its position is that the various racial and ethnic groups have the right and, indeed, should be encouraged to retain their ancestral languages, that there is no reason why there must be only one official language, and that all members of the national polity should be encouraged, perhaps even compelled, to become bilingual or multilingual. The large growth in numbers and political activism of the Hispanic population in the United States and the consequent demand for bilingual education in the public schools have brought aspects of this issue to the fore in recent years in the American context. Canadian society, with its English-speaking and French-speaking populations, is an example of an institutionally bilingual nation with its attendant controversies which are still in the process of attempted resolution.

CONCLUSION

The preceding six dimensions serve to define the differences between liberal pluralism and corporate pluralism. By their conceptualization and use I have tried to make it clear that there is now an important dilemma before the American people and that this dilemma is not simply a choice between isolated and fragmented policies, but rather that there is an inherent logic in the relationship of the various positions on these public issues which makes the choice one between two patterns—two overall types of racial and ethnic pluralism each with distinctly different implications for the American way of life. Those who favor the liberal form of pluralism emphasize in their arguments the ethical and philosophical value of the idea of individual meritocracy and the notion that current generations should not be expected to pay for the sins of their fathers—or at least, those who lived here before them, whether genetically related or not. They also point to functional considerations such as the possibility that measures such as forced busing and affirmative action to ensure group quotas will create white backlash and serve as a continuing major irritant in the relationships between racial and ethnic groups. Those who favor policies which fall, logically, under the rubric of corporate pluralism emphasize, in return, the moral and philosophical position which posits group rights as well as individual rights, and the need for major compensatory measures to make up for the massive dimensions of racial discrimination in the past.

And so the argument is joined. This article has been written with the distinct conviction that the argument is a momentous one and that its resolution, in whatever form, will be best served by as much intellectual clarity, thoughtfulness, and good will as we can all muster in the process. Certainly, what the American people decide about this patterned complex of issues in the last 20 years of the twentieth century will have much to do with determining the nature, shape, and destiny of racial and ethnic relations in America in the twenty-first century which will then follow.

NOTES

1. Gunnar Myrdal, with the assistance of Richard Sterner and Arnold Rose, *An American Dilemma* (New York: Harper and Brothers, 1944), particularly, chs. 1 and 45.

2. Milton M. Gordon, *Assimilation in American Life* (New York: Oxford University Press, 1964); see also my *Human Nature, Class, and Ethnicity* (New York: Oxford University Press, 1978).

3. See Herbert J. Gans, "Symbolic Ethnicity: The Future of Ethnic Groups and Cultures in America," in *On the Making of Americans: Essays in Honor of David Riesman,* eds. Herbert J. Gans, Nathan Glazer, Joseph R. Gusfield, and Christopher Jencks (Philadelphia: University of Pennsylvania Press, 1979).

4. See Milton M. Gordon, *Assimilation in American Life,* passim.

5. Milton M. Gordon, "Toward A General Theory of Racial and Ethnic Group Relations," in *Ethnicity: Theory and Experience,* eds. Nathan Glazer and Daniel P. Moynihan (Cambridge, MA: Harvard University Press, 1975). This paper is reprinted in my *Human Nature, Class, and Ethnicity.* The terms "liberal pluralism" and "corporate pluralism" were chosen because they appear to me to portray accurately and nonpejoratively the salient and historically appropriate characteristics of each type of pluralist society. It is true that many liberals today support measures which fall in the "corporate" variety of pluralism. But there has been a longer historical association of the term "liberal" with those measures and conditions which I am grouping under the term "liberal pluralism."

6. See Nathan Glazer, *Affirmative Discrimination* (New York: Basic Books, 1975), ch. 1, for a presentation of such a viewpoint.

20

Alien Nation

PETER BRIMELOW

From time to time while struggling with this book, and earlier, while writing the humongous "Time to Rethink Immigration?" *National Review* cover story that preceded it,[1] I've broken off to experience once again—it will be for such a short, short time—the inexpressible joy of changing my infant American son's dirty diaper.

Alexander James Frank Brimelow is an American although I was still a British subject, and his mother a Canadian, when he shot into the New York Hospital delivery room, yelling indignantly, one summer dawn in 1991. This is because of the Fourteenth Amendment to the U.S. Constitution. It states in part:

> All persons born or naturalized in the United States, and subject to the jurisdiction thereof, are citizens of the United States and of the State wherein they reside.

The Fourteenth Amendment was passed after the Civil War in an attempt to stop Southern states denying their newly freed slaves the full rights of citizens. But the wording is general. So it has been interpreted to mean that any child born in the United States is automatically a citizen. Even if its mother is a foreigner. Even if she's just passing through.

This "birthright citizenship" is by no means the rule among industrialized countries. Even if you are born in a manger, the Japanese, French and Germans say in effect, that still doesn't make you a bale of hay. The British used to have birthright citizenship, but in 1983 they restricted it—requiring for example that one parent be a legal resident—because of problems caused by immigration.

I am delighted that Alexander is an American. However, I do feel slightly, well, guilty that his fellow Americans had so little choice in the matter.

But at least Maggy and I had applied for and been granted legal permission to live in the United States. There are currently an estimated 3.5 to 4 million foreigners who have just arrived and settled here in defiance of American law.[2] When these illegal immigrants have children in the United States, why, those children are automatically American citizens too.

And right now, *two thirds* of the births in Los Angeles County hospitals are to illegal-immigrant mothers.[3]

In fact, a whole minor industry seems to have been created by those twenty-eight words added to the U.S. Constitution. One survey of new Hispanic mothers in California border hospitals found that 15 percent had crossed the border specifically to give birth, of whom a quarter said that their motive was to ensure U.S. citizenship for their child.[4]

All of which is just another example of one of this [chapter's] central themes:

- **The United States has lost control of its borders—in every sense.** A series of institutional accidents, of which birthright citizenship is just one, has essentially robbed Americans of the power to determine who, and how many, can enter their national family, make claims on it . . . and exert power over it.

The heart of the problem: immigration.

THE IMMIGRATION INUNDATION

In 1991, the year of Alexander's birth, the Immigration and Naturalization Service reported a total of over 1.8 million legal immigrants. That was easily a record. It exceeded by almost a third the previous peak of almost 1.3 million, reached eighty-four years earlier at the height of the First Great Wave of Immigration, which peaked just after the turn of the century.

The United States has been engulfed by what seems likely to be the greatest wave of immigration it has ever faced. The INS estimates that 12 to 13 million legal and illegal immigrants will enter the United States during the decade of the 1990s. The Washington, D.C.–based Federation for American Immigration Reform (FAIR), among the most prominent of the groups critical of immigration policy, thinks the total will range between 10 and 15 million. An independent expert, Daniel James, author of *Illegal Immigration: An Unfolding Crisis,* has argued that it could be as high as 18 million.[5]

And the chaotic working of current U.S. immigration law has created a peculiar, but little-understood, reality. *The extraordinary truth is that, in almost all cases, Americans will have little more say over the arrival of these new claimants on their national community—and voters on their national future—than over the arrival of Alexander.*

This is because it's not just illegal immigration that is out of control. So is legal immigration. *U.S. law in effect treats immigration as a sort of imitation civil right, extended to an indefinite group of foreigners who have been selected arbitrarily and with no regard to American interests.*

Whether these foreigners deign to come and make their claim on America—and on the American taxpayer—is pretty much up to them.

AMERICA'S ONE-WAY IMMIGRATION DEBATE

Everyone knows that there are two sides to every question, except the typical American editor ordering up a story about immigration, for whom there is only one side: immigration good, concern about immigration bad.

This results in the anecdotal happy-talk good-news coverage of immigration that we all know and love:

> *XYZ was just Harvard's valedictorian—XYZ arrived in the U.S. speaking no English three months ago—XYZ PROVES THE AMERICAN DREAM IS STILL ALIVE!—despite those nasty nativists who want to keep all the XYZs out.*

Now, the achievement of immigrants to the United States (more accurately, of some immigrants to the United States) is indeed one of the most inspiring, and instructive, tales in human history. Nevertheless, there are still two sides to the question. Thus we might, equally reasonably, expect to see balancing anecdotal coverage like this:

> *In January 1993, a Pakistani applicant for political asylum (and, simultaneously, for amnesty as an illegal immigrant) opens fire on employees entering CIA headquarters, killing two and wounding three! In February 1993, a gang of Middle Easterners (most illegally overstaying after entering on non-immigrant visas—one banned as a terrorist but admitted on a tourist visa in error) blow up New York's World Trade Center, killing six and injuring more than 1,000!! In December 1993, a Jamaican immigrant (admitted as a student but stayed, illegal status automatically regularized after marriage to a U.S. citizen) opens fire on commuters on New York's Long Island Rail Road, killing six and wounding 19!!! WHAT'S GOING ON??!!?*

The case of Colin Ferguson, arrested in the Long Island Rail Road shootings, is particularly instructive. With a little help from President Clinton, talking the very next day at a lunch for journalists, it was rapidly converted into another argument for gun control.

Which missed the point completely. You can be for or against gun control. Arguably, the proposed federal legislation would not have helped here because Ferguson bought his gun legally, in California, which already requires proof of identity and a fifteen-day waiting period.

But Ferguson's own writings showed him to be motivated by hatred of whites. And this racial antagonism is a much deeper problem. In any rational mind, it must raise the question: *Is it really wise to allow the immigration of people who find it so difficult and painful to assimilate into the American majority?*

Because the fact cannot be denied: if Ferguson and the others had not immigrated, those fourteen Americans would not have been killed.

Although we might reasonably expect to see such balancing media coverage of immigration, don't hold your breath. There are powerful taboos preventing it. The result, however, is that the American immigration debate has been a one-way street. Criticism of immigration, and news that might support it, just tends not to get through.

This is no mere journalism-school game of balancing anecdotes. It involves the broadest social trends. For example, the United States is in the midst of a serious crime epidemic. Yet almost no Americans are aware that *aliens make up one quarter of the prisoners in federal penitentiaries*—almost three times their proportion in the population at large.[6]

Indeed, many problems that currently preoccupy Americans have an unspoken *immigration dimension.* Two further instances:

- *The health-care crisis.* Americans have been told repeatedly that some 30 to 40 million people in the country have no health insurance at any one point in time. Typically, nobody seems to know how many are immigrants. But immigrants certainly make up a disproportionate share—particularly of the real problem: the much smaller hard core, perhaps 6 million, that remains uninsured after two years.

We know that about 6 million of the 22 million U.S. Hispanics are uninsured at any one point. Since almost a third of U.S. Hispanics are foreign-born, it's obvious that immigrants and their children must be some and perhaps most of them. The hard core of uninsured, experts confirm, is substantially Hispanic. That probably includes many of the estimated nearly 2 million uninsured illegal immigrants permanently settled here, a heavily Hispanic group.[7]

- *The education crisis.* Americans are used to hearing that their schools don't seem to be providing the quality of education that foreigners get. Fewer of them know that the U.S. education system is also very expensive by international standards.[8] Virtually none of them know anything about the impact of immigration on that education system.

Yet the impact of immigration is clearly serious. For example, in 1990 almost one child in every twenty enrolled in American public schools either could not speak English or spoke it so poorly as to need language-assistance programs. This number is increasing with striking speed: only six years earlier, it had been one child in thirty-one.[9] Current law is generally interpreted as requiring schools to educate such children in their native language. To do so, according to one California estimate, requires spending some 65 percent more per child than on an English-speaking child.[10] And not merely money but, more importantly, teacher time and energy are inevitably being diverted from America's children.

(And it's not working anyway. The Bureau of the Census recently reported for the first time, because the phenomenon was previously unheard of, that 2.3 percent of native-born Americans now do not speak English "very well" and that 1.2 percent are "linguistically isolated"—living in households where no one aged fourteen or over speaks only English or speaks English "very well." Astonishingly, nearly a third of the immigrants who entered the country between 1980 and 1990 *and had become U.S. citizens* were "linguistically isolated"—although until 1990, English proficiency was usually a condition of naturalization.[11])

In this book, I show that the immigration resulting from current public policy

1. is dramatically larger, less skilled, and more divergent from the American majority than anything that was anticipated or desired
2. is probably not beneficial economically—and is certainly not necessary
3. is attended by a wide and increasing range of negative consequences, from the physical environment to the political
4. is bringing about an ethnic and racial transformation in America without precedent in the history of the world—an astonishing social experiment launched with no particular reason to expect success. . . .

RACISTS . . .

Some of my American readers will be stirring uneasily at this point. They have been trained to recoil from any explicit discussion of race. *And anyone who says anything critical of immigration is going to be accused of racism.* This is simply a law of modern American political life.

When you write a major article in a national magazine, you in effect enter into a conversation with Americans. And part of the conversation I got into by writing my *National Review* cover story illustrated this law. It was a muttering match with Virginia Postrel, editor of the libertarian *Reason* magazine.

Virginia flipped out at the word *experiment,* as used in point 4 above, and launched into a rendition of the pro-immigration moldy oldie "America Is an Experiment That Works." (This often happens.) I pointed out gently that the experiment in question was *not* America—but instead the 1965 Immigration Act and its imminent, unprecedented, ethnic and racial transformation of America. She replied angrily in print:

> . . . he [*me!*] thus defines authentic Americans not by their values or actions but by their blood. This is nonsense and, though I hate to use the term, profoundly un-American.[12]

Thus Virginia, like many modern American intellectuals, is just unable to handle a plain historical fact: that the American nation has always had a specific ethnic core. And that core has been white.

A nation, of course, is an interlacing of ethnicity and culture. Individuals of any ethnicity or race might be able to acculturate to a national community. And the American national community has certainly been unusually assimilative. But nevertheless, the massive ethnic and racial transformation that public policy is now inflicting on America is totally new—and in terms of how Americans have traditionally viewed themselves, quite revolutionary. Pointing out this reality may be embarrassing to starry-eyed immigration enthusiasts who know no history. But it cannot reasonably be shouted down as "racist." Or "un-American."

. . .

First, it is universally agreed that whatever impact immigration has must fall first on unskilled workers. *And in the United States, that means blacks.* Nor is this the first time that immigration has adversely affected these poorest of Americans.

"Immigrants are revitalizing American cities," say the immigration enthusiasts—genuinely unaware, it seems, that they are in effect expressing coded horror at the earlier effects of the great black migration from the rural South to the industrial urban North. Perhaps it is immigration enthusiasts, not immigration critics, who should be examining their motives.

Second, I have indeed duly examined my own motives. And I am happy to report that they are pure. I sincerely believe I am not prejudiced—in the sense of committing and stubbornly persisting in error about people, regardless of evidence—which appears to me to be the only rational definition of "racism." I am also, however, not blind.

Race and ethnicity are destiny in American politics. And, because of the rise of affirmative-action quotas, for American individuals too.

My son, Alexander, is a white male with blue eyes and blond hair. He has never discriminated against anyone in his little life (except possibly young women visitors whom he suspects of being babysitters). But public policy now discriminates against him. The sheer size of the so-called "protected classes" that are now politically favored, such as Hispanics, will be a matter of vital importance as long as he lives. And their size is basically determined by immigration. . . .

IMMIGRATION AND QUESTIONS OF MORALITY

American intellectuals approach the issue of immigration in a highly moralistic way. And their morality works in only one direction. For example, the huge academic industry has produced *not one* serious philosophical treatment of this topic that is other than pro-immigration.[13]

The illegal-immigration scandal on the border, of course, is only part of the problem. These intellectuals seem to view all of immigration policy as an opportunity for public displays of exquisite sensibility. The immigration debate provides them with the equivalent of a revivalist meeting. They get to fall on the floor and speak in tongues.

It definitely slows things down. At other people's expense.

For example, after my *National Review* cover story came out, I found myself invited to the University of Cincinnati Law School to debate immigration. I love this sort of thing. As a provincial from a small country, I am fascinated by the way in which America really is a federal society. The different urban centers of commerce, culture and politics are genuinely independent from—and, indeed, positively indifferent to—each other.

Plus, of course, you could never on your own think up all the weird questions people ask.

The weird question I remember these American law students asking on this occasion went directly to the morality of immigration:

QUESTION: *Isn't immigration a civil right?*
[ANSWER: *No! Are you serious?*]

Isn't immigration a *what?* Well, I should have anticipated it, I suppose. Current U.S. policy, as we have seen, does indeed treat legal immigration as a sort of bastard civil right, extended to relatives of the arbitrarily selected group of foreigners who happen to have shouldered through the door first since the 1965 Immigration Act.

But that was not what the students meant. They meant that all foreigners just have a right, a civil right, to emigrate to the United States. (In fact, I suspect that, like many Americans, the students didn't realize foreigners have an independent existence at all. They just viewed them as an exotic type of American minority. Like Hollywood's Maurice Chevalier or Charles Laughton.)

And on this level, needless to say, the proposition is hopelessly incoherent, logically and morally. How can foreigners have civil rights when they are not members of the *civitas?* And why *these* foreigners—at the expense of the infinite number of other foreigners? . . .

I don't think I shook their simple faith.

QUESTION: *Aren't we morally obliged to accept immigrants?*
[ANSWER: *Even if we are, that's just the start of the problem.*]

If immigration to the United States is not a civil right, then maybe it's an overriding moral right? This notion is particularly popular among the men and women who staff the major American religious organizations.

(The laity is notably less enthusiastic. A 1992 Gallup Poll found that self-reported Christians, Catholics and Protestants alike were not only heavily opposed to current mass immigration—but were actually *more* opposed than those respondents who professed no religion.[14])

Curiously, morality seems to have reversed itself completely since the 1960s. In 1967, 1968 and 1972 the United Nations passed resolutions condemning the developed nations for seducing away the educated of the Third World—the so-called "brain drain."

Some splendid scripture gets quoted to support immigration. Leviticus 19:33–34 has resonance for Jews in particular:

> *If a stranger sojourn with thee in your land, ye shall not vex him. But the stranger that dwelleth with you shall be unto you as one born among you, and thou shalt love him as thyself; for ye were strangers in the land of Egypt.*

It's a curious passage, because elsewhere in the Old Testament the Children of Israel are instructed to be very careful indeed about those alien influences. For example, many Americans might see more relevance to their country's current plight in the dire warning of Deuteronomy 28:43–44:

> *The stranger that is within thee shall get up above thee very high; and thou shalt come down very low. He shall lend to thee, and thou shalt not lend to him; he shall be the head and thou shalt be the tail.*

Mainline Christian denominations often cite a New Testament text to justify immigration: Matthew 25:31–46—the Last Judgment. Christ describes a time when "the Son of Man" will divide the nations, and condemn one group to hell, saying—

> *For I was an hungred, and ye gave me no meat; I was thirsty, and ye gave me no drink. I was a stranger, and ye took me not in; naked, and ye clothed me not; sick, and in prison, and ye visited me not.*

Naturally, the condemned nations get upset:

> *Then shall they also answer him, saying, 'Lord, when saw we thee an hungred, or athirst, or a stranger, or naked, or sick, or in prison, and did not minister unto thee?'*

* * *

> *Then shall he answer them, saying, Verily I say unto you, inasmuch as ye did it not to one of the least of these, ye did it not to me.*

This text is interpreted surprisingly literally by liberal theologians, who usually view fundamentalism with disdain. They suggest that any "stranger" prevented from entering the United States may be, in effect, well, Jesus.

The problem, however, is this: *there are rather a lot of Jesuses out there.* No conceivable U.S. immigration policy can "minister" to all of them.

Once again, the sensibility is exquisite. But it is not a practical guide to action.

Let's look at the practicalities. Suppose that the United States does have an obligation to "minister" to the poor of the world. Then, obviously, it must do so *effectively.*

How could the United States "minister" effectively? There are two possibilities, depending upon your understanding of the way the world works.

Either: *1. Americans are sitting on a pile of wealth. They should simply share it.*

* * *

Or: *2. Americans have created a system that produces wealth. They can only share wealth to the extent that sharing it does not impair the system.*

From an economist's standpoint, there is simply no argument about which of these possibilities is right. Quite obviously, wealth is not a matter of resources: it is a matter of resourcefulness.

Some countries with large populations and great natural riches, like Brazil—or Mexico—are poor. Other countries with few resources and small populations, like Switzerland, are rich. And countries with no resources but fairly large, hardworking and ingenious populations, like Japan, can become very rich indeed.

In other words, the United States is not a pile of wealth but a fragile system—a lifeboat. And lifeboats can get overcrowded and sink.

On the other hand, lifeboats can tow large numbers of survivors along in their wake. In fact, this is usually what happens in shipwrecks.

The lifeline everyone can hang on to, in this case, is trade. By buying and importing straw hats (or whatever), the wealth generated by the American system can penetrate the remotest fastnesses of China (or wherever).

But it is not at all necessary for Chinese peasants to come in person to America in order for the American system to "minister" to them effectively.

In fact, it may be easier if they don't.

It's worth remembering that in the last century, the same religious moralists who now support immigration provided much of the motivating force behind imperialism. The partition of the world by the Western powers was quite often in response to missionaries' demands that Something Be Done about slavery, starvation and assorted degradations beyond the frontiers of civilization. The great poet of the British Empire, Rudyard Kipling, was not being at all ironic when he wrote his famous lines applauding the U.S. seizure of the Philippines:

Take up the White Man's burden,
Send forth the best ye breed—
Go, bind your sons to exile
To serve your captives' need.

A hundred years later, the White Person's Burden is apparently that the same "captives" be brought here. It amounts to an inverted imperialism. It confirms the United States as a colony of the world.

QUESTION: *What about the American tradition of accepting refugees?*
[ANSWER: *What tradition?*]

It's just another manufactured immigration myth. The truth is that almost the first federal legislation affecting immigration, the Alien and Sedition Acts of 1798, was largely motivated by fear of refugees from the French Revolution. Subsequently, some immigrants arriving in America were fleeing disruption at home (although that can be exaggerated—contrary to the general impression, for example, relatively few Germans came to the United States as a direct result of the collapse of the democratic revolutions of 1848[15]). But there was no explicit recognition of refugees as such until select groups began to be admitted in the years following World War II. The United States did not acquire a comprehensive refugee policy until the Refugee Act of 1980. And, as we have seen, that was promptly captured and debauched by special interest groups.

QUESTION: *But didn't the United States cause all these refugees because of its foreign policy?—look at El Salvador/Nicaragua/Vietnam.*
[ANSWER: *Does that mean you want to accept 5 million white South Africans?*]

People who make this argument seem to mean only those foreign policy controversies where they disagree with the United States and want to punish it. Thus, resisting communism was always pretty controversial with a small but vocal group of Americans. Forcing the whites to give up power in South Africa was not.

Nevertheless, it cannot be denied that U.S. policy played a key role in breaking the white South African government's will. And the country might easily become another Lebanon.

Well—where's the welcome mat?

The reality is this: the United States is the only global superpower. It is the central pillar of world order. This means there is practically nothing for which U.S. action, or inaction, cannot be blamed. And there will always be Americans ready to do the blaming. . . .

The United States, however, is the flower that the rest of the world is struggling to pluck. Should it not at least ensure that its native-born citizens are treated equally in exchange?

GIVING IMMIGRATION CRITICS A GOOD NAME

Critics of current U.S. immigration policy worry about what to call themselves. They think their inability to get a public hearing is partly because they don't, quite literally, have a good name.

Being "anti-immigration" just doesn't sound very good. (Besides being inaccurate: most critics merely want reform.) Too much like being "anti-immigrant."

Negative. Nasty. Possibly—aargh!—nativist. No decent TV news director wants anything to do with *that.*

As an immigrant, I have a modest proposal for these critics of immigration.

As we have seen, any general moral obligation to minister to strangers is met, and more than matched, by the specific and even stronger moral obligation to protect our own family.

And on the political level, the equivalent of the family is the nation-state—every one of them, in Aleksandr Solzhenitsyn's words, a particular facet of God's design.

So I suggest that the critics of immigration adopt a name that has a long and honorable role in American history.

They should call themselves—"Patriots."

NOTES

1. Peter Brimelow, "Time to Rethink Immigration?" *National Review,* June 22, 1992.

2. Interview with Bureau of the Census spokesman; unofficial preliminary estimate as of April 1993.

3. *Los Angeles Times,* January 6, 1992.

4. Judith T. Fullerton and Company, *Access to Prenatal Care for Hispanic Women of San Diego County.* Latina/Latino Research Program, California Policy Seminar (Berkeley: Regents of the University of California, 1993).

5. Daniel James, *Illegal Immigration—An Unfolding Crisis* (Lanham, Md.: University Press of America, 1991); interview.

6. Senate Committee on Government Affairs, Permanent Subcommittee on Investigations, *Investigation of the INS Criminal Alien Program,* minority staff statement, November 10, 1993.

7. Bureau of the Census, *Population Profile of the U.S.: 1993,* prepared by the Bureau of the Census (Washington, D.C., 1993), 32–33; "Assessment of Potential Impact of Undocumented Persons on Health Reform: Report by National Health Foundation to Presidential Task Force on Health Reform," *New York Times,* May 3, 1993.

8. See, for example, Peter Brimelow, "American Perestroika?" *Forbes,* May 14, 1990.

9. Spokesman interview. Center for Education Statistics, Department of Education, Washington, D.C.

10. Orange County Grand Jury, Human Services Committee, *Impact of Immigration on the County of Orange,* Report of July 16 (Santa Ana, Calif., 1993), 5.

11. Bureau of the Census, *Census of Population and Housing: The Foreign-Born Population in the U.S.,* prepared by the Bureau of the Census (Washington, D.C., 1990), CP-3-1.

12. Virginia Postrel, editorial, *Reason,* May–October 1993.

13. John Lachs, Professor of Philosophy, Vanderbilt University, Nashville, Tennessee, interview.

14. Roy Beck, "Religions and the Environment: Commitment High Until U.S. Population Raised," *Social Contract,* Winter 1992–93, 87.

15. Stephan Thernstrom, Ed., *Harvard Encyclopedia of American Ethnic Groups* (Cambridge, Mass: Belknap Press, Harvard University Press, 1980), 410.

21

Five Myths About Immigration

DAVID COLE

For a brief period in the mid-nineteenth century, a new political movement captured the passions of the American public. Fittingly labeled the "Know-Nothings," their unifying theme was nativism. They liked to call themselves "Native Americans," although they had no sympathy for people we call Native Americans today. And they pinned every problem in American society on immigrants. As one Know-Nothing wrote in 1856: "Four-fifths of the beggary and three-fifths of the crime spring from our foreign population; more than half the public charities, more than half the prisons and almshouses, more than half the police and the cost of administering criminal justice are for foreigners."

At the time, the greatest influx of immigrants was from Ireland, where the potato famine had struck, and Germany, which was in political and economic turmoil. Anti-alien and anti-Catholic sentiments were the order of the day, especially in New York and Massachusetts, which received the brunt of the wave of immigrants, many of whom were dirt-poor and uneducated. Politicians were quick to exploit the sentiment: There's nothing like a scapegoat to forge an alliance.

I am especially sensitive to this history: My forebears were among those dirt-poor Irish Catholics who arrived in the 1860s. Fortunately for them, and me, the Know-Nothing movement fizzled within fifteen years. But its pilot light kept burning, and is turned up whenever the American public begins to feel vulnerable and in need of an enemy.

Although they go by different names today, the Know-Nothings have returned. As in the 1850s, the movement is strongest where immigrants are most concentrated: California and Florida. The objects of prejudice are of course no longer Irish Catholics and Germans; 140 years later, "they" have become "us." The new "they"—because it seems "we" must always have a "they"—are Latin Americans (most recently, Cubans), Haitians and Arab-Americans, among others.

But just as in the 1850s, passion, misinformation and shortsighted fear often substitute for reason, fairness and human dignity in today's immigration debates. In the interest of advancing beyond know-nothingism, let's look at five current myths that distort public debate and government policy relating to immigrants.

America is being overrun with immigrants. In one sense, of course, this is true, but in that sense it has been true since Christopher Columbus arrived. Except for the real Native Americans, we are a nation of immigrants.

It is not true, however, that the first-generation immigrant share of our population is growing. As of 1990, foreign-born people made up only 8 percent of the population, as compared with a figure of about 15 percent from 1870 to 1920. Between 70 and 80 percent of those who immigrate every year are refugees or immediate relatives of U.S. citizens.

Much of the anti-immigrant fervor is directed against the undocumented, but they make up only 13 percent of all immigrants residing in the United States, and only 1 percent of the American population. Contrary to popular belief, most such aliens do not cross the border illegally but enter legally and remain after their student or visitor visa expires. Thus, building a wall at the border, no matter how high, will not solve the problem.

Immigrants take jobs from U.S. citizens. There is virtually no evidence to support this view, probably the most widespread misunderstanding about immigrants. As documented by a 1994 A.C.L.U. Immigrants' Rights Project report, numerous studies have found that immigrants actually *create* more jobs than they fill. The jobs immigrants take are of course easier to see, but immigrants are often highly productive, run their own businesses and employ both immigrants and citizens. One study found that Mexican immigration to Los Angeles County between 1970 and 1980 was responsible for 78,000 new jobs. Governor Mario Cuomo reports that immigrants own more than 40,000 companies in New York, which provide thousands of jobs and $3.5 billion to the state's economy every year.

Immigrants are a drain on society's resources. This claim fuels many of the recent efforts to cut off government benefits to immigrants. However, most studies have found that immigrants are a net benefit to the economy because, as a 1994 Urban Institute report concludes, "immigrants generate significantly more in taxes paid than they cost in services received." The Council of Economic Advisers similarly found in 1986 that "immigrants have a favorable effect on the overall standard of living."

Anti-immigrant advocates often cite studies purportedly showing the contrary, but these generally focus only on taxes and services at the local or state level. What they fail to explain is that because most taxes go to the federal government, such studies would also show a net loss when applied to U.S. citizens. At most, such figures suggest that some redistribution of federal and state monies may be appropriate; they say nothing unique about the costs of immigrants.

Some subgroups of immigrants plainly impose a net cost in the short run, principally those who have most recently arrived and have not yet "made it." California, for example, bears substantial costs for its disproportionately large undocumented population, largely because it has on average the poorest and least educated immigrants. But that has been true of every wave of immigrants that has ever reached our shores; it was as true of the Irish in the 1850s, for example, as it is of Salvadorans today. From a long-term perspective, the economic advantages of immigration are undeniable.

Some have suggested that we might save money and diminish incentives to immigrate illegally if we denied undocumented aliens public services. In fact, undocumented immigrants are already ineligible for most social programs, with the exception of education for schoolchildren, which is constitutionally required, and benefits directly related to health and safety, such as emergency medical care and nutritional assistance to poor women, infants and children. To deny such basic care to people in need, apart from being inhumanly callous, would probably cost us more in the long run by exacerbating health problems that we would eventually have to address.

Aliens refuse to assimilate, and are depriving us of our cultural and political unity. This claim has been made about every new group of immigrants to arrive on U.S. shores. Supreme Court Justice Stephen Field wrote in 1884 that the Chinese "have remained among us a separate people, retaining their original peculiarities of dress, manners, habits, and modes of living, which are as marked as their complexion and language." Five years later, he upheld the racially based exclusion of Chinese immigrants. Similar claims have been made over different periods of our history about Catholics, Jews, Italians, Eastern Europeans and Latin Americans.

In most instances, such claims are simply not true; "American culture" has been created, defined and revised by persons who for the most part are descended from immigrants once seen as anti-assimilationist. Descendants of the Irish Catholics, for example, a group once decried as separatist and alien, have become Presidents, senators and representatives (and all of these in one family, in the case of the Kennedys). Our society exerts tremendous pressure to conform, and cultural separatism rarely survives a generation. But more important, even if this claim were true, is this a legitimate rationale for limiting immigration in a society built on the values of pluralism and tolerance?

Noncitizen immigrants are not entitled to constitutional rights. Our government has long declined to treat immigrants as full human beings, and nowhere is that more clear than in the realm of constitutional rights. Although the Constitution literally extends the fundamental protections in the Bill of Rights to all people, limiting to citizens only the right to vote and run for federal office, the federal government acts as if this were not the case.

In 1893 the executive branch successfully defended a statute that required Chinese laborers to establish their prior residence here by the testimony of "at least one credible white witness." The Supreme Court ruled that this law was constitutional because it was reasonable for Congress to presume that nonwhite witnesses could not be trusted.

The federal government is not much more enlightened today. In a pending case I'm handling in the Court of Appeals for the Ninth Circuit, the Clinton Administration has argued that permanent resident aliens lawfully living here should be extended no more First Amendment rights than aliens applying for first-time admission from abroad—that is, none. Under this view, students at a public university who are citizens may express themselves freely, but students who are not citizens can be deported for saying exactly what their classmates are constitutionally entitled to say.

Growing up, I was always taught that we will be judged by how we treat others. If we are collectively judged by how we have treated immigrants—those who appear today to be "other" but will in a generation be "us"—we are not in very good shape.

22

Lingo Jingo

English-Only and the New Nativism

GEOFFREY NUNBERG

Since Slovakia became an independent state a few years ago, the Slovak majority has been imposing increasingly stringent language restrictions on the ethnic Hungarian minority, whom they suspect of irredentist leanings. Hungarian place-names must be changed to accord with Slovak spellings, all official business must be transacted in Slovak even in districts that are almost entirely Hungarian-speaking, and so forth. It's a familiar enough pattern in that part of the world, where antique ethnic antagonisms are routinely fought out on the field of language, except that in this case, the Slovakians have insisted that their policies are in fact thoroughly modern—even American. By way of demonstrating this, the Slovak State Language Law of 1995 cites the example of American official-English bills, and the drafters of the law made a point of entertaining a delegation from the U.S. English organization. In American eyes, though, the similarities might lead to another, more disquieting conclusion: What if it's we who are becoming more like them?

For most of our history, language has not been a major theme in American political life. The chief reason for that, to be sure, is that God in his wisdom has given us a single dominant language, with few real dialects or patois of the sort that European nations have had to deal with in the course of their nation building. (One notable exception is the post-Creole variety spoken by many African Americans.) It's true that America has always had substantial communities of speakers of non-English languages: indigenous peoples; groups absorbed in the course of colonial expansion, like the Francophones of Louisiana and the Hispanics of the Southwest; and the great flows of immigrants from 1880 to 1920 and during the past 30 years. And since the eighteenth century there have been recurrent efforts to discourage or suppress the use of other languages by various minorities, particularly at the time of the nativist movement of the turn of the century. But the focus on language has always been opportunistic, a convenient way of underscoring the difference between us and them: the issue has always subsided as minorities have become anglicized, leaving little symbolic residue in its wake. Unlike the Slovakians, the Italians, the Germans, or those paragons of official orality, the French, we have not until now made how we speak an essential element of what we are.

* * *

Given the minor role that language has played in our historical self-conception, it isn't surprising that the current English-only movement began in the political margins, the brainchild of slightly flaky figures like Senator S.I. Hayakawa and John Tanton, a Michigan ophthalmologist who co-founded the U.S. English organization as an outgrowth of his involvement in zero population growth and immigration restriction. (The term "English-only" was originally introduced by supporters of a 1984 California initiative opposing bilingual ballots, a stalking horse for other official-language measures. Leaders of the movement have since rejected the label, pointing out that they have no objection to the use of foreign languages in the home. But the phrase is a fair characterization of the goals of the movement so far as public life is concerned.)

Until recently, English-only was not a high priority for the establishment right. President Bush was opposed to the movement, and Barbara Bush once went so far as to describe it as "racist." And while a number of figures in the Republican leadership have been among the sponsors of official-language bills, most did not become vocal enthusiasts of the policy until the successes of English-only measures and of anti-immigrant initiatives like California's Proposition 187 persuaded them that anti-immigrant politics might have broad voter appeal. Senator Dole endorsed English-only in the 1996 presidential campaign, and Newt Gingrich recently described bilingualism as a menace to American civilization.

The successes of English-only are undeniably impressive. Polls show between 65 percent and 86 percent of Americans favoring making English the official language, and the U.S. English organization currently claims more than 650,000 members. Largely owing to its efforts, 18 states have adopted official-language measures via either referenda or legislative action, with legislation pending in 13 more (four other states have official-language statutes that date from earlier periods). The majority of these laws are largely symbolic, like the 1987 Arkansas law—which President Clinton now says it was "a mistake" to sign—that states merely, "The English language shall be the official language of the state of Arkansas." But a few are more restrictive, notably the measure adopted by Arizona voters in 1988, which bars the state or its employees from conducting business in any language other than English, apart from some narrow exceptions for purposes like health and public safety. In 1996 the House passed H.R. 123, which is similar in most respects to the Arizona law. (Its title is the "English Language Empowerment Act," which as the writer James Crawford has observed is a small assault on the language in its own right.) The Senate did not act on the bill, but it has been reintroduced in the current session; given the present makeup of the Congress, there is a fair chance that some legislation will be enacted in this session—though perhaps in the watered-down version preferred by some Senate Republicans who are apprehensive about offending Hispanic constituents. In that form, as little more than a symbolic affirmation of the official status of English, the bill would likely win the support of some Democrats, and might prove difficult for President Clinton to veto.

In any case, to the extent that the bill is symbolic, its adoption is more or less facultative; the movement achieves most of its goals simply by raising the issue. At the local level, the public discussion of English-only has encouraged numerous private acts of discrimination. In recent years, for example, dozens of firms and institutions have adopted English-only workplace rules that bar employees from using foreign languages even when speaking among themselves or when on breaks. More generally, the mere fact that politicians and the press are willing to take the proposals of English-only seriously tends to establish the basic premise of the movement: that there is a question about the continued status of English as the common language of American public discourse. In the end, the success of the movement should be measured not by the number of official-language statutes passed, but by its success in persuading people—including many who are unsympathetic to the English-only approach—to accept large parts of the English-only account of the situation of language in America.

IS ENGLISH REALLY ENDANGERED?

In rough outline, the English-only story goes like this: The result of recent immigration has been a huge influx of non-English speakers, who now constitute a substantial proportion of the population. Advocates of English-only often claim that there are 32 million Americans who are not proficient in English, a figure that will rise to 40 million by the year 2000. Moreover, these recent arrivals, particularly the Hispanics, are not learning English as earlier generations of immigrants did. According to Senator Hayakawa, "large populations of Mexican Americans, Cubans, and Puerto Ricans do not speak English and have no intention of learning."

The alleged failure to learn English is laid to several causes. There are the ethnic leaders accused of advocating a multiculturalist doctrine that asserts, as Peter Salins describes it, that "ethnic Americans [have] the right to function in their 'native' language—not just at home but in the public realm." Government is charged with impeding linguistic assimilation by providing a full range of services in other languages, even as bilingual education enables immigrant children to complete their schooling without ever making the transition to English. Moreover, it is claimed, the peculiar geographic situation of Hispanics creates communities in which linguistic or cultural assimilation is unnecessary. For example, Paul Kennedy (himself no supporter of English-only) writes of an impending "Hispanicization of the American Southwest," where

> Mexican-Americans will have sufficient coherence and critical mass in a defined region so that, if they choose, they can preserve their distinctive culture indefinitely. They could also undertake to do what no previous immigrant group could ever have dreamed of doing: challenge the existing cultural, political, legal, commercial, and educational systems to change fundamentally not only the language but also the very institutions in which they do business.

Once you accept all this, it is not hard to conclude, as Congressman Norman Shumway puts it, that "the primacy of English is being threatened, and we are moving to a bilingual society," with all the prospects of disorder and disunity that bilingualism seems to imply. As Senator Hayakawa wrote:

> For the first time in our history, our nation is faced with the possibility of the kind of linguistic division that has torn apart Canada in recent years; that has been a major feature of the unhappy history of Belgium, split into speakers of French and Flemish; that is at this very moment a bloody division between the Sinhalese and Tamil populations of Sri Lanka.

A U.S. English ad makes the point more graphically: A knife bearing the legend "official bilingualism" slashes through a map of the United States.

* * *

But the English-only story is nonsense from beginning to end. Take, for starters, the claim that there are 32 million Americans who are not proficient in English. To see how wild that figure is, consider that the total number of foreign-born residents over five years old is only 18 million, some of them immigrants from other English-speaking countries and most of the rest speaking English well. The actual Census figure for residents over five who speak no English is only 1.9 million—proportionately only a quarter as high as it was in 1890, at the peak of the last great wave of immigration. And even if we include people who report speaking English "not well," the number of residents with limited English proficiency stands at around six million people in all. This is not a huge figure when you consider the extent of recent immigration and the difficulty that adults have in acquiring a new language, particularly when they are working in menial jobs that involve little regular contact with English speakers. (Or to put it another way: More than 97 percent of Americans speak English well, a level of linguistic homogeneity unsurpassed by any other large nation in history.)

What is more, recent immigrants are in fact learning English at a faster rate than any earlier generations of immigrants did—and by all the evidence, with at least as much enthusiasm. Whatever "multiculturalism" may mean to its proponents, it most assuredly does not involve a rejection of English as the national lingua franca. No ethnic leaders have been crazy enough to suggest that immigrants can get along without learning English, nor would any immigrants pay the slightest attention to such a suggestion if it were made. According to a recent Florida poll, 98 percent of Hispanics want their children to speak English well. And the wish is father to the deed: Immigrants of all nationalities are moving to English at a faster rate than ever before in our history. The demographer Calvin Veltman has observed that the traditional three-generation period for a complete shift to English is being shortened to two generations. A recent RAND Corporation study showed that more than 90 percent of first-generation Hispanics born in California have native fluency in English, and that only about 50 percent of the second generation still speak Spanish.

That latter figure suggests that for recent Hispanic arrivals, as for many groups of immigrants that preceded them, becoming American entails not just mastering English but also rejecting the language and culture of one's parents. It is a regrettable attitude (and the very one that English-only has battened on), but the process seems inevitable: Relatively few Hispanics display the fierce religious or patriotic loyalty to their mother tongue that the Germans did a hundred years ago. The only exception is the Cubans, who have a special political motivation for wanting to hang on to Spanish, but even here the preference for English is increasingly marked—a survey of first- and second-generation Cuban college students in Miami found that 86 percent preferred to use English in speaking among themselves. It is only the assimilated third- and fourth-generation descendants of immigrants who feel the loss of languages keenly, and by then it is almost always too late. (For a linguist, there is no more poignant experience than to watch a class of American college freshmen struggling to master the basic grammar of the language that their grandparents spoke with indifferent fluency.)

* * *

A number of factors contribute to the accelerated pace of language shift among immigrants: the increased mobility, both social and geographical, of modern life; the ubiquity of English-language media; universal schooling; and the demands of the urban workplace. In the nineteenth century, by contrast, many immigrants could hold on to their native language for several generations at no great cost: some because they lived in isolated farming communities and required very little contact with English speakers, others because they lived in one of the many states or cities that provided public schooling in their native tongues. At the turn of the century, in fact, more than 6 percent of American schoolchildren were receiving most or all of their primary education in the German language alone—programs that were eliminated only around the time of the First World War.

All of this underscores the irony of the frequent claims that unlike earlier generations, modern immigrants are refusing to learn English—or that modern bilingual education is an "unprecedented" concession to immigrants who insist on maintaining their own language. In point of fact, there's a good chance that great-grandpa didn't work very hard to learn English, and a fair probability that his kids didn't, either. Today, by contrast, all publicly supported bilingual education programs are aimed at facilitating the transition to English. The programs are unevenly implemented, it's true, owing to limited funding, to the resistance of school administrators, and to the shortage of trained teachers. (An early study found that 50 percent of teachers hired in "bilingual" programs lacked proficiency in their students' native languages.) And in any case such programs are available right now for only about 25 percent of limited English students. Still, the method clearly works better than any of the alternatives. An extensive 1992 study sponsored by the National Academy of Sciences found that, compared with various types of "immersion" programs, bilingual education reduces the time to reach full English fluency by between two and three years.

* * *

What of the other government programs that critics describe as opening the door to "official bilingualism"? Measured against the numerous social and economic motivations that limited-English immigrants have for learning English, the availability of official information in their own language is a negligible disincentive, and there are strong arguments for providing these services. To take an example that the English-only people are fond of raising, why in the world would we want to keep immigrants with limited English from taking their driver's license tests in their native languages? Do we want to keep them from driving to work until they have learned the English word *pedestrian?* Or to be more realistic about it—since many of them will have no choice but to drive anyway—do we want to drive to work on roads full of drivers who are ignorant of the traffic laws?

In any event, these programs are extremely, even excessively, limited. Federal law mandates provision of foreign-language services only in a handful of special cases—interpreters must be provided for migrant worker health care centers and for certain Immigration and Naturalization Service procedures, for example—and a recent General Accounting Office survey found that the total number of federal documents printed in languages other than English over the past five years amounted to less than one-tenth of 1 percent of the total number of titles, hardly a sign of any massive shift to multilingualism in the public realm.

LANGUAGE AS SYMBOLISM

Considered strictly in the light of the actualities, then, English-only is an irrelevant provocation. It is a bad cure for an imaginary disease, and moreover, one that encourages an unseemly hypochondria about the health of the dominant language and culture. But it is probably a mistake to try to engage the issue primarily at this level, as opponents of these measures have tried to do with little success. Despite the insistence of English-only advocates that they have launched their campaign "for the immigrants' own good," it's hard to avoid the conclusion that the needs of non-English speakers are a pretext, not a rationale, for the movement. At every stage, the success of the movement has depended on its capacity to provoke widespread indignation over allegations that government bilingual programs are promoting a dangerous drift toward a multilingual society. The movement's supporters seem to have little interest in modifying that story to take the actual situation of immigrants into account. To take just one example, there are currently long waiting lists in most cities for English-language adult classes—around 50,000 people in Los Angeles County alone—but none of the English-only bills that have been introduced in the Congress make any direct provision for funding of such programs. Who, after all, would care about that?

One indication of just how broadly the movement transcends any immediate, practical concerns about immigrants is the success it has had in regions where issues like immigration and multiculturalism ought by rights to be fairly remote concerns. Of the states that have passed official-English laws in recent years, only four (California, Florida, Arizona, and Colorado) have large immigrant populations. The remainder consist of western states like Montana, North and South Dakota, and Wyoming; Indiana and New Hampshire; and all of the southern and border states except Louisiana (apart from Florida, the only state in the region with substantial numbers of non-English speakers). The breadth of support for these measures seems to increase as its local relevance diminishes, as witness the 89 percent majority that the measure won in an Alabama referendum and the unanimous or near-unanimous legislative votes for English-only measures in states like Arkansas, Georgia, Tennessee, Kentucky, and Virginia. These are not the sorts of places where voters could feel any imminent threat to English from the babel of alien tongues, or indeed, where we would expect to see voters or legislators giving much attention to immigration at all.

* * *

At the national level, then, English-only is not strictly comparable to explicit anti-immigrant measures like Proposition 187, which raise genuine substantive issues. The English-only movement has been successful because it provides a symbolic means of registering dissatisfaction with a range of disquieting social phenomena—immigration, yes, but also multiculturalism, affirmative action, and even public assistance. (Not missing a trick, U.S. English advocates like to describe bilingual programs as "linguistic welfare.") By way of response, the movement offers an apparently minimal conception of American identity: We are at the very least a people who speak English.

It seems an unexceptionable stipulation. Even Horace Kallen, who introduced the notion of "cultural pluralism" 70 years ago as a counter to the ideology of the melting pot, readily acknowledged that all Americans must accept English as "the common language of [our] great tradition." But the decision to invest a language with official status is almost never based on merely practical considerations. Language always trails symbolic baggage in its wake and frames the notion of national identity in a particular way. That is why the designation of a national language is controversial wherever the matter arises.

However, the actual significance varies enormously from one nation to the next. Sometimes language is made the embodiment of a liturgical tradition, as in various Balkan countries, and sometimes of a narrowly ethnic conception of nationality, as in Slovakia or the Baltic states. In the recent French debates over the status of the language and the use of English words, the language is standing in more than anything else for the cultural authority of traditional republican institutions—a recent constitutional amendment declared French not the national language, but *la langue de la Republique.*

* * *

Even in the American context, the case for English has been made in very different ways over the course of the century. For the nativists of Kallen's time, language was charged with a specifically ideological burden. The imposition of English was the cornerstone of an aggressive program of Americanization, aimed at sanitizing immigrant groups of the undemocratic doctrines they were thought to harbor. The laws passed in this period undid almost all the extensive public bilingualism of the late nineteenth century, particularly in the civic and political domains. The ability to speak English was made a condition for citizenship in 1906, and in 1915 an English-literacy requirement was added, over President Wilson's veto. A 1919 Nebraska statute stipulated that all public meetings be conducted in English; Oregon required that foreign-language periodicals provide an English translation of their entire contents. More than 30 states passed laws prohibiting or restricting foreign-language instruction in primary schools.

The justification provided for these measures was a peculiar doctrine about the connection between language and political thought, which held that speaking a foreign language was inimical to grasping the fundamental concepts of democratic society. The Nebraska supreme court, for example, warned against the "baneful effects" of educating children in foreign languages, which must "naturally inculcate in them the ideas and sentiments foreign to the best interests of their country." English was viewed as a kind of "chosen language," the consecrated bearer of "Anglo-Saxon" political ideals and institutions. A New York official told immigrants in 1916: "You have got to learn our language because that is the vehicle of the thought that has been handed down from the men in whose breasts first burned the fire of freedom." (Like many other defenders of this doctrine, he dated the tradition from the Magna Carta, a text written, as it happens, in Latin.)

Taken literally, the chosen-language doctrine does not stand up under scrutiny, either linguistically or philosophically. Nothing could be more alien to the Enlightenment universalism of the Founders than the notion that the truths they held to be "self-evident" were ineffable in other languages. But it is almost always a mistake to take talk of language literally. It was not our democratic ideals that seemed to require expression in English, but the patriotic rituals that were charged with mediating the sense of national identity in the period, such as the obligatory schoolroom declamations of the sacred texts of American democracy, and more broadly, the Anglo culture in which those rituals were embedded. Theodore Roosevelt made the connection clear when he said: "We must . . . have but one language. That must be the language of the Declaration of Independence, of Washington's Farewell Address, of Lincoln's Gettysburg speech and second inaugural." The list is significant in its omissions. English might also be the language of Shakespeare, Emerson, and Melville, but its claim to merit official recognition had to be made on political grounds, as the only cloth from which our defining ideals could be woven.

* * *

In this regard, the "new nativism" is greatly different from the old. The modern English-only movement makes the case for a national language in what seem to be apolitical (or at least, nonideological) terms. English is important solely as a lingua franca, the "social glue" or "common bond" that unites all Americans. Indeed, advocates are careful to avoid suggesting that English has any unique virtues that make it appropriate in this role. A U.S. English publication explains: "We hold no special brief for English. If Dutch (or French, or Spanish, or German) had become our national language, we would now be enthusiastically defending Dutch." (It is hard to imagine Theodore Roosevelt passing over the special genius of English so lightly.)

On the face of things, the contemporary English-only movement seems a less coercive point of view. Indeed, the movement often seems eager to discharge English of any cultural or ideological responsibility whatsoever. Its advocates cast their arguments with due homage to the sanctity of pluralism. As former Kentucky Senator Walter Huddleston puts it, Americans are "a generous people, appreciative of cultural diversity," and the existence of a common language has enabled us "to develop a stable and cohesive society that is the envy of many fractured ones, without imposing any strict standards of homogeneity." At the limit, advocates seem to suggest that Americans need have nothing at all in common, so long as we have the resources for talking about it.

That is misleading, though. Language is as much a proxy for culture now as it was at the turn of the century, except that now neither English nor Anglo culture needs any doctrinal justification. This explains why English-only advocates are so drawn to comparisons with polities like Canada, Belgium, and Sri Lanka. Turn-of-the-century nativists rarely invoked the cases of Austria-Hungary or the Turkish empire in making the case against multilingualism, not because such scenarios were implausible—after all, the nativists had no qualms about invoking equally implausible scenarios of immigrant hordes inciting revolution—but because they were irrelevant: What could Americans learn about their national identity from comparisons with places like those? And the fact that Americans are now disposed to find these specters plausible is an indication of how far the sense of national identity has moved from its doctrinal base. The ethnic divisions in Canada and Belgium are generally and rightly perceived as having no ideological significance, and the moral seems to be that cultural differences alone are sufficient to fragment a state, even this one.

* * *

There are a number of reasons for the shift in emphasis. One, certainly, is a generally diminished role for our particular political ideology in an age in which it seems to lack serious doctrinal rivals. Over the long term, though, the new sense of the role of a common language also reflects the emergence of new mechanisms for mediating the sense of national community—radio, film, television—which require no direct institutional intervention. And the effects of the new media are complemented by the techniques of mass merchandising, which ensure that apart from "colorful" local differences, the material setting of American life will look the same from one place to another. ("To be American is to learn to shop," Newt Gingrich observed not long ago, without apparent irony.)

As Raymond Williams noted, the broadcast media aren't direct replacements for traditional institutions: They do not inculcate an ideology so much as presuppose one. In this sense they are capable of imposing a high degree of cultural and ideological uniformity without explicit indoctrination, or indeed, without seeming to "impose" at all. This may help to explain why the English-only movement appears indifferent to the schools or the courses in citizenship that played such an important part in the program of the turn-of-the-century Americanization movement, as well as to the theories about the special mission of English that were so prominent then. It's hard to imagine anyone making the case for English as the language of Washington's farewell speech or Lincoln's second inaugural, when students are no longer required to memorize or even read those texts anymore. Of all our sacred texts, only the Pledge of Allegiance and the national anthem are still capable of rousing strong feelings. But these are, notably, the most linguistically empty of all the American liturgy (schoolchildren say the first as if it were four long words, and I have never encountered anybody who is capable of parsing the second), which derive their significance chiefly from their association with the non-linguistic symbol of the flag.

CHERISHED CONFORMITY

It is inevitable, then, that modern formulations of the basis of national identity should come to focus increasingly on the importance of common experience and common knowledge, in place of (or at least, on an equal footing with) common political ideals. Michael Lind, for example, has argued that American identity ought to be officially vested in a national culture, which has native competence in American English as its primary index but is also based on American "folkways" that include:

> particular ways of acting and dressing; conventions of masculinity and femininity; ways of celebrating major events like births, marriages, and funerals; particular kinds of sports and recreations; and conceptions of the proper boundaries between the secular and religious spheres. And there is also a body of material—ranging from historical events that everyone is expected to know about to widely shared but ephemeral knowledge of sports and cinema and music—that might be called common knowledge.

Once we begin to insist on these cultural commonalities as necessary ingredients of national identity, it is inevitable that the insistence on English will become more categorical and sweeping. Where turn-of-the-century Americanizationists emphasized the explicitly civic uses of language, English-only casts its net a lot wider. It's true that the movement has tended to focus its criticism on the government bilingual programs, but only because these are the most accessible to direct political action; and within this domain, it has paid as much attention to wholly apolitical texts like driver's license tests and tax forms as to bilingual ballots. Where convenient, moreover, English-only advocates have also opposed the wholly apolitical private-sector uses of foreign languages. They have urged the California Public Utilities Commission to prohibit Pac Tel from publishing the Hispanic Yellow Pages; they have opposed the FCC licensing of foreign-language television and radio stations; they have proposed boycotts of Philip Morris for advertising in Spanish and of Burger King for furnishing bilingual menus in some localities. For all their talk of "cherished diversity," English-only advocates are in their way more intolerant of difference than their nativist predecessors. "This is America; speak English," English-only supporters like to say, and they mean 24 hours a day.

The irony of all this is that there was never a culture or a language so little in need of official support. Indeed, for someone whose first allegiance is to the English language and its culture, what is most distressing about the movement is not so much the insult it offers to immigrants as its evident lack of faith in the ability of English-language culture to make its way in the open market—and this at the very moment of the triumph of English as a world language of unprecedented currency. (A Frenchman I know described the English-only measures as akin to declaring crabgrass an endangered species.) The entire movement comes to seem tainted with the defensive character we associate with linguistic nationalism in other nations. I don't mean to say that English will ever acquire the particular significance that national languages have in places like Slovakia or France. But it's getting harder to tell the difference.

PART 5

Education

Education has been seen as both part of the solution to race and ethnic conflict and part of the problem. On the one hand, upward mobility opportunities in education have been viewed as part of the solution to racial inequality. Getting more minorities through the increasingly meritocratic educational institutions should bring them more economic equality, the argument goes. On the other hand, a variety of racial barriers in education are said to keep minorities from getting through the educational system. In addition to the barriers of prejudice and discrimination, say critics, the educational system is structured in a way that works to the disadvantage of most minority students.

THE STATISTICS

The available data can be used to support both views. On the one hand, the level of educational inequality between whites and minorities has dramatically declined. On the other hand, whites and Asians continue to receive more years of schooling than other minorities. The most recent data comparing the educational attainment of people twenty-five years and older from all race/ethnic groups were collected by the U.S. Bureau of the Census (1997) for 1990. The following figures show the percentage of each group that had graduated from high school and college:

	High School Graduate Or More	College Graduate Or More
Asian/Pacific Islander	78%	37%
White	78%	22%
Black	63%	11%
Native American	66%	9%
Hispanic	50%	9%

This illustrates the high level of education among Asians and whites, relative to other race/ethnic groups.

The American Council on Education (ACE) publishes more recent data on high school completion rates (Carter and Wilson 1997). In 1995, for example, 82 percent of the white 18- to 24-year-olds completed high school, compared with 77 percent of comparable blacks and 59 percent of comparable Hispanics. The black high school completion rate was 94 percent of the white rate (77/82 = 94%). The Hispanic high school completion rate, however, was only 72 percent of the white rate.

The ACE data clearly indicate that the black-white gap in high school completion rates for 18- to 24-year-olds has been narrowing substantially; it went from 70 percent in 1970 to 94 percent in 1994. The Hispanic-white gap, on the other hand, has diminished more slowly, going from 64 percent in 1972 to 72 percent in 1994.

The ACE also provides data on the rates of completing four years of college that show even greater inequality. In 1995, 26 percent of whites, 25–29 years old, had graduated from college, compared with 15 percent of blacks and 9 percent of Hispanics. The black college graduation rate is 58 percent of the white rate and the Hispanic rate is 35 percent of the white rate. The data also show that the black-white gap has diminished from 48 percent in 1975 to 58 percent in 1995. The Hispanic-white gap, on the other hand, has *increased* somewhat from 39 percent in 1975 to 35 percent in 1995.

Finally, there exist huge *class* differences in educational inequality. In 1994, for example, only 8 percent of the population from families in the lowest income quartile (earning below $22,033 annually) had a bachelor's degree by the time they were 24 years old. The comparable figure for people in the richest income quartile (earning above $67,881 annually) was 79 percent. Comparable data for the second and third quartiles (15 percent and 29 percent, respectively) are much closer to the bottom quartile than to the top (*Postsecondary Education Opportunity* 1995).

Even more significant is that the bachelor's degree gap between the top and bottom income quartiles is getting *larger*. In 1994, people in the top income quartile were almost ten times more likely to have a bachelor's degree than those from the bottom quartile. In 1970, those in the top quartile were "only" four times more likely to have a bachelor's degree than those in the bottom quartile.

These data show that educational inequality is still quite substantial, especially in terms of college graduation rates. Whites are almost twice as likely as blacks and three times as likely as Hispanics to graduate from college, even though the gap has been declining for blacks. Upper-income students are ten times more likely to graduate from college than lower-income students, and the gap has been getting larger.

THE EXPLANATION

Although all sides acknowledge these data, there are dramatically different explanations of why the group differences in education exist. There are at least three major explanations: (1) differences in culture and academic skills, (2) racial discrimination, and (3) structural inequalities of education. Each is briefly considered below.[1]

Skills/Culture

Most conservatives, and some liberals, argue that the reason that whites and Asians do better in school than blacks, Hispanics, and Native Americans is that they are more skilled. There is overwhelming evidence that at any given year in elementary and secondary school, whites and Asians are better than blacks and Hispanics at reading, writing, math, and so on. The racial/ethnic differences in academic skills can be seen in grades, scores on achievement tests, and virtually any other measure of academic achievement.

The important question, of course, is *why* whites and Asians tend to have superior academic skills to those of other minorities. Many social scientists attribute the skill differences to cultural variables. The better academic performance of whites and Asians is attributed to cultural factors such as stable homes, high levels of encouragement from parents and significant others, future orientation, a strong emphasis on personal discipline, and the development of a linear intellectual process that emphasizes rationality and logic. White and Asian families are also said to be more active in their children's schools than black and Hispanic families.

The lower level of achievement of non-Asian minorities, on the other hand, is said to be due to cultural factors that are less conducive to educational achievement, including family disorganization, present orientation, feelings of powerlessness, anti-intellectualism, low levels of parental encouragement and involvement in education, a lack of emphasis on personal discipline, and a nonlinear intellectual style. Language problems are also said to be impediments, especially for Hispanics. In part, this is a continuation of the culture of poverty argument discussed in Part Three.

The solution to educational inequality, according to the skills/culture explanation, is to help minority students cope more effectively with existing schools. In addition to providing minority students with academic skills and study habits, skills/culture theorists would encourage schools to intervene in the students' culture by emphasizing respect for authority, the ability to defer gratification, the belief in the ability to control one's own life, and the need for more parental involvement and more stable families. Schools would also increase the academic demands placed on minority students.

Racial Discrimination

All analysts agree that racial discrimination in education has existed in the past, especially prior to the 1954 *Brown v. Board of Education* decision of the U.S. Supreme Court, which outlawed legal segregation in the public schools. Many also argue that segregation is a continuing problem in schools and colleges, even though it may not be as obvious as it was in the past.

The overwhelming majority of black and Hispanic students still attend predominantly minority public schools. In 1994, two-thirds of black students and three-quarters of Hispanic students attended segregated schools, that is, schools where the student population was at least half minority. From 1970 to 1991, the segregation rate of black students had declined somewhat. Since 1991, it has begun to increase again. The segregation rate of Hispanics, on the other hand, has steadily increased since 1970 (Applebome 1997).

Predominantly minority schools tend to be older and underfunded relative to schools in white communities. Some white teachers are still prejudiced toward minority students and treat them unfairly. The schools often have low expectations of minority students and offer less rigorous curricula. Students often conform to those expectations by performing poorly. Ethnoviolence, which includes everything from name-calling to physical attacks that are a result of prejudice, is also said to poison the atmosphere of schools and colleges.

The solutions to educational inequality, according to the discrimination explanation, include more racial integration in public schools and colleges, more equal funding of white and minority schools, and the removal of prejudiced teachers and staff members. Ethnoviolence, whether it originates from other students or from teachers, should not be tolerated.

Structural Inequalities

According to this explanation, the structure of education has evolved in such a way that it perpetuates educational inequality. So-called meritocratic schools sort out the winners from the losers, and minority students are disproportionately found among the losers.

Because of their relatively low grades and test scores, for example, minority students tend to be disproportionately placed in lower tracks in public schools and are not prepared to attend college. In a national study of eighth grade math classes in 1988, for example, more than one-third of blacks and American Indians and one-quarter of Hispanics were in the "low-ability" classes, compared with 15 percent of whites and 17 percent of Asians. In contrast, only 10 percent of blacks, 15 percent of American Indians, and 18 percent of Hispanics were in the "high-ability" classes, compared with 35 percent of the whites and 47 percent of the Asians ("Education Life" 1992).

The curriculum in schools and colleges tends to be "Eurocentric" in that it focuses on the white historical and cultural traditions that can be traced back to Western Europe. The cultural and historical traditions of Africa, Asia, and Latin America tend to be ignored or downplayed. In addition, the problems faced by minorities in the United States in the 1990s tend to be ignored or minimized.

Given the family income differences between white and minority families, minority students find it difficult to afford expensive college-prep private schools. In addition, both white and minority students are finding it more and more difficult to finance college education due to increases in the cost of tuition, housing, books, and supplies. Because of political decisions made by conservative administrations in Washington, the amount of financial aid for students has declined, and most of the available aid has been in the form of loans rather than grants. This has created additional barriers for minority students who try to complete four years of college.

In order to turn things around, say structural theorists, the meritocratic structure of education, which emphasizes sorting over learning, must be transformed. Tracking in public schools must be eliminated. The transition from two-year to four-year colleges must be made easier. Adequate financial aid, in the form of grants rather than loans, must be made available to all who need it. Finally, the curricula of schools and colleges must reflect the history, culture, and present experience of students from all racial and ethnic groups.

Each of these three explanations focuses on a different facet of the problem. The result is that they each lead to different social policies.

* * *

What is the relationship of education to prejudice? There is a widespread belief that increased education decreases prejudice. A central part of the faith in education that most Americans hold is that formal education instills tolerance. There is a kernel of truth to the belief. A small correlation between years of schooling and prejudice does exist: As years of schooling go up, prejudice goes down. That correlation, however, is so small that it is clear that other, more important factors are involved.

The most important factor is, not surprisingly, the *content* of what gets taught. Obviously people can and do go through many years of school with little or no positive intergroup contacts and with little formal education in intergroup relations and cultural differences. During the 1960s, curricular reform was a major social issue as the prevailing movements for change sought to correct for the absence of minority concerns both in curriculum materials and in the telling of history. These reform issues are again before us, although the struggles are now more directed toward the universities, where the issue has come to be identified as "multiculturalism" and "diversity" in higher education.

The three articles in this section discuss two of the issues mentioned above—ethnoviolence and multiculturalism—and how they affect college campuses. Howard J. Ehrlich ("Campus Ethnoviolence") reviews research showing that ethnoviolence by whites against minorities is a major problem at colleges and universities. He then discusses some of the underlying causes of this problem.

Thomas Sowell ("'New Racism' and Old Dogmatism") also acknowledges the racial/ethnic tensions on college campuses, especially at large northern elite universities. Instead of pointing to ethnoviolence, however, Sowell believes that the causes of tension are the campus policies that favor minority students over whites. Campus administrators punish white students for any actions that offend even a single minority student but ignore similar actions by minority students toward whites. In addition, says Sowell, affirmative action causes resentment among whites.

Ronald Takaki ("Multiculturalism: Battleground or Meeting Ground?") analyzes the struggle over the university curriculum. Minorities want to broaden the curriculum to include the experiences of their own group, much of which involves past and current oppression. Academic conservatives, on the other hand, either try to protect Eurocentrism or call for a "safe" multiculturalism in which minority contributions are added on to the white majority experience.

NOTES

1. A small number of social scientists have put forward a contemporary version of a long-discredited argument that some race/ethnic groups are genetically more intelligent than others. Since this argument has been thoroughly discredited, we will not discuss it in this book.

REFERENCES

Applebome, Peter (1997) "Schools See Reemergence of 'Separate but Equal.'" *New York Times*, April 8: A1, 10.

Carter, Deborah J., and Reginald Wilson (1997) *Minorities in Higher Education, 15th Annual Status Report*. Washington, D.C.: American Council on Education.

"Education Life" (1992) *New York Times*, November 1: A4.

Postsecondary Education Opportunity (1995) No. 41: 1–8.

U.S. Bureau of the Census (1997) "Educational Attainment of the U.S. Population by Racial and Ethnic Group, 1990." *Chronicle of Higher Education*, August 29: 19.

U.S. Department of Education (1996) *Digest of Education Statistics, 1996*. Washington, D.C.: U.S. Government Printing Office.

23

Campus Ethnoviolence

HOWARD J. EHRLICH

The front page headline of the weekly *Chronicle of Higher Education* read: "New Outbreak of Cross-Burnings and Racial Slurs Worries Colleges." The dateline was January 12, 1981. The story reported ethnoviolent incidents at Harvard, Purdue, Williams, Wesleyan, Cornell, Iowa State, Wisconsin, and Massachusetts. You could easily mistake this story—in terms of the incidents described and the rhetoric of the college administrators quoted—for a story that had been written today.

The major news media were not ready to put campus ethnoviolence on their agenda, and the story did not break in the major news media until the last half of the 1985–1986 academic year. Three dramatic incidents received slight national coverage: the destruction of anti-apartheid shanties at Dartmouth, an attempt by white University of Texas students (wearing Ronald Reagan masks) to throw a black student out of a dormitory window, and a cross-burning in the yard of a black sorority house at the University of Alabama in Tuscaloosa. But it was not until the start of the following school year, 1986–1987, that an incident at the Citadel in Charleston, South Carolina, became the starting point for the news media's expanded coverage of campus ethnoviolence. The incident was a perfect scenario for a media morality play: a cross-burning and harassment of a black student at a southern military school with residues of Civil War regalia, a history of intergroup conflict, and a student victim who dropped out presumably because of his harassment.

Today, on college campuses across the United States—regardless of size, prestige, type of school, or region of the country—intergroup hostilities are being played out in traditional as well as newer patterns. Racist posters, signs, and fliers, spray-painted graffiti, and even T-shirts bearing group slurs are common. Minority students, as well as staff and faculty, have received intimidating and threatening mail, e-mail, and telephone calls. Physical assaults and property damage, although less common, have done serious harm.

This report addresses the multifaceted dimensions of ethnoviolence on campus. Reviewing systematic studies that have been done on thirty-two campuses since the National Institute Against Prejudice and Violence (now The Prejudice Institute) initiated this research in 1986, I will cover the following: the extent of ethnoviolent behaviors on campuses and the differences by ethnicity, race, religion, gender, and sexual orientation; the extent of revictimization, that is, how frequently the same students are targeted for attack; the prevalence of covictimization, that is, how an incident of ethnoviolence affects those who see or hear about it; the unique traumatic effects of being a victim of prejudice-motivated acts; what we know about the perpetrators of these acts; and why victimized students do not report these incidents. I close with a discussion of the ultraconservative undercurrents of intergroup conflicts on campus and with an analysis of the new targets of campus bigotry.

SURVEYS OF CAMPUS ETHNOVIOLENCE

In the spring of 1987, my associates and I undertook a systematic study of ethnoviolence on the campus of the University of Maryland Baltimore County (UMBC). The school, which is a part of the state system, is a mainly undergraduate institution of (then) approximately 9,000 students located in a predominantly white suburb of Baltimore. Several highly publicized incidents had occurred on the campus, and a sit-in protesting administrative inaction overlapped with the period of study (Ehrlich, Pincus, and Morton 1987).

Close replications of this original study have been conducted on fifteen campuses, all using variants of the same survey questionnaire (Ehrlich 1995). There have also been numerous case studies and five national surveys yielding comparable and supporting data. In addition, I include the findings of more specialized studies, which have dealt with prejudice-motivated violence directed at people because of their gender or sexual orientation.

"Ethnoviolence," which is our primary concern here, is defined as an act that is motivated by prejudice and intended to do psychological or physical harm to people because of their ethnic group membership. (I use *ethnic group* in its modern, inclusive sociological sense, which includes, among others, groups identified by their sexual orientation as well as the more traditional groups of race, religion, nationality, and national origin.) In general, we determine campus ethnoviolence rates by sampling students and asking them to report on their experiences.

THE BASIC FINDINGS

I now turn to what I think are some of the more reliable and replicated findings. As might be expected, there are substantial differences across campuses in the percentage of students reporting victimization based on prejudice. These differences may be attributable, in part, to campus size, the diversity of the campus population, and whether it is a residential or a commuter campus. Certainly each campus has its own history of intergroup relations as well as some unique subcultural dimensions.

There are general patterns to the findings of campus ethnoviolence research. I present here the major findings that emerged from the studies of middle-sized to large public universities.

One out of four students is the victim of at least one ethnoviolent incident during the school year. These findings include reports based on race/ethnicity, gender, age, sexual orientation, religion, national origin and citizenship, and disability. The actual proportion of students varies across campuses and it depends on the number of groups included in the survey design. Among white students, 5 to 18 percent report being victimized (the latter figure comes from the University of Hawaii at Manoa, where Asian Pacific students are in the majority). The corresponding figures for racial/ethnic minorities range from 12 to 60 percent with an estimated median of 25 percent. For those who were not directly victimized, the majority have seen or heard about incidents on campus.

The most common category of action is verbal aggression, which includes insults and name-calling, harassment and intimidation, threats, and insulting phone calls or mail. (E-mail appears to be a growing channel of insult and harassment.) Although there is a tendency for casual observers to downplay the significance of verbal and written forms of violence, our data indicate that people experience significant trauma from acts of verbal aggression. Words do wound.

In the more recent studies, *depersonalization* also emerges as a primary category of prejudice-motivated behavior, accounting for approximately 20 percent of student reports. This category refers to experiences of being treated as if you were invisible and did not exist. Property damage and acts of physical intimidation or assault are less frequent.

The groups who are victimized vary by campus. Past research suggests that the size and visibility of a minority group are the best predictors of whether its members will be victimized (Ehrlich 1973). What happened to these students? Here are some examples:

- A Chinese-American student sat down at the end of a library table. At the other end, a group of students who had been sitting there began telling ethnic jokes and directing anti-Asian slurs at her. She left. She was angry, hurt, badly upset, and afraid to return to the library alone.
- A gay male, at a time of intimate conversation with his two roommates, told them of his affectional orientation. They became verbally abusive and physically assaulted him.
- Sixty e-mail messages were sent to Asian American students threatening to kill Asian American students and staff if they did not leave the university. The message read "I personally will make it my life career to find and kill every one of you personally."
- A fraternity sent its pledges out on a "scavenger hunt" in which they were to return with photos of themselves with "Oriental girls." Another fraternity sent its members on a scavenger hunt for thirty-nine items, including "the biggest bra you can find," "pictures of two chicks making out," and a picture of "any funny looking Mexican." This was part of a hazing ritual for recruits.
- Two female cadets were forced to stand in a closet while they were shoved, kicked, and forced to drink alcohol in what was supposedly a hazing ritual. Their clothes were set on fire.
- A black columnist on a student newspaper depicted white people as "irredeemable racists" and called for blacks to "unite, organize and execute" whites who pose a threat.
- A theater piece about Walt Whitman, written by a noted gay historian, was rejected for production by the head of a university's playwriting

department, who asserted that a publicly supported university should not be expected to stage a play that celebrates "the virtues of homoeroticism."

- The Sigma Chi fraternity was found burning crosses and wearing Confederate uniforms. This was part of their ritual celebrating the founding of the fraternity.
- Swastikas were painted on two cars and a walkway outside of a predominately Jewish fraternity. One student whose car was vandalized complained that the police did not take his case seriously. He said that an officer told him, "Go to the federal government. I deal with criminals." Another officer told him that this was not a racial incident because "Jews aren't another race."
- Two organizations representing minority students, the United Coalition Against Racism and Latin American Solidarity Committee, received a flier that said, "Faggots, Niggers and Spic Lovers—BEWARE! You have gone beyond acceptable criticism. Never again will you go unpunished." The fliers were slipped under their office doors.
- One campus newspaper ran a racist editorial cartoon; another paper published a letter praising Hitler's eugenics programs; a campus radio program conducted a call-in ethnic joke fest; a computer bulletin board was used for displaying various epithets and slogans of bigotry.
- Native American students were subjected to racial taunts during the annual Indian Days Pow Wow. The American Indian Club filed a formal complaint, charging that participants were subjected to abusive comments and racial slurs, including war whoops.
- Members of a fraternity painted "KKK" and "We hate niggers" on the chests of two white pledges and then dumped them on the grounds of a nearby, predominantly black college. On being observed, the two naked white students were chased across campus until they found sanctuary in the college security office.
- On the second day of an exhibit by a gay artist at a campus art gallery, about thirty students entered the gallery and made hostile, homophobic comments. One woman said, "I think [the artist] is fucking psycho and I hope he dies." That night, vandals broke into a theater adjoining the gallery and unsuccessfully attempted to break into the gallery. They used shaving cream to spray anti-gay slurs inside the theater and on windows outside the gallery.
- Racial epithets were written on the walls and mirror of a residence hall room assigned to a Latino student.
- A sign of a black fraternity was defaced with the message "KKK—Go back to Africa."
- Leaflets proclaiming that the Holocaust was a hoax were passed out in front of the Hillel Foundation, a Jewish student organization.
- A music professor told his class that black music is dirty and that blacks were better off as slaves because they ate regularly and had roofs over their heads.
- A man with a red swastika painted on his forehead verbally assaulted a Jewish professor.

- A fraternity held a "border party." In order to gain entrance, guests had to crawl under a barbed wire barrier.
- A faculty member who required crutches in order to be ambulatory was besieged by subscriptions taken out in her name for magazines such as *Runner's World* and *Bicycling.*
- About a dozen members of a White Student Union, wielding clubs and chains, attacked three white antiracist protestors who were picketing outside the campus radio station.

REVICTIMIZATION AND COVICTIMIZATION

Some students can go through the school year never experiencing a single act of ethnoviolence; others are *revictimized,* that is, they become victims more than once. Most typically the incidents are unrelated, but some students are the continuing targets of one or more perpetrators. Revictimization may be especially important on a campus where size and closeness make a victim easily accessible to a perpetrator. Two studies at Maryland universities indicate that the average victim has experienced two incidents during the school year (Ehrlich, Pincus, and Lacy 1997; Ehrlich and others 1997). Often the motivation for the incidents differs; a student may be victimized once on the basis of race and again on the basis of gender. The matter is important because the traumatic effects of revictimization are considerably greater than the effects of a single incident.

Covictimization refers to the fact that one does not have to be directly attacked to experience the distress of someone else's victimization. We use the term covictim to describe the status of persons who (1) are aware that others who share their ethnic identity have been attacked and (2) have been emotionally affected by this. Covictims may have directly witnessed an ethnoviolent attack on another person, or they may have heard about it from the victim or from others. For the covictim, attacks on their peers are seen as danger signals to the entire group, as well as potential threats to their personal well-being. Potential covictims are all of those persons who have seen or heard about an ethnoviolent incident regardless of whether they have been emotionally affected by it.

Looking at all students—black, white, Latino, Asian, and so on—the 1986–1987 UMBC study suggests a potential covictimization rate as high as 48 percent. In a survey on a State University of New York (SUNY) campus, the covictimization rate was 61 percent, and almost all of the potential covictims (96 percent) said the incident affected them to some degree (Ehrlich 1995). Of course, different ethnic groups have different rates. These vary by their group self-awareness and solidarity. The more cohesive groups are able to communicate about incidents with greater speed and coverage.

In the UMBC (1987) study, for example, 64 percent of the black students were covictims as were 60 percent of the Jewish students. Studies of anti-gay violence at Yale, Rutgers, and Pennsylvania State reveal covictimization rates among gay and lesbian students of 76 percent, 57 percent, and 66 percent, respectively (Berrill 1992). These rates of victimization and covictimization are part of the substructure of group tensions. Stories go round, incidents are magnified and distorted, and listeners and storytellers become anxious, angry, and maybe even frightened.

As the campus atmosphere changes, the perceptions of students change, resulting in heightened sensitivity and increased group tensions.

GENDER, SEXUAL ORIENTATION, AND SEXUAL HARASSMENT

Studies in the 1980s indicated that 30 percent to 92 percent of women undergraduates reported experiencing some form of unwanted sexual attention. Women graduate students appear more likely than undergraduates to be harassed; and more than half of women medical students report sexual harassment (Baldwin, Daugherty, and Eckenfels 1991). One study reports a 48 percent rate of women faculty harassed by male students (McKinney and Maroules 1991).

Because there are a variety of ways to operationalize sexual harassment, it is difficult to compare victimization rates across campuses. (See the various methodological studies in the *Journal of Social Issues,* Spring 1995.) In the campus ethnoviolence research, a number of incidents have been indexed, including being subject to unwanted teasing, jokes, or remarks of a sexual nature; pressure for dates; letters and phone calls of a sexual nature; pressure for sexual activity; touching, pinching, or cornering; and attempted or actual rape. Although these behaviors are not gender specific, women on campus seem twice as likely as men to be sexually harassed and even more likely to be subjected to more than one type of harassing behavior (Hippensteele, Chesney-Lind, and Veniegas 1996; Ehrlich, Pincus, and Lacy 1997). There is some evidence to suggest that younger women living on campus are more likely to be victims of sexual harassment. Further, women are more likely than men to be victimized more than once during the school year.

Gender-based ethnoviolence, that is, incidents where the basis of prejudice is gender and the incident does not entail an apparent sexual motivation, has not yet been well studied in this domain of research. It does appear that sexual harassment is more common than gender victimization, although the distinction between the two is often difficult. In the UMBC study, for example, one-third of the gender victims did not report any incident of sexual harassment.

Studies focusing exclusively on violence against gay, lesbian, or bisexual students have been conducted at Pennsylvania State, Yale, Rutgers, the University of Illinois, Oberlin College, and the University of Massachusetts at Amherst. These studies find rates of verbal harassment to range from 45 percent to 76 percent. Threats of physical violence ranged from 15 percent to 26 percent, while actual assaults were 5 percent to 6 percent (Berrill 1992). Although the gay, lesbian, and bisexual student campus population is small, proportionately more of these groups are attacked and attacked more frequently than other student groups (Ehrlich and others 1997; Ehrlich, Pincus, and Lacy 1997; Hippensteele, Chesney-Lind, and Veniegas 1996; Hippensteele 1997). The frequency and intensity of homophobic violence seem even more pronounced than gender-based or other ethnoviolent attacks.

EFFECTS OF ETHNOVIOLENCE

There are two important facets of ethnoviolent victimization. First, persons victimized for reasons of prejudice do, in fact, suffer more than those victimized for other reasons. The second facet of ethnoviolent victimization is that, as an observer, one cannot predict the level of victim trauma simply by noting the nature of the act itself. Certainly the act is not irrelevant, but its effect is interwoven with the past experiences and personality of the victim, the status of the perpetrator, and even the historical context of the act. Furthermore, in the context of increased group tensions, what at one time might have been construed as an awkward or insensitive act may now be construed as a blatant violation of civil or social relations. Therefore one student may become traumatized by a single instance of name-calling in an incident on campus, whereas another endures and struggles through a semester of harassment, threats, and property damage in her dormitory.

The Prejudice Institute's studies of victimization, which include national, campus, and workplace samples, indicate that people who are physically or psychologically attacked for reasons of prejudice are more traumatized than people who are victims of other sorts of similar incidents or crimes (Weiss, Ehrlich, and Larcom 1992; Ehrlich, Larcom, and Purvis 1995). Black and white victims of ethnoviolence, for example, report more symptoms of psychophysiological stress than do black and white victims of similar incidents not motivated by prejudice. As an example of parallel incidents consider the case of two people bumping into each other and exchanging unpleasantries. In one instance they merely snarl at each other; in the other instance one of them also utters a racial/ethnic epithet.

In one national survey, for example, on thirty-four out of thirty-five symptoms of post-traumatic stress, black respondents who were victimized for reasons of prejudice displayed greater psychophysiological symptomatology than did those respondents who were victimized for other reasons. Campus studies show similar results. Among the most frequent responses are anger, thinking about the incident over and over, nervousness, fear, withdrawal, and revenge fantasies. Many victims develop problems in sleeping, eating, and the use of alcohol and drugs.

In the UMBC and Hawaii studies, one-fourth to one-third of student victims reported that the incident had seriously affected their interpersonal relations on campus. In the SUNY study, almost 15 percent of victim responses reflected a withdrawal from social relationships, while another 11 percent indicated difficulty in relations with family, friends, and significant others as a result of the ethnoviolent incident. As many as one out of three students indicates that the experience affected his or her classroom performance.

The politics of victimization on campus is not much different than it is in other settings (Elias 1986). Victims tend to be ignored; their fright, anger, and suffering are trivialized. The student victim sometimes becomes a spectacle, often subtly revictimized in the political struggle to affirm or reconstruct the moral order of the campus. In this struggle, the matter of victim rights and services is underplayed.

THE PERPETRATORS

There are two more dimensions of campus ethnoviolence. Who did it and did the victims report it? On the matter of perpetrators, we know very little. At least half of the incidents are committed covertly, or if committed publicly, the victims are unfamiliar with their assailants.

There are some strong impressions, however, that perpetrators are more likely to be male students and that members of fraternities are overrepresented among the known perpetrators. Fraternity houses as well as dormitories seem to be key sites at which incidents occur. The sexist, elitist, and anti-intellectual socialization of fraternity members has been well-documented (see Martin and Hummer 1989; Moffat 1989; Sanday 1991; Bausell, Bausell, and Siegel 1991).

In the UMBC study (Ehrlich, Pincus, and Lacy 1997), we were able to query victims about their observations of those who attacked them. What they reported was that the perpetrators were predominantly students who were known to them and acted alone. Multiple perpetrators were far more common in anti-gay incidents, and single perpetrators were more common in gender and sexual harassment incidents. Gender victimization and sexual harassment seem more likely to occur in situations where the victim and victimizer know each other.

Three studies inquired about faculty and staff as perpetrators—Hawaii, Towson, and UMBC. Students cited them as perpetrators in a surprising 10 to 16 percent of the incidents.

We also noted that the race/ethnicity of *self-identified* perpetrators tended to be congruent with the ethnic background of UMBC students, although they were slightly younger than the average student. Perpetrators perceived a more violent campus experience than others. That is, they reported observing more ethnoviolence and sexual harassment and being more often personally victimized. Student perpetrators expressed greater anger and were more likely to report revenge fantasies than others.

Much more research is needed to understand the motivations of perpetrators of ethnoviolence. Ethnoviolent acts, like all behaviors, are a consequence of multiple motives and situational factors. For some people, the act is an end in itself—*expressive acts* committed for "thrills." These are acts typically done in groups, often involving alcohol. The targets tend to be opportunistic. Some sociologists have considered these to be acts of "recreational violence."

Instrumental acts—acts that are a means to some end—are likely more frequent and more complex. These acts are generally responsive to a sense of threat to the person's status, territory, or central beliefs. Sometimes the responses are *realistic,* that is, are based on real incidents correctly perceived. From the standpoint of the actor, a violent response was not inappropriate. More likely, the responses are *unrealistic,* that is, are based on perceptions of threat that have no grounding in fact. Instrumental acts of ethnoviolence are built on prevailing stereotypes and feed off the propaganda of ultraconservative and right-wing groups.

There are, of course, some students who belong to such groups or who have come to accept their program. Their motivation is ideological and their end in view is to drive the target group from campus (or some campus activity or event) and to affirm their own group's superiority.

Finally, for some students, engaging in an ethnoviolent act is a means to some end unrelated to group prejudice (a *collateral response*). Typically such acts involve students who are acting in order to achieve or maintain peer group acceptance. The fraternity pledge who engages in a sexist or other act of discrimination in order to achieve membership is a classic example of a collateral response.

REPORTING THE INCIDENTS

Who reports their victimization to campus police or student affairs offices or residence hall advisors—or to any other school official? The answer is practically no one. Data from eleven campus studies indicate that the median percentage of students who do not report being victimized is 90 percent. The range is from 80 percent to 95 percent.

Certainly some incidents are difficult to report—for example, being sneered at or being leered at. Some incidents—for example, being called an insulting name by someone in a passing car—hardly seem worth the effort of reporting. Nevertheless, much of what goes unreported is serious, and the level of underreporting is outstanding. By illustration, in the Towson State University study, in which 95 percent of the victimized students did not tell any campus authority about their experiences, we estimated that one-fourth of the incidents were likely civil rights violations (Ehrlich and others 1997).

In the National Crime Survey, a regular household sample asking people about criminal victimization and whether they reported the incident to the police, about 60 percent of crime victims indicate that they did not report the incident to the police. It is apparent that students are even less likely than the general population to report their victimization.

There are three central sets of reasons that students give for not reporting what happened. The first and most frequent is that the incident was not serious or important. (It is our inference from the data that this statement is a form of detachment and denial.) The second is that authorities would do nothing or that there was nothing they could do. Whereas these two sets of reasons contain a great deal of denial on the part of the victim, the third set is based on fear. People fear retaliation by the perpetrator, or they fear that reporting the incident would only create more trouble for them.

Aside from the reasons presented by victimized students, it is our observation that *on most campuses,* even if students were willing to report an incident, neither they nor most of their advisors would know how or where to make such a report. Such formal procedures are typically obscure or nonexistent, and there are no easily articulated norms that support student disclosure.

THE UNDERCURRENTS OF THE CAMPUS CLIMATE

For the most part, students arrive at college without significant intergroup or multicultural experiences. Their life experiences have been generally confined to segregated neighborhoods and predominantly segregated schools. Their friendship circles are almost exclusively racially homogeneous. Their vicarious intergroup experiences through the media of mass education or mass entertainment provide little compensation or correction.

With little background, the incoming students enter a world of some greater diversity than what they left. But it is an age-segregated world of essentially equally naive actors, all now removed from the observability and constraints of their families and significant others. On most campuses whites are not likely to encounter many black or Hispanic or other minority students, and they will have even less exposure to minority faculty. Even so, intergroup contacts will be more frequent and likely more intimate than in their home situation.

Past research indicates that students who had multi-ethnic friendships in high school had such friendships in college as well. A key factor in both high school and college friendships was the ethnic composition of the schools. That is, the opportunity for friendships was a pivotal determinant of actual friendships. The motivation for friendships is also pivotal. The Diversity Project at the University of California, Berkeley, suggests "that while both African American and white freshman students want more interracial experiences and contacts, they want them on different *terms.* African Americans want more classes and programs and institutional commitments and responses. Whites want more individual, personal contacts developed at their own time and leisure" (Institute for the Study of Social Change 1991, 14).

Minority students also perceive the climate of the campus quite differently. Whereas white students perceive the campus atmosphere as friendly and accepting of minority students, minority students are often twice as likely to perceive the climate as unfriendly and not accepting. The exact figures vary by campus and by minority group, but the pattern seems constant across studies. (See, for example, Ehrlich, Pincus, and Lacy 1997; Ehrlich and others 1997; Eimers and Pike 1997; and Nora and Cabera 1996.) There is further evidence to indicate that the perception of a negative campus climate has a harmful effect on students' academic involvement and success (Eimers and Pike 1997; Nora and Cabera 1996).

Certainly college educators can play a significant role in influencing the attitudes and values of their students. In part, this can be done through manipulating the opportunities for sociable interaction, the control of ethnoviolence, and the opportunities for working together on educationally meaningful projects. Both of these appear to require changes in traditional approaches to education. These attempts to institute changes have resulted in the change agents—the faculty and staff involved in the intergroup and multicultural education of students—becoming the targets of a conservative response to maintain the status quo.

The role of right-wing and ultraconservative organizations has been a somewhat understated dimension of campus ethnoviolence. It is not that organizations are necessarily or directly implicated in ethnoviolent events. Rather, these organizations function (sociologically) to provide the intellectual and moral justification for social inequalities, including ethnoviolence. They promote values of individualism, meritocracy, and hierarchy that are essentially authoritarian. These organizations sometimes have actual chapters on campus (for example, Students for America, Students in Free Enterprise, White Student Union). More typically, though, the major players operate by providing financial support, maintaining a base for networking across campuses, providing training opportunities, and sometimes supplying stock propaganda.

Probably the most significant networks are, among faculty, the National Association of Scholars (NAS) and, among students, the Intercollegiate Studies Institute (Diamond 1991; Center for Campus Organizing 1997). The NAS is a directed effort at organizing ultraconservative faculty. It has official state affiliates and members across the United States with an estimated 4,500 members. It has also established its own research center and an employment service and has formed caucuses in several academic societies. Begun in 1987, it is funded by conservative corporate foundations and has an estimated budget of $2 million.

The Intercollegiate Studies Institute (ISI), the oldest and largest of the ultraconservative campus groups, receives its support from the major conservative foundations such as Coors, Mobil, Olin, Scaife, and Smith-Richardson. The ISI has a membership of approximately 50,000 students and a budget of $3.5 million, as reported in 1995. They produce a widely distributed magazine, *Campus,* which features student critiques of progressive events and trends on college campuses. It has also financially supported conservative campus newspapers and magazines and provided them with technical assistance and formal training (Seligman and Simpson 1991). There were fifty-five such publications operating in 1995 according to the Center for Campus Organizing (1997). Many are disruptive forces on their campuses, promoting intergroup hostility, authoritarian solutions, and elitist values. As Diamond's research indicates, the NAS and the ISI have a systematic strategy for right-wing organizing and activism (Diamond 1991). A current catalog of these groups is available in *Uncovering the Right on Campus* (Center for Campus Organizing 1997).

A more subtle part of the undercurrent of the campus climate is the proliferation of campus institutes and endowed chairs funded by the major conservative foundations. At the least, these institutes and professorships require a conservative posture, and many demand an adherence to economic or political commitments that promote social inequalities. To the extent that their inquiries are limited to outcomes that are in keeping with the sponsoring ideologies, they are violative of the principles of academic inquiry and are instruments for legitimating their sponsors. In *Leasing the Ivory Tower,* Lawrence Soley (1995) provides a social history of these right-wing influences on the campus climate. The financial power of their work is demonstrated in a report by the National Committee for Responsive Philanthropy. The report indicates that "a dozen foundations with combined 1994 assets of $1.1 billion have provided key support in training right-wing scholars and in building a network of conservative think tanks and law firms. These dozen foundations, including Bradley, the John M. Olin Foundation, and the Sarah Scaife Foundation, gave away $300 million from 1992 to 1994. Of that, a staggering 70 percent—$210 million—went to promote conservative policy groups and educational efforts" (Stehle 1997).

THE NEW TARGETS

Institutional and faculty responses to ethnoviolence have included the reconsideration of university methods for recruiting and retaining minority faculty and students, redesigning freshman orientation programs, revising student codes of conduct, and changing course content and curricula. These reformist responses came under strong attack at the beginning of the decade, with the reform movement being dubbed by the news media as a movement for "political correctness."

The reforms proposed for course and curricular changes have been oriented toward reducing ethnocentrism both in course content and in methods of instruction. In the jargon of college educators, they have sought to replace a "monocultural" approach with a "multicultural" approach. This movement for multicultural educational reform has two serious obstacles. Internally, the movement has not achieved a consensus on its goals. This lack of consensus results in a wide range of proposals being put forth in the name of "multiculturalism." Although this lack of consensus is expectable in the beginning stages of a reform movement, it also makes that movement more vulnerable to attack. Externally, multiculturalism has been viewed as corrupting both "traditional" values and existing educational practices. As *Newsweek* magazine editorialized, multiculturalism "is an attack on the primacy of the Western intellectual tradition" (December 24, 1990). By implication it is also an attack on the conservative faculty who control the university departments and divisions at many schools as well as academic professional associations. Related to this is another, sometimes explicit, dimension to the movement for multiculturalism. Many of its proponents see it as an integral part of a movement for the democratization of education. Although colleges and academic societies have strong democratic elements, they are essentially hierarchical and somewhat authoritarian institutions. Even though reformists' ideas of institutional democracy seem even less well developed than the curriculum reforms, just their suggestion has threatened not only the conservative faculty but other institutions that have had increasing influence on college curricula (Dickson 1984; Ehrlich 1985; Soley 1995).

On May 4, 1991, President George Bush, in a commencement address at the University of Michigan, told the nation that this movement for political correctness had led to political intolerance. "Political extremists," he said, "roam the land, abusing the privilege of free speech, setting citizens against one another on the basis of their class or race." This extraordinary act of political doublethink by the president—whereby the victims and their advocates are labeled as the victimizers—did not originate in the White House. The president had merely given his seal to the "anti-PC" movement defined by a year of mass media coverage. This included cover stories in *Newsweek,* the *Atlantic Monthly*, and the *New Republic* and extensive accounts in the *New York Times, Time, Fortune,* and the *Wall Street Journal,* as well as substantial coverage by conservative columnists and periodicals. A word search of "political/politically" with "correct/correctness" was conducted by Charles Whitney and Ellen Wartella (1992) for 33 U.S. metropolitan newspapers as well as 435 general interest U.S. and Canadian magazines. The term's appearance increased by 600 percent in 1991 over 1990 in newspapers and by more than 700 percent in magazines. Three years earlier there had been no magazine coverage and 97 percent fewer references in newspapers.

Newsweek (December 24, 1990) ended the year with a vitriolic, eight-page cover story on the "tyranny of PC." The story concluded that PC was a plot of Marxist origin and was essentially "a totalitarian philosophy." Its grip on the campus was so great, *Newsweek* reported, that "one defies it at one's peril." The PC peril, however, seemed far less apparent in the annual survey of senior campus administrators conducted by the American Council on Education (El-Khawas 1991). After adding questions about political correctness to its 1990–1991 questionnaire, the ACE found that conflicts involving political correctness were not especially commonplace. Administrators were asked: "In the past year, this institution has experienced significant controversy over the political or cultural content of___." This was followed by a checklist: "course texts," "information presented in the classroom," and "invited speakers or lecturers." The percentage of respondents checking these conflicts were, respectively, 3 percent, 4 percent, and 10 percent. In addition, the questionnaire asked if the administration had "received complaints from faculty or pressure to alter the political or cultural content of their courses." Only 5 percent said "yes."

In an earlier day, many of those who opposed school desegregation argued that their opposition was not based on prejudice but on their concern with the behavioral effects of riding on a bus. In an analogous and similarly specious fashion, the opponents of "political correctness" argue for their own freedom from bigotry and their concern with academic freedom. They see campus programs for the reduction of ethnoviolence as unnecessary, and they redefine as bigots the advocates of ethnic and feminist studies and multiculturalism in curricula. As conservatives manipulate the campus political process, the activists in the movements for equality and multiculturalism are becoming the new targets of ethnoviolence.

NOTES

This paper was first presented, in part, at the annual meeting of the American Sociological Association in Cincinnati, Ohio, August 1991. An abridged and revised version was presented to the National Conference on Racial and Ethnic Relations in American Higher Education in San Francisco, California, June 1992. An updated and expanded version was published in the first edition of this anthology. The version published here has been further updated and revised (December 1997).

REFERENCES

Baldwin, De Witt C., Steven R. Daugherty, and Edward J. Eckenfels. 1991. "Student Perceptions of Mistreatment and Harassment During Medical School: A Survey of Ten United States Schools." *Western Journal of Medicine* 155 (2): 140–145.

Bausell, R. Barker, Carole R. Bausell, and Dorothy G. Siegel. 1991. *The Links Among Alcohol, Drugs, and Crime on American College Campuses: A National Followup Study*. Towson, MD: Campus Violence Prevention Center (Towson State University).

Berrill, Kevin T. 1992. "Anti-Gay Violence and Victimization in the United States: An Overview." In Gregory M. Herek and Kevin T. Berrill, eds., *Hate Crimes: Confronting Violence Against Lesbians and Gay Men*. Newbury Park, CA: Sage Publications.

Center for Campus Organizing. 1997. *Uncovering the Right on Campus*. Cambridge, MA.: The Center.

Diamond, Sara. 1991. "Readin', Writin', and Repressin'." *Z Magazine*, February, pp. 45–48.

______. 1995. *Roads to Dominion: Right-Wing Movements and Political Power in the United States*. New York: Guilford Press.

Dickson, David. 1984. *The New Politics of Science*. New York: Pantheon Books.

Ehrlich, Howard J. 1973. *The Social Psychology of Prejudice*. New York: John Wiley & Sons.

______. 1985. *The University-Military Connection* (Research Group One Report No. 30). Baltimore: Vacant Lots Press.

______. 1990. *Campus Ethnoviolence and the Policy Options* (Institute Report No. 4). Baltimore: National Institute Against Prejudice and Violence.

______. 1995. "Prejudice and Ethnoviolence on Campus." *Higher Education Extension Service Review* 6, Winter (the whole issue).

Ehrlich, Howard J., Barbara E. K. Larcom, and Robert D. Purvis. 1995. "The Traumatic Impact of Ethnoviolence." In Laura Lederer and Richard Delgado, eds., *The Price We Pay: The Case Against Racist Speech, Hate Propaganda, and Pornography*. New York: Hill and Wang.

Ehrlich, Howard J., Fred L. Pincus, and Deborah Lacy. 1997. *Intergroup Relations on Campus—UMBC: The Second Study.* Baltimore: The Prejudice Institute.
Ehrlich, Howard J., Fred L. Pincus, and Cornel Morton. 1987. *Ethnoviolence on Campus: The UMBC Study* (Institute Report No. 2). Baltimore: National Institute Against Prejudice and Violence.
Ehrlich, Howard J., and others. 1997. *Ethnoviolence on Campus: The Towson Study.* Baltimore: The Prejudice Institute.
Eimers, Mardy T., and Gary R. Pike. 1997. "Minority and Nonminority Adjustment to College: Differences or Similarities?" *Research in Higher Education* 38: 77–97.
Elias, Robert. 1986. *The Politics of Victimization.* New York: Oxford University Press.
El-Khawas, Elaine. 1991. *Campus Trends, 1991.* Washington, DC: American Council on Education.
Hippensteele, Susan K. 1997. "Toward a 'Shared Reality' of Campus Ethnoviolence: Data as a Tool for Combatting Victim Isolation." *Social Process in Hawai'i* 38: 72–91.
Hippensteele, Susan K., Meda Chesney-Lind, and Rosemary Veniegas. 1996. "On the Basis of . . . : The Changing Face of Harassment and Discrimination in the Academy." *Women and Criminal Justice* 8: 4–26.
Institute for the Study of Social Change. 1991. *The Diversity Project: Final Report.* Berkeley: University of California Press.
Journal of Social Issues. "Gender Stereotyping, Sexual Harassment, and the Law," 51, Spring 1995 (the whole issue).
Martin, Patricia Yancey, and Robert A. Hummer. 1989. "Fraternities and Rape on Campus." *Gender and Society* 3: 457–473.
McKinney, Kathleen, and Nick Maroules. 1991. "Sexual Harassment." In E. Grauerholz and M. Koralewski, eds., *Sexual Coercion.* New York: Lexington Books.
Moffat, Michael. 1989. *Coming of Age in New Jersey: College and American Culture.* Newark, NJ: Rutgers University Press.
Newsweek, December 24, 1990.
Nora, Amaury, and Alberto F. Cabera. 1996. "The Role of Perceptions of Prejudice and Discrimination on the Adjustment of Minority Students to College." *Journal of Higher Education* 67: 119–148.
Sanday, Peggy Reeves. 1991. *Sex, Brotherhood, and Privilege on Campus.* New York: New York University Press.
Seligman, Miles, and Cymbre Simpson. 1991. "Behind Right-Wing Campus Newspapers." *Extra,* September–October.
Soley, Lawrence C. 1995. *Leasing the Ivory Tower.* Cambridge, MA: South End Press.
Stehle, Vince. 1997. "Righting Philanthropy." *The Nation*, June 30, pp. 15–20.
Weiss, Joan C., Howard J. Ehrlich, and Barbara E. K. Larcom. 1991–1992. "Ethnoviolence at Work" (Institute Report No. 6). *Journal of Intergroup Relations* 18 (4): 21–33.
Whitney, D. Charles, and Ellen Wartella. 1992. "Media Coverage of the 'Political Correctness' Debate." *Journal of Communication* 42 (2): 83–94.

24

"New Racism" and Old Dogmatism

THOMAS SOWELL

Increasing hostility toward blacks and other racial minorities on college campuses has become so widespread that the term "the new racism" has been coined to describe it. For example, a dean at Middlebury College in Vermont reported that—for the first time in 19 years—she was now being asked by white students not to assign them black room mates. There have been reports of similar trends in attitudes elsewhere. A professor at the University of California at Berkeley observed: "I've been teaching at U.C. Berkeley now for 18 years and it's only within the last three or four years that I've seen racist graffiti for the first time." Another Berkeley professor, recalling support for the civil rights movement on the campuses of the 1960s and 1970s, commented: "Twenty years later, what have we got? Hate mail and racist talk."

Much uglier incidents, including outright violence, have erupted on many campuses where such behavior was unheard of, just a decade or two earlier. At the University of Massachusetts, for example, white students beat up a black student in 1986 and a large mob of whites chased about 20 blacks. A well-known college guide quotes a Tufts University student as saying, "many of my friends wouldn't care if they never saw a black person again in their lives."

Racism, as such, is not new. What is new are the frequency, the places, and the class of people involved in an unprecedented escalation of overt racial hostility among middle-class young people, on predominantly liberal or radical campuses. Painful and ugly as these episodes are, they should not be surprising. . . .

The passing years have seen an ever-widening double standard of behavior, by race, on many campuses. At the University of California at Berkeley, for example, when some partying fraternity members pinned a confederate flag outside the frat house, the administration imposed "sensitivity" training on the whole fraternity and asked them to seek more minority members, but it took a very different view when the feelings of Jewish students were involved:

Editors' note: Footnotes deleted. See original source for documentation.

> Two female members of the Jewish Student Union were recruiting for the organization when members of the Black Muslim Union spotted them, and began loudly harassing them with anti-Semitic remarks. A small crowd gathered and egged the Muslims on. The women, in tears, fled and reported the incident to the Student Conduct Office, wanting the fighting words code invoked. They were told that they ought to develop "thicker skins" and nothing was done.

On many other college campuses as well, the standards for "racism" themselves vary by race. For example, when a white woman at the University of Pennsylvania expressed her "deep regard for the individual and my desire to protect the freedoms of *all* members of society," she was chided by an administrator who said that the word "individual" is "considered by many to be RACIST." The reason is that emphasis on the individual could be construed as "opposition to group entitlements." At Stanford, an even more strained use of the word "racist" grew out of a conflict that had nothing to do with race. When a fraternity student was punished for insulting a homosexual resident advisor, a few of his fraternity brothers staged a silent, candlelight vigil as a protest, wearing hockey masks to shield their identity and avoid having this protest be seen as a fraternity-sponsored action. Some observer decided that this silent, candlelight vigil was reminiscent of the Ku Klux Klan and contacted the Black Students Union, 30 of whose members then appeared on the scene.

Although the fraternity protesters expressed surprise at the racial interpretation put on their vigil, an altercation was only narrowly averted. The fraternity men were condemned as "insensitive" by Stanford President Donald Kennedy for not realizing the racial implications of their actions, even though those actions were not directed at any racial or ethnic minorities and involved entirely different issues. But the Stanford administration had no such condemnation when the head of the Black Students Union publicly declared, "I do not like white people." He said:

> Unfortunately, for blacks, we only get our pictures in the paper when we protest or fail and not when we succeed.
>
> My response, and you may quote me, is "kiss my black behind!"

No one in the Stanford administration called him "insensitive"—or said anything at all publicly. Had a white student made similar remarks concerning blacks, he would be lucky to escape expulsion—not only at Stanford, but at many other colleges and universities across the country. Formal prohibitions on statements that can be construed as racist (or sexist or homophobic) have become common, along with stringent penalties for violations of their broad and vague provisions. What has also become common are double standards in applying these codes. The latitude permitted members of minority groups (or homosexuals, feminists, and others) has been extremely broad. Moreover, the students themselves know that such double standards exist.

At Vassar College, a black student had a public outburst that included such epithets as "dirty Jew" and "f—king Jew." He was neither suspended nor expelled, as the Vassar administration focused its efforts on keeping the story from being published by the *Vassar Spectator*, a student-run publication, which became a target of intense criticism—and retribution—when it published the story anyway.

A number of black student organizations on various college campuses have invited as a speaker Louis Farrakhan, noted for his fiery denunciations of Jews. However, Minister Farrakhan is by no means unique in this respect. Other speakers invited to address black student groups on various campuses have made such comments as "the Jew hopes to one day reign forever," that Jews are a "violent people," that the "best Zionist is a dead Zionist," or have referred to "Columbia Jewniversity in Jew York City." Official condemnations of "racism," which are freely proclaimed in other situations, are seldom if ever forthcoming when minority students, faculty, or invited speakers attack other racial or ethnic groups.

Double standards extend not only to words but also to actions. When dozens of minority students have invaded classrooms to shout down the professor, intimidate the students, and prevent the lecture from being given, they have done so with impunity at San Francisco State University, at Berkeley, and at the City College in New York. On the campus of the State University of New York at Binghamton, a public lecture by a 70-year-old retired professor was invaded and disrupted by dozens of students—mostly minority—carrying sticks. One of the black students blew his nose on a tissue, which he then deposited in a cup of coffee from which the professor had been drinking—to the cheers of the mob, while an administrator sat silently in the audience, grinning.

Despite a readiness of university officials to interpret all sorts of words and deeds by whites as racist, even outright physical assaults by blacks against whites are unlikely to be labeled that way. When two white students at Brown University were victims of unprovoked street attacks by blacks, according to the student newspaper the head of campus security "was quick to point out that 'There is nothing at all that would tend to indicate that this is a racially motivated incident.'" After a similar unprovoked street attack on two white students by five blacks at the University of Wisconsin (Madison), the student newspaper there similarly reported that campus police "do not believe the attack was racially motivated, although 'racial slurs' were used." Indeed, when the students asked why they were being attacked, the answer was: "Because we're black and you're white." But, officially, it was still not considered a racial attack. At Wesleyan University, where thinly-veiled hints of violence from black student activists both preceded and followed a fire-bombing of the university president's office, the president of Wesleyan likened the arson to an "automobile accident" and called for "healing."

A series in the *Christian Science Monitor* on campus racial problems included this episode:

> When a dozen black youths crashed a Theta Delta Chi fraternity party at Berkeley last fall, pulling knives, hurling epithets, and putting two whites in the hospital, the student paper didn't cover the story. "There were 11 cops and two ambulances—and *we* were the ones worried about a lawsuit!" says fraternity member Jon Orbik. "Can you imagine the media if it had been the other way around?"

Double standards and hypocrisy are recurring complaints about the way racial issues are handled on campuses across the country. The specifics range from double standards of admission to charges of racism by minority students or faculty who make racist statements themselves, to self-segregation by students who claim to be "excluded."

As regards preferential admissions, Dartmouth professor Jeffrey Hart wrote:

> The white student who gains admissions to a good college has undoubtedly worked hard for four years in secondary school and experienced the heavy anxiety of filing application for admission and waiting for acceptance or rejection. Such a student is very likely to be a competitive personality. That a black skin or a Hispanic surname is worth several hundred Scholastic Aptitude Test points sticks in the craw.

Even those who are themselves admitted often feel resentment on behalf of relatives or friends who were not admitted, despite better records than minority students admitted preferentially. As a Rutgers University undergraduate said on the MacNeil/Lehrer news program: "The reason why we have racial tensions at Rutgers is they have a very strong minority recruitment program, and this means that many of my friends from my hometown were not accepted, even though they are more qualified." This was not peculiar to Rutgers. When two Californians from the same preparatory school applied to the University of California at Berkeley, this was the result:

> Student A was ranked in the top third of his class, student B in the bottom third. Student A had SAT scores totaling 1290; student B's scores totaled 890. Student A had a record of good citizenship while student B was expelled the previous winter for breaking a series of major rules. Student A was white; student B was black. Berkeley rejected student A and accepted student B.

Similar stories abound. At Dartmouth, a student with uninspiring SAT scores and poor high school grades was admitted, even though students with far better academic records have been turned away. This young man had some trace of American Indian ancestry, though he was blond and blue-eyed.

Whatever resentments grow out of this issue are compounded when college authorities stifle any complaints about it. At U.C.L.A., for example, a comic strip in the student newspaper contained an episode in which a student sees a rooster on campus and asks how he got admitted. "Affirmative action" was the rooster's reply. The editor was removed from his job—and when the student newspaper at Cal State Northridge criticized this action editorially, illustrating the editorial with the comic strip in question, that editor was also removed.

At the University of Wisconsin (Eau Claire) a cartoon in the student newspaper showed two white students with faces darkened from a bucket of paint labeled "Minority in a Minute" and "E-Z 2-ITION." One student says: "Who needs to work so hard to get a perfect G.P.A. or money for tuition, when ya have this stuff?" The other sings "Free tuition here we come." A Michigan State University student who displayed this cartoon on his dormitory door was suspended.

Self-segregation by minorities is another common complaint. Sometimes this extends from eating together—the "black table" is a common phenomenon at many colleges—to socializing exclusively within one's own racial or ethnic group, to having separate dormitories. Nor is all this spontaneous. Often there are social pressures, sometimes abetted by college administrators in various ways.

The process begins even before the minority student sets foot on campus. Racial identity information on the admissions application form triggers racially separate listings of students, with these lists then being shared with the local Black Students Union or other minority organizations on campus. Students may be invited to campus as individuals, only to discover after arrival that the gathering is all-black, all-Hispanic, etc. In short, they do not join minority organizations the way Jewish students may join Hillel or Catholics may join Newman clubs; they are *delivered* to campus minority organizations.

Pressures to self-segregate and adopt groupthink attitudes begin early. As an observer at Washington University in St. Louis said:

> The minute they get on campus, the Legion of Black Collegians tells them that they are going to be discriminated against. So they stick together and ostracize any that might get involved on campus.

Mark Mathabane, black South African author of *Kaffir Boy,* traveled to America to go to college and escape apartheid—only to discover its philosophy flourishing here:

> When I was in college, I and a few other black students were labeled Uncle Toms for sitting with whites in the cafeteria, sharing with them black culture, working with them on projects and socializing with them.

Similar attitudes can be found among other minority groups, including Asians on some campuses. An Asian American student at Carleton College reported:

> Students of color are looked down upon and sometimes openly criticized by their peers for having too many white friends, not doing enough for their respective multicultural groups, or just being too "Americanized" or trying too hard to blend in. Using the Asian American experience as an example, terms like "banana" (yellow on the outside, white on the inside) are sometime used and questions like "How come you don't have an Asian first name?" come up in everyday conversation.

The term "banana" for Asians who reject separatism parallels the use of the term "Oreo" (black on the outside, white on the inside) for blacks and "coconut" (brown on the outside, etc.) for Mexican Americans who reject separatism. In short, campus political activists in various groups attempt to stigmatize those students of their own race who do not join their political constituency and share its groupthink. Such activism is, however, less common and less extreme among Asian Americans, though the general pattern is similar in those cases where Asian campus activists are at work.

The cumulative effects of self-segregation pressures eventually take their toll on many minority youngsters. An observer described the process among black students at Dartmouth:

> Most have a healthy attitude when they come here. They want to meet all kinds of people, and expand their intellectual and cultural horizons. Yet, if they happen to make more white friends than black ones, they quickly learn the ugly reality of Dartmouth's reverse racism. Normally-adjusted blacks are called "incogs" and "oreos," meaning that they are "black on the outside and white on the inside." Most frequently, it is blacks themselves who call other blacks by these hateful names.
>
> Many black freshmen can't withstand the pressure. . . . They begin to eat together, live together, and join all-black fraternities and sororities. . . . At first, they resisted the pressure to abandon their well-integrated circle of friends, yet were unable to keep up the resistance.

As on other campuses, the Dartmouth administration abetted this process, not only by arranging a special orientation weekend for blacks (at first not so labeled) and then by providing *de facto* segregated housing:

> Dartmouth participates in the segregation process by providing Cutter Hall for black housing and the Afro-American Society. Although housing in Cutter is ostensibly available for anyone who wants it, the last time a white student lived there was the winter of 1986. Cutter's militant, ingrown atmosphere ensures that few whites will ever cross the threshold, let alone consider living there.

At Berkeley, self-segregation is achieved by matching room mates by race. "I came here expecting to have friends, even room-mates, of other races," a white student at Berkeley said. Of the minority students she said, "They go around calling everybody 'racist,' but they're the ones insisting on being separate." She added: "If white students got together on the basis of race, they'd be considered Nazis."

Sometimes self-segregation endures right on through to graduation itself. The Stanford *Campus Report* for June 13, 1990, listed a "Black Baccalaureate," a "Native American Graduation Dinner" and an "Asian American Graduation Reception" at separate locations.

Minority students who insist on going their own way as individuals, not only socially but ideologically, face special pressures and even physical threats—often to the complete disinterest of college administrations. In Allan Bloom's *Closing of the American Mind,* he reports going to Cornell University's provost on behalf of "a black student whose life had been threatened by a black faculty member when he refused to participate in a demonstration." The provost expressed sympathy but did nothing, because (1) the administration was preoccupied with current racial tensions on campus and (2) campus politics in general were such that "no university in the country could expel radical black students or dismiss the faculty members who incited them."

At about the same time, black educator Kenneth B. Clark resigned from Antioch College's board of directors in protest against the administration's silence as militant black students "intimidate, threaten, and in some cases physically assault" other black students who disagreed with them. Similar patterns can still be found on elite college campuses today. Threats of violence against a black student who was also editor of the conservative *Dartmouth Review* evoked a similar lack of interest on the part of the Dartmouth administration, even though the student named names and had faculty witnesses. At Stanford, Hispanic students who complained of intimidation by more militant, organized Hispanic students found a similar indifference on the part of the administration. Moreover, a copy of their letter of complaint, complete with signatures of the complaining students, was turned over to the militant Hispanic organization.

Often, college administrators deal with the most vocal minority organization as if it represents "the" blacks, "the" Hispanics, etc.—regardless of whether it does in fact. Hispanic students at Stanford, for example, claimed that "only 15.2 percent of Chicano/Latino students have ever participated in any way whatsoever" in any of the activities of the organization which speaks in their name. Nevertheless, such organizations tend to monopolize administrators' attention, whether because of ideological affinity, administrative convenience, or because they represent a credible threat to campus tranquility.

Because college officials respond to the organized and vocal elements within each minority group, the whole racial atmosphere on campus tends to reflect the issues raised by these vocal elements and by administrators' policy responses to their charges and demands. What *most* minority students think may carry far less weight. Sad as it is to have tensions between two racial groups when they disagree, it is tragic insanity to have racial tension when these groups as a whole are in fundamental agreement. For example, a survey of 5,000 students at 40 colleges showed that, at predominantly white colleges, 76 percent of black students and 93 percent of white students agreed that all undergraduates should be admitted by meeting the same standards. At predominantly black colleges, more than 95 percent of the students of both races agreed. This divisive issue inflames campuses across the country because college officials respond to the vocal activists.

Another factor not to be overlooked in explaining college policies is the sheer, blind imitativeness of the academic world. Even colleges and universities which have lagged behind in the developments which have brought turmoil to other campuses often decide later to imitate their less fortunate compatriots. For example, Whitman College, a somewhat traditional institution which escaped much of the turmoil and fashions of the 1960s, nevertheless chose later to establish a Director of Minority Affairs, and he in turn chose to invite to campus a speaker on racism, described—by the speaker's own promotional literature—as someone who "draws out anger," who is "loud, verbally brutal, demeaning, cold and oppressive."

Why invite such a man to Whitman College? According to an official of Whitman's Multi-Ethnic Student Organization: "Just because we don't have any real problem (at Whitman) doesn't mean there is no problem. . . . Racial sensitivity is what we're after." In other words, they could not resist stirring up problems, instead of leaving well enough alone. This is all too typical of the mindset which has led to escalating racial polarization on many campuses—a polarization which, however, enhances the visibility and importance of people associated with "multicultural" and minority affairs.

Bringing on campus people who are specialists in emotional confrontations on race relations is not a practice unique to Whitman College. There is in fact a whole industry of "diversity consultants" or race relations specialists who give talks or conduct seminars on campus, advise administrators on racial matters, participate in freshman orientation programs, hold off-campus retreats for faculty members and administrators, prepare films, videotapes, or other materials, hold conferences around the country, and publish newsletters and magazines devoted solely to "diversity." While individual styles vary, a common theme is that *everyone* white is racist, with the only distinction being between those who are overt and those who do not realize their own racism, those who admit it and those who engage in psychological "denial." To minority individuals, the message is: Racism is pervasive around you, whether you realize it or not. Ambiguous situations should always be interpreted as racial affronts. "Never think that you imagined it," one speaker at a Harvard workshop said, "because chances are that you didn't." This speaker was an official of the university.

Colleges and universities across the country utilize race relations consultants. Tulane University, for example, has subjected its administrators to two-day seminars off campus, operated by an Atlanta organization which uses methods described as "confrontational" and based on the usual *a priori* presumption of racism that has to be rooted out by these consultants. This Atlanta organization has also received money from the Ford Foundation to bring together high officials of universities throughout the region for similar sessions. Yale University paid several thousand dollars to a New York–based firm to conduct workshops on its campus, with one of the consultants suggesting that students who had chosen to go to class rather than attend the workshops were racist. At a week-long series of workshops at Harvard, the presumed breakdown of racism was quantified as 85 percent subtle racism and 15 percent overt racism. Yet, despite this air of scientific precision, an observer found that the atmosphere surrounding the keynote address "resembled a religious revival meeting." This too is not uncommon. Psychological techniques used by old-time itinerant revival-meeting preachers have proved effective in evoking feelings of guilt and repentance in academia. At the University of Wisconsin, for example, an itinerant race relations specialist evoked "the repentant sobs of white students" at one of his workshops, while pushing his message that virtually all white people are racists and all black people are angry. Sometimes the old-fashioned revival meeting techniques are combined with modern psychological devices like role-playing.

The very possibility that self-interest might be involved in consultants' commercial promotion of polarization on campus never seems to be mentioned, even though these secular Elmer Gantrys have made a career for themselves by practicing an art requiring little academic qualification and facing no empirical check regarding either assertions or consequences.

As with so many other non-academic intrusions into education at all levels, the problem is not that these activities will necessarily succeed at their avowed purpose, but that they can do enormous damage in the process. Perhaps the most ironic venue for racial polarization has been Oberlin College, whose long tradition of liberalism (in the original sense) on racial issues goes far back into the nineteenth century, when Oberlin was a stop on the "underground railroad" that helped blacks escape from slavery. Today, while workshops are being held on the Oberlin Campus with such themes as "fighting oppression" and "celebrating diversity," blacks and whites go their separate ways, letters to the student newspaper are filled with angry recriminations among the various fractionalized groups, and there is a search for "ever more rarefied units of racism," according to the college's own president.

The prevalence of the idea that frequent and sweeping charges of racism are going to improve intergroup relations cannot be explained either by its plausibility or its track record. On the contrary, it feeds the polarization which benefits only those minority activists and apparatchiks who promote this approach. Increasingly, white students are becoming not only hardened against such denunciation but openly resentful of it. As a student at the University of Texas (Austin) wrote:

> Racism has become an epithet against which there is no defense. The charge of racism needs little support, is nearly impossible to refute, and is more damaging to a person than any other label. It has become the insult-of-choice to many liberals.

A University of Michigan student said, "the word *racism* is thrown around so often that it is in danger of losing its meaning." Certainly the term had lost its sting for the *University Review of Texas,* which responded to accusations of racism by calling them "boring and uncreative." A recently graduated Stanford law student referred to "panhandlers for minority representation" on campus and to "minority advocates who greet any opposition to their agenda of quotas and preferences with charges of racism." At colleges around the country, there have been bitter complaints about the double standards used in determining what is and is not racism. A student at the University of Virginia, for example, noted:

> Apparently there is a double standard for racism at the University. When a sign was found on Route 29 containing a racial slur, the entire University was up in arms. However, when a black fraternity distributed a flyer with a picture of a black man holding a sword in one hand and the decapitated head of a white man, entrails and all, aloft in the other, no one seemed concerned. The same was true when a representative from the Nation of Islam speaking at the University claimed to have words only for black students saying, "to hell with the rest of them."

A Stanford undergraduate likewise declared that the racism on his campus was a racism "against whites." He added:

> There is a quiet, powerful resentment growing among whites here who feel that they are paying an increasingly burdensome toll for the crimes of their, or someone else's, ancestors. The fact that this resentment is not expressed in campus literature or open conversation does not mean it is not there; on the contrary, its lack of expression will ensure that it festers and grows.

An observer at an "anti-racism" seminar at Oberlin reported:

> Throughout the three-and-a-half hour session, no participant raised an objection, yet I subsequently heard that many were dismayed. Why had they not spoken out? "It's not worth it," one senior told me. "You just get attacked."

A professor at Kenyon College said:

> Black students . . . are regularly permitted the most outrageous expressions of anti-white racism and, increasingly, antisemitism, while white students must be extraordinarily careful in their choice of words and in their actions lest they be accused of racism and punished accordingly.

The student newspaper at Bryn Mawr and Haverford reported a "backlash" at these colleges against the *a priori* charges levelled against white students:

> From the moment they arrived on campus, they have been called racist, sexist or classist.

Not all the students take it. A white student at Haverford, responding to a complaining and accusatory article by a black classmate, said:

> You come off in your article as a most embittered person—"pity me" you write: "pity me more because I am Black." Though you make good points about disadvantages Blacks have, I found your letter offensive to me as a person who happens to be white. I did not choose to be this color any more than you chose to be Black; and I respect that which is distinct in the Black culture, but I refuse to be ashamed because I am white.

Some white students at Berkeley complain that it is a problem just to avoid setting off criticism by not being up to date on ever-changing names for different groups:

> It's Chicano now, or Chicana, or Mexican, Latina, Hispanic, I mean . . . every year it changes. . . . If you say the wrong thing you're either racist or they yell at you. . . . But we're always the white honky . . . we don't get to change our name every year.

Another Berkeley student complained of "whites hearing all year they are racists." He said:

> I grew up with white, yellow, black. I mean half my buddies on the football team were black, and I come here and read every other day in the paper I'm a racist. It irritates me.

Neither whining nor breast-beating are sounds that anyone wants to hear incessantly. Nevertheless, the search for grievances over racism remains unabated. In some cases, charges are fabricated. The Tawana Brawley hoax in New York has had a number of campus counterparts. A black instructor at Ohio Dominican College resigned after claiming to have received racial hate mail from one of her students—and after detectives found evidence suggesting that she had forged the letters herself. Other reports of racial incidents at Tufts University, at Smith College, at Emory University, and at the University of Texas have also turned out to be false, and an incident at Columbia University was described by more than 20 eyewitnesses very differently from the way it was first reported in the media. The attorney for the black students in the Columbia University case was C. Vernon Mason, who was also an attorney for Tawana Brawley.

Both false and true racial incidents reveal something of the atmosphere on college campuses, an atmosphere whose complex cross-currents derive ultimately from the needless pressures generated by double standards and double talk, both of which poison the atmosphere required for people to get along. As race relations have worsened in the wake of policies designed to make them better, there has been no re-thinking of the original assumptions on which these policies were based. On the contrary, there has been a renewed insistence on more of the same dogmas. In addition, the escalating racial and ethnic strife has generated some new dogmas as well, based on the same general vision as the old.

NEW DOGMAS FOR "NEW RACISM"

Three responses to the growing backlash of insulting, harassing, and violent incidents against blacks and other minorities across the country have been common among academics:

1. Blaming it on the racism of the past, continuing into the present
2. Blaming it on the racism of the larger society, spilling over onto college campuses
3. Blaming it on the conservative mood of the times, exemplified by the election and re-election of President Ronald Reagan

What these three explanations have in common is that they wholly ignore *the very possibility* that the policies and practices of the colleges themselves may have been responsible for the hostile racial climate on campus. They also completely ignore facts which go counter to each of these three explanations. In addition, the "remedies" suggested or taken extend or accentuate the racial double standards which have been so much resented. Moreover, the "experts" consulted in such matters have often been ethnic studies professors and minority affairs administrators, who have the most blatantly obvious vested interest in continuing and expanding these double standards.

Typical of the closed mind on such issues in academia was a long feature article in *The Chronicle of Higher Education* of January 27, 1988, focusing exclusively on the views of those with the three explanations already noted. Of the thousands of words in its story, not one was from anyone with a different perspective, challenging the prevailing social vision or the policies based on it. According to *The Chronicle of Higher Education,* "black students are finding that white campuses are often hostile environments in which vestiges of the 'old' racism persist." But the "vestige" argument is contradicted by the fact that the racial outbreaks on many campuses are both more numerous and more severe than anything witnessed in past decades on these same campuses, even though minority students have been attending such colleges for generations. By definition, a vestige is not larger or worse than what it is a vestige of. Nuclear bombs are not a vestige of bows and arrows. Moreover, the geographical distribution of racial incidents also belies the "vestige" argument.

In the 1960s, there were many violent resistances to the racial integration of colleges and universities in the South, while today such violence is far more prevalent in the North. Tabulations of outbreaks of racial or ethnic violence by the National Institute Against Prejudice and Violence in 1988 and 1989 both found more such incidents in the state of Massachusetts alone than in the entire region of the South.* Yet the "vestige" doctrine is by no means confined to *The Chronicle of Higher Education.* It is part of a far more general dogmatism in academia, which refuses even to consider the possibility that its own policies have contributed to the disasters it is experiencing.

Professor Troy Duster of Berkeley echoed a widespread view among academics when he blamed racial strife on "the society that generated the students who come here." This ignores the observations of others who have said that the racial strife on campus is more severe than that normally encountered in the larger society, as well as more severe than in the past. A professor at San Jose State University noted among his painful experiences hearing a black woman who "said she'd never been called a nigger till she got to this campus." An Hispanic student at Cornell likewise said that she "had never experienced racism in my face before I came to Ithaca." When 70 percent of the graduating seniors at Stanford say that racial tensions have *increased* during their time on campus, that does not suggest a "vestige," if only because a growing "vestige" is a contradiction in terms.

On most campuses, however, the very possibility that institutional policies are themselves adding to racism is not even mentioned. Instead, it is dogmatically assumed that the racism on campus must have originated off campus. When Dr. Ira M. Heyman, then chancellor at Berkeley, blamed racial hostilities on that campus on "the larger framework of the general mood in the U.S.," he ignored Berkeley's own racial quota policies under his administration—policies which turned away more than 2,000 white and Asian students with straight A averages in one year, in order to admit black students who overwhelmingly failed to graduate.

Professor Duster, while likewise blaming campus racial problems on "the mood in the country," more explicitly blamed a "conservative era," in which "Reagan has made racism a more legitimate thing." Similar views have been echoed by many others, including Professor Philip G. Altbach of the State University of New York at Buffalo, who said that "the racial crisis on campus is very much a part of the legacy of Reaganism." But Massachusetts has never been Reagan country and the problems plaguing liberal or radical institutions like Berkeley or the University of Massachusetts have seldom erupted on more conservative campuses.

Very conservative Pepperdine University, for example, has a higher percentage of non-white students than the more liberal or radical University of Massachusetts—and yet it is U. Mass which has had headline-making racial violence. The conservative University of Oklahoma, with a predominantly white undergraduate student body, elected a black woman president of the student body by a majority vote—which is to say, a larger vote than that received by the three other candidates combined. At a time when black students at many liberal Northern campuses express alienation and dissatisfaction, and engage in self-segregation, a college admissions counselor visiting conservative Rhodes College in Memphis found the black students on that Southern campus expressing feelings of being

*Editors' note: The National Institute data showed more newspaper stories about University of Massachusetts incidents. One incident alone was repeated in almost 250 stories.

part of the campus community. While this evidence is suggestive rather than decisive, the larger point is that the very concept of evidence is not applied by those who repeat the academic dogma that racial polarization is caused by conservatism, wholly ignoring the possibility that this polarization may be a backlash against double standards promoted by liberals and radicals.

The argument is often made that what really angers white students is the loss of coveted places in elite colleges to blacks and other minorities, and their consequent loss of numerical predominance or "cultural hegemony" on various campuses, as the numbers of minority students has increased. But, although this theory is often asserted, it is almost never tested empirically. For example, on many elite campuses, Asian students often substantially outnumber black students and are a significant percentage of the total student body, without provoking nearly as much hostility or violence as that directed against blacks, Hispanics, and others who are admitted under double standards—and who are permitted double standards of behavior.

Asian students outnumber blacks at seven of the eight Ivy League colleges and on all nine campuses of the University of California, as well as at Stanford, Case Western Reserve, Union College, Haverford, Davidson College, Franklin & Marshall, the Illinois Institute of Technology, Lehigh University, and Whitman College, among other places. They outnumber black, Hispanic, and American Indian students—put together—at Cal Tech, the University of Chicago, Harvey Mudd College, Renssealaer Polytechnic, Cooper Union, the Rose-Hulman Institute, and Worcester Polytechnic. Asians are more than 20 percent of the student body at more than a dozen institutions.

Why does this large-scale taking of places from whites not provoke the same reactions against Asians as against other nonwhites? As an old song said: "It ain't what you do, it's the way that you do it." Asians have done it by outperforming whites. A white student at San Jose State University expressed the different reactions to the two kinds of minority admissions:

> Just because 150 years ago some people were treated poorly doesn't mean I have to repay their descendents. Simply because I'm white, should somebody who's not white get my slot?
>
> I think it stinks. The Asian with a better grade point average—that person should have that slot.

Neither Asians nor Jews have been wholly immune to all forms of student resentment and Asians have been adversely affected to some extent, like the Jews, in the racial backlash and polarization which has struck many campuses. It has been a common pattern in a number of countries, and in various periods of history, that heightened group hostility between groups *A* and *B* also adversely affects attitudes toward groups *C, D,* and *E*—who have nothing to do with the strife between *A* and *B.* Increased group chauvinism is a threat to everyone. Nevertheless, Asians have seldom been targets of outright violence, even on campuses where they are a large presence. If whites' real resentments were over a loss of slots or a loss of "cultural hegemony," the Asians would be their prime targets on elite campuses across the country.

On any of these issues revolving around the "new racism," people might differ and argue—but they almost never do in academia. Views contrary to the prevailing ideology are simply not mentioned, much less debated. That is the essence of the dogmatism which makes any solution, or even improvement, in the campus racial scene unlikely for many years to come.

The obviously self-serving nature of the usual administrative responses to racial incidents—free speech restrictions, making ethnic studies courses mandatory, larger quotas for minority students and faculty—provide an impetus to new and ever-escalating rounds of double standards and racial backlash. Where will this self-reinforcing spiral end? In other countries, group preferences and quotas in higher education have led to widespread bloodshed (as in India) or to outright civil war (as in Sri Lanka). The growing evidences of racial hostility and sporadic outbreaks of violence which we in the United States call "the new racism" may be an early warning that we are heading in the same direction as other countries which have promoted preferences and quotas longer and more strongly. But the prevailing dogmatism among academics suggests that the real meaning of these early warnings may not be understood until long after it is too late.

25

Multiculturalism

Battleground or Meeting Ground?

RONALD TAKAKI

It is very natural that the history written by the victim does not altogether chime with the story of the victor.

—Jose Fernandez of California, 1874[1]

In 1979, I experienced the truth of this statement when I found myself attacked by C. Van Woodward in the *New York Review of Books.* I had recently published a broad and comparative study of blacks, Chinese, Indians, Irish, and Mexicans, from the American Revolution to the U.S. war against Spain. But, for Woodward, my *Iron Cages: Race and Culture in Nineteenth-Century America* was too narrow in focus. My analysis, he stridently complained, should have compared ethnic conflicts in the United States to those in Brazil, South Africa, Germany, and Russia. Such an encompassing view would have shown that America was not so "bad" after all.

The author of scholarship that focused exclusively on the American South, Woodward was arguing that mine should have been cross-national in order to be "balanced." But how, I wondered, was balance to be measured? Surely, any examination of the "worse instances" of racial oppression in other countries should not diminish the importance of what happened here. Balance should also insist that we steer away from denial or a tendency to be dismissive. Woodward's contrast of the "millions of corpses" and the "horrors of genocide" in Nazi Germany to racial violence in the United States seemed both heartless and beside the point. Enslaved Africans in the American South would have felt little comfort to have been told that conditions for their counterparts in Latin America were "worse." They would have responded that it mattered little that the black population in Brazil was "17.5 million" rather than "127.6 million" by 1850, or whether slavery beyond what Woodward called the "three-mile limit" was more terrible and deadly.

What had provoked such a scolding from this dean of American history? One might have expected a more supportive reading from the author of *The Strange Career of Jim Crow,* a book that had helped stir our society's moral conscience during the civil rights era. My colleague Michael Rogin tried to explain Woodward's curious reaction by saying that the elderly historian perceived me as a bad son. History had traditionally been written by members of the majority population; now some younger scholars of color like me had received our Ph.D.'s and were trying to "re-vision" America's past. But our critical scholarship did not chime with the traditional version of history. Noting my nonwhiteness, Woodward charged that I was guilty of reverse discrimination: my characterization of whites in terms of rapacity, greed, and brutality constituted a "practice" that could be described as "racism." Like a father, Woodward chastised me for catering to the "current mood of self-denigration and self-flagellation." "If and when the mood passes," he lamented, "one would hope a more balanced perspective on American history will prevail."[2]

Looking back at Woodward's review today, we can see that it constituted one of the opening skirmishes of what has come to be called the culture war. Some of the battles of this conflict have erupted in the political arena. Speaking before the 1992 Republican National Convention, Patrick Buchanan urged his fellow conservatives to take back their cities, their culture, and their country, block by block. This last phrase was a reference to the National Guard's show of force during the 1992 Los Angeles riot. On the other hand, in his first speech as President-elect, Bill Clinton recognized our ethnic and cultural diversity as a source of America's strength.

But many of the fiercest battles over how we define America are being waged within the academy. There minority students and scholars are struggling to diversify the curriculum, while conservative pundits like Charles J. Sykes and Dinesh D'Souza are fighting to recapture the campus.[3]

The stakes in this conflict are high, for we are being asked to define education and determine what an educated person should know about the world in general and America in particular. This is the issue Allan Bloom raises in his polemic, *The Closing of the American Mind.* A leader of the intellectual backlash against cultural diversity, he articulates a conservative view of the university curriculum. According to Bloom, entering students are "uncivilized," and faculty have the responsibility to "civilize" them. As a teacher, he claims to know what their "hungers" are and "what they can digest." Eating is one of his favorite metaphors. Noting the "large black presence" at major universities, he regrets the "one failure" in race relations—black students have proven to be "indigestible." They do not "melt as have *all* other groups." The problem, he contends, is that "blacks have become blacks": they have become "ethnic." This separatism has been reinforced by an academic permissiveness that has befouled the curriculum with "Black Studies" along with "Learn Another Culture." The only solution, Bloom insists, is "the good old Great Books approach."[4]

Behind Bloom's approach is a political agenda. What does it mean to be an American? he asks. The "old view" was that "by recognizing and accepting man's natural rights," people in this society found a fundamental basis of unity. The immigrant came here and became assimilated. But the "recent education of openness," with its celebration of diversity, is threatening the social contract that had defined the members of American society as individuals. During the civil rights movement of the 1960s, Black Power militants had aggressively affirmed a group identity. Invading college campuses, they demanded "respect for blacks as blacks, not as human beings simply," and began to "propagandize acceptance of different ways." This emphasis on ethnicity separated Americans from each other, shrouding their "essential humankindness." The black conception of a group identity provided the theoretical basis for a new policy, affirmative action, which opened the doors to the admission of unqualified students. Once on campus, many black students agitated for the establishment of black studies programs, which in turn contributed to academic incoherence, lack of synopsis, and the "decomposition of the university."[5]

Bloom's is a closed mind, unwilling to allow the curriculum to become more inclusive. Fortunately, many other educators have been acknowledging the need to teach students about the cultural diversity of American society. "Every student needs to know," former University of Wisconsin chancellor Donna Shalala has explained, "much more about the origins and history of the particular cultures which, as Americans, we will encounter during our lives."[6]

This need for cross-cultural understanding has been grimly highlighted by recent racial tensions and conflicts such as the black boycott of Korean stores, Jewish-black antagonism in Crown Heights, and especially the 1992 Lost Angeles racial explosion. During the days of rage, Rodney King pleaded for calm: "Please, we can get along here. We all can get along. I mean, we're all stuck here for a while. Let's try to work it out." But how should "we" be defined?[7]

Earlier, the Watts riot had reflected a conflict between whites and blacks, but the fire this time in 1992 Los Angeles highlighted the multiracial reality of American society. Race includes Hispanics and Asian Americans. The old binary language of race relations between whites and blacks, *Newsweek* observed, is no longer descriptive of who we are as Americans. Our future will increasingly be multiethnic as the twenty-first century rushes toward us: the western edge of the continent called California constitutes the thin end of an entering new wedge, a brave new multicultural world of Calibans of many different races and ethnicities.[8]

If "we" must be more inclusive, how do we "work it out"? One crucial way would be for us to learn more about each other—not only whites about peoples of color, but also blacks about Koreans, and Hispanics about blacks. Our very diversity offers an intellectual invitation to teachers and scholars to reach for a more comprehensive understanding of American society. Here the debate over multiculturalism has gone beyond whether or not to be inclusive. The question has become, How do we develop and teach a more culturally diverse curriculum?

What has emerged are two perspectives, what Diane Ravitch has usefully described as "particularism" versus "pluralism." But, by regarding each as exclusive, even antagonistic, Ravitch fails to appreciate the validity of both viewpoints and the ways they complement each other.[9]

Actually, we need not be forced into an either-or situation. Currently, many universities offer courses that study a particular group, such as African Americans or Asian Americans. This focus enables students of a specific minority to learn about their history and community. These students are not necessarily seeking what has been slandered as self-esteem courses. Rather, they simply believe that they are entitled to learn how their communities fit into American history and society. My grandparents were Japanese immigrant laborers, and even after I finished college with a major in American history and completed a Ph.D. in this field, I had learned virtually nothing about why they had come to America and what had happened to them as well as other Japanese immigrants in this country. This history should have been available to me.

The particularistic perspective led me to write *Strangers from a Different Shore: A History of Asian Americans.* This focus on a specific group can also be found in Irving Howe's *World of Our Fathers: The Journey of the East European Jews to America,* Mario Garcia's *Desert Immigrants: The Mexicans of El Paso, 1880–1920,* Lawrence Levine's *Black Culture and Black Consciousness,* and Kerby Miller's *Emigrants and Exiles: Ireland and the Irish Exodus to North America.*[10]

Increasingly, educators and scholars are recognizing the need for us to step back from particularistic portraits in order to discern the rich and complex mosaic of our national pluralism. While group-specific courses have been in the curriculum for many years, courses offering a comparative and integrative approach have been introduced recently. In fact, the University of California at Berkeley has instituted an American cultures requirement for graduation. The purpose of this course is to give students an understanding of American society in terms of African Americans, Asian Americans, Latinos, Native Americans, and European Americans, especially the immigrant groups from places like Ireland, Italy, Greece, and Russia.

What such curricular innovations promise is not only the introduction of intellectually dynamic courses that study the crisscrossed paths of America's different groups but also the fostering of comparative multicultural scholarship. This pluralistic approach is illustrated by works like my *Different Mirror: A History of Multicultural America* as well as Gary Nash's *Red, White, and Black: The Peoples of Early America,* Ivan Light's *Ethnic Enterprise in America: Business and Welfare among Chinese, Japanese, and Blacks,* Reginald Horsman's *Race and Manifest Destiny: The Origins of American Racial Anglo-Saxonism,* and Benjamin Ringer's *"We the People" and Others: Duality and America's Treatment of Its Racial Minorities.*[11]

Even here, however, a battle is being fought over how America's diversity should be conceptualized. For example, Diane Ravitch avidly supports the pluralistic perspective, but she fears national division. Stressing the importance of national unity, Ravitch promotes the development of multiculturalism based on a strategy of adding on: to keep mainstream Anglo-American history and expand it by simply including information on racism as well as minority contributions to America's music, art, literature, food, clothing, sports, and holidays. The purpose behind this pluralism, for Ravitch, is to encourage students of "all racial and ethnic groups to believe that they are part of this society and that they should develop their talents and minds to the fullest." By "fullest," she means for students to be inspired by learning about "men and women from diverse backgrounds who overcame poverty, discrimination, physical handicaps, and other obstacles to achieve success in a variety of fields." Ravitch is driven by a desire for universalism: she wants to affirm our common humanity by discouraging our specific group identities, especially those based on racial experiences. Ironically, Ravitch, a self-avowed proponent of pluralism, actually wants us to abandon our group ties and become individuals.[12]

This privileging of the "unum" over the "pluribus" has been advanced more aggressively by Arthur Schlesinger in *The Disuniting of America.*

In this jeremiad, Schlesinger denounces what he calls "the cult of ethnicity"—the shift from assimilation to group identity, from integration to separatism. The issue at stake, he argues, is the teaching of "*bad* history under whatever ethnic banner." After acknowledging that American history has long been written in the "interests of white Anglo-Saxon Protestant males," he describes the enslavement of Africans, the seizure of Indian lands, and the exploitation of Chinese railroad workers. But his discussion on racial oppression is perfunctory and parsimonious, and he devotes most of his attention to a defense of traditional history. "Anglocentric domination of schoolbooks was based in part on unassailable facts," Schlesinger declares. "For better or worse, American history has been shaped more than anything else by British tradition and culture." Like Bloom, Schlesinger utilizes the metaphor of eating. "To deny the essentially European origins of American culture is to falsify history," he explains. "Belief in one's own culture does not require disdain for other cultures. But one step at a time: no culture can hope to ingest other cultures all at once, certainly not before it ingests its own." Defensively claiming to be an inclusionist historian, Schlesinger presents his own credentials: "As for me, I was for a time a member of the executive council of the *Journal of Negro History*. . . . I have been a lifelong advocate of civil rights."[13]

But what happens when minority peoples try to define their civil rights in terms of cultural pluralism and group identities? They become targets of Schlesinger's scorn. This "exaggeration" of ethnic differences, he warns, only "drives ever deeper the awful wedges between races," leading to an "endgame" of self-pity and self-ghettoization. The culprits responsible for this divisiveness are the "multicultural zealots," especially the Afrocentrists. Schlesinger castigates them as campus bullies, distorting history and creating myths about the contributions of Africans.[14]

What Schlesinger refuses to admit or is unable to see clearly is how he himself is culpable of historical distortion: his own omissions in *The Age of Jackson* have erased what James Madison had described then as "'the black race within our bosom'" and "'the red on our borders.'" Both groups have been entirely left out of Schlesinger's study: they do not even have entries in the index. Moreover, there is not even a mention of two marker events, the Nat Turner insurrection and Indian Removal, which Andrew Jackson himself would have been surprised to find omitted from a history of his era. Unfortunately, Schlesinger fails to meet even his own standards of scholarship: "The historian's goals are accuracy, analysis, and objectivity in the reconstruction of the past."[15]

Behind Schlesinger's cant against multiculturalism is fear. What will happen to our national ideal of "*e pluribus unum?*" he worries. Will the center hold, or will the melting pot yield to the Tower of Babel? For answers, he looks abroad. "Today," he observes, "the nationalist fever encircles the globe." Angry and violent "tribalism" is exploding in India, the former Soviet Union, Indonesia, Guyana, and other countries around the world. "The ethnic upsurge in America, far from being unique, partakes of the global fever." Like Bloom and Ravitch, Schlesinger prescribes individualism as the cure. "Most Americans," he argues, "continue to see themselves primarily as individuals and only secondarily and trivially as adherents of a group." The dividing of society into "fixed ethnicities nourishes a culture of victimization and a contagion of inflammable sensitivities." This danger threatens the "brittle bonds of national identity that hold this diverse and fractious society together." The Balkan present, Schlesinger warns, may be America's prologue.[16]

Are we limited to a choice between a "disuniting" multiculturalism and a common American culture, or can we transform the "culture war" into a meeting ground? The intellectual combats of this conflict, Gerald Graff suggests, have the potential to enrich American education. As universities become contested terrains of different points of view, gray and monotonous cloisters of Eurocentric knowledge can become brave new worlds, dynamic and multicultural. On these academic battlegrounds, scholars and students can engage each other in dialogue and debate, informed by the heat and light generated by the examination of opposing texts such as Joseph Conrad's *Heart of Darkness* and Chinua Achebe's *Things Fall Apart*. "Teaching the conflicts has nothing to do with relativism or denying the existence of truth," Graff contends. "The best way to make relativists of students is to expose them to an endless series of different positions which are *not* debated before their eyes," Graff turns the guns of the great books against Bloom. By viewing culture as a debate and by entering a process of intellectual clashes, students can search for truth, as did Socrates "when he taught the conflicts two millennia ago."[17]

Like Graff, I welcome such debates in my teaching. One of my courses, "Racial Inequality in America: A Comparative Historical Perspective," studies the character of American society in relationship to our racial and ethnic diversity. My approach is captured in the phrase "from different shores." By "shores," I intend a double meaning. One is the shores from which the migrants departed, places such as Europe, Africa, and Asia. The second is the various and often conflicting perspectives or shores from which scholars have viewed the experiences of racial and ethnic groups.

By critically examining these different shores, students address complex comparative questions. How have the experiences of racial minorities such as African Americans been similar to and different from those of ethnic groups such as Irish Americans? Is race the same as ethnicity? For example, is the African American experience qualitatively or quantitatively different from the Jewish American experience? How have race relations been shaped by economic developments as well as by culture—moral values about how people think and behave as well as beliefs about human nature and society? To wrestle with these questions, students read Nathan Glazer's analysis of assimilationist patterns as well as Robert Blauner's theory of internal colonialism, Charles Murray on black welfare dependency as well as William Julius Wilson on the economic structures creating the black underclass, and Thomas Sowell's explanation of Asian American success as well as my critique of the "myth of the Asian-American model minority."[18]

The need to open American minds to greater cultural diversity will not go away. Faculty can resist this imperative by ignoring the changing racial composition of student bodies and the larger society, or they can embrace this timely and exciting intellectual opportunity to revitalize the social sciences and humanities. "The study of the humanities," Henry Louis Gates observes, "is the study of the possibilities of human life in culture. It thrives on diversity. . . . The new [ethnic studies] scholarship has invigorated the traditional disciplines." What distinguishes the university from other battlegrounds, such as the media and politics, is that the university has a special commitment to the search for knowledge, one based on a process of intellectual openness and inquiry. Multiculturalism can stoke this critical spirit by transforming the university into a crucial meeting ground for different viewpoints. In the process, perhaps we will be able to discover what makes us an American people.[19]

Whether the university can realize this intellectual pursuit for collective self-knowledge is uncertain, especially during difficult economic times. As institutions of higher learning face budget cuts, calls for an expansion of the curriculum often encounter hostility from faculty in traditional departments determined to protect dwindling resources. Furthermore, the economic crisis has been fanning the fires of racism in society: Asian Americans have been bashed for the seeming invasion of Japanese cars, Hispanics accused of taking jobs away from Americans, and blacks attacked for their dependency on welfare and the special privileges of affirmative action.

This context of rising racial tensions has conditioned the culture war. Both the advocates and the critics of multiculturalism know that the conflict is not wholly academic; the debate over how America should be defined is related to power and privilege. Both sides agree that history is power. Society's collective memory determines the future. The battle is over what should be remembered and who should do the remembering.

Traditionally excluded from the curriculum, minorities are insisting that America does not belong to one group and neither does America's history. They are making their claim to the knowledge offered by the university, reminding us that Americans originated from many lands and that everyone here is entitled to dignity. "I hope this survey do a lot of good for Chinese people," an immigrant told an interviewer from Stanford in the 1920s. "Make American people realize that Chinese people are humans. I think very few American people really know anything about Chinese." As different groups find their voices, they tell and retell stories that liberate. By writing about the people on Mango Street, Sandra Cisneros explained, "the ghost does not ache so much." The place no longer holds her with "both arms. She sets [Cisneros] free." Indeed, stories may not be as innocent or simple as they might seem. They "aren't just entertainment," observed Native American novelist Leslie Marmon Silko.[20]

On the other side, the interests seeking to maintain the status quo also recognize that the contested terrain of ideas is related to social reality. No wonder conservative foundations like Coors and Olin have been financing projects to promote their own political agenda on campuses across the country, and the National Association of Scholars has been attacking multiculturalism by smearing it with a brush called "political correctness." Conservative critics like Bloom are the real campus bullies: they are the ones unwilling to open the debate and introduce students to different viewpoints. Under the banner of intellectual freedom and excellence, these naysayers have been imposing their own intellectual orthodoxy by denouncing those who disagree with them as "the new barbarians," saluting Lynne Cheney, the former head of the National Endowment for the Humanities, for defending traditional American culture, and employing McCarthyite tactics to brand ethnic studies as "un-American."[21]

How can the university become a meeting ground when the encounter of oppositional ideas is disparaged? What Susan Faludi has observed about the academic backlash against women's liberation can be applied to the reaction to multiculturalism. "The donnish robes of many of these backlash thinkers cloaked impulses that were less than scholarly," she wrote. "Some of them were academics who believed that feminists had cost them in advancement, tenure, and honors; they found the creation of women's studies not just professionally but personally disturbing and invasive, a trespasser trampling across *their* campus." Her observation applies to multiculturalism: all we need to do is to substitute "minority scholars" for "feminists," and "ethnic studies" for "women's studies." The intellectual backlashers are defending "their" campuses against the "other."[22]

The campaign against multiculturalism reflects a larger social nervousness, a perplexity over the changing racial composition of American society. Here Faludi's insights may again be transferrable. The war against women, she notes, manifests an identity crisis for men: what does it mean to be a man? One response has been to reclaim masculinity through violence, to "kick ass," the expression George Bush used to describe his combat with Geraldine Ferraro in the 1984 vice-presidential debate. Eight years later, during the Persian Gulf war against Saddam Hussein, Bush as President demonstrated masculine power in Desert Storm. In a parallel way, it can be argued, the expanding multicultural reality of America is creating a racial identity crisis: what does it mean to be white?[23]

Demographic studies project that whites will become a minority of the total U.S. population some time during the twenty-first century. Already in major cities across the country, whites no longer predominate numerically. This expanding multicultural reality is challenging the traditional notion of America as white. What will it mean for American society to have a nonwhite majority? The significance of this future, *Time* observed, is related to our identity—our sense of individual self and nationhood, or what it means to be American. This demographic transformation has prompted E. D. Hirsch to worry that America is becoming a "Tower of Babel," and that this multiplicity of cultures is threatening to tear the country's social fabric. Nostalgic for a more cohesive culture and a more homogeneous America, he contends, "If we *had* to make a choice between the *one* and the *many,* most Americans would choose the principle of unity, since we cannot function as a nation without it." The way to correct this fragmentization, Hirsch argues, is to promote the teaching of "shared symbols." In *Cultural Literacy: What Every American Needs to Know,* Hirsch offers an appendix of terms designed to create a sense of national identity and unity—a list that leaves out much of the histories and cultures of minorities.[24]

The escalating war against multiculturalism is being fueled by a fear of loss. "Backlash politics may be defined as the reaction by groups which are declining in a felt sense of importance, influence, and power," observed Seymour Martin Lipset and Earl Raab. Similarly, historian Richard Hofstadter described the impulses of progressive politics in the early twentieth century in terms of a "status revolution"—a widely shared frustration among middle-class professionals who had been displaced by a new class of elite businessmen. Hofstadter also detected a "paranoid style in American politics" practiced by certain groups such as nativists who suffered from lost prestige and felt besieged by complex new realities. Grieving for an America that had been taken away from them, they desperately fought to repossess their country and "prevent the final destructive act of subversion."[25]

A similar anxiety is growing in America today. One of the factors behind the backlash against multiculturalism is race, what Lawrence Auster calls "the forbidden topic." In an essay published in the *National Review,* he advocates the restriction of immigration for nonwhites. Auster condemns the white liberals for wanting to have it both ways—to have a common culture and also to promote racial diversity. They naively refuse to recognize the danger: when a "critical number" of people in this country are no longer from the West, then we will no longer be able to employ traditional reference points such as "our Western heritage" or speak of "our Founding Fathers." American culture as it has been known, Auster warns, is disappearing as "more and more minorities complain that they can't identify with American history because they 'don't see people who look like themselves' in that history." To preserve America as a Western society, Auster argues, America must continue to be composed mostly of people of European ancestry.[26]

What Auster presents is an extreme but logical extension of a view shared by both conservatives like Bloom and liberals like Schlesinger: they have bifurcated American society into "us" versus "them." This division locates whites at the center and minorities at the margins of our national identity. "American," observed Toni Morrison, has been defined as "white." Such a dichotomization denies our wholeness as one people. "Everybody remembers,"' she explained, "the first time they were taught that part of the human race was Other. That's a trauma. It's as though I told you that your left hand is not part of your body."[27]

In their war against the denied parts of American society, the backlashers are our modern Captain Ahabs. In their pursuit of their version of the white whale, they are in command; like Ahab directing his chase from the deck of the *Pequod,* they steer the course of the university curriculum. Their exclusive definition of knowledge has rendered invisible and silent the swirling and rich diversity below deck. The workers of the *Pequod* represent a multicultural society—whites like Ishmael, Pacific Islanders like Queequeg, Africans like Daggoo, Asians like Fedallah, and American Indians like Tashtego. In Melville's powerful story, Ishmael and Queequeg find themselves strangers to each other at first. As they labor together, they are united by their need of mutual survival and cooperation. This connectedness is graphically illustrated by the monkey-rope. Lowered into the shark-infested water to secure the blubber hook into the dead whale, Queequeg is held by a rope tied to Ishmael. The process is perilous for both men. "We two, for the time," Ishmael tells us, "were wedded; and should poor Queequeg sink to rise no more, then both usage and honor demanded that, instead of cutting the cord, it should drag me down in his wake." Though originally from different shores, the members of the crew share a noble class unity. Ahab, however, is able to charm them, his charisma drawing them into the delirium of his hunt. Driven by a monomanic mission, Ahab charts a course that ends in the destruction of everyone except Ishmael.[28]

On college campuses today, the voices of many students and faculty from below deck are challenging such hierarchical power. In their search for cross-cultural understandings, they are trying to re-vision America. But will we as Americans continue to perceive our past and peer into our future as through a glass darkly? In the telling and retelling of our particular stories, will we create communities of separate memories, or will we be able to connect our diverse selves to a larger national narrative? As we approach a new century dominated by ethnic and racial conflicts at home and throughout the world, we realize that the answers to such questions will depend largely on whether the university will be able to become both a battleground and a meeting ground of varied viewpoints.

NOTES

1. David J. Weber, ed., *Foreigners in Their Native Land: Historical Roots of the Mexican Americans* (Albuquerque: University of New Mexico Press, 1973), p. vi.

2. C. Van Woodward, "America the Bad?" *New York Review of Books,* 22 Nov. 1979; Ronald Takaki, *Iron Cages: Race and Culture in Nineteenth-Century America* (New York: Knopf, 1979).

3. Charles J. Sykes, *The Hollow Men: Politics and Corruption in Higher Education* (Washington, DC: Regnery Gateway, 1990); Dinesh D'Souza, *Illiberal Education: The Politics of Race and Sex on Campus* (New York: Free Press, 1991).

4. Allan Bloom, *The Closing of the American Mind: How Higher Education Has Failed Democracy and Impoverished the Souls of Today's Students* (New York: Simon & Schuster, 1987), pp. 19, 91–93, 340–341, 344.

5. Ibid., pp. 27, 29, 33, 35, 89, 90, 347.

6. *University of Wisconsin—Madison: The Madison Plan* (Madison: University of Wisconsin, 1988).

7. Rodney King's statement to the press; see *New York Times,* 2 May 1992, p. 6.

8. "Beyond Black and White," *Newsweek,* 18 May 1992, p. 28.

9. Diane Ravitch, "Multiculturalism: E Pluribus Plures," *American Scholar,* 59(3): 337–354 (Summer 1990).

10. Ronald Takaki, *Strangers from a Different Shore: A History of Asian Americans* (Boston: Little, Brown, 1989); Irving Howe, *World of Our Fathers: The Journey of the East European Jews to America and the Life They Found and Made* (New York: Simon & Schuster, 1976); Lawrence W. Levine, *Black Culture and Black Consciousness: Afro-American Folk Thought from Slavery to Freedom* (New York: Oxford University Press, 1977); Mario T. Garcia, *Desert Immigrants: The Mexicans of El Paso, 1880–1920* (New Haven, CT: Yale University Press, 1981); Kerby A. Miller, *Emigrants and Exiles: Ireland and the Irish Exodus to North America* (New York: Oxford University Press, 1985).

11. Ronald Takaki, *A Different Mirror: A History of Multicultural America* (New York: Little, Brown, 1993); Gary Nash, *Red, White, and Black: The Peoples of Early America* (Englewood Cliffs, NJ: Prentice-Hall, 1974); Ivan Light, *Ethnic Enterprise in America: Business and Welfare among Chinese, Japanese, and Blacks* (Berkeley: University of California Press, 1972); Reginald Horsman, *Race and Manifest Destiny: The Origins of American Racial Anglo-Saxonism* (Cambridge, MA: Harvard University Press, 1981); Benjamin Ringer, *"We the People" and Others: Duality and America's Treatment of Its Racial Minorities* (New York: Tavistock, 1983).

12. Ravitch, "Multiculturalism," pp. 341, 354.

13. Arthur M. Schlesinger, Jr., *The Disuniting of America: Reflections on a Multicultural Society* (Knoxville, TN: Whittle Communications, 1991), pp. 2, 24, 14, 81–82.

14. Ibid., pp. 58, 66.

15. James Madison, quoted in Takaki, *Iron Cages,* p. 80; Arthur M. Schlesinger, Jr., *The Age of Jackson* (Boston: Little, Brown, 1945); idem, *Disuniting of America,* p. 20.

16. Schlesinger, *Disuniting of America,* pp. 2, 21, 64.

17. Gerald Graff, *Beyond the Culture Wars: How Teaching the Conflicts Can Revitalize American Education* (New York: Norton, 1992), p. 15.

18. Nathan Glazer, *Affirmative Discrimination: Ethnic Inequality and Public Policy* (New York: Basic Books, 1975); Robert Blauner, *Racial Oppression in America* (New York: Harper & Row, 1972); Charles Murray, *Losing Ground: American Social Policy, 1950–1980* (New

York: Basic Books, 1984); William Julius Wilson, *The Truly Disadvantaged: The Inner City, the Underclass, and Public Policy* (Chicago: University of Chicago Press, 1987); Thomas Sowell, *Ethnic America: A History* (New York: Basic Books, 1981); Takaki, *Strangers from a Different Shore.* For an example of the debate format, see Ronald Takaki, *From Different Shores: Perspectives on Race and Ethnicity in America* (New York: Oxford University Press, 1987).

19. Henry Louis Gates, Jr., *Loose Canons: Notes on the Culture Wars* (New York: Oxford University Press, 1992), p. 114.

20. Pany Lowe, interview, 1924, Survey of Race Relations, Hoover Institution Archives, Stanford, CA; Sandra Cisneros, *The House on Mango Street* (New York: Vintage, 1991), pp. 109–110; Leslie Marmon Silko, *Ceremony* (New York: New American Library, 1978), p. 2.

21. Dinesh D'Souza. "The Visigoths in Tweed," in *Beyond PC: Towards a Politics of Understanding,* ed. Patricia Aufderheide (St. Paul, MN: Graywolf Press, 1992), p. 11; George Will, "Literary Politics," *Newsweek,* 22 Apr. 1991, p. 72; Arthur Schlesinger, Jr., "When Ethnic Studies Are Un-American," *Wall Street Journal,* 23 Apr. 1990.

22. Susan Faludi, *Backlash: The Undeclared War against American Women* (New York: Doubleday, 1992), p. 282.

23. Ibid., p. 65.

24. William A. Henry III, "Beyond the Melting Pot," *Time,* 9 Apr. 1990, pp. 28–31; E. D. Hirsch, Jr., *Cultural Literacy: What Every American Needs to Know* (Boston: Houghton Mifflin, 1987), pp. xiii, xvii, 2, 18, 96, 152–215.

25. Lipset and Raab quoted in Faludi, *Backlash,* p. 231; Richard Hofstadter, *The Age of Reform: From Bryan to F.D.R.* (New York: Random House, 1955), pp. 131–173.

26. Lawrence Auster, "The Forbidden Topic," *National Review,* 27 Apr. 1992, pp. 42–44.

27. Toni Morrison, *Playing in the Dark: Whiteness in the Literary Imagination* (Cambridge, MA: Harvard University Press, 1992), p. 47; Bonnie Angelo, "The Pain of Being Black," *Time,* 22 May 1989, p. 121. Copyright © 1989 Time Inc. Reprinted by permission.

28. Herman Melville, *Moby Dick* (Boston: Houghton Mifflin, 1956), pp. 182, 253, 322–323.

PART 6

Selected Topics

The economics of book size and the limits of a college semester place constraints on how many different selections and topics we can cover in a collection such as this. In the previous edition, we had a small section on the civil disorders in Los Angeles. It was current and a hot topic: There were many lessons for intergroup relations that could be learned from such large-scale ethnoviolence.

In this edition, we selected three topics for special focus. The first is the social function of the news media. The second deals with the conflict over the control of education, and the third concerns the role of the right wing.

In the first essay, Howard J. Ehrlich details the role of the news media in reporting on issues of conflict and ethnoviolence. Using many case illustrations, he builds a sociological picture of the news media as a central institution in creating and maintaining intergroup tensions.

We continue with Mike Long's essay on "ebonics." In exploring the struggle over language usage, Long places it in the context of discrimination, of assimilation, and of the efforts of the state to control education. "The elites speak the official state language . . . which they made official or standard; the oppressed groups are decreed by the same elites to speak a less acceptable . . . language."

In the final essay, Abby Ferber reviews the right-wing, white supremacist movement in America—in a sense, the logical sociological extreme of prejudice and discrimination. She describes the range and history of this movement, exposes its ideology, and sketches the major hate groups.

26

Reporting Ethnoviolence

Newspaper Treatment of Race and Ethnic Conflict

HOWARD J. EHRLICH

There were four of us at the Baltimore-based National Institute Against Prejudice and Violence who routinely handled press inquiries. Over the past seven years, before the Institute closed, we provided interviews and information to most of the major print and electronic news media in the United States. My media contact log indicates that I have spoken to over 200 reporters. My guess is that only a few had any serious knowledge of race relations—or any form of intergroup relations. My associates share my estimate.

We had another source of information not easily accessible to most people. For five years, the Institute's press clipping service sent us about 100–150 clips a week which they drew from close to 500 newspapers and news magazines. They all told stories about conflict and ethnoviolence. The clips make transparent the operation of the American newspaper.

Newspapers are the major source of news about racial, religious, and ethnic group relations in the cities. The daily newspaper reaches an estimated 113 million readers. Based on a nationwide poll of over 2,000 people, Michael J. Robinson and Andrew Kohut concluded, in their *Public Opinion Quarterly* article, that the majority of Americans believe "most of what it hears, sees, or reads in the nation's press." Television is a less useful way of conveying news. There have been 15 studies of news learning that show that newspaper readers are more informed than TV viewers. Both of these facts are alarming.

There are many people in the news media who believe that all they must do is master the form. You don't need to have any special knowledge about your subject, you just need to know how to "research" the story and then how to present it. When I suggested in an op-ed piece that there really is a body of social science knowledge about prejudice and intergroup conflict that reporters should learn, the op-ed page editor wrote me a personal note in which he called my suggestion "intellectually arrogant."

For most newspaper writers, research means talking to as many "experts" and other people as their deadline permits. Typically, the story form becomes an interrelated set of paragraphs which are basically quotes. When the quotes are drawn from people with differing opinions or perspectives, the story takes on the appearance of "objectivity."

These quotes, by the way, are important data. First, most of what a source person tells a reporter is not printed. Second, what is printed is used to legitimate the story being composed by the reporter or news organization. This selective display of the source's "inkbites" are framed by special reference to the source's credibility. The frame takes the form of pointing to their expert status and organizational affiliation. It is the source's status that provides the legitimacy to the story. With a skilled journalist, the story that emerges often appears to be constructed by the experts—virtually a story that tells itself. In fact, the writer and editor have fabricated the story through their selective choice of sources and their skillful use of quotes. While much derision has been directed at the brevity of television "soundbites," the newspaper equivalents may be worse. Martin Plissner, political director of CBS News, writes that "the average inkbite in one day's political stories in [the *New York Times* and the *Washington Post*] . . . was about 15 words—a six-second soundbite if you read them aloud" (*Washington Post, National Weekly Edition,* March 27–April 2, 1989).

For the working journalist, special knowledge or training about subjects they are writing on is seen as irrelevant. For example, when one of my associates asked the assistant city editor of the *Miami Herald* whether the reporters who were regularly assigned stories about minority group conflict had any special training, he replied: "No. They are not there to resolve conflicts; they are journalists." In calls to 14 major newspapers, we found only two instances where reporters had received any special training. In answer to our query, several did indicate that they were Black or Hispanic and thus, presumably, not in need of any further training.

Probably the most knowledgeable writers on any newspaper are those who write about sports. That's their beat and they work on it year after year. Science is often another well-defined beat; most major papers have a science writer. In fact, major papers have a slew of specialized writers in music, film, cooking, business, politics, and even local gossip.

Send out a reporter who knows nothing about intergroup relations and the results are often disastrous. One reporter, writing in the Baltimore *Sun,* made four errors in the lead paragraph of a story about race relations. Among other things, he confused the distinction between prejudice and discrimination. This is the metaphorical equivalent of confusing Iodine with its isotope, Iodine 131. A second reporter from the same paper was shocked to hear from us that prejudice was not instinctive. She was so disbelieving that she argued with me and the Institute's executive director over the assertion that "prejudice is learned." In writing her feature, the reporter treated the statement in her story as if it were an idiosyncratic personal opinion of the director.

In an extraordinary piece on "bias crime" (May 29, 1990), Daniel Goleman, *New York Times* science writer, contradicted the statements of six experts he interviewed on the growth of bias crimes, totally misconstrued the findings of the study which he made the centerpiece of the article, reduced the causes of prejudice to a combination of bizarre psychological processes and the state of the economy, and concluded by resting bias crime on the backs of working class kids and unemployment.

IS THIS A GOOD TIME TO CALL?

Most reporters who contact us start out with the wrong questions. Asking the wrong question is the critical difference between someone who is and someone who is not knowledgeable about a subject. In a typical call to the Institute, reporters have a repertory of three questions. Is the incidence of X increasing? (X could be campus violence, housing incidents, or whatever is going on in their city.) How many Xs occurred? And, what is the cause? This last question is usually asked with the expectation that you will cite a single cause, two at best. When you cite more, the reporters choose those causes which are on their agenda.

On the matter of counting Xs, we usually tell reporters that these are only estimates and not scientifically precise counts. The real issue, we counter, is the tragic frequency of these incidents and their effects on victims. Many reporters get upset with such an answer, repeating their question as if we didn't understand it or are trying to keep the data secret. Aggressive reporters have sometimes called another Institute staffer in an effort to obtain these secret figures. I have occasionally received return calls from reporters who tell me that their editor insists that they come up with a figure.

As a result of their search for numbers, reporters have written or asserted some strange figures. Commonly we read or hear a statement such as, "According to the National Institute Against Prejudice and Violence . . . 300 racial incidents . . . have occurred on college campuses during the past three years." In fact, there are likely over a million ethnoviolent incidents that take place every year. A knowledgeable reporter would not have made such an error.

The figure of one million campus incidents in an academic year is our estimate based on seven years of research done by independent investigators on many different campuses. That figure is almost never reported.

"GROUP BLAMES REAGAN"

On May 31, 1990, we staged our first major press conference. The Institute was releasing my report, "Campus Ethnoviolence and the Policy Options." There were three important things about the report. It summarized all of the research to date on the incidence of ethnoviolence on American campuses; it offered a detailed explanation as to why it was occurring; and it suggested what campus administrators could do in response.

I made up a press packet. It contained the full report, a summary of the report, and a point-by-point outline of the remarks I was to make (a different and shorter form of the summary). The packet also contained biographical and institutional data. I had, in fact, done everything but write the story for them.

We held the conference at the National Press Club in downtown Washington, DC. The president of our board of directors, former Indiana Senator Birch Bayh, was featured following my presentation of the report. Most of the major newspaper and radio groups came; only CNN among the television outlets taped the proceedings. The only major newspaper that didn't show up was the *Washington Post.* Apparently they could spare only one reporter at the Press Club that morning, and he went down the hall to cover the National Water Coolers Association press conference. With few exceptions, the reporters all pulled out one or two points that became the pegs for their stories. The best of these, oddly enough given their time limitations, were National Public Radio's "All Things Considered" and Pacifica National News. The worst was the Associated Press. The story that made the wire was that the Institute had indicted Ronald Reagan as the cause of campus ethnoviolence. (I had asserted that civil rights had been devalued under the Reagan administration, and that the President's actions had served to delegitimize the issue. My assertion was obviously not newsworthy.) The reporter ended his story with a disclaimer from a Reagan spokesperson, Mark Weinberg, who declared, "To Ronald Reagan there is no greater sin than prejudice." Many Indiana papers used the wire service report to bash Senator Bayh, whose liberalism had always been an anathema and whose son, Evan Bayh, is now the state's governor. By and large the major policy recommendations of the report received no coverage in the major newspapers, and the small conservative papers had a field day with their versions and response to the AP story. After all, who was more credible—a Reagan spokesperson or, as the *Phoenix Gazette* labeled us, "a five-year-old fringe group"?

IMPLICIT THEORIES

Reporters, like most people in this society, have an implicit theory of prejudice and group relations. Through their own reading and life experiences they have come to formulate some ideas about race, about ethnicity, about how and why people are prejudiced, and so on. It would be naive to expect that journalists, by virtue of their job, should be much different from anyone else. The issue, however, is not that some journalists have an "implicit theory" that is false. The issue is that news operatives, because of their job, are expected to "set aside" their preconceived ideas, at least when they write a straight news story. For me, there is a fairly simple test of how well reporters have been able to do this. Tell them something they don't want to hear, something that is outside their preconceived mind set, and see whether it makes its way into print.

Sometimes editorial theory and fantasy result in the reorganization of facts. On Monday, August 8, 1988, the Baltimore *Evening Sun* ran this headlined story: "Poll: Many feel racism abating." The same set of facts ran the next morning in the *New York Times:* "Poll Finds Majority Believe Race Prejudice is Still Strong." The stories were almost the same, but the *Evening Sun* had placed the only "positive" finding of the survey in the two lead paragraphs and headline. The *Times,* in contrast, provided a cryptic but more accurate representation of the actual poll. The *Times,* however, like all newspapers, is not beyond putting a distorted frame around such stories. "Blacks Found Lagging Despite Gains," was one of their headlines on July 28, 1989. The thrust of the article was that "the status of blacks relative to whites has stagnated or regressed since the early 1970s." The "gains" cited in the headline occurred between 1945 and 1970.

There is an "official consensus" among editors and writers. Some people are positive authorities and some are not; some explanations are acceptable and some are not; and some subjects are acceptable and some are not. The newspaper, after all, is a major corporate enterprise. "Freedom of the press," Robert Maxwell told us after purchasing the New York *Daily News,* "cannot be maintained if you don't make a profit." That newspapers defend this political economic system which enables its writers, stockholders, and managers to accumulate wealth and the resources of power, surely, should not be a surprise. Yet, I think, it continues to surprise people. There are many reasons why. One is that the news media maintain a constant campaign to socially reinforce their image as "objective," that is, as presenting all sides fully. "Objectivity" has achieved mystical status in professional journalism. Even the appearance of bias may be sanctioned. Some newspaper managers consider it inappropriate for their reporters to be active in civic associations including such groups as the PTA. Of course, such restrictions serve a dual purpose. They display reporters as people with no allegiances and at the same time they help isolate the reporter from a community of conscience.

A second reason is that reporters who move beyond the official consensus and who attempt to criticize the structure of elite privilege and power are discharged, often publicly, for their poor judgment or lack of objectivity. Critical reporting of elite corruption or scandals is permissible, but criticism of the underlying political and economic structure seems allowable only in some papers on some Sundays on the op-ed page.

Third, on issues which are of little consequence to the news organization, a wider range of people and ideas is permitted in the news. This, of course, helps provide a view of the media as being open and objective.

Finally, we need to recall that the elites themselves are at times in conflict on major issues. When that occurs the newspaper can reflect that range of difference. The range is highly limited, yet it is often enough to provide the appearance of diversity. W. L. Bennett, writing in the *Journal of Communication,* noted that when the level of elite opposition to an administration policy goes up, so does the proportion of opposing stories and op-ed page opinion.

There is a cultural pattern of denial that characterizes the American perception of intergroup relations, especially Black-White relations. Like all cultural patterns it is transmitted across people and authorized and maintained by the legitimate authorities of society. Elite denial is President Reagan declaring that civil rights leaders exaggerate racial problems, or Presidents Bush and Clinton refusing to engage in political dialogue over the four days of intergroup violence which occurred in Los Angeles during their political campaign. Certainly, if issues are not mentioned, they do not become part of the public agenda.

The denial of problems of group relations has permeated American thought and policy. For example, national polls reveal that more than one out of every two White Americans believe that Blacks are as well off or have the same life chances as do Whites.

This denial has also characterized the newsroom. The consequence is that most reporters and editors do not want to hear about the pervasiveness of racism and ethnoviolence. The most facile technique for maintaining this denial is simply not covering the story.

At a media panel convened by the Institute, the panelists all agreed that poverty, racism, and the pathologies of everyday life were not news. The panel included representatives of the Mutual Broadcasting System, *Baltimore Evening Sun, Los Angeles Times,* and the *Washington Journalism Review.*

Yet another dimension of denial is the manner in which the news organization defines "news." Joann Byrd, the *Washington Post* ombudsman, wrote in her column of March 28, 1993, "One way of viewing 'news' is as today's status report on our commonly held values." Byrd presumably means the values of *Post* editors and writers. What of a lack of agreement on basic values or genuine conflict rooted in value differences?

TECHNIQUES OF DISTORTION

Newspaper executives have frequently expressed their perceived obligation to protect the public from unworthy news. For example, Katherine Graham, owner of the *Washington Post* and *Newsweek,* asserted: "There are some things the general public does not need to know and shouldn't. I believe democracy flourishes when the government can take legitimate steps to keep its secrets and when the press can decide whether to print what it knows" (cited in *Regardies* magazine, April 4–10, 1990).

Among the values which editors bring to this protective custody is an absence of concern for openmindedness. Certainly when a person's statement is deliberately distorted, we can infer a propagandistic intent on the part of an editor. My associate, Robert Purvis, documented this transparent distortion in a letter he wrote to the editor. The letter was not answered.

"Recently the *Evening Sun* carried a *New York Times* news service report about welfare mothers' struggle to gain employment and break free of welfare. The original report included a case study of a particular woman's struggle, coupled with substantial information about the national scope of the problem. The *Evening Sun*'s edited version served to trivialize the issue by eliminating the national perspective and focusing solely on the limited, anecdotal case study.

"One pernicious piece of editing in this piece is worth mentioning. At one point the report focused on the mother's inability to provide adequate day care for her children while she worked. In the original report, the mother 'shrugged helplessly' in response to this dilemma. In the *Evening Sun,* she merely 'shrugged.' The former description conveys the mother's anguish, while the edited version equally suggests indifference. If you doubt that many of your readers will incorrectly infer the mother's indifference from your edited version, then you are seriously out of touch with some of the most powerful forces at work in our society today."

There is another dimension to what gets reported and to how well it is reported. Assigning a story to a reporter who has no knowledge of the subject is a political decision, a decision that says that this story doesn't warrant any special concern. When the policies of a newspaper do not give priority to multicultural issues or ethnoviolence, the result is a lack of commitment to provide the necessary training for reporters who cover these stories. A self-perpetuating cycle of incompetence results.

When reporters write about ethnoviolent conflict, it is seldom placed in any social context. Why? Because to place it in its social context means doing research and looking carefully at complex social trends, which requires a fair level of knowledge and sophistication. It also requires time for research. Perhaps, more important, if issues of minority disparities or intergroup conflict were placed in their social context, the reporter would transgress the paper's official consensus.

I don't want to overstate the case. Stories about ethnoviolence are often easy to get at, and if they challenge any official consensus, it is one that says let's not report anything which may rock the boat. Any enterprising reporter can go to the official records of the police department or human relations commission to see what's happening. Two researchers at Northwestern, David L. Protess and James S. Ettema, did just that. They went to the records of bias crimes reported to the Chicago Commission on Human Relations and to the reports of these events in Chicago's weekly and daily newspapers. They looked at a one-year period from mid-1988 to mid-1989. They found that only 9 percent of the bias crimes reported to the Commission were mentioned in the press.

The incidents selected for coverage were most likely to be the more serious crimes. It was the spectacular character or the "newsworthiness" of the incident rather than the pervasiveness of ethnoviolence that framed the story. The report noted that during the year only two stories "offered a glimpse of the big picture." These stories, which appeared in the *Tribune* and the *Sun-Times* the day after the mayoral election, were hung on a news peg of bias crimes which took place during the campaign.

Following the model of the Northwestern researchers, I compared the *Sunpapers* coverage of Maryland bias incidents over the past three and one-half years with reports made to the state Human Relations Commission by local police departments. I found that for every 82 incidents only one appeared in either of the *Sunpapers.* There were no "big picture" stories in the entire period, which covered January 1990 through July 1993.

The fragmentation of stories is another way of masking the explicit bias of the news organization. Take the case of the Stockton, California, elementary school shootings. On January 18, 1989, Patrick Edward Purdy entered the Cleveland Elementary schoolyard in Stockton, California. He let loose with more than 100 rounds of ammunition from a semiautomatic assault rifle at 300 youngsters, most of whom were the children of Southeast Asian refugees. Five students were killed; 29 students and one teacher were injured. Newspapers across the country gave the story front-page coverage.

Purdy killed himself before he was caught, and he left behind no letter or explicit statement of his motives. Was this just another random act of violence or was it an act of ethnoviolence deliberately directed at Asian Americans? Because of the ambiguity and political pressure, the California attorney general, John Van de Kamp, initiated an investigation. In early October of the same year, Van de Kamp issued a report stating that "Purdy attacked Southeast Asian immigrants out of a festering sense of racial resentment and hatred." This conclusion to the event appeared as a three-inch story in the back pages of the *Washington Post* and was not reported by many papers which had featured the event as front-page news earlier in the year.

This fragmentation of news, that is the reporting of events without a context or without an ending, is ultimately confusing. Even the careful reader becomes unable to complete stories or establish some understanding of discrete events.

Stories can be fragmented internally, although I don't think this is very common. Here is how the *Baltimore Sun* fragmented a story that they would not normally run. On March 13, 1990, toward the end of an analytic piece by Ron Harris of the *Los Angeles Times,* the editor inserted four paragraphs of local commentary designed clearly to neutralize Harris's main points. This story-within-a-story is certainly a novel technique of media control. It may be a new form of journalistic distortion.

The "peg" of Harris's story was the Howard University student protest that forced the resignation of then Republican Party National Chair Lee Atwater from the university's board of trustees. On his peg the writer hung three observations. One was that there is a rising level of Black pride and militancy, not just on campuses but everywhere. Harris wrote: "It was evident in their dress, their music, their conversation and their attitude." The second observation was on the incidence of Black poverty, unemployment, crime, and other pathologies of racism. The third observation was stated in a quote from Walter Allen, a well-known African-American sociologist. Commenting on the state of intergroup relations, Allen said, "What we have is a kettle that is on the verge of boiling over, an explosion waiting to happen."

That was Harris's story, but it was not the story the *Sun* normally prints. Why did they print it? I don't know. But what they did do, following the Allen quotation, was to add four paragraphs of local quotes all denying the points made by the *Los Angeles Times* writer.

VIOLATIONS OF CIVILITY

There is a difference between Black crime and White crime. The pathologies of White America are underreported. In simple numbers, alcoholism, crime, drugs, poverty, homelessness, welfare, child abuse, and teenage pregnancy—virtually the range of recognized social pathologies—occur more often among Whites. The news media focus quite clearly on their manifestations among Blacks and on rates. Differences in rates are not unimportant, if you are an epidemiologist or a community organizer. Teenage pregnancy, for example, is important, and Black women have a higher rate. But how many people know that two-thirds of teenage mothers are White? Or, take the case of drug use: how clear is it from news media depictions that White users outnumber Black users by almost 5 to 1?

Such subtle stereotyping occurs with all groups. Take the repeated media depiction of the affluence of Asian Americans. How many people are aware of the high levels of poverty among the recent immigrants from Southeast Asia?

By overstating pathology in one case and affluence in the other, the media misdirects public attention, adding to the general confusion about social policy.

Prejudice often leads reporters to emphasize Black separatism and anger. The selective focus on Black anger often conveys an imagery threatening to Whites and it distracts the reader from the events which caused the anger. The focus on the psychological state of Black bystanders or demonstrators may reflect bad reporting and bad editing, rather than the underlying prejudice of the reporter. I think not. You can see the same pattern of reporting in class-based disputes. Workers on strike are always depicted as angry, while the psychological states of managers are never portrayed. When strikes become rancorous, the conflict becomes the story, not the conditions of work that led to the strike. The same is true in prison protests. The conditions of prison life and the specific demands of the inmates are always secondary to the spectacle of protest. There is an underlying principle here: if you focus on the anger of those at the bottom, you distract the reader from a social critique.

NEWSPAPERS AS PERPETRATORS

In our effort to look for external and structural reasons for media bias and neglect we certainly shouldn't overlook the fact that some forms of bias reflect institutional discrimination. Complaints of discrimination have been filed against newspapers across the country, from the *Sacramento Bee,* the flagship paper of the McClatchy chain, to the elite *Washington Post.* The *Washington Post* may be a good example. In mid-1988, the Newspaper Guild filed a class-action suit against the *Post* charging systematic discrimination against women, Blacks, Hispanics, other minority groups, and employees over the age of 40. In 1987, the paper was boycotted by Black community leaders in protest over the *Post*'s stereotyping and their neglect of Black issues. Jill Nelson, a *Post* reporter for four and one-half years and a central figure in the Guild's class action suit, wrote of her experience: "When it comes to Black folks, we exist mostly as potential sociological, pathological, or scatological slices of life waiting to be chewed, digested, and excreted into the requisite number of column inches in the paper" (*Volunteer Slavery: My Authentic Negro Experience,* Noble Press, 1993).

Although the *Post*'s recent coverage of Black-White issues seems improved, an astounding myopia still obscures their editorial views. Their editorial on the Supreme Court's decision on statutes which enhance penalties for crimes motivated by bias is an example (June 14, 1993). The editorial asserts: "The justices unanimously cite the reasoning of the Wisconsin legislature that penalties should be greater for hate crimes because 'this conduct is thought to inflict greater individual and societal harm . . . provoke retaliatory crimes . . . and incite community unrest.' This is speculative at best." Considering that numerous *amicus* briefs presented to the Court cited specific evidence that bias-motivated crimes did inflict greater harm, the editorial can be characterized as misguided at best.

According to an American Newspaper Publisher's Association report, in June 1990, 64 percent of daily newspapers had no active affirmative action plan. Their employee survey indicated that 90 percent of all news and editorial personnel were White. The American Society of Newspaper Editors annual newsroom survey, released in March 1993, reports a 10 percent level of minorities in the newsroom. Their survey, however, indicates that approximately 45 percent of all newspapers do not have any minorities on staff.

Although increasing the numbers of minority journalists may have some impact on news coverage and on news sources, the complexion of the newsroom may have no impact on the underlying social functions of the newspaper. There is an explicit argument being made in some minority journalist circles that newspapers are losing ground because they have failed to adapt their coverage to their changing readership (Some newspapers have attempted to adapt by changing their readership. This has been accomplished by paying telemarketers lower royalties on subscriptions in poor or Black neighborhoods or by offering special subscription rates in more affluent neighborhoods. This was a core issue in the case of the "Gazette Seven," marketing employees who took on the *Arkansas Gazette* in Little Rock in 1988–89.)

"Once Hispanics start appearing in the newsroom," wrote Michelle Heller in the November 1992 magazine *Hispanic,* "perhaps the Hispanic community will start appearing in the paper." Perhaps it will. But Heller, like so many others, confuses the issue by viewing coverage of minority middle-class affairs along with a de-emphasis on crime and conflict news as an end in itself. One can look, for example, at the *Miami Herald* with its 35 percent minority-staffed newsroom and find little difference between it and other large dailies in their reports on matters of social justice and group conflict.

There is one way in which changing the ethnicity of the newsroom population may change newspaper coverage. Erna Smith, a journalism professor at San Francisco State University, reports in her study of Bay area news media that stories by minority writers were more likely than stories written by Whites to use minority news sources. She writes: "Most of the stories (90 percent) reported by Blacks used minority news sources."

What is missing in the focus on numbers is the sociological perspective that tells you that the news of race and ethnic affairs is reported so as to validate the power relations among groups in society. Within the context of the large corporate newspaper, you will not achieve tenure as a reporter if you challenge the existing structure of power. Even among columnists, and certainly among those widely syndicated, the advocacy of genuine social reform is rare. David Croteau and William Hoynes concluded their study of columnists: "The political tilt of the most widely distributed columnists is clearly to the right, articulating a consistent conservative perspective while providing only fragments of a liberal position. First-rate political analysis from a consistent progressive position is entirely absent" (*EXTRA!*, June 1992).

There are clear class interests involved. The average editor of a major metropolitan newspaper is earning around $265,000 a year. A beginning reporter for a major newspaper can start at $50,000. Half of all families in the United States don't make that much money even with two incomes. Since crude economics may not be sufficient to channel the social motives of reporters, management has begun to screen out the potential rebels. Ben Bagdikian, writing in *Mother Jones* (May–June 1992), describes this recruitment: "More than ever before, major news corporations are conducting systematic screenings of new reporters to keep out journalists who might not readily comply with company wishes or who might join newsroom unions. Some major news companies, including the nation's second-largest newspaper chain, Knight-Ridder, do the screening through mandatory, lengthy psychological questionnaires of all potential new reporters. Others, including some papers in the largest newspaper chain, Gannett, order editors to be deliberately blunt in interviews so that applicants know the company wants only 'team players' who will not rock the boat and are not in favor of unions."

THE PICTURES LOST

Critical aspects of ethnoviolent incidents are never reported. Sometimes the missing details are substantive. For example, only a handful of stories about the problem of ethnoviolence have paid serious attention to the victims. Only a few reporters have ever asked, or printed when my associates and I have prompted them, the story of the effects of prejudice-motivated violence on people. That may appear odd since reporters often dwell embarrassingly on victim suffering, especially, it seems, on television. But our experience has been that most reporters don't recognize the psychological devastation that ethnoviolence causes, and so only victims of extreme personal violence or property damage are given serious attention. Further, from an elite standpoint, since most victims of ethnoviolence are unworthy victims, their trauma is also not worthy of news coverage.

The news media also frequently lose sight of underlying issues. For instance, few stories have considered how unprepared most community agencies have been to deal with the high levels of immigration of foreign-born nationals. This past decade has been the second largest period of immigration in American history. Yet, neither the issues of acculturation, nor the capacity of communities to absorb new cultural groups, nor the inevitable conflicts and ethnoviolence that follow rapid immigration have been appropriately planned for in most cities.

Often what doesn't get reported does not get put on the public agenda. The mainstream news organizations have to be viewed as agents of social control. Routine acts of bigotry are assumed by the journalist to be glitches in the normally smooth operation of a just and consensual system. A "responsible press" keeps the coverage within the boundaries of legitimate political discourse. To be sure, the boundaries shift marginally in response to external crises, and sometimes the political elites themselves become divided. Such crises and divisions are what allows other groups to force themselves on to the agenda.

Since everyday ethnoviolence is perceived generally as glitch and not newsworthy, why is it covered at all? There are two reasons. One is that the story itself is often cast as a representation of how well the "system" is operating. That is, people care and the perpetrators are stigmatized. The second is that these reports keep the victims in their place. That is, the reporting of routine ethnoviolence is a social reminder that group conflict persists and that the dominant participants are still dominant. And probably deserve to be.

The underlying effect of the newspaper reporting of prejudice, group conflict, and ethnoviolence is to reaffirm the subordinate status of women, of the "traditional" minorities, and of political and cultural dissidents. In doing so, it fragments and distorts the news of intergroup problems and generally alienates the underrepresented, minorities, and those members of the dominant groups who are genuinely civicly concerned.

The most insidious form of news control is silence. Silence is a form of rewriting history; it transforms events into non-events. Consider the case of the Hate Crime Statistics Act of 1990 and the Baltimore *Sunpapers.* On April 23, 1990, President Bush signed this act into law. Under this new law, the Justice Department was charged with collecting and publishing statistics on crimes motivated by prejudice based on race, religion, ethnicity, or sexual orientation.

The story was newsworthy for two major reasons: (1) it was the first federal law of its kind, and (2) it was the first time that "sexual orientation" had been included in a federal civil rights law. There were several other reasons why this law was newsworthy: it's a new law; it was signed by the President in a White House ceremony; it was the first civil rights bill signed by him after repeated opposition to more substantial bills; it was likely the first time that gay and lesbian activists were invited to a White House ceremony; it was the outcome of the work of an extraordinary coalition of national organizations. In Baltimore, there were even local angles that gave the story a higher priority. For example, Maryland was the first state to enact a local hate crimes statistics act, and several Marylanders testified at the original Congressional hearings in support of the bill's passage.

The *New York Times* gave the story 15 column inches. The *Washington Post* gave the story 10 column inches and a 2-column photo. *USA Today* gave the story 15 column inches and a 1-column photo.

The Baltimore *Sun* and the *Evening Sun* both gave the story zero inches. For the people of Baltimore, it was a non-event. Both *Sunpapers* editors made the decision not to report this event. Both editors did not respond to my inquiries about their decision.

Given the wrong information, including no information, people can't think very constructively about the issues of race and ethnicity. Given the wrong information, people are often left with the illusions of knowledge. Those media-generated illusions do not lead to knowing.

27

Ebonics, Language, and Power

MIKE LONG

Modern education not only corrupts the heart of our youth by the rigid slavery to which it condemns them, it also undermines their reason by the unintelligible jargon with which they are overwhelmed in the first instance, and the little attention that is given to accommodating their pursuits to their capacities in the second.

—William Godwin, *An Account of the Seminary* (1783), p. 31

The current furor and confusion in the United States over the role of "Ebonics" in education is but a recent skirmish in a long-running struggle. It is not new, not confined to "Black English," or to English in general, not confined to education, and certainly not confined to the United States. It is a controversy that surfaces in North America and around the world time and time again. On all five continents, coercive power relationships between socioeconomic elites wielding state power and oppressed groups wielding little or none find linguistic reflexes. The elites speak the "official" state language or the "standard" variety of a language—in the present case, "Standard English" (SE)—which *they made* official or standard; the oppressed groups (not necessarily minorities, as in the present case) are decreed by the same elites to speak a less acceptable or unacceptable language or a socially stigmatized variety of the same language, such as "Black English." Very real objective linguistic differences thus provide yet another excuse for discrimination in many areas of public life, including education, (so-called) criminal justice systems, employment, media access, and even labor unions. The public policy decisions in different countries that result from these periodic convulsions, often enshrined in statute and case law, concern linguistic human rights, and they have wide-ranging social consequences for hundreds of millions of people. The rhetorical barrage surrounding the present struggle serves to confuse the real issues, or to ensure that they are not discussed at all, which benefits only one side in the status quo.

For these reasons and because the role of language in education is but one of several examples of the critical nexus of language and state power, the Ebonics issue is a vital one for working people everywhere. The radical right in the United States recognizes its importance and is all over the mass media using it to push its own domestic agenda, that is, a relentless attack on the burgeoning U.S. underclass, spiced with obvious racism, one manifestation of which is the defunding of public education. Symptomatic of the level of confusion, misinformation, and disinformation, at least one supposedly radical left group, the (Trotskyist) International Socialist Organization, has unwittingly aligned itself, albeit for different reasons, with radical conservative demagogues such as Rush Limbaugh, William Raspberry, and George Will. The ISO opposes attention to Ebonics because it sees such attention as an irrelevant distraction from the "real issues" in U.S. education—racism and lack of funding. And usually well-meaning liberals such as Kweisi Mfume, Maya Angelou ("incensed"), Jesse Jackson ("ungrammatical English"), and Ellen Goodman ("legitimizing slang") have come out with reactionary, ill-informed public pronouncements. Some familiarity with the basic linguistic concepts involved and with research findings on (in this case, educational) solutions is required for an informed and appropriately targeted response and also in order to initiate a long overdue discussion of libertarian approaches to language education and language in education.

EBONICS

Ebonics is a term coined by Robert Williams at a 1973 conference, the proceedings of which, edited by Williams, were published two years later as *Ebonics: The True Language of Black Folks.* He defined it as

> the linguistic and paralinguistic features which on a concentric continuum represent the communicative competence of the West African, Caribbean, and United States idioms, patois, argots, idiolects, and social forces of black people. . . . Ebonics derives its form from ebony (black) and phonics (sound, the study of sound) and refers to the study of the language of black people in all its cultural uniqueness. (1975, p. vi)

The *Journal of Black Studies* devoted a special issue (June 1979) to Ebonics, but other terms more often employed by linguists are "Black English," "Black English Vernacular" (BEV), and "African-American Vernacular English" (AAVE). AAVE is the term that will be used here, except when citing those who refer to Ebonics.

The other terms more accurately reflect the fact that we are concerned not just with the sounds, or pronunciation, of "Black English," such as final consonant deletion (*goo* for 'good'), final consonant cluster reduction (*yo daw* for 'your dogs'), or 'th'/'f' substitution (*wif* for 'with'), but with its grammar (morphology and syntax), meaning (lexicon and semantics), and use (discourse and pragmatics), as well. With considerable variation both within and across speakers, common morpho-syntactic differences between AAVE and SE, for example, involve subject-verb agreement (*She like, They like*), copula (*He/They be mighty fine*), copula deletion (*They feels as though they even*), past time reference (*He done seen him*), negative inversion (*Don't nobody see*), and double (sometimes even triple) negatives (*I ain' never doin tha no moa*) (see, e.g., Fasold 1972; Labov 1972; Wolfram 1969). There is nothing inferior (or superior) about any of these constructions. If some varieties of AAVE can give expression to an idea about time much earlier than the time of speaking by use of a nifty auxiliary, "I *bin* read that book," whereas most "white" varieties have to use a clumsier adverbial construction, "I read that book *a long time ago*," to say the same thing (example courtesy of Ralph Fasold), it is not that AAVE is better or the white varieties worse but that they are *different*.

The fact that most AAVE speakers are intelligible to speakers of other varieties most of the time, and vice versa, does not alter the fact that some differences do nevertheless cause communication breakdowns and that those can occur without speaker or hearer, for example, teacher and student, understanding either that or why they have occurred. The late Charlene ("Charlie") Sato (1989) showed, moreover, that the *degree* of difference and its import for instruction often go unrecognized, affecting both comprehension and classroom participation in hidden ways. For example, many an SE-speaking immigrant in Hawaii has interpreted Hawaii Creole English (HCE) *neva*, in *I neva see him*, as SE 'never', instead of what it really means, that is, 'didn't', in 'I didn't see him', *neva* functioning as a past time marker in HCE. Similarly, the African-American child who writes *I be fighting*, which is true, only to have a white SE-speaking teacher correct it to *I am fighting*, which is false, for example (courtesy of Ralph Fasold), is frustrated and confused, and his teacher blissfully unaware of the fact (or the facts).

Numerous linguistic studies of AAVE over the years have documented its richness, expressiveness, and communicative adequacy (see, e.g., Labov 1969, 1995). Like any other natural human language or language variety, AAVE is systematic and rule-governed, its rules sometimes less complex than those of SE, sometimes more so. To illustrate the greater complexity (example courtesy of Ralph Fasold), AAVE offers three tenses *(He thinking about it, He be thinking about it,* and *He think about it)* for two in SE in the same domain *(He is thinking about it* and *He thinks about it),* allowing more precision. Those rules and the varieties are, again, not better or worse, just different. AAVE is not a separate language (as the original Oakland, California, School Board resolution unfortunately implied, allowing opponents another opening for their attacks) but simply a variety of English. Although there are no hard and fast rules, the usual criterion for distinguishing separate languages from separate varieties of the same language (including geographically, ethnically, or social class–based dialects) is mutual intelligibility. If 80 percent or more of what speaker A says is comprehensible to speaker B, they are usually held to speak different varieties of the same language, not different languages (there are exceptions; Danish, Norwegian and Swedish, for example, are much closer than this, yet are referred to as separate languages). Which of two or more varieties of a language is considered the prestige variety is not a linguistic issue but a sociolinguistic one, that is, a function of the prestige of its speakers. In the often quoted words of the linguist Max Weinreich, "A language is a dialect with an army and a navy."

The stigmatization of AAVE reflects not its linguistic qualities but negative attitudes toward AAVE *speakers*. For example, it so happens that a number of features of AAVE are also common in several varieties of American English spoken by some whites in southern states, for example, Arkansas, Georgia, Alabama, Mississippi, and the Carolinas, yet they are not considered problematic when produced by the likes of such fine moral guardians as Bill Clinton, Jimmy Carter, Howell Hefflin, Strom Thurman, or Jesse Helms. It would be a mistake, however, to dismiss negative attitudes toward AAVE as simply one more manifestation of racism.

Although much of the criticism and many of the critics may well be racially motivated, the same stigmatization is often performed by speakers of a "standard" language or dialect at the expense of speakers of a "nonstandard" one who are members of the same ethnic group. Obvious examples include speakers of "Standard" British English and "cockney" English or of "restricted" and "elaborated" codes in the United Kingdom, "Standard" American English and Appalachian English, "high" and "low" German, and "standard" French and Quebecois or Cajun French. Power is at least roughly distributed along racial lines in many societies, including the United States, and in turn with linguistic differences, but it is the *power* to discriminate along racial, linguistic, or any other lines that is the real issue.

Even so-called "Standard" English varies considerably with geography, ethnicity, social class, and other factors, as well as over time. Compare, for instance, what is considered SE by elites in New York, California, and Alabama, or in India, Australia, Singapore, and Nigeria, or in London, Liverpool, and Edinburgh. It quickly becomes apparent that the ruling classes (of different ethnic backgrounds) in English-speaking countries around the world all have their own peculiar local notions of SE, which always happen to coincide with the way they and their friends speak, and which they proceed to exploit as one more means of discriminating against those who speak differently. In fact, if anything approaching a universal "standard" variety exists at all, it is found only in the *written* form of English or any other language. Discriminating against people for the way they speak is even more unwarranted than might be obvious to any rational person, for nobody speaks either "English" or "Standard English"; *everyone* speaks a variety of English, and SE speakers speak but one *variety* of SE.

LANGUAGE AND IDENTITY

AAVE is the variety of American English, itself taking several distinct forms, that is spoken by many, but by no means all, African Americans, particularly, but not only, in the inner cities, as well as by a few other groups in the United States, such as some Southeast Asian refugees who grew up in African-American neighborhoods. AAVE is usually identified with the race and ethnicity of its speakers, but many African Americans, especially members of the black middle classes, seldom experience it as children, and others do so but choose not to speak it, or do so only rarely and only in certain settings in which they consider its use appropriate. AAVE is better seen as not simply a matter of race, therefore, but of social class and, to some degree, also of age, for it tends to be especially strong and salient among the young urban poor. Among black youth, linguists have found evidence of AAVE's increasing divergence from "standard" (i.e., currently mostly white, middle-class) spoken American English, especially in its pronunciation and intonation, apparently as a marker of group solidarity and resistance (see, e.g., Bailey 1987, 1993; Bailey and Maynor 1989; Labov and Harris 1986).

The same trend was reported by Sato (1991) among adolescents in Hawaii. Most Hawaiian children, like (this time) the *majority* of people who grow up in the Hawaiian Islands, especially those from working-class backgrounds and educated in public schools, are speakers of another "nonstandard" (albeit, this time, again, *majority*) variety, Hawaii Creole English (HCE), often referred to locally as

"Pidgin." Paralleling disputes over AAVE, the status of HCE in Hawaii's classrooms has also been the subject of a long, continuing struggle (see Sato 1985).

To sum up so far, AAVE, like HCE and like language everywhere, is a conscious part of people's identity. To attack a language or language variety by discriminating against it in education, for example, by forcing students to be educated through someone else's language or language variety, is to attack its speakers. It is an effective way of breaking down resistance and of rendering communities and cultures more vulnerable to state control. As the current rapid spread of English as a vehicle for international capitalism worldwide illustrates, the spread of an "official" language or "standard" language variety increases the influence of its existing speakers and facilitates absorption of new ones into an English-speaking (especially, now, U.S. capitalist) worldview. Linguistic dependency quickly translates into political, economic, and cultural dependency, or as Pennycook (1995) puts it, "English in the world" quickly becomes "the world in English."

Governments know all this. It is no accident that, as part of the fascist dictatorship's brutal suppression of the Basques after 1939, Franco made it illegal to speak Basque and an imprisonable offense to teach it, or that the indigenous Hawaiian language (now being revived through school immersion programs) was suppressed by the plantation owners and missionaries to the point of extinction, or that the same politicians, for example, Dole and Gingrich, and forces behind current movements to make English the (only) official language of the United States are those on the wrong side of every other struggle for social justice, or that Israel obliges Arabic-speaking university students to take their classes and exams in Hebrew (despite Arabic being an official language in Israel), or that the United States, Britain, France, Germany, and now Japan consider it so important to spend so much (of other people's) time and money on teaching their national languages overseas.

What is true of languages is true of language varieties. Governments and elites understand the gatekeeping opportunities afforded them by support of a "standard" variety as a requirement for access to power, too. The fact that discrimination against speakers of other languages and of nonstandard dialects is often carried out by people of the *same* race, upper class against working class and/or regional dialect–speaking white children in Germany and the United Kingdom, for example, shows that the issue is fundamentally one of power, not race. Although power imbalances are often strongly correlated with racial differences, as in the present U.S. case, it would be a mistake to dismiss the attack on Ebonics as *simply* another manifestation of racism, as some have done, and to lose sight of the important linguistic issues in the process. Racism and underfunding may be more important overall than language issues in public education in the United States, but as explained earlier, there is ample independent evidence of the importance of linguistic discrimination in education for African-American and many white children, too.

THE OAKLAND SCHOOL BOARD RESOLUTION

According to a January 15, 1997, article in *Education Week*, approximately 53 percent of the 52,300 K–12 student population in the Oakland, California, School District is black, and 47 percent Asian or Latino. There are very few white students. A plurality of the teaching staff is white, the next largest group is black. Oakland teachers had not had a raise in five years and in February 1996 went on a two-month strike over pay and conditions, especially class size, black and white teachers standing shoulder to shoulder on the picket lines. They won a partial victory over wages but little else. The schools themselves, like public schools almost everywhere in the United States, are underfunded and run down. Student test scores are low and getting worse; of the 28,000 black students, 71 percent are in special education classes, 64 percent have been held back a grade, and on a four-point scale, their collective grade point average is a meager 1.8.

Against this background, on December 18, 1996, the seven-member Oakland School Board unanimously adopted a resolution recognizing Ebonics as a legitimate "genetically based" (sic) "language" (sic) spoken by many of its African-American students and proposed seeking state and federal funds in order to mount additional training programs. (Some programs, costing $200,000 a year in state and federal funding, were already in effect for 3,000 students in the district.) Their purpose was not, as has often been asserted, to "teach Ebonics" (which the students already know, after all) but initially to teach *in* Ebonics, as the resolution clearly stated, "for the combined purposes of maintaining the legitimacy and richness of such language . . . and to facilitate [African-American students'] acquisition and mastery of English-language skills." Like the successful five-year Ebonics program in the Dallas public schools recently shut down due to funding cuts, the Oakland resolution's first objective was to help sensitize teachers to linguistic differences between AAVE and Standard English (SE). On a par with programs designed to help immigrants who speak a different language to learn English, the second aim was to help AAVE speakers learn SE and to do so without denigrating or (as if this were possible by fiat) eradicating the home (AAVE) variety. The third goal was to *begin* instruction in reading, mathematics, and so forth, in AAVE, on the usually unchallenged pedagogic principle of starting where the students are and then gradually making the transition to SE. Subsequent public comments by school board members suggested that the resolution was an honest, well-intentioned (not to mention, for the most part, scientifically supportable) attempt to do something tangible to help a large group of underachieving students in their care.

A few voices were raised publicly in support of the general thrust, at least, of the board's proposal during the weeks that followed, including that of the country's preeminent professional association for linguists, the Linguistics Society of America (LSA), which at the end of its annual conference, fortuitously meeting in Chicago early in January 1997, issued a formal resolution broadly supportive of the Oakland initiative. The LSA resolution stressed AAVE's well-documented rule-governed systematicity, appending a list of nearly thirty scientific books on the subject, noted that the distinction between "language" and "dialect" is usually made more on social and political than linguistic grounds and termed recent public characterizations of Ebonics as "slang," "mutant," "lazy," "defective," "ungrammatical," and "broken English" as "incorrect and demeaning." The resolution further noted evidence from Sweden, the United States, and other countries to the effect that pedagogical approaches that recognize the legitimacy of nonstandard varieties of a language help their speakers learn the standard variety. The LSA resolution concluded that "the Oakland School Board's decision to recognize the vernacular of African-American students in teaching them Standard English is linguistically and pedagogically sound." A resolution to expand language programs for African-American students was introduced in January by a member of the Los Angeles School Board, the second largest in the United States.

Supporters, however, were simply overwhelmed by an immediate and intense barrage of angry, often blatantly racist, sometimes close to hysterical, criticism from all sides. Different interest groups singled out different aspects of the resolution, parts of which really were open to criticism because they were linguistically uninformed or poorly communicated. With hardly a pause for breath, let alone unwanted debate or hearings on the real issue, and obviously relieved at the easy "out" the resolution allowed his agency, U.S. Department of Education Secretary Richard W. Riley quickly issued a statement saying USDOE would certainly not be funding any education programs for AAVE speakers or their teachers, since, contrary to what the Oakland resolution had stated, Ebonics was not a "separate language"—about which, since AAVE is simply one *variety* of English, the USDOE was right. Others reacted negatively to the idea that Ebonics, or any other "language," was "genetically based," and in this, too (see below), they were right, while managing to avoid the real issue.

For numerous right-wing commentators with their usual surfeit of airtime in the mainstream media—often their own regular newspaper columns and whole television shows—a common approach was simply to assert that support for Ebonics was an unfounded, minority, "liberal" position, just one more dangerous example of divisive "Afrocentrism," and then quickly to lose the original language-in-education issue amidst a melange of baseless, sweeping charges about "European" civilization and "white" history and culture being under threat in the curriculum. Aristotle was Greek and white, for instance, but how many students learned that at school, an irate George Will demanded to know within minutes of the start of an early ABC current affairs "debate" supposedly on Ebonics. To make matters worse, the ideologues' task was facilitated by the shield provided them in the form of the strong condemnations of the Oakland resolution issued by prominent black liberals, notably Maya Angelou, who has credibility as the current U.S. poet laureate. Such pronouncements on the issue were given exceptionally good media coverage. For instance, perhaps because of his increasingly more reactionary political stances on a number of issues in recent years, the Reverend Jesse Jackson is often sought out and presented by mainstream journalists as if he were an official spokesperson for all African Americans; meanwhile, more radical (although often equally reactionary) African-American leaders with large followings, such as the Reverend Louis Farrakhan, are marginalized.

Faced with the media onslaught, on January 15, the Oakland School Board unanimously adopted a somewhat modified version of their original resolution. While continuing to maintain (falsely) that Ebonics is not a dialect of English, and stating (correctly) that some linguistic features of Ebonics have their origins in West African and Niger-Congo languages, references to Ebonics as "genetically based" were removed. The earlier call to have children educated in their "primary language," Ebonics, was also modified to clarify the intention of the original resolution, which was for education to begin where children were at linguistically—an uncontroversial proposition in any other aspect of education—and to move them toward SE over time.

As should be obvious by now, however, the details and fate of the Oakland resolutions themselves are not the real issue. If the Oakland initiative is stymied and eventually goes away, as currently (February 1997) seems likely, the critical role of language and of language varieties in education will not. It is useful, therefore, to continue the debate (and this chapter) a little further in the hope that our own response can be that much better informed and "ready to go" whenever and wherever the language police strike next, as they assuredly will, as well for the purpose of stimulating long overdue discussion among those more seriously interested in libertarian approaches to both language education and language in education. A useful place to start, given the critical relevance of each to the current debate, is with a sketch of (1) the relationship between genetics and the environment in language and language learning, and (2) educational options for "unofficial" or "nonstandard" language or dialect school-age populations.

NATURE AND NURTURE IN LANGUAGE

It is clear that every child, whatever his or her ethnic or social class origin, is born with the same innate capacity to learn whichever language(s) he or she is exposed to, to do so at a very young age, and to do so remarkably fast. There is some evidence that children first exposed to a second dialect of a language after age six, like those first attempting second language acquisition after that age, are unable to master the new variety to native-like standards, with the prognosis deteriorating markedly for those first exposed as teenagers, and with morpho-syntax also problematic for starters older than the midteens (see, e.g., Chambers 1992). If second dialect acquisition really is subject to the same putative maturational constraints that seem to affect second language acquisition, the linguistic flexibility routinely demanded of ethnolinguistic minority schoolchildren is even more discriminatory than previously thought. Requiring a radical change of accent by adults for certain kinds of employment could be demanding the biologically impossible and so could constitute a violation of civil rights law in some countries, although, of course, one that few courts are likely to recognize, whatever the merits, for fear of the socioeconomic consequences of offering legal protection for the linguistic rights of people other than those that judicial systems primarily serve to protect.

This much is due to nature. *Which* language(s) or language varieties are learned during this period, conversely, is determined by nurture, that is, the linguistic environment. In other words, it is the ability and timetable for acquiring language that is genetically based, not the languages themselves. Caucasian or African-American children born to English-speaking parents in Chicago will learn whatever varieties of English they hear spoken around them, principally those of their parents, other caretakers, and age peers. A child of whatever ethnicity born to a linguistically mixed couple can learn both languages (say, English and Spanish) if both are used with him or her sufficiently, although overwhelming exposure to one of them outside the home often leads to that language being "dominant" or to the child's ability in it being stronger. Any child whose family moves early enough to an environment where another language is spoken will learn that second or third language (say, German or Japanese) instead of, or in addition to, English and/or Spanish, given sufficient exposure. The genetic inheritance for language acquisition is equal and universal, regardless of the social class origin or ethnicity of the child and regardless of the language or language variety in the environment.

Language acquisition is thus a product of both nature and nurture. Every child comes into the world innately equipped to learn one or more languages. Members of any particular ethnic group are genetically programmed to speak not a particular language or language variety but, rather, whichever one(s) they are exposed to early enough. An important corollary of this for the Ebonics debate is that *every* language or language variety is a reflection of the same human capacity and, as such, inevitably of equal communicative potential. This is the case regardless of any differences two languages or varieties of a language may exhibit at any one point in time in such areas as their "technical" vocabulary for discussing the colors of tropical foliage, personal computers, or sumo wrestling and, of course, regardless of their current *social* prestige.

EDUCATIONAL OPTIONS

The importance of the home-to-school language switch has long been documented in numerous countries. The vast majority of children throughout the world enter primary school with at least some degree of mismatch between what they have grown used to linguistically by listening to their caretakers and playmates in and around the home and the language of schooling. In many parts of Africa, Asia, and Latin America, children have to learn a new language if they want any formal education at all, and sometimes a third language in order to continue on to secondary or tertiary education. The fact that *some* of those children succeed both in mastering the language(s) required and in their education does not make the task less of an imposition, nor does it compensate for the vast numbers of others who fail at both or do less well because of the extra linguistic burden with which they are confronted.

With varying degrees of subtlety, the usual solution favored by states everywhere is *submersion* in the official language or prestige "standard" dialect as soon as children enter school. This favors the children of parents who speak the language or dialect concerned, disfavors those who do not, and increases the likelihood of linguistic, political, and cultural *assimilation* of groups, such as immigrants or racial blocks, which, left linguistically intact, might eventually threaten the hegemony of current elites. Submersion programs should not be confused with the widely successful *immersion* programs, such as French immersion for English-speaking Canadians, in which children who speak the dominant national language, English, receive all or part of their curriculum delivered through the other official, but minority, language, French (their L2), and, as evaluation studies show, typically graduate with a good command of French (comparable to native speakers in listening and reading, somewhat weaker in speaking and writing), with no adverse effects on their achievement in other subjects. In immersion, all students start as a linguistically and educationally homogeneous group, usually as beginners, making it possible for teachers to adapt their (L2 French) speech appropriately and keep content instruction comprehensible. In submersion, on the other hand, non-English-speaking or limited English-speaking children are thrown in with English-speaking children in English-medium classrooms. The speech they hear around them is initially incomprehensible because it is addressed primarily to children who already speak English, making it difficult for the non-native speakers to learn either the language or the subject matter being taught through it. Submersion programs are also known as "sink or swim." Countless immigrant and other linguistic minority children sink (see, e.g., Schinke-Llano 1983). These are the programs favored by the "English-only" movements.

Slightly less obviously coercive are various kinds of *transition* models, which allow use of the home language or dialect in the early stages, but quickly introduce the official language or standard variety, and move children from one to the other, such that the home language or dialect is replaced by the new one, a process known as *subtractive bilingualism* (adding the second language but losing the first). In theory, for example, so-called transitional, or "early-exit," bilingual education programs in some parts of the United States allow classroom use of Spanish for some subjects, while gradually introducing English for others, in the first one to three years of school, after which Spanish is dropped. In practice, studies show that Spanish, the most widely spoken minority language in the United States, is rarely used or survives even that long in such programs. The fate of less-supported languages is even worse.

Much more respectful of linguistic rights, as well as of students' identities and cultural backgrounds, are models that seek to add the second language or dialect while validating and preserving the first, so-called *maintenance* bilingual programs. Examples include what are known in the United States as "late-exit" bilingual education programs, which, in theory, allow classroom use of Spanish (or some other L1) for up to the first six years of schooling, while gradually introducing English in selected subjects, before transitioning to English. These programs aim to maintain the students' first language and add the second, that is, *additive bilingualism,* graduating bilinguals, not monolingual L2 English–speakers. Continuation of Hawaiian for the first six years of the fledgling Hawaiian immersion programs was recently approved after intense pressure and not a little direct action on the part of parents, Hawaiian activists, and their supporters. In practice, unfortunately, true maintenance programs are extremely rare, as it seems there is a vast difference between rhetoric and practice when it comes to school boards digging up the money, curricular materials, and personnel to implement true six-year maintenance bilingual education.

Evaluation research in this area has been scant and often of poor quality, but a five-year, three-way comparative study (Ramirez 1992; Ramirez et al. 1991) of (1) early-exit and (2) late-exit Spanish bilingual programs and (3) programs for Spanish-speakers that were English-medium from the outset at twenty-seven sites around the United States found fairly consistent positive relationships between the length of time classroom Spanish use continued and children's eventual attainment in other subjects, including reading, mathematics, *and* L2 English. Ramirez et al. (1991) and others suggest that bilingual education can work quite well, yet it is precisely bilingual programs, and especially maintenance bilingual programs—which have hardly ever been given a chance to show what they can do—that are under attack from the "English-only" forces and the likes of Gingrich, Dole, and Buchanan, as part of the more general onslaught on immigrants, ethnolinguistic minorities, and public education in the United States and elsewhere.

A general methodological principle, noted earlier, that is apparent in the relatively successful immersion and bilingual programs is that a good teacher or educational program starts where the students are. This is not questioned in the case of subject matter instruction. Few people would suggest trying to teach the tennis serve before the forehand, multiplication before addition, or cardiac surgery before anatomy. The same principle applies with language. There is a vast body of literature documenting the way caretakers (typically parents and elder siblings) adapt their speech and/or conversation to the current linguistic abilities of children acquiring their first language and then, while conversing with them at their level and thereby making *what* they say comprehensible, simultaneously provide them with models of *how* to say it in an increasingly native-like, adult manner. The same phenomena have repeatedly been observed in child and adult second language acquisition (for review, see Long 1996). In a very real sense, in other words, if given the opportunity, people of all ages use their innate language-acquisition capacity to learn languages by using what they know so far to try to communicate and in the process learn a little more. As Hatch (1978, p. 404) put it, "language learning evolves *out of* learning how to carry on conversations."

Starting where the students are is essentially what the Oakland resolution proposed. Quite apart from the above rationale for doing so, there is a fair amount of evidence (although not nearly as much or as good evidence as one would like) of the effectiveness of the same principle applied to education through a second dialect. Simkins and Simkins (1981), for example, compared reading gains by 530 AAVE-speaking children, grades 7 through 12, in twenty-one classes in five parts of the United States using Houghton Mifflin's three-stage *Bridge* reading program (see Labov 1995 for a useful critique of these and other reading materials) with gains by AAVE students in six classes using traditional SE materials in remedial reading classes. The treatment group first learned to read using a text written in AAVE, then a transitional reader, and finally an SE reader. The average gain in reading scores for students in the *Bridge* program was 6.2 months for the four months of instruction. The control group students gained only 1.6 months in the same period. It should be noted, however, that there were several methodological problems with the study, which unfortunately was suspended after four months due to the objections of some African-American community members, including the use of different curricula for black and white children.

After reviewing work by Boggs, Watson-Gegeo, Speidel, and others documenting a wide variety of dialect-based problems in the classroom, Sato (1989) went on to describe several programs, such as those in the Kamehameha [Schools] Early Education Program (KEEP), that have been used with children in Hawaii and elsewhere to address both the comprehension and classroom participation problems arising from both dialect differences and differences in teachers' and students' interactional styles. The latter involve such phenomena as culturally based differences in the significance of pauses and silence in talk, notions of "precision" and "relevance," an orientation toward trusted peers rather than adult authority figures, a preference for cooperation rather than competition, the function and interpretation of various kinds of questions, and the perceived appropriateness of various kinds of responses (e.g., "direct" or "indirect") to those questions.

These and many other linguistic differences affect comprehension, participation patterns, and learning in classrooms but are important far beyond classrooms, of course. Eades (1992, 1995), for example, has shown how there are also differences that have cost Aboriginal defendants dearly in Australian courts on more than one occasion.

The problems, Sato argued, must first be recognized and understood. They can then be addressed successfully at a variety of levels, both inside and outside the classroom. What is called for

> is not simply consciousness-raising, that is, informing teachers about sociolinguistic diversity. . . . The bureaucracy of the school system itself should be analyzed. . . . Working in organizations such as teachers' unions and parent-teacher associations can also lead to a more sympathetic treatment of minority schooling issues. A recent controversy in Hawai'i over the State Board of Education's proposed "English Only" policy [see Sato 1991] illustrates how effective collective action by teachers, students, parents and researchers can be against reactionary views toward sociolinguistic diversity. (Sato 1989, p. 276–277)

Overall, where educational outcomes turn partly on differences in varieties of a language, Sato advocated models where children's home variety, for example, HCE or AAVE, is validated and preserved, while a second—usually "standard"—variety is added, to graduate students who command two, or in practice, a range of speech levels and styles, and whose attainment in content areas will not have been impeded by instruction that was delivered from the outset through a variety that was initially unfamiliar to them. If additive bilingualism, as in the case of French immersion programs in Canada, is a worthy linguistic and educational goal for the children of dominant language groups, why not use this approach for the children of Oakland, Hawaii, and elsewhere? Sato's recommendations eight years ago are just as apt today:

> It has been argued that understanding of the political context of teaching SESD [standard English as a second dialect] and greater familiarity with differences in varieties and the classroom experiences of minority students are necessary for both policy making and pedagogy. The "nonstandard" approach to the teaching of SESD advocated here takes as fundamental (a) the social and linguistic integrity of minority varieties of English and, therefore, (b) the need to design sociolinguistically appropriate pedagogy for speakers of such varieties. Rather than remediation of students' language and replacement of minority varieties with "proper" English, the teaching of SESD may prove more successful if systematically practiced as *additive bidialectalism*. (Sato 1989, pp. 276–277, emphasis added)

A BROADER DEBATE

As indicated earlier, the above discussion not only is preliminary but has been conducted within the stifling constraints entailed in the continued existence of imperialist nation states, whether monopoly capitalist or authoritarian socialist.

Many current problems with language in education around the world are epiphenomena, nasty by-products of such things as the need of states everywhere for "national unity" (i.e., acceptance of the status quo, or their legitimacy), one manifestation of which is a fear of linguistic diversity among their own (or, increasingly, the world's) peoples. The useful gatekeeping function of official languages and standard dialects for those wielding state power, likewise, has already been noted. Hierarchical power structures, centralized authority, and state control over (compulsory) education systems are among the mechanisms that make state-mandated violations of students' and teachers' identities and language rights possible in the first place. State coercion, often in the form of punishment and "failure" at school and ultimately involving brute force and imprisonment in some countries, is what sanctions the discriminatory language policies. Likewise, some proposed solutions advocated within the same restricted terms of reference are equally clearly illusory. Struggles to force governments, or even the United Nations, to recognize linguistic human *rights,* for instance, as the Israeli, Australian, and many other far worse cases show, are really no more than struggles for just as easily revokable, temporary *licenses* and simultaneously serve to legitimize states as the arbiters in such matters, when it is governments that are often the problem, not the solution.

What is needed among those seriously interested in language issues, in education, and in areas where the two intersect is a far broader debate than has been initiated here. For example, what are the generally accepted principles, assuming such principles exist, that underlie libertarian educational theory and practice? In sum, would most problems of linguistic human rights, in education and elsewhere, simply disappear with the advent of voluntary communities, *l'education integrale,* a radically learner-centered educational symbiosis of mental and manual work, voluntary schooling, informal education, control of their workplaces by education workers (including students) and their industrial unions, and other promises of anarchism and anarcho-syndicalism, or might there still be at least a few problems in paradise?

REFERENCES

Avrich, P. (1980) *The modern school movement: Anarchism and education in the United States.* Princeton: Princeton University Press.

Bailey, G. (1987) Decreolization? *Language and Society* 16, 449–473.

Bailey, G. (1993) A perspective on African-American English. In D. Preston (ed.), *American dialect research* (pp. 287–318). Philadelphia: John Benjamins.

Bailey, G., and N. Maynor (1989) The divergence controversy. *American Speech* 64, 12–39.

Bernstein, B. (1971) *Class, codes, and control.* London: Routledge and Kegan Paul.

Chambers, J. K. (1992) Dialect acquisition. *Language* 68, 4, 673–698.

Chomsky, N. (1959) Review of "Verbal Behavior" by B. F. Skinner. *Language* 35, 26–58.

Chomsky, N. (1988) *Language and problems of knowledge: The Managua lectures.* Cambridge: MIT Press.

Eades, D. (1992) *Aboriginal English and the law.* Brisbane: Queensland Law Society.

Eades, D. (1994) A case of communicative clash: Aboriginal English and the legal system. In J. Gibbons (ed.), *Language and the law* (pp. 234–264). London: Longman.

Fasold, R. (1972) *Tense marking in Black English.* Arlington, VA: Center for Applied Linguistics.

Hatch, E. M. (1978) Discourse analysis and second language acquisition. In E. M. Hatch (ed.), *Second language acquisition: A book of readings* (pp. 401–435). Rowley, MA: Newbury House.

Hymes, D. (1992) Inequality in language: Taking for granted. *Working Papers in Educational Linguistics* (University of Pennsylvania) 8, 1, 1–30.

Labov, W. (1969) The logic of non-standard English. *Georgetown Monographs on Language and Linguistics* 22. Washington, DC: Georgetown University, Center for Applied Linguistics.

Labov, W. (1972) *Language in the inner city.* Philadelphia: University of Pennsylvania Press.

Labov, W. (1995) Can reading failure be reversed? A linguistic approach to the question. In P. Gadsden and D. Wagner (eds.), *Literacy among African-American youth.* Cresskill, NJ: Hampton Press.

Labov, W., and W. A. Harris (1986). De facto segregation of black and white vernaculars. In D. Sankoff (ed.), *Diversity and diachrony* (pp. 45–58). Philadelphia: John Benjamins.

LoBianco, J. (1987) *National policy on languages.* Canberra: Australian Government Publishing Service.

Long, M. H. (1990) Maturational constraints on language development. *Studies in Second Language Acquisition* 12, 3, 251–285.

Long, M. H. (1993) Second language acquisition as a function of age: Substantive findings and methodological issues. In K. Hyltenstam and A. Viberg (eds.), *Progression and regression in language* (pp. 196–221). Cambridge: Cambridge University Press.

Long, M. H. (1996) The role of the linguistic environment in second language acquisition. In W. C. Ritchie and T. K. Bhatia (eds.), *Handbook of second language acquisition* (pp. 413–468). New York: Academic Press.

Luke, A., A. W. McHoul, and J. L. Mey (1990) On the limits of language planning: Class, state, and power. In R. Baldauf and A. Luke (eds.), *Language planning and education* (pp. 25–44). Clevedon, Avon: Multilingual Matters.

Malcolm, I. G. (1994) Aboriginal English inside and outside the classroom. *Australian Review of Applied Linguistics* 17, 1.

Marshall, P. (ed.) (1986) *The anarchist writings of William Godwin.* London: Freedom Press.

McGroarty, M. (1991) English instruction for linguistic minority groups: Different structures, different styles. In M. Celce-Murcia (ed.), *Teaching English as a second or foreign language.* Second edition (pp. 372–385). Cambridge, MA: Newbury House; Harper and Row.

Michaels, S. (1981) "Sharing time": Children's narrative style and differential access to literacy. *Language in Society* 10, 423–442.

Pennycook, A. (1995) English in the world/The world in English. In J. W. Tollefson (ed.), *Power and inequality in language education* (pp. 34–58). Cambridge: Cambridge University Press.

Phillipson, R. (1992) *Linguistic imperialism.* Oxford: Oxford University Press.

Ramirez, J. D. (1992) Executive summary [Special Issue]. *Bilingual Research Journal* 16, 1–2.

Ramirez, J. D., S. D. Yuen, and D. R. Ramey (1991) Executive summary final report: Longitudinal study of structured English immersion strategy, early-exit, and late-exit transitional bilingual education programs for language-minority children. San Mateo, CA: Aguirre International.

Sato, C. J. (1985) Linguistic inequality in Hawai'i: The post-creole dilemma. In N. Wolfson and J. Manes (eds.), *Language of inequality* (pp. 255–272). Berlin: Mouton de Gruyter.

Sato, C. J. (1989) A non-standard approach to Standard English. *TESOL Quarterly* 23, 2, 259–282.

Sato, C. J. (1991) Language attitudes and sociolinguistic variation in Hawai'i. In J. Cheshire (ed.), *English around the world: Sociolinguistic perspectives* (pp. 647–663). Cambridge: Cambridge University Press.

Schinke-Llano, L. (1983) Foreigner talk in content classrooms. In H. W. Seliger and M. H. Long (eds.), *Classroom-oriented research in second language acquisition* (pp. 146–164). Rowley, MA: Newbury House.

Shotton, J. (1993) *No master high or low: Libertarian education and schooling, 1890–1990.* Bristol: Libertarian Education.

Simpkins, G. and C. Simpkins (1981) Cross-cultural approach to curriculum development. In G. Smitherman (ed.), *Black English and the Education of Black Children and Youth.* Proceedings of the National Invitational Symposium on the King Decision. Detroit: Center for Black Studies. Wayne State University. pp. 212–240.

Skutnabb-Kangas, T., R. Phillipson, and M. Rannut (eds.) (1995) *Linguistic human rights: Overcoming linguistic discrimination.* Berlin: Mouton de Gruyter.

Smith, M. P. (1980) *The libertarians and education.* London: Methuen.

Spring, J. (1975) *A primer of libertarian education.* New York: Free Life Editions.

Tollefson, J. W. (ed.) (1995) *Power and inequality in language education.* Cambridge: Cambridge University Press.

Ward, C. (1995) *Talking schools.* London: Freedom Press.

Williams, R. (1975) *Ebonics: The True Language of Black Folks.* St. Louis, MO: Institute of Black Studies.

Wolfram, W. (1969) *A sociolinguistic description of Detroit Negro speech.* Arlington, VA: Center for Applied Linguistics.

Wright, N. (1989) *Assessing radical education: A critical review of the radical movement in English schooling, 1960–1980.* Milton Keynes: Open University Press.

28

The White Supremacist Movement in the United States Today

ABBY L. FERBER

THE CONTEMPORARY ORGANIZED HATE MOVEMENT

Prior to the April 19, 1995, bombing of the Oklahoma City federal building and the deaths of 168 people, few Americans were concerned about the organized hate movement in America. This was not, however, an isolated incident. Organizations that monitor the movement have tallied the violence for decades. Klanwatch, one of these organizations, has identified 329 white supremacist groups in existence throughout the United States. Although it is difficult to estimate the often concealed membership of these groups, the general membership in white supremacist organizations is estimated to be around 40,000, while hard-core members number 23,000 to 25,000. An additional 150,000 people purchase movement literature and take part in movement activities, and an additional 450,000 read the movement literature, even though they do not purchase it themselves (Daniels 1997; Ezekiel 1995). The Anti-Defamation League, an organization that monitors hate groups, estimates that fifty white supremacist periodicals publish on an ongoing basis (Anti-Defamation League 1988, 1). In addition to traditional forms of communication, white supremacists are increasingly turning to the internet to spread their hate, through bulletin boards and worldwide web sites, such as the Stormfront's *White Pride, World Wide* home page.

Despite commonly held assumptions that white supremacists are uneducated or especially hard-hit victims of economic upheaval, contemporary white supremacist group members are similar to the U.S. population in general in terms of education, income, and occupation (Aho 1990; Ezekiel 1995). Additionally, there are white supremacist periodicals, such as *Instauration,* that target highly educated audiences.

The white supremacist movement is overwhelmingly a movement of and for *men.* White men make up the bulk of the membership, hold all positions of leadership, and serve as the writers, publishers, and editors of their publications. Recently, however, many groups have begun recruiting women into their ranks. Kathleen Blee estimates that women now make up 25 percent of the membership and as much as 50 percent of the new recruits in many Klan and neo-Nazi groups. She argues that "women now play a highly visible and significant role in the racist movement" (Blee 1996).

Why are these organizations targeting women? One southern Klan leader's description of his rationale for pursuing women recruits is illustrative: "The men will follow the women. If a wife is against the husband's being involved, you can just about . . . forget the husband hanging around for long. . . . The other way, if the wife is into it, she'll drag the husband along" (Blee 1996, 682).

Although the numbers of women in the movement are increasing, women are seldom found in positions of power within these organizations. Some groups, such as Christian Identity organizations, assign women to separate, subordinate roles, as helpmates to the men. In *The Racist Mind,* Raphael Ezekiel found that tasks within the organizations he observed are strictly segregated by gender. He notes, "A few women are around, never as speakers or leaders; usually they are wives, who cook and listen. Highly traditional ideas of sex roles, and fears of losing male dominance, fill the conversation and speeches" (Ezekiel 1995, xxvii). Other groups, such as skinheads and some Klan groups, are more inclusive of women, but women are still largely excluded from positions of power and leadership. It will be important in future research to explore whether the movement and its ideology changes in response to the growing numbers of women in these organizations.

THE CONTEMPORARY MOVEMENT IN CONTEXT

The contemporary movement is a response to the shift in racial and sexual politics since the 1960s. Contemporary American society has witnessed a wide-ranging backlash to the civil rights, women's, and gay and lesbian movements, which have challenged traditional notions of race, gender, and sexual identity and inequality. Certainly the white supremacist movement constitutes only one small part of this broad-based backlash, manifest in attacks on affirmative action, welfare, bilingual education, immigrant rights, homosexual rights, and the birth of a reactionary men's movement, which includes organizations such as the Promise Keepers. These are all attempts to roll back the clock and reverse the gains of women and minorities. Responding to what is perceived as a threat to white male privilege, the contemporary white supremacist movement is primarily concerned with rearticulating white masculinity and is situated within a continuum of backlash.

Because white men benefit most from the traditional race and gender order, they are most likely to respond to change with fear and anger. This is clearly demonstrated in white supremacist publications. For example, an article in the *White Patriot* argues that "the White people of America have become an oppressed majority. Our people suffer from discrimination in the awarding of employment, promotions, scholarships, and college entrances" (*White Patriot* no. 56, 6). Similarly, an article in *Instauration* echoes, "We are now becoming a minority in a land which we tore from the vines and tangle of the wilderness" (*Instauration* February 1985, 14).

As these passages suggest, the contemporary white supremacist movement depicts the white race, and men in particular, as under attack. Their ideology trivializes and dismisses the enduring reality of both race and gender oppression and portrays white men as the real victims.

FROM THE KU KLUX KLAN TO THE POSSE COMITATUS: THE RANGE OF CONTEMPORARY ORGANIZATIONS

The various organizations that make up the contemporary white supremacist movement have a great deal in common, and their memberships often overlap. As Ezekiel found in his study of members of the movement, "the agreement on basic ideas is the glue that holds the movement together. . . . The white racist movement is about an idea" (Ezekiel 1995, xxix). However, although the various organizations share a common worldview, it is often personality conflicts and infighting that divides them. The contemporary movement, therefore, contains a variety of hybrid organizations drawing and expanding upon four traditions: the Ku Klux Klan, the American Nazi Party, the Christian Identity Church movement, and the Militia movement.

Ku Klux Klan

The Ku Klux Klan, historically the most influential white supremacist group in the United States, was founded in Pulaski, Tennessee, in 1865, as a secret fraternal order for Civil War veterans of the Confederate states. The Klan developed into a political organization with thousands of members who feared emancipated blacks as well as northern carpetbaggers. The Klan grew to incorporate anti-Semitic and antiforeigner beliefs into its antiblack platform. The Klan has reemerged at various junctures throughout American history, with as many as four million members in 1925. The Klan experienced a resurgence in the late 1970s and early 1980s and has been declining since, as newer white supremacist groups have sprung up, attracting many Klan members; however, key Klansmen have been implicated in a number of violent crimes.

The Knights of the Ku Klux Klan, led by Thom Robb, is the largest, most active Klan group. Robb has urged followers to abandon overtly racist language in order to attract more members, suggesting that the Klan is not about hate but "love of the white race" (Anti-Defamation League 1996). Beneath this kindler, gentler facade, Robb draws upon the racist, anti-Semitic Identity doctrine (described below) and has proclaimed, "I hate Jews. I hate race-mixing Jews. We've let anti-Christ Jews into our country and we've been cursed with abortion, inflation, homosexuality and the threat of war" (Anti-Defamation League 1996).

Neo-Nazis

The American Nazi Party was founded in 1958 by George Lincoln Rockwell to honor the legacy of Hitler and the German Nazis.

The New Order has been one of the strongest and most stable neo-Nazi organizations in recent years. Formerly the National Socialist White People's Party, it is the direct descendant of the original American Nazi Party. Under the leadership of Matthias Koehl, this organization remains the most strictly committed to Nazi ideals, has new members pledge their loyalty to a statue of Hitler, and maintains international contacts through the World Union of National Socialists.

The second most active neo-Nazi organization is the National Alliance, headed by former Oregon State University physics professor and longtime Nazi activist William Pierce. Pierce is the author of the white supremacist utopian novel *The Turner Diaries,* which has been identified as the model for the Oklahoma City bombing.

Neo-Nazi skinheads are perhaps the most violent wing of the white supremacist movement today, with over 70,000 youths active in thirty-three countries, linked by traveling skinhead rock bands and their recordings, a variety of publications known as skinzines, and, increasingly, through the use of the internet. Skinhead gangs of teenagers are often highly visible with their closely shaven heads, combat boots, and Nazi tattoos. Skinheads have been responsible for dozens of murders in the United States, most recently the murder of a police officer and a West African man in two separate incidents in Denver, Colorado. Resistance Records, in Detroit, is a popular producer of skinhead music and publishes a magazine with a self-proclaimed publication of over 12,000. The words of a song by skinhead band Nordic Thunder is typical of the skinhead racist, anti-Semitic message: "I know the truth and I know what is right. To destroy the zionist way and keep my land White . . . I've sworn to protect my people, For that I am crucified, I live for my Race and for my Race I will die" (Anti-Defamation League 1996).

Christian Identity Church Movement

The Identity Church movement was not recognized as a strong presence within the U.S. white supremacist movement until the 1970s and early 1980s. The racist and anti-Semitic Identity doctrine provides theological underpinnings for a variety of white supremacist organizations. Identity doctrine teaches that Jews are the children of Satan and that other nonwhites are "pre-adamic mud people," people without souls, closer to animals. White Anglo-Saxons are presented as the Bible's "chosen people," destined to establish God's kingdom on earth, and they consider the United States and Great Britain to be their birthright.

Aryan Nations, a paramilitary organization with several hundred followers, is led by Reverend Richard Butler of the Church of Jesus Christ Christian, an Identity church. On its compound in Hayden Lake, Idaho, it hosts a "World Congress" as well as youth gatherings each year, drawing together white supremacists from numerous organizations throughout the world and especially attracting young skinheads. A virulently anti-Semitic organization, it seeks to establish a white homeland in the northwestern United States.

Militia Movement

Since the first militias began appearing in 1994, their numbers have expanded to include 15,000 members in at least forty states. Militia members believe that the federal government is eroding the constitutional rights of American citizens, and they have established common-law courts, self-appointed vigilante groups to carry out their own version of the law. They declare themselves exempt from state and federal law and reserve the right to arrest and murder the opposition. Although the militia movement is not as overtly racist and anti-Semitic as other white supremacist organizations, it is "a tool for furthering the white supremacist struggle for the erection of a white Christian republic on U.S. soil" (Crawford and Burghart 1997, 190). It constitutes an alternative government, representing the interests of white supremacists. Militias are the direct descendants of the Posse Comitatus, a group of activists who embrace Christian Identity doctrine and join it with an antigovernment agenda. Refusing to pay taxes, counterfeiting money, and stockpiling arms, they recognize the county sheriff as the only legal law enforcement officer (Crawford and Burghart 1997; Anti-Defamation League 1996). Some militia organizations, such as the Montana Freemen, believe that the true Constitution protects only whites, and they do not recognize the Thirteenth and Fourteenth Amendments.

Although overall membership in white supremacist organizations has declined since the early 1980s, the threat they pose has not. The movement has become increasingly violent. Dozens of white supremacists have been convicted of murders, robberies, fire bombings, and conspiracies to overthrow the government. Organizations have been found stockpiling weapons and bombs, providing paramilitary training for their members, and planning actions designed to provoke a race war. It is this increasing crusade of violence that culminated in the bombing of the Oklahoma City federal building and continues to take lives.

While certain wings of the hate movement have become increasingly violent, other white supremacists, including the well-publicized case of David Duke, have moved further into the mainstream by entering electoral politics. Although the contemporary movement is certainly diverse, it is united by a shared ideology and a commitment to maintaining white supremacy.

EXAMINING WHITE SUPREMACIST IDEOLOGY

White supremacists share a number of unquestioned beliefs. They argue that humans can be classified into biological racial categories and that the races are essentially and eternally different not only in terms of visible characteristics but also in terms of behavior, character, and culture.

Despite decades of scholarship by sociologists, anthropologists, and biologists that supports race as a social construct, with no grounding in genetics, white supremacist discourse adamantly claims that race is a biological and/or God-given essence. Throughout white supremacist discourse, whiteness is constructed in terms of visible, physical differences in appearance. According to one article, true whites are Nordics, "the thin, fair and symmetric race originating in Northern Europe" (*Instauration* February 1980, 13). For some of the organizations, white skin and European heritage are the only requirements to be included in the category white, whereas elsewhere Aryans are defined as strictly *Northern* Europeans, and there is debate over exactly where to draw the line in Europe.

In this discourse, physical characteristics and culture are linked, both unchanging and determined by race, and this racial essence is defined as immutable. Those who would attempt to change these racial natures are ridiculed. For example, a *White Power* article admonishes:

> Perhaps the cruelest hoax is the liberal lie of telling the Negro he's the equal of the White man and expecting to make an instant White man out of him by sending him to college, giving him a federal handout. . . . Let's have the honesty and decency to recognize the Negro for what he is, and not make impossible demands of him. . . . This has nothing to do with "hate" or "bigotry." I love my dog, for example, but I'm not about to recognize her as my equal. (*White Power* March 1973, 3–6)

As this passage demonstrates, races are ranked hierarchically based on these supposedly innate differences. The white race is believed to be superior and responsible for all of the advances of Western civilization. For example, a *Thunderbolt* article asserts that

> The White Race has created and developed most of the world's present and past civilizations . . . responsible for almost all of the scientific, engineering and productive know-how that has raised the world's standard of living . . . the only race which has been able to maintain a free democratic government. Liberty, justice and freedom only exist in White nations. . . . The charity and goodness of the White Race have time and again saved the non-White peoples of the world from famine and plague. The White Race in the past has established moral codes, rules and laws, and educational systems for the advancement of society that have been unsurpassed by any other race in the world. (*Thunderbolt* May 30, 1975, 8)

White supremacists also mobilize against a common threat. While white supremacists demonize African Americans and all nonwhites, Jews are defined as the ultimate enemy. As an article in the white supremacist *New Order* argues, "the single serious enemy facing the White man is the Jew. The Jews are not a religion, they are [a] *race*, locked in mortal conflict with Aryan man which has lasted for millennia, and which will continue until one of the two . . . is extinct" (*The New Order* March 1979, 3).

As the *Thunderbolt* proclaims, it is a "WAR OF EXTERMINATION—God's seed against Satan's seed" (*Thunderbolt* January 1974, 10). Jews are defined as nonwhite and made identifiable by physical markers such as "long kinky curls and typical hooked nose, thick fleshy lips, slant eyes and other typical Jew features" (*Thunderbolt* no. 301, 6). White supremacists assert that Jews control all facets of society, including the media and the government (frequently referred to as "ZOG," Zionist Occupied Government).

Once again turning reality on its head, white supremacists deny that the Holocaust ever happened, labeling it the "Holy Hoax," and argue instead that it is Jews who are conspiring to exterminate the white race. They believe this genocidal plan is being carried out through forced race-mixing. Interracial relationships are considered even deadlier than outright war because "even a global war in which the Jews were victorious would leave a few Whites to breed back the race. Their final solution is MONGRELIZATION. A mongrel can only breed more mongrels" (*Thunderbolt* January 1974, 10).

Jews are held responsible for all forms of integration and race-mixing. For example, the white supremacist publication *Thunderbolt* has published articles with titles such as "Jewish Leaders Supporting Race-Mixing," "Jews Finance Race-Mixing Case," and "Jewish Organizations Back Interracial Marriage" (*Thunderbolt* no. 297, 1, 3).

Separation of the races is the end goal for the wide range of white supremacist groups. Geographical apartheid is presented as the only way to guarantee racial purity and prevent the threat of racial mixing. Various groups argue over whether to support the deportation of nonwhites or to settle for carving up the country into separate homelands for each race.

INTERSECTIONS OF RACE AND GENDER

Although race is the most overt preoccupation of the white supremacist movement, gender identity is central to the discourse and is intertwined with the construction of racial identities (Ferber 1995, 1998). Gender is depicted in oppositional and complementary terms: Men are in control, active, aggressive; women are passive possessions, fought over by men.

Like race, gender is constructed as an immutable essence. A *White Power* author explains that "our ancestors wisely realized that women were different from men not just biologically but psychologically and emotionally as well. They recognized that the sexes had distinct but complementary roles to play in society . . . ordained by natural law" (*White Power* no. 105, 4).

Beliefs about gender are not merely an addendum to the racist, anti-Semitic ideology of the movement, they are intertwined. Gender is an integral component of the belief system. Throughout white supremacist publications, gender difference is defined as a key component of racial difference. For example, the differences between white and nonwhite females is emphasized as a feature distinguishing the white race and signaling its superiority. The belief that white women represent the ideal of female beauty is widespread and considered commonsense knowledge in this discourse. For example, *Instauration* asserts that "25,000 years of tough natural selection on the edge of glaciers" produced "these beauteous products of a very special kind of evolution . . . these magnificent-looking [Aryan] women" (*Instauration* May 1981, 36). And the *National Vanguard* argues, "The White woman stands at the apex of beauty. . . . But what about the Black woman? Alas, she is truly a pitiable creature. Whites have never found her attractive, and Blacks began to scorn her after they caught a glimpse of a White woman" (*National Vanguard* May 1979, 11).

Gender is also central to white supremacist discourse because the fate of the race is posited as hinging on the sexual behavior of white women. Interracial sexuality is defined as the "ultimate abomination," and the greatest threat to white people. Images of white women stolen away by black men are the ever present symbol of this threat (Ridgeway 1990, 19). The protection of white womanhood, therefore, comes to symbolize the protection of the race. Interracial relationships not only threaten the illusion of white purity and the propagation of the white race, they represent a threat to white male authority (i.e., the "natural" hierarchy), usurping their control over both white women and black men. For example, in the *National Vanguard,* beneath a photograph of a black man and white woman, nude and embracing, the caption reads, "SHAME of White men is their loss of control over their women. This German girl is one of thousands who have sought sexual fulfillment with blacks in Jamaica" (*National Vanguard* January 1983, 17).

All forms of integration are depicted as part of a great plan to encourage interracial relationships. For example, one typical article argues that "integration is just a code word for racemixing. Civil rights for Black men do not really mean equal employment opportunities; they mean equal enjoyment opportunities with White women" (*National Vanguard* May 1979, 11).

White supremacist publications berate white men for failing to protect white women. For example, a typical article argues that

> Northern European males have traditionally tended throughout history to be dominant by nature, but . . . they are becoming submissive and passive. This phenomenon is especially obvious in the declining strength of their opposition to the interracial sexual transgressions of non-Northern European males with Northern European females. [Northern European men] repress the natural inborn tendencies of exclusivity which played an important role in preserving the biological integrity of their race during its evolution. Many carry their altruism to the point of even seeming to approve of, and to encourage, the sexual trespasses of non-Northern European males upon Northern European females whom their more vigorous and race-conscious ancestors would have defended from such defilements with their very lives. (*Instauration* June 1980, 8)

This demasculinization is frequently blamed on feminism and minority social movements for challenging racial and gender inequality. In an article titled "Sexuality in a Sick Society" and subtitled "The changing relationship between men and women is leading to ominous racial consequences for the West," we are told that feminism and the sexual revolution has led to the

> demasculinization of the Western male, [and] together with the reaction of the Western female to this, [it] is a cause for grave concern. . . . [Men] are constrained from expressing their maleness in any of the ways which were natural in the past. One of the most important of those ways was protecting a mate . . . [but now he is no longer] the master in his house. (*National Vanguard* January 1983, 17)

The problem, then, is the perversion of the "natural" racial and gender order, where white men rule over women and nonwhites. So what is the solution? White supremacists argue that we need more "real men" to reclaim white women and reassert control and that the separation of the races is the only way to secure the future of the white race.

The white supremacist project, then, is primarily concerned with forging white male identity and restoring the "natural relationship that existed between the sexes [and races] in earlier times" (*National Vanguard* January 1983, 21). Clearly, the contemporary white supremacist movement organizes to maintain not only white power but white *male* power. Conversely, those seeking to organize against racist and misogynist injustice must work together to combat these movements.

CONCLUSION

Contemporary scholars are increasingly arguing that white supremacist ideology is not as "extremist" as we like to think (Daniels 1997; Ferber 1995, 1998). In many ways white supremacist discourse rearticulates traditional American racial ideology. After all, it was not until 1967 that laws forbidding interracial marriage were declared unconstitutional, and throughout the nineteenth and early twentieth centuries, American scientists argued that racial intermixture with "inferior stock" would lead to the degeneration of the white race. In fact, it was American eugenicists who developed the ideas that Hitler appropriated to justify his goal of racial "purity."

The white supremacist movement is able to successfully attract new recruits whose ideas about race have been cultivated by what we consider "mainstream" society. For example, the baseless assumption that people can be classified into biological racial categories and that race and gender identity are immutable and rooted in nature are widespread, yet these assumptions provide the foundation for white supremacist views about race and gender.

As the Anti-Defamation League points out in its report on the skinhead problem, "in those instances where the Skins have had a major impact, it is largely because their views were shared by a broader segment of the population" (Anti-Defamation League 1996). It is crucial, then, that we explore the ways in which white supremacist ideology is similar to mainstream racial ideologies. I believe that if we are to combat white supremacist activity, the only way to begin is by attacking our own racist assumptions. These may be less overt, but they are far more dangerous.

REFERENCES

Aho, James A. 1990. *The Politics of Righteousness: Idaho Christian Patriotism.* Seattle: University of Washington Press.

Anti-Defamation League of B'nai B'rith. 1988. *Hate Groups in America: A Record of Bigotry and Violence.* New York.

______. 1995. *The Skinhead International: A Worldwide Survey of Neo-Nazi Skinheads.* New York.

______. 1996. *Danger: Extremism, the Major Vehicles and Voices on America's Far-Right Fringe.* New York.

Blee, Kathleen. 1996. "Becoming a Racist: Women in Contemporary Ku Klux Klan and Neo-Nazi Groups." *Gender and Society* 10 (6): 680–702.

Crawford, Robert, and Devin Burghart. 1997. "Guns and Gavels: Common Law Courts, Militias, and White Supremacy." In *The Second Revolution: States Rights, Sovereignty, and Power of the County,* ed. Eric Ward. Seattle: Peanut Butter Publishing.

Daniels, Jessie. 1997. *White Lies: Race, Class, Gender, and Sexuality in White Supremacist Discourse.* New York: Routledge.

Ezekiel, Raphael S. 1995. *The Racist Mind: Portraits of American Neo-Nazis and Klansmen.* New York: Viking.

Ferber, Abby. 1995. "'Shame of White Men': Interracial Sexuality and the Construction of White Masculinity in Contemporary White Supremacist Discourse." *Masculinities* 3 (2): 1–24.

______. 1998. "Constructing Whiteness: The Intersections of Race and Gender in U.S. White Supremacist Discourse." *Ethnic and Racial Studies* 21 (1): 48–63.

Ridgeway, James. 1990. *Blood in the Face.* New York: Thunder's Mouth Press.

PART 7

Electoral Politics or Direct Action?

This section concerns politics and activism. When most people think of "politics," they probably think of working within the traditional structure of government to achieve some end. The main political action, in this view, is selecting representatives for office at the local, state, or federal levels by means of elections.

Racial and ethnic minorities, according to this view, can achieve more power in the society by participating in the political process. Thus, minority candidates should run for office, and minority communities should organize voter registration campaigns to support candidates who are sympathetic to their interests. The underlying assumption here is that the electoral system will be responsive to the needs of minority communities once those communities get mobilized.

When politics are defined more broadly, the traditional conception seems far too restrictive. We define politics as any collective action that is intended to support, influence, or change social policy or social structures. This goes beyond simply working within the existing system of government. Consider the following list of political actions:

- Predominantly black and Latino hospital workers go out on strike against a national chain of private nursing homes to force their employer to recognize their union. After two weeks, the employer agrees to collective bargaining.
- Asian students at a large West Coast university refuse to leave the president's office until he agrees to provide funds for an Asian studies program. After several days of negotiation, the students are arrested by police and charged with trespassing.
- A multiracial group decides to establish an alternative school for adults who want to learn more about how left-wing perspectives and political activities can lead to racial equality. Classes are held in teachers' homes, and the small tuition is divided between the teachers and the school organizers.
- Armed Native Americans in the Northeast patrol roads leading into their reservation to prevent state police from entering in search of a Native American activist. They claim that the reservation is a sovereign nation and that the state police have no jurisdiction. After several days, the police leave.

- Thousands of blacks and Hispanics in Los Angeles burn and loot stores and attack motorists after the acquittal of four white police officers who were videotaped brutally beating a black motorist suspected of drunk driving. In three days, an estimated fifty-one people are killed and the property damage is estimated at $800 million.

All of these actions, we assert, are deeply political even though they do not involve the electoral process. The hospital workers use traditional collective bargaining channels to redress their grievances. The assumption is that through the union, they can get better wages and fringe benefits and have more control over their own labor.

The Asian sit-in employs nonviolent but illegal tactics to force decisionmakers to listen to the wishes of minority groups. The underlying premise of the students is that the system would not be responsive if they went through legitimate organizational channels (or they had already exhausted these channels). Therefore, they chose civil disobedience as a tactic.

The organizers of the multiracial alternative school believe in the importance of creating alternative institutions under the direct control of those who participate in them. The existing educational structure simply could not cede such power under law.

The armed action by Native Americans provokes a direct confrontation with the armed representatives of the state in order to protect the sovereignty of the reservation. The assumption here is that force is the only way to oppose an illegitimate political system.

Finally, the urban disorder in Los Angeles represents, in part, a spontaneous outpouring of anger against a political system that is perceived as illegitimate. These acts of rage, usually illegal and often violent, often force political leaders to take notice of minority problems when they otherwise would ignore them.

The question of what kind of political participation is most effective in representing and protecting minority interests is critical, and not surprisingly, there is no consensus on the answer. Stephen Thernstrom and Abigail Thernstrom ("Politics") are optimistic about minority participation in electoral politics. They argue that the number of blacks holding elected political office has increased because the black community is becoming more politically mobilized and because whites are more willing to vote for black candidates than in the past.

Two other readings raise questions about the limits of electoral politics. Howard Zinn ("Representative Government: The Black Experience") argues that blacks have gained concessions from the federal government only after fighting for it, most often outside of the electoral process. He expects that blacks will have to continue this struggle of nonviolent civil disobedience in coming years. Mark Toney ("Power Concedes Nothing Without a Demand") describes the process of building multiracial political organizations in the 1990s that focus on direct action at the local level.

A wide variety of policies have been suggested to combat racial inequality. Liberal and conservative policies suggest various ways of reducing racial and ethnic inequality within the existing capitalist economic system and the two-party political system. Radical policy, on the other hand, holds that both capitalism and the two-party political system must be eliminated in order to achieve racial and ethnic equality.

Liberals have traditionally called for more government involvement at the federal level in the form of civil rights legislation and administrative regulations to prevent discrimination. They have also called for more government spending to provide more services for the largely disadvantaged minority populations in terms of better education, job training, health care, and housing for poor and minority communities.

Conservatives, on the other hand, are wary of social programs funded by the federal government and call for policies that provide incentives for the business community to expand and to hire minority workers. They support enterprise zones, where businesses would receive tax incentives to locate in poor inner-city neighborhoods and hire neighborhood workers. Rather than providing aid to public schools in poverty areas, conservatives suggest providing educational vouchers to enable more poor parents to send their children to better public schools and to private and parochial schools.

Radicals differ from both liberals and conservatives by viewing the capitalist system as the root cause of poverty and racial inequality. Their policies are intended to mobilize people of all racial and ethnic groups to take control over their own lives. The power of the capitalist class and government bureaucrats would be replaced by a more democratically controlled economy and political system.

As the Thernstroms point out in "Politics," black voters have overwhelmingly supported liberal political candidates since the 1960s. They also argue that since many blacks hold conservative attitudes on social issues such as abortion and crime, it may be possible for conservative political candidates to appeal to black voters. For the past fifteen years there has been a small group of black intellectuals and businesspeople who have articulated conservative viewpoints in the mainstream press, including Thomas Sowell, Shelby Steele, Glen Lowery, Robert Woodson, and Ward Connerly.

Deborah Toler ("Black Conservatives") criticizes this black conservative perspective. She sees their call for self-help as a reiteration of the American myth of individualism. It would both cut off government programs and replace progressive attempts at community mobilization. Toler argues that this might be a useful strategy for the small black elite that is associated with powerful conservative think tanks, but it would be a disaster for the black poor and working-class majority.

Finally, we turn our attention to the small group of whites who are actively involved in the struggle for racial equality. Eileen O'Brien ("Privileged Polemics: White Antiracist Activists") examines the lives of a small group of activists, many of whom are political radicals, to see how they became activists while growing up in a racist society.

29

Politics

STEPHEN THERNSTROM AND
ABIGAIL THERNSTROM

In two cities in Maine—Augusta and Lewiston—blacks have captured the mayor's seat. Maine! Blacks are barely a presence in the state. "No one gives a squat" about skin color, says the mayor of Lewiston, John Jenkins, who won a runoff in 1993 against an incumbent councilman by a three-to-one margin in a city that is over 99 percent white. In Augusta, William Burney was first elected mayor in 1988 and has been reelected twice since then. He was a "hometown hero" (in the words of his predecessor)—a basketball star in high school and a graduate of the University of Maine Law School. Evidently, "no one gives a squat" about race there, either.

"As Maine goes, so goes the nation," ran an old political saying. And, while there are plenty of places where color still does matter, perhaps those black electoral victories in a state 0.4 percent black do tell us something. When it comes to polities, the importance of color may finally be fading. Black mayors are popping up all over. The conventional wisdom has it that most are elected in majority-black cities. True—and misleading. That count includes victories in many tiny municipalities in the South. Eliminate those small dots on the urban map and the picture looks quite different. Between 1967 and 1993, African Americans won the mayor's seat in eighty-seven cities with a population of 50,000 or more. A remarkable two-thirds of those mayors were elected in cities in which blacks were a minority of the population. Half of them, in fact, were in municipalities less than 40 percent black, and over a third in cities in which no more than three out of ten residents were African-American. . . .

Lani Guinier has described blacks as "still the pariah group: systematic losers in the political marketplace." That certainly was true once, but it is no longer the case. "People in political life are reluctant to say how much progress has been made . . . ," the black journalist Juan Williams has noted. "In fact . . . ," he went on, "segregationist politics is out; race-baiting is gone. Yes, there is racially tainted politics, but nothing like it was." His point, of course, was primarily about the South. And indeed a political revolution swept the South in the wake of the passage of the 1965 Voting Rights Act. In 1962, George Wallace won the Alabama gu-

---

Footnotes have been deleted. See original text for references.

bernatorial race by "out-segging" his opponent; in 1970, he was still warning white voters, "If I don't win, them niggers are going to control this state." But by 1974 he had begun to solicit black votes, and by 1982 he was asking black Alabamians to forgive his past. Four years later, in a survey of Alabama black opinion. Wallace came off as the best governor in the history of the state. One year after that, Jesse Jackson, running for president, made time to pay his political respects to a man he once loathed.

Wallace was not alone in seeing the political light. . . . White supremacists always knew that fundamental change would follow once blacks acquired the right to vote. And it did [in] part by forcing those politicians to change their tune or retire from politics. Demography made the South a good place for blacks to run and win. In each of the five Deep South states—South Carolina, Georgia, Alabama, Mississippi, and Louisiana—blacks are more than a quarter of the population. In four more states—Virginia, North Carolina, Maryland, and Delaware—the black population is in the 16 to 25 percent range. No northern state has concentrations of African-American residents that large.

In 1968 in the entire South there were 3 black mayors, by 1978 the number had risen to only 38, and in 1996 it stood at 290. As late as 1970, no African Americans held elective office in state government in Alabama, Arkansas, or South Carolina, while Florida, Louisiana, Mississippi, and North Carolina each had a single black member of the state legislature. The total for the eleven ex-Confederate states was just 32. By 1993 those states had almost ten times that many black state legislators—a total of 312—and 16 African Americans represented them in Congress. In fact, 69 percent of all black elected officials in the nation in 1993 were southerners, with the largest numbers in Alabama and Mississippi, the most hard-core of the segregationist states not so long ago.

A NATIONAL STORY

Of course the South is not the only region in which blacks roam the corridors of political power. . . . The information available on black elected officials is quite scanty before 1970, but their numbers were very small. Just 4 African Americans were members of the U.S. House of Representatives in 1960; in 1964, there were 5. Detailed data are not available, but we know that when the historic Civil Rights Act was passed, a black population of 20 million people could claim no more than 103 elected officials at any level of government—national, state, or local.

The picture changed suddenly and dramatically thereafter. By 1975, 18 African Americans were in Congress; nearly 300 were sitting in a state legislature; 135 occupied the mayor's office in a city; close to 400 were judges, sheriffs, or other elected local officials. In the two decades since, the pace of change has not slowed. The number of blacks in Congress has more than doubled: the number in state legislatures has almost doubled; and the number serving as mayors has tripled. Thus, the U.S. House of Representatives, after the 1994 elections, had 40 black members, 9.2 percent of the total—a figure actually a bit higher than the group's 8.5 percent share of the ballots cast in 1994. The number was reduced by one as a result of the November 1996 elections. Furthermore, in several state legislatures today, African Americans hold a higher proportion of seats than their share of the voting-age population. As of 1993, this was true in nine states, including California, Florida, Ohio and Wisconsin.

Although the number of blacks holding elected office has grown impressively, overall black officeholding still falls far short of proportionality. Some take this as proof that the electoral system is not racially fair. Blacks are 11.8 percent of the voting-age population, and yet the nearly 8,000 elected offices African Americans held in 1993 were only 1.6 percent of the total. In fact, that number is quite misleading. Black candidates are almost invariably Democrats—usually liberal Democrats. They're very weak competitors in places where Republicans generally win. Thus, the real question is: What proportion of those offices held by Democrats (or more specifically, liberal Democrats) do blacks occupy? And for how many of those offices have they made a run?

To the first question, we do have a partial answer. In 1992, blacks made up 14 percent of the voters in Democratic Party primaries. After the 1992 general election, African Americans held 14.4 percent of the seats occupied by Democrats in the U.S. House of Representatives. The 1994 congressional elections resulted in a loss of seats by the Democrats, which increased the black percentage of the party's total strength to 18. It declined slightly as a result of the 1996 elections, which returned a few more Democrats but the same number of black Democrats to the House. If one focuses on the party to which almost all blacks belong, in other words, their representation in the lower house of Congress has been strong.

At the state level, black success is less impressive but still notable. Nationwide in 1992, blacks averaged 10 percent of the Democratic presence in the lower state legislative chambers and had 8.1 percent of the seats in the state senates. But these figures include, of course, a great many states in which blacks are a tiny fraction of the population. In 1992, in the states with sizable black populations, the percentage of black Democratic state legislators was proportionate to the black voting-age population.

African Americans are residentially concentrated—in certain cities as well as certain states—and that, too, has affected the likelihood of their winning office. The 1990 Census showed that over four out of ten (41 percent) of all blacks in the United States lived in the central cities of metropolitan areas of 1 million or more, as compared with only 15 percent of the white population. There are forty such metropolitan areas, and blacks hold the mayor's seat in the central cities of sixteen of them. But the total number of black faces in office may be disproportionately low in part precisely because African Americans are such an urban people. In big cities the ratio of population to the number of elected offices tends to be lower than in smaller communities and rural areas. For instance, the school committee in Lexington, Massachusetts, a town of 29,000 with only a small black population, is roughly the same size as that serving all of Boston.

Furthermore, blacks still disproportionately reside in the South; over half the black population is southern, while the figure for whites is just under one-third. Historically, the southern political system has had fewer elective offices than other regions of the nation. Outside the South there is nothing equivalent to the Charlotte-Mecklenburg School District, which spans 542 square miles: in Illinois an area that size would contain a multitude of independent school systems, each with an elected governing body. Atlanta is 67 percent black, but it has fewer elected offices than an older, multilayered, big public-sector city of a similar size—Pittsburgh, for example, which is only 26 percent African-American. In short, where the white population is concentrated, there are more elective offices to fill. Even if African Americans in every town and city held public office in proportion to their numbers, the national picture would still seem suspiciously white. Blacks would appear, in the aggregate, underrepresented in political office.

The national data on black officeholding, in short, paint a deceptively dreary picture. Blacks have become major players in the American political process and in the years since the 1960s have advanced more impressively in politics than in any other arena. In Alabama in 1956 the State Senate unanimously passed a resolution asking Congress for the funds to move the entire black population out of the state. Today that Senate is 11 percent black, and in Birmingham, Montgomery, Selma, and elsewhere, memorials celebrate the civil rights revolution that Governor Wallace and others once so brutally opposed.

THE POWER OF THE BLACK VOTE

Those memorials are testimony to the power of the black vote—its impact on white as well as black officeholding. Blacks are the nation's most solidly Democratic voting bloc. Few Americans realize it, but the Democratic Party would have lost every presidential election from 1968 to the present if only whites had been allowed to vote. Jimmy Carter carried only 47 percent of the white vote in 1976, but was elected because his 83 percent support from blacks more than made up the deficit. Bill Clinton did even worse among white voters, getting only 39 percent of their vote in 1992 and 43 percent in 1996. But Clinton, too, got five out of six black votes, and that was enough to give him wins over George Bush in 1992 and Bob Dole in 1996.

That white senators know how to count black ballots was evident in the 1991 vote on the appointment of Judge Clarence Thomas to the U.S. Supreme Court. Despite the opposition of many civil rights groups, polls demonstrated that a majority of blacks supported Thomas. Crucial votes for his confirmation came from three southern Democrats who had been supported by only a minority of white voters in 1986—Democrats who were up for reelection in 1992 and who needed every African-American vote they could get. Even a small drop in black support might have made a difference in those Senate contests.

Blacks are becoming more powerful politically both because their numbers are growing and because they have become politically mobilized. In the three decades following the passage of the Voting Rights Act of 1965, the total black population of the United States increased by 56 percent, double the rate of increase for whites, raising the black share of the total population from 10.8 percent to 12.5 percent. In those same decades, the number of African Americans registered to vote increased even more rapidly. The number of blacks on the voting rolls rose 7 million—from under 6 million in 1964 to nearly 13 million in 1994, 2.4 times the white rate of increase.

Despite these advances, however, African Americans are still somewhat less likely to be registered than whites. In 1968, the percentage point gap was 9 points—75 percent of whites as compared with 66 percent of blacks had signed up to vote. The gap narrowed a little in the mid-1980s to 4 points in 1984 and just 1 point in 1986, but then it gradually widened again, and was 6 points in both 1992 and 1994. In the South, however—where 55 percent of the black population currently lives—the clear trend has been toward greater equality. In 1968, the black-white gap in the southern states was 9.2 percentage points; by 1992 it had fallen to 3.8 points. That was the year that the Voter Education Project—once at the forefront of the civil rights struggle—died a natural death. Its job was done.

Not only are African-American registration rates a few points lower than those for whites, the rate at which blacks who are registered actually turn up at a polling place is also lower. In 1980, for example, 61 percent of whites on the voting lists cast a ballot on election day; for African Americans the figure was 51 percent. In 1984 the turnout gap dropped to 5 points, and to 4 points in 1986, but then it widened again. In both 1992 and 1994 the turnout difference was 10 points. In the South, however, the trend was once again clearly toward equality. In 1968 blacks who were registered (most of them first-time voters) were 20.3 points behind whites in their actual voting rate; by 1992 the gap was down to just 6.5 points. When racial differences in registration and turnout are controlled for income, education, and the like, they shrink further or even vanish. . . .

Black political participation will rise and fall in response to particular candidates. When voters care, they reach for a ballot. When white supremacist David Duke ran for governor of Louisiana in 1991, the black turnout reached a record 80 percent, exceeding that for whites. The high level of participation of blacks in the 1989 mayoral election in New York was affected by the fact that David Dinkins was the first serious black candidate to run for the post. In the New Orleans mayoral race in 1994, a heavy black turnout was attributed in good part to the circulation of anonymous antiblack campaign fliers linked to the white candidate. In Chicago prior to the state and congressional elections of 1982, before Harold Washington had decided to enter the mayoral fray, black antagonism toward both President Reagan and Mayor Jane Byrne seems to have been one element in a wildly successful black registration drive that helped convince Washington to run.

In turn, Harold Washington himself—like other well-organized strong black candidates—pulled in still more voters. His own campaign conducted a massive and effective voter registration drive, involving over two hundred grassroots groups. In one black church the minister admonished his parish that it was a "sin" not to register to vote. The combined result: black registration went from being 10 points lower than white registration to being almost 6 points higher. Black turnout also rose—to an impressive 73 percent of those who were eligible, 6 points higher than the white figure, an increase of 25 percent over 1979.

The point extends to a variety of races. In the 1989 Virginia gubernatorial race, L. Douglas Wilder used the black churches to reach the black electorate. He also earmarked $750,000 for a "get out the vote" drive that targeted 190,000 households. Voter registration drives also accompanied Jesse Jackson's two presidential bids, and seem to have been particularly effective in 1984. In that year, in the seven states for which we have reliable data, black turnout in the Democratic primaries in which Jackson ran almost doubled.

Harold Washington, Douglas Wilder, and Jesse Jackson all ran ground-breaking campaigns, and the fact that they were "firsts" almost certainly inspired black participation. In 1967, when Carl Stokes was first elected mayor in Cleveland, turnout in the predominantly black wards reached almost 82 percent. As the political scientist Katherine Tate has noted, "Black officeseeking, particularly in elections involving Blacks as political newcomers, seems to be associated with astoundingly high Black turnouts." The reasons are obvious: group loyalty, racial pride, and the assiduous courting of black voters. As one observer has remarked, "To black Chicagoans, Washington embodied the hopes and dreams of centuries of struggle." Across the black economic spectrum, from Hyde Park to the Cabrini Green housing project, "it was not uncommon to see the red, black, and green flag of black unity flying high with Washington's name displayed in bold print." On the other hand, when the novelty wears off or voters' expectations are not met, black turnout for a black incumbent can drop. Katie Hall was elected to Congress from Indiana's majority-white first district in 1982 with an impressive 57 percent of the vote; two years later she went down to defeat when many black constituents failed to show up at the polls. . . .

The power of the black vote has changed American politics—and will bring more change if the remaining still significant racial gap in political participation can be closed. In 1994 blacks were 11.5 of the voting-age population but only 8.5 percent of those who voted. They were riding down the political road with only three out of their four cylinders operating. Black electoral power was about a quarter less than it would have been if their registration and turnout rates had matched those of whites. It is estimated that in the 1996 elections the proportion of the total vote coming from African Americans rose to one-tenth. If this finding is not the result of mere sampling error, it hints at advances in black political mobilization.

WINNING IN MAJORITY-BLACK COMMUNITIES

Black enfranchisement in the South after 1965 changed the political identity of towns, cities, and counties throughout the region. Majority-black settings governed by whites became places in which blacks lived, worked—and, for the first time, voted. And where blacks voted, black candidates sought public office. In 1976 there were 150 black mayors nationwide; 50 were in southern towns of less than 1,000 inhabitants. Over half (84 out of 150) were in southern towns of less than 15,000. By 1993 the number of black mayors had risen to 356, with 253 in the South. In Mississippi alone that year, 32 towns had black mayors, and, again, almost all were majority-black and very small. In May 1996 the membership of the National Conference of Black Mayors stood at 405, with 65 percent from southern states.

For the most part, these are places that blacks came to govern because black residents, long a majority, could finally vote. But other cities—in North and South—are now majority-black for a different reason. Their demography has changed. The urban landscape is blacker, which means more blacks are likely to run and win. In 1940 no large American city had a black majority. By now the list of majority-black cities includes Detroit, Baltimore, Memphis, Washington, D.C., New Orleans, Atlanta, Newark, and Birmingham.

The results have been predictable: black mayors elected where black residents are a majority. And mayors aren't the only story. Black cities elect blacks to Congress, state legislatures, county offices, and the judiciary. That stands to reason. Generally only a very small percentage of blacks fail to vote for black candidates (perhaps a consequence of the relative novelty of their political power), and in majority-black settings, there are always blacks in a race. "In Birmingham, I mean if you're not black, then you're [politically] nobody," one resident said in 1993. It has become true in politics (at least with respect to the mayor's seat) in a variety of places: Washington, D.C., Atlanta, Detroit, and Newark, among others.

In such cities black politics are the only true game in town. "White candidates are no longer taken seriously in Detroit," the journalist Ze'ev Chafets wrote in 1989. White politics went out when Coleman Young came in. That was in 1973, the same year that Atlanta got rid of its last white mayor. It's not that whites have lost all potential power in such cities; with a divided black electorate, whites become the swing vote. But the mayor's office and a majority of the city council seats are safely black.

WHEN WHITES VOTE FOR BLACKS

There's a final reason for the increase in black officeholding in recent decades—one to which we have already alluded. Whites are voting for blacks. In increasing numbers. To a degree that was unimaginable thirty years ago. And not just in places (like Detroit) where only blacks run. In a contest that pits a black against a white, blacks will generally vote for one of their own, but whites won't necessarily support the candidate who is white. That is, while black candidates can usually count on almost every black vote, whites who run in a racially diverse setting have no such advantage. . . .

In 1996, 67 of the nation's cities with populations of 25,000 or more had black mayors. Many of those cities are majority-black, but most are not. Almost six out of ten (58 percent) of the black mayors of these urban centers were elected in places in which whites outnumbered African Americans. And if we look only at cities outside of the South—two-thirds of the total—70 percent of those with black mayors do not have black population majorities. African-American candidates needed significant white support to win—and they got it.

It is not only in mayoral races that white voters often choose black candidates over those who are white. L. Douglas Wilder, in his successful gubernatorial run in 1989, got an estimated 40 to 43 percent of the vote of Virginia whites. Skeptics will say that that figure still represents less than half of the white electorate, but Charles Robb, the Democratic governor who preceded Wilder, did only a shade better—45 percent.

When Virginians size up a candidate, a euphoric Douglas Wilder said right after his victory, they "don't care what that person looks like, what that person's religion would be or what that person's gender is." It was the politic thing to say, and perhaps, in the flush of an historic victory, he even meant it. The truth is more complicated. Of course race determines how some whites vote some of the time. In the 1991 Memphis mayoral contest, 97 percent of the whites voted for the white candidate, 99 percent of the blacks for the black one. In the March 1994 New Orleans mayoral election, the black candidate won an estimated 90 percent of the black vote, while 91 percent of whites supported his white opponent. Despite the fact that the white had worked for years to build a biracial political coalition and had kicked off his campaign in a black church, there was very little crossover voting. But the mayoral race that year was unusually dirty; anonymous campaign fliers with antiblack and anti-Semitic slogans were widely circulated. That's not an everyday occurrence. It now makes news; it has become the unexpected—even in New Orleans where black mayoral candidates in earlier races had picked up more than 20 percent of the white vote.

Voting rights experts frequently argue that almost all elections in which blacks run are "polarized"; black and white voters form, in effect, opposing teams. But that conclusion rests on a definition of polarization very much open to argument—one that depicts whites and blacks as separate and hostile in any election in which black voters support black candidates in proportionally greater numbers than do white voters. By this dubious logic the Douglas Wilder election in Virginia was racially "polarized" even though at least 40 percent of whites voted for him; his black support was greater. In fact, blacks and whites had come together in Virginia to elect a governor.

Race cuts both ways. Although it is rarely acknowledged, in some races and with some white voters, it's actually a political asset to be black. To begin with as journalist Michael Barone has pointed out, political newcomers need to get noticed and black candidates are clearly visible. More important, a portion of the white electorate is often eager to vote for an African American. In 1989 in New York, race-conscious voting, particularly by whites on the Upper West Side of Manhattan, undoubtedly put David Dinkins over the top. "One reason Mr. Dinkins did so well among whites was wishful thinking," the *New York Times* noted. White voters hoped "he would be able to say and do things . . . that a white mayor would not say or do"—on the subject of black crime, for instance. In addition, New York had just been torn apart by a racially motivated killing, and Dinkins, with his soothing low-key style, promised to heal the wounds. In 1992, Carol Moseley-Braun, too, was certainly helped by the color of her skin when she won the Illinois Senate race by ten points over her white GOP opponent. As the *Economist* observed at the time, "Ms. Braun's supporters [were] less enamored of her than of what she represent[ed]"—a racial first. . . .

Hers is not a unique story; whites have been both casting ballots and writing checks in support of black candidates. Harvey Gantt, who made unsuccessful bids to unseat North Carolina senator Jesse Helms in 1990 and 1996, held fund-raisers in New York and Los Angeles, among other cities, and raised the bulk of his large war chest from contributors outside the state, with much of the money undoubtedly coming from whites. Two blacks made the runoff in the 1991 Denver mayoral election; the white business community picked its candidate and helped raise $1.5 million for his unsuccessful campaign. In May 1995, Ron Kirk was elected mayor of Dallas; a lawyer and former Texas secretary of state, he was able to raise $700,000, twice the amount collected by either of his two major opponents. The business establishment in the city had endorsed Kirk and filled his coffers.

The change in white attitudes extends to the highest office in the land. In 1957 a national sample of whites was asked whether they would vote for a well-qualified black candidate for president if he were nominated by their party; 63 percent said no. In 1994 just 10 percent of whites held to that view. Growing white receptivity to a black presidential candidate opened the door to General Colin Powell, though he has not yet chosen to walk through it. In the 1995 presidential primary season Powell was the nation's most wanted political candidate; in an October 1995 *Time*/CNN poll, he beat Clinton 51 to 34 percent. Moreover, exit polls conducted on election day in November 1996 suggest that he would have defeated President Clinton by 11 points. Another poll shortly after had Powell smashing Vice President Gore by 28 points in the presidential contest in 2000. . . .

THE NEW BLACK MAYORS

A deep divide separates those black politicians who (like Wilder) make an effort to appeal to white voters and those who don't. The difference is often generational. In Prince George's County, Maryland, a new crop of leaders arrived on the political scene in 1994. They're young, they're black and "their favorite color is green," a local lawyer and mentor said. "They want to see prosperity."

The description fits a number of black mayors as well. In Cleveland in 1989 two black candidates made it into a nonpartisan runoff. One was fifty-eight-year-old George L. Forbes, who, by his own admission, found soliciting votes in white neighborhoods "very painful." "My generation came out of a strong black civil rights movement," he explained, "and we always went back to black issues." His opponent, twenty years younger, was Michael White, who knew, he said, that "you don't make progress standing outside throwing bricks." He was the first black elected student body president at Ohio State, and described himself as never having "been a radical in my entire life about anything." He won.

Other black mayors, too, have been stressing clean streets, reduced crime, a balanced budget, and even the cost to blacks of court-ordered busing. Take Detroit. For twenty years Coleman Young dominated that city's politics. He did "more than broaden access to the pork barrel," writer Ze'ev Chafets noted. "Under him, Detroit [became] not merely an American city that happen[ed] to have a black majority, but a black metropolis, the first major Third World city in the United States. The trappings [were] all there—showcase projects, black-fisted symbols, an external enemy and the cult of personality."

Dennis Archer, elected in 1993, was a definite change. As one columnist put it, "'Our turn' platforms with the symbolic rhetoric of racial justice [took] a back seat to the more practical demands of governing." Throughout the campaign Archer had intimated that the business of Detroit was business, and as mayor-elect, he spent his first morning with the Republican governor of the state. In Atlanta, too, in 1993 there was a changing of the guard; Bill Campbell rode to victory promising more police, efficient government, economic growth, and no new taxes. He was the first black mayor of that majority-black city without close ties to the city's illustrious civil rights community.

Old-style black politicians are still around. Marion Barry, mayor of Washington, D.C., is a man cast in the Coleman Young mold. In small cities and towns—the places that only the locals know and scholars and media ignore—there could be others. Nor do all black mayors fit one mold or the other. The urban political scene is full of variety. Politicians are idiosyncratic, and consequently often hard to classify.

THE CONGRESSIONAL BLACK CAUCUS

If some mayors have dropped the rhetoric of racial empowerment and veered from the straight and narrow liberal path, that rhetoric and those programs have remained very much alive among the members of the Congressional Black Caucus—the CBC. For many black representatives in Congress time has stood still; they remain old-school civil rights warriors, whose power base is typically so heavily African-American that they need display little concern for white sensibilities. Coleman Young no longer occupies City Hall in Detroit, but Congressman John Conyers, Jr., is cut from the same cloth. First elected in 1964, he has been a militant voice for racial justice who demands that the United States pay reparations to all descendants of slaves. The *Congressional Quarterly's* 1996 *Politics in America* described him as "sarcastic and abrasive," seemingly "less interested in becoming a power broker than in being a liberal voice of protest."

Not all members of the CBC have Conyers's views or style, but they have tended to be markedly more ideological and racially militant than the typical black mayor. Part of the explanation may lie in the composition of the electorate that puts them in office. In early 1996, 82 percent of the African-American members of Congress—in contrast to 42 percent of the black mayors of cities of 25,000 or more—were elected by constituencies in which African Americans were a majority. The average congressional district that elected an African American was 56 percent black; the average city that voted a black mayor into office was only 42 percent black. A fourteen-point difference, in other words, the result of which is that the many black candidates who seek the mayor's seat in majority-white cities are forced to fight for the white vote. And those who survive have the desire and ability to put together biracial or multiethnic coalitions—to reach across racial and ethnic lines. . . .

Had black mayoral candidates been unwilling or unable to gather white support, there would have been many fewer African Americans elected, and in all likelihood, a much higher proportion with the ideological profile of most members of the CBC. For the majority-white settings that encourage biracial coalitions also encourage—as part of the same political package—a less racially strident style. By the same token, the constituency that is heavily black is likely to promote candidates whose main appeal is the stress they place on racial identity.

Most of the districts sending blacks to Congress have, in fact, been heavily black—although Supreme Court decisions that declared unconstitutional some of those most obviously racially gerrymandered have altered the picture somewhat. Those decisions brought about a steep drop in the proportion of African-American members of Congress who came from majority-black districts in the 1996 elections, a fall from 82 percent to 62 percent. But the typical black member of the House still had a considerably blacker constituency than the typical African-American mayor. . . .

The racial composition of the average CBC district may not be the only reason its members have generally been politically left and racially militant. The job of a member of Congress is more ideological than that of a mayor; move a Michael White to Congress and he might sound different. Mayors are managers; they need to get the trash off the streets, and will be held accountable if they don't. They can't so easily afford the luxury of advocating policies that depress economic growth and send the middle class (black and white) scurrying to the suburbs. Their greater need for white support is thus only one part of the story. Voters who might go for a left-leaning African-American candidate for Congress may not be equally receptive to the standard liberal fare at the municipal level. Thus, in Detroit's 1993 mayoral election Dennis Archer, a business-oriented coalition-builder, did well among both whites and educated, employed blacks. Representative John Conyers, Jr., ran against him and got just 3 percent of the vote. The man the city's voters were still willing to send to Congress was not even seriously considered when he went for the mayor's seat.

This is not to say that members of the Congressional Black Caucus are politically indistinguishable. Not only the racial composition of their districts, but the region makes a difference. It used to be that African Americans in Congress were mostly from the urban North. The southern membership of the CBC stood at six before the 1992 elections; by 1993, the number had risen to nineteen. The racially gerrymandered districts created after the 1990 census, in other words, had a dramatic impact; the caucus grew by almost 50 percent, with every one of the additional members from the South. Those Southerners "have agricultural and rural interests that frequently put them on a collision course with assumed positions of the caucus," Representative Conyers has said. "We never had a problem with taking away tobacco subsidies before."

Regional differences aside, it nevertheless remains the case that, as *Newsweek* reporter Howard Fineman noted in 1993, the Congressional Black Caucus "may be the only place on Capitol Hill where entitlements are still spoken of with reverence."

POLITICAL DISSENT

The only deviations from the monolithically liberal stance of African Americans in Congress have been on the part of two Republicans, Gary Franks of Connecticut and J. C. Watts of Oklahoma. Franks was first elected in 1990, from a district less than 5 percent black, but was defeated in 1996; Watts arrived in 1994, elected by a district only 7 percent black. Their maverick politics put both at odds with the CBC, which Watts declined to join ("I didn't come to Congress to be a black leader or a white leader, but a leader," he said). Franks became a member, but in the fall of 1993 was briefly barred from the weekly luncheon meetings—or rather told he could eat but not meet. He was allowed to participate in the group's deliberations only after a flurry of negative publicity threatened to turn a political nonconformist into a full-fledged martyr.

The expectation of ideological conformity within the CBC—a conformity that the majority-black districts helped create—was revealed in a July 1993 "Open Letter" to Congressman Franks from Missouri representative William Clay. The letter charged that Franks had shown a "callous disregard for the basic rights and freedoms of thirty-five (35) million black Americans." His greatest crime, was his support for the appointment of Judge Clarence Thomas to the Supreme Court, which exposed "millions of individuals, mostly black and poor, . . . [to] the ravishes [*sic*] of now Supreme Court Justice Clarence Thomas's indecent, cynical, distorted vision of equal justice under law." . . .

Their extraordinarily scarce numbers make black Republicans elected to office particularly vulnerable to the charge of being racially incorrect. As of 1996, according to data compiled by the Joint Center for Political and Economic Studies, only about 60 of the more than 8,000 black elected officials in the nation identified themselves as Republican. The only black Republicans holding statewide office were J. Kenneth Blackwell, the state treasurer in Ohio, and Victoria Buckley, secretary of state in Colorado. Out of the 550 black state legislators in the country, a mere 11 were Republican. . . .

Such blacker-than-thou, not-one-of-us rhetoric works—or works in the right setting. As did whiter-than-thou charges in the Jim Crow South, where white racial moderates often found themselves labeled "Nigger-lovers." And for the same reasons. Rallying 'round the racial flag feeds on racial distrust—of which there is always plenty.

THE POLITICS OF BLACK VOTERS

Black allegiance to the Democratic Party—across social classes—has been extremely stable since 1964. In presidential elections, at least five out of six African-American voters have cast their ballots for the Democratic candidate. Furthermore, fewer than 10 percent of blacks identify themselves as Republican.

Nevertheless, Democratic candidates cannot take black support absolutely for granted. Black support for GOP presidential candidates has been quite unwaveringly low, but that is not the case when it comes to congressional races. Thus, in 1990, 21 percent of black voters (a record high) cast their ballots for Republicans running for House seats. That's an average; some individual GOP candidates have done better. For instance, Senator John Danforth got 27 percent of the black vote in Missouri in 1988, while Senator Richard Lugar picked up 25 percent of the black vote in Indiana that same year. In 1990, 24 percent of African Americans in Texas supported Phil Gramm, and in 1992, 30 percent cast their ballots for Arlen Specter in Pennsylvania.

Black defectors from the Democratic Party have helped white Republicans running for state or local offices as well. . . .

When black voters cast their ballots for a Thomas Kean or a John Danforth, it makes news. And yet it has long been a bit of a puzzle why more African Americans are not attracted to the GOP. The Joint Center's January 1996 survey found that 31 percent of blacks identified themselves as liberals, 32 percent as moderates, and 30 percent as conservatives (most of the latter "Christian" conservatives). A year earlier Gallup had asked blacks whether they thought the political views of the Republican Party too conservative, too liberal, or just about right. Only 53 percent said "too conservative." Those findings are not surprising: polling data indicate that on a number of issues, substantial numbers of blacks favor "Republican" policies. For instance, in the 1996 Joint Center poll, 76 percent of black respondents favored a constitutional amendment allowing prayer in public schools; 49 percent wanted no benefit increases for single mothers on welfare who had additional children; 48 percent supported school vouchers; and a whopping 73 percent were enthusiastic about "three strikes and you're out" laws that sentence to life imprisonment violent criminals convicted of a third offense.

Conservatism on significant social issues, however, does not translate into political support for conservative candidates. Part of the reason is surely the fact that on other questions, blacks live up to their reputation as liberal Democrats. For instance, asked in the fall of 1995 whether they thought "that the federal government can do something to help those African Americans with severe problems," 70 percent of blacks said yes, whereas only 38 percent of whites agreed. In 1994, on the issue of government assistance to blacks, 74 percent of African Americans but only 16 percent of whites said too little was being spent. There is also a marked racial divide on questions such as: Would you rather have the federal government provide more services, even if it means more in taxes? Is it the responsibility of government to reduce the differences in income between people? And, do you agree that the government has an obligation to help people when they're in trouble? The affirmative action issue likewise splits blacks and whites—to different degrees, depending on how the question is asked.

A high degree of commitment to an expansive, protective federal government clearly separates blacks from whites. The historic sense of vulnerability continues to affect black political attitudes. Even the middle class views its hard-won status as fragile, with the consequence that individual blacks see their own fate as tied to that of the race, the political scientist Michael Dawson has persuasively argued. In believing that the fate of the race depends on the helping hand of government—that only its forceful presence keeps the enemies of racial justice at bay—most blacks remain in the Democratic camp. Whites are all over the political map; blacks disagree among themselves, but generally vote left. "The perceived economic domination of blacks by whites became intertwined with a sense of political domination as well," Dawson has suggested.

Perhaps it is the status anxiety of African Americans and their unshakable commitment to big government and the Democratic Party that frees black elected officials (to an unusual degree) from concern about the views of their constituents. . . . In the summer of 1994, the CBC (with the exception of Ron Dellums and Gary Franks) pushed hard for an invasion of Haiti, although their own constituents weren't with them. In a survey taken in July only 21 percent of the black respondents said they supported sending in troops. The black leadership was eager for action, but clearly had no mandate for military action from its own constituents. Apparently that didn't matter; they could count on incumbency and racial solidarity to provide political cover.

The strong allegiance of African-American voters to the Democratic Party does not mean that black Democrats always stick together. In the 1991 Chicago mayoral race, for instance, the white incumbent, Richard M. Daley, carried 26 percent of the black vote, even though his opponent was an African American running on the Harold Washington party line. That same year, Edward Rendell (white) became mayor of Philadelphia after he took 20 percent of the black vote in a Democratic primary in which there were three black candidates. Seven years earlier New Orleans voters casting their ballots in a congressional district that was 55 percent black had chosen Representative Lindy Boggs over a serious black candidate; black turnout was higher than white, but Boggs was a trusted incumbent, endorsed by a wide variety of black organizations.

Boggs had found her black support both in housing projects (where her staff held office hours) and in upscale black neighborhoods in New Orleans. In 1990,

Donald Mintz, a white mayoral candidate in that same majority-black city, was not a popular incumbent and managed to win only 14 percent of the total African-American vote. But in the more affluent black precincts, his black support went as high as 39 percent. Social class, in other words, can send black Democratic voters heading in quite different political directions. That's particularly apparent in all-black contests. . . .

It's not class alone that splits the black vote. In ethnically complex cities like New York, whites have never been one group. Working-class Catholics in Queens have little in common with Manhattan's Upper West Side Jews, and those Jews don't share much with their ultra-Orthodox brethren in Brooklyn. By now the black "community" is also ethnically fragmented. Racial incidents will still unite black voters—behind the candidacy of Mayor Dinkins in 1993, for instance. But even in that election, significant differences simmered beneath the surface consensus. "West Indian blacks in Flatbush and Crown Heights," a reporter noted at the time, ". . . consider themselves politically and culturally distinct from American-born blacks one neighborhood over in Bedford-Stuyvesant." New York politics have become "post black-white." Even among the American-born, all is not politically harmonious. Admirers of the demagogic style of an Al Sharpton are not likely to lick envelopes for conventional black politicians running for the city council. In New York and elsewhere, if Louis Farrakhan and other black Muslims enter the electoral arena, they are likely to further divide the African-American vote.

WHEN BLACK CANDIDATES LOSE

Differences among black voters can spell trouble for black candidates; competition can sink them all. For example, in the 1989 Chicago mayoral race two African-American candidates split the black vote and turned that black-run city over to a white, Richard M. Daley, "Son of Boss" (Daley), as the reporters had dubbed him five years earlier. But most often when black candidates don't win, the reason is whites voting for whites. Needed white votes aren't there. And when that happens, the explanation most commonly given is white racism.

Which means what? The answer is not obvious. Take the 1982 California gubernatorial race between Tom Bradley and George Deukmejian. Bradley, the black mayor of Los Angeles lost—by a whisker. (The margin for Deukmejian was 93,000 votes out of 7.8 million cast.) Some called it "racism as usual." Voters who swung to Deukmejian at the last minute, California Assembly speaker Willie Brown said, were driven by a "great fear of anything that is different from what is considered WASP."

In fact, Bradley did stunningly well, polling 48 percent of the vote in a state that was only 7 percent black, and winning nearly 3 million white votes. But neither blacks nor whites saw Bradley as a black candidate, polling data suggested, and low black turnout cost him the election. His race, per se, had not generated the enthusiastic black turnout that he needed. In addition, he had a problem with white voters: he was viewed as a liberal Democrat, which was not to his advantage. Four years earlier California voters had passed a cap on property tax in the state, and a year after that they had voted to amend the state constitution to stop all busing for purposes of school integration. In 1982 they didn't go either for Bradley or for Jerry Brown (running for the U.S. Senate). Nor did they back handgun control, also on the ballot, favored by Bradley, and important in drawing conservatives to the polls. . . .

Political convictions that defeat a black candidate are not necessarily racist. The failure to distinguish the one from the other marred much of the discussion not only of the Bradley race but of New York's 1993 mayoral election as well. Even before 3 November the contest between David Dinkins and Rudolph Giuliani had been declared race-driven. In campaigning for Dinkins in September, President Clinton had charged that many New Yorkers are "still too unwilling to vote for people who are different than we are." Dinkins's loss was indeed noteworthy; he was alone among black mayors of big cities in having been tossed out of office after only one term. But the president's view was both a rush to judgment and a warped view of the electorate.

As it turned out, most whites did cast their ballots against Dinkins. But was that fact alone "a stark reminder" of the importance of race, as a *New York Times* reporter, among others, argued? . . . And yet, while color had clearly been the first consideration among African-American voters, roughly one out of four whites had stuck with the mayor, and those who did not had plenty of reasons other than race for choosing Giuliani. Dinkins had been tried and found wanting, survey data suggested. In a *New York Times*/WCBS-TV poll taken just before the November election, 59 percent of New Yorkers said life in the city had gotten worse on the mayor's watch, and only 8 percent thought it had improved. The city was on the economic skids; its streets, subways, and parks were not safe; a sense of civil disorder was pervasive; and the old formulas, to which Dinkins was wedded, no longer worked. In addition—and perhaps most important—the mayor had managed, as columnist Jim Sleeper wrote, "to deepen racial and other differences in the name of respecting them. . . . "

. . . Race undoubtedly played some part in the outcome in New York; in a variety of ways, Dinkins himself made color an issue. But where race still plays a role, it is usually but one element in a subtle, complicated picture, and its impact is hard to judge. That has become true even of races in the Deep South. For instance, in the 1990 gubernatorial race in Georgia, the lieutenant governor, Zell Miller, trounced Andrew Young in the Democratic primary. That was no picture-perfect, racially polarized contest, however. In a crowded primary field Miller won roughly 20 percent of the black vote in Atlanta (although Young had been the city's mayor), and was endorsed by three black Georgia state senators. In other respects as well, Young was at a political disadvantage. He failed to get the support of U.S. Representative John Lewis, black and highly respected; his reputation as a mayor had been tarnished by an explosion of crime and Miller had proposed a state lottery, a popular idea.

WHERE RACE MATTERS

In New York, California, and even Georgia, skin color seems to have taken a backseat to other issues in these elections. But obviously there are contests in which race does figure prominently. Some voters turn to race as a "cue" when black and white candidates are either equally appealing or equally unknown. Race is also clearly a factor in those now very rare elections in which explicit racial appeals are made. David Duke's campaigns for the U.S. Senate in 1990 and in 1991 for the Louisiana governor's seat are the obvious examples. A one-time Klan leader, a Nazi sympathizer, and the founder of the National Association for the Advancement of White People, Duke ran (in effect) against black citizens and the white Democrats for whom they voted.

There are no other David Dukes in the 1990s, however. In the 1983 Chicago mayoral race, Bernard Epton ran unsuccessfully against Harold Washington with a racially charged slogan: "Epton for Mayor. Before It's Too Late." His followers sang "Bye Bye Blackbird" at rallies and sported buttons featuring a crossed-out watermelon. He thus had a reprehensible slogan and a racist following. Nevertheless, Epton was no former Nazi. Yet, like Duke's, his campaign made news precisely because that sort of racism had become so unusual. Moreover, it was the last mayoral race of its kind in the city; by 1989 the leading white candidate, Richard M. Daley, was working hard to attract black votes.

Racist campaigns have almost entirely disappeared because they cost votes. In Chicago, Epton's loss was followed five years later by that of the white Republican candidate for the recorder of deeds in Cook County (Chicago). He had asked reporters to "just run a picture" of his black opponent, Carol Moseley-Braun—a request to which voters did not respond kindly. Likewise, in the New Orleans mayoral race in 1994, the white candidate, Donald Mintz, used (but probably did not create) anti-black and anti-Semitic fliers. In the waning days of the campaign, those fliers galvanized black votes that tipped the balance against him.

Explicitly racist campaigns—blatant appeals to antiblack prejudice—are out. But what about references to controversial public policies that involve race? In North Carolina in 1990 the former mayor of Charlotte, Harvey Gantt, made a bid for the U.S. Senate seat held for eighteen years by Jesse Helms. Helms had been behind in the polls until mid-October, when he began to run racially charged advertisements that raised his ratings. One of the ads showed a pair of white hands crumpling a job notice while an off screen voice said, "They had to give your job to a minority." Another charged that Gantt had used "his office and minority status" to make a $450,000 profit on a $679 investment in a television station license that was then sold to a white corporation. It was the last that seems to have been the real killer. Labeled "racist" by Helm's opponents, it was in fact accurate.

The television spot that linked the Democratic candidate to affirmative action employment preferences got a great deal of national attention, and was indeed questionable. On the other hand, whether it made a difference to the outcome is doubtful. Gantt was an unabashed liberal in a relatively conservative state. He refused to come out against an increase in the tax on cigarettes, a North Carolina staple; he opposed the death penalty, was pro-choice, and hedged on the question of tough sentencing for drug dealers and other criminal offenders. In addition, Helms was a tough man to beat. In 1984 his white Democratic opponent had done a mere 1 percent better than Gantt did in 1990, even though he was a former governor who had won his gubernatorial races with huge margins.

More often the subject of race is raised more subtly, as Cleveland mayor Michael R. White observed in 1992. "You hear code words like welfare, crime, drugs, and unwed mothers in the inner city. . . ." In other words, "crime" (surely an issue worthy of debate) is a "code word" for blacks—and as such, out of bounds. In Mayor White's view, a great many important topics are off-limits. To discuss them is to appeal to prejudice at a time when explicit racism is off-limits.

Code words are thus said to be "rhetorical winks" that have allowed a variety of candidates—for instance, Barry Goldwater, with his talk of states' rights—to play on white racial resentment. A willingness to exploit racial resentment, it is charged, was also central to the 1988 campaign of George Bush for president. Bush won the backing of racially conservative whites through coded appeals—most notably, the two "Willie Horton" ads attacking Michael Dukakis as soft on crime. One showed convicts moving through a revolving door, but with a picture sufficiently grainy as to make the men racially unidentifiable. The other—not produced by the Bush campaign itself, but by an independent Republican activist named Floyd Brown—had a mug shot of Horton, who was black.

Horton was a Massachusetts prison inmate, convicted of murder and sentenced to life in prison, who was nevertheless granted a weekend furlough in 1986. On that weekend out, he broke into a house, pistol-whipped a man at home, sliced him twenty times with a knife, and tied him up in the basement. When the victim's fiancée arrived at the house, Horton tied her up and raped her twice. Dukakis was governor at the time, and had vetoed a bill that would have ended the furlough program. After this appalling incident, he had refused to meet with Horton's victims. The Bush campaign did not pull the story out of a bag of dirty tricks, as frequently alleged; the Lawrence, Massachusetts, newspaper had run it right after Horton was captured in Maryland. Although Democrats denounced it as racist when employed by Republicans, the name of Willie Horton was actually first used as a club against Michael Dukakis by none other than Senator Al Gore, running in New York as a Democratic contender in the 1988 primaries.

The Willie Horton ads were thus factually sound, and they raised a serious policy issue: the risks to the public that furlough programs entail. Nevertheless, the racial identification of Horton in the Floyd Brown ad improperly played on deep popular fears linking blacks with crime, and thus reinforced a stereotype that had no place in political discourse. Democrats, of course, said precisely that—at every possible opportunity. In fact, the ads were still an issue in the 1996 presidential season, often referred to in the media. The Willie Horton story is so often cited as an example of the indelible racism of white America, and yet clearly Democrats have calculated that they gain more than they lose by reminding the public of the sort of racially inflammatory ad that a GOP activist was willing to run in 1988. Apparently they believe that white revulsion against negative racial stereotypes is greater than white fears of black crime. It is one more sign of heartening racial change.

30

Representative Government

The Black Experience

HOWARD ZINN

Amid the enthusiastic celebrations in 1987 surrounding the Bicentennial of the Constitution, novelist James Michener wrote,

> The writing of the Constitution of the United States is an act of such genius that philosophers still wonder at its accomplishment and envy its results. Fifty five typical American citizens . . . fashioned a nearly perfect instrument of government. . . . Their decision to divide the power of the government into three parts—Legislative, Executive, Judicial—was a master stroke.[1]

In the abolitionist movement of the early nineteenth century, there was no such enthusiasm. William Lloyd Garrison, editor of *The Liberator,* held up a copy of the Constitution before several thousand people at a picnic of the New England Anti-Slavery Society and burned it, calling it "a covenant with death and an agreement with hell," and the crowd shouted "Amen!"

Ex-slave Frederick Douglass, invited to deliver a Fourth of July speech in 1852, told his white audience,

> The rich inheritance of justice, liberty, prosperity and independence, bequeathed by your fathers, is shared by you, not by me. The sunlight that brought light and healing to you, has brought stripes and death to me. This Fourth of July is yours, not mine. You may rejoice, I must mourn.

During our 1987 celebrations, former Chief Justice Warren Burger, chairman of the Bicentennial Commission, delivered the usual superlatives to the Founding Fathers and the Constitution. But the sole black Supreme Court Justice Thurgood Marshall spoke this way:

> In this bicentennial year, we may not all participate in the festivities with flag-waving fervor. Some may more quietly commemorate the suffering, struggle, and sacrifice that has triumphed over much of what was wrong with the original document, and observe the anniversary with hopes not realized and promises not fulfilled.[2] . . .

Today, Americans still celebrate the Constitution; they learn in school about checks and balances and what Michener called "the master stroke" of dividing the government into Executive, Legislative, and Judicial branches. We hold elections, vote for president and representatives in Congress, and think *that* is democracy. Yet for black people in this country, none of those institutions—not the Constitution, not the three branches of government, not voting for representatives—has been the source of whatever progress has been made toward racial equality. . . .

The history of blacks in the United States exposes dramatically the American political system. What that history makes clear is that our traditional, much-praised democratic institutions—representative government, voting, and constitutional law—have never proved adequate for solving critical problems of human rights. . . .

The American revolutionists . . . were moved by . . . the necessity to overthrow monarchical rule, to put forth a rhetoric that would win popular support, and then to set up a government that would be more democratic than a monarchy. It would be a representative government (a revolutionary idea at the time), but one that would represent the interests of the wealthy classes most of all. And so, the Declaration of Independence, a masterpiece of rhetorical idealism, was followed by the Constitution, a masterpiece of ambiguous practicality.

That combination of rhetoric and ambiguity appeared in the Bill of Rights itself, in the Fifth Amendment, which says no person shall be deprived of "life, liberty, or property" without due process of law. The white person might be thankful that "liberty" was safe, but the black slave, knowing he or she was "property," might well be unimpressed. Indeed, when the Supreme Court in 1857 had to decide between Dred Scott's liberty and his former master's property, it decided for property and declared Dred Scott a nonperson, to be returned to slavery.

Those were not "fifty five typical American citizens" (James Michener's phrase) who drew up the Constitution. At that convention, there was no representation of black people, who at that time numbered about one-fifth of the population of the states. There was no representation of women, who were about half the population, and certainly no representation of Indians, whose land all of the colonists were occupying. . . .

The Constitution was blatant in its representation of the interests of the slaveholders. It included the provision (Article IV, Section 2) that escaped slaves must be delivered back to their masters. Roger Sherman pointed out to the Convention that the return of runaway horses was not demanded with such specific concern, but he was ignored.

In eighty-five newspaper articles *(The Federalist Papers)*, arguing for the ratification of the Constitution among New York State voters (blacks, women, Indians, and whites without property were excluded), James Madison, Alexander Hamilton, and John Jay were quite frank. Madison wrote . . . that representative government was a good way of calming the demand of people "for an equal division of property, or for any other improper or wicked object." It would accomplish this by creating too big a nation for a revolt to spread easily and by filtering the anger of rebels through their more reasonable representatives. . . .

[While modern representative government is indeed] an improvement over monarchy, and may be used to bring about some reforms, it is chiefly used by those holding power in society as a democratic facade for a controlled society and a barrier against demands that threaten their interests.

The experience of black people reveals this most clearly, but there is instruction in it for every citizen. The Constitution did not do away with slavery; it legalized it. Congress and the president (including later the antislavery but politically cautious Abraham Lincoln) had other priorities that came ahead of abolishing slavery. Billions of dollars were invested in southern slaves, and northern political leaders, wanting to keep what power they had, did not want to rock the national boat.

It became clear to those who wanted to abolish slavery that they could not depend on the regular structures of government. So they began to agitate public opinion. This was dangerous not just in the South, where blacks were enslaved, but in the North, where they were segregated and denied the right to vote, their children excluded from public schools, and they were treated as inferiors in every way.[3]

A free black man in Boston, David Walker, wrote the pamphlet *Walker's Appeal,* a stirring call for resistance, in 1829:

> Let our enemies go on with their butcheries. . . . Never make an attempt to gain our freedom . . . until you see your way clear—when that hour arrives and you move, be not afraid or dismayed. . . . They have no more right to hold us in slavery than we have to hold them. . . . Our sufferings will come to an end, in spite of all the Americans this side of eternity. . . . 'Every dog must have its day,' the American's is coming to an end.

Georgia offered $1,000 to anyone who would kill David Walker. One summer day in 1830, David Walker was found dead near the doorway of the shop where he sold old clothes. The cause of death was not clear.

From the 1830s to the Civil War, antislavery people built a movement. It took ferocious dedication and courage. White abolitionist William Lloyd Garrison, writing in *The Liberator,* breathed fire: "I accuse the land of my nativity of insulting the majesty of Heaven with the greatest mockery that was ever exhibited to man." A white mob dragged him through the streets of Boston in chains, and he barely escaped with his life.

The Liberator started with twenty-five subscribers, most of them black. By the 1850s, it was read by more than 100,000. The movement had become a force.

Black abolitionists were central to the antislavery movement. Even before Garrison published *The Liberator,* a black periodical, *Freedom's Journal,* had appeared. Later, Frederick Douglass, ex-slave and abolitionist orator, started his own newspaper, *North Star.* A conference of blacks in 1854 declared, "it is emphatically our battle; no one else can fight it for us."

The Underground Railroad brought tens of thousands of slaves to freedom in the United States and Canada. Harriet Tubman, born into slavery, had escaped alone as a young woman. She then made nineteen dangerous trips back into the South, bringing over 300 slaves to freedom. She carried a pistol and told the fugitives, "You'll be free or die." . . .

No more shameful record of the moral failure of representative government exists than the fact that Congress passed the Fugitive Slave Act, the president signed it, and the Supreme Court approved it.

The act forced captured blacks to prove they were not someone's slave; an owner claiming him or her needed only an affidavit from friendly whites. For instance, a black man in southern Indiana was taken by federal agents from his wife and children and returned to an owner who claimed he had run away nineteen years ago. Under the act more than 300 people were returned to slavery in the 1850s.

The response to it was civil disobedience. "Vigilance committees" sprang up in various cities to protect blacks endangered by the law. In 1851 a black waiter named Shadrach, who had escaped from Virginia, was serving coffee to federal agents in a Boston coffeehouse. They seized him and rushed him to the federal courthouse. A group of black men broke into the courtroom, took Shadrach from the federal marshals, and saw to it that he escaped to Canada. Senator Webster denounced the rescue as treason, and the president ordered prosecution of those who had helped Shadrach escape. Four blacks and four whites were indicted and put on trial, but juries refused to convict them.[4] . . .

In Christiana, Pennsylvania, in September 1851, a slaveowner arrived from Maryland with federal agents to capture two of his slaves. There was a shoot-out with two dozen armed black men determined to protect the fugitives, and the slaveowner was shot dead. President Fillmore called out the marines and assembled federal marshals to make arrests. Thirty-six blacks and five whites were put on trial. A jury acquitted the first defendant, a white Quaker, and the government decided to drop the charges against the others.

Rescues took place and juries refused to convict. In Oberlin, Ohio, a group of students and one of their professors organized the rescue of an escaped slave; they were not prosecuted.

A white man in Springfield, Massachusetts, had organized blacks into a defense group in 1850. His name was John Brown. In 1858, John Brown and his band of white and black men made a wild, daring effort to capture the federal arsenal at Harper's Ferry, Virginia, and set off a slave revolt throughout the South. Brown and his men were hanged by the collaboration of the state of Virginia and the national government. He became a symbol of moral outrage against slavery. The great writer Ralph Waldo Emerson, not an activist himself, said of John Brown's execution: "He will make the gallows holy as the cross."

What Garrison had said was necessary—"a most tremendous excitement" was shaking the country. The abolitionist movement, once a despised few, began to be listened to by millions of Americans, indignant over the enslavement of 4 million men, women, and children.

Nevertheless when the Civil War began, Congress made its position clear, in a resolution passed with only a few dissenting votes: "This war is not waged . . . for any purpose of . . . overthrowing or interfering with the rights of established institutions of those states, but . . . to preserve the Union."

As for President Lincoln, his caution, his politicking around the issue of slavery (despite his personal indignation at its cruelty) had been made clear when he campaigned for the Senate in 1858. At that time he told voters in Chicago: "Let us discard all this quibbling about . . . this race and that race and the other race being inferior, and therefore they must be placed in an inferior position."

But two months later, in southern Illinois, he assured his listeners: "I will say, then, that I am not, nor ever have been, in favor of bringing about in any way the social and political equality of the white and black races. . . . I as much as any other man am in favor of having the superior position assigned to the white race."[5]

The abolitionists went to work. To their acts of civil disobedience and of armed resistance, they added more orthodox methods of agitation and education. Petitions for emancipation poured into Congress in 1861 and 1862. Congress, responding, passed a Confiscation Act, providing for the freeing of slaves of anyone who fought with the Confederacy. But it was not enforced.

When the Emancipation Proclamation was issued at the start of 1863, it had little practical effect. It only declared slaves free in states still rebelling against the Union. Lincoln used it as a threat to Confederate states: if you keep fighting, I will declare your slaves free; if you stop fighting, your slaves will remain. So, slavery in the border states, on the Union side, [was] left untouched by the proclamation. . . .

By the summer of 1864 approximately 400,000 signatures asking legislation to end slavery had been gathered and sent to Congress. The First Amendment's right "to petition the government for a redress of grievances" had never been used so powerfully. In January 1865 the House of Representatives, following the lead of the Senate, passed the Thirteenth Amendment, declaring slavery unconstitutional.

The representative system of government, the constitutional structure of the modern democratic state, unresponsive for eighty years to the moral issue of mass enslavement, had now finally responded. It had taken thirty years of antislavery agitation and four years of bloody war. It had required a long struggle—in the streets, in the countryside, and on the battlefield. Frederick Douglass made the point in a speech in 1857:

> Let me give you a word of the philosophy of reforms. The whole history of the progress of human liberty shows that all concessions yet made to her august claims have been born of struggle. . . . If there is no struggle there is no progress. Those who profess to favor freedom and yet deprecate agitation, are men who want crops without plowing up the ground. They want rain without thunder and lightning. They want the ocean without the awful roar of its many waters. The struggle may be a moral one; or it may be a physical one; or it may be both moral and physical, but it must be a struggle. Power concedes nothing without a demand. It never did and it never will.[6]

A hundred years after the Civil War, Frederick Douglass's statement was still true. Blacks were being beaten, murdered, abused, humiliated, and segregated from the cradle to the grave and the regular organs of democratic representative government were silent collaborators.

The Fourteenth Amendment, born in 1868 of the Civil War struggles, declared "equal protection of the laws." But this was soon dead—interpreted into nothingness by the Supreme Court, unenforced by presidents for a century.

Even the most liberal of presidents, Franklin D. Roosevelt, would not ask Congress to pass a law making lynching a crime. Roosevelt, through World War II, maintained racial segregation in the armed forces and was only induced to set up a commission on fair employment for blacks when black union leader A. Philip Randolph threatened a march on Washington. President Harry Truman ended segregation in the armed forces only after he was faced with the prospect—again it was by the determined A. Philip Randolph—of black resistance to the draft.

The Fifteenth Amendment, granting the right to vote, was nullified by the southern states, using discriminatory literacy tests, economic intimidation, and violence to keep blacks from even registering to vote. From the time it was passed in 1870 until 1965, no president, no Congress, and no Supreme Court did anything serious to enforce the Fifteenth Amendment, although the Constitution says that the president "shall take care that the laws be faithfully executed" and also that the Constitution "shall be the Supreme Law of the land."

If racial segregation was going to come to an end, if the century of humiliation that followed two centuries of slavery was going to come to an end, black people would have to do it themselves, in the face of the silence of the federal government. And so they did, in that great campaign called the civil rights movement, which can roughly be dated from the Montgomery Bus Boycott of 1955 to the riot in Watts, Los Angeles, in 1965, but its roots go back to the turn of the century and it has branches extending forward to the great urban riots of 1967 and 1968.

I speak of roots and branches, because the movement did not suddenly come out of nowhere in the 1950s and 1960s. It was prepared by many decades of action, risk, and sacrifice; by many defeats; and by a few victories. The roots go back at least to the turn of the century, to the protests of William Monroe Trotter; to the writings of W.E.B. DuBois; to the founding of the National Association for the Advancement of Colored People (NAACP); to the streetcar boycotts before World War I; to the seeds sown in black churches, in black colleges, and in the Highlander Folk School of Tennessee; and to the pioneering work of radicals, pacifists, and labor leaders.[7]

It is a comfort to the liberal system of representative government to say the civil rights movement started with the Supreme Court decision of 1954 in *Brown v. Board of Education of Topeka.* That was when the Supreme Court finally concluded that the Fourteenth Amendment provision of "equal protection of the laws" meant that public schools had to admit anyone, regardless of color. But to see the origins of the movement in that decision gives the Supreme Court too much credit, as if it suddenly had a moral insight or a spiritual conversion and then read the Fourteenth Amendment afresh.

The amendment was no different in 1954 than it had been in 1896, when the Court made racial segregation legal. There was just a new context now, a new world. And there were new pressures. The Supreme Court did not by itself reintroduce the question of segregation in the public schools. The question came before it because black people in the South went through years of struggle, risking their lives to bring the issue into the courts.

Local chapters in the South of the NAACP had much to do with the suits for school desegregation. The NAACP itself can be traced back to an angry protest in Boston in 1904 of the black journalist William Monroe Trotter against Booker T. Washington. Washington, a black educator, founder of Tuskegee Institute, favored peaceful accommodation to segregation. Trotter's arrest and his sentence of thirty days in prison aroused that extraordinary black intellectual W.E.B. DuBois, who wrote later, "when Trotter went to jail, my indignation overflowed. . . . I sent out from Atlanta . . . a call to a few selected persons for organized determination and aggressive action on the part of men who believe in Negro freedom and growth."

That "call to a few persons" started the Niagara Movement—a meeting in Niagara, New York, in 1905 that led to the founding of the NAACP in 1911. . . .

It seems a common occurrence that a hostile system is made to give ground by a combination of popular struggle and practicality. It had happened with emancipation in the Civil War. In the case of school desegregation, the persistence of blacks and the risks they took became joined to a practical need of the government. The *Brown* decision was made at the height of the cold war, when the United States was vying with the Soviet Union for influence and control in the Third World, which was mostly nonwhite.

Attorney General Herbert Brownell, arguing before the Supreme Court, asked that the "separate but equal" doctrine, which allowed segregation in the public schools, "be stricken down," because "it furnishes grist for the communist propaganda mills, and it raises doubt, even among friendly nations, as to the intensity of our devotion to the democratic faith."[8] . . .

By the provision of the Fourteenth Amendment for equal protection, there should have been no segregation of the buses in Montgomery, Alabama, in 1955. If the amendment had meaning, Rosa Parks should not have been ordered out of her seat to give it to a white person; she should not have been arrested when she refused. But the federal government was not enforcing the Constitution. The checks and balances were check-mated and out of equilibrium, and the black population of Montgomery had to get rid of bus segregation by their own efforts.

They organized a citywide boycott of the buses. Black people, old and young, men and women, walked miles to work. One of those people, an elderly lady who walked several miles to and from her job, was asked if she was tired. She replied, "My feets is tired, but my soul is rested." . . .

Finally, the government responded. In November 1956, a year after the boycott began, the Supreme Court outlawed segregation on local bus lines.[9] . . .

Why did four black college students have to sit at a "whites only" lunch counter in Greensboro, North Carolina, on February 1, 1960, and be arrested? Why did there have to be a "sit-in movement" to end discrimination in restaurants, hotels, and other public places throughout the South? Was it not the intent of the Thirteenth Amendment, as Justice John Harlan said back in 1883, to remove not only slavery but the "badges" of slavery? Was it not the intent of the Fourteenth Amendment to make all blacks citizens, and did not the Constitution (Article IV, Section 2) say that "the citizens of each State shall be entitled to all privileges and immunities of citizens in the several States"?[10] . . .

So it would take a struggle to relieve black parents of the problem of telling their little children that they could not sit at *this* lunch counter, use *this* water fountain, enter *this* building, or go to *this* movie theater. It would take sit-ins in city after southern city. There would be beatings and arrests. There would be in the year 1960 sit-ins and demonstrations in a hundred cities involving more than 50,000 people, and over 3,600 demonstrators would spend time in jail. . . .

There was an electric effect of all this on black people around the country. Bob Moses, who would later become an organizer of the movement in Mississippi, told how, sitting in his Harlem apartment, he saw on television the pictures of the Greensboro sit-in:

> The students in that picture had a certain look on their faces, sort of sullen, angry, determined. Before, the Negro in the South had always looked on the defensive, cringing. This time they were taking the initiative. They were kids my age, and I knew this had something to do with my own life.[11]

The young black veterans of the sit-ins from the Deep South, along with some blacks from the North and a few whites, formed a new organization, the Student Nonviolent Coordinating Committee (SNCC). They became the "point" people (to use a military term: those who go ahead into enemy territory) for the civil rights movement in the Deep South.

In the spring of 1961 the Congress of Racial Equality (CORE) organized the "Freedom Rides": whites and blacks rode together on buses throughout the South to try to break the segregation pattern in interstate travel. The two buses that left Washington, D.C., on May 4, 1961, headed for New Orleans, never got there. In South Carolina, riders were beaten. In Alabama, a bus was set afire. Freedom Riders were attacked with fists and iron bars. The southern police did not interfere with any of this violence, nor did the federal government. FBI agents watched, took notes, did nothing.

CORE decided to call off the rides. SNCC, younger, more daring (more rash, some thought) decided to continue them. Before they started out, they called the Department of Justice in Washington to ask for protection. A SNCC staff member, Ruby Doris Smith (one of my students at Spelman College), told me about the phone call: "The Justice Department said no, they couldn't protect anyone, but if something happened, they would investigate. You know how they do." . . .

The law was clear. Presumably, representative government had done its work by enacting the Fourteenth Amendment, which called for equal protection of the law. In 1887 Congress had enacted the Interstate Commerce Act, which barred discrimination in interstate travel, and the courts had reinforced this in the 1940s and 1950s. But it took the Freedom Rides and the embarrassing publicity surrounding them that went around the world to get the federal government to do something. In November 1961, through the Interstate Commerce Commission, it issued specific regulations, asking that posters be put on all interstate terminals and establishing the right of travel without segregation.

Even that was not seriously enforced. Two years later, in Winona, Mississippi, a group of blacks who used the white waiting room were arrested and brutally beaten. Constitutional government did not exist for them. . . .

I had another opportunity to see if the federal government would enforce its own laws in November 1963 when I traveled to Selma, Alabama, to participate in Freedom Day. It was a day when black people in Dallas County were being organized to come to Selma, the county seat, and register to vote. It was a dangerous thing for a black person to do in Dallas County, and so a mass meeting was held the evening before in a black church, with speeches designed to build people's courage for the next day. Novelist James Baldwin came and so did comedian Dick Gregory, who tried to diminish fear with laughter. And there were the thrilling voices of the Selma Freedom Singers.

The next day, black men and women, elderly people, and mothers carrying babies lined up in front of the county courthouse where the voting registrar had his office. The street was lined with police cars. Colonel Al Lingo's state troopers were out in force, carrying guns, clubs, gas masks, and electrified cattle prods. Sheriff Jim Clark had deputized a large group of the county's white citizens, who were there, also armed. It looked like a war.

The federal building in Selma was across the street from the county courthouse. When two SNCC workers climbed up on the steps of the building and held up signs facing the courthouse that read Register to Vote, Sheriff Jim Clark and his deputies mounted the steps and dragged them off into police cars.

That federal building also housed the local FBI. Two FBI agents were out on the street taking notes. Two representatives of the Justice Department's Civil Rights Division were also there. We were all watching the arrest of two men for standing on federal property urging people to register to vote; I turned to one of the Justice Department lawyers. "Don't you think federal law has just been violated?" I asked.

The Justice man said, "Yes, I suppose so."

"Are you going to do something about that?"

"Washington is not interested." . . .

The FBI has the power to make arrests when federal law is violated before its eyes. Would its agents let a bank robber do his work and just watch and take notes? They would apprehend a bank robber, but not a local southern policeman violating a black man's constitutional rights. When I wrote an article for the *New Republic* on what happened in Selma, pointing to the failure of the U.S. government to enforce its own laws, Burke Marshall of the Justice Department replied. He defended the federal government's inaction, speaking mystically of "federalism," which refers to the division of power between states and federal government. But the Fourteenth Amendment had made a clear statement about that division of power and gave the federal government the right to forbid the states from doing certain things to its citizens. And a number of laws were on the books to buttress the Fourteenth Amendment. . . .

[President] Kennedy had not planned to introduce new civil rights legislation. But in the late spring of 1963 he put his force behind a new, sweeping civil rights law, designed to outlaw segregation in public accommodations, eliminate segregation in state and local facilities, provide for fair employment regardless of race, and also put a bit more teeth into the federal government's actions against discrimination in schools and in voting.

What had changed Kennedy's mind was the mass demonstrations in Birmingham, Alabama, in the spring of 1963. These were organized by Martin Luther King and the Southern Christian Leadership Conference, along with local black leaders like Fred Shuttlesworth. Thousands of children marched in the streets, against firehoses and billy clubs and police dogs. The photos of police brutality, of children being smashed against the wall by high-power hoses, of a boy being attacked by a police dog, went around the world.

The demonstrations spread beyond Birmingham. In the ten weeks following the children's march, over 3,000 people were arrested in 758 demonstrations in 75 southern cities. By the end of 1963, protests had taken place in 800 cities across the country. Congress debated furiously the provisions of the new civil rights law, which it finally passed, after a year of debate and filibuster—the longest debate on any bill in history. That became the Civil Rights Act of 1964.

The same summer that the new law was being debated, events in Mississippi revealed the limits of the federal government's commitment to racial equality, how little meaning there was to that end product of representative government, the federal statute.

The civil rights groups working together in Mississippi—SNCC, CORE, and SCLC—decided that they needed help and that they should call on young people from all over the country to come to Mississippi in the summer of 1964. The plan was to engage in an all-out effort to end segregation, to register black Mississippians to vote, to encourage local black people by showing how much national support they had.

Everyone connected with the plan knew it would be dangerous. Black people in Mississippi faced that danger every day, all their lives. . . .

Three young people with the summer project—a black Mississippian named James Chaney and two whites from the North, Michael Schwerner and Andrew Goodman—disappeared while on a trip to Neshoba County, Mississippi, to investigate the burning of a black church. Chaney and Schwerner were staff members of CORE. Goodman was a summer volunteer and had just arrived in Mississippi hours before.

Two days later their burned station wagon was found, but no trace of the three men. On August 4, forty-four days after their disappearance, their bodies were found buried on a farm. James Chaney had been brutally beaten, so badly that a pathologist examining him said he had "never witnessed bones so severely shattered, except in tremendously high speed accidents such as aeroplane crashes." All three had been shot to death.[12]

In 1988 a film called *Mississippi Burning* was seen throughout the country. It was the story of the FBI search for the murderers of Chaney, Goodman, and Schwerner. It portrayed the FBI as the heroes of the investigation that led to the discovery of the bodies and the prosecution of a number of Neshoba County men. One of those prosecuted was Deputy Sheriff Cecil Price, who had arrested them for speeding and then released them from jail in a prearranged plan to have them murdered. Price and several others were found guilty, spent a few years in prison.[13]

Those of us who were involved in the Mississippi Summer were angered by the movie. We knew how the FBI, again and again, had failed to do its duty to enforce federal law where the rights of black people in the South were at stake, how many times they had watched bloody beatings and done nothing, how the law had been violated before their eyes and they made no move. And we knew how outrageously they had behaved, along with the entire federal government, when the three young men disappeared. . . .

It may well be that there was no way of saving the lives of the three young men after their disappearance. But there had certainly been a way of *preventing* what happened, if the government had only met the movement's request that it station federal marshals in Mississippi, to be on the spot, to accompany people into dangerous situations like Neshoba County. Don't they send police to guard the payrolls of banks?

Most of all, the behavior of the FBI and the Justice Department in that situation tells something about the moral and emotional remoteness of liberal constitutional government from the deepest grievances of its citizens. It tells us how important is Frederick Douglass's admonition that those who want the rain of freedom must themselves supply the thunder and lightning.

Later that same summer the Democratic party refused to seat a black delegation from Mississippi that claimed 40 percent of the seats (the percentage of blacks in the state). Instead the Credentials Committee voted to give 100 percent of the Mississippi seats to the official white delegates. It was representative government for whites, exclusion for blacks.

By 1965 it was clear that despite the Fifteenth Amendment, which said that citizens could not be denied the right to vote on grounds of race, and despite the civil rights acts of 1957, 1960, and 1964, all concerned with voting in some way, blacks in the Deep South were still not being allowed to vote.

A little-noticed clause of the Fourteenth Amendment, Section 2, says that if citizens are unfairly denied the right to vote, the representation in Congress of that state can be reduced. This would be the job of the president, who officially gets the census and decides on the number of representatives from each state. But no president, liberal or conservative, Republican or Democrat, had ever invoked this part of the Constitution—although it would have been a powerful weapon against racial discrimination in voting.

In the spring of 1965 the Southern Christian Leadership Conference began a campaign for voting rights in Selma, Alabama, around the same time that President Lyndon Johnson was discussing with Congress a new voting rights bill. Martin Luther King, Jr., went to Selma to join the action.

On March 7, later called "Bloody Sunday," a column of civil rights activists, beginning the long walk from Selma to the state capital in Montgomery, was confronted by state troopers demanding they turn back. They continued to walk, and the troopers set on them with clubs, beating them viciously, until they were dispersed and the bridge was splattered with blood.

During that campaign in Selma, Jimmie Lee Jackson, a black man, was shot in the stomach by a state trooper and died hours later. James Reeb, a white minister from the North, was clubbed to death by angry whites as he walked down the street. . . .

The Voting Rights Act of 1965, for the first time, took the registration of blacks out of the hands of racist registrars in areas with a record of discrimination and put the force of the federal government behind the right to vote. David Garrow, in his book *Protest at Selma,* calls the new law "a legislative enactment that was to stimulate as great a change in American politics as any one law ever has."[14] It resulted in a dramatic increase in black voters and the election of black officials all through the Deep South.

What is clear from Garrow's careful study is how the protest movement in Selma was crucial in bringing about the Voting Rights Act. He gives some credit to the federal courts, but he says, "black southerners were unable to experience truly substantial gains in voting rights until, through their own actions, they were able to activate the federal executive and Congress." Furthermore, "the national consensus in favor of that bill . . . was primarily the result of the very skillful actions of the SCLC in Selma."[15]

Voting brought some black Americans into political office. It gave many more the feeling that they now had political rights equal to that of whites. They were now *represented* in local government and in Congress, at least more than before.

But there were limits to what such representation could bring. It could not change the facts of black poverty or destroy the black ghetto. After all, black people in Harlem or the South Side of Chicago had the right to vote long ago; they still lived in Harlem or the South Side, in broken-down tenements, amid rats and garbage. Thirty to 40 percent of young blacks were unemployed. Crime and drugs are inevitable in that atmosphere.

So it is not surprising that almost exactly at the time the Voting Rights Act was being enacted in 1965, the black ghetto of Watts, Los Angeles, erupted in a great riot. Or that in 1967 there were disorders, outbreaks, and uprisings in over a hundred cities, leaving eighty-three people dead, almost all blacks. And in 1968, after Martin Luther King was assassinated, there were more outbreaks in cities all over the country, with thirty-nine people killed, thirty-five of them black.[16]

But riots are not the same as revolution. The *New York Times* reported in early 1978: "The places that experienced urban riots in the 1960s have, with a few exceptions, changed little, and the conditions of poverty have spread in most cities."

The constitutional system set up by the Founding Fathers, a system of representation and checks and balances, was a defense in depth of the existing distribution of wealth and power. By arduous struggle and sacrifice, blacks might compel it to take down its "whites only" signs here and there. But poverty remained as the most powerful barrier to equality.

That is the barrier Madison spoke of when he said the system being set up in the new United States of America would prevent "an equal division of property or any other improper or wicked object." It is the fact of *class,* however disguised it is by the procedures of modern liberal societies. . . .

No representative can adequately represent another's needs; the representative tends to become a member of a special elite; he has privileges that weaken his sense of concern over his constituents' grievances. The anger of the aggrieved loses force as it is filtered through the representative system (something Madison saw as an advantage in *Federalist #10*). The elected official develops an expertise that tends toward its own perpetuation. Representatives spend more time with one another than with their constituents, become an exclusive club, and develop what Robert Michels called "a mutual insurance contract" against the rest of society.[17]

We can see the difficulties in the United States, which has one of the most praised systems of representative government in the world. People have the right to vote, but the choices before them are so limited, they see so little difference between the candidates, they so despair of their vote having any meaning, or they are so alienated from society in general because of their own misery that roughly 50 percent of those eligible to vote do not vote in presidential elections and over 60 percent do not vote in local elections.

Money dominates the election process. The candidate for national office either has to have millions of dollars or have access to millions of dollars. (In 1982 a senator from Minnesota spent $7 million on his campaign.) Money buys advertising, prime time on television, a public image. The candidates then have a certain obligation to those with money who supported them. They must *look* good to the people who voted for them, but *be* good to those who financed them.[18]

Voting is most certainly overrated as a guarantee of democracy. The anarchist thinkers always understood this. As with Rousseau, we might not be sure of their solutions, but their critique is to the point. Emma Goldman, talking to women about their campaign for women's suffrage, was not *opposed* to the vote for women, but did want to warn against excessive expectations:

> Our modern fetish is universal suffrage. . . . I see neither physical, psychological, nor mental reasons why woman should not have the equal right to vote with man. But that can not possibly blind me to the absurd notion that woman will accomplish that wherein man has failed. . . . The history of the political activities of men proves that they have given him absolutely nothing that he could not have achieved in a more direct, less costly, and more lasting manner. As a matter of fact, every inch of ground he has gained has been through a constant fight, a ceaseless struggle for self-assertion, and not through suffrage.[19]

Helen Keller, who achieved fame for overcoming her blindness and deafness and displaying extraordinary talents, was also a socialist, and wrote the following in a letter to a woman suffragist in England:

> Are not the dominant parties managed by the ruling classes, that is, the propertied classes, solely for the profit and privilege of the few? They use us millions to help them into power. They tell us, like so many children, that our safety lies in voting for them. They toss us crumbs of concessions to make us believe that they are working in our interest. Then they exploit the resources of the nation not for us, but for the interests which they represent and uphold. . . . We vote? What does that mean? It means that we choose between two bodies of real, though not avowed, autocrats. We choose between Tweedledum and Tweedledee.[20]

[Elsewhere] I noted how the vote for president means so little in matters of foreign policy; after the president is elected he does as he likes. We should also note that voting for members of Congress is meaningless for the most important issues of life and death. That is not just because it is impossible to tell at election time how your representative will vote in a future foreign policy crisis. It is also because Congress is a feeble, often nonexistent factor in decisions on war and peace, usually following helplessly along with whatever the president decides. That fact makes a shambles of "representative" government. . . .

Direct democracy is possible in small groups, and a wonderful idea for town meetings and neighborhood meetings. There could be discussions in offices and factories, a workplace democracy that neither the commissars of the Soviet Union nor the corporate executives of the United States and often not even the trade union leaders in these countries allow today.

To make national decisions directly is not workable, but it is conceivable that a network of direct democracy groups could register their opinions in a way that would result in some national consensus. Lively participation and discussion of the issues by the citizenry would be a better, more democratic, more reliable way of representing the population than the present stiff, controlled system of electoral politics.

There is already experience with special democratic procedures. Many states have provisions for initiatives and referenda. Citizens, by petition, can initiate legislation, call for general referenda, change the laws and the Constitution. That leads to a lively discussion among the public and something close to a real democratic decision. Except that so long as there are wealthy corporations dominating the media with their money, they can virtually buy a referendum the way they now buy elections.

There is also the idea of proportional representation, so that instead of the two-party system of Democrats and Republicans monopolizing power (after all, a two-party system is only one party more than a one-party system), Socialists and Prohibitionists and Environmentalists and Anarchists and Libertarians and others would have seats in proportion to their following. National television debates would show six points of view instead of two.

The people who control wealth and power today do not want any real changes in the system. (For instance, when proportional representation was tried in New York City after World War II and one or two Communists were elected to the City Council, the system was ended.) Also, when one radical congressman, Vito Marcantonio, kept voting against military budgets at the start of the cold war era, but kept getting elected by his district time after time, the rules were changed so that his opponent could run on three different tickets and finally beat him.

Someone once put a sign on a bridge over the Charles River in Boston: If Voting Could Change Things, It Would Be Illegal. That suggests a reality. Tinkering with voting procedures—proportional representation, initiatives, etc.—may be a bit helpful. But still, in a society so unequal in wealth, the rich will dominate any procedure. It will take fundamental changes in the economic system and in the distribution of wealth to create an atmosphere in which councils of people in workplaces and neighborhoods can meet and talk and make something approximating democratic decisions.

No changes in procedures, in structures, can make a society democratic. This is a hard thing for us to accept, because we grow up in a technological culture where we think: If we can only find the right mechanism, everything will be okay, then we can relax. But we can't relax. The experience of black people in America (also Indians, women, Hispanics, and the poor) instructs us all. No Constitution, no Bill of Rights, no voting procedures, no piece of legislation can assure us of peace or justice or equality. *That* requires a constant struggle, a continuous discussion among citizens, an endless series of organizations and movements, creating a pressure on whatever procedures there are.

The black movement, like the labor movement, the women's movement, and the antiwar movement, has taught us a simple truth: The official channels, the formal procedures of representative government, have been sometimes useful, but never sufficient, and have often been obstacles, to the achievement of crucial human rights. What has worked in history has been *direct action* by people engaged together, sacrificing, risking together, in a worthwhile cause.

Those who have had the experience know that, unlike the puny act of voting, being with others in a great movement for social justice not only makes democracy come alive—it makes the people engaged in it come alive. It is satisfying, it is pleasurable. Change is difficult, but if it comes, that will most likely be the way.

NOTES

1. James Michener, "The Secret of America," *Parade*, Sept. 15, 1985.
2. "Remarks of Thurgood Marshall at the Annual Seminar of the San Francisco Patent and Trademark Law Association in Maui, Hawaii," May 6, 1987.

3. See Leon Litwack, *North of Slavery* (University of Chicago Press, 1961).

4. For excellent accounts of the resistance to the Fugitive Slave Act, see James McPherson, *Battle Cry of Freedom* (Oxford University Press, 1988), 82–83.

5. Quoted by Richard Hofstadter, *The American Political Tradition* (Vintage, 1974), 148.

6. Ibid., 169–170.

7. Alden Morris, *The Origins of the Civil Rights Movement* (The Free Press, 1985), traces the complex and fascinating roots of the civil rights movement.

8. Quoted by John Hope Franklin, *From Slavery to Freedom* (Knopf, 1967), 556. Also in William Strickland, "The Road Since Brown," [*The Black Scholar* (Sept.-Oct. 1979)].

9. *Browder v. Gayle* 352 U.S. 903 (1956).

10. *Civil Rights Cases* 109 U.S. 3 (1883).

11. See the chapter "Out of the Sit-ins" in Howard Zinn, *SNCC: The New Abolitionists* (Greenwood Press, 1985).

12. *Post Mortem Examination Report of the Body of James Chaney,* by David Spain, M.D. (in my personal files).

13. See Seth Cagin and Philip Dray, *We Are Not Afraid: The Story of Goodman, Schwerner, and Chaney and the Civil Rights Campaign for Mississippi* (Macmillan, 1988).

14. Quoted by David Garrow, *Protest at Selma: Martin Luther King, Jr. and the Voting Rights Act of 1965* (Yale University Press, 1978), 236.

15. Ibid., 235.

16. On the Watts riots, see Robert Conot, *Rivers of Blood, Years of Darkness* (William Morrow, 1968). On the 1967 and 1968 uprisings, see the report of the National Advisory Committee on Civil Disorders (Bantam, 1968).

17. Robert Michels, *Political Parties* (Free Press, 1966).

18. See Philip M. Stern, *The Best Congress Money Can Buy* (Pantheon, 1988).

19. Emma Goldman, "Woman Suffrage," in *Anarchism and Other Essays* (Dover, 1969), 195–211.

20. Philip Foner, ed., *Helen Keller: Her Socialist Years* (International Publishers, 1967).

31

Black Conservatives

DEBORAH TOLER

THE ORIGINS OF BLACK CONSERVATISM

In order to understand Black conservatism, it is important to understand the character of the Black bourgeoisie. Developing as it did within the context of white cultural oppression, it is not surprising that the values identified by Black conservative intellectuals such as Shelby Steele and Thomas Sowell as "traditional American values" are hallmarks of both American conservative mythology and Black bourgeois mythology. The ethic of "individual initiative" and "strong families" are values intimately related to the stereotypes that locate Black poverty in the misbehavior of those Blacks who do not make progress.

Black bourgeois mythology is a powerful theme in the African American community, one that exists on two layers. First, like the conservative Horatio Alger myth, Black bourgeois mythology asserts that values and behavior determine economic success. Second, the myth maintains that middle-class African Americans are different from other African Americans. The development of the Black bourgeoisie is rooted in its apartness from the Black mass majority.

Prior to desegregation, African Americans of all socioeconomic groups lived in the same segregated communities. The economic and political position of the Black bourgeoisie depended on the business and political support of poorer Blacks living under segregated circumstances. Nonetheless, most of the Black bourgeoisie historically has seen itself (even when white America has not) as different from the Black masses, in attitude and behavior as well as in economic success.

Histories of the socio-cultural development of the Black middle class emphasize the pivotal role played by schooling for newly freed slaves, schooling which often would make them members of an incipient Black bourgeoisie in the immediate post–Civil War era. Initially, most of this schooling was carried out by white missionaries and abolitionists from the north, and later by Black graduates of their schools. These white instructors were intent on imparting the Puritan work ethic and morality prevalent in white schools of the day. Thus, among other things, the schooling emphasized "proper" sexual behavior. Schools demanded that students be chaste, especially the girls, and all students were expected to marry and live "conventional" family lives.

The emphasis on "moral" sexual behavior had special significance in the case of Black students. White northern teachers emphasized it because, using paternalistic and implicitly racist reasoning, they believed it the best way to disprove Southern white racists' belief that the Negro's "savage instincts" prevented him from conforming to puritanical sex behavior.

"Moral" sexual behavior resonated with newly freed slaves for a number of reasons—among them, the sexual exploitation and denial of the right to family life under slavery, and the teachings of the Black Church.

In addition to insisting on high moral standards, schooling for the incipient Black middle class added the classist and racist concept that only "common Negroes" engaged in "unconventional" sexual behavior and a wide array of other "dysfunctional," "primitive" behaviors, such as laziness, boisterousness, improvidence, and drunkenness. Thus, it was their values and their behaviors that made Black elites elite and set them apart from the Black masses.

It is no accident that today both liberal and conservative Black elites are preoccupied by what is, in reality, a nonexistent "epidemic" of Black teen pregnancies, or that poor, female-headed households receive special opprobrium. In part, this stems from the overall patriarchal character of U.S. culture—one in which white ethnic groups' poverty is also largely blamed on female-headed households. But sexual behavior has long been a touchstone of Blacks' civilized status.

Indeed, it is important to recognize that a historical strain in Black political agitation was that elite Blacks were being denied the rights they deserved by virtue of having proved themselves "civilized," *i.e.*, better than and separate from "common Negroes." In the words of Adolph Reed, Jr.: "Race spokespersons commonly have included in their briefs against segregation (or discrimination in other forms) an objection that its purely racial character fails to differentiate among blacks and lumps the respectable, cultivated, and genteel in with the rabble."

I emphasize this because far too little attention has been paid to the extent to which Black conservatives' arguments—whether delineating the causes of Black oppression, locating the causes of Black poverty, or (as will be seen) making the case against affirmative action—all come back to issues of distinguishing middle class from poor Blacks. This holds also for Black conservatives as individuals, and their need to distinguish themselves, their status, and their identity from negative Black stereotypes.

THE ROLE OF INTERNALIZED OPPRESSION

Apart from their classic Black bourgeois perspectives, Black conservative intellectuals also consistently demonstrate they have personally internalized negative stereotypes about poor African Americans and about African American culture. The evidence for this lies in the underlying assumptions of their written work, the descriptions of poor African Americans in that work, and their personal biographies.

In 1986 Glenn Loury wrote: "But it is now beyond dispute that many of the problems of contemporary black American life lie outside the reach of effective government actions and these can only be undertaken by the black community itself. These problems involve at their core the values, attitudes, and behaviors of individual blacks. They are exemplified by the staggering statistics on pregnancies among young, unwed black women and the arrest and incarceration rates among black men."

Yet Loury's personal history includes fathering two out-of-wedlock children, a jailing for non-payment of child support, and 1987 arrests for cocaine and marijuana possession and for assaulting the young mistress he had established in a separate household. Referring to that past history Loury has said: "I thought if I hung out in the community and engaged in certain kinds of social activities, in a way I was really being black."

English professor Shelby Steele complains that African Americans suffer from a collective self-image that prefers victimization to success and imposes a suffocating racial conformity that ostracizes nonconformists like him. He discusses his own dissociation from images of lower-class Black life when it was represented by an imaginary character named Sam, created by his childhood family. Sam embodied all the negative images of Blacks his father had left behind because "they were 'going nowhere.'"

Steele succinctly states his concern about being confused with poor Blacks when he admits: "The stereotype of the lazy black SOB is common, and the fear is profound that I'll be judged by that stereotype. They will judge our race by him [an unemployed young Black man]—and they'll overlook me, quietly sitting on that bus grading those papers."

Nowhere in the array of Black conservatives' positions are the themes of traditional Black bourgeois attitudes and personal individual status and identity more prevalent than in Black conservatives' opposition to affirmative action. As we have seen earlier, in their analyses of Black oppression and the Black culture of poverty the foundation of their arguments comes from white conservatives and neoconservatives.

BLACK CONSERVATIVES AND AFFIRMATIVE ACTION

Nathan Glazer's 1975 book, *Affirmative Action, Ethic Inequality and Public Policy,* summarized white neoconservatives' objections to affirmative action: that by the end of the 1960s, discrimination was no longer a major obstacle to minorities' access employment, education and other social mobility mechanisms; affirmative action has not benefited the poor who need it most, but has primarily benefited middle-class Blacks and other minorities; and affirmative action fuels white resentment against minorities.

In his 1984 book, *Civil Rights: Rhetoric or Reality?,* Thomas Sowell repeats each of Glazer's basic objections. Quoting statistics from the Moynihan Report, Sowell insists: "The number of blacks in professional, technical, and other high level occupations more than doubled in the decade preceding the Civil Rights Act of 1964. . . . The trend was already under way." Also, like Glazer and other white conservatives, Sowell maintains that: "The relative position of disadvantaged individuals within the groups singled out for preferential treatment has generally declined under affirmative action."

Sowell and the other Black conservatives insist affirmative action programs violate whites' "constitutional rights" in general and those of white males in particular. Not only is this seen as unfair, but, like Glazer, Black conservatives worry about the resulting white resentment. In Sowell's words: "There is much reason to fear the harm that it is currently doing to its supposed beneficiaries, and still more reason to fear the long-run consequences of polarizing the nation. . . . Already there are signs of hate organizations growing in more parts of the country and among more educated classes than ever took them seriously before."

What is most interesting about Sowell's affirmative action critique, however, is not that he repeats the standard white conservative critique, but that he adds a self-esteem component to that critique. It is this self-esteem component that reflects the personal status concerns of Sowell and other Black conservatives.

Sowell argues that while accomplishing few positive results, affirmative action actually undermines the efforts of successful minority individuals by creating a climate in which it will be assumed that their achievements reflect not individual worth, talent, or skill, but special consideration. "Pride of achievement is also undermined by the civil rights vision that assumes credit for minority and female advancement. This makes minority and female achievement suspect in their own eyes and in the eyes of the larger society."

Other Black conservative intellectuals follow Sowell's position, first making the same criticisms as white conservatives but adding self-esteem, personal diminishment, and status issues. . . .

In *Reflections of an Affirmative Action Baby,* Stephen Carter denies being a conservative. But his discussion of affirmative action is a mirror image of the standard neoconservative critique. Like Glazer, Carter argues that: "What has happened in America in the era of affirmative action is this: middle-class black people are better off and lower class black people are worse off." Carter's "best black syndrome" is the most quoted Black conservative status/self-esteem statement about affirmative action: "The best black syndrome creates in those of us who have benefited from racial preferences a peculiar contradiction. We are told over and over that we are the best black people in our profession. And we are flattered. . . . But to professionals who have worked hard to succeed, flattery of this kind carries an unsubtle insult, for we yearn to be called what our achievements often deserve: simply the best—no qualifiers needed!"

Carter and the other Black conservative intellectuals say they object to the fact that affirmative action benefits those minorities who are already middle income. They do not produce convincing statistical evidence to support this contention. Nor do they recognize that affirmative action was designed to address discrimination, not economic disadvantage, or that most government programs benefit middle and, especially, high income groups. Nor do Black conservatives ever recommend that affirmative action become a program for all poor people, including the more than ten million poor whites in this country.

What Black conservatives do argue for is that Blacks compete on merit and merit alone. Their "merit only" policy is clearly an idealized paradigm. It ignores the fundamental reality that any selection process is always a combination of some imperfect assessment of merit (skills and talent) and purely personal filtering processes. To assume that race and/or gender considerations are neutral at the level of personal filtering is naive to say the least. . . .

THE THEME OF SELF HELP

Black conservative intellectuals' solutions for improving race relations are very much tied to the classic attitudes of the Black bourgeoisie, and to issues of identity and status. Further, their solutions always assign leadership roles to the Black middle class. Consistent with their analysis of the causes of Black oppression and Black poverty, they return to the "slavery damaged" theme, and locate the solutions within individual Blacks and the Black community. The reasoning behind their proposed solutions represents some of the most reactionary of their thinking.

Loury and the other Black conservatives insist "self help" is the only viable solution to Black dilemmas. They argue we have to rely on ourselves because, as Loury states referring to Booker T. Washington, "[Washington] understood that when the effect of past oppression has been to leave people in a diminished state, the attainment of true equality with their former oppressor cannot much depend on his generosity but must ultimately derive from an elevation of their selves above the state of diminishment."

In addition, Loury and others have developed the profoundly subversive notion, as described by Adolph Reed, that "it is somehow illegitimate for black citizens to view government action and public policy as vehicles for egalitarian redress." Unlike all other American citizens, African Americans, according to Black conservatives, must win white approval by proving ourselves worthy of the rights of citizenship.

"The progress that must now be sought is that of achieving respect, the equality of standing in the eyes of one's political peers, of worthiness as subjects of national concern," Loury argues. Loury frequently acknowledges his intellectual debt to Booker T. Washington's controversial philosophy. He concedes Washington's approach may not have been entirely appropriate for the political and social contexts of his time, but Loury firmly believes the Washington approach is relevant in the post–civil rights era. "The point on which Booker T. Washington was clear, and his critics seem not to be, is that progress of the kind described above must be earned, it cannot be demanded."

Consistent with their belief in the superiority of the Black middle class, Black conservatives argue that instead of relying on government programs and civil rights legislation, middle class Blacks should make economic investments in Black communities, Blacks should support Black businesses, and most important, the Black middle class needs to teach poor African Americans proper behavior and values. This self-help language, cloaked as it is in Black cultural nationalist rhetoric, has been among the most warmly received of the Black conservative messages in the African American community.

This is not surprising. First of all, self help literally defines how African Americans have managed to survive slavery, Reconstruction, and a series of trials and travails right up through the present day. Black conservatives and those praising them on this point sound as though African American history has not always included such famous proponents and practitioners of self help as Martin Delaney, Edward Blyden and Alexander Crummel, Marcus Garvey, the Nation of Islam, the Black Panthers, Jesse Jackson's Operation PUSH, and the thousands of Black women's clubs, Black Greek and professional associations and Black church-based organizations, among others. But African Americans' long heritage of self-help activities has tended to see self help as a supplement to, not a replacement for, deserved government services and full employment at family-sustaining wages.

In addition to its historical resonance for African Americans, the Black conservative promotion of self help flatters the Black middle class, casting it as the salvation for poor African Americans. It is noteworthy that even some liberal and progressive middle class Blacks have endorsed the Black conservatives' "culture of poverty" analysis and their call for self help to address the problem.

What is missed about Black conservatives' self-help advocacy is that, unlike the cultural Black nationalist tradition whose rhetoric they borrow, theirs is neither an organic, collective model of self help, nor one intended to enhance Black unity and Black cultural integrity. It is based on a savage individualism, advocating a laissez-faire formula for Black progress through the commitment of individual Blacks to economic wealth and cultural assimilation.

As stated by Shelby Steele: "The middle class values by which we [the Black middle class] were raised—the work ethic, the importance of education, the value of property ownership, of respectability, of 'getting ahead,' of stable family life, of initiative, of self reliance, *et cetera*—are, in themselves, raceless and even assimilationist. They urge us toward participation in the American mainstream, toward integration, toward a strong identification with the society, and toward the entire constellation of qualities that are implied in the word individualism."

Steele's comments illustrate another subversive aspect of Black conservatives' proposed solutions—the call to subsume our racial identity and to forgo collective racial action in favor of individualistic pursuits and a nationalistic American identity. Black conservatives issued this call during the 1980s, at a time when overt racist (and frequently violent) attacks on Blacks were at a post–civil rights era high, when the national political leadership of the country implicitly signaled its approval of racist attitudes, and when government and corporate policies were decimating poor and middle class African Americans alike with last hired/first fired policies. Given the political climate of the 1980s, Black conservatives were calling for no less than Black acquiescence and appeasement in their own oppression.

BLACK CONSERVATIVES' TIES TO WHITE CONSERVATIVES

Black conservatives are few in number, with few exceptions have no name recognition in the African American community, have little to no institutional base in our community, have no significant Black following, and no Black constituency. Indeed Black conservatives' highest visibility is in the white, not the Black community. It is due primarily to their ties to white conservative institutions that Black conservatives have come to be viewed as spokespersons for the race, despite lacking a base in the African American community. Conservative think tanks such as the Hoover Institution on War, Revolution, and Peace, the American Enterprise Institute and the Heritage Foundation (which has even implemented a minority outreach program), and conservative foundations such as the Olin Foundation, the Scaife Foundation, and the Bradley Foundation sponsor Black conservatives in numerous ways.

White conservative institutions award Black conservatives fellowships, consultant work, directorships, and staff positions. They also provide public relations services which get Black conservatives television and radio appearances, help get editorials, opinion pieces, and articles by Black conservatives into mainstream, even liberal, newspapers and magazines, publish articles and books by Black conservatives, and sponsor workshops and conferences by and for Black conservatives.

Conservative and neoconservative publications such as *The Wall Street Journal, Human Events, The Washington Times, Commentary, The Public Interest, The National Interest, American Scholar,* and *The New Republic* have played a major role in promoting Black conservatives' visibility, publishing articles by and about them. And finally, the Republican Party, especially during the years of the Reagan Administration but also during the Bush Administration, rewarded Black conservatives with high-visibility government appointments and with financing for Black conservative electoral campaigns.

The Institute of Contemporary Studies, a conservative research organization established by former aides to Ronald Reagan after Reagan left the statehouse in Sacramento, sponsored the first conference of Black neoconservatives in San Francisco in December 1980. Called The Fairmont Conference, it attracted about 125 conservative Black lawyers, physicians, dentists, ivy league professors, and commentators. It remains the best-known gathering of Black conservative thinkers and policy makers.

A review of prominent Black conservatives' careers reveals the extent to which they have benefited from their corporately funded presence in white conservative foundations, think tanks, and publications.

Thomas Sowell is a senior fellow at the conservative Palo Alto think tank, The Hoover Institution on War, Revolution, and Peace. Sowell is the most prolific of the Black conservative intellectuals; his fourteen books have been widely reviewed in conservative and mainstream publications alike. Conservative publications such as *Commentary, The American Spectator, Human Events, The Wall Street Journal, Barron's,* and *Businessweek* consistently provide the most glowing reviews. Articles by and/or about Sowell have appeared in numerous mainstream publications such as *Time, Newsweek, The Washington Post,* and *The New York Times,* among others.

When Sowell decided in 1981 to start a (short-lived) organization explicitly intended to counter the NAACP, the Black Alternatives Association, Inc., he reportedly received immediate pledges totaling $1,000,000 from conservative foundations and corporations.

Glenn Loury's reputation and influence rest on only one book and a series of articles that have appeared in most of the major mainstream publications, as well as the conservative *Wall Street Journal, Commentary,* and *The Public Interest.* The Heritage Foundation published one of his best known essays, "Who Speaks for American Blacks," as a monograph in *A Conservative Agenda for America's Blacks.* Boston University's rightist President John Silber hired Loury when Loury left Harvard University's Kennedy School of Government.

Robert Woodson has served in several capacities at the American Enterprise Institute. Woodson is also an adviser for the Madison Group, a loose affiliation of conservative state-level think tanks, launched in 1986 by the American Legislative Exchange Council or ALEC. ALEC is an association of approximately 2,400 conservative state legislators and is housed in the Heritage Foundation's headquarters in Washington, D.C. The conservative John M. Olin Foundation gave $25,000 to Woodson's National Center for Neighborhood Enterprise. Woodson's 1987 book, *Breaking the Poverty Cycle: Private Sector Alternatives to the Welfare State,* was published by the conservative National Center for Policy Analysis in Dallas, then reissued in 1989 by the conservative Commonwealth Foundation, on whose board he sits.

Walter Williams is the John M. Olin Distinguished Professor of Economics at George Mason University, has been a fellow at the Hoover Institution and at the Heritage Foundation, and received funding for one of his books from the Scaife Foundation.

The importance of these ties is not white conservative patronage *per se*. Black liberals benefit from similar ties to liberal institutions. A critical intellectual difference, however, is that Black liberals' analyses and policy ideas originated in their experiences in the Civil Rights and Black Power movements, movements that emerged from the African American community. Black liberals' analyses, limited though they are, continue to be shaped by their Black constituents, who help fund civil rights organizations and elect them to office. It is important to question the implications of the fact that Black conservatives' arguments originate in white conservatives' arguments, and that Black conservatives are in no way answerable to a Black constituency.

The historical distinction between white liberals and white conservatives is also a critical one. White liberal patrons and allies have historically allied themselves with, not against, Black interests. During the civil rights struggles, the only place white conservatives could be found was implicitly or explicitly beside Bull Connor, Strom Thurmond, Lester Maddox, and George Wallace. The white conservatives with whom Black conservatives are allied tried to obstruct the very civil rights legislation which even Black conservatives concede was necessary to create what they insist is now a largely discrimination-free America.

Today Black conservatives belong to a Republican Party thoroughly tainted by racism, whose leadership openly pursues a "southern strategy," employing racially polarizing tactics. Ironically, even today white conservatives remain ambivalent over the desirability of attracting more Blacks to conservative causes and to the Republican Party. Those favoring outreach to Blacks and other minorities have various motives. Pragmatic Republican strategists want to capture at least some of the solid Black support for the Democratic Party. Further, many conservatives recognize that sometime in the 21st century a majority of the U.S. population will be people of color. Given the historical role played by the traditionally politically liberal African American community as a catalyst for change, many mainstream white conservatives believe conservatism must become more inclusive if it is to survive.

Additionally, many Jewish conservatives seek an alliance with Black conservatives, who represent a sector within the African American community that will unite with them in support of Israel. The result is to diminish African American support for Palestinian and Arab causes and the related criticism of military ties between Israel and South Africa.

The more extreme conservatism of Patrick Buchanan and the extreme right wing of the Republican Party is, however, explicitly racialist. As Margaret Quigley and Chip Berlet detailed in the December 1992 issue of *The Public Eye*, the right has always seen the African-American civil rights movement as part of a secular humanist plot to impose communism on the United States. This faction identifies sexual licentiousness and "primitive" African American music with subversion.

Patrick Buchanan wrote a well-known column titled "GOP Vote Search Should Bypass Ghetto" in which he argued that Blacks have been grossly ungrateful for efforts already made on their behalf by Republicans, who had already done more than enough to obtain their support.

It says much about his willingness to "sleep with the enemy" that, even after this notorious column and after Buchanan's outspoken racism during his 1992 run for the Republican Party's presidential nomination, Thomas Sowell could still write in a 1992 column: "If and when he [Buchanan] becomes a viable candidate on his own, perhaps in 1996, that will be time enough to start scrutinizing his views and policy proposals on a whole range of issues."

As crucial as white conservative patronage has been to the careers and visibility of Black conservatives, it should not be viewed as their sole support. Mainstream, liberal, and even progressive institutions also have promoted them to their present-day status and levels of influence.

Robert Woodson's most notable award came from the moderately liberal MacArthur Foundation, which awarded him a $320,000 "genius" grant in 1990. Walter Williams is a featured commentator on National Public Radio's "All Things Considered." Both Williams and Sowell are syndicated columnists. Shelby Steele produced and hosted a public television documentary on Bensonhurst in 1990. Articles by or about Sowell, Loury, Steele, and Carter appear regularly in such established outlets as *The New York Times,* the *Boston Globe, Dissent, Time,* and *Newsweek.* Shelby Steele, Glenn Loury, and Tony Brown were among those featured in the January/February and the March/April 1993 issues of *Mother Jones* magazine, in a two-part article on urban poverty.

It is similarly noteworthy that while Black conservatives received an exceptional amount of publicity throughout the 1980's, the most intellectually sophisticated and nuanced group of African American scholars and theorists—progressives such as bell hooks, Angela Davis, June Jordan, Manning Marable, Adolph Reed, and Cornel West—received next to none.

Between January 1980 and August 1991 three prominent newspapers, *The New York Times, The Washington Post,* and *The Philadelphia Inquirer,* published eleven op-eds, fourteen articles, and thirty reviews by or about Thomas Sowell, Shelby Steele, and Walter Williams. However during this same period, three prominent progressive African American scholars, bell hooks, Manning Marable, and Cornel West, had no op-eds, no articles and no stories by or about them in these same three newspapers.

This is, in part, a reflection of the conservatism that pervaded the political culture of the United States throughout the 1980's. But the question remains: How and why did a group of African Americans so unrepresentative of Black majority political opinion and so uninvolved in the affairs of the African American community come nonetheless to be anointed as race spokespeople, even by white institutions claiming to reflect liberal democratic ideals? From the perspective of the African American community, there is nothing democratic about the ascendancy of Blacks who demand that we acquiesce in fundamentally racist interpretations of who we are.

CONCLUSION

The principal complaint of most African Americans against Black conservatives, particularly the intellectuals featured here, is that they provide cover for policies that do grievous harm to Black people. But the potential harm inherent in Black conservatism is a danger to all Americans.

June Jordan has observed that problems which first appear in poor African American communities—substandard schools, AIDS, violent crime—always eventually appear in middle income white communities. At that point they leave the realm of the "culture of poverty" and become an "American problem."

The United States has never allowed full citizenship rights for all its citizens. It has never built a social culture devoid of racism, sexism, anti-Jewish bigotry, homophobia, or classism. Our economic system has never provided full employment at a sustainable wage. As a nation, we have never committed ourselves to providing as basic human rights a quality education for each and every child, universal high-quality health care, and a decent place to live for all people.

So long as the devastating inequities that characterize American society persist, and racism continues to exacerbate these inequities, there is absolutely no way to make meaningful, much less provable, statements correlating peoples' values with their socioeconomic status.

By tying poor African Americans' poverty to race and our supposed slavery-flawed culture, Black conservatives insult African Americans. They also divert attention from June Jordan's observation that Black problems inevitably become problems of the larger society. At some point, white Americans and middle income Americans in general are going to be forced to confront the fundamental problems caused by this country's severe maldistribution of resources and its intolerance of diversity. Black conservatives delay that confrontation and in so doing, they do the entire country a grave disservice.

By uncritically promoting Black conservatives, liberal and progressive institutions not only undermine their own stated principles, they exhibit a not-so-subtle form of racism. As Adolph Reed Jr. points out: Who would listen if the word "Italian" or "Jew" were substituted in Black conservatives' characterizations of African Americans? We should be clear that stereotyping and victim-blaming is not more respectable because it is done by a member of the group being demeaned.

32

Power Concedes Nothing Without a Demand

Building Multiracial Organizations with Direct Action

MARK TONEY

Even our friends said it couldn't be done. They said that we couldn't start a community group from scratch with no start-up funds, no connections with established local groups, and no big shots on our board. They said that we couldn't bring together Black, Latino, Asian, and white families in low-income neighborhoods to take strong action to confront big shots in their offices—and still get foundation support. Good thing we're so hard of hearing.

—Mattie L. Smith, Co-founder Direct Action for Rights and Equality, Providence, Rhode Island

In the 1980s, in an inner-city neighborhood on the poor side of Providence, Rhode Island, small children played in the streets, dodging the cars that raced by. Sometimes their parents would look over at the nearby abandoned city playground—overgrown with weeds, taken over by drug dealers, and full of broken equipment—and wonder why the city didn't fix it up. Everyone knew the answer, of course. Providence doesn't pay much attention to poor people—at least, not until they get organized.

In 1987, Direct Action for Rights and Equality, or DARE[1], organized families who lived near the playground to demand that the city of Providence renovate it for the neighborhood's young children. At its high point, a group of 75 parents and children carrying signs (and accompanied by the news media) marched into the private office of the Parks Commissioner. Preschool children chanted, "We want a tot lot, we want a tot lot." In the end, DARE forced the city to clean the playground, install new play equipment, and put in a fence. Eventually, the playground was renamed the "Mattie L. Smith Tot Lot" to honor the leader of DARE's campaign to improve neighborhood conditions in Providence.

DARE went on to replicate this campaign elsewhere in the city, organizing families who lived near abandoned playgrounds or vacant lots to take collective action by confronting city officials, either in their offices or in the "hot seat" at community meetings. Over the ensuing six or seven years, the tot lot campaign persuaded the city to build or renovate ten playgrounds in low-income Providence neighborhoods, as well as clean up over 200 vacant lots.

DARE's reputation and organizing success soon reached the point at which a simple phone call from the DARE office would be sufficient to get the city to clean up a vacant lot or repair a playground—after all, what city official likes to see 40 or 50 people crowding into his or her office unannounced, or wants to attend a community meeting of angry residents on a hot summer night? But DARE continues to organize families to take collective action to make demands of people in power, almost always using confrontational tactics.

DARE continues to use collective direct action as the primary tactic for winning community issues because of its commitment to transforming victims into victors, to forcing a redistribution of decisionmaking power and to building an organizational base of power for low-income Providence families. To DARE, simply having "a seat at the table" or "a voice" is not the same thing as exercising power. "Empowerment" is not something that staff organizers can carry around in their hip pockets to pass out to active members of their organization. The most effective way for a low-income person to become empowered is to see how people in power treat them differently when they are with a group of angry neighbors with clear demands.

According to DARE, a victory achieved by one person making a phone call is a victory for one individual. A victory achieved by 100 people who organize a public hearing and get a solid commitment from a public official is a collective victory. Through collective action, low-income families learn that their most potent weapon is their collective ability to disrupt the normal course of business in a disciplined, organized fashion.

DARE, along with many other effective community organizations, has turned the tactic of confrontation with people in power into a tool for building organization, and thus the power of the community as a whole. More than simply a method of social justice organizing, it is a philosophy that undergirds how DARE builds its multiracial membership and how the group defines itself to the outside world.

The consistent use of confrontation has allowed DARE to articulate a new kind of politics in Providence, one that does not rely on calls for solidarity based on race, gender or sexuality, but instead shows how multiculturalism works in the most practical sense. The character of American society is such that it is hard to build organizations of low-income people by appealing solely to their class interests (although this seems to work very well for the rich). For DARE, the use of direct action—the philosophy of direct confrontation—is the glue that holds people together across the boundaries of race, language, gender, age, and all the rest.

Besides, nothing else wins victories and builds organizations like direct action. As community organizations, labor unions, civil rights groups, workers centers[2], women's organizations, AIDS activists, and every other historically oppressed group has found, direct action can get you what you want. Since its founding in 1986, DARE has used collective action to win improved benefits and working conditions for daycare providers, greater access to bilingual education for immigrant students, the restoration of key human services lost in budget-cutting, a moratorium on winter shut-offs from the utility company, and fresher food at local supermarkets.

MORE THAN GUTS

Building effective community organizations takes more than sheer determination, raw guts, and blind ambition. Unlike the little engine that could, many communities' best efforts to build lasting local groups to represent their common interests have been thwarted, often by internal conflicts such as racial divisions or disagreements over strategies and tactics, an unwillingness to make long-term organizational investments, weak membership and leadership development, and a lack of internal and external funding. While the past ten years have been especially difficult for emerging organizing projects, some of the groups that beat the odds have not only survived, but thrived, building powerful vehicles for their communities.

The recipe for DARE's success is a little like the stone soup recipe in which everyone puts in a little of something to create a meal for the entire community—a dollop of membership dues, a bunch of organizing campaigns, a helping of leadership development, and a measure of grassroots fundraising, along with a dash of technical assistance, a touch of strategic planning, and a healthy dose of collective vision. But the three key ingredients that are the meat and potatoes of the DARE soup are:

- Building a multiracial organization (primarily of women), reflecting the racial diversity within the local low-income neighborhoods;
- Using confrontation through direct action as the primary form of collective activity to win demands from "targets";[3]
- Developing a comprehensive, though informal, marketing plan to guide everything the organization does.

These three ingredients have been essential during the past ten years, helping DARE grow from a group of five community residents sitting around a kitchen table with little more than a vision into a powerful community organization with experienced leadership, skilled staff, and a diverse membership committed to working and winning improvements in a broad array of neighborhood conditions. Since 1986, DARE has recruited over 800 low-income families in communities of color in Rhode Island to take collective action on issues that affect their everyday lives, increased its annual budget to $300,000, and conducted a successful capital campaign to purchase and renovate a building that serves as headquarters for DARE's organizing activities.

POWER THROUGH DIVERSITY

Much of DARE's organizational strength and legitimacy comes from its multiracial composition, achieved through years of cultivating a membership, board, and staff to reflect the racial diversity within low-income families in Providence.

When DARE goes to make demands on the city or on local private businesses, the organization can truly claim to represent the community and is immune to attempts to pit one part of the community against another, a tactic at which city administrations are especially adept.

While many organizations in DARE's environment viewed race as essentially a bipolar Black/white issue, DARE leaders wanted to include the large Latino population in Providence, as well as the smaller Southeast Asian population. While DARE started out as a primarily Black organization with significant participation from low-income whites, its 1995 membership was about 55 percent Black, 30 percent Latino, 10 percent white, and 5 percent Asian—and 80 percent women. DARE's board of directors and staff composition closely corresponds to the racial and gender composition of its membership.

Simply wanting to diversify is generally not enough. In Providence, there are a few groups (outside of Latino-specific organizations) that have attempted to increase involvement from Latino communities with limited tactics that required limited resources. For example, a mailing or flyer is translated and printed in Spanish to invite Latino families to a community meeting. Latinos attending such meetings often found that the meetings were conducted in English with no translation or agendas in Spanish. Organizations willing to commit greater resources provided interpreters to welcome the participation of Spanish-speaking people at community meetings.

During DARE's first couple of years, it became clear that translated flyers and interpreters at membership meetings were not doing enough to increase DARE's Spanish-speaking members beyond a small number. Perhaps the most troubling problem was that even with interpreters, most Latino members would listen attentively, but would seldom speak at meetings. At a strategy session to discuss this problem, Latino leaders suggested that DARE develop a membership committee whose explicit goal would be to increase Latino membership in DARE. This committee would develop organizing campaigns around priority issues in the Latino community, conduct all its meetings in Spanish, and elect a representative to the DARE board of directors. Thus Comité Latino was founded.

As a membership committee, Comité Latino conducted monthly meetings and developed its own organizing campaigns to galvanize and recruit local Latino families. To promote multiracial solidarity, Black and Anglo DARE members were encouraged to attend activities organized by Comité Latino, and vice versa. One of the Comité Latino campaigns, the Bilingual Education Campaign, organized the first large conference in Providence at which low-income Latino parents, as opposed to middle-class Latino professionals, developed plans to improve bilingual education and English as a Second Language programs (ESL). Within three years, the campaign forced the school department to initiate bilingual/ESL programs in all college-bound public schools and education programs, increase parents' rights to choose a bilingual, ESL, or mainstream program for their children, and contribute to DARE's publication of the first parent's guide to bilingual/ESL programs in seven languages.

Perhaps the most significant progress occurred in the fall of 1993 with the purchase of multi-channel translating machines that permit simultaneous translations in multiple languages. Using these machines significantly increased the involvement of Spanish-speaking members in general DARE meetings, and also facilitated the participation of members who spoke Hmong or Cambodian. In 1994, DARE Latino leaders held a series of discussions and presented the DARE board with a proposal, which was accepted, to dissolve Comité Latino because it had met its goals of transforming DARE into a multiracial and multilingual organization. By then, over 150 Latino families had become members of DARE, monthly membership meeting attendees were usually one-third Latino, and two Latinos served on the DARE board, in addition to the Comité Latino representative.

The first lesson from DARE's experience is that it takes a considerable investment of financial resources, staff time, and strategic planning to build a multiracial organization. It took DARE five years and over $100,000 to build significant Latino membership and participation. The second is that a comprehensive strategy that incorporates the translation of all printed materials, interpretation at meetings, and the formation of an independent development committee is necessary to overcome cultural, linguistic, and physical barriers to multiracial alliances. Finally, it is critical that a cross-fertilization and exchange take place between the independent language committee and the rest of the organization to avoid the risk that the committee simply spin off and form its own organization. At DARE, leaders kept making it clear that an issue for Latino parents was an issue for all parents, and that all DARE parents needed to show support.

PRESSURING THE TARGET

Very few organizations in South Providence use direct action as a strategy to achieve change because of their different theoretical assumptions about how people in power make decisions. Community-based organizations usually ascribe to one of three theories about what motivates people in positions of power to respond to community demands:

- Morality. People in power evaluate policies on the basis of their sense of right and wrong or out of a moral obligation to society. *We will build your playground because kids in low-income neighborhoods should have the same services as kids in high-income neighborhoods.*
- Rationality. People in power evaluate the effectiveness and efficiency of policies to reach stated goals and measure the cost/benefit to society. *We will build your playground because keeping kids off the streets reduces the chances that they will get hit by cars or join gangs.*
- Organizational self-interest. *People in power evaluate policies based on whether they will make their institution look good or bad. We will build your playground because it will eliminate the negative media coverage and disruptive unannounced visits from angry residents.*

These different assumptions about how people in power make decisions influenced the strategic approaches that organizations would advocate in coalition work with DARE. Organizations that assumed that morality guided decisionmaking would approach targets with a friendly attitude, follow an institutional chain of command, and focus on the art of persuasion with appeals to moral character.

Organizations that assumed that rationality guided decisionmaking would approach targets with a civil attitude, providing fact sheets, charts, and calculations showing them how much they could save in the long run, if they but invested a little in the short run. DARE would approach targets with a confrontational attitude, believing that the most effective way to affect the behavior of people in power is to make the cost of doing business as usual greater than the cost of doing business the way DARE wants it done.

A key form of DARE's direct action is the accountability session, in which the target is invited to a meeting at a time and place chosen by DARE, and confronted with a list of demands. For example, at one accountability session, each DARE member dumped a piece of trash from abandoned lots near their homes on the table in front of the Director of Public Works. The city responded by cleaning up 75 vacant lots within six weeks.

While the target of an accountability session squirms on the hot seat, DARE members and local reporters wait for the response. Any hedging by the target is met by chants of "yes or no, yes or no!"—quite an exchange and different from the usual ones between low-income people and powerful local politicians, businesspeople, and bureaucrats! DARE was often accused of not being "nice" or "polite," but members figured out pretty quickly that being nice got them nothing when dealing with the representatives of power. While people might not like DARE's militancy, they respected it.

Another example of DARE's direct action is its campaign to force Almacs, the largest supermarket chain in Rhode Island, to upgrade their Elmwood Avenue store. For years, people had complained that the Elmwood Almacs, the only Almacs located in Providence's low-income neighborhoods, was selling rotten meat and produce, was filthy, and treated customers rudely. Involving people in collective actions was extremely effective in pressuring Almacs to make rapid changes to the store.

On July 3, 1992, a DARE press conference drew 40 neighborhood presidents and representatives from the news media. At the press conference, DARE put its reputation on the line with a bold public accusation that Almacs was selling spoiled meat. Almacs' initial response was to deny the accusation and counterattack, calling the action a "sucker punch," saying that some of the charges "border on libelous," and that "none of these conditions really exist."[4] Later that same day, after receiving a copy of DARE's press release, the Health Department conducted a surprise inspection of the Elmwood Almacs, and ordered them to throw out 273 items of food due to improper storage and spoilage, including "green meat."[5] Immediately after the press conference, twenty-five DARE members conducted an action at Almacs corporate headquarters in East Providence. The members charged into the office and refused to leave without talking to the president. By demanding to speak to Almacs President/CEO Greg Mays, and by using the traditional tactics of collective disruptive behavior, DARE commanded the attention of Almacs officials, who agreed to attend a DARE community hearing scheduled for July 15.

On July 15, 80 people attended DARE's community hearing on Almacs. For three hours, community residents, small business owners, local elected officials, and others complained about unsanitary conditions at the Elmwood Almacs. By the end of the meeting, Almacs officials agreed to meet eleven of DARE's fourteen original demands.[6] Within four weeks, the roof, floor, lighting, refrigerators, and freezers had been upgraded; the general manager, meat manager, and produce manager were replaced; and multilingual signs were installed throughout the store.

Thus, in less than two weeks, with three well-organized actions, a small community organization transformed the behavior of a corporation with $500 million in annual sales. Almacs made a 180 degree turn from denial and counterattack to actively seeking solutions and cooperating with community organizations to clean up their Elmwood Avenue store.

By the time the campaign was over, Almacs had made far more concessions than DARE had originally asked for—such as conducting major interior and exterior renovations, hiring a new management team, and establishing a consumer advisory committee with DARE representation.[7] DARE received heavy coverage in television, radio, and print media, building the group's reputation as fearless and successful throughout the area, and forty-seven new families joined the organization that summer.

Direct action meets goals and also helps to build community organizations by involving members in leadership roles. New leaders emerge in the heat of confrontation. People get a sense of their own power in numbers, and the organization gains respect from members, targets, and the public. Finally, as members start to exercise power and leadership and see the concrete victories that result, a sense of enthusiasm and pride develops that allows members to transcend petty bigotries and prejudices that so frequently corrode relationships in our society and our organizations.

STRATEGIC MARKETING

A great deal of DARE's strength was built by developing a comprehensive strategic marketing plan that guided everything from how organizing campaigns were chosen and how the phone was answered to how relations with private funders and the media were cultivated. A deliberate marketing strategy enabled DARE to become a United Way partner agency, conduct a traditional capital campaign, and receive funding from sources that seldom fund community organizing—such as Masonic organizations, banks, and the news media. DARE did all this while still maintaining a militant reputation.

Developing deliberate marketing strategies among community organizations is virtually unheard of. The lack of coherent marketing strategies leads many community groups to adopt self-destructive behaviors and attitudes, such as the belief that begging for money is the most effective technique for fundraising. Who hasn't heard of an organization that threatens to cut back its services, or even to close down, if you don't immediately send them a check? Many people hold the belief that their organizations should look and act poor to reflect and express solidarity with low-income families who are the membership. Another common attitude among community organizations is that every penny has to be pinched until it screams.

At times money is tight and it simply isn't possible to do things the way you know they should be done. But DARE always took the view that the organization was going to be around for the long haul, that organizers were building a sophisticated, strategic, pro-active, and capable organization.

DARE leaders took a look around the political scene in the late 1980s and did not see any successful political organizations following the organizational internalization of poverty, which seems to guarantee that the group will remain small and ineffectual. DARE leaders asked themselves, How much sense does it really make to spend the time and expense of running to a copy shop several times a day instead of investing in a photocopier? In the long run, is a donated computer that is obsolete and nearly impossible to run really cheaper than paying for a modern computer system that meets your organizational needs? DARE decided to look and act like a dedicated professional organization. For example, DARE developed catchy names for organizing campaigns to communicate an image of innovation. A campaign with a catchy name is remembered and talked about by members, funders, and the media. DARE received much more support for its organizing against illegal dumping in vacant lots when it changed its campaign from Neighborhoods Now to Project GREEN (Grassroots Revival for the Environmental Empowerment of Neighborhoods). When the state proposed to eliminate dental care for disabled adults, DARE asked organizations to join the Bite Back Alliance for Dental Care, the slogan of which was: Bite back—while you still can. Perhaps the most successful name DARE used was for its campaign for multicultural education: Education = Multicultural Core Curriculum ($E = MC^2$).

DARE's standard stationery was printed on heavy cotton bond paper with custom color ink—the kind of stationery that a successful business might use. Flyers advertising meetings were always laser-printed and sharp-looking, and incorporated graphics. Newsletters were typeset, contained photographs, and recognized contributors, as well as members, for their support.

DARE developed a fiscally conservative long-range financial management strategy to communicate an image of fiscal responsibility and stability. Funders were thrilled to find out that DARE ran a budget surplus during every year of its existence—and staff members could feel more secure and focused because they didn't have to worry about being paid. DARE invested heavily in computer equipment and cutting-edge technology such as the translating machines. They also adopted a principle of making all organizational investments in cash (even the DARE building has no mortgage), as opposed to loans or leases, which gave members and funders confidence that the organization would not go out of business due to debt, a fate more than one community organization has suffered.

Strategic marketing can help community organizations expand the universe of people who support and contribute to their work far beyond the rather small world of organizational members and community activists. It is the little things that count. The things that DARE did on a day-to-day basis, such as send "thank you" letters to donors within two days, and tape an answering machine message that said "The folks at DARE, Direct Action for Rights and Equality, are out on the streets organizing for justice," are things that people remember.

The bottom line, however, is always the people and the power. Direct action organizing and a real commitment to building a multiracial membership make DARE unusual and account for its power in Providence. Creatively blending these elements with strategic marketing is the recipe for DARE's overall success and provides an effective model for any social justice organization to follow. Of course, these elements cannot by themselves build successful community organizations. Organizations must also incorporate a membership dues system, organizing campaigns that meet the needs of the community, persistent leadership development, effective grassroots fundraising activities, annual strategic planning sessions, and a commitment to building collective vision. But if we are ever going to get past the endless appeals for cross-racial political solidarity into a national movement for social and economic justice, some combination of direct action, multiracial organizing, and strategic marketing are important first steps.

NOTES

1. Not to be confused with the front for the Los Angeles Police Department known as Drug Abuse Resistance Education or D.A.R.E.

2. Meaning independent organizations of workers, often immigrants, that fight for the rights of the membership without forming a union. Examples include Asian Immigrant Workers Advocates in Oakland, California, and Black Workers for Justice in Rocky Mount, North Carolina.

3. A target in organizing terms is the person who can give you what you want, the one with the power to make a decision in your favor.

4. "Activists Representing Immigrants Protest Conditions at Almacs Store," *Providence Journal-Bulletin,* July 4, 1992.

5. *Retail Food Inspection Report,* Division of Food Protection and Sanitation, Rhode Island Department of Health, July 3, 1992.

6. "Almacs Agrees to DARE's Demands," *The Providence American,* August 1, 1992.

7. David Paulhus, Almacs Public Relations Director, Correspondence to DARE, August 25, 1992.

33

Privileged Polemics

White Antiracist Activists

EILEEN O'BRIEN

Malcolm [X] gave a speech and a white woman went up to him afterwards and said, "I really loved your speech and I loved what you said and I agree with what you believe and I want to help. How can I help? What can I do?" And he looked at her and said, "nothing!" and walked away. And then, years later, he was self-critical in the way that real revolutionaries are—sincere and blunt towards yourself like you would be towards someone else—and said, "I'm not proud of that answer. I should have talked to her about working in the white community." . . . The problem exists among white people.

—Steve, an antiracist activist

Luckily, there are individual non-black people who have divested of their racism. . . . We have yet to have a significant body of writing from these individuals that gives expression to how they have shifted attitudes and daily vigilantly resist becoming reinvested in white supremacy.

—bell hooks

In the wake of the recent and ongoing backlash against racial equality in the United States, it has become evident that whites of all backgrounds play a role in orchestrating the daily rituals of white racism that keep this hostile racial climate intact (Feagin and Vera 1995). From actions as blatant as cross-burnings, killings, and inflammatory racial remarks to the subtle messages of "you-don't-belong-here" directed at African Americans and other people of color throughout their daily existence, white Americans assist in keeping racism alive and well in this country. If Frederick Douglass was right in saying "power concedes nothing without demand," we might expect that this white racism has no hope of becoming eradicated, especially not by way of voluntary concessions by white Americans. Yet there is a considerable presence of antiracist white Americans who are doing just that. Although these individuals are the exception rather than the rule, it seems imperative that we begin to understand how it is that white Americans willingly divest themselves of racism. It is only by understanding the processes that these whites have undergone that we might be able to look to a day when more and more, and perhaps even all, white Americans will work toward ending racism.

When I use the term "white antiracist," I am speaking about an individual who actively works against racism in her or his daily life. This is considerably different from, although does not automatically exclude, those who would register as "unprejudiced" or "nonracist" on a survey about white racial attitudes. Although survey researchers have identified a slow but steady decline in white "racial prejudice" over the past several decades (e.g., Carmines and Champagne 1990; Schuman, Steeh, and Bobo 1985), it is not improbable, and is perhaps even likely, that these same whites whose prejudice has appeared to have decreased are also the ones who stand back and passively observe when racism goes on in their midst. These are people who have learned the socially desirable or so-called politically correct responses to such surveys but do little or nothing to interrogate their own racism and that of those around them. For example, a recent study demonstrates that, although more-educated whites were more likely to support integrated housing and schools on survey questions, those same whites were *least* likely to live in or send their children to school in such integrated settings (Emerson and Sikkink 1997). White antiracists, in contrast, are those who do not only answer a survey in a desirable manner but rather actively take on the task of challenging the racism perpetrated by other whites, as well as the unearned race privilege they are offered as whites in their daily lives. This obviously takes considerably more effort than answering a survey question in a politically correct fashion.

Although this considerable effort may seem too much of a chore for most whites to handle, the fact is that there are a handful of whites across the country who take on this challenge now. There are antiracist organizations with predominantly white memberships sprouting up all over the country, as well as individuals who are not organizationally affiliated but who prioritize antiracist work, as defined above, as a fundamental part of their lives. This study takes a look at these individuals and asks the questions (1) Who are they? (2) What do they do? (3) How do they think about race?

LITERATURE REVIEW

Lest the reader be fooled by the present study of contemporary white antiracists, it should be noted that such work on the part of white Americans extends as far back into our history as white racism itself. This is what Herbert Aptheker (1992) concluded in his historical review of the first two hundred years of white antiracism in the United States. Although these antiracist voices of protest have always been in the minority and have often been overlooked or downplayed by historians, the fact remains that they have been there nonetheless. Aptheker's work also provides information as to who antiracists are. He writes: "My study has persuaded me that the following generalizations are valid: (1) anti-racism is more common among so-called lower classes than among the so-called upper class; (2) anti-racism especially appears among people who have had significant experiences with people of African origin; and (3) anti-racism seems to be more common among women than men" (Aptheker 1992:xiv). Although Aptheker does not further theorize about why these whites are more prone to be antiracist than others, more recent work by Joe Feagin and Hernan Vera (1995) provides more of an answer to this question. Based on their own focus groups with white Americans and selected interviews done by their graduate students, the authors find that whites who have had "some personal experience with exploitation, discrimination or oppression are more likely than other whites to understand the situation of and empathize with African-Americans" (1995:175). The role of empathy is stressed by these authors as important for whites in coming to terms with racism. Thus, for the individuals in Aptheker's study, those whites who had experienced classism or sexism, as well as those who had important relationships with people of color, were in a better position to develop empathy with the victims of, and respond to, racism.

However, other work presented by Feagin and Vera (1995) challenges the notion that women were automatically more prone to being antiracist. Relying on the work of Hogan and Netzer, they find that "just being female did not necessarily increase understanding of racial oppression, although sometimes it did. But white women who were socially stigmatized in additional ways (for example, lesbians) were better able than other white women to empathize with the discrimination faced by African-Americans" (1995:176). Thus, white women who are doubly stigmatized in some way seem to be more likely to participate in antiracism than others. Further, Hogan and Netzer also come up with the concept of "approximating experiences" to describe the way in which people can draw upon their own or others' experiences to develop empathy with people of color and develop an antiracist awareness.

Jennifer Eichstedt (1997) extends this concept to her own interview data with white antiracist women, and she finds three types of approximating experiences. In addition to having relationships with people of color and experiencing stigmatization of being Jewish, Eichstedt's third approximating experience is unique to her study: having experienced sexual abuse or incest in their lives. This made these women more conscious of "abuses of power" and thus enabled them to more closely approximate the experience of racism, another abuse of power. Ruth Frankenberg (1993) also examines white antiracist women and adds "other routes to awareness of racism," including feminist networks, college campuses, and the influence of friends and family.

If little has been done in the way of investigating who white antiracists are, fewer still are the inquiries into what antiracists do. Aptheker's (1992) historical review of antiracist action demonstrated that it ranged from risking one's political reputation (by way of expressing one's opinion verbally) to facing imprisonment or even death (upon breaking the law to harbor fugitive slaves, for example). Feagin and Vera (1995) also observe a particular willingness to risk one's own livelihood in the course of taking antiracist action, as in the case of a woman who risks her job. (Also see Ignatiev and Garvey 1996.)

Another question that researchers of white antiracists have been interested in is the way(s) in which these individuals think about race. This question is so crucial because, as bell hooks (1995) has noted, the mainstay of white supremacy is keeping whiteness from being named or examined. Thus, the extent to which these whites name whiteness and locate it in a racist power structure is an important first step in dismantling racism itself. In fact, Frankenberg (1993) describes "race-cognizant" individuals as those who clearly identify whiteness as a position of privilege in a racial hierarchy, standing in direct contrast to "color- and power-evasive" individuals who profess to "ignore" race and hence racism along with it. Some of the race-cognizant women described in explicit terms their own passage out of color-"blindness" and into race cognizance (1993:157), using terms like "'awakening' and 'coming to' (as from unconsciousness or a coma) to describe their newfound perceptions about race and racism" (1993:160).

One important dimension of this race-cognizant discourse that Frankenberg (1993) mentions is the willingness to accept responsibility for racism as white people. The race-cognizant women in this study "insisted racism was something in which *they* had a part: 'my racism' was a phrase used as frequently by . . . these women as the claim that 'there is no difference' was made by color- and power-evasive women" (Frankenberg 1993:167). Similarly, Feagin and Vera (1995), relying on the work of Holly Hanson, note that white antiracists demonstrate a need to admit to their own racism and to constantly "self-criticize" in a constructive and ongoing manner. (Also see Eichstedt 1997.) Thus, as whites in a racist society, we should expect white antiracists to view themselves, like former alcoholics, as "recovering" racists and to be candid and up-front about their own racism.

METHODOLOGY

The data for this study were collected using an in-depth interview method. Snowball sampling was used to locate sixteen white antiracists in several communities, including a large city in the Midwest, one in the South, one in Canada, and one in New England, as well as two smaller college towns (one in the South and one in New England). About half of the respondents were members of antiracist organizations and half were not. The two organizations I have sampled from thus far are Anti-Racist Action (ARA), which has several chapters all over the country, and the People's Institute for Survival and Beyond, which is based out of New Orleans. There are nine women and six men in the sample who are from their early twenties to sixties.

The interviews were "active" as all interviews are—that is, they involved active meaning-making on the part of both myself as the interviewer and the respondent. As such, I did not approach my respondents as "vessels of knowledge" that could be "contaminated" by introducing them to the ideas of other respondents (Holstein and Gubrium 1995:8). In fact, they had *no problem* letting me know if they did not agree with certain things I had told them that other respondents had previously said. These respondents were very interested in expressing their own views, sometimes reformulating their thoughts on antiracism as they went along, and often thanking me afterward for the opportunity to clarify their own thought processes on these issues with someone else who understood. I should add here that I made no secret of identifying as a white antiracist myself. My background knowledge facilitated the flow of the interviews and even contributed to the many hours of off-tape conversation long after the interviews (which lasted anywhere from forty minutes to a little over two hours) were over.

RESULTS

Who Are They?

The respondents in my study had similarities with as well as differences from white antiracists in previous literature. In terms of social class I found, contrary to Aptheker (1992), that my respondents were spread across class in terms of education and household income. With respect to highest level of education attained, four had some graduate work, two had an undergraduate degree, two had one to three years of college, and two had a high school degree. As far as household income went, four had less than $21,000, two had $21,000–$30,000, two had $31,000–$40,000, one had over $71,000, and one was unknown.

Like Feagin and Vera (1995), I found that a majority of the white women in my sample (four out of six) were "doubly stigmatized" in some way. One was bisexual, one was lesbian, one was Jewish (her parents were from Yemen), and one had previously been involved in both lesbian and heterosexual relationships. As Claire put it, "I could never experience the pain and the . . . intimidation that an African American person [would face]. . . . The closest I've ever come to that myself is like, I'm bisexual myself, and I've gotten a lot of intimidation from people like that and I've had a lot of pain." Although, I found some support for the idea of developing empathy through approximating experiences, it was not enough *just* to have relationships with people of color, or *just* to be a lesbian/bisexual. Tracing the life stories of how they saw themselves coming to an antiracist awareness, I observe a sort of "two-pronged" awareness occurring with many of the respondents. In other words, one experience "planted the seed," so to speak, followed up by another experience that allowed that seed to take root. For example, Mike, an elementary school teacher in his thirties, had become aware of racial inequality through his experiences with the children of color he taught in the inner city but did not see himself as an active antiracist until he took a People's Institute Undoing Racism workshop. Similarly, two different women in the sample (Angela and Lori) were involved in interracial relationships while in high school, which heightened their awareness, but neither of them saw themselves as antiracist until they developed a sense of institutionalized racism in an academic environment—Angela through sociology and Lori through women's studies. Additionally, Lori also attributed coming out as a lesbian (additional stigmatization) as a part of her process.

Others also look back to early childhood experiences as the first "prong" of their two-pronged awareness. Betty, in her sixties, attributed some of her awareness to a grandfather who was a minister to black churches and who educated her when she was very young about black history (pretty amazing for Jim Crow days!). She then sees her friendships with people of color as a way she became further aware of atrocities and willing to act.

Men seem less likely to fall into the "approximating experiences" idea. According to my own work, the *generation* that these men are from, more than anything else, seems to affect how they became aware. Men in their thirties did tend to have some sort of approximating experience (e.g., Mike, above) but not necessarily two-pronged. Travis remembers his mother dating a black man and the resistance that they faced as a family. Scott defended the lone black boy in junior high in a fight against some big bullies—who happened to be his football buddies. From that point on he was ostracized, his football career went downhill, and he began to seek out the companionship of people of color throughout his life, including his wife, who is Mexican.

All three men in their forties had essentially the same story of how they became involved. They did not talk about relationships with people of color, but rather anti–Vietnam War activism and other leftist causes that made them aware of racism. For example, Steve said:

> So they took working-class kids [because of the student deferment], and there was a much larger percentage of non-white people who fought in the Vietnam War than of the white young people. . . . Anything I say should not be taken to be a knock on white people, I am one, I love 'em, my parents are white people, my children are all white kids, I love 'em very much—but . . . we can still, having said that, say—recognize the fact that, by and large, black folks have gotten the wrong end of the stick for a long time, and it's not even that hard to prove. So the Vietnam War was an example of it.

Steve, along with the two other men in their forties, tended to see antiracism as just one of the axes of activism in which they were involved (in addition to anti-sexism/feminism, the peace movement, etc.). Similarly, Jason, the only man in his twenties I have spoken with so far, did not speak of relationships with people of color. He says he became antiracist largely through joining an antiracist group. His motivation to join it was simply that it seemed like "basically the best way to do the right thing, in my mind."

What Do They Do?

As previous research shows, white antiracists show a willingness to take risks and sacrifice their white privilege in certain situations. A couple of respondents were articulate about this process. Said Scott, "Being white and being antiracist is to, in a lot of ways, cut yourself off from that; in a lot of ways, you aren't part of the good ol' boy network anymore 'cause a lot of these friends that you knew are a part of this good ol' boy social club network."

Similarly, in Angela's words:

> Maybe even a white person is trying to give you privilege and you aren't taking it, and they're looking at you like, "What's wrong with you? We're white, aren't we? What's going on? Why aren't you joining into, like, accepting what I'm trying to give you here?" . . . It's like we've got to have this common front against outsiders, against black people, and if you don't, then I'm going to cut you off too, if you've made the choice to be with him [an African American] then you're cut off.

Clearly, these respondents know what it is like to reject white privilege, understanding the meaning of what they are doing in terms of the implications for the racial power structure. They also recognize that whites will be willing to pose sanctions for their "treason"-like behavior, thus implying consequences for their actions.

The most common such consequence that appeared among my sample was loss of friends. Most did not lament this but instead shrugged it off as a necessary sacrifice for the cause. Scott says that after he defended the lone black boy in his school from a racist attack perpetrated by his football team buddies, his friends gave him

> that kind of reaction, "why don't you stick to your own kind?" . . . and they started to dissociate themselves from me because I was not "one of them" anymore. I wasn't part of the gang anymore, and you could see that in the interaction, even playing football. . . . I was kind of ostracized from them but I really didn't care because I thought that was a bunch of bullshit basically.

There were a couple of fortunate people in the bunch—Kristin claimed she had not lost any friends because "I wouldn't be friends with them in the first place probably," and Steve, another longtime radical, proclaimed, "No, I've been the luckiest antiracist you've ever met." So generally speaking, although most had lost friends when they became antiracists, they viewed it as par for the course.

A few of my respondents reported more serious consequences due to their antiracist actions. Betty, a retired newspaper reporter, who had been arrested and jailed during the march on Selma, had repeated complications on the job due to her antiracism: "The new publisher came in . . . and he said we should have more coverage on the black community, and I got assigned to do it. And so I wrote it like it is. And I quoted black people on the racism that made it necessary to set up programs of one kind or the other and my editors hated me, I mean, they hated me! They were rednecks, real rednecks."

Of another job, she commented:

> I wrote a story about health care, what the blacks were getting and not getting in [name] County, and I included the fact that the local hospital wasn't serving any black people. Because we also complained to Washington after that happened and they sent somebody in, and the hospital straightened up. But anyway, I got fired. . . . It turned out the publisher was on the hospital board.

Because of her community actions, Betty had actually had to move continually just to be able to find a job.

Although these were consequences suffered during the civil rights era, younger respondents reported more recent dangers of being a white antiracist. Said Claire, "I have friends who are pretty much marked by hate groups, who could lose their lives by not being careful." Lori suffered death threats as a result of one antiracist action protesting a fraternity that was originally started as "the academic arm of the KKK":

> We were going to hang signs that said . . . "The Confederate Flag: 400 Years of Oppression or a [frat name] Tradition? You Decide." And we hung them up all over campus one night when everyone was asleep. . . . Like an idiot, I wrote, "for more information, contact [her name]" [laughs]. And I wrote my number on it, right?! And my P.O. Box, so of course, what do I get? Millions of harassing phone calls, and [frat

name]'s telling me they're going to sue me for defamation! And I'm like, well, it's true, it was their symbol! I don't know what they thought they were going to sue me for, but so I had all these people like calling me up, and all these people leaving me notes in my mailbox telling me I was going to die and I started getting death threats and stuff, whatever, people saying they were going to burn a cross and shoot me.

Lori ended up moving home and finishing her degree by taking classes at home and transferring them over because of the issue of her safety on campus. Again, even with these more serious consequences, respondents preferred not to dwell on them, and probing was often necessary to find out more about these high-risk situations.

Privileged Polemics

Taking into account the risks and sacrifices of their position, these respondents overwhelmingly saw their position as a privileged one, particularly in relationship to how vocal they could be about challenging racism. They repeatedly saw themselves as more able to challenge racism without the fear of repercussions that people of color would face. As a result, several of my respondents professed an unrelenting creed of constantly challenging the racism they observed in their lives:

> I won't let it [racism] just pass by me. . . . It's real important to me to not let things that are said and done slip by me. (Kristin)

> How do I deal with it [white racism]? I tell them I don't agree! I tell them what I think of what they said and that I think it's really screwed up and that they need to examine their own thinking about that subject and that there are other ways of thinking about it and that maybe they've been taught something all their lives and need to reexamine. (Lori)

This posture on confronting racism stands in direct contrast to the African-American respondents quoted in Feagin and Sikes (1994), who stated that they gave an incident a great amount of deliberation and reevaluation before responding, if they responded at all, so as not to confirm the stereotype of paranoid and overreacting blacks. Thus, whites stand in a particularly advantaged position to challenge white racism and be heard and to engage in what I call privileged polemics. My respondents were significantly aware of this position:

> You still have privilege and people will listen . . . like a white person being antiracist or a man being antisexist—then it's considered sort of validated and the voice of authority, whereas if a person of color expresses an antiracist opinion, they're just being overly sensitive. So, I would say that's one big difference is that people will listen to me more. (Lori)

> And I think too that the reason that white antiracists may do the things that they do is because I think that in a lot of ways they won't be subjected to a lot of the same kinds of things that African Americans do. If you're an African American and you're

> involved in an antiracist rally and you hit a police officer, the trial's going to be biased from the start. I think there's a difference there as far as tactics go. (Claire)

> I'm coming from a privileged position. And in my privileged position I can take more risks than a person of color who is antiracist. (Kristin)

In addition, Scott reports repeated conflicts with his Mexican wife over whether or not she should confront the racism she experiences and acknowledges that he is more confrontational than she because he has less to lose in doing so.

Although practice of privileged polemics was the norm among my respondents, there was one notable exception. Steve shared this point of view:

> I am more skilled as a revolutionary now than I was when I believed that every time somebody said "nigger" I had to throw a fit. I do not have to throw a fit. I don't have to do anything, except whatever is the most effective thing right then to get them closer to fixing it. . . . We have to get people's ideas to change. And ranting sometimes pushes them the other way [to being more racist instead of less so].

His response sounds more like that of an African American from Feagin and Sikes's (1994) study than most of the other whites in my study. Interestingly, Steve is the one (quoted earlier) who also says he is "the luckiest antiracist you've ever met" in terms of not facing many serious consequences for his actions. However, the divergent methods of addressing racism that characterize most white antiracists could be one reason why white and black antiracists, for the most part, work separately.

How Do They Think About Race?

The respondents who discussed their relatively privileged position in terms of action tactics were race cognizant because they recognized the power they had as whites relative to people of color in a racist society. When I asked them the meaning of whiteness, they acknowledged this:

> To be white is to be part of the race that is in power. . . . To be white is to be part of the group that is in charge. . . . To be white in America is to have the upper hand. . . . [Some white people] have the audacity and the ability to say, "Oh well, affirmative action, it's preferential." The system the way it stands now, you get your preference when you're white. (Scott)

> Just in a word would be . . . easy! . . . to be able to be oblivious to a whole lot of things unless you really seek it out and want to know . . . not having to dress up nice to go into a store, being able to look like a bum and expect nobody to follow you around while you're in there. . . . I can expect not to be bothered, I can expect when a policeman pulls me over, he will be polite to me. There's so many things you can expect to have just because you're white. (Angela)

These respondents, then, clearly take a step toward dismantling white supremacy by naming whiteness and the power and privilege associated with it.

Some respondents, however, also saw whiteness as being mediated by a number of other factors. Ani, a Jewish respondent, described her experience as being "white but not quite white" because of her ethnicity. In addition, being a woman mediates what being white is for some respondents:

> I can expect to be considered to be fairly intelligent until I show myself not to be—except for the fact that there's the woman thing involved too. (Angela)

> It means different things to be a white male and a white female in America. . . . So, in general it means privileged institutionalized power, but it means it in very different ways for different people. And it can mean, like, power for white men, whereas it can mean power through white men, for white women, I think. So it's hard. Does it really mean power for white women? In ways it does, but it's different. (Lori)

In addition, some respondents saw class as a mediating factor. Finally, Steve thought it was very important to get away from thinking about race as a privilege:

> Racism is not good for most white people. It's good for a few people, most of whom are white. Still doesn't mean that white people on average don't do better than black people in almost every circumstance [because] they do, 'cause of this institution that's put on everybody. But seeing most white people as victims of it as well is more accurate than to emphasize the privilege element of white racism in the United States.

Evidently, these whites have clearly given a lot of thought to their whiteness. They acknowledge the power and privilege inherent in it, as well as its varying dimensions, and the need to do away with its precarious position if the goal of racial equality is to be truly realized.

Organizational Culture

There were a minority of respondents, however, that mixed elements of both color- and power-evasive discourse with race cognizance. Incidentally, these were all members of the antiracist action group. On being white:

> It's that section on your driver's license that says skin color—that's about all it is to me. I'm not proud, I'm not not-proud, I'm just—that's just the way I was born. When my page came up in the coloring book they whipped out the flesh-colored crayon. And I'm not green, I'm not blue, I'm not any other color, I'm the color I was given. [pause] I look at everybody as human beings first, and that's really all that needs to be looked at. (Jason)

> In terms of dating somebody of color, it really makes no difference if they're of color or not. I've dated, you know, people that are white, you know, I mean, I date—it doesn't matter, the color itself. . . . It's got nothin' to do with the pigment of your skin. . . . To me, to me, there's racists in every nationality, every color, every religion, there's racists everywhere. . . . It—the hatred itself that is—is the monster, the evil

> thing, right? . . . So I—there's hatred everywhere and there's good people everywhere. (Travis)

Based on the literature, we would not expect antiracists to turn a blind eye to issues of race in this manner. Frankenberg (1993) and others (e.g., Carr 1997) would argue that "colorblindness" is a way to ignore racism and thus perpetrate it. Notice in the first quote Jason's reference to the "flesh-colored crayon" that ignores the fact that Crayola's "flesh" corresponds only to white skin color. But how do we reconcile this with the active work they have been doing against racism and their willingness to acknowledge white privilege in many facets of their lives?

The explanation for the variation I find between different antiracists and how they think about race rests largely with the organizational culture to which they belong. Jaber Gubrium and James Holstein (1997) refer to organizational culture as the stock of knowledge that group members draw upon for their ways of interpreting their situation and the world around them. The ideologies of the members of antiracist groups were clearly influenced by the culture of the group to which they belonged. Jason and Travis (quoted directly above) both belong to Anti-Racist Action (ARA), a direct action group that has set up more than sixty independent chapters in cities all over the United States and Canada. Many of the members are young, often in their teens, and they are looking for a way to fight against racism and neo-Nazi organizing in their schools and communities. In direct response to such racist organizing, members of larger ARA chapters often travel with touring bands, setting up a table at every show where they distribute their literature (including ways to start your own local chapter) as well as signing people up for the mailing list for their free newsletter, *ARA News*.

As I worked one of these tables one night alongside Steve, an ARA organizer in his forties, a curious white boy approached the table tentatively, asking Steve if ARA also focused on "black racism." Expecting Steve to rattle off the sociological definition of "power + prejudice = racism" and to explain how only white people can be racist, I was surprised at what happened instead. Steve assured the boy that ARA was against hate in *any* form. But Steve also picked up a copy of *ARA News* to show him the preponderance of newspaper clippings collected that month on racist violence, all of it white-on-black. He mentioned that although ARA condemns hate in any form, they have noticed no black group that even approaches the equivalent of the KKK and other white groups with genocidal missions. This boy, who was not going to sign up on the mailing list before this exchange, then signed his name and picked up some information.

This story illustrates how crucial ARA feels it should *not* be hypocritical in claiming that one group can be racist and another cannot, because they want to get people's "foot in the door," so to speak ("hey, come join this fun organization!"), to then hear their larger message. Giving me numerous examples, Steve pointed out how many of these kids are just as likely to go to a neo-Nazi group instead if their initial message sounds more consistent. This is why he feels it is imperative that ARA not take an aggressively race-cognizant stance up-front but rather send the message more subtly in presenting the evidence of a white racist society through their publications and allow them to draw their own conclusions.

Contrast this with the People's Institute, another antiracist group, which is very race cognizant in its philosophy. This group makes it explicit that the movement should be led by people of color, and whites within the organization have developed a group-within-the-group called European Dissent, which, in Lisa's words, is "just dissenting what has been done in the European name." Mike's comments suggest that this group might deal very differently with the "questioning" teen above:

> Unfortunately most white people aren't able to handle the analysis that the People's Institute uses because it's much too real. You know, it tells it like it is, and the truth about white privilege is very, very hard for most white people to take. . . . They don't *want* people that aren't ready to confront reality because people of color live in this reality every day, and they don't really have time to coddle white people.

The antiracists I met through the Institute had all attended a two-and-a-half-day Undoing Racism workshop, which they administer all around the country, where they learned that all whites are racist, but they can also be antiracist and work against racism as part of their daily lives. For all those who attended, this workshop was a transformative experience. These antiracists more closely fit the understandings of antiracists in other literature: They are race cognizant and they are self-critical of their own racism.

Another interesting difference in the organizational culture of the two groups is the way that they viewed organizing against other types of oppression, such as lesbian/gay/bisexual rights and feminism. Both organizations happen to have flyers that list the "four principles" of their organization, and both of them have a "principle" that addresses the question of whether fighting other "isms" is a part of their program. Steve, an ARA member, summed up the ARA outlook on other "isms" as follows:

> ARA itself is only successful to the extent that we don't be exclusive to race. Our fourth principle says: "ARA network intends to do the hard work necessary to build a broad strong movement against racism"—we start with that, and it's a good place to start—"sexism, anti-Semitism, homophobia, discrimination against the disabled, the oldest, the youngest and the weakest of our people"—that's a pretty broad statement. . . . We passed that over a year ago on purpose so that it would be clear from the beginning that Anti-Racist Action is about sexism too. Anti-Racist Action is about homophobia too. Anti-Racist Action is about people in wheelchairs having access to a better life too. And anybody who confuses 'em doesn't know us.

On the other hand, the Institute affiliates seemed to have a different take on placing other "isms" at the same level of importance as racism. The Institute's first principle reads, "*Racism* has historically been the most critical barrier to unity in this country. It continues to be the primary cause of our failure to overcome poverty and bring about justice." Other "isms" are not mentioned. Lisa explained why this is the case: "When they start the workshop, you buy into a contract for the two days, and one of the things that they say is that we can talk about sexism, we can talk about classism, we can talk about homophobism [*sic*], whatever, as long as it's in the context of racism because too often we focus on other 'isms' as escapism, like from trying to get out of racism." The Institute was described as seeing racism as the primary "ism" and that racism shapes all of the other "isms" one could possibly want to talk about. Thus, anyone who did not subscribe to this philosophy was trying to "escape" or avoid dealing with issues of racism.

I bring up the differences in the organizational cultures of various antiracist groups to show that white antiracists, like any other group, are not monolithic. They are negotiating a better path in a culture that is extremely oppressive along the lines of race as well as many other issues. Hence, there are few places to look for guidance. As another white antiracist group, White Women Challenging Racism, has recently written, "While many sports stars, Hollywood actors, and cartoon characters are household names, few of us could name even five white antiracists—in this generation, decade, *or* century. The effect of this historical amnesia is that few white people have role models or ways of knowing what has worked before—and not" (Thompson et al. 1997:354). As Steve put it:

> So I started trying to be not racist and was totally unsuccessful at it, and still I am not skilled at it, because you get programmed at an early age and then deprogramming your uncontrollable mental processes as a white person that grew up in this culture—or as a male, for that matter—is not that easy! So this is why it's a lifelong kind of evolution. But if you're trying, who gives a shit? [laughs] That's the most you can do!

The white antiracists I have talked to are forging ahead the best way they know how, in the absence of any nationally based antiracist organization.

CONCLUSION

The data presented here suggest several possible answers to the questions of who white antiracists are, what they do, and how they think about race. The white antiracists here were heterogeneous with respect to social class, and most were brought to antiracist action through some sort of empathic experience. As with other work of this nature, double-stigmatization on the part of white women seemed to heighten their awareness about racial issues, but more commonly a two-pronged type of awareness occurred. Although many use approximating experiences to develop empathy with people of color, it usually took more than one experience for that to develop, in a "two-pronged" pattern. Some men, in particular, do not use approximating experiences but instead are affected by organizational culture, depending on their generation. Men who grew up in the seventies came up into an antiwar culture that made radical activism imperative across the board for all types of issues. For younger men, coming into contact with an organization such as ARA might be all that is needed to prompt them to action.

Although they downplayed the importance of their sacrifices and losses, several white antiracists had experienced them due to their actions, including loss of friends and job security and threats on their lives. White antiracists also appear very different from people of color in terms of their readiness and willingness to aggressively challenge racist incidents. Many of them were also aware that, as whites in a white supremacist society, they were afforded the power and privilege to be able to take such a stand, engaging in "privileged polemics." This finding might be a site of future research in terms of what the role of white people should be in combating racism. The question of whether separate tactics for white and black people is the best way to go remains to be addressed. Clearly, the divergent tactics show the potential of difficulty of different races working together on these issues, which may or may not be a desired goal.

It is evident that white antiracists are aware of their power and privilege as whites, and in this respect they think about race in a race-cognizant manner. However, they also point out factors that mediate the power of being white, such as gender and class, and also see an advantage in de-emphasizing privilege so that whites will realize they too have something to gain by ending racism. In addition, it seems that whites who are members of antiracist organizations are deeply affected by organizational culture in terms of how they think about race. Institute members were closer to the idealized type of "race cognizance" than were ARA members, who also saw the world in some "colorblind" ways even as they recognized white privilege. These differing outlooks on race had directly to do with the goals of the organizations and the ways in which those groups viewed how to go about reaching people. Further, ARA members saw fighting other "isms" along with racism as not only compatible goals but *necessary* goals, whereas Institute members interpreted this plurality of goals as "escapism" from racism and yet another dimension of white privilege. The data clearly point to a *diversity* of white antiracist "coming out" experiences, tactics, and philosophies. I look forward to assessing this diversity and making recommendations as my research continues.

REFERENCES

Aptheker, Herbert. 1992. *Antiracism in U.S. History: The First Two Hundred Years.* New York: Greenwood Press.

Bonilla-Silva, Eduardo, Tyrone A. Forman, and Jose Padin. 1997. "'I Am Not a Racist but . . . ': The Contemporary Contours of White Racial Ideology." Paper presented at the annual meetings of the American Sociological Association, Toronto, Ontario.

Carmines, Edward G., and Richard A. Champagne, Jr. 1990. "The Changing Content of American Racial Attitudes: A Fifty Year Portrait." *Research in Micropolitics* 3:187–208.

Carr, Leslie. 1997. *Colorblind Racism.* Thousand Oaks, CA: Sage.

Eichstedt, Jennifer L. 1997. "White Identities and Anti-Racism Activism." Paper presented at the annual meetings of the American Sociological Association, Toronto, Ontario.

Emerson, Michael O., and David H. Sikkink. 1997. "What People Say, What People Do: Education, Racial Attitudes, and Racial Realities." Paper presented at the annual meetings of the American Sociological Association, Toronto, Ontario.

Feagin, Joe R., and Melvin P. Sikes. 1994. *Living with Racism: The Black Middle-Class Experience.* Boston: Beacon Press.

Feagin, Joe R., and Hernan Vera. 1995. *White Racism: The Basics.* New York: Routledge.

Frankenberg, Ruth. 1993. *White Women, Race Matters: The Social Construction of Whiteness.* Minneapolis: University of Minnesota Press.

Gubrium, Jaber F., and James A. Holstein. 1997. *The New Language of Qualitative Method.* New York: Oxford University Press.

Holstein, James A., and Jaber F. Gubrium. 1995. *The Active Interview.* Thousand Oaks, CA: Sage.

hooks, bell. 1995. *Killing Rage: Ending Racism.* New York: Henry Holt.

Ignatiev, Noel, and John Garvey. 1996. *Race Traitor.* New York: Routledge.

Schuman, Howard, Charlotte Steeh, and Lawrence Bobo. *Racial Attitudes in America: Trends and Interpretations.* Cambridge: Harvard University Press.

Thompson, Becky, and White Women Challenging Racism. 1997. "Home/Work: Antiracism and the Meaning of Whiteness." Pp. 354–366 in *Off White: Readings on Race, Power, and Society*, Michelle Fine, Lois Weis, Linda C. Powell, and L. Mun Wong, eds. New York: Routledge.

PART 8

Toward Change

We end this book by addressing the issue of change. Social scientists often emphasize identifying a problem and analyzing its causes, but they spend much less time dealing with solutions. It is not uncommon for enthusiastic students to come up to an instructor of race and ethnic relations and say something like, "We want to do something to help. What can we do?" We think that it is important to have some answers.

Earlier in the book, we described our dual emphasis on the social psychological emphasis on attitudes (a micro-level analysis) and the sociological emphasis on structure (a macro-level analysis). We want to discuss change in the same way.

At the micro-level, attitudes must be changed. We must find ways to reduce the level of prejudice. In reducing prejudice, we reduce its behavioral manifestations of discrimination and ethnoviolence. Although there is not a simple relationship between prejudice and discrimination, reducing prejudice is certainly a step in the right direction.

At the macro-level, institutions must change. Economic, educational, political, cultural, and legal policies that have a detrimental effect on minorities or that unnecessarily exacerbate intergroup tensions should be changed. This should be done at both the public and private levels of society. Institutional discrimination should be eliminated. Structural discrimination (i.e., policies that are race-neutral in intent but that have negative effects on minorities) should be reevaluated to find acceptable alternatives.

Of course, there are interconnections between micro- and macro-level policies. Reducing prejudiced attitudes will make people more receptive to changing institutional policy. If, for example, whites believed that black poverty was caused more by institutional barriers than by cultural defects, whites would be more receptive to government programs to help the poor and to eliminate discrimination.

On the other hand, institutional change can lead to attitude change. Prior to the 1954 *Brown* decision outlawing school segregation, for example, it was inconceivable to think that black and white students would attend major state universities in the South. Now it is an accepted way of life. When the white South was forced to dismantle Jim Crow segregation and white southerners were forced to change their behavior, attitudes gradually changed.

Regardless of whether one is emphasizing the macro- or micro-level of analysis, the specific change strategy depends, in part, on one's political perspective.

Conservatives, for example, would rather rely on market forces than on government intervention in order to achieve change. Liberals, on the other hand, would call for more federal government spending and enforcement of antidiscrimination guidelines to achieve change. Both liberals and conservatives, of course, believe that change can be achieved within the context of the American version of capitalism.

Radicals, on the other hand, argue that capitalism is an integral part of the race relations problem. They would like to see the development of a new society based on cooperation rather than competition, democratic planning rather than relying on market forces, and grassroots democracy rather than a political process that is democratic in form but not in essence. Some believe that large-scale multiracial social movements are necessary to achieve these goals. Others look to a decentralized movement and the budding of alternative institutions.

* * *

The three readings in this section address the issue of change in different ways. Dinesh D'Souza ("Rethinking Racism") brings a conservative analysis to structural change. D'Souza calls for strong laws preventing discrimination by governments but *no* laws preventing discrimination by individuals or in the private sector. Since discrimination is economically irrational, he argues, private employers who discriminate will be hurt economically because they will not have the services of talented minority employees. Those employers who are meritocratic or who prefer talented minority employees, on the other hand, will prosper.

Arthur Salz and Julius Trubowitz ("It Was All of Us Working Together: Resolving Racial and Ethnic Tension on College Campuses") take a different approach and describe one successful program that is based on social psychological research on attitude change.

Finally, Charles Jaret ("Changing the Whole System") describes several liberal and radical strategies for macro-level change. He talks about ways to increase racial integration, transform capitalism, and increase the number of social democratic entitlement programs. He also explores the pros and cons of more racial/ethnic separatism.

We hope that these three readings will stimulate class discussion and provide lots of food for thought. In the end, you will be the agents of change.

34

Rethinking Racism

DINESH D'SOUZA

So what about racism? The conclusion of our inquiry into the history and nature of racism suggests that it is not reducible to ignorance or fear. Not only is the liberal remedy for racism incorrect; the basic diagnosis of the malady is wrong. Racism is what it always was: an opinion that recognizes real civilizational differences and attributes them to biology. Liberal relativism has been based on the denial of the differences. Liberals should henceforth admit the differences but deny their biological foundation. Thus liberals can continue to reject racism by preserving the Boasian distinction between race and culture. This is not a denial of the fact that individuals do differ or even the possibility that there are some natural differences between groups. Yet liberals can convincingly argue that whatever these may be, they are not significant enough to warrant differential treatment by law or policy. In other words, intrinsic differences are irrelevant when it comes to the ability of citizens to exercise their rights and responsibilities. Liberals can explain group differences in academic and economic performance by pointing to cultural differences, and acknowledging that some cultures are functionally superior to others. The racist fallacy, as Anthony Appiah contends, is the act of "biologizing what is culture."[14]

Yet this new liberal understanding should not make the present mistake—duplicated in thousands of sensitivity classes—of treating racism the way a Baptist preacher considers sin. Rather, it should recognize racism as an opinion, which may be right or wrong, but which in any case is a point of view that should be argued with and not suppressed. Antiracist education is largely a waste of time because it typically results in intellectual and moral coercion. Heavy-handed bullying may produce public acquiescence but it cannot compel private assent. Increasingly it appears that it is liberal antiracism that is based on ignorance and fear: ignorance of the true nature of racism, and fear that the racist point of view better explains the world than its liberal counterpart.

For a generation, liberals have treated racism as a form of psychological dementia in need of increasingly coercive forms of enlightenment. But liberal societies should not seek to regulate people's inner thoughts, nor should they outlaw ideas however reprehensible we find them. Hate speech and hate crime laws that impose punishment or enhanced penalties for proscribed motives and viewpoints are inherently illiberal and destructive of intellectual independence and conscience. Americans should recognize that racism is not what it used to be; it does exist, but we can live with it. This is not to say that racism does not do damage, only that the sorts of measures that would be needed to eradicate all vestiges of racist thought can only be totalitarian. Efforts to root out residual racism often create more injustice than they eliminate.

The crucial policy issue is what to do about discrimination. Irrational discrimination of the sort that inspired the civil rights laws of the 1960s is now, as we have seen, a relatively infrequent occurrence. Although such discrimination continues to cause harm, it is irrelevant to the prospects of blacks as a group because it is selective rather than comprehensive in scope. For a minority like African Americans, discrimination is only catastrophic when virtually everyone colludes to enforce it. Consider what would happen if every baseball team in America refused to hire blacks. Blacks would suffer most, because they would be denied the opportunity to play professional baseball. And fans would suffer, because the quality of games would be diminished. But what if only a few teams—say the New York Yankees and the Los Angeles Dodgers—refused to hire blacks? African Americans as a group would suffer hardly at all, because the best black players would offer their services to other teams. The Yankees and the Dodgers would suffer a great deal, because they would be deprived of the chance to hire talented black players. Eventually competitive pressure would force the Yankees and Dodgers either to hire blacks, or to suffer losses in games and revenue.[15] As Gary Becker has pointed out, in a free market, selective discrimination imposes the heaviest cost on the discriminator, which is where it should be. Some people will undoubtedly continue to eschew blacks because of their "taste for discrimination," but most will continue to deal with them because of their taste for profit.[16] Rational discrimination, on the other hand, is likely to persist even in a fully competitive market.

There are four possible policy remedies for dealing with persistent discrimination: the first two embrace the one-drop rule, the last two reject it. The first approach is to maintain the status quo, perhaps even to expand the logic of proportional representation for all racial groups. The approach, as we have seen, is a radical application of cultural relativism, which becomes the basis for an enforced egalitarianism between racial groups. This approach, which necessarily entails racial preferences, was perhaps necessary and inevitable in the late 1960s—it sought to eliminate comprehensive discrimination against blacks in many areas, to kick in a closed door. Now such comprehensive discrimination, which stretches across entire sectors of the workforce, is nonexistent, yet we have become used to doing business through the legerdemain of preferences and relaxed standards. Proportional representation also entails administrative benefits: it establishes an enforceable arithmetical standard for implementing civil rights laws. These paltry benefits, however, are overridden by the destructive impact of proportional representation.

First, the concept is incoherent. As we have seen, there is no reason whatsoever to believe that in the absence of discrimination, all groups would perform equally in every area. Equality of rights for individuals does not necessarily translate into equality of result for groups. Just as racism is a distortion of the principle of merit, so proportional representation is a distortion of the principle of equality. If different groups of runners hit the finishing tape at different times, it does not follow that the race has been rigged. Our current civil rights laws, therefore, are built on an intellectual foundation of quicksand.

In addition, proportional representation fails the test of social justice. Columnist Michael Kinsley argues that race is a "rough and ready short-hand for disadvantage,"[17] but that facile equation does not hold true any more. When W. E. B. Du Bois wrote in the early part of this century, the vast majority of blacks were indeed poor. But now the African American community has bifurcated into a middle class and an underclass. There is no justification for giving a university admissions preference to the government official's son who attends a private school in Washington, D.C., just because he belongs to an underrepresented group, over the daughter of an Appalachian coal miner or a Vietnamese refugee. Another problem with proportional representation is that it frequently subsidizes the children of new immigrants, who have played no part in American history, at the expense of the sons and daughters of native-born citizens. Those who are not disadvantaged should not get preferences, and debts that are not owed should not be paid.

Proportional representation also erodes the principle of merit which constitutes the only unifying principle for a multiracial society. People can live with inequality of result if they are assured equality of rights, just as we can endure losing a race as long as all competitors started on the same line. James Fallows writes that "America's radius of trust is expanded not by racial unity but by the belief that everyone is playing by the same rules."[18] Majorities, no less than minorities, need the assurance that they are being treated fairly, otherwise they are sure to mobilize through democratic channels to affirm their interests. By not only tolerating racial nepotism for minorities but enshrining it in law, proportional representation is rapidly balkanizing the country along racial lines, destroying the confidence of citizens that the law will treat them equally and provoking a strong and largely justified backlash.

Finally proportional representation assures an unceasing racialization of American society. By seeking to fight discrimination by practicing it, proportional representation multiplies the wounds inflicted by race-based decisions. Far from compensating old victims, it creates new ones. Proportional representation seeks to institutionalize race and make it a permanent feature of American public life. It has normalized and legitimized a neurotic obsession with race that maims our souls. If Americans acquiesce in this prescription, it will set them on a perpetual treadmill of racial recrimination and conflict. At least the old discrimination existed anomalously with the American creed; the new discrimination, embedded in law and policy, corrupts the nation's institutions and makes them purveyors of injustice.

What, then, sustains proportional representation? I believe it is the liberal conviction that the social outcomes produced by merit alone would prove painful and humiliating for blacks. If the Massachusetts Institute of Technology selected students solely based on merit, the number of blacks at MIT might well fall to around 2 percent.[19] Similarly blacks would be scarce in some professions, and virtually absent from others. Proportional representation will end only when we have the courage to say that we are willing to live with these outcomes, until blacks are able to raise their own standards to compete at the highest levels.

A second option, favored by some scholars, is to abolish racial preferences for all groups except one: African Americans. Andrew Kull writes, "The moral awkwardness of asking black Americans to be content with nondiscrimination should not stop us from giving that answer to everyone else."[20] Orlando Patterson,

Nathan Glazer, and Eugene Genovese argue that blacks have faced a unique history in this country which does not place them in the same position as other immigrants.[21] Genovese argues that African Americans should be permitted to identify themselves as culturally (as opposed to racially) black and benefit from a carefully selected range of preferences restricted to that group. This approach has the advantage of acknowledging the absurdity of preferring newcomers from Paraguay over locals from Peoria. It sensibly seeks to narrow the range of beneficiaries to the group that has suffered the unmitigated evils of slavery, segregation, and widespread discrimination. It would preserve preferences as exceptional, rather than typical. And it would continue to view them as temporary.

The problem with this attractive strategy is that while it has a chance of working in a black and white milieu, it is increasingly unsustainable in a multiracial society. When there are many groups with different ancestral histories, there are bound to be competing claims. These can be rejected out of hand, but it we are going to insist that middle-class blacks deserve preference for admissions and jobs over the poorest members of all other groups, this will not only produce acute resentment, it will probably stigmatize African Americans as inherently inferior. Whites, Hispanics, Asians, and native Americans would all be competing together, with a kind of Special Olympics held for blacks. The moral and psychological damage wrought by such an approach would almost certainly outweigh any tangible short-term benefits, so that the only workable scheme is one proposed by Lawrence Fuchs: limit affirmative action now to African Americans and set a date, perhaps 2010, when "all counting by race should be phased out."[22]

The two remaining options for dealing with discrimination reject the one-drop rule and thus avoid the risk, as Hugh Davis Graham puts it, of "our racist past being institutionalized in the present and hence poisoning the future."[23] Both options are premised on an embrace of equality of rights rather than equality of result. Both proceed from the belief that for government to judge people on the basis of race or other arbitrary features is immoral and illegal. Thus they would require the agencies of government to stop classifying citizens by race and forbid race-based decisions by the state. As African American writer Itabari Njeri puts it, "If our interest is in the elimination of oppression, then the elimination of classifications based on race is the only solution that makes sense. We should be challenging the nomenclature of oppression and attacking the philosophical underpinnings of racism."[24]

The first option is a blanket nondiscrimination rule, which establishes a right not to be discriminated against; consequently, it requires the enforcement of color-blind principles in both the private and the public sector. This is the approach that Martin Luther King favored, and the one that was written into law in the Civil Rights Act of 1964. Many liberals such as Jim Sleeper, Randall Kennedy, William Julius Wilson, and Clarence Page, as well as conservatives such as Newt Gingrich and Jack Kemp, are trying to revive this approach now, typically combined with a demand for class-based affirmative action.[25] This approach concedes that race can provide the basis for private identity, but not for public forms of conduct. Thus it is perfectly fine for persons to insist that they will date only members of their own race—obviously in the process discriminating against members of all other groups—but it would be illegal to discriminate in hiring for a job or selling a home. . . .

One difficulty with a broad-based color-blind rule is that it is not easy to enforce. Private discrimination is hard to prove when the discriminator seeks to conceal his motives. Yet the obstacle is not insurmountable. Courts could use an intent standard and yet examine all available circumstantial evidence to determine whether an act of illegal discrimination has occurred. Thus if companies treat black applicants differently from similarly situated whites, that discrepancy provides strong prima facie proof of intentional discrimination. Although such an approach requires case-by-case prosecution that some enforcement agencies consider cumbersome, it is justified by the fact that it is discriminators rather than the entire workforce that the law seeks to penalize.

A more serious problem with the Martin Luther King approach is that if applied consistently and even-handedly, it would require the government to make it illegal for minority companies to give preferences to members of their own group. Peek into the back of a Korean grocery store and you often see Korean workers in addition to the owners. Similarly, many black-owned businesses insist upon hiring African American employees. Should the government prohibit these obvious displays of minority ethnocentrism? I am reluctant to approve of such interference. Yet I am also unwilling to live with a double standard that forces whites to be race neutral while minorities are allowed to discriminate in favor of their own group. Thus I am forced to conclude that while a broadly enforced color-blind rule would be a great improvement over current policy, it would not be the best approach for a civil rights policy that seeks to be principled as well as pragmatic.

What we need is a long-term strategy that holds the government to a rigorous standard of race neutrality, while allowing private actors to be free to discriminate as they wish. In practice, this means uncompromising color blindness in government hiring and promotion, criminal justice, and the drawing of voting districts. Yet individuals and companies would be allowed to discriminate in private transactions such as renting an apartment or hiring for a job. Am I calling for a repeal of the Civil Rights Act of 1964? Actually, yes. The law should be changed so that its nondiscrimination provisions apply only to the government.

In a recent book, legal scholar Richard Epstein argues for precisely such an approach, which has so far remained outside the mainstream of the race debate. Arguing that "discrimination laws represent the antithesis of freedom of contract," Epstein asserts that people should be free to hire and fire others for good reason, bad reason, or no reason at all. Epstein challenges the strongly held belief of many Americans that they have a right not to be discriminated against: in a free society, he counters, people have a right to enter into voluntary transactions that other parties should be at liberty to accept or refuse. Epstein admits that while competitive markets would make irrational discrimination costly and relatively rare, companies would continue to practice rational discrimination. He argues that it is not unjust for an employer to refuse to hire even the most qualified black because the job is the employer's to give and the rejected applicant is no worse off than before applying for the job.[27]

Without putting it this way, Epstein is defending ethnocentrism as not only natural but also justifiable. As we have seen, it is a universal practice to prefer members of one's own group over strangers. Epstein implies, and I agree, that this is a defensible and in some cases even admirable trait. What is the argument for preventing people from giving jobs and benefits, which are theirs to give, to those whom they favor? Admittedly in some cases the job goes to the nephew of the boss. This, in the boss's mind, is his nephew's "merit"—to be related to him. Such nepotism, although reprehensible in the public sector where the government has an obligation to treat citizens equally, need not be restricted in the competitive private sector where the economic cost of selecting the less competent falls on the individual or company making the selection.

At this point I can already hear the gasps of civil rights activists. Absent legal penalties, they will warn, many companies would simply refuse to hire blacks even when they have demonstrated that they are the best-qualified candidates for jobs. Since such behavior makes no economic sense, we can expect that it would be relatively infrequent in a competitive market. Some employers undoubtedly would discriminate against blacks. Precisely how many is unknown, although after a generation of hiring preferences in favor of minorities, sometimes without external coercion, there is no reason to believe that comprehensive discrimination will make a comeback. Indeed I would go further: based on existing evidence, today's corporate culture exhibits more discrimination in favor of blacks than against blacks. Consequently, faced with the alternative of an enforced race-blind approach that would outlaw discrimination in either direction, many African Americans who recognize the pervasiveness of contemporary minority preferences might well prefer to see those private benefits continue, and would be willing to pay the price of tolerating a few relatively isolated employers who would refuse to hire backs. Thus we arrive at the greatest paradox of all: the best way for African Americans to save private-sector affirmative action is to repeal the Civil Rights Act of 1964.

The issue of private discrimination is important, but whichever way it is settled, the central choice facing American society is whether its agencies of government are going to embrace the one-drop rule and practice racial discrimination, or reject it and treat citizens equally under the law. The one-drop rule reveals the way in which our current antidiscrimination policy is premised upon the ideological foundation established by the old racists. It endorses and perpetuates racial discrimination, even while purporting to fight it. Although current policy professes to promote "benign" discrimination, all discrimination is benign for its beneficiary and invidious for its victim. America will never liberate itself from the shackles of the past until the government gets out of the race business. . . .

NOTES

14. Anthony Appiah, *In My Father's House: Africa in the Philosophy of Culture,* Oxford University Press, New York, 1992, p. 45.

15. Christopher Jencks, *Rethinking Social Policy: Race, Poverty, and the Underclass,* Harvard University Press, Cambridge, 1992, p. 41.

16. Gary S. Becker, *The Economics of Discrimination,* University of Chicago Press, Chicago, 1971.

17. Michael Kinsley, "The Spoils of Victimhood," *New Yorker,* March 27, 1995, p. 66.

18. James Fallows, *More Like Us,* Houghton Mifflin, New York, 1989, p. 49.

19. Theodore Cross, "Suppose There Was No Affirmative Action at the Most Prestigious Colleges and Graduate Schools," *Journal of Blacks in Higher Education,* No. 3 (Spring 1994), pp. 44–51.

20. Andrew Kull, *The Color-Blind Constitution,* Harvard University Press, Cambridge, 1992, p. 223.

21. Orlando Patterson argues that "our traditional liberal conception that one simply creates opportunities and assumes everything will work itself out . . . works very well for most people, including black immigrants, but the problem with black Americans is unique." Orlando Patterson, "American Dilemmas Revisited," *Salmagundi,* Fall 1994–Winter 1995, p. 42. See also Nathan Glazer, "Race, Not Class," *Wall Street Journal,* April 5, 1995, p. A12.

22. Cited in "A Race-Neutral Helping Hand," *Business Week,* February 27, 1995, p. 121.

23. Hugh Davis Graham, "Race, History, and Policy: African Americans and Civil Rights Since 1964," *Policy History,* Pennsylvania State University Press, Vol. 6, No. 1, 1994, p. 34.

24. Itabari Njeri, "Sushi and Grits: Ethnic Identity and Conflict in a Newly Multicultural America," in Gerald Early, ed., *Lure and Loathing: Essays on Race, Identity, and the Ambivalence of Assimilation,* Penguin, New York, 1993, p. 40.

25. See, e.g., Jim Sleeper, *The Closest of Strangers,* W. W. Norton, New York, 1990; Wilson, *The Truly Disadvantaged;* Cass Sunstein, "Voting Rites," *The New Republic,* April 25, 1994; Rod Dreher, "Kemp Urges Affirmative Action Based on Economics," *Washington Times,* February 20, 1995, p. A1; Clarence Page, "Salvation Based on Need," *Washington Times,* February 21, 1995, p. A16.

27. Richard Epstein, *Forbidden Grounds: The Case Against Employment Discrimination Laws,* Harvard University Press, Cambridge, 1992.

35

It Was All of Us Working Together

Resolving Racial and Ethnic Tension on College Campuses

ARTHUR SALZ AND
JULIUS TRUBOWITZ

The *New York Times* headline of 25 October 1995 defined the issue: "Nation's Campuses Confront an Expanding Racial Divide." According to the author (Applebome 1995, A1), racial issues are especially divisive "on college campuses, where Blacks and Whites live and work together to a degree they seldom do elsewhere, [and] where racial division has become increasingly institutionalized in separate dormitories or dormitory floors." Indeed, we see a disquieting picture of the deteriorating state of relations between ethnic and racial groups on college campuses (Applebome 1995):

- a newspaper column at Columbia University charged, "Lift up the yarmulke and what you will find is the blood of billions of Africans weighing on their heads";
- a flyer at the University of Southern California alerted European Americans that "the niggers are taking over. Take up arms and defend yourselves, my brothers";
- at Emory University, notes were placed under the doors of several African-American students that threatened, "You niggers never sleep," and swastikas were marked on the clothing of a Jewish student;
- at Kent State University, racial slurs were directed toward African-American students; and
- on the unofficial bulletin board at Pomona College, comments called for violence against Asians, African Americans, and homosexuals.

While serious problems of race and ethnic relations on college campuses is nothing new, there is a widespread sense that conditions have exacerbated recently (People for the American Way 1991). Increasingly, ignorance, bigotry, and hatred on today's campuses pose a problem of huge dimensions.

THE BACKGROUND

However, a service-learning project originally developed to ameliorate the devastating effects of homelessness on children offers a model for healing the rift between college students of different ethnic and racial backgrounds. The Queens College Big Buddy program, initiated in 1989, has addressed the affective and cognitive needs of youngsters by providing a college mentor who would serve as a friend, educational and cultural guide, confidant, and role model. As the program continued over a number of years, it became clear that it was having a marked and dramatic impact not only on the children but on the college students as well (Salz and Trubowitz 1992). For mentors, the experience of participating together in the program profoundly affected their feelings, attitudes, and behavior across ethnic and racial lines.

THE PROBLEM

Our nation's first colleges were guided by a vision of uniformity, and for the first 200 years students were socially and economically very much alike. Campuses were populated by men drawn primarily from the privileged class. Virtually no minority students were enrolled and at most of these colleges even a female student was "as unwelcome as any uninvited guest" (Horowitz 1987, 68; Carnegie Foundation for the Advancement of Teaching 1990).

Diversity has significantly changed the culture of U.S. higher education. In the past 20 years there has been a notable increase in the number of minority students attending universities. Today men and women students come from almost every racial and ethnic group in the country and from every nation in the world.

Although surveys of undergraduate students indicate that a majority express a wish for more involvement with people of different backgrounds, the picture of campus life that emerges today is one of limited and often tense interaction between ethnically different students (Sampson 1986; Magner 1990). While colleges and universities celebrate pluralism, discrete enclaves of separatism have in fact developed. Increasingly, college and university presidents have become concerned about the loss of community on campus; colleges are so divided that common purposes are blurred or lost forever.

The term "balkanization" is now used to describe undergraduate life on many campuses. Throughout higher education, religious, racial, and ethnic students have organized themselves into separate student associations. With sub-groups established along these lines, students do little else together other than attending the same classes or rooting for their football team on Saturday. Lunch tables, intramural sports teams, and even dormitory residences are homogeneously grouped along religious, racial, and ethnic lines (Sampson 1986).

A notable example is the continued segregation of Cornell University's student housing. Ujamaa College was established as an all-African-American dormitory in 1972 in an atmosphere of racial ferment and threats of violence. At that time, students of other races were excluded from the dormitory. Ujamaa remains overwhelmingly segregated today and, indeed, "balkanization" of the Cornell campus has increased with the opening of the Latino Living Center and the Akwe:Kon for Native Americans (Clark and Meyers 1995).

This fragmentation has resulted in an increasing number of students experiencing feelings of isolation with little contact outside of their own group. Frequent reports from students portray a badly splintered campus life. Many college students openly acknowledge that they have no friends of another race, religion, or ethnic group (Magner 1990). This isolation has bred feelings of distrust and fear, fertile soil for the rise in hate crimes on college campuses today, as well as more complex, persistent social intolerance (People for the American Way 1991).

Queens College has not been immune to this separatism. On a diverse campus with students identifying with 108 different countries and speaking 66 different languages, the potential for cross-cultural interaction is enormous. However, very little of it takes place, either on a formal or informal basis. The special circumstance of Queens as a commuter institution reduces student identification with the college. Nearly all of the students work part-time, averaging 25 hours per week. Two-thirds of Queens College students report spending six hours or less per week on campus outside of class attendance and no involvement in any extracurricular activities. Of those students involved, many are members of campus clubs organized along ethnic and/or religious lines (Savage 1992). While these clubs contribute to student's cultural and social enrichment, they also serve to reinforce barriers between these groups. Club hour on Mondays and Wednesdays, when students meet in their separate groups, is the most segregated time on the Queens College campus. Again and again students note the separateness based on ethnicity: "How can you get to know other students if they all break off into separate clubs?" Students even eat in segregated groups, speaking in distinct language groups. As one student noted, "It's hard to just walk over."

While most students reported feeling comfortable on the Queens College campus, 40 percent of African-American students perceived other students as not friendly. Overall, 60 percent of students felt that other students have different values from their own; 75 percent of African Americans and Asians expressed this feeling. Furthermore, a majority of African-American students described feeling out of place on the Queens College campus. While most students believed that different racial groups "get along" at Queens College, "almost 40 percent felt that racial tension exists on campus" and 32 percent stated that they had witnessed or experienced discrimination at the College (Queens College 1992).

Despite the potential for cross-cultural interaction and education on this amazingly diverse campus, little takes place. Even for those who stay on campus, too many interact with culturally similar acquaintances rather than with those who are different.

THE PROGRAM

By contrast, the Big Buddy program brings 50 college students together from various ethnic and racial backgrounds for protracted periods of time in a service-learning endeavor. Big Buddies represent a cross-section of the diverse Queens College population: African Americans of various backgrounds; Latinos; a Filipino male; a Jewish woman in her 60s from Long Island; a young Irish woman;

Asian women; and others who trace their roots to Iran, Yemen, Greece, Italy, Romania, Czechoslovakia, and the former Soviet Union.

Their involvement with each other is considerable. The program begins with an all-day training session in which Big Buddies discuss their goals, expectations, and concerns for the year. On the following Saturday, an orientation session takes place at the college; mentors share in the experience of meeting children and parents, discuss the program, and have lunch together. Throughout the year, each Big Buddy meets his or her youngster at the residence for homeless families each Saturday morning. Together, they spend the entire day visiting sites of educational, cultural, or recreational interest. Frequently, several Buddies and their youngsters go on outings together. Pairs also provide community service every third week. There are frequent contacts between Big Buddies apart from time spent with the children, including phone conversations and informal meetings. Every other week, all Big Buddies meet with college coordinators to discuss common concerns and problems. At mid-year an all-day retreat is held for Big Buddies to assess the program and refocus energy for the second semester. Buddies participate in cooperative problem solving and trust-building activities. They openly discuss their work with youngsters, sharing triumphs and concerns.

The experience that has the greatest impact on children and college students alike is the two-day, overnight trip to the Queens College Environmental Center at Caumsett State Park. In this beautiful setting, college students and children live together for two days, participate in exciting ecological studies, cooperate in dining-room chores for five meals, and clean their rooms; Big Buddies stay up late "shooting the bull." For students at a commuter college, this rare opportunity to bond has considerable impact. The final experience of the program for mentors is the Recognition Night Dinner at which students receive an honor certificate signed by the college president. The camaraderie and warmth among the Big Buddies is palpable. When they leave the restaurant at the end of the evening, it is not unusual to see them with arms around each other. The emergence of such powerful, positive feelings in college students across ethnic and racial lines, in such sharp contrast to mainstream student life on campus, makes it imperative to examine the dynamics of intergroup contact theory as it applies to the Big Buddy program.

THE MODEL IN THEORY

We know what does not work. As Schofield (1995, 264) noted, "If there is one thing that social psychological theory and research have taught us about racially and ethnically diverse environments during the last forty years it is that simply putting children [and youth] from different backgrounds together is not enough to ensure positive social outcomes." Gerard and Miller (1975) found that, long after the schools had been desegregated, children grouped in their own ethnic clusters. Moreover, anxiety among ethnic minorities had increased and remained high long after desegregation had occurred. Indeed, careful scholarly reviews of the research show few, if any, benefits to integration (Stephan 1978; St. John 1975).

Thus, early support for the naive idea that contact between different ethnic and racial groups would automatically produce positive attitude and behavior changes has been tempered by the knowledge that direction of change is highly dependent on conditions surrounding the contact (Amir 1976). What, then, are the necessary factors that facilitate positive change of attitude and behavior?

Allport's (1954) multidimensional model has identified those conditions in the intergroup contact situation necessary to produce positive social outcomes. The first facilitative factor is that sufficient opportunity be offered for the development of personal, satisfying interaction between people of diverse ethnic backgrounds (acquaintance potential). The second necessary requirement is for the participants in the intergroup contact to be of equal status. The third condition is that the person or institution of authority supports and validates the intergroup contact (authority norm). Finally, the fourth condition is that the nature of the contact fosters cooperation in the pursuit of common goals.

THE MODEL IN PRACTICE

Significant differences emerge as we compare the nature of most student contact on campus with the type of interaction among participants in the Big Buddy Program. Participants experienced positive growth in acquaintance potential, sense of equal status, authority norm, and the pursuit of common goals.

Acquaintance Potential

The typical contact between different group members on college campuses offers limited opportunity for students to get to know each other. Merely attending the same class or eating in the same cafeteria restricts communication and the development of more meaningful personal relationships. The Big Buddy program, by contrast, provides a year-long setting in which students interact with each other closely on a personal level.

As a young man from Romania related, "On campus it's not easy to meet people of different backgrounds. Most people don't get involved in activities in school. It was different in the Big Buddy program. . . . Big Buddies really got to know each other."

A Hispanic woman said, "I was always alone; everything I did was alone. . . . I didn't have many opportunities to meet other students, to share with others. I'd be all by myself in the cafeteria. In the Big Buddy program, I interacted with everyone. . . . There were really nice people in the program, really friendly people from different cultures."

An African-American male said, "On campus it's hard to meet people. . . . We'd have different schedules, meet for ten minutes and then disperse. But in the program, especially with Caumsett, we'd sit around for hours and just talk. We'd learn about everybody else."

A young Greek woman stated, "When you're on campus you really just pass people to and fro; the only thing that brings you together are the classes. I never got relationships or friendships going from my classes. . . . But the Big Buddy program brings out a more humanistic self; it's different. It's like a little family; it creates that family aura. It's much easier to develop a more intense friendship in the program. . . . You exchange numbers, talk about your problems with the kids, help each other out, and solve problems together. . . . I found the program had caring, emotional, sensitive people. . . . We all got to know each other; it brought us closer together."

Equal Status

When individuals of different backgrounds lack the opportunity for personal contact as equals, they tend to view each other in more stereotypic terms rather than as individual personalities. Among students engaged in impersonal classroom contact, perceptions of each other tend to be based on the two most salient characteristics of today's university students—social class background and academic ability (Sampson 1986). In such limited contact, stereotypes regarding ethnic and racial groups tend to remain intact as students maintain their long-held prejudices and negative associations. However, in working with homeless youngsters in the Big Buddy program, college students provide the same valuable community service, assume mentoring responsibility, and view themselves as equals. The endeavor places all students in the same role, and neither academic ability nor social class seems of significance in the interaction.

As a young Jewish woman related, "A bunch of us would go out together and share in the activity for the day. . . . I really got to know them all; we'd have a great time."

An African-American male said that "the biweekly meetings were a real catharsis. Everybody talked about their kids, the good things, their problems, their gripes, and we all tried to help each other out. I really felt we were in this thing together."

An Eastern-European woman noted, "Everybody had the same spirit; easy, no conflict. . . . After a while you didn't notice where people were from. It seems like we were all there with our concerns, all there with the same problems of working with the kids."

As a European-American male said, "At first I was concerned . . . about how I would be received because I'm White and many of the Big Buddies were Black and Hispanic. It never became an issue. Even though we were a diverse group, the bonds were very strong."

Authority Norm

On campuses with established ethnic and racial dormitories and/or strong religious or ethnic clubs, the college, as authority figure, has given its imprimatur to these organizations, fostering separatism among students. If equal emphasis is not accorded efforts to bring diverse groups together, the college administration sends a clear, albeit unfortunate, educational message to its student body. In contrast, Big Buddies receive a very different message: their work with homeless children and their close and cooperative involvement with each other has the consistent support and validation of their college administration and faculty, the parents of their youngsters, social workers, and the outside community.

The Queens College Faculty Committee has been integrated since its inception, providing a model for close cooperation across racial and ethnic lines. The Committee works closely with Big Buddies, encouraging them to share and help each other in their work with homeless children. The admiration and appreciation demonstrated by parents also contribute to the pride mentors feel in being part of the program.

As one Big Buddy related, "It was terrific the way the parents looked at us. It was a nice feeling. You felt like you were doing good when you saw them. . . . They treated us like we were something great; it was a nice feeling."

Another Big Buddy who remained in contact with his youngster after the family moved to permanent housing said, "I got to know the mother a little bit. . . . She told me how good it made her feel that I was with Tyrone. I really felt I was doing something important."

Another young man said that his youngster's mother "trusted me a lot and wanted me to be with him every Saturday. Jose's mother would always come to me for advice, about problems in school, should she send him to the Dominican Republic for the summer, and other things."

One woman related how the Big Buddy program's impact was felt at graduation: "Being in the Big Buddy program was really the only way I connected with Queens College; it gave meaning to my time in school, I guess you could say. And then the college president mentioned the Big Buddy program for homeless kids in her speech, and a big cheer went up. Did I feel great!"

In Pursuit of Common Goals

In the college classroom, students are almost never engaged in the pursuit of common goals. In the vast majority of cases, the process of education is highly competitive. Students vie with one another for good grades and for the respect of the teacher. On the other hand, Big Buddies join together in achieving the common goal of providing a positive growth experience for homeless children. Big Buddies perceive each other as partners, discussing, sharing, and helping each other with problems and concerns as they guide their youngsters.

As one woman related, "Everybody in the program was just working together, doing things together, helping each other. If you didn't know what you were doing or where you wanted to go, another person had an idea."

One of the men noted that "basically everyone in the program had the same interest, the same goal with the kids. If someone went to a place they found interesting, they would recommend it to another Big Buddy. What was good was when we were all out together, we all looked out for each other's Little Buddies."

An African-American participant said, "It was great, the diversity of students, people of different backgrounds all concerned about the kids. . . . There was great diversity—Indian, Jewish, Black, White—working toward a common goal. Occasionally a Big Buddy was unable to take her child out. I remember helping out and taking a child along with my Little Buddy. It was kind of like it was reciprocity."

THE IMPLICATIONS

Race and ethnic relations on college campuses throughout the country are facing a crisis. Increasingly, communication and contact between groups continue to deteriorate. Campus life has become more and more polarized, creating an atmosphere of tension and mistrust, posing a potentially explosive situation. What is most distressing is the paucity of attention devoted to effectively address this problem. As Hamburg (1995) noted, "while research on improving interracial and interethnic relations flourished after World War II, it has declined rapidly over the past two decades despite the rapid increase in our nation's diversity."

The Queens College Big Buddy program offers a successful model bridging the chasm of misunderstanding and fear existing among college students. It does so because the basic characteristics of the program are grounded in Allport's intergroup contact theory, recognized as necessary to bring about positive change in attitude and behavior. Within the program the college students interact with each other on a personal level, closely and supportively over an extended period of time (acquaintance potential). In working with homeless youngsters, college students assume the same role, provide the same valuable guidance, and view themselves as having equal status. Big Buddies know that the work they do cooperatively with homeless youngsters is valued at the highest level by the college administration, its faculty, parents, social workers, and the community. In pursuing the common goal of providing a positive growth experience for homeless children, these college students share the same interests, concerns, and activities, are mutually interdependent, and are actively involved in a give and take situation, providing the most effective way to induce lasting attitude changes among participants (Schild 1962).

As we have noted before (Salz and Trubowitz 1992, 556), "The model employed by the Queens College Big Buddy Program has proved to be workable and appropriate, and we highly recommend it to other colleges interested in giving their students an opportunity to serve their communities." We have now revisited this model and have discovered that it also has inherent in it the mechanism for building positive, supportive relationships among college students of very different ethnic and racial backgrounds.

The implications are obvious. Service-learning programs that are grounded in Allport's theoretical construct "provide opportunities for students to work cooperatively and learn about each other across racial and ethnic lines," thus "foster[ing] positive intergroup relations" (Jackson 1995, 448). If schools and colleges wish to improve intergroup attitudes and behaviors, neither preaching nor ethnic food tasting parties will accomplish those goals (Banks 1989). Rather, the college must create activities and projects that bring students of diverse backgrounds together cooperatively in order to accomplish tasks that participants deem valuable. These may be organized around college courses, internships related to academic majors, or independent service-learning projects. Colleges may even make participation in these types of activities part of the graduation requirement. We urge a major commitment on the part of colleges to improve race and ethnic relations on their campuses. Given the seriousness of the situation, college administrations must make a choice. Either they continue to live with tensions simmering just below the surface and periodic racist explosions or they take action to change the climate on their campuses. Instead of racist epithets on college bulletin boards, intergroup campus life could have the quality expressed in the words of one of the Big Buddies: "Instead of it being just one group it was more diversified. It was kind of nice that everybody got along. The program was hard, but it was worth it. It was one of the biggest parts of my education here at Queens. It wasn't a class, but it was a fulfilling time for me. It was one of the most memorable experiences because, through it all, with all those different people, it was just like making friends." The choice is ours.

REFERENCES

Allport, G. W. 1954. *The nature of prejudice.* Cambridge, Mass.: Addison Wesley.

Amir, Y. 1976. The role of intergroup contact in change of prejudice and ethnic relations. In *Towards the elimination of racism,* ed. P. A. Katz, 245–308. New York: Pergamon.

Applebome, P. 1995. Nation's campuses confront an expanding racial divide. *New York Times,* 25 October, A1, B9.

Banks, J. A. 1989. Integrating the curriculum with ethnic content. Approaches and guidelines. In *Multicultural education issues and perspectives,* ed. J. A. Banks and C. A. McGee Banks, 189–207. Boston: Allyn and Bacon.

Carnegie Foundation for the Advancement of Teaching. 1990. *Campus life: In search of community.* Princeton, N.J.: CFAT.

Clark, K. B., and M. Meyers. 1995. Separate is never equal. *New York Times,* 1 April, A19.

Gerard, H. B., and N. Miller. 1975. *School desegregation: A long-term study.* New York: Plenum Press.

Hamburg, D. 1995. Letter to Allen Sessoms, President of Queens College.

Horowitz, H. L. 1987. *Campus life: Undergraduate cultures from the end of the eighteenth century to the present.* New York: Knopf.

Jackson, A. W. 1995. Toward a common destiny: An agenda for further research. In *Toward a common destiny: Improving race and ethnic relations in America,* ed. W. D. Hawley and A. W. Jackson, 435–53. San Francisco: Jossey-Bass.

Magner, D. K. 1990. Amid the diversity racial isolation remains at Berkeley. *The Chronicle of Higher Education* 37(11): A37–39.

People for the American Way. 1991. Hate in the ivory tower: A survey of intolerance on college campuses and academia's response. Washington, D.C.: PAW. ERIC ED 340 818.

Queens College. 1992. Multicultural diversity study. Unpublished.

St. John, N. H. 1975. *School desegregation: Outcomes for children.* New York: Wiley.

Salz, A., and J. Trubowitz. 1992. You can see sky from here: The Queens College Big Buddy program. *Phi Delta Kappan* 73(7): 551–56.

Sampson, W. A. 1986. Desegregation and racial tolerance in academia. *Journal of Negro Education* 55(2): 171–84.

Savage, D. The Queens College and beyond: Longitudinal study of the seniors of 1989, 1992. Unpublished.

Schild, E. O. 1962. The foreign student, as stranger, learning the norms of the host-culture. *Journal of Social Issues* 18(1): 41–54.

Schofield, J. W. 1995. Promoting positive intergroup relations in school settings. In *Toward a common destiny: Improving race and ethnic relations in America,* ed. W. D. Hawley and A. W. Jackson, 257–89. San Francisco: Jossey-Bass.

Stephan, W. G. 1978. School desegregation: An evaluation of predictions made in *Brown v. Board of Education. Psychological Bulletin* 85(2): 217–38.

36

Changing the Whole System

CHARLES JARET

In this section, we consider four approaches, each of which would make a marked change in the American social order. Each is touted by its supporters as having the potential to greatly reduce racial inequality and improve intergroup relations. These are (a) policies that increase residential integration among racial-ethnic groups, (b) radical or socialist proposals to redistribute power and wealth, (c) "universal entitlements," that is, the idea of extending a broad range of social and economic benefits to the entire population, and (d) racial-ethnic separatism, that is, limiting contact with out-groups in order to develop cohesion within a group and strengthen its resources and institutions.

RESIDENTIAL INTEGRATION

For the most highly segregated groups, a good argument can be made that an effective way to reduce racial inequality (e.g., access to jobs, schools, and medical care) is by taking actions and adopting policies that greatly increase the number of stable integrated neighborhoods in a metropolitan area. The Kerner Commission, back in 1968, explicitly recommended policies of school, residential, and employment integration, coupled with "enrichment" services for minority neighborhoods, as the best response to overcome the underlying problems and causes of the 1960s ghetto riots.

More recently, DeMarco and Galster (1993:143) strongly affirmed the urgent need for stable, racially integrated neighborhoods rather than the status quo. They said that

> segregation means restricting minorities' opportunities for social and economic advancement and full participation in the American Dream. Segregation forms the key link in what may be called a vicious circle of self-perpetuating racial prejudice and inequality.

To analyze that vicious circle, Galster and Keeny (1988) worked out a statistical model that tried to estimate the mutual interactions and effects of prejudice, housing discrimination, economic inequality, and housing costs. Their hypothetical computer simulations suggested that a 10% reduction in black-white residential segregation would be associated with an 18% decrease in occupational inequality between blacks and whites and a 5% gain in black household income relative to white household income.

Residential integration would also bring educational benefits, in that it would make racial-ethnic integration in the schools more effective and less costly. With integrated neighborhoods, children would not have to be bused long distances to desegregate schools, which would save money and lower parental opposition. It would also facilitate minority parental involvement in the local school, PTA, and the like, and this is associated with better performance by students.

Rather than continuing to discuss theoretical and empirical aspects of the housing segregation "vicious circle," our purpose in this subsection is to look at and evaluate several important attempts to create racially integrated neighborhoods. We'll examine the actions or policies that fair housing advocates have tried, giving special attention to the legal status and overall effectiveness of these efforts.

Working for Residential Integration

Creation and maintenance of racial-ethnic integration in residential areas often require two related advocacy efforts. One involves working for "open" or "fair" housing, and the other involves neighborhood "stabilization." The first tries to "open up" housing units in areas where minority group members have been unable to live because of the high cost of housing there, discrimination, or a mixture of the two. Neighborhood "stabilization" comes after a minority group gains access to an area and is aimed at preventing excessive turnover (e.g., "white flight"). It seeks to create a community with real racial-ethnic diversity, rather than having the area become resegregated as former occupants are totally replaced by the newly arriving group. Often, both of these advocacy efforts are necessary to create a stable integrated community, and people work cooperatively in them. But sometimes they can and have come into conflict, as in Oak Park, Illinois, and Starrett City, New York, when numerical limits were put on the number of blacks who could move into the area (or parts of it) to try to maintain racial balance.

Efforts to attain residential integration have been studied in works by Bradburn, Sudman, and Glockel (1971), Molotch (1972), Saltman (1990, 1991), and R.A. Smith (1993). We'll summarize some of this material, begining with Juliet Saltman's (1990) study of the rise and decline of a group called National Neighbors. She looked at it as a social movement in which individuals and groups work for a cause—residential integration—and must mobilize resources to overcome internal and external problems.

In 1969 a dozen neighborhoods from different parts of the United States, each of which was trying on its own to deal with the prospect of racial integration, banded together to create an organization called National Neighbors. Its purpose was to be a private, nonprofit agency that could help neighborhoods going through the process of racial integration. The kinds of help that it gave included publishing a newsletter and serving as a network to aid communication among geographically distant neighborhoods that shared a positive orientation toward interracial living; sponsoring conferences and research and doing consulting work on racial steering, property values, housing discrimination audits, and methods of attracting or retaining multiracial residents; drafting and lobbying for fair housing laws; assembling and publishing case studies of successful and failed attempts at integration; and doing public relations work on the benefits of interracial neighborhoods. By the 1980s, however, National Neighbors was struggling to survive. Probably its biggest problem was its perpetual financial crisis, which left it unable to pay staff salaries and bills or to support programs, although internal power struggles and federal administrations that have not strongly advocated integration or civil rights also fueled its decline (Saltman, 1990).

The legacy of National Neighbors and other organizations advocating integrated residential areas (e.g., the National Committee Against Discrimination in Housing, which existed between 1950 and 1987, the Oak Park Exchange Congress, and Cleveland's East Suburban Council for Open Communities) is a host of methods and strategies for integrating and maintaining racial diversity in neighborhoods. We'll outline these and then suggest which, if any, are effective and also comment on other factors influencing racial integration.

The following methods have been used to either initiate integration or maintain it once the process has begun:

A. *Affirmative Marketing.* To reverse the effects of "racial steering," special efforts (e.g., brochures, housing referral services, tours of homes) show or tell whites about good housing opportunities in mixed or black areas and show or tell blacks about good housing in white areas.

B. *Financial Incentives for Prointegrative Moves.* This approach was first proposed in 1972, and a revised version of it was implemented in the 1980s by the Ohio Housing Finance Agency and the Fund for the Future of Shaker Heights (Saltman, 1990:356; DeMarco & Galster, 1993). The basic idea is that some form of financial benefit is made available to someone who moves into an area in which most of the other residents are of another race. Financial benefits take the form of below-market-level mortgage loan rates, grants or low-interest loans for down payments, or monthly mortgage payment supplements.

C. *Restrictions Placed on the Real Estate Industry.* A number of towns have passed laws limiting the size, number, and placement of "For Sale" signs in residential neighborhoods. In special circumstances, courts have even upheld total bans on "For Sale" signs (R.A. Smith, 1993:127). Restrictions have also been put on the number or types of solicitations that realtors can make to residents. These are designed to reduce the possibility of "block busting" and "panic peddling," which might otherwise cause rapid racial turnover in a neighborhood. In some cases, fair housing advocates have pressured real estate boards to label racial steering and inducing residential turnover based on racial fears as unethical business conduct.

D. *Numerical Restrictions (Quotas) on Who Can Move In.* Undoubtedly, this is the most controversial method of trying to maintain racial stability, and in recent years the higher courts have not allowed it. In the highly publicized case of Starrett City, an initial settlement proposing to limit minority occupancy to 37% of the apartments and expand integrated housing opportunities for minorities in other parts of the city was overturned (Saltman, 1990:392). More ambiguous is the situation in Oak Park, a suburb of Chicago, where real estate companies are encouraged to voluntarily refrain from selling homes to blacks in subareas of the town that already have a large number of blacks.

E. *Coordination Between the School System and the Housing Market.* An intimate connection exists between residential choices and conditions in neighborhood schools. In light of this, Orfield (1981) and others have argued that school policy and housing supply decisions cannot continue to be made in isolation; instead, they should be made to further the goal of integration. For example, students in integrated neighborhoods should be exempted from busing programs; special efforts must be made to ensure high-quality academic programs in schools in integrated neighborhoods; school attendance zones might be redrawn to maximize integration even as racial housing patterns shift in neighborhoods; school administrators could get more involved with property developers to push for housing at varied price levels to attract more of a racial-ethnic mix. In Shaker Heights, Ohio, the school board helps to support stable racial integration by contributing a substantial sum to the local fair housing advocacy organization.

F. *Frequent Audits of Housing Market Discrimination.* A recent survey of housing discrimination against minorities indicated that "no measurable progress has been made in reducing housing discrimination" since a similar survey done in 1979 (Urban Institute, 1992). It is recommended that frequent, systematic audits be done, and when evidence shows that real estate agents or apartment managers are violating state or federal fair housing laws, it should be given to the appropriate authorities for aggressive prosecution.

G. *Scatter-site Housing in Suburban Areas.* A number of government-sponsored programs have tried to enable poor minority residents to find better-quality housing outside of ghetto neighborhoods. Besides better housing and safer neighborhoods, this dispersal could put minority group members in areas where better schools, more jobs, and higher-quality medical care are available. During the 1970s, some obtained private homes and apartments via the Title 235 and 236 programs (but administrative corruption helped to destroy these efforts). In 1976, as a result of a consent decree in a Chicago housing discrimination case, the "Gautreaux experiment" used Section 8 federal housing subsidies to help low-income blacks who wished to move from all-black housing projects to apartments in mixed or predominantly white parts of the city or the suburbs. In evaluating the Gautreaux experiment, Rosenbaum and Popkin (1991) found that blacks who moved to suburban areas were considerably more likely to find jobs and work at them than were blacks who remained in public housing or those who moved to other parts of the city of Chicago.

Although there are some legal difficulties with a number of these methods of increasing racial residential integration, for only one of them—residential quotas—are the legal problems really major obstacles. Metropolitan areas across the country can and should experiment with various mixes of these approaches. The federal government might encourage such experimentation, perhaps by offering incentives to the communities that successfully do so. At present, what we really lack is the vision and collective will that would put the creation of racially integrated neighborhoods near the top of the political agenda. The policy tools are at hand; the question is "Are we willing to use them?"

After surveying the situation in the late 1980s, Saltman (1990:393) concluded that "racially transitional urban neighborhoods do not inevitably become resegregated. Whether they do or don't depends on a number of critical factors; some are related to internal organized efforts, but more are external to those efforts." R.A. Smith (1993:131) more cautiously concluded that "integrated neighborhoods are very difficult to maintain" and described several reasons why. The most important factors that distinguish neighborhoods that have experienced stable racial integration from those that have not, according to Saltman (1990, 1991), are listed below. She believes that items (c) and (d) are so crucial that she dubbed them the "killer variables."

A. *Amenities:* There is good-quality housing in the area, along with other attractions or important institutions (e.g., a park, university, governor's mansion).
B. *City Government:* The local government plays an active, positive role (e.g., by making housing rehabilitation grants available; by devoting Community Development Block Grant or Urban Development Action Grant money to neighborhood business or housing programs; by supporting neighborhood anticrime or antiblockbusting efforts).
C. *School Desegregation:* The school board's or a court's policy enables the neighborhood school to remain "racially balanced" (i.e., schools in this neighborhood should not tip to a higher percentage of minority students than other schools in the system).
D. *Public Housing Deconcentration:* There is no large concentration of public housing located in the neighborhood.

As suggested above, with residential integration come greater opportunities for children to attend integrated schools. A vast number of studies have been done on the outcome of school desegregation—whether or not it is beneficial for students and the conditions under which integration can be maintained over time. Among the most positive findings are those of Crain and Weisman (1972) and Braddock, Crain, and McPartland (1984), which showed that blacks who attended integrated schools were more likely to go on to college, obtain more stable or higher-status jobs, have stable marriages, own their own homes, live in integrated areas, and have white friends. Many other studies of school integration have found less evidence of positive results, though the positive outcomes outnumber the negative . . .

REDISTRIBUTING POWER AND WEALTH: RADICAL MOVEMENTS

Historically, individuals and groups on America's "left wing" (e.g., socialist and communist parties) joined in the struggle against racism earlier and more actively than did the "mainstream" Democratic and Republican parties. In the policy decisions of the dominant parties there has been a tendency to see the needs and interests of American racial minorities as being distinct from or opposed to what leaders of the dominant parties have defined as the broader national interest, and the parties have often favored the latter over the former. In contrast, radical or left-wing parties have usually seen themselves as representing society's underdogs and the exploited classes. At times this has led them to see racism and racial-ethnic inequality as one of the key props supporting general inequality in U.S. society. Therefore a great deal of radical writing and action has been aimed at getting rid of it.

For example, long before most "respectable" white Americans cared to face the issue of racial segregation and take a stand against it, college students with communist affiliations rallied against it (e.g., picketing in the 1930s when the University of Michigan gave in to the University of Alabama's segregation policy and did not let a black Michigan football player appear in the game against Alabama). The Communist Party was quite active in the 1930s protests during the trial of the "Scottsboro boys" (in which nine black youths in Alabama were falsely convicted of raping two white women on a train). In the 1940s and 1950s, left-wing activists gave aid and support to civil rights groups while most established Democratic and Republican leaders were unresponsive to attempts to enlist them in the civil rights struggle. Despite these and other actions, the role of left-wing groups in the struggle against racism has been, and remains, controversial. We'll explore why and then evaluate the approaches offered by radical groups.

Perhaps the most important point of controversy is the basic idea held by many radicals of what it will ultimately take to resolve our greatest racial-ethnic inequalities. For those who take a Marxist position, the accumulation of wealth by capitalists is what provokes the exploitation and impoverishment of laborers, and this is more easily accomplished if people of color are the most exploited, impoverished, feared, and hated of all. According to Gomes and Fishman (1989), the ultimate solution to the problem of African American or Hispanic inner-city poverty, unemployment on Native American reservations, or any other form of poverty, is *not* piecemeal tinkering or reform of the system through legislative or social changes (though these may be useful tactical steps toward the solution). Instead, if minorities' demands for the necessities of life (i.e., jobs, food, housing, education, and health care) are to be met, "it will require the dismantling of the capitalist political apparatus and market system and the reorganization of society to distribute to the masses the glut of goods and services that exist and are being produced daily" (Gomes & Fishman, 1989:92) or, as Newby (1989:132) puts it, "replacing a system that places profits before people with a more humane system."

Calling for an end to the capitalist system is obviously controversial. It sparks denial and repression from those who benefit (or think they benefit) from capitalism, as well as disagreement from those who believe that less drastic or more feasible solutions exist. The recent collapse of the noncapitalist systems created by communist parties in Eastern Europe and what was the Soviet Union makes American radicals' task of convincing the public that a socialist economy is the best solution more difficult now than it was earlier.

When radical groups actively participate in racial-ethnic conflicts, a second controversy often arises. It grows out of attempts to discredit or impugn the motives of people who are active in or leading the struggle against racism. In some cases it is the radicals' motives that are called into question, and in other cases it's those of the racial-ethnic group's national or local leaders. Sometimes it's both, and a situation of mutual distrust and recrimination is produced that hurts the progress of the antiracist efforts. For example, many whites who opposed the civil rights movement of the 1950s and 1960s tried to discredit the entire movement (or specific individual leaders) by saying that many communist agents were involved in it. They hoped, in making this charge, to get the public to believe that there was an ominous "anti-American" hidden agenda in the civil rights movement and that its leaders really wanted (or were unknowingly being duped into) a revolt against democracy and capitalism. In reality, some former and current communist activists did participate in civil rights organizations and protests, but they had neither the power nor necessarily the motives that the prosegregationist forces attributed to them. Nevertheless, the accusation of leftist or communist involvement in the civil rights movement did hinder it. . . .

This rancorous debate continued, and even today radical and moderate groups sometimes engage in similar questioning of each other's motives. Some Marxist theorists assert that black workers are in a strategic position to radicalize the rest of the working class and will be in the vanguard as the proletariat begins an "American Socialist Revolution." In contrast, many black moderates and nationalists skeptically think that African Americans are being used by radical and mainstream political parties and are dubious of the "solutions" that they prescribe.

We should now take a more concrete look at the actions and proposals for attaining racial equality advocated by radical political movements. If we go beyond the apocalyptic rhetoric ("batter the fortress of American capitalism . . . until one day the whole edifice will come crashing down" [Bonacich, 1990:205]), what do we see?

For one thing, we find enthusiastic advocacy and dedicated workers supporting many of the same social justice initiatives that liberals favor. For example, Cloward and Piven (1989) propose reforms that make it easier for racial-ethnic minorities and the poor to become registered voters. They believe that the poverty of the U.S. underclass (in which racial minorities are overrepresented) will not be eliminated without government intervention in education, job training and employment, housing, and social welfare. They argue that politicians won't pursue these policies as long as vast numbers of the poor and minorities remain unregistered and cannot vote for them. James Geschwender (1989) favors drastically altering the opportunity structure, and since he thinks that the underpayment of employed females is responsible for much of the racial-ethnic income inequality, he advocates "comparable worth" legislation and other measures designed to reduce the gender income gap. Other changes favored by many radicals include raising the minimum wage, reforms in day labor pools, and legislation aimed at curbing the activities of "hate groups."

While efforts like those just cited are seen as progressive and useful, they leave leftist scholars and activists unsatisfied, for these reforms don't seem to go far enough. In reflecting on the constraints of professional social policy research and "political reality," Bonnie Thorton Dill (1989:74) said with frustration, "Must the result—in order for us to be heard and have any hope of having our ideas implemented—be a band-aid of some sort rather than fundamental economic reorganization?" She argued that unless an active radical political constituency develops that can force an expansion of the policy choices, radical social scientists will remain stuck with proposals that "keep us from going as far as we really know we need to go."

Where do they want to go? Since they view capitalism as a pathological economic system (because it causes the privileged classes to treat more and more people as superfluous [Newby, 1989]), they envision an alternative economic order (e.g., see Luria and Russell's [1984] plan to revitalize Detroit's manufacturing economy while giving workers and the community a stronger position in running and benefiting from the new industries). Indeed, Bonacich (1989:53) explicitly rejected as an answer increasing the number of good jobs available to racial-ethnic minorities and individual upward mobility into the white middle-class mainstream. Jobs in the existing white-dominated capitalist order, she said, only replicate the continued exploitation of people of color. Instead, she called on African Americans to regain control over their own resources and build alternative, noncapitalistic economic institutions. Perhaps she would advise other racial-ethnic groups that have not already been "bought off" by the system to do likewise. A major problem, of course, is the absence of a clear plan for this and lack of strong political support for it. Rather than offering a blueprint for attaining that goal, however, Bonacich (1989, 1990) suggested what university faculty and students should do. She encouraged us to look at our communities, see where class, gender, and racial inequities lie, and direct our talents toward eliminating them. She believes that the university community should be more willing to listen to the needs and goals of the masses in the racial-ethnic communities and then put its energies into serving their needs rather than the needs of the elite.

Similarly, Manning Marable (1984) insisted that even if racial-ethnic minorities are successful in business, gain the mayor's office, or do well in school, the masses of people will still have no real power and will therefore remain disadvantaged. His idea of racial equality requires severely restricting the prerogatives of capitalists (e.g., preventing them from arbitrarily closing or relocating factories, limiting the private accumulation of wealth) and transferring power from propertied elites to the working class in their work and residential settings. Marable (1984:212) asserted that only in a society in which power is held by the "labouring classes, national minorities, and all of the oppressed" will people's rights to a job, decent housing, a full education, and good medical care become realities. Therefore he advocated support for socialist parties and black or other minority "nationalist" groups with a radical agenda.

In contrast to this path of rebellion, which has often floundered because of external repression and internal conflicts, we now consider a "reform" approach to attaining some of these same "people's rights."

"UNIVERSAL" ENTITLEMENTS

People who call for "universal entitlements" argue that the best way to eliminate the socioeconomic problems of racial-ethnic minorities in the United States is to adopt "nonracial" programs that enhance human capital (better schools and job training), create a tight labor market ("full" employment), stimulate broad economic growth, and meet the health, housing, and child-care needs of the entire population. They contend that *most* Americans need better health care, more economic security, better schools, and less crime and pollution. They then claim that the only politically viable way to bring these things to the people who need them the most (the so-called racial-ethnic minority underclass) is by convincing political-economic leaders to establish policies and programs that bring these to *all* Americans who need them. The reason given by advocates of this approach is that a majority of the electorate and/or the power structure would not support a program that seemed to be mainly or only for the benefit of a particular group (e.g., African Americans, the working poor) and not themselves.

The strongest advocate of this approach in recent years has been William J. Wilson (1987, 1991), who has argued that the most feasible way to improve the life chances of America's ghetto dwellers is by implementing programs that also bring benefits to the more advantaged segments of all races. He proposed a social democratic public policy agenda modeled on the systems in place in Sweden, Austria, Norway, and what was West Germany. Specifically, this means extensive "rational" governmental involvement in economic activity and planning (to promote high employment rates, wage and price stability, and some wealth redistribution), along with programs ensuring that citizens' social needs are adequately met.

Some readers may object to the placement of this approach in the "Changing the Whole System" section, since the so-called universal entitlement measures that the United States has adopted (e.g., Social Security, unemployment insurance) seem to be reform measures that do not actually cover the entire population that needs their benefits. While this is true, I believe that we should not limit our thinking to how things have been done in the past and should instead realize that *if* the changes advocated by Wilson really were put in place, they would produce major changes in U.S. society. The fact that these will be very difficult to bring about is not ignored by Wilson and is not the real issue. If it were, then we should have not discussed some of the ideas advocated by radicals in the previous section, since some of them (e.g., Newby, 1989:131–132) criticize Wilson's social democratic position for being politically unrealistic but then propose a solution (eliminating capitalism) that has an even lower probability of occurring.

Wilson's basic point (1987:139) is that the problems of people living in high-poverty areas require

> a far more comprehensive program of economic and social reform than what Americans have usually regarded as appropriate or desirable. In short, it will require a radicalism that neither Democratic nor Republican parties have as yet been realistic enough to propose.

He hopes that a coalition of whites and racial-ethnic minorities with moderate to radical political views can develop and create a strong enough social movement to make the political-economic powers that be adopt policies that will enable every American's social and economic needs to be met.

In suggesting this coalition strategy, Wilson touches on but does not do justice to the important debate between advocates of coalition and those who favor a more separatist approach. The arguments of Bayard Rustin (1966) for the former approach and of Stokely Carmichael and Charles Hamilton (1967) for the latter are still relevant today. For now we will limit ourselves more narrowly to the pros and cons of the idea of universal entitlements.

The most widely cited advantage of this approach seems to be the appeal it may have among the white majority, given that it promises to reduce the effects of poverty on racial-ethnic minorities in a way that does *not* give them "special treatment" (i.e., advantages or opportunities that are unavailable to other nonaffluent members of society). The white majority, apparently, is seen as unalterably opposed to a program of social and economic reform unless it is included as a major beneficiary along with the racial-ethnic minorities. Herbert Gans (1991:274), for example, argued that even though racial factors (e.g., discrimination) are the primary cause of black poverty, white support for programs that are designed to make up for the disadvantages inflicted on blacks is so low that race-specific policies are not the best solutions to the problem.

In calling for economic and social welfare reforms that improve the quality of life for the vast majority of Americans, supporters of the universal entitlements approach borrow and place much faith in the old nautical cliche "a rising tide lifts all boats." They imply that general economic growth, a national health insurance program, or a program that gives all families a housing subsidy would raise the quality of life for Americans of every ethnicity. The problem with this is that while it may sound reasonable, in a number of cases it is not true. Newman et al. (1978) made a convincing case that a high rate of general economic growth is a necessary but not sufficient condition for minority employment gains and that even during periods of economic expansion, racial minorities need protection against discrimination. In addition, given the complex, multisegmented nature of the modern U.S. economy and the fact that American racial-ethnic groups are concentrated in certain sectors of it, there is no guarantee that prosperous conditions "in general" will spread into the sector(s) where the poorer groups are concentrated.

There is another problem with entitlement programs that are supposed to aid the universe of people who need the programs' benefits. In practice, most programs fail to achieve complete coverage, that is, many people who want and qualify for the benefits do not get them. Medicaid, unemployment insurance, Social Security, and Aid to Families with Dependent Children all, in varying degrees, leave out certain categories of needy people. Racial-ethnic minorities, it is important to realize, are overrepresented among those who are underserved by the so-called "universal programs." This happens for a variety of reasons, which may or may not be racially motivated. In some cases, to make the program easier to administer, a class of people is made ineligible. In other cases the reason given is to lower the program's total cost or to reduce its inflationary impact. Additionally, in a program such as Medicaid, which relies heavily on private caregivers (doctors and hospitals), eligible people are sometimes not served because the caregivers find that they can earn more money by serving non-Medicaid patients.

The main point of these criticisms, however, is not to declare universal entitlements to be a flawed or useless approach. On the contrary, many of them are valuable. There are, however, real limitations in viewing them as the sole answer to the problem of racial-ethnic inequality. First, unless special efforts are made to encourage and ensure their inclusion in the programs, racial-ethnic minorities easily fall or get pushed through the "cracks" in the service delivery system. Indeed, there is a danger that if social welfare benefits are broadened to serve more of the middle- and working-class population, the poor and "truly disadvantaged" will get lost in the shuffle and not benefit as much as is necessary. Second, although extending the services and benefits of entitlement programs to whites makes this approach more popular politically, it lessens the degree to which racial-ethnic inequality per se is reduced and arguably fails to channel the most assistance to where the most serious needs and degrees of victimization exist. If the violence and rhetoric surrounding the Los Angeles riots are an indication, many in the minority community believe that the approaches that are politically popular among whites are *not* acceptable. They say that through conflict and confrontation the dominant group can be jolted into targeting many more resources specifically to the poor inner-city minorities.

In conclusion, several social policy analysts now believe that programs targeted at specific, high-need categories of people must be used in conjunction with universal entitlement programs. William J. Wilson (1991:478) himself agrees with this but qualifies it by saying that the targeted needy populations should not be defined simply in racial terms.

SEPARATISM

The most dramatic mode of changing the whole system of racial-ethnic relations occurs when two or more groups that were formerly connected by social, economic, and political relationships go their separate ways. When separation occurs, it is usually the culmination of efforts by a nationalist social movement. It involves severe conflict and agitation growing out of widespread feelings of exploitation, relative deprivation, inequality, distrust, and hatred. Currently, the various ethnic groups that formed the nations of Yugoslavia and Czechoslovakia have split up and are creating new independent states, and in Canada a revival of secessionist sentiment is taking place among many French-speaking inhabitants of Quebec. U.S. history contains several attempts at racial-ethnic separatism of this sort. Among the more interesting are those of the Germans in Texas who hoped to create an independent country in the mid-1800s; the African Americans who migrated to places in Central America, Africa, and Oklahoma in hopes of building a separate society free from racism; and the Mormons who fled west, settled around the Great Salt Lake, and established their domain in what later became Utah. An effort at political separatism in the United States today is the movement to change the status of Puerto Rico to that of an independent country.

In cases in which an actual separation occurs, regardless of whether the decision is made unilaterally (i.e., by just one ethnic group) or is mutually agreed on, the social, psychological, and economic consequences for each racial-ethnic group and subgroups within them vary greatly. In this sense it is similar to the breakup of a family through separation or divorce, in that the husband's and wife's psychological and economic costs and benefits are usually different, as are those of the children and other relatives.

Separatism is sometimes conceptualized in another way in the United States, in a less dramatic but still somewhat controversial form in which members of a racial-ethnic group cut off or greatly reduce their relations with out-group members, especially the dominant group. This is usually done so that the racial-ethnic group can better maintain or elaborate its culture and/or gain control over its own communities while still remaining within the political jurisdiction of the U.S. government. The two major examples of this are calls for greater levels of self-determination by Native Americans on reservations and the demands for community control issued by black power advocates (e.g., Malcolm X, Stokely Carmichael). In both, separatism is seen as an antidote for the problems associated with internal colonialism, although in practice an outcome resembling "neocolonialism" is a real possibility.

Separatism, in the sense of reduced contact with out-groups and greater control over local institutions by a racial-ethnic group, is common in the field of education and has generated much debate. Beginning in the 1970s, a number of Native American tribes began establishing their own schools (often out of frustration with the poor quality of education offered by the Bureau of Indian Affairs or church-sponsored schools), and a few established their own colleges. . . .

Some Jewish and Chinese Americans have long had their own separate day schools for essentially the same purposes, and more recently, some African Americans have argued that many black students would be better served in an all-black school environment specifically designed to serve their needs. Obviously, this approach differs markedly from the "mainstreaming" approach advocated by proponents of racial-ethnic integration. Space limitations do not permit our delving into the merits of each side's arguments and evidence, but it appears that while schools that are designed to meet the needs of students from a specific racial-ethnic group are not necessarily a good choice for every child, they can be a useful option for many.

Finally, we should summarize and consider the position taken by many black nationalists, who reject the idea of joining the kinds of coalitions suggested by Bayard Rustin (1966) and William J. Wilson (1987). They assert that blacks should lead and work in black organizations to build a stronger community, and whites should support those efforts and work within the white community to press for racial change. Stokely Carmichael and Charles Hamilton (1967) gave a classic statement of this position. They called for wholesale change in the system: "the political and economic institutions of this society must be completely revised if the political and economic status of black people is to be improved" (Carmichael & Hamilton, 1967:178). Why then did they propose to work almost completely within the African American community rather than pursuing institutional change via a coalition with liberal whites, labor unions, church groups, and an established political party (e.g., the Democrats)? Carmichael and Hamilton (1967:188) answered by saying, "advocates of Black Power are not opposed to coalitions per se" and Black Power "has no connotation of 'go it alone.'" They did, however, oppose joining a coalition if it involves blacks only as dependent "junior partners" and if it does not place a very high priority on achieving specific goals that would benefit the black masses in this country. On the basis of the historical record, Carmichael and Hamilton contended that the kind of coalition proposed above would not be the "right kind"—it would not be in the real interests of blacks because it is based on three myths.

Carmichael and Hamilton, in the mid-1960s, concluded that the time was not ripe for a viable coalition of blacks and other more affluent and privileged Americans. They believed that the first order of business was to organize and mobilize African Americans so that they could more clearly define their mutual interests and goals. The next step would then be building a strong, independent political and economic base in America's black communities. Carmichael and Hamilton advised that only when these political and economic resources were available should blacks select allies and enter into coalitions with them based on shared areas of self-interest, clearly defined goals, and a mutual respect for each other's own needs and power. As they put it, "Black Power simply says: enter coalitions only *after* you are able to 'stand on your own'" (Carmichael & Hamilton, 1967:188). Although Carmichael and Hamilton were concerned with black-white relations, they implied that the same conclusions apply to other poor racial-ethnic minority groups. Looking to the future, they saw a need for a coalition between poor blacks and poor whites but believed that a lot of education and organization had to be done by black and white leaders in their own communities before such a coalition could emerge and transform American society.

Should separatism in the form proposed by Carmichael and Hamilton be given a high priority in today's struggle against racism, or is the time now ripe for something like the racial-ethnic "Rainbow Coalition" promoted by Jesse Jackson? Multiethnic coalitions are difficult to create or maintain, and evidence suggests that the competition for jobs, political power, and other scarce resources is producing more antagonism and conflict than unity and cooperation among American urban ethnic groups. But if the separatist alternative just means each group gaining control over its own local institutions, the problem may remain, for as Robert Allen (1970:33) noted, "black control of black communities will not mean freedom from oppression so long as the black communities themselves are subservient to an outside society which is exploitative." Furthermore, today's minority groups that have made economic progress via an "ethnic enclave" approach (e.g., Cubans in Miami, Koreans in Los Angeles and New York) cannot be used as examples of successful separatism for the simple reason that these groups do not really limit themselves to their own communities in terms of where and with whom they do business; they successfully tap into larger markets than just their own group. The idea of each racial-ethnic group guarding its own turf, relying just on its own internal resources, and putting its own narrow self-interest ahead of everything else seems less like a progressive strategy and more like a throwback to the days when dominant groups used a "divide and conquer" approach to keep racial-ethnic minorities in disadvantaged positions.

CONCLUSION

Finding productive ways to solve the interlocking problems of prejudice, discrimination, and inequality is the most important task facing people who are interested in racial-ethnic relations. [I believe] that most available means of fighting racism have not been adequately evaluated or tested, and those that have need to have their potential and problems widely discussed. We [have] examined four ways in which our whole society might change to produce greater racial-ethnic equity.

Ironically, these four changes seem to consist of two sets of polar opposites. In the first, residential integration and separatism seem to be at odds with each other. Perhaps they could be reconciled in a system that encouraged mixed racial-ethnic residential living in many parts of the city and suburbs but also encouraged a few areas to remain largely in the hands of a single group. In the other, universal entitlements may be a way of widely extending beneficial services and scarce resources without completely redistributing power and wealth through a revolutionary struggle. It may be, however, that without the threat of the latter, elite members of the racial-ethnic majority will not be willing to move toward the former.

Finally, we should realize that although we have arrayed strategies on changing the whole society, these useful analytic distinctions are less important in actual practice. Changing the whole system inevitably involves changing individual attitudes, and for individual attitude changes to have much positive impact, they must be harnessed to behavioral changes in large, powerful social groups and institutions. Now that we know what our racial-ethnic problems are and what many proposed solutions involve, it is our responsibility to creatively figure out what to do so that the mistakes of the past, or new racial-ethnic patterns that are just as bad, do not overwhelm us.

REFERENCES

Allen, R.L. 1970. *Black Awakening in Capitalist America.* Garden City, NY: Doubleday.

Bonacich, E. 1989. "Racism in advanced capitalist society: comments on William J. Wilson's The Truly Disadvantaged." *Journal of Sociology and Social Welfare* 16(4):41–56.

Bonacich, E. 1990. "Inequality in America: the failure of the American system for people of color." In G.E. Thomas (Ed.), *U.S. Race Relations in the 1980s and 1990s,* pp. 187–208. New York: Hemisphere.

Bradburn, N., S. Sudman, and G. Glockel. 1971. *Side by Side: Integrated Neighborhoods.* Chicago: Quadrangle Books.

Braddock, J.H, R.L. Crain, and J.M. McPartland. 1984. "A long-term view of school desegregation." *Phi Delta Kappan* 66(4): 259–264.

Carmichael, S., and C. Hamilton. 1967. *Black Power: The Politics of Liberation in America.* New York: Random House.

Clark, W.A.V. 1993. "Neighborhood transition in multi-ethnic/racial contexts." *Journal of Urban Affairs* 15(2):161–172.

Cloward, R.A., and F.F. Piven. 1989. "Poverty and electoral power" *Journal of Sociology and Social Welfare* 16(4):99–106.

Crain, R.L., and C.S. Weisman. 1972. *Discrimination, Personality, and Achievement.* New York: Seminar Press.

DeMarco, D.L., and G.C. Galster. 1993. "Prointegrative policy: theory and practice." *Journal of Urban Affairs* 15(2):141–160.

Dill, B.T. 1989. "A limited proposal for social reform: a response to William J. Wilson's The Truly Disadvantaged." *Journal of Sociology and Social Welfare* 16(4):69–76.

Galster, G.C., and W.M. Keeney. 1988. "Race, residence, discrimination, and economic opportunity: modeling the nexus of urban racial phenomena." *Urban Affairs Quarterly* 24(1):87–117.

Gans, H.J. 1991. *People, Plans, and Policies.* New York: Columbia University Press.

Geschwender, J.A. 1989. "The Truly Disadvantaged: structuring an agenda for change." *Journal of Sociology and Social Welfare* 16(4):107–122.

Gomes, R.C., and W.K. Fishman 1989. "A critique of The Truly Disadvantaged: A historial materialist perspective." *Journal of Sociology and Social Welfare* (16)4: 77–98.

Goodwin, C. 1979. *The Oak Park Strategy.* Chicago: University of Chicago Press.
Luria, D., and J. Russell. 1984. "Motor city changeover." In L. Sawers & W.K. Tabb (Eds.), *Sunbelt/Snowbelt: Urban Development and Regional Restructuring,* pp. 271–312. New York: Oxford University Press.
Marable, M. 1984. *Race, Reform and Rebellion: The Second Reconstruction in Black America, 1945–1982.* Jackson, MS: University Press of Mississippi.
Molotch, H. 1972. *Managed Integration.* Berkeley: University of California Press.
Newby, R.G. 1989. "Problems of pragmatism in public policy: a critique of William J. Wilson's The Truly Disadvantaged." *Journal of Sociology and Social Welfare* 16(4):123–132.
Newman, D.K, N.J. Amidei, B.L. Carter, D. Day, W.J. Druvant, and J.S. Russell. 1978. *Protest, Politics, and Prosperity.* New York: Pantheon Books.
Orfield, G. 1981. *Toward a Strategy for Urban Integration.* New York: Ford Foundation.
Rosenbaum, J.E. and S.J. Popkin. 1991. "Employment and Earnings of Low-Income Blacks Who Move to Middle-Class Suburbs." In C. Jencks and P.E. Peterson (Eds.), *The Urban Underclass,* pp. 342–356. Washington, D.C.: The Urban Institute.
Rustin, B. 1966. "'Black Power' and coalition politics." *Commentary* 42(Sept.):35–40.
Saltman, J. 1990. *A Fragile Movement: The Struggle for Neighborhood Stabilization.* Westport, CT: Greenwood Press.
Saltman, J. 1991. "Maintaining racially diverse neighborhoods." *Urban Affairs Quarterly* 26(3):416–441.
Smith, R.A. 1993. "Creating stable racially integrated communities: a review." *Journal of Urban Affairs* 15(2):115–140.
Urban Institute. 1992. "New evidence of urban housing discrimination." *The Urban Institute Policy and Research Report* 22(1):4–6.
Wilson, W.J. 1987. *The Truly Disadvantaged: The Inner City, the Underclass, and Public Policy.* Chicago: University of Chicago Press.
Wilson, W.J. 1991. "Public policy research and The Truly Disadvantaged." In C. Jencks & P.E. Peterson (Eds.), *The Urban Underclass,* pp. 460–481. Washington, D.C.: Brookings Institution.

Statistical Appendix

TABLE A.1 Median Family Income by Race/Ethnicity, 1959–1996

Year	*Race/Ethnicity of Family* White	Black	Hispanic*	*Black as % of White*	*Hispanic as % of White*	*Black as % of Hispanic*
1959	$5,893	$3,047	—	54	—	—
1970	10,236	6,279	—	61	—	—
1980	21,904	12,674	14,717	58	67	87
1990	36,915	21,423	23,431	58	63	92
1996	44,756	26,522	26,179	59	58	101
1996**	50,190	41,943	31,930	84	64	131

*Hispanics can be of any race.

**Refers to married couple families only; other data refers to all families.

SOURCE: U.S. Bureau of the Census, Current Population Reports, Series P-60, No. 193. *Money Income in the United States, 1995.*

TABLE A.2 Median Income for Year-Round Full-Time Workers in 1996 by Race/Ethnicity and Gender

Race/ Ethnicity	*Sex*				*Women as % of Men*
	Male		*Female*		
	Income	*% of White*	*Income*	*% of White*	
White	$34,741	—	$25,358	—	73
Black	27,136	78	21,990	87	81
Hispanic*	21,265	61	19,272	76	91
All Workers	33,538	—	24,935	—	74

*Hispanics can be of any race.

SOURCE: U.S. Bureau of the Census, Current Population Reports, Series P-60, No. 197. *Money Income in the United States, 1996.*

TABLE A.3 Percentage of Population That Is Poor* by Race/Ethnicity, 1959–1996

Year	*Race/Ethnicity* White	Black	Hispanic**	*Black % / White %*	*Hispanic % / White %*	*Black % / Hispanic %*
1959	18.1%	55.1%	—	3.0	—	—
1966	11.3	41.8	—	3.7	—	—
1970	9.9	33.5	—	3.4	—	—
1980	10.2	32.5	25.7	3.2	2.5	1.3
1990	10.7	31.9	28.1	3.0	2.6	1.1
1996	11.2	28.4	29.4	2.5	2.6	1.0

For example, in 1996, 11.2% of the white population was poor, 28.4% of the black population was poor, and 29.4% of the Hispanic population was poor. Blacks were 3 times more likely to be poor than whites (55.1/18.1=3.0); Hispanics were 2.6 times more likely to be poor than whites; blacks and Hispanics were equally likely to be poor.

*A nonfarm family of four was defined as "poor" if their annual income was $16,036 in 1996. In the same year, 13.7% of the population (36.5 million people) was defined as poor. There were more poor whites than poor blacks—24.7 million poor whites, 9.7 million poor blacks, and 8.7 million poor Hispanics.

**Hispanics can be of any race.

SOURCE: U.S. Bureau of the Census, Current Population Reports, Series P-60, No. 198. *Poverty in the United States, 1996.*

TABLE A.4 Median Net Worth of Households in 1988 and 1993 by Race/Ethnicity

Race/ Ethnicity	*1988* Net Worth	*1988* % of White	*1993* Net Worth	*1993* % of White
White	$43,279	—	$45,740	—
Black	4,169	9.6	4,418	9.7
Hispanic*	5,524	12.7	4,656	10.2

*Hispanics can be of any race.

For example, in 1993, the median net worth for a white household was $45,740 and for a black household was $4,418. Black households had only 9.7% of the net worth of white households.

SOURCE: U.S. Census Bureau, "Asset Ownership of Households: 1993 Highlights." Available: http://www.census.gov/hhes/www/wealth/highlite.html.

TABLE A.5 Unemployment Rates for Whites, Nonwhites, and Blacks, 1955–1996

	Race				
Year	*White*	*Nonwhite**	*Black*	*Nonwhite/White*	*Black/White*
1948	3.5	5.9	—	1.7	—
1955	3.9	8.7	—	2.2	—
1960	4.9	10.2	—	2.1	—
1965	4.1	8.1	—	2.0	—
1970	4.5	8.2	—	1.8	—
1975	7.8	13.9	—	1.8	
1981	6.7	14.2	15.6	2.1	2.3
1990	4.7	—	11.3	—	2.5
1996	4.7	—	10.5	—	2.2

*The division "white/nonwhite" was originally employed by the U.S. Department of Labor in its regular surveys and reports.

SOURCE: U.S. Dept. of Labor, *Employment and Earnings,* various issues.

TABLE A.6 Unemployment Rates of 16- to 24-Year-Olds Not Enrolled in School by Race/Ethnicity and Education, 1996

	Level of Education			
Race/Ethnicity	*High School Dropouts*	*High School Graduates*	*Some College*	*College Graduates*
Whites	18.5	9.9	5.9	5.3
Blacks	43.0	23.0	13.3	5.3
Hispanics*	17.7	13.4	9.6	8.1
Black/White	2.3	2.3	2.3	1.0
Hispanic/White	1.0	1.4	1.6	1.5

*Hispanics can be of any race.

SOURCE: U.S. Dept. of Labor, *Employment and Earnings,* January 1997.

TABLE A.7 Educational Attainment Rates for Whites, Blacks, and Hispanics,* 1975–1995

	*High School Graduation or More***					*College Graduation or More****				
Year	*White*	*Black*	*Hispanic*	*Black/White*	*Hispanic/White*	*White*	*Black*	*Hispanic*	*Black/White*	*Hispanic/White*
1975	83.2	64.8	57.5	78	69	22.8	10.7	8.8	47	39
1980	82.6	69.7	54.1	84	65	23.7	11.6	7.7	49	32
1985	83.6	75.6	62.9	90	75	23.2	11.5	11.1	50	48
1990	82.5	77.0	54.5	93	66	24.2	13.4	9.2	55	38
1995	81.9	76.9	58.6	94	72	26.0	15.3	8.9	59	34

*Hispanics can be of any race.

**18–24-year-olds

***24–29-year-olds

For example, in 1995, 26.0% of whites and 15% of blacks were college graduates. The black college graduation rate was 59% of the white rate (15.3/26.0=59%).

SOURCE: Deborah J. Carter and Reginald Wilson, *Minorities in Higher Education, 1996–1997: Fifteenth Annual Status Report* (Washington, D.C.: American Council on Education, 1997).

About the Editors and Contributors

Marc Bendick, Jr. is a principal in Bendick & Eagan Economic Consultants, Inc. and a consultant to the Fair Employment Council of Greater Washington, Inc.

Bob Blauner teaches sociology at the University of California at Berkeley.

Clairece Booher Feagin is an independent writer.

Peter Brimelow is senior editor at *Forbes* magazine and *The National Review.*

Prince Brown, Jr. teaches in the Sociology and Anthropology Department at Northern Kentucky University.

David Cole teaches at the Georgetown University Law Center.

Dinesh D'Souza is a research fellow at the American Enterprise Institute.

Howard J. Ehrlich, a sociologist and social psychologist, directs the Prejudice Institute and is the 1994 recipient of the Sociological Practice Award of the Society for Applied Sociology.

Joe R. Feagin teaches sociology at the University of Florida.

Abby L. Ferber teaches sociology at the University of Colorado at Colorado Springs.

Joan Ferrante teaches in the Sociology and Anthropology Department at Northern Kentucky University.

Charles A. Gallagher teaches sociology at Georgia State University.

Milton M. Gordon is a retired sociologist.

Lawrence E. Harrison teaches at the Center for International Affairs at Harvard University.

Karen J. Hossfeld teaches sociology at San Francisco State University.

Charles W. Jackson is an attorney in Boston and formerly worked with the Fair Employment Council of Greater Washington, Inc.

Charles Jaret teaches sociology at Georgia State University.

James M. Jones teaches social psychology at the University of Delaware.

Joleen Kirshenman is a graduate student in sociology at the University of Chicago.

Mike Long teaches linguistics at the University of Hawaii at Manoa.

Douglas S. Massey teaches sociology at the University of Pennsylvania.

Joan Moore teaches sociology at the University of Wisconsin at Milwaukee.

Kathryn M. Neckerman teaches sociology at Columbia University.

Geoffrey Nunberg teaches linguistics at Stanford University.

Eileen O'Brien is a graduate student in sociology at the University of Florida.

Fred L. Pincus is associate professor of sociology at the University of Maryland, Baltimore County.

Raquel Pinderhughes teaches urban studies at San Francisco State University.

Pyong Gap Min teaches sociology at Queens College and the CUNY Graduate Center.

Victor A. Reinoso is a management consultant. He formerly worked with the Fair Employment Council of Greater Washington, Inc.

Byron M. Roth teaches psychology at Dowling College.

Arthur Salz teaches elementary education at Queens College (CUNY).

Saskia Sassen teaches urban planning at Columbia University.

Thomas Sowell is a senior fellow at the Hoover Institution.

Ronald Takaki teaches ethnic studies at the University of California at Berkeley.

Abigail Thernstrom is a senior fellow at the Manhattan Institute.

Stephen Thernstrom teaches history at Harvard University.

Deborah Toler is senior research analyst at the Institute for Food and Development Policy (Food First) in Oakland, California.

Mark Toney is the director of Strategic Tools, Inc.

Julius Trubowitz teaches elementary education at Queens College (CUNY).

William Julius Wilson teaches African American studies at Harvard University.

Howard Zinn, a retired political scientist, formerly taught at Boston University.